_____

_____

_____

_____

_____

GLENCOE
McGraw-Hill

and

SHEPARD'S
McGRAW-HILL

proudly announce their cooperative effort to publish
textbooks and other instructional material
of the highest quality and integrity
for paralegal education.

Shepard's/McGraw-Hill, located in Colorado Springs, Colorado, has been long
known for its legal citation services. It also publishes single- and multi-volume
practice sets, specialty newsletters and law reporters, legal directories, demon-
strative videos, and document drafting software. Shepard's publications cover a
wide range of legal practice at the state and federal levels. Each publication is
kept current by a series of periodic updates, revisions, or supplements to keep
pace with constantly evolving changes in the law and legal procedures.

ABOUT THE AUTHOR

Deborah L. Kutzavitch *is an adjunct professor in the Paralegal Institute at Duquesne University in Pittsburgh, Pennsylvania, where she currently teaches corporate law. She has been a corporate legal assistant since 1981 and has worked for small and large law firms and corporations. She is a past president of the Pittsburgh Paralegal Association; is the coordinator of the Allegheny County Bar Association Homeless Project; and has lectured widely.*

Deborah Kutzavitch's educational background includes receiving a B.S. in finance and a Paralegal Certificate from Robert Morris College.

LEGAL STUDIES SERIES

B A S I C
CORPORATE
LAW
AND
BUSINESS
ORGANIZATIONS

DEBORAH L. KUTZAVITCH
Paralegal Institute
Duquesne University

GLENCOE
McGraw-Hill

New York, New York
Columbus, Ohio
Mission Hills, California
Peoria, Illinois

SHEPARD'S
McGRAW-HILL

Colorado Springs, Colorado

Titles in the Glencoe/Shepard's Legal Studies Series

Basic Law Office Management
Basic Legal Writing
Basic Legal Research
Basic Legal Research and Writing
Introduction to Legal Assisting

Basic Family Law
Basic Civil Litigation
Defining the Law
Basic Wills, Trusts, and Estates
Basic Corporate Law and Business Organizations

Library of Congress Cataloging-in-Publication Data

Kutzavitch, Deborah L.
   Basic corporate law and business organizations / Deborah L. Kutzavitch.
      p.   cm. — (Legal studies series)
   Includes index.
      ISBN 0-02-801348-4 (text). — ISBN 0-02-801356-5 (study guide). —
ISBN 0-02-801357-3 (instructor's manual). — ISBN 0-02-801358-1
(tests)
      1. Business enterprises—Law and legislation—United States.
2. Corporation law—United States. 3. Legal assistants—United States—Handbooks,
manuals, etc.   I. Title.   II. Series.
KF1365.K84   1994
346.73'065—dc20
[347.30665]
                                                                94-35101
                                                                CIP

Basic Corporate Law and Business Organizations

1996 Imprint

Certificates in figures 4–4, 6–13, 10–1, and 15–4 are used with permission of Goes Lithographing
Company of Chicago. All rights reserved. Several styles are available for corporate use from Goes
Litho, Chicago, IL 60621–3999.

Send all inquiries to:
Glencoe/McGraw-Hill
936 Eastwind Drive
Westerville, OH 43081

ISBN: 0–02–801348–4

Printed in the United States of America.

2 3 4 5 6 7 8 9 POH 01 00 99 98 97 96

PREFACE

Corporate Law provides the fundamentals necessary for a student to begin work towards a career as a corporate paralegal. This basic text illustrates ideas with sample forms, agreements, and documents. Yet it does not lose the forest for the trees, backing up complex concepts with practical discussions. Further, although the text emphasizes the Model Business Corporation Act, it references state peculiarities where appropriate.

Organization of the Text

The first three chapters cover sole proprietorship, general partnership, and limited partnership.

Subsequent chapters help students gain an understanding of how to form, operate, and maintain a corporation.

For example, chapters 4–7 cover types of corporations and organizations; ownership and management structure; the formation of business corporations; professional, nonprofit, and close corporations; and the limited liability company. The student will learn how to hold meetings and how to document the actions of the shareholders and board of directors.

Further chapters highlight the extraordinary activities of the corporation, such as amending the articles of incorporation and bylaws; qualifying to do business in a foreign jurisdiction; financing by selling securities and issuing debt instruments; and distributing profits.

The final chapters detail the statutes that regulate the offer and sale of securities; merger, share exchange, consolidation, and sale of stock and assets; dissolution and liquidation; and the issuance and sale of shares in closely held corporations.

Additionally, students can gain invaluable experience with model statutes in the appendices, including the Model Business Corporation Act, the Uniform Partnership Act, and the Revised Uniform Limited Partnership Act.

Text Design

The text has been structured to keep students on track. Each chapter begins with an outline of its key concepts and a vignette to show how the concepts apply on the job. What can be learned in the chapter is clearly listed in the student objectives section. Further, each chapter highlights in feature sections the practical use of the material, illustration of the concepts with case discussions, and advice on how to handle trouble spots. These unique features are aptly titled "Practical Considerations," "Legal Links," and "Paralegalert!"

End-of-chapter study aids include a summary keyed to the chapter sections, review and discussion questions, and activities to expand learning. Comprehension is supported within the chapter by the bold key terms, which are listed at the ends of the chapters and defined in the glossary at the back of the book.

Other Resources

Students will appreciate the practice available in the accompanying *Study Guide,* which may help them improve test scores and help develop their critical thinking skills. Numerous exercises review the course objectives in a way that is related to real-life situations. Its format begins with a fill-in chapter outline, followed by a corporate concepts section, a vocabulary activity, yes/no statements, and a case study.

For the teacher, the *Instructor's Manual* offers model course syllabi (for quarter system or semester schedules), answer keys to the text, and tests for each chapter.

A computer test bank, with over a thousand questions, is also available to instructors.

State-Specific Supplements

Because the rules applicable to each state often differ in the details, supplements are available for certain states. The supplements discuss the laws and procedures applicable in these states. For more information about the supplements, contact the publisher.

Acknowledgments

I would like to thank the following reviewers whose efforts, suggestions, ideas, and insights made this text more valuable:

Jerold E. Aubry, Attorney at Law, Jacksonville Beach, FL; Jeffrey A. Helewitz, Attorney at Law, Adjunct Faculty, Paralegal Program, Queens College, Flushing, NY; Herbert G. Feuerhake, Attorney at Law, Norwalk, CT; R. Rudy Filek, Jr., Attorney at Law, Paralegal Program Coordinator, Bradford School, Pittsburgh, PA; Eugene N. Lindenbaum, J.D., Instructor, Paralegal Program, University of San Francisco, San Francisco, CA; Donald C. Lubner, Attorney at Law, Adjunct Faculty, Paralegal Program, Milwaukee Area Technical College, Milwaukee, WI; Professor Claudia D. Richardson, Paralegal Program, University of Hartford, Hartford College for Women, Hartford, CT; Lori J. Trofemuk, Attorney at Law, Coordinator of Paralegal Studies, Kelsey-Jenney College, San Diego, CA; Jefferson H. Weaver, Attorney at Law, Davie, FL; Dana M. Zupanovich, Corporate Services International, Instructor, Paralegal Program, University of California, Los Angeles and University of West Los Angeles, Los Angeles, CA.

I wish to acknowledge the continued support of my editor, Rick Adams, who gave me the optimism and confidence to complete this book.

Special thanks go to my patient family, friends, and to the Lord's guidance.

CONTENTS

About the Author _____ iv

Preface _____ v

CHAPTER 1   Sole Proprietorship _____ 1

1–1   Characteristics _____ 2
1–2   Formation and Operation _____ 3
    Registration of a Name _____ 3
    Regulatory Filings _____ 6
1–3   Liability of the Sole Proprietorship _____ 7
1–4   Taxation of the Sole Proprietorship _____ 8
1–5   Termination of the Sole Proprietorship _____ 8
1–6   Practical Considerations _____ 9

Chapter 2   General Partnership _____ 12

2–1   Characteristics _____ 13
2–2   Formation and Operation _____ 15
    The Partnership Agreement _____ 15
    Registration of Name _____ 16
    Regulatory Filings _____ 19
    Management of the Partnership _____ 20
2–3   Ownership of Partnership Property _____ 22
2–4   Partners' Liability _____ 23
    Liability of Incoming and Terminating Partners ___ 23
    Criminal Activity _____ 24
2–5   Taxation of the Partners _____ 24
2–6   Distribution of Profits and Losses _____ 26
2–7   Termination of the General Partnership _____ 29
2–8   Practical Considerations _____ 32

CHAPTER 3   Limited Partnership ——————————— 37

3–1   Characteristics ————————————————— 38
    Uniform Limited Partnership Acts ——————— 39
    Definition of a Limited Partnership ——————— 39

3–2   Formation and Operation ——————————— 39
    Certificate of Limited Partnership ——————— 40
    The Limited Partnership Agreement ——————— 43
    Merger, Consolidation, and the Foreign Limited Partnership — 45
    Partners' Participation in Management ——————— 45

3–3   Liability of the Partners ——————————— 46

3–4   Taxation of the Partners ——————————— 47

3–5   Changes in Partnership Interests ——————— 48
    Addition and Withdrawal of General Partners ——— 48
    Addition and Withdrawal of Limited Partners ——— 48

3–6   Termination of the Limited Partnership ————— 49

3–7   Practical Considerations ——————————— 50

**CHAPTER 4   Corporations and Other Forms of
Business Organizations** ——————————— 54

4–1   The Corporation —————————————— 55
    Characteristics ———————————————— 55
    Advantages and Disadvantages ——————————— 56
    Statutory Creation and Powers ——————————— 59

4–2   Types of Corporations ————————————— 61
    Business Corporation ————————————— 61
    Professional Corporation ———————————— 61
    Nonprofit Corporation ————————————— 62
    Close Corporation ——————————————— 63

4–3   Other Forms of Business Organizations ————— 64
    Limited Liability Company ———————————— 64
    Business Trust ———————————————— 66

4–4   Practical Considerations ——————————— 68

CHAPTER 5   Business Corporation ——————————— 71

5–1   Ownership and Management Structure ————— 72
    Shareholders ————————————————— 73
    Directors —————————————————— 78
    Officers ——————————————————— 81

5–2   Liability ——————————————————— 83
    Limited Liability of Shareholders ————————— 83
    Liability of Directors and Officers ————————— 84
    Indemnification of Directors and Officers ————— 87

5–3   Taxation of Corporations ——————————— 88
    Federal Income Taxation ————————————— 88
    Double Taxation ——————————————— 89
    Subchapter S Election ————————————— 92
    State Income Taxation ————————————— 94

5–4   Dissolution of Corporations —————————————— 95

5–5   Practical Considerations ———————————————— 96

CHAPTER 6   Formation of Corporations ——————— **100**

6–1   Statutory Requirements for Incorporation ——————— 101
- *Statutory Filing Documents* ————————————— 103
- *Filing Procedures* ——————————————————— 103

6–2   Preincorporation Activities and Considerations —————— 105
- *Subscription for Shares* ————————————————— 105
- *State of Incorporation* ————————————————— 107
- *Corporate Name* ——————————————————— 108
- *Fictitious Name* ———————————————————— 111

6–3   Articles of Incorporation: Statutory Provisions —————— 112
- *Corporate Name* ——————————————————— 112
- *Capital Structure* ——————————————————— 113
- *Registered Agent and Address* ———————————— 114
- *Incorporator* ————————————————————— 115

6–4   Articles of Incorporation: Optional Provisions —————— 116
- *Initial Directors* ——————————————————— 116
- *Corporate Purposes and Powers* ———————————— 116
- *Period of Existence* —————————————————— 117
- *Preemptive Rights* —————————————————— 117
- *Cumulative Voting for Directors* ———————————— 118
- *Quorum and Vote of Shareholders* ——————————— 119
- *Indemnification of Directors and Officers* ———————— 120

6–5   Postincorporation Activities ——————————————— 121
- *Organizational Meeting* ———————————————— 121
- *Payment of Capital* —————————————————— 121
- *Minute Book, Stock Book, and Corporate Seal* —————— 122
- *Legal Advertisement* ————————————————— 122
- *Securities Law Considerations* ————————————— 123
- *Subchapter S Election* ————————————————— 124

6–6   Bylaws ———————————————————————— 124

6–7   Incorporating Other Forms of Business Organizations ——— 126
- *Professional Corporation* ———————————————— 126
- *Nonprofit Corporation* ————————————————— 128
- *Close Corporation* ——————————————————— 129
- *Limited Liability Company* ——————————————— 131

6–8   Practical Considerations ———————————————— 134

CHAPTER 7   Corporate Meetings and Actions ——————— **140**

7–1   Types of Meetings ——————————————————— 141
- *Organizational Meetings* ———————————————— 143
- *Directors' Meetings* —————————————————— 143
- *Shareholders' Meetings* ————————————————— 144

7–2   Organizational Meetings ———————————————— 144
- *Business Transacted at Meetings* ———————————— 145

Incorporators' Organizational Meeting ———— 145
Directors' Organizational Meeting ———— 145
Location of the Meeting ———— 147
Calling the Meeting and Satisfying Quorum Requirements —— 147

7–3   Requirements of Directors' Meetings ———— 148
Annual, Special, and Regular Meetings ———— 149
Location of Meetings ———— 149
Notice ———— 150
Waiver of Notice ———— 151
Quorum and Voting ———— 152

7–4   Requirements of Shareholders' Meetings ———— 153
Annual and Special Meetings ———— 153
Location of Meetings ———— 154
Setting the Record Date ———— 154
Notice and Waiver of Notice ———— 155
Proxy ———— 158
Quorum ———— 159
Voting of Shares ———— 160

7–5   Other Procedures and Types of Meetings ———— 161
Distinction Between Call and Notice of Meetings ———— 161
Meetings by Conference Telephone ———— 162
Meetings of Committees of the Board ———— 162

7–6   Documenting Business Conducted at Meetings ———— 162
Resolutions ———— 164
Meeting Minutes ———— 168
Action Without a Meeting ———— 170

7–7   Organization of the Corporate Minute Book ———— 172

7–8   Practical Considerations ———— 173

CHAPTER 8   Amendments to Articles of Incorporation
and Bylaws ———— 179

8–1   Amendment to the Articles of Incorporation ———— 180
Board of Directors' Approval ———— 181
Limited Power of Board of Directors to Authorize Amendments 182
Shareholders' Approval ———— 182
Preparation and Filing of Articles of Amendment ———— 183
Amendment Prior to Issuance of Shares ———— 184

8–2   Postamendment Formalities ———— 184
Effectiveness of Amendment ———— 185
Postamendment Procedures ———— 185

8–3   Restated Articles of Incorporation ———— 186

8–4   Amendment to the Bylaws ———— 186

8–5   Practical Considerations ———— 188
Articles of Amendment ———— 188
Restated Articles of Incorporation ———— 189
Amendment to the Bylaws ———— 189

**CHAPTER 9   Qualification of Corporations in
                Foreign Jurisdictions** ———————————— **192**

9–1   Foreign Corporations ———————————————— 193
        Qualifying to Do Business ———————————— 193
        What Constitutes Doing Business ——————— 194

9–2   Certificate of Authority ——————————————— 196
        Application for Certificate of Authority ——— 196
        Filing Requirements ———————————————— 196
        Board of Directors' Approval ————————— 198
        Corporate Name ——————————————————— 200
        Registered Address and Agent ——————— 202

9–3   Postqualification Requirements ———————— 203
        Taxes and Annual Reports —————————— 203
        Amendment to the Certificate of Authority — 204
        Merger of the Foreign Corporation ————— 206
        Legal Advertising —————————————————— 206

9–4   Penalties for Failure to Qualify ——————— 207
9–5   Withdrawal of Authority ——————————————— 208
9–6   Revocation of Authority ——————————————— 210
9–7   Practical Considerations ——————————————— 211

CHAPTER 10   Financing the Corporation ——————— **215**

10–1   Capitalization of the Corporation ——————— 216
10–2   Types of Corporate Securities ————————— 217
        Equity Securities —————————————————— 218
        Debt Securities ——————————————————— 218
        Variations Between Equity and Debt ———— 219

10–3   Equity Securities ———————————————————— 221
        Authorized, Issued, and Outstanding Shares — 222
        Treasury Shares ——————————————————— 223
        Class and Series of Shares ————————— 224
        Par Value and Market Value of Shares —— 225
        Issuance of Share Certificates ——————— 227
        Consideration Paid for Shares ——————— 229

10–4   Common Stock ———————————————————— 231
        Voting Rights ———————————————————— 231
        Liquidation Rights ———————————————— 232
        Dividend Rights ——————————————————— 232
        Preemptive Rights ————————————————— 233

10–5   Preferred Stock ———————————————————— 234
        Voting Rights ———————————————————— 234
        Liquidation Rights ———————————————— 236
        Dividend Rights ——————————————————— 237
        Redemption Rights and Sinking Fund —— 238
        Conversion Rights ————————————————— 239
        Creation of Preferred Stock ————————— 240

10–6   Debt Securities _____ 241
    Secured and Unsecured Debt _____ 242
    Short-Term and Long-Term Debt _____ 243

10–7   Types of Debt Securities _____ 243
    Promissory Note _____ 243
    Bond _____ 244
    Debenture _____ 245
    Provisions of Debt Securities _____ 245
        Redemption _____ 245
        Conversion _____ 247
        Subordination _____ 247

10–8   Practical Considerations _____ 247

CHAPTER 11   Corporate Dividends and Distributions ____ 253

11–1   Dividends and Distributions _____ 254
    Authorization to Make Distributions _____ 254
    Corporation's Repurchase of Shares _____ 256

11–2   Sources of Funds for Distribution as Dividends ____ 256
    Corporation's Balance Sheet _____ 257
    Sources from Which Dividends May Be Declared ___ 259
    Restrictions on Payment _____ 260

11–3   Cash and Property Dividends _____ 260
    Right to Receive Dividends _____ 260
    Procedure for Payment _____ 261
    Accounting Procedures _____ 261
    Tax Implications _____ 262

11–4   Share Dividends _____ 262
    Procedure for Issuance _____ 263
    Accounting Procedures _____ 264
    Reasons for Paying Share Dividends _____ 264
    Tax Implications _____ 265

11–5   Stock Split _____ 265
    Procedure for Issuance _____ 266
    Accounting Procedures _____ 267
    Reasons for Effecting Stock Splits _____ 268
    Tax Implications _____ 268

11–6   Reverse Stock Split _____ 269
    Procedures _____ 269
    Accounting Procedures _____ 270
    Reasons for Effecting Reverse Stock Splits ___ 270

11–7   Practical Considerations _____ 271

CHAPTER 12   Securities Regulation _____ 276

12–1   Introduction to Securities Regulation _____ 277
    Laws Governing the Issuance of Securities ___ 278
    Uniform Securities Act _____ 280
    Commonly Used Definitions in the Securities Industry ___ 280

What Is a Security? — 281
Securities Markets — 283

12–2 Securities Act of 1933 — 283
Registration Statement — 284
Registration Process — 286
Exemptions from 1933 Act Registration — 288
Liability and Antifraud Provisions — 290

12–3 Securities Exchange Act of 1934 — 291
Securities and Exchange Commission — 291
Registration Under the 1934 Act — 292
Reporting and Disclosure Requirements — 293
Insider Short-Swing Profits — 295
Liability and Antifraud Provisions — 299

12–4 Blue-Sky Laws — 300
Registration Process — 301
Exemptions from Registration — 302
Antifraud Provisions and Enforcement — 303

12–5 Practical Considerations — 304

CHAPTER 13 Merger, Share Exchange, Consolidation, and Sale and Purchase of Stock and Assets — **308**

13–1 Corporate Structural Changes — 309
13–2 Merger, Share Exchange, and Consolidation — 310
Merger — 311
Short-Form Merger — 313
Share Exchange — 313
Consolidation — 314

13–3 Procedures for Merger, Share Exchange, and Consolidation — 315
Plan of Merger — 315
Plans of Share Exchange and Consolidation — 315
Directors' and Shareholders' Approval — 318
Statutory Filing Requirements — 321

13–4 Sale and Purchase of Stock — 323
Negotiating the Transaction — 323
Procedures — 324
Stock Purchase Agreement — 325

13–5 Sale and Purchase of Assets — 327
Negotiating the Transaction — 328
Procedures — 328
Bulk Transfer Law — 329
Asset Purchase Agreement — 330

13–6 Dissenting Shareholders' Rights — 333
13–7 Practical Considerations — 334

CHAPTER 14 Dissolution and Liquidation — **341**

14–1 Dissolution and Liquidation — 342
14–2 Voluntary Dissolution — 343

		Prior to Commencement of Business	343
		After Commencement of Business	344
14–3	Articles of Dissolution		346
		Board of Directors' Approval	347
		Shareholders' Approval	348
		Filing Requirements	349
14–4	Postdissolution Procedures and Requirements		351
		Winding Up and Liquidating	351
		Tax Considerations	352
		Revocation of Dissolution	353
14–5	Involuntary Dissolution		354
		Administrative Dissolution	355
		Judicial Dissolution	356
14–6	Practical Considerations		357

CHAPTER 15 Shareholders' Agreements — 362

15–1	Closely Held Corporations		363
15–2	Characteristics of a Shareholders' Agreement		364
15–3	Share Transfer Restrictions		370
		Protection of Shareholders' Interests	372
		Share Certificate Legend	372
15–4	Procedures for Selling Shares Under a Shareholders' Agreement		373
		Mandatory Obligation to Purchase and Sell	373
		Option to Purchase	374
15–5	Mechanisms for Pricing Shares		375
15–6	Practical Considerations		377

Appendix A	**Model Business Corporation Act (1984)**	**381**
Appendix B	**Uniform Partnership Act**	**405**
Appendix C	**Revised Uniform Limited Partnership Act (1985)**	**419**
Glossary		**435**
Index		**455**

CHAPTER 1   Sole Proprietorship

OUTLINE

1–1   Characteristics
1–2   Formation and Operation
        Registration of Name
        Regulatory Filings
1–3   Liability of the Sole Proprietorship
1–4   Taxation of the Sole Proprietorship
1–5   Termination of the Sole Proprietorship
1–6   Practical Considerations

APPLICATIONS

Harriet Johnson's dream has been to have her own antique shop someday. Now that she has taken an early retirement and received a substantial pay-out from her employer for doing so, her day has finally come. She has always known she wanted complete control over her business. She realizes that if she wants complete control, she must also assume all the risk.

Consideration of the following factors will help Harriet Johnson decide whether she should operate as a sole proprietorship, a general partnership, a limited partnership, or a corporation:

1. The amount of risk she is willing or able to assume.
2. The amount of control over managing the business she wants to maintain.
3. The proportion of income (or loss) of the business she is willing to tolerate.
4. The tax considerations of operating the business as a sole proprietorship.

As a paralegal, you will usually become involved with someone like Harriet Johnson only after she has decided to operate her business as a sole proprietorship. This chapter will help you identify the areas in which you can assist a sole proprietor in the organization and operation of a business.

OBJECTIVES

It is important to understand the different characteristics of the four types of business entities—the sole proprietorship, the general partnership, the limited partnership, and the corporation—and the ways in which they are organized and operated. Succeeding chapters will cover the general partnership, the limited partnership, and the corporation. After completing Chapter 1, which covers the sole proprietorship, you will be able to:

1. Define *sole proprietorship*.
2. Identify the characteristics of a sole proprietorship.
3. Determine when the sole proprietor is required to register the name of the business.

4. Describe the circumstances under which the sole proprietor may have to register with regulating authorities in order to operate the business.
5. Explain the extent to which liability may be incurred by the sole proprietor.
6. Explain how income and losses are treated for tax purposes.
7. Identify the events that would cause the sole proprietor to terminate the business.

1–1 Characteristics

The **sole proprietorship** is a form of business organization owned and managed by one individual. It is the simplest and oldest form of business organization. The significant distinction between the sole proprietorship and other business entities is that it is owned by one person. The ultimate responsibility for the operation, management, liability, and for all decisions affecting the business lies with the individual owning the business, or the **sole proprietor.** An example of a person operating a business as a sole proprietorship might be the enterprising teenager who delivers your newspaper, the industrious person who cleans your home every other week, or the creative individual who sells homemade gifts and crafts at local fairs.

Even though a sole proprietorship is owned and managed by one individual, the sole proprietor may hire employees for support in the operation of the business and may delegate authority to those employees. Any acts performed by an employee in the scope of his or her employment are the full responsibility of the employer. For example, suppose that while making a pizza delivery in the van owned by Mr. Pepe, the sole proprietor of Pepe's Pizza Parlor, Sam, the delivery boy, strikes a pedestrian. Because Sam was acting within the scope of his employment for Mr. Pepe, Mr. Pepe will be held liable and is personally responsible for Sam's actions. In addition, most courts have held that ownership of the vehicle is irrelevant. The sole proprietor is still liable.

Unlimited liability is one of the disadvantages of operating as a sole proprietor. This and other disadvantages, as well as the advantages of operating a sole proprietorship, are explained in this chapter. A summary of more significant advantages and disadvantages of the sole proprietorship is provided in Figure 1–1.

Figure 1–1   Advantages and Disadvantages of the Sole Proprietorship

Advantages of the Sole Proprietorship

- Ease of formation and termination.
- Flexibility in control and management.
- Sole possession of all profits.
- Freedom from sharing of financial information about the business.

Disadvantages of the Sole Proprietorship

- Unlimited liability for all debts and liabilities of the business.
- Limited access to capital for expanding (or starting) the business.
- Multiple talents required of owner.
- Termination on death of owner (instability and impermanence).

Because of its ease of formation, the sole proprietorship is the most common form of business entity. No formal filings must be made with any state or federal agency before a sole proprietor can do business; therefore, the cost and time involved in forming the sole proprietorship are insignificant. Laws governing sole proprietorships vary from state to state; however, there are some exceptions:

1. If the sole proprietor plans to do business under a name that does not include his or her surname, registration of the name to be used usually is required.
2. For some types of business, the sole proprietor may have to file an application for a sales tax license or other license.
3. The city or county in which the business will be located may require a local business permit or license.
4. If a special service mark or trademark will be used in connection with the business, the sole proprietor may want to protect it by registering it with a state or federal agency or both.

The ultimate responsibility for the success or failure of the business lies with the sole proprietor; hence, the business is *dependent* on the strengths and weaknesses of the sole proprietor. For example, Jonathan Smith, a carpenter for 30 years, would in all likelihood have a difficult time operating a retail clothing store. He may be unfamiliar with the latest clothing styles, be unaccustomed to dealing with others in the clothing business, and have little interest in operating a clothing store. Since Jonathan Smith's strength is carpentry, he would probably not be able to operate a profitable clothing business.

The personal nature of the sole proprietorship is evident in the way the reputation of the business depends on the honesty and integrity of its owner, the sole proprietor. The actions of an employee of a sole proprietorship may also positively or negatively affect the business's reputation. In addition, all sole proprietorships require the owners to possess many talents and skills. A sole proprietor must fill many roles, which may include those of manager, accountant, accounts payable and receivable clerk, receptionist, delivery person, and maintenance engineer. Whatever these roles are, however, the sole proprietor is also compelled to maintain a careful watch over all activities of the business, since he or she alone is responsible for all aspects of the business.

The availability of capital to expand or enhance the business may be limited. The owner's personal assets and the profit-making capability of the business are normally the only forms of security available to secure a loan from a bank or lending institution. This is an important *disadvantage* when the sole proprietor is relying on loans to fund expansion. Expansion of the business usually depends on the reinvestment of the earnings of the business. The inability of the sole proprietorship to obtain large amounts of capital will often prevent the growth of the business into a large enterprise.

Registration of Name

A sole proprietor may conduct business under a name other than his or her own, but state statutes generally require the sole proprietor to register the **fictitious name** (referred to as an **assumed name** in some states) with the secretary of state in the state in which the sole proprietor will be doing business. A **fictitious name registration,** an **affidavit of assumed name,** or a similar document must be filed if the sole proprietor intends to conduct business under a name that does not include his or her surname.

Consider the following example. Victoria Rogers owns and operates a dance studio, which she calls Rogers Dance Studio. She is not required to register this name as a fictitious name or an assumed name, because she is using her surname in the name of the business. If she used the name Tap Dance Studio, statutes in most states would require some form of registration. In Figure 1–2 is a fictitious name registration that Victoria Rogers would be required to file with the secretary of the commonwealth of Pennsylvania if she wanted to operate her business under the name Tap Dance Studio in Pennsylvania. The information provided to the secretary of the commonwealth of Pennsylvania in Figure 1–2 is similar to the information required by the statutes of most other states. You will find, however, that many states refer to the fictitious name registration as a "fictitious name statement."

Registration requirements vary from state to state. Most states, counties, or other local governments require some form of registration. Therefore, it is important to research both state and local statutes and regulations to determine the filing requirements, if any, in those jurisdictions. For example, suppose Harriet Johnson, the sole proprietor in our example at the beginning of this chapter, wants to sell antiques in Pulaski County, Arkansas, under the name Harriet's Antique Shop. A corporate paralegal will probably be assigned the task of researching the statutes of the state of Arkansas and of Pulaski County to determine the filing requirements of both of those jurisdictions.

If registration of the fictitious name is required, an inquiry to the governing jurisdiction should be made to determine whether the fictitious name is available for use by the sole proprietor. In general, a sole proprietor will *not be permitted* to use a name that is deceptively similar to the name of any corporation registered

Figure 1–2   Fictitious Name Registration

Filed with the Department of State on _____

_____

Fictitious Name Registration

In compliance with the requirements of 54 Pa. C.S. §311 (relating to registration), the undersigned, desiring to register a fictitious name under 54 Pa. C.S. Ch. 3 (relating to fictitious names), hereby states that:

1. The fictitious name is: TAP DANCE STUDIO.
2. The address, including street and number, of the principal place of business is 123 America Street, Pittsburgh, Pennsylvania 15222, Allegheny County.
3. A brief statement of the character or nature of the business is: Operation of dance studio to offer lessons in various forms of dance.
4. The name and address, including street and number, of the individual interested in the business is: Victoria Rogers, 234 First Street, Pittsburgh, Pennsylvania 15222, Allegheny County.
5. The applicant is familiar with the provisions of 54 Pa. C.S. §332 (relating to effect of registration) and understands that filing under the Fictitious Names Act does not create any exclusive or other right in the fictitious name.

The undersigned has caused this fictitious name registration to be executed this 24th day of January, 1994.

_____

Victoria Rogers

International Inventors Incorporated, East v. Martin Berger

In the action *International Inventors Incorporated, East v. Martin Berger*, 242 Pa. Super. 265, 363 A.2d 1262 (1976), International Inventors, a Virginia corporation, brought an action against an individual, Martin Berger, for an injunction barring him from using the corporation's name in Pennsylvania. The Court of Common Pleas, Allegheny County, granted an injunction, and Martin Berger appealed.

In a 1973 agreement, the plaintiff and defendant had agreed to form a corporation and to choose a corporate name containing the words "International Inventors." By agreement in 1975, both parties terminated their relationship, and they declared the 1973 agreement null and void. Before the effective date of the 1975 agreement to terminate the relationship, Martin Berger filed a fictitious name registration in accordance with the statutes of the commonwealth of Pennsylvania to do business under the name International Inventors. The secretary of the commonwealth of Pennsylvania had not precluded Berger's use of the name because the plaintiff had not registered to do business in Pennsylvania.

In June 1975, plaintiff International Inventors filed a complaint claiming that Berger, by conducting business under the name International Inventors, had appropriated its business name. The lower court issued an order enjoining Berger "from using the name International Inventors, International Inventor's, International Inventors Incorporated, International Inventors Incorporated, East, or other names similar to that of the Plaintiff."

On appeal, the Superior Court of Pennsylvania reversed the lower court's decision. The plaintiff, International Inventors Incorporated, East, had failed to obtain a certificate of authority to conduct business in the commonwealth of Pennsylvania before the defendant, Martin Berger, filed his fictitious name registration. Therefore, the Superior Court held, the defendant was entitled to use the name International Inventors for his business in Pennsylvania.

---

in the state. However, many jurisdictions permit the registration of similar names by sole proprietorships or by general partnerships. You must review state and local statutes and regulations before advising a client whether the name he or she has selected is available for use in a particular jurisdiction. Again, and most importantly, the regulations vary from state to state *and* from county to county regarding registration and the procedure for determining name availability. For example, most states require registration with the state, but in California, the sole proprietor need only register with the county.

The importance of timely and proper filing of a fictitious name registration is emphasized in the *Legal Links* in this chapter.

Several states require the official publication of a notice by the sole proprietor of the filing of a fictitious name application or of his or her intention to file one. The notice is usually required to be placed in a newspaper of general circulation in the county in which the principal office or place of business of the sole proprietorship is located. In Figure 1–3 is an example of a notice that Victoria Rogers would be required to place if she wanted to do business under the fictitious name Tap Dance Studio.

P**ARALEGALERT!**

In most states, the availability of a business name to be used by a sole proprietor can be determined by calling the state's corporation division. It is usually the paralegal's responsibility to call the appropriate state agency to determine whether the name is available for use. Beware: telephone confirmation that the name is available for use is, in most cases, not a guarantee that the name will be available when the fictitious name registration is filed.

Figure 1–3   Notice for Publication by a Sole Proprietor upon Filing a Fictitious Name Registration

---

Notice

Notice is hereby given that an application for registration of a fictitious name has been filed under the Fictitious Names Act of the Commonwealth of Pennsylvania for the conduct of business under the fictitious name of **Tap Dance Studio** with its place of business at 123 America Street, Pittsburgh, Pennsylvania. The name and address of the person party to the registration is: Victoria Rogers, 234 First Street, Pittsburgh, Pennsylvania.

Regulatory Filings

Depending on the nature of the business being conducted, the sole proprietor may be required to make certain other filings with federal, state, or local agencies. For example, a lawyer is required to obtain a license from the State Bar of the state in which he or she is practicing. The lawyer may also have employees for whom he or she is required to withhold federal, state, and local income taxes; make deposits of taxes withheld; and contribute under state unemployment compensation regulations. Quarterly and final tax reports must also be filed with the Internal Revenue Service and the departments of revenue of the state and the city or county in which the sole proprietorship employs individuals. In addition, any number of other possible filings may be required by local, state, and federal agencies.

One form that a sole proprietor may need to file is Internal Revenue Service Form SS-4, Application for Employer Identification Number. This form is used to apply for an **employer identification number,** or **EIN,** a nine-digit number assigned to a sole proprietorship for filing and reporting purposes. The sole proprietor who pays wages to one or more employees must apply for an EIN and use the EIN on any return, statement, or other document filed with the IRS. An applicant will receive an EIN by mail approximately four to five weeks after the IRS receives the application. In addition, an EIN is also assigned to partnerships, corporations, estates, trusts, and other entities upon filing Form SS-4. Figure 1–4 is a copy of IRS Form SS-4, which is used by all entities when applying for an EIN.

An applicant may also apply for an EIN by telephone. The IRS will instantly assign an EIN, which the applicant can use immediately to file a return or make a federal tax deposit. Only certain authorized individuals may request an EIN by telephone. For example, in the case of a sole proprietorship, the individual himself or herself must initiate the telephone call to request the EIN and should have a Form SS-4 completed before making the telephone call.

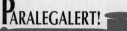

PARALEGALERT!

A paralegal is very often given the task of determining the filing requirements, if any, for a sole proprietor operating a specific business. This is where the paralegal's organizational and creative skills will prove invaluable. The paralegal will be assigned this task because the attorney responsible for this client may also be unfamiliar with local, state, and federal regulating authorities.

PARALEGALERT!

The corporate paralegal may be asked to prepare and file Form SS-4 or to instruct the sole proprietor on the procedures for obtaining an EIN by telephone. In some cases, the sole proprietor's accountant will take responsibility for obtaining the EIN.

Figure 1–4   Form SS-4, Application for Employer Identification Number

| Form **SS-4** (Rev. December 1993) Department of the Treasury Internal Revenue Service | **Application for Employer Identification Number** (For use by employers, corporations, partnerships, trusts, estates, churches, government agencies, certain individuals, and others. See instructions.) | EIN OMB No. 1545-0003 Expires 12-31-96 |

Please type or print clearly.

1   Name of applicant (Legal name) (See instructions.)

2   Trade name of business, if different from name in line 1 | 3   Executor, trustee, "care of" name

4a   Mailing address (street address) (room, apt., or suite no.) | 5a   Business address, if different from address in lines 4a and 4b

4b   City, state, and ZIP code | 5b   City, state, and ZIP code

6   County and state where principal business is located

7   Name of principal officer, general partner, grantor, owner, or trustor—SSN required (See instructions.) ▶

8a   Type of entity (Check only one box.) (See instructions.)
☐ Sole Proprietor (SSN)   ☐ Estate (SSN of decedent)   ☐ Trust
☐ REMIC   ☐ Personal service corp.   ☐ Plan administrator-SSN   ☐ Partnership
☐ State/local government   ☐ National guard   ☐ Other corporation (specify)   ☐ Farmers' cooperative
☐ Other nonprofit organization (specify)   ☐ Federal government/military   ☐ Church or church controlled organization
☐ Other (specify) ▶   (enter GEN if applicable)

8b   If a corporation, name the state or foreign country (if applicable) where incorporated ▶ | State | Foreign country

9   Reason for applying (Check only one box.)
☐ Started new business (specify) ▶   ☐ Changed type of organization (specify) ▶
☐ Hired employees   ☐ Purchased going business
☐ Created a pension plan (specify type) ▶   ☐ Created a trust (specify) ▶
☐ Banking purpose (specify) ▶   ☐ Other (specify) ▶

10   Date business started or acquired (Mo., day, year) (See instructions.) | 11   Enter closing month of accounting year. (See instructions.)

12   First date wages or annuities were paid or will be paid (Mo., day, year). **Note:** *If applicant is a withholding agent, enter date income will first be paid to nonresident alien. (Mo., day, year)* . . . . ▶

13   Enter highest number of employees expected in the next 12 months. **Note:** *If the applicant does not expect to have any employees during the period, enter "0."* . . . . ▶ | Nonagricultural | Agricultural | Household

14   Principal activity (See instructions.) ▶

15   Is the principal business activity manufacturing? . . . . ☐ Yes ☐ No
If "Yes," principal product and raw material used ▶

16   To whom are most of the products or services sold? Please check the appropriate box.   ☐ Business (wholesale)
☐ Public (retail)   ☐ Other (specify) ▶   ☐ N/A

17a   Has the applicant ever applied for an identification number for this or any other business? . . . . ☐ Yes ☐ No
Note: *If "Yes," please complete lines 17b and 17c.*

17b   If you checked the "Yes" box in line 17a, give applicant's legal name and trade name, if different than name shown on prior application.
Legal name ▶   Trade name ▶

17c   Enter approximate date, city, and state where the application was filed and the previous employer identification number if known.
Approximate date when filed (Mo., day, year) | City and state where filed | Previous EIN

Under penalties of perjury, I declare that I have examined this application, and to the best of my knowledge and belief, it is true, correct, and complete. | Business telephone number (include area code)

Name and title (Please type or print clearly.) ▶

Signature ▶   Date ▶

Note: *Do not write below this line.   For official use only.*

Please leave blank ▶ | Geo. | Ind. | Class | Size | Reason for applying

For Paperwork Reduction Act Notice, see attached instructions.   Cat. No. 16055N   Form **SS-4** (Rev. 12-93)

1–3   Liability of the Sole Proprietorship

The biggest disadvantage of operating a business as a sole proprietorship is that a sole proprietor is **personally liable** *for all losses that the business incurs.* Unlike the shareholder of a corporation or a limited partner in a limited partnership, where the extent of financial risk is limited to the total investment made in the business, the sole proprietor places personal assets at risk, including his or her home, car, savings, and bank accounts. Because personal assets must be available to satisfy any debts or losses of a sole proprietorship, an individual may elect to incorporate the business to limit this risk.

A sole proprietor may offset the extent to which his or her personal assets are at risk by purchasing insurance to cover the cost of any unforeseen liabilities. However, the cost of such insurance often makes this an unattractive alternative.

1–4 Taxation of the Sole Proprietorship

The sole proprietorship is *not* a separate taxpaying entity. In other words, the sole proprietorship itself is a **nontaxed entity.** All revenues and expenses of the business are reported by the sole proprietor on a special schedule in his or her personal tax return. Therefore, the sole proprietor *personally* will pay tax on the income and will deduct any losses of the business.

The sole proprietorship is, however, a tax-reporting entity. It is required to report employees' income and the amount of tax withheld from each employee's pay to the Internal Revenue Service and to any other state or local taxing authority.

All business income of the sole proprietorship is combined with other income of the sole proprietor, and the individual income tax rates are applied. Any loss that the business incurs can be applied to offset any other income of the sole proprietor, generally resulting in a tax savings to the sole proprietor. It may or may not be advantageous for the sole proprietor to be taxed at the individual tax rates, rather than to incorporate the business and pay tax at the corporate income tax level.

Just as the sole proprietor is required to deposit with the IRS any income tax withheld from employees' pay, he or she must also make prepayments of his or her own income tax. The sole proprietor must generally make estimated federal income tax payments each quarter. State and local governments that impose income taxes also generally require a sole proprietor to estimate his or her income and make deposits with the appropriate taxing authority.

1–5 Termination of the Sole Proprietorship

A sole proprietorship will terminate upon the death or bankruptcy of the sole proprietor. In addition, a sole proprietor may decide at any time on a **voluntary termination** or sale of the business. Just as no formal filings are required by any state or federal agency when a sole proprietor begins a business, *no filings* are required when the sole proprietor decides to terminate or sell the business. But, again, there may be exceptions, depending on the type of business the sole proprietor operates. For example, the sale to another individual or to a partnership or corporation of a license to sell liquor may require the approval of the state's liquor licensing authority.

The sale of the business is simple in that the sole proprietor does not need the approval of partners or other shareholders as in a partnership or a corporation. The sole proprietor is free to sell the business whenever and to whomever he or she desires.

The sole proprietor may will his business to a family member, a business associate, or an employee, but there is no guarantee that, upon death of the sole proprietor, the beneficiary will continue operating the business. In fact, the business will most likely be **liquidated;** that is, the assets will be sold, all liabilities and bills will be satisfied, and any remaining cash or property will be delivered to the beneficiary under the sole proprietor's will. Even if the business continues to operate, under a new owner it is a different sole proprietorship, or the new owner may decide to use another form of business organization.

1–6 Practical Considerations

Your involvement in the organization and operation of a sole proprietorship will probably not be extensive. One of the significant advantages of operating a business as a sole proprietorship is its ease of formation. This advantage is one of the main reasons an individual operates a business as a sole proprietorship: it requires very little initial organizational activity. However, there are tasks that can be performed by the paralegal, including:

- Reviewing the state and local statutes and determining requirements for registering a fictitious name with the state or county where the sole proprietor is doing business
- Preparing and filing a fictitious name registration or assumed name affidavit with the appropriate state and county agencies
- Determining whether publication of the fictitious name registration is required
- Filing Form SS-4, Application for Employer Identification Number, with the IRS
- Determining the requirements of federal, state, and local agencies for registering or licensing a particular business to be conducted by the sole proprietor

SUMMARY

1–1

The sole proprietorship is owned and managed by one individual, the sole proprietor. The sole proprietor is responsible for the operation, management, and liability of the business; for all decisions affecting the business; and for all acts performed by employees on behalf of the business.

1–2

Even though no formal filings are required before the sole proprietor begins doing business, there are some exceptions. The sole proprietor may be required to register the name of the business if it does not include his or her surname. The type of business in which the sole proprietor will engage may require certain other filings with federal, state, or local agencies. The hiring of one or more employees will require the sole proprietor to apply for a federal employer identification number and to deposit income tax withheld from any employee's pay. A sole proprietor may be at a disadvantage in having to rely only on his or her own talents, business strengths, and profit-making capability.

1–3

All debts and losses that a business incurs are the full responsibility of the sole proprietor, whose personal assets are at risk to satisfy any of the debts and losses. This unlimited liability is the biggest disadvantage of operating a business as a sole proprietorship.

1–4

All revenues and expenses of the business are reported by the sole proprietor on his or her personal tax return, because the sole proprietorship is not a separate tax-paying entity.

1–5

The sole proprietorship will terminate upon the death or bankruptcy of the sole proprietor or upon his or her voluntary termination or sale of the business. Even if the business is willed to a beneficiary and the business continues to operate, it will do so as a different business entity from that of the deceased sole proprietor. A sole proprietor is free to sell the business at any time and to whomever he or she chooses.

1–6

Because of the ease of formation of a sole proprietorship, the owner usually takes it upon himself or herself to apply for an employer identification number or file a fictitious name registration. Therefore, your involvement in the organization of a sole proprietorship will usually be minimal.

REVIEW GUIDE

Key Terms

Before proceeding, review the key terms listed below to be sure you understand each one. If necessary, read over the corresponding section of the chapter. When you are ready to test your understanding, answer the review questions.

sole proprietorship (p. 2)
sole proprietor (p. 2)
fictitious name (p. 3)
assumed name (p. 3)
fictitious name registration (p. 3)
affidavit of assumed name (p. 3)
employer identification number (p. 6)
EIN (p. 6)
personally liable (p. 7)
nontaxed entity (p. 8)
voluntary termination (p. 8)
liquidated (p. 8)

Questions for Review and Discussion

1. Define *sole proprietor*.
2. Of the numerous characteristics of a sole proprietorship discussed in this chapter, list and discuss three.
3. Under what circumstances would a sole proprietor be required to file a fictitious name registration or an assumed name affidavit?
4. Describe a situation in which a sole proprietor may be required to apply for an employer identification number.
5. What is the biggest disadvantage of operating a business as a sole proprietorship?
6. How is tax paid on the income generated by a sole proprietorship?
7. What must a sole proprietor do if he decides to terminate his business voluntarily?
8. Outline the advantages and disadvantages of operating a business as a sole proprietorship.

Activities

1. Select a business you would like to operate, and determine the county and state requirements for registering such a business.
2. For the business that you selected in Activity 1, determine whether the business name you selected is available for use in the state in which you will be doing business.
3. Joseph Johnson, a sole proprietor, hires an employee to deliver groceries to customers. The employee will use Mr. Johnson's truck. Discuss the liability Mr. Johnson may incur if his employee is involved in an accident while making a delivery.

CHAPTER 2   General Partnership

OUTLINE

2–1   Characteristics
2–2   Formation and Operation
    The Partnership Agreement
    Registration of Name
    Regulatory Filings
    Management of the Partnership
2–3   Ownership of Partnership Property
2–4   Partners' Liability
    Liability of Incoming and Terminating Partners
    Criminal Activity
2–5   Taxation of the Partners
2–6   Distribution of Profits and Losses
2–7   Termination of the General Partnership
2–8   Practical Considerations

APPLICATIONS

Harriet Johnson has successfully operated her antique shop out of a side-street storefront for three years now. She believes that with greater exposure to customer traffic, she could double her business. But she realizes that she needs a partner or several partners who can supply the additional skills and capital she needs to expand the business. Harriet Johnson needs a partner or partners to share the risk of doing business, provide additional management skills, and ultimately share the profits of the business.

The formation and operation of a general partnership is a bit more complex than the formation and operation of a sole proprietorship. Nevertheless, Ms. Johnson decides to form a partnership with two of her close friends who are interested in participating in the business. We want to be sure that Ms. Johnson is aware of a partner's rights and responsibilities so that she and her business associates may avoid unnecessary problems or disagreements in the future.

OBJECTIVES

As you work through this chapter, you will recognize greater complexity in the characteristics of the general partnership than in those of the sole proprietorship. After completing Chapter 2, which covers the general partnership, you will be able to:

1. Define *general partnership*.
2. Identify the characteristics of a general partnership.
3. Describe the role of the Uniform Partnership Act in governing the manner in which partnerships operate.
4. List the issues generally covered by a partnership agreement.

5. Determine when the partners of a general partnership are required to register the name of the business.
6. Identify the circumstances under which partners may have to register with regulating authorities in order to operate the business.
7. Describe the partners' involvement in managing the business.
8. Explain the extent to which liability is incurred by a partner of the general partnership.
9. Explain how income and losses incurred by the partnership are treated for tax purposes.
10. Explain what is meant by the profit/loss-sharing scheme of a general partnership.
11. Distinguish between the dissolution and the winding up of the business of a partnership.

2–1 Characteristics

The **general partnership** is a form of business organization owned and managed by two or more persons, or **partners.** It is similar in many ways to the sole proprietorship: the partners are taxed individually on the profits and losses of the partnership; the partners equally share the ultimate responsibility for the operation and management of the business, unless (as you will see later in this chapter) there is an agreement by the partners to the contrary or a managing committee is selected to operate the partnership; and the partnership is dissolved upon the death of a partner. Another characteristic of a general partnership, similar to one of a sole proprietorship, is that *each partner is personally liable for all losses that the partnership incurs.* This is an important disadvantage of a general partnership. See Figure 2–1 for a list of the more significant advantages and disadvantages of the general partnership. Obviously, this is not an all-inclusive list, but it indicates the major issues to consider when forming a general partnership.

The characteristic that distinguishes the general partnership from the sole proprietorship is *the partnership agreement,* which governs the relationship between the partners and the manner in which the partnership conducts its business. The agreement may be written or oral. A formal, written agreement is not always needed, but a written agreement will clarify and provide evidence of the partners' intentions if a dispute arises in the future.

Figure 2–1 Advantages and Disadvantages of the General Partnership

Advantages of the General Partnership

- Relative ease and low cost of formation
- Enhanced access to capital for expanding (or starting) the business.
- Use of the managerial and business skills of all partners.
- Freedom from taxation as an organization.

Disadvantages of the General Partnership

- Unlimited liability of each partner for all debts and liabilities of the partnership.
- Dissolution upon the death, bankruptcy, or unlawful act of a partner.
- Possible disagreements between partners.

The existence of a partnership may be implied or express. If it is an express partnership, the partners' agreement will be either written or oral. For an implied partnership to exist, specific elements must exist: joint interest, common investment, and sharing in the profits, losses, and management of the partnership.

Even without a written or an oral agreement, which would evidence an **express partnership,** a partnership may legally exist. The existence of a partnership may be implied by the acts of the partners and evidence of their intent to form the partnership. If an express agreement (written or oral) does not exist, there may be an **implied partnership** if all the following elements exist:

1. The partners share a joint interest in the business.
2. The partners make a common investment in the business.
3. The partners share in the profits and losses of the business.
4. The partners share in the management of the business.

The **Uniform Partnership Act** (this act will be referred to as the **UPA**) is a model for statutes governing partnerships. The preparation of a uniform law governing partnerships was commissioned by the National Conference of Commissioners on Uniform State Laws in 1902. By 1914 the UPA was completed. It promoted consistency in state partnership laws. The National Conference of Commissioners first modified the 1914 version of the UPA in 1992, and only Montana and Wyoming have adopted this version. The UPA was further modified in 1994, and to date, no states have adopted the 1994 version. It is anticipated that in the coming years, states will begin to adopt the 1994 version. The 1914 version of the UPA has been adopted in every state except Louisiana, and the 1992 version has been adopted by Montana and Wyoming. Therefore, because of the similarities between the 1914 version of the UPA and the laws of the states governing partnerships, we will refer to the 1914 version of the UPA in our discussion. The full text of the 1914 version of the UPA is reproduced in Appendix B.

In the eyes of the law, a partnership exists if it has all the elements contained in the definition of a partnership. The UPA defines a partnership and provides rules for determining whether a partnership exists. Section 6(1) of the UPA defines a partnership as "an association of two or more persons to carry on as co-owners a business for profit." Specific aspects of this definition deserve discussion. First, a partnership requires "an association," which implies the voluntary association of persons who want to become members of the partnership. No person can become a partner without his or her consent. In addition, according to Section 18(g) of the UPA, "no person can become a member of a partnership without the consent of all the partners."

Second, a partnership requires the association "of two or more persons." The term **persons,** defined in Section 2 of the UPA, includes "individuals, partnerships, corporations, and other associations." Therefore, not only individuals, but corporations, associations, or other partnerships, can be members of a partnership. The power of a corporation to become a member of a partnership is, however, governed by state corporate statutes and by the corporation's articles of incorporation—not by partnership law.

Third, the criterion that the partners be "co-owners" distinguishes the partners from employees, agents, or other representatives acting on behalf of the partnership, none of whom share in the profits or the control of management of the partnership. The co-owners of a partnership must share in the profits (or losses) *and* must share control or management of the partnership. Section 7(2) of the UPA provides that "joint tenancy, tenancy in common, tenancy by the entireties, joint property, common property, or part ownership does not of itself establish a partnership, whether such co-owners do or do not share any profits made by the use of the property." For example, Mary and Joe Farmer, sister and brother, inherit land on the death of their father. For 20 years Mr. Farmer used this land to grow corn, which he sold to local farmers for their cattle. Joint ownership of this land by Mary and Joe on the death of their father does not make them partners. To be partners they must also satisfy the other elements of a partnership discussed in this section.

Fourth, the "business for profit" element of the definition of a partnership excludes unions, fraternal clubs, and other nonprofit organizations and associations from being treated as a partnership. To qualify as a partnership, an association of two or more persons must be organized with an expectation of enjoying a profit. However, the failure to earn a profit does not extinguish the existence of a partnership. The partnership must merely be organized to expect a profit.

In summary, a partnership exists if the following essential elements are present:

- An association of two or more persons.
- The intent to carry on a business.
- The sharing of profits (or losses) by the partners.
- Joint control of management by the partners.
- The expectation of enjoying a profit.

PARALEGALERT!

Persons is defined in the Uniform Partnership Act to include "individuals, partnerships, corporations, and other associations." Therefore, not only individuals, but corporations, associations, and even other partnerships, can be partners in a partnership.

2–2 Formation and Operation

Except that a sole proprietorship has one owner and a general partnership has two or more owners, the formation of a general partnership is almost indistinguishable from that of a sole proprietorship. One distinction is the general partnership's most important element: the **general partnership agreement.** In addition, some states require the filing of a partnership certificate with the office of the secretary of state. Usually the certificate must include the name of the partnership, the general nature of the business, and the names and residence addresses of all the partners. Requirements for such filings will be discussed in greater detail later in this chapter.

The requirements outlined in Section 1–2 in relation to the formation of a sole proprietorship apply also to a general partnership. That is, a general partnership may be required to file a fictitious name registration or an assumed name affidavit and to make other regulatory filings. Situations requiring such filings will also be discussed in greater detail later in this chapter.

The Partnership Agreement

As we have already discussed, the agreement between the parties may be written or oral. Usually, when persons form a partnership, it is because they have made a conscious decision to carry on a business together. But as circumstances change and business problems arise, the partners often find it difficult to work amicably. Therefore, you can imagine the importance of entering into a *written* agreement when the partners are rational and reasonable and before disputes occur. However, partnerships may be formed with an oral agreement.

PARALEGALERT!

When drafting the partnership agreement, you need not reinvent the wheel. You are not the first person to be given the task of drafting a partnership agreement. Form books, collections of sample agreements, will prove helpful in drafting the partnership agreement. Such books also contain sample paragraphs or provisions that may apply to particular points that you know must be included in your agreement.

The partnership agreement should contain all the provisions needed to carry on the management, operation, and liquidation of the partnership. Although no two agreements will be identical in all respects, there are several major issues and points that should be covered in a general partnership agreement. Generally, the paralegal will be asked to prepare the initial draft of the general partnership agreement. The best place to start is with a checklist of the issues to be covered in the agreement. Figure 2–2 is a list of the major issues and points that should be covered in an agreement. Figure 2–3 is an example of a simple general partnership agreement that incorporates most of the issues identified in Figure 2–2.

Registration of Name

State statutes generally provide that if the surnames of all the partners are not included in the name of the business, the partners must register the name of the business as a **fictitious name** or an **assumed name.** A fictitious name registration, a fictitious business name statement, an affidavit of assumed name, or a similar document must be filed if the partners will conduct business under a name that does not include the surnames of all the partners. For example, Andrew Adams, Robert Bianco, and Christopher Care own and operate a partnership for the preparation of tax returns and call their business Adams, Bianco, and Care Returns. They are not required to register this name as a fictitious name or an assumed name, because their surnames are included in the name of the business. If they operated the business under the name Tax Return Associates, state statutes would require some form of registration similar to that shown in Figure 1–2 in Chapter 1. It is important to mention that, in some jurisdictions, a fictitious name registration may *not* be required if a certificate of partnership is filed or recorded with the state or the county. You will need to check the state statutes to determine the filing requirements in a particular jurisdiction. The circumstances under which a certificate of partnership must be filed will be discussed in the next subsection.

Figure 2–2 Major Issues and Points in a General Partnership Agreement (Checklist)

____ Name of the partnership and nature of the business to be conducted.

____ Names and addresses of the partners.

____ Duration of the partnership.

____ Location(s) in which the partnership will conduct its business.

____ Initial capital contributions of the partners and valuation of any property contributed by each partner; specific identification of partnership property.

____ Obligation of the partners to make additional contributions to the partnership, including procedures for changes in capital (withdrawals and additions).

____ Scope of partners' authority in the partnership and partners' ability to bind the partnership.

____ Financial and accounting matters, including fiscal year, accounting method, compensation of partners.

____ Method for admitting new partners.

____ Method for distributing partnership profits and capital.

____ Method for dissolving the partnership, including special circumstances that will cause a dissolution of the partnership.

____ Provision for method of settling disputes that may arise.

Figure 2–3   General Partnership Agreement

General Partnership Agreement
of
ABC Property Associates

This General Partnership Agreement (the "Agreement") is made and entered into this _____ day of _____, 199__, by and among the persons who have executed this Agreement on the signature page hereof and all other persons who hereafter become a party hereto by executing an addendum to this Agreement (referred to collectively as the "Partners" and each individually as a "Partner").

Recitals

WHEREAS, the parties hereto desire to form a partnership (the "Partnership") to purchase, develop, and lease certain real property located in Alabama County, Anystate (the "Property");

NOW, THEREFORE, in consideration of the mutual covenants herein contained and intending to be legally bound hereby, the Partners hereby agree as follows:

Name, Place of Business, and Purpose

1.1. The activities and business of the Partnership shall be conducted under the name of ABC PROPERTY ASSOCIATES.

1.2. The principal office of the Partnership shall be 123 America Drive, Alabama County, Anystate, or at such other places within or without the state as the Partners may determine.

1.3. The purpose of the Partnership shall be to acquire, develop, lease, own, and sell the Property; to enter into agreements of purchase, lease, and sale and other undertakings as may be related to the Property; to obtain such loans, make such pledges or security assignments, or to enter into such other financing or refinancing arrangements or rearrangements as may be necessary or desirable in carrying out any or all of the foregoing purposes; and to carry on such activities as may be necessary or incidental to the foregoing purposes.

Term of the Partnership

2.1. The term of the Partnership shall begin on the date hereof and shall continue until terminated as specifically provided in this Agreement.

Contributions to the Partnership

3.1. The Partners shall make cash contributions from time to time to the capital of the Partnership in accordance with the respective percentages set forth in Section 4.3.

3.2. If any Partner makes a disproportionate advance of any funds to or for the account of the Partnership in excess of his or her percentage interest in the Partnership, such advance, in the absence of a written agreement of the Partners to the contrary, shall be considered a loan to the Partnership and shall not result in an increase in the percentage interest of such Partner in the Partnership.

3.3. A capital account shall be maintained for each Partner, reflecting his or her capital contributions, allocation of net income or losses, withdrawals, and all other appropriate adjustments.

Profits and Losses and Drawings by the Partners

4.1. The net income and losses of the Partnership shall be determined in accordance with the cash receipts and disbursements method of accounting used by the Partnership for federal income tax purposes.

continued

Figure 2–3, continued

4.2. Drawings of income shall be made by each Partner from Partnership funds in such amounts and at such times as all the Partners shall agree upon.

4.3. The net income or losses of the Partnership shall be allocable to the Partners in the proportions set forth here:

James Bond	25%
Karen Ellison	25%
Diane Hastings	30%
Suzanne Southwick	20%

Partnership Property

5.1. All right, title, and interest to real or personal property acquired by the Partnership, including all improvements placed or located on such property, and all rents, issues, and profits arising therefrom, shall be owned by the Partnership.

Fiscal Matters

6.1. Proper and complete books and records shall be kept with reference to all Partnership transactions and property, and each Partner shall at all reasonable times during business hours have access thereto. The books shall be kept by a cash receipts and disbursements method of accounting. The books and records of the Partnership shall be reviewed annually at the expense of the Partnership by an accountant selected by the Partnership, who shall prepare and deliver to the Partnership, for filing, appropriate partnership income tax returns and such other information as may be necessary to enable each Partner to file his or her personal federal, state, and local tax returns.

Management of the Partnership

7.1. All material Partnership decisions, including, without limitation, those specified in Section 7.2, shall be made jointly unless such authority is otherwise delegated by one Partner to the others in a particular instance.

7.2 No Partner, without the consent of the other Partners, may:

(i)   Do any act in contravention of this Agreement;
(ii) Do any act that would make it impossible to carry on the business of the Partnership;
(iii) Affiliate, employ, or terminate professional or nonprofessional personnel of the Partnership;
(iv) Possess Partnership property or assign the right of the Partnership or the Partners in specific Partnership property for other than a Partnership purpose;
(v)   Make, execute, or deliver any general assignments for the benefit of creditors;
(vi) Assign, transfer, pledge, compromise, or release any claim of the Partnership except for full payment;
(vii) Make, execute, or deliver any deed, long-term lease, or contract to sell all or substantially all of the Partnership property;
(viii) Make, execute, or deliver for the Partnership any note, bond, mortgage, deed of trust, guaranty, indemnity bond, or surety bond if such document creates any personal liability for any Partner other than that personal liability to which the Partner may have agreed in writing;
(ix) Make any expenditures or disbursement in excess of $ _____ ;
(x)   Borrow monies to the extent such borrowing would cause the aggregate amount of indebtedness to exceed $ _____ ; and
(xi) Purchase or acquire real property.

Figure 2–3, continued

7.3. An account or accounts in the name of the Partnership may be maintained in such bank or banks as the Partnership may select from time to time, and checks drawn thereon may be signed on behalf of the Partnership by any two Partners, except as provided in Section 7.2(ix).

7.4. No salaries or other compensation shall be paid to the Partners.

Dissolution and Liquidation

8.1. The Partnership shall be dissolved upon the occurrence of any of the following:
 (a) The mutual consent of the Partners; or
 (b) The sale, abandonment, or disposal by the Partnership of all or substantially all of its assets; or
 (c) The entry of a final judgment, order, or decree of a court of competent jurisdiction adjudicating the Partnership to be a bankrupt; or
 (d) The bankruptcy of a Partner; or
 (e) The death of a Partner.

8.2. Upon the dissolution of the Partnership, the Partner charged with winding up the Partnership affairs shall proceed to liquidate its assets, wind up its affairs, and apply and distribute the proceeds, after debts and expenses and subject to reasonable reserves, to the Partners or their personal representatives in cash according to their respective percentage interests in the Partnership.

Miscellaneous

9.1. All notices, statements, or other documents required or contemplated by this Agreement shall be in writing and shall either be personally delivered to the person entitled thereto or mailed, postage prepaid, to such person at his or her last known mailing address.

9.2. This Agreement shall be interpreted and construed in accordance with the laws of the State of Anystate.

9.3. The Partners agree that they will execute any further documents or instruments and perform any acts that are or may become necessary to effectuate and to carry on the Partnership created by this Agreement.

9.4. This Agreement may be executed in any number of counterparts, each of which may be executed by one or more of the Partners, and all such counterparts when executed and delivered shall together constitute one and the same instrument.

IN WITNESS WHEREOF, the parties hereto have executed this Agreement on the day and year first above written.

Witnesses: *Partners:*

_____   _____
                                                   James Bond

_____   _____
                                                   Karen Ellison

_____   _____
                                                   Diane Hastings

_____   _____
                                                   Suzanne Southwick

Regulatory Filings

As with a sole proprietorship, a general partnership may be required to make certain filings with federal, state, or local agencies because of the nature of the business conducted by the partnership. For example, partners who form a general partnership to operate a liquor store will be required to register with the state's liquor licensing agency.

A certificate of partnership may be required to be filed with the state and the county or counties where the partnership is doing business. To determine if such a filing is required, you must review the statutes of the state in which the general partnership intends to do business. The following are examples of some state requirements for filing a certificate:

1. Minnesota statutes require a general partnership to file with the Secretary of State a certificate setting forth the names of the partners, unless the names appear in the partnership's name.
2. Nebraska statutes require the partners to record a certificate in the office of the county clerk of the county where the place of business is located. The certificate must be signed by all the partners and must show the name of the partnership, the general nature of the business, the principal place of doing business, and the full names and residence addresses of each partner.
3. New York statutes permit no persons to carry on or transact business as members of a partnership unless they file, in the office of the clerk of the county or counties where business is to be transacted, a certificate executed and acknowledged by all the partners. The certificate must set forth the name and address of the partnership, the names and residence addresses of all partners, and the ages of any infant partners (those who are minors).

Figure 2–4 is an example of a certificate that a general partnership would have to file to do business in the state of Minnesota, unless the surnames of all the members of the partnership were included in the name of the partnership.

It is important to emphasize that after you have determined the county and state in which the partnership will do business, *you should always check the state statutes to determine the filing requirements in that particular state.* Filing requirements are different in virtually every one of the states. Complying with statutes and regulations in some states is cumbersome, some states' requirements are simple, and some states have no criteria at all. Because of the diversity of filing requirements, it is not feasible to list every state's requirements here. It is important to check the state statutes to determine the filing requirements.

For tax purposes, the partnership must apply for an employer identification number with the Internal Revenue Service. Taxes will be discussed in detail later in this chapter.

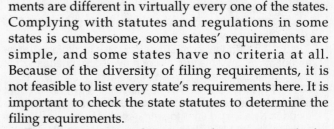

PARALEGALERT!

Once you know the state in which the partnership will be doing business, you should look to that state's statutes and regulations to determine the filing requirements, if any, in that state.

Management of the Partnership

Unless another arrangement is agreed on and spelled out in the partnership agreement, all the partners have equal voices in the management of the business, regardless of their proportionate shares of interest in the partnership. Thus, each partner has one vote on any matter concerning the partnership. For example, if one partner contributes 75 percent of the capital of the partnership and five other partners each contribute 5 percent of the capital of the partnership, each of the six partners will have one vote. All six partners will have equal authority in the management of the business. In addition, Section 18(h) of the UPA provides that any decisions on ordinary matters connected with the partnership business are to be made by a majority of the partners.

The partners will often recognize one partner, sometimes called the **managing partner,** or a committee of two or three partners, usually called the **managing committee,** to manage the daily operations of the partnership. The partnership agreement will specify the duties that the managing partner or committee may or

Figure 2–4   Certificate Required to Be Filed with the Secretary of State of Minnesota

Certificate

Pursuant to Chapter 333.01, Minnesota Statutes, the undersigned, who is or will be conducting or transacting a commercial business in the State of Minnesota under an assumed name, hereby certifies that:

1. The assumed name under which the business is or will be conducted is:

_____

2. The address of the principal place of business in Minnesota is or will be:

_____

3. The true name(s) of each person conducting or transacting or intending to conduct business is (are):

Name	Address
_____	_____
_____	_____
_____	_____

IN WITNESS WHEREOF, the person(s) conducting or transacting or intending to conduct business have executed this Certificate this _____ day of January, 199__.

_____

_____

_____

State of _____

County of _____

The foregoing instrument was acknowledged before me this _____ day of _____, 199__, by _____, _____, and _____.

_____
Notary Public

may not perform on behalf of the partnership. Further, Section 9(3) of the UPA prohibits certain acts by a managing partner or a managing committee unless all partners consent. These acts include:

1. Assigning partnership property in trust for creditors.
2. Disposing of the goodwill of the business.
3. Performing any act that would make it impossible to carry on the ordinary business of the partnership.
4. Confessing a judgment.
5. Submitting a partnership claim or liability to arbitration.

In addition, it is advisable to require the managing partner or the managing committee to submit all consequential matters to the entire partnership for approval. This requirement can be accomplished by a provision in the partnership agreement. For example, the managing partner could be prevented from borrowing more than $10,000 or from hiring or firing employees without the approval of the partnership. In any event, the managing partner's or committee's authority to act on behalf of the partnership should be explicitly provided in the partnership agreement.

2–3 Ownership of Partnership Property

Unlike the sole proprietorship, in which the segregation of business assets and personal assets is not important, a partnership must make a clear distinction between partnership property and the personal assets of the partners. **Partnership property** is acquired through contributions by the partners and is generally in the form of cash, real property (land), personal property (furniture and motor vehicles), or intellectual property (trademarks, patents, or service marks). The partnership agreement should itemize by description and monetary value all the property contributed to the partnership by each partner.

Section 8(1) of the UPA provides that "all property originally brought into the partnership stock or subsequently acquired by purchase or otherwise, on account of the partnership, is partnership property." For example, a partner may still hold title to property in his or her name, even after bringing the property into the partnership as his or her capital contribution to the partnership. Even though the property remains in the name of the individual partner, it is partnership property.

In addition, Section 8(2) provides that "property acquired with partnership funds is partnership property." A partner might purchase a delivery truck for the partnership and put title to the truck in his own name. If the truck is purchased with partnership funds, it will be considered partnership property.

The property rights enjoyed by a partner are provided for in Section 24 of the UPA: "The property rights of a partner are (1) his rights in specific partnership property, (2) his interest in the partnership, and (3) his right to participate in the management." The partner's rights to partnership property and to a voice in the management of the partnership are rights that he or she is not permitted to assign, except when *all the partners* of the partnership assign their rights in the same property. The only partnership property right that a partner may assign, separately from all the other partners of the partnership, is his or her interest in the partnership, or the claims to the profits and capital contributions that were made by that partner.

Partnership assets or property are held in a type of ownership called **tenancy in partnership,** in which all the partners are co-owners but they have limited ownership rights. Characteristics of the ownership of property as tenants in partnership, as provided in Section 25 of the UPA, include the following:

1. A partner has an equal right with the other partners to possess specific partnership property for partnership purposes, but a partner has no right to possess such property for any other purpose, unless the other partners consent.
2. A partner may not assign his or her right in partnership property, "except in connection with the assignment of rights of all the partners in the same property," as provided in Section 25(2)(b) of the UPA.
3. A creditor of a partner of the partnership may not attach or execute a claim against any specific partnership property. The partnership's property may, however, be seized to satisfy a claim made against the partnership.
4. A partner's heirs or assigns have no interest in partnership assets. Section 25(2)(d) of the UPA specifically provides that "on the death of a partner his right in specific partnership property vests in the surviving partner or partners, except where the deceased was the last surviving partner."

PARALEGALERT!

A basic problem in partnership law is distinguishing partnership property from property that belongs to an individual partner. This has been the cause of much litigation, and courts will look to the titleholder of the property (as with real estate, automobiles, share certificates, etc.) or to the person who pays for taxes, repairs, and insurance on the property.

2–4 Partners' Liability

Sections 13, 14, and 15 of the UPA prescribe a partner's liability for acts by and on behalf of the partnership. Under Section 15(a) of the UPA, partners are **jointly and severally liable**—that is, liable as a group and as individuals—for the following:

1. Any wrongful act or omission of any partner acting in the ordinary course of the business of the partnership.
2. Loss or injury caused to any person who is not a partner in the partnership.
3. Any penalty imposed on the partnership.
4. Misapplication of any money or property of a third person.

And, under Section 15(b) of the UPA, partners are **jointly liable** "for all other debts and obligations of the partnership."

Under joint and several liability, which may be incurred by the partnership, the partners are bound as one unit (jointly) and individually or personally (severally). First, if the partnership is unable to satisfy a claim out of partnership assets, the creditor or injured party can look to the personal assets of an individual partner, regardless of the proportion of that partner's contribution to the partnership and regardless of that partner's involvement in incurring the liability. Second, if the personal assets of one partner are not sufficient to satisfy the claim, the creditor may look to the other partners to satisfy the claim. Often the creditor will attempt to collect on a claim from a partner who has extensive personal assets before attempting to collect from partners with insufficient personal assets. In any case in which a partner is required to pay more than his or her share of any loss, that partner has the right to compel the other partners to contribute their share of the loss.

In effect, under joint and several liability, one individual partner may be required to satisfy a claim if the partnership and the other partners have no assets out of which to satisfy the claim.

The extent to which joint and several liability may be imposed upon partners in a partnership is underscored in the case reported in the *Legal Links* at the end of this section.

Under joint liability, which may be incurred by the partnership, the partners share any debts or liabilities incurred by the partnership. In this case, when a creditor must be paid, the assets of the partnership are used first. If an amount is still owing, it is settled out of each partner's personal assets in proportion to his or her share in the partnership. In addition, the personal creditors of the individual partners must be satisfied prior to the creditors of the partnership.

Whether a partner is held jointly and severally liable or jointly liable, every partner in a general partnership has unlimited liability to pay all the debts and obligations of the partnership. Even though the partners usually agree to share equally in the losses of the partnership, creditors of the partnership are not bound by this agreement. A creditor may collect its debt of the partnership from any one partner, upon whom the burden then exists to collect from the other partners. Creditors don't care who pays a debt; they only care that they are paid.

Liability of Incoming and Terminating Partners

A person admitted as a partner to an existing partnership will be liable for all the obligations of the partnership that arose prior to that partner's admission to the partnership. However, such liability will extend only to his or her capital contribution to the partnership. Section 17 of the UPA provides that "a person admitted as a partner into an existing partnership is liable for all the obligations of the partnership arising before his admission as though he had been a partner when such obligations were incurred, except that this liability shall be satisfied only out of partnership property."

When a partner leaves the partnership for any reason, he or she remains liable for any debts or obligations incurred by the partnership while he or she was a partner.

Criminal Activity

Liability for any partner's criminal act performed on behalf of the partnership is generally not imposed on the other partners. Only partners who participated in the crime or authorized or approved it will be held liable for another partner's criminal activity. The partnership, however, may be found guilty and fines may be levied against partnership assets for a crime committed for which no criminal intent exists. For example, if the partnership illegally sells alcohol to a minor, the partnership will be held liable for this act and other acts involving strict liability.

2–5   Taxation of the Partners

The general partnership is not a taxpaying entity; it pays no organization, franchise, or income tax. There are some exceptions: a partnership may be liable for property taxes on any property held in the partnership's name, and a partnership may have to pay other taxes imposed by the state or by local jurisdictions.

The partnership is only an avenue for passing through its income, deductions, and credits to its partners. Nevertheless, the partnership must file a partnership return on **Form 1065,** showing its income or loss, deductions and credits, and the names and addresses of the partners entitled to receive a distributive share of the

---

LEGAL *LINKS* LEGAL *LINKS* LEGAL *LINKS* LEGAL *LINKS*

Moseley v. Commercial State Bank

In *Moseley v. Commercial State Bank*, 457 So.2d 967 (Ala. 1984), the bank brought an action against a partnership and its partners for money due on several promissory notes. Moseley, one of four partners of the partnership, apparently had no knowledge of the day-to-day operations of the partnership, and he did not find out about the note until the bank brought the action in this case. Moseley had considered his $100,000 contribution to the partnership's capital account a loan. However, he had executed an agreement granting him all the rights of a general partner in the firm and authorizing the other partners in the firm to obligate him as a general partner.

Another twist to this case is Moseley's contention that the note on which the bank demanded payment was a note issued in exchange for existing notes. The existing notes had been issued by the partnership prior to Moseley's being admitted as a partner. Moseley unsuccessfully contended that the debt preexisted his admission to the partnership.

The Supreme Court of Alabama held that the partners who entered into the partnership agreement were "competent business men dealing at arm's length, who presumably have ample access to counsel. If Moseley had wished to limit his exposure to liability, he should have taken steps to do so when he chose to become involved in the enterprise." In addition, the court found that "the partnership agreement was not an adhesion contract entered into by parties with unequal bargaining strength."

income. The purpose of Form 1065 is to report the income, deductions, gains, and losses from the operation of the partnership. According to Internal Revenue Service (IRS) regulations, Form 1065 will not be considered a return unless a general partner signs the return on behalf of the partnership. A copy of Form 1065, U.S. Partnership Return of Income, is reproduced in Figure 2–5, pp. 26–29.

In addition to filing Form 1065 with the IRS, the partnership is required to provide to each partner a **Schedule K-1,** which will show each partner's distributive share of the partnership's income or loss, credit, and deduction to use in calculating the partner's individual taxable income. The partners then report the items from Schedule K-1 on their personal income tax return and pay tax at the individual income tax rate. A copy of Schedule K-1, Partner's Share of Income, Credits, Deductions, etc., is reproduced in Figure 2–6, pp. 30–31.

A penalty will be assessed against a partnership if the partnership fails to furnish Schedule K-1 to a partner or fails to include on Schedule K-1 all the information required. In addition, the inclusion of any incorrect information is a violation for which a penalty may also be imposed against the partnership. The penalty for each violation is $50, but it increases to $100 for intentional disregard of the requirement to report correct information. A partnership can incur a maximum penalty of $100,000 for violations of these IRS regulations.

Each partner reports his or her proportionate share of the income, credits, deductions, and other items that are reported on Schedule K-1 on his or her personal tax return filed with the IRS. A partner's share of each separately listed item is treated as if the partner had realized it directly (Internal Revenue Code of 1986, as amended, §702; Treas. Reg. §1.702.1). A partner's share of the partnership's taxable income or loss is treated as ordinary income or loss.

Because the partnership is required to make certain filings with the IRS, it must apply for an employer identification number (EIN). The form and process for applying for an EIN were discussed in detail in Section 1–2 of Chapter 1. Refer to that section, and review Form SS-4 and the requirements for filing it.

A partnership's hiring of employees triggers an array of filing requirements under the Internal Revenue Code. Not all forms required to be prepared and filed under IRS statutes and regulations can be mentioned here, but the more common employment-related forms include the following:

PARALEGALERT!

Under most circumstances, tax matters relating to the partnership are taken care of by the partnership's accountant or tax counsel. However, it is important for a paralegal to have an understanding of the requirements imposed on the partnership.

1. Form W-2, Wage and Tax Statement.
2. Form W-3, Transmittal of Income and Tax Statements.
3. Form 940, Employer's Annual Federal Unemployment (FUTA) Tax Return. The partnership may be liable for federal unemployment tax if it paid wages of $1,500 or more in any calendar quarter or if one or more employees worked for the partnership for some part of a day in any 20 different weeks during the calendar year.
4. Form 941, Employer's Quarterly Federal Tax Return. Any employer, including a partnership, must file this form quarterly to report income tax withheld and employer and employee social security and Medicare taxes.

A partnership may also have to file Form 720, Quarterly Federal Excise Tax Return. Form 720 is used to report environmental excise taxes, communications and air transportation taxes, fuel taxes, luxury tax on passenger vehicles, manufacturers' taxes, ship passenger tax, and certain other excise taxes.

Figure 2–5 Internal Revenue Service Form 1065, U.S. Partnership Return of Income

Form **1065**
Department of the Treasury
Internal Revenue Service

U.S. Partnership Return of Income

For calendar year 1993, or tax year beginning ...., 1993, and ending ...., 19 ....
▶ See separate instructions.

OMB No. 1545-0099

1993

A Principal business activity	Use the IRS label. Otherwise, please print or type.	Name of partnership	D Employer identification number
B Principal product or service		Number, street, and room or suite no. (If a P.O. box, see page 9 of the instructions.)	E Date business started
C Business code number		City or town, state, and ZIP code	F Total assets (see Specific Instructions) $

G Check applicable boxes: (1) ☐ Initial return (2) ☐ Final return (3) ☐ Change in address (4) ☐ Amended return
H Check accounting method: (1) ☐ Cash (2) ☐ Accrual (3) ☐ Other (specify) ▶ ....
I Number of Schedules K-1. Attach one for each person who was a partner at any time during the tax year ▶ ....

Caution: *Include **only** trade or business income and expenses on lines 1a through 22 below. See the instructions for more information.*

Income	1a Gross receipts or sales	1a			
	b Less returns and allowances	1b		1c	
	2 Cost of goods sold (Schedule A, line 8)			2	
	3 Gross profit. Subtract line 2 from line 1c			3	
	4 Ordinary income (loss) from other partnerships and fiduciaries *(attach schedule)*			4	
	5 Net farm profit (loss) *(attach Schedule F (Form 1040))*			5	
	6 Net gain (loss) from Form 4797, Part II, line 20			6	
	7 Other income (loss) (see instructions) *(attach schedule)*			7	
	8 **Total income (loss).** Combine lines 3 through 7			8	
Deductions (see instructions for limitations)	9a Salaries and wages (other than to partners)	9a			
	b Less employment credits	9b		9c	
	10 Guaranteed payments to partners			10	
	11 Repairs and maintenance			11	
	12 Bad debts			12	
	13 Rent			13	
	14 Taxes and licenses			14	
	15 Interest			15	
	16a Depreciation (see instructions)	16a			
	b Less depreciation reported on Schedule A and elsewhere on return	16b		16c	
	17 Depletion **(Do not deduct oil and gas depletion.)**			17	
	18 Retirement plans, etc.			18	
	19 Employee benefit programs			19	
	20 Other deductions *(attach schedule)*			20	
	21 **Total deductions.** Add the amounts shown in the far right column for lines 9c through 20			21	
	22 **Ordinary income (loss)** from trade or business activities. Subtract line 21 from line 8			22	

Please Sign Here

Under penalties of perjury, I declare that I have examined this return, including accompanying schedules and statements, and to the best of my knowledge and belief, it is true, correct, and complete. Declaration of preparer (other than general partner) is based on all information of which preparer has any knowledge.

▶ Signature of general partner ▶ Date

Paid Preparer's Use Only	Preparer's signature ▶	Date	Check if self-employed ▶ ☐	Preparer's social security no.
	Firm's name (or yours if self-employed) and address ▶		E.I. No. ▶	
			ZIP code ▶	

For Paperwork Reduction Act Notice, see page 1 of separate instructions. Cat. No. 11390Z Form **1065** (1993)

2–6 Distribution of Profits and Losses

The partners are not entitled to receive any form of compensation—such as salaries, rents, or interest—from the partnership for their services, unless specifically provided for in the partnership agreement. A partner's compensation for devotion and services to the partnership is a share in the distribution of the profits. Section 18(f) of the UPA provides that "no partner is entitled to remuneration for acting in the partnership business, except that a surviving partner is entitled to reasonable compensation for his services in winding up the partnership affairs."

Figure 2–5, continued

Schedule A   Cost of Goods Sold

1	Inventory at beginning of year	1
2	Purchases less cost of items withdrawn for personal use	2
3	Cost of labor.	3
4	Additional section 263A costs (see instructions) *(attach schedule)*	4
5	Other costs *(attach schedule)*	5
6	**Total.** Add lines 1 through 5	6
7	Inventory at end of year	7
8	**Cost of goods sold.** Subtract line 7 from line 6. Enter here and on page 1, line 2	8

9a Check all methods used for valuing closing inventory:

    (i) ☐ Cost

    (ii) ☐ Lower of cost or market as described in Regulations section 1.471-4

    (iii) ☐ Writedown of "subnormal" goods as described in Regulations section 1.471-2(c)

    (iv) ☐ Other (specify method used and attach explanation) ▶

  b Check this box if the LIFO inventory method was adopted this tax year for any goods *(if checked, attach Form 970)* . ▶ ☐

  c Do the rules of section 263A (for property produced or acquired for resale) apply to the partnership? . ☐ Yes ☐ No

  d Was there any change in determining quantities, cost, or valuations between opening and closing inventory? ☐ Yes ☐ No

    If "Yes," attach explanation.

Schedule B   Other Information

		Yes	No
1	What type of entity is filing this return? Check the applicable box ▶ ☐ General partnership ☐ Limited partnership ☐ Limited liability company		
2	Are any partners in this partnership also partnerships?		
3	Is this partnership a partner in another partnership?		
4	Is this partnership subject to the consolidated audit procedures of sections 6221 through 6233? If "Yes," see **Designation of Tax Matters Partner** below		
5	Does this partnership meet **ALL THREE** of the following requirements?		
a	The partnership's total receipts for the tax year were less than $250,000;		
b	The partnership's total assets at the end of the tax year were less than $600,000; **AND**		
c	Schedules K-1 are filed with the return and furnished to the partners on or before the due date (including extensions) for the partnership return. If "Yes," the partnership is not required to complete Schedules L, M-1, and M-2; Item F on page 1 of Form 1065; or Item J on Schedule K-1		
6	Does this partnership have any foreign partners?		
7	Is this partnership a publicly traded partnership as defined in section 469(k)(2)?		
8	Has this partnership filed, or is it required to file, **Form 8264,** Application for Registration of a Tax Shelter?		
9	At any time during calendar year 1993, did the partnership have an interest in or a signature or other authority over a financial account in a foreign country (such as a bank account, securities account, or other financial account)? (See the instructions for exceptions and filing requirements for form TD F 90-22.1.) If "Yes," enter the name of the foreign country. ▶		
10	Was the partnership the grantor of, or transferor to, a foreign trust that existed during the current tax year, whether or not the partnership or any partner has any beneficial interest in it? If "Yes," you may have to file Forms 3520, 3520-A, or 926		
11	Was there a distribution of property or a transfer (e.g., by sale or death) of a partnership interest during the tax year? If "Yes," you may elect to adjust the basis of the partnership's assets under section 754 by attaching the statement described on page 5 of the instructions under **Elections Made By the Partnership**		

Designation of Tax Matters Partner (See instructions.)

Enter below the general partner designated as the tax matters partner (TMP) for the tax year of this return:

Name of designated TMP ▶   Identifying number of TMP ▶

Address of designated TMP ▶

continued

Thus, providing services during the termination or liquidation of the partnership is the one exception to the prohibition of compensation from the partnership. In addition, the partnership must reimburse a partner for making payments from his or her own funds on behalf of the partnership for the preservation of the partnership's business and property. Such reimbursement is required by Section 18(b) of the UPA.

The right to share in the profits also brings with it the obligation to share in the losses. Unless otherwise agreed by all the partners and set forth in the partnership agreement, the profits *and* the losses incurred by the partnership are shared equally.

The **profit/loss-sharing scheme** of the general partnership need *not* have any relation to the proportion of the original contributions made by each partner.

Figure 2–5, continued

Form 1065 (1993)   Page **3**

Schedule K | Partners' Shares of Income, Credits, Deductions, etc.

	(a) Distributive share items		(b) Total amount
Income (Loss)	**1** Ordinary income (loss) from trade or business activities (page 1, line 22)	**1**	
	2 Net income (loss) from rental real estate activities (attach Form 8825)	**2**	
	3a Gross income from other rental activities ... **3a**		
	b Expenses from other rental activities (attach schedule) ... **3b**		
	c Net income (loss) from other rental activities. Subtract line 3b from line 3a	**3c**	
	4 Portfolio income (loss) (see instructions): **a** Interest income	**4a**	
	b Dividend income	**4b**	
	c Royalty income	**4c**	
	d Net short-term capital gain (loss) (attach Schedule D (Form 1065))	**4d**	
	e Net long-term capital gain (loss) (attach Schedule D (Form 1065))	**4e**	
	f Other portfolio income (loss) (attach schedule)	**4f**	
	5 Guaranteed payments to partners	**5**	
	6 Net gain (loss) under section 1231 (other than due to casualty or theft) (attach Form 4797)	**6**	
	7 Other income (loss) (attach schedule)	**7**	
Deductions	**8** Charitable contributions (see instructions) (attach schedule)	**8**	
	9 Section 179 expense deduction (attach Form 4562)	**9**	
	10 Deductions related to portfolio income (see instructions) (itemize)	**10**	
	11 Other deductions (attach schedule)	**11**	
Investment Interest	**12a** Interest expense on investment debts	**12a**	
	b (1) Investment income included on lines 4a, 4b, 4c, and 4f above	**12b(1)**	
	(2) Investment expenses included on line 10 above	**12b(2)**	
Credits	**13a** Credit for income tax withheld	**13a**	
	b Low-income housing credit (see instructions):		
	(1) From partnerships to which section 42(j)(5) applies for property placed in service before 1990	**13b(1)**	
	(2) Other than on line 13b(1) for property placed in service before 1990	**13b(2)**	
	(3) From partnerships to which section 42(j)(5) applies for property placed in service after 1989	**13b(3)**	
	(4) Other than on line 13b(3) for property placed in service after 1989	**13b(4)**	
	c Qualified rehabilitation expenditures related to rental real estate activities (attach Form 3468)	**13c**	
	d Credits (other than credits shown on lines 13b and 13c) related to rental real estate activities (see instructions)	**13d**	
	e Credits related to other rental activities (see instructions)	**13e**	
	14 Other credits (see instructions)	**14**	
Self-Employment	**15a** Net earnings (loss) from self-employment	**15a**	
	b Gross farming or fishing income	**15b**	
	c Gross nonfarm income	**15c**	
Adjustments and Tax Preference Items	**16a** Depreciation adjustment on property placed in service after 1986	**16a**	
	b Adjusted gain or loss	**16b**	
	c Depletion (other than oil and gas)	**16c**	
	d (1) Gross income from oil, gas, and geothermal properties	**16d(1)**	
	(2) Deductions allocable to oil, gas, and geothermal properties	**16d(2)**	
	e Other adjustments and tax preference items (attach schedule)	**16e**	
Foreign Taxes	**17a** Type of income ▶ .... **b** Foreign country or U.S. possession ▶		
	c Total gross income from sources outside the United States (attach schedule)	**17c**	
	d Total applicable deductions and losses (attach schedule)	**17d**	
	e Total foreign taxes (check one): ▶ ☐ Paid ☐ Accrued	**17e**	
	f Reduction in taxes available for credit (attach schedule)	**17f**	
	g Other foreign tax information (attach schedule)	**17g**	
Other	**18a** Total expenditures to which a section 59(e) election may apply	**18a**	
	b Type of expenditures ▶..................		
	19 Tax-exempt interest income	**19**	
	20 Other tax-exempt income	**20**	
	21 Nondeductible expenses	**21**	
	22 Other items and amounts required to be reported separately to partners (see instructions) (attach schedule)		

Analysis	**23a** Income (loss). Combine lines 1 through 7 in column (b). From the result, subtract the sum of lines 8 through 12a, 17e, and 18a			**23a**		

b Analysis by type of partner:	(a) Corporate	(b) Individual i. Active	(b) Individual ii. Passive	(c) Partnership	(d) Exempt organization	(e) Nominee/Other
(1) General partners						
(2) Limited partners						

However, Section 18(a) of the UPA does provide that contributions by the partners toward the losses sustained by the partnership are to be in proportion to the profits distributed.

Generally, income, gains, losses, deductions, and credits of the partnership are allocated among the partners according to the partnership agreement. If all the partners agree, specific items may be allocated in a ratio different from the ratio for sharing income and loss. For example, if the net income of the partnership is divided evenly among three partners, special items such as interest, dividends, or capital gains *may be* allocated 50 percent to Partner A, 30 percent to Partner B, and 20 percent to Partner C. Such a deviation from the typical treatment of special items would be addressed in the partnership agreement.

Figure 2–5, continued

Note: If Question 5 of Schedule B is answered "Yes," the partnership is not required to complete Schedules L, M-1, and M-2.

Schedule L   Balance Sheets

Assets	Beginning of tax year		End of tax year	
	(a)	(b)	(c)	(d)
1 Cash				
2a Trade notes and accounts receivable				
b Less allowance for bad debts				
3 Inventories				
4 U.S. government obligations				
5 Tax-exempt securities				
6 Other current assets (attach schedule)				
7 Mortgage and real estate loans				
8 Other investments (attach schedule)				
9a Buildings and other depreciable assets				
b Less accumulated depreciation				
10a Depletable assets				
b Less accumulated depletion				
11 Land (net of any amortization)				
12a Intangible assets (amortizable only)				
b Less accumulated amortization				
13 Other assets (attach schedule)				
14 Total assets				
Liabilities and Capital				
15 Accounts payable				
16 Mortgages, notes, bonds payable in less than 1 year				
17 Other current liabilities (attach schedule)				
18 All nonrecourse loans				
19 Mortgages, notes, bonds payable in 1 year or more				
20 Other liabilities (attach schedule)				
21 Partners' capital accounts				
22 Total liabilities and capital				

Schedule M-1   Reconciliation of Income (Loss) per Books With Income (Loss) per Return (see instructions)

1 Net income (loss) per books

2 Income included on Schedule K, lines 1 through 4, 6, and 7, not recorded on books this year (itemize): ....

3 Guaranteed payments (other than health insurance)

4 Expenses recorded on books this year not included on Schedule K, lines 1 through 12a, 17e, and 18a (itemize):
a Depreciation $ ....
b Travel and entertainment $ ....

5 Add lines 1 through 4

6 Income recorded on books this year not included on Schedule K, lines 1 through 7 (itemize):
a Tax-exempt interest $ ....

7 Deductions included on Schedule K, lines 1 through 12a, 17e, and 18a, not charged against book income this year (itemize):
a Depreciation $ ....

8 Add lines 6 and 7

9 Income (loss) (Schedule K, line 23a). Subtract line 8 from line 5

Schedule M-2   Analysis of Partners' Capital Accounts

1 Balance at beginning of year

2 Capital contributed during year

3 Net income (loss) per books

4 Other increases (itemize): ....

5 Add lines 1 through 4

6 Distributions: a Cash
                 b Property

7 Other decreases (itemize): ....

8 Add lines 6 and 7

9 Balance at end of year. Subtract line 8 from line 5

Printed on recycled paper   ☆ U.S. GPO:1993-345-264

2–7   Termination of the General Partnership

The **dissolution** and **winding up** of the business of a partnership leads to the **termination** of a partnership. A partnership's existence will cease only after dissolution, winding up, and termination, a three-step process.

Under Section 29 of the UPA, "dissolution of a partnership is the change in the relation of the partners caused by any partner ceasing to be associated in the carrying on as distinguished from the winding up of the business." Except as may be necessary to wind up the partnership affairs and complete any unfinished

Figure 2–6   Internal Revenue Service Schedule K-1, Partner's Share of Income, Credits, Deductions, etc.

SCHEDULE K-1 (Form 1065)
Department of the Treasury
Internal Revenue Service

Partner's Share of Income, Credits, Deductions, etc.
► See separate instructions.
For calendar year 1993 or tax year beginning   , 1993, and ending   , 19

OMB No. 1545-0099

1993

Partner's identifying number ►   Partnership's identifying number ►

Partner's name, address, and ZIP code   Partnership's name, address, and ZIP code

A   This partner is a ☐ general partner ☐ limited partner ☐ limited liability company member
B   What type of entity is this partner? ► ....
C   Is this partner a ☐ domestic or a ☐ foreign partner?
D   Enter partner's percentage of: (i) Before change or termination   (ii) End of year
    Profit sharing . . . . %   .... %
    Loss sharing . . . . %   .... %
    Ownership of capital . . . . %   .... %
E   IRS Center where partnership filed return:

F   Partner's share of liabilities (see instructions):
    Nonrecourse . . . . $ ....
    Qualified nonrecourse financing . . $ ....
    Other . . . . . . $ ....
G   Tax shelter registration number . ► ....
H   Check here if this partnership is a publicly traded partnership as defined in section 469(k)(2) . . . . ☐
I   Check applicable boxes: (1) ☐ Final K-1 (2) ☐ Amended K-1

J   **Analysis of partner's capital account:**

(a) Capital account at beginning of year	(b) Capital contributed during year	(c) Partner's share of lines 3, 4, and 7, Form 1065, Schedule M-2	(d) Withdrawals and distributions	(e) Capital account at end of year (combine columns (a) through (d))
			( )	

	(a) Distributive share item		(b) Amount	(c) 1040 filers enter the amount in column (b) on:
Income (Loss)	1	Ordinary income (loss) from trade or business activities . . .	1	See Partner's Instructions for Schedule K-1 (Form 1065).
	2	Net income (loss) from rental real estate activities	2	
	3	Net income (loss) from other rental activities	3	
	4	Portfolio income (loss):		
	a	Interest	4a	Sch. B, Part I, line 1
	b	Dividends	4b	Sch. B, Part II, line 5
	c	Royalties	4c	Sch. E, Part I, line 4
	d	Net short-term capital gain (loss)	4d	Sch. D, line 5, col. (f) or (g)
	e	Net long-term capital gain (loss)	4e	Sch. D, line 13, col. (f) or (g)
	f	Other portfolio income (loss) (attach schedule) . .	4f	Enter on applicable line of your return.
	5	Guaranteed payments to partner	5	See Partner's Instructions for Schedule K-1 (Form 1065).
	6	Net gain (loss) under section 1231 (other than due to casualty or theft)	6	
	7	Other income (loss) (attach schedule)	7	Enter on applicable line of your return.
Deductions	8	Charitable contributions (see instructions) (attach schedule) . .	8	Sch. A, line 13 or 14
	9	Section 179 expense deduction	9	See Partner's Instructions for Schedule K-1 (Form 1065).
	10	Deductions related to portfolio income (attach schedule) . . .	10	
	11	Other deductions (attach schedule)	11	
Investment Interest	12a	Interest expense on investment debts	12a	Form 4952, line 1
	b	(1) Investment income included on lines 4a, 4b, 4c, and 4f above	b(1)	See Partner's Instructions for Schedule K-1 (Form 1065).
		(2) Investment expenses included on line 10 above	b(2)	
Credits	13a	Credit for income tax withheld	13a	See Partner's Instructions for Schedule K-1 (Form 1065).
	b	Low-income housing credit:		
		(1) From section 42(j)(5) partnerships for property placed in service before 1990	b(1)	
		(2) Other than on line 13b(1) for property placed in service before 1990	b(2)	Form 8586, line 5
		(3) From section 42(j)(5) partnerships for property placed in service after 1989	b(3)	
		(4) Other than on line 13b(3) for property placed in service after 1989	b(4)	
	c	Qualified rehabilitation expenditures related to rental real estate activities (see instructions)	13c	
	d	Credits (other than credits shown on lines 13b and 13c) related to rental real estate activities (see instructions)	13d	See Partner's Instructions for Schedule K-1 (Form 1065).
	e	Credits related to other rental activities (see instructions) . . .	13e	
	14	Other credits (see instructions)	14	

For Paperwork Reduction Act Notice, see Instructions for Form 1065.   Cat. No. 11394R   Schedule K-1 (Form 1065) 1993

business of the partnership, the authority of an individual partner to act for the partnership ceases upon dissolution. Section 30 of the UPA does provide, however, that "on dissolution the partnership is not terminated, but continues until the winding up of partnership affairs is completed."

Section 31 of the UPA spells out specific causes for dissolution of a partnership, which include the following:

1.   Death or bankruptcy of a partner.
2.   Agreement of the partners.
3.   Act of the partners in violation of the partnership agreement.

Figure 2–6, continued

Schedule K-1 (Form 1065) 1993 — Page **2**

	(a) Distributive share item		(b) Amount	(c) 1040 filers enter the amount in column (b) on:
Self-employment	**15a** Net earnings (loss) from self-employment	15a		Sch. SE, Section A or B
	b Gross farming or fishing income	15b		See Partner's Instructions for Schedule K-1 (Form 1065).
	c Gross nonfarm income	15c		
Adjustments and Tax Preference Items	**16a** Depreciation adjustment on property placed in service after 1986	16a		See Partner's Instructions for Schedule K-1 (Form 1065) and Instructions for Form 6251.
	b Adjusted gain or loss	16b		
	c Depletion (other than oil and gas)	16c		
	d (1) Gross income from oil, gas, and geothermal properties	d(1)		
	(2) Deductions allocable to oil, gas, and geothermal properties	d(2)		
	e Other adjustments and tax preference items (attach schedule)	16e		
Foreign Taxes	**17a** Type of income ▶			Form 1116, check boxes
	b Name of foreign country or U.S. possession ▶			
	c Total gross income from sources outside the United States (attach schedule)	17c		Form 1116, Part I
	d Total applicable deductions and losses (attach schedule)	17d		
	e Total foreign taxes (check one): ▶ ☐ Paid ☐ Accrued	17e		Form 1116, Part II
	f Reduction in taxes available for credit (attach schedule)	17f		Form 1116, Part III
	g Other foreign tax information (attach schedule)	17g		See Instructions for Form 1116.
Other	**18a** Total expenditures to which a section 59(e) election may apply	18a		See Partner's Instructions for Schedule K-1 (Form 1065).
	b Type of expenditures ▶			
	19 Tax-exempt interest income	19		Form 1040, line 8b
	20 Other tax-exempt income	20		See Partner's Instructions for Schedule K-1 (Form 1065).
	21 Nondeductible expenses	21		
	22 Recapture of low-income housing credit:			
	a From section 42(j)(5) partnerships	22a		Form 8611, line 8
	b Other than on line 22a	22b		

Supplemental Information

23 Supplemental information required to be reported separately to each partner (attach additional schedules if more space is needed):

✪ Printed on recycled paper

4. Any event that makes it unlawful for the partnership to continue doing business.
5. Court decree.

Circumstances under which a court may issue a decree dissolving a partnership are the insanity, incapacity, or misconduct of a partner or the continuing inability of the partnership to make a profit. A temporarily unprofitable business would not justify a dissolution by decree of court.

As already mentioned, a partnership dissolves upon the death of a partner. Typically, the partnership interest of the deceased partner passes to his or her heirs or beneficiaries. To provide continuity in the business, however, the partnership agreement may provide for the continuation of the partnership after the death of a partner. In such cases the agreement generally also provides for the buyout of the deceased partner's interest from his or her heirs. Then, even though the partnership dissolves by operation of law upon a partner's death, the partnership does not wind up its business and affairs. It continues to operate the business until a new partnership agreement is executed by the remaining partners.

After dissolution, the partnership continues with the winding up, or liquidation, of the business. During this process the partnership should not enter into any new contracts, but any business required to be performed under existing contracts should be completed. The partnership should not purchase property or engage in any new activities. Section 37 of the UPA gives the right to wind up the partnership affairs to any partner who has not wrongfully dissolved the partnership.

The winding-up procedures normally include completing unfinished business, liquidating partnership property (converting all the partnership's assets to cash), paying outstanding debts, and collecting outstanding accounts. Once these activities have been completed, the remaining assets are used to satisfy all other claims in this order:

1. Claims of individual partners for repayment of loans made to the partnership.
2. Claims of individual partners for return of capital contributions made to the partnership.

Any assets remaining after these claims are satisfied are distributed to the partners as profits according to the profit/loss-sharing scheme in the partnership agreement. In the unfortunate event that the partnership has sustained a loss, the loss is shared equally by the partners, unless the partnership agreement states otherwise.

Upon completion of the winding-up procedures, the partnership is terminated and its existence ceases. State or local regulations may require that an appropriate government office be notified of the dissolution or termination of the partnership.

PARALEGALERT!

The cessation of a partnership's existence takes place in a three-step process: dissolution, winding up (or liquidation), and termination.

2–8   Practical Considerations

Every task you perform as a paralegal in corporate and business law will require your analytical and organizational skills. For example, many of your assignments will consist of drafting agreements, reviewing federal and state statutes and regulations, and preparing documents or forms in compliance with those statutes or regulations. It may feel overwhelming at first, but properly analyzing the task assigned to you and organizing the steps to complete the job will help you master the process.

You may be asked to draft a partnership agreement, to research the state regulations governing fictitious name registrations, or to prepare a partnership certificate. First, begin your inquiry with the attorneys and paralegals in your office, or call upon your paralegal colleagues working in the business or corporate area at other firms. Second, locate the form books or form files kept by your firm or company in the library or a central filing location. Third, review other client files in your office for documents prepared by attorneys and other paralegals. And, fourth, put your personal analytical and organizational skills to work for you.

Tasks that you may be asked to perform in connection with the formation and operation of the general partnership include the following:

- Draft partnership agreement.
- Arrange for the execution of the partnership agreement by all the partners.
- File Form SS-4 with the IRS to obtain an employer identification number for the partnership.
- Review state law to determine if a certificate of general partnership must be filed.
- Prepare and file a certificate of general partnership, and determine the appropriate fees for filing with the state's corporation division and, if needed, with the county in which the business will operate.
- Review state law to determine if a fictitious name registration or an assumed name affidavit must be filed.
- Prepare and file a fictitious name registration or an assumed name affidavit, and determine the appropriate fees for filing with the state's corporation division and with the county in which the business will operate.

SUMMARY

2–1

The general partnership is a form of business organization owned and managed by two or more persons or partners. *Persons* is defined to include individuals, partnerships, corporations, and other associations, so another partnership or a corporation may be a partner in a general partnership. The general partnership has many of the same characteristics as the sole proprietorship, the most important of which is the unlimited liability incurred by the owners of the business. The Uniform Partnership Act governs the manner in which general partnerships operate.

2–2

One element distinguishes the general partnership from the sole proprietorship: the general partnership agreement. The agreement, which may be written or oral, covers the major issues of operating the partnership, including provisions for valuing property contributed by the partners to the partnership, admitting new partners, distributing partnership profits and capital, dissolving the partnership, and settling disputes among the partners. Just as in the sole proprietorship, the business conducted by the general partnership will dictate the necessity of certain filings with federal, state, or local agencies. Often a certificate of partnership must be filed in the state or the county or counties where the partnership is doing business. If the partners' surnames are not all included in the name of the business, a fictitious name registration or an assumed name affidavit is usually required, even if a certificate of partnership is not required to be filed. Unless otherwise specifically stated in the partnership agreement, all partners have equal voices in the management of the business. A managing partner or a managing committee may be designated by the partners to manage the daily operations of the partnership.

2–3

The partnership must make a clear distinction between partnership property and the personal assets of the individual partners. Partnership property is acquired from the partners as their contributions to the partnership, and the partnership agreement identifies the property contributed and the value of such property. All partnership assets and property are held by the partners as tenants in partnership. No individual partner has an absolute right of ownership to any specific property of the partnership.

2–4

Partners are jointly and severally liable for wrongful acts, for losses or injuries to third parties, for any penalties incurred by the partnership, and for the misapplication of property owned by a third party. Partners are jointly liable for the debts and liabilities of the partnership. A partner admitted to a partnership after its formation is responsible for its obligations incurred before his or her admission, but only to the extent of the capital contribution made. A partner who leaves the partnership remains liable for any debts incurred while he or she was a partner. Generally, any claims by creditors are satisfied first out of partnership assets and property, then out of the personal assets of the partners.

2–5

The partnership is not a taxpaying entity. It is only a conduit for passing income, deductions, and credits directly to the partners. The partnership files with the Internal Revenue Service a Form 1065, which shows the partnership's income or loss, deductions and credits, and the names and addresses of all the partners. The Schedule K-1, provided by the partnership to each partner, shows the partner's proportionate share of income (or loss), deduction, and credit, which the partner then uses to complete his or her personal tax return. The partnership must apply for a federal employer identification number, and it must file other forms if it has employees.

2–6

A partner's compensation for intangible contributions and services to the partnership is his or her share in the distribution of the partnership's profits. Unless otherwise spelled out in the partnership agreement, the profits and losses incurred by the partnership are shared equally by the partners. The profit/loss-sharing by the partners has no relation to the contributions made by the partners, unless such a relation is specified in the partnership agreement.

2–7

The partnership is not terminated on dissolution. It continues until the winding up of partnership affairs is complete. Then the partnership is terminated. Specific causes for dissolution of a partnership include death or bankruptcy of a partner, agreement of the partners to dissolve the partnership, an act of the partners in violation of the partnership agreement, an event that makes it unlawful for the partnership to continue doing business, and court order or decree. Winding-up procedures, which include the conversion of partnership assets to cash and the collection and payment of outstanding debts, follow the event that caused the dissolution of the partnership. After these procedures have been carried out, all remaining assets of the partnership are distributed to satisfy the following claims in order: claims of creditors for debts and liabilities, claims of partners for loans to the partnership, claims of partners for capital contributions, and claims of partners for the profits of the partnership.

2–8

Proficiency in analysis and organization will prove very useful in the tasks assigned to you in the formation of the general partnership.

REVIEW GUIDE

Key Terms

Before proceeding, review the key terms listed below to be sure you understand each one. If necessary, read over the corresponding section of the chapter. When you are ready to test your understanding, answer the review questions.

general partnership (p. 13)
partners (p. 13)
express partnership (p. 14)
implied partnership (p. 14)
Uniform Partnership Act (UPA) (p. 14)
persons (p. 14)
general partnership agreement (p. 15)
fictitious name (p. 16)
assumed name (p. 16)
managing partner (p. 20)
managing committee (p. 20)
partnership property (p. 22)
tenancy in partnership (p. 22)
jointly and severally liable (p. 23)
jointly liable (p. 23)
Form 1065 (p. 24)
Schedule K-1 (p. 25)
profit/loss-sharing scheme (p. 27)
dissolution (p. 29)
winding up (p. 29)
termination (p. 29)

Questions for Review and Discussion

1. What is the relationship between the general partnership and the partners?
2. State at least five points that should be covered in a partnership agreement.
3. What conditions exist in an implied partnership?
4. Summarize the advantages and disadvantages of operating a business as a general partnership.
5. Explain when a certificate of partnership is required to be filed.
6. List the business activities of a partnership to which all partners must consent.
7. Identify the partnership property rights a partner may assign and those he or she may not assign.
8. Explain why a creditor would rather execute a judgment against a partnership under joint and several liability than under joint liability.
9. How does a partnership pay tax on its income?
10. How are the profits and losses of a partnership distributed to the partners?
11. List the reasons for which a partnership would dissolve.

12. How are the assets of the partnership distributed after the winding-up procedures are complete?

Activities

1. Find out whether your state has adopted the Uniform Partnership Act (UPA). If so, determine whether any modifications or revisions were made to the UPA by your state.
2. Review the statutes of your state, and determine the requirements with which a general partnership must comply to operate a dry cleaning business in that state. After you have identified the requirements and procedures, call the office of the secretary of state to confirm the information and procedures you have identified.
3. Visit the local law library, locate a form book, and become familiar with the contents of the book. Find a sample general partnership agreement, and review the paragraphs that apply specifically to the distribution of partnership profits and capital.

CHAPTER 3   Limited Partnership

OUTLINE

3–1   Characteristics
    Uniform Limited Partnership Acts
    Definition of a Limited Partnership
3–2   Formation and Operation
    Certificate of Limited Partnership
    The Limited Partnership Agreement
    Merger, Consolidation, and the Foreign Limited Partnership
    Partners' Participation in Management
3–3   Liability of the Partners
3–4   Taxation of the Partners
3–5   Changes in Partnership Interests
    Addition and Withdrawal of General Partners
    Addition and Withdrawal of Limited Partners
3–6   Termination of the Limited Partnership
3–7   Practical Considerations

APPLICATIONS

Several of Harriet Johnson's friends and business associates are interested in making investments in Harriet's antique shop. The store has grown to more than 15,000 square feet of display area, and Harriet now employs 10 people to help her run the business. The potential investors, however, are not interested in managing the business, nor do they want to be held responsible for any liabilities the shop might incur. Harriet's lawyer advises her that the limited partnership is the avenue through which her needs and those of the investors can be met.

    The attorney asks you to gather all the necessary information to prepare the certificate of limited partnership and to draft the limited partnership agreement.

OBJECTIVES

You have learned in the last two chapters the varying complexities and differences in the organization and operation of the sole proprietorship and the general partnership. Here we will examine the same characteristics of the limited partnership; you will find that the limited partnership shares characteristics with both the general partnership and the corporation, which will be discussed in greater detail beginning in Chapter 4. After completing this chapter, you will be able to:

1. Define *limited partnership.*
2. Identify the characteristics of a limited partnership.
3. Describe the role of the Revised Uniform Limited Partnership Act in governing the operation of partnerships.
4. Identify the components of the limited partnership agreement.

5. Determine the necessary filing requirements for the proper formation of a limited partnership.
6. Describe the involvement of both the general partners and the limited partners in managing the business.
7. Identify the persons responsible for the liabilities incurred by the limited partnership.
8. Explain how income and losses incurred by a limited partnership are treated for tax purposes.
9. Explain the logistics involved when a general or limited partner is added or withdrawn from the partnership.
10. List the events that will dissolve a limited partnership.
11. State the order in which the assets of a limited partnership are distributed on dissolution.

3–1 Characteristics

The **limited partnership** is a form of business organization having one or more general partners and one or more limited partners. The limited partnership shares many characteristics with the general partnership and the corporation. For example, a **general partner** of a limited partnership is governed in the same manner as a partner of a general partnership. A **limited partner** of a limited partnership shares some of the characteristics of a shareholder of a corporation, as the liability of the limited partner is limited to the amount of his or her investment in the business.

This limitation of liability makes the limited partnership an attractive investment vehicle for many investors. A limited partnership may be able to obtain investment capital from individuals, other partnerships, and corporations that would not otherwise consider investing in a partnership.

After a brief discussion of the responsibilities, duties, and powers of a general partner of a limited partnership, most of this chapter will be devoted to the unique characteristics of the limited partner and the limited partnership.

The limited partnership must have *at least one* general partner, who has active responsibility for the management and operation of the partnership and has unlimited liability for the debts and obligations of the partnership (just as a general partner of a general partnership does). The general powers and liabilities of a general partner are specifically provided for by state statutes governing limited partnerships. In part, Sections 403(a) and 403(b) of the uniform statute governing limited partnerships (discussed in the next subsection) state that "a general partner of a limited partnership has the rights and powers and is subject to the restrictions of a partner in a partnership without limited partners" and "a general partner of a limited partnership has the liabilities of a partner in a partnership without limited partners to persons other than the partnership and the other partners."

The limited partnership must have *at least one* limited partner, who is essentially a passive investor. The primary characteristics that distinguish the limited partner from the general partner are that:

1. The liability of the limited partner is limited to the amount invested in the partnership.
2. The limited partner is restricted from participating in the management of the partnership and must not exercise control of such management.

Liability of and management by the partners in a limited partnership are more fully discussed in upcoming Sections 3–2 and 3–3.

Uniform Limited Partnership Acts

The first limited partnership statute was adopted by the state of New York in 1822, and many states followed with similar legislation. To assist in creating nationwide uniformity in governing limited partnerships, the **National Conference of Commissioners on Uniform State Laws** (hereinafter referred to as NCCUSL) adopted the **Uniform Limited Partnership Act** (hereinafter referred to as **ULPA**) in 1916. By 1973 every state except Louisiana had adopted the ULPA in its entirety, with no changes or with minor changes. However, during the 1970s many states adopted significant changes from the original ULPA.

In 1976 the NCCUSL issued the **Revised Uniform Limited Partnership Act** (hereinafter referred to as **RULPA**), which clarified vague provisions of the ULPA and provided practical solutions to problems arising from the ULPA. Most states and the District of Columbia have adopted the RULPA. However, Delaware and California have adopted major revisions of the RULPA.

In 1985 the NCCUSL adopted significant changes to the RULPA, incorporating many of the changes that had been made by Delaware and California. The 1985 amendments, which substantially changed the 1976 RULPA, have been adopted in whole or in part by more than half the states.

To summarize, every state (except Louisiana) has adopted in whole or in part the ULPA issued in 1916, the RULPA issued in 1976, or the RULPA with the 1985 amendments. Most states have adopted the RULPA with the 1985 amendments, but many have made modifications or adopted amendments, some substantial, to one or more of its provisions. Because most states have adopted the RULPA with the 1985 amendments, most references in this chapter are to the RULPA approved in 1985. Hereafter this act will be referred to as the 1985 RULPA. The 1985 RULPA is reproduced as Appendix C to this text.

PARALEGALERT!

When organizing a limited partnership in any state, you must always find out which version of the uniform limited partnership act that particular state enacted and whether the state adopted amendments or revisions to that version.

Definition of a Limited Partnership

Section 101(7) of the 1985 RULPA defines a limited partnership as "a partnership formed by two or more persons under the laws of this State and having one or more general partners and one or more limited partners." The term *person* is defined by the 1985 RULPA as "a natural person, partnership, limited partnership, trust, estate, association, or corporation." This means that not only can individuals act in the capacity of a general or limited partner, but any general partnership, limited partnership, or other entity named in the definition of *person* can be a general or limited partner in a limited partnership.

See Figure 3–1 for a list of the significant advantages and disadvantages of the limited partnership, all of which will be discussed in this chapter.

3–2   Formation and Operation

Virtually any lawful business activity may be conducted by a limited partnership. An exception is that many states prohibit partnerships from carrying on banking and insurance business. Limited partnerships have been formed to

Figure 3–1 Advantages and Disadvantages of the Limited Partnership

Advantages of the Limited Partnership

- Limited liability of the limited partners.
- Enhanced access to capital resources.
- Flexibility in the transfer of partnership interests.
- Freedom from taxation as an organization.

Disadvantages of the Limited Partnership

- Unlimited liability of each general partner.
- Organizational formalities and expenses.
- Full control of the business by the general partner(s).

engage in numerous types of businesses, which include, but are not limited to, the operation of hotels, shopping centers, restaurants, and apartment complexes; the exploration and mining of natural resources; the manufacture of computers, chemicals, and medical equipment; the ownership of professional sports franchises; and the business of acting as a holding company.

Certificate of Limited Partnership

The legal formation of a limited partnership occurs upon the filing of a **certificate of limited partnership.** This certificate *must* be filed with the office of the secretary of state in the state where the limited partnership is being formed. Section 201(a) of the 1985 RULPA prescribes the information that must be included in the certificate of limited partnership as follows:

1. The name of the limited partnership.
2. The address of the office of the limited partnership and the name and address of the agent for service of process.
3. The name and business address of each general partner.
4. The latest date on which the limited partnership is to dissolve.
5. Any other matters the general partners determine to include therein.

The filing fee and the number of executed copies to be filed vary from state to state. Before filing the certificate of limited partnership, or any amendment or cancellation of the certificate, you should verify the number of copies to be filed and the proper filing fee required by that state. The amount of the filing fee is the one area in which the states are not consistent.

Section 206 of the 1985 RULPA requires that two executed copies of the certificate of limited partnership and all appropriate filing fees must be delivered to the secretary of state for a limited partnership to be formed in the state. See Figure 3–2, which is an example of a certificate of limited partnership prepared in accordance with the provisions of the 1985 RULPA.

Generally, the certificate of limited partnership will contain only the minimum amount of information required under the state statute. Only a few states require the filing of the limited partnership agreement (discussed in the next section) as an exhibit or attachment to the certificate of limited partnership. It will be necessary to call the office of the secretary of state to verify the requirements for properly filing the certificate of limited partnership.

Figure 3–2 Certificate of Limited Partnership

Certificate of Limited Partnership

ABC Limited Partnership, a limited partnership organized under the Revised Uniform Limited Partnership Act of [state] (the "Act"), for the purpose of filing its Certificate of Limited Partnership pursuant to Section 201 of the Act, hereby certifies that:

1. The name of the limited partnership is ABC LIMITED PARTNERSHIP.
2. The address of the principal place of business of the limited partnership is:

   _____.

3. The name and address of the agent for service of process is:

   _____.

4. The name and business address of each general partner is:

   Name   Address

   _____

5. The latest date upon which the limited partnership is to dissolve is:

   _____.

IN WITNESS WHEREOF, this Certificate of Limited Partnership has been duly executed by each general partner this _____ day of _____, 199__.

General Partner(s):

_____

_____

Care must be taken to use the most current statute enacted by a state when preparing the certificate of limited partnership. For example, a Delaware limited partnership is *not* required to list its limited partners in the certificate of limited partnership. However, many other states require the identification of the limited partners in the certificate. When a limited partnership formed in Delaware desires to qualify to do business in another state, it must comply with that state's limited partnership statute. Therefore, although it is not required to identify its limited partners in Delaware, it may be required to do so under other states' statutes.

Special attention needs to be given to the limited partnership name and the **agent for service of process,** both of which must be included in the certificate of limited partnership.

Section 102(1) of the 1985 RULPA requires that the **limited partnership name,** as set forth in the certificate of limited partnership, contain the words *limited partnership.* For example, the name Real Estate Holdings would not be permitted, but Real Estate Holdings Limited Partnership would. Some states permit the use of the abbreviation *L.P.* in lieu of the words *limited partnership.* The principal reason the name of the limited partnership must contain the words *limited partnership* or, in some states, the abbreviation *L.P.* is to put the public on notice that the business organization is a limited partnership.

Section 102(3) of the 1985 RULPA specifies that the name of the limited partnership "may not be the same as, or deceptively similar to, the name of any corporation or limited partnership organized under the laws of this State or licensed or registered as a foreign corporation or limited partnership in this State." Therefore, before filing a certificate of limited partnership, you must check with the office of the secretary of state to make sure the name the limited partnership intends to use is not deceptively similar to other entities formed in that state.

Additionally, Section 104(2) of the 1985 RULPA requires that "each limited partnership shall continuously maintain in this State: . . . (2) an agent for services of process on the limited partnership, which agent must be an individual resident of this State, a domestic corporation, or a foreign corporation authorized to do business in this State." A limited partnership may organize and file a certificate of limited partnership in a state in which it has no business address. In that case, most state statutes require that it maintain an agent for service of process in that state. As indicated in Section 104(2) of the 1985 RULPA, any individual or corporation may act as the agent for a limited partnership. **Service companies** exist for the specific purpose of providing this service to limited partnerships and corporations. They act in the capacity of **registered agent** in the state in which they offer the service. The requirements for maintaining an agent for service of process, or registered agent, for corporations are discussed in Chapter 6.

For its service, a service company charges the limited partnership an annual fee. The fees range from $50 to $200, depending on the type of service provided. The service company accepts all service of process on behalf of the limited partnership. It immediately delivers all documents it accepts on behalf of the limited partnership to whomever the limited partnership has designated to receive such documents.

The 1985 RULPA permits the reservation of the name to be used by the limited partnership. The name can be reserved by filing an application with the office of the secretary of state, who will in turn confirm that the name is reserved for a specified period. Then, when the certificate of limited partnership is filed, the partnership will be sure that the name it has selected is available.

The 1985 RULPA provides for the amendment or cancellation of a certificate of limited partnership. After the original certificate of limited partnership has been filed, certain events may require the amendment or cancellation of the certificate as originally filed. When such an event occurs, an **amendment to certificate of limited partnership** or a **certificate of cancellation of limited partnership,** whichever is appropriate, must be filed with the secretary of state.

Generally, the certificate of limited partnership must be amended any time the information reported in the certificate no longer accurately reflects the agreement among the partners. Section 202 of the 1985 RULPA deals with amendments to the certificate of limited partnership. Specifically, Section 202(c) of the 1985 RULPA provides that "a general partner who becomes aware that a statement in a certificate of limited partnership was false when made or that arrangements or other facts described have changed, making the certificate inaccurate in any respect, shall promptly amend the certificate." In addition, Section 202(d) of the 1985 RULPA states that "a certificate of limited partnership may be amended at any time for any other proper purpose the general partners determine." Amendment of the certificate is required upon the admission or

Figure 3–3   Certificate of Amendment to Certificate of Limited Partnership

---

Certificate of Amendment to Certificate of Limited Partnership

ABC Limited Partnership, a limited partnership organized under the Revised Uniform Limited Partnership Act of [State] (the "Act"), for the purpose of amending its Certificate of Limited Partnership pursuant to Section 202 of the Act, hereby certifies that:

1. Paragraph 1 of the Certificate of Limited Partnership is amended to read in its entirety as follows:

    _____

    _____

2. Paragraph 4 of the Certificate of Limited Partnership is amended to reflect the addition of a general partner having the following name and business address: Diane Coll, 123 America Street, Anytown, Anystate

    IN WITNESS WHEREOF, this Certificate of Amendment to Certificate of Limited Partnership has been duly executed by a general partner thereunto duly authorized and by the general partner designated herein as a new general partner and is being filed this 26th day of April, 1995.

                              ABC LIMITED PARTNERSHIP

                    By: ABC Manager, Inc., a General Partner

                          By: _____
                                Harriet Johnson, President

                    By: _____
                          Diane Coll, a General Partner

---

withdrawal of a general partner or upon a change in any other provision of the certificate as it was originally filed. Figure 3–3 is a certificate of amendment to certificate of limited partnership, prepared in accordance with the provisions of the 1985 RULPA.

A certificate of limited partnership must be canceled upon the dissolution and winding up of the business affairs of the partnership or at any time when there are no limited partners. The dissolution and termination of the limited partnership will be discussed in greater detail in Section 3–6 of this chapter.

The Limited Partnership Agreement

To supplement the limited partnership information that must be included in the limited partnership certificate, in most instances the parties in a limited partnership also enter into a comprehensive agreement that governs the principal aspects of the business relationship among the partners. This agreement among the partners may be called the **limited partnership agreement,** the agreement of limited partnership, the articles of partnership, or some similar term readily recognizable by the partners. The limited partnership agreement is the foundation of the limited partnership. In effect, it gives the partners the ultimate discretion to define all aspects of the organization, operation, and management of the limited partnership.

As we have already stated, the limited partnership is formed upon the filing of a certificate of limited partnership with the secretary of state. It is important to note that an agreement among the partners does *not* form a limited partnership. If a certificate of limited partnership is not filed with the secretary of state, the state will consider the partnership a general partnership and will treat it as such. In other words, the filing of a certificate of limited partnership *and* the entering into of an agreement among the general and limited partners constitutes the proper formation of a limited partnership. However, the limited partnership agreement will usually *not* be included with the certificate of limited partnership when it is filed with the secretary of state.

The provisions of the certificate of limited partnership will prevail over any inconsistent provisions of the limited partnership agreement if disagreements arise among the partners. Therefore, it is important that the limited partnership agreement and the certificate of limited partnership are carefully drafted in accordance with the limited partnership statute enacted in the state in which the limited partnership is formed.

The paralegal is often asked to prepare the initial draft of the limited partnership agreement. Although no two agreements will be identical in all respects, there are several major issues and points that should be covered in a limited partnership agreement. Figure 3–4 is a checklist of items to consider when drafting a limited partnership agreement. Obviously, this is not an all-inclusive list, but it presents the major issues to consider.

Figure 3–4 Components of a Limited Partnership Agreement (Checklist)

____ Name of the partnership and nature of the business to be conducted.

____ Names and addresses of all general and limited partners.

____ Duration of the partnership.

____ Location(s) in which the partnership will conduct its business.

____ Capital contributions of the general and limited partners and valuation of any property contributed by each partner.

____ Obligation of the partners to make additional contributions to the partnership, including guidelines for changes in capital (withdrawals and additions).

____ Indemnification of the general and limited partners.

____ Duties and rights of the general partners, including:

    ____ Liability to the limited partners and third parties.

    ____ Management and control of the business.

    ____ Limitation of powers.

    ____ Compensation.

____ Duties and rights of the limited partners, including:

    ____ Liability to the general partners and third parties.

    ____ Review of business records.

    ____ Substitution of limited partner.

____ General business and accounting procedures and policies.

____ Method for distributing partnership profits and capital to general and limited partners.

____ Sale or purchase of a limited partnership interest.

____ Addition or withdrawal of general and limited partners.

____ Method for dissolving and winding up the affairs of the partnership, including special circumstances that will cause a dissolution of the partnership.

____ Provision for settling disputes that may arise, including arbitration.

Merger, Consolidation, and the Foreign Limited Partnership

The statutes of most states permit limited partnerships to merge or consolidate with other limited partnerships and even to merge or consolidate with other forms of business organizations (e.g., corporations, trusts, or other associations). A **merger** is the combination of two or more entities (including limited partnerships and corporations) into one of the merging entities; only one of the merging entities remains after the merger. A **consolidation** is the combination of two or more entities (including limited partnerships and corporations) into one entirely new entity; none of the consolidating entities remain after the consolidation.

The states that permit such mergers and consolidations specifically spell out in their limited partnership statutes the requirements and procedures for merging or consolidating the limited partnership with other limited partnerships or with other forms of organizations. The 1985 RULPA does not, however, provide for the merger or consolidation of limited partnerships. We will discuss merger and consolidation in more detail with respect to corporations in Chapter 13, as the merger or consolidation of limited partnerships is not frequently done.

Limited partnerships are not restricted from transacting business in states other than the one in which they initially registered. Article 9 of the 1985 RULPA permits the formation and registration of a **foreign limited partnership** under the laws of a state that is not the state of the limited partnership's initial formation and registration. Registration requirements, similar to those of the initial certificate of limited partnership, must be met by the foreign limited partnership before it is permitted to transact business in the **foreign state.** Generally, a **certificate of foreign limited partnership** must be filed in the foreign state.

In every state in which the limited partnership files a certificate of limited partnership or a certificate of foreign limited partnership, the limited partnership must maintain a registered office and an agent for service of process. As we discussed in a previous subsection, service companies provide the service of acting as the registered agent for limited partnerships in the state in which they were originally organized. Service companies will also act as the agent for service of process for foreign limited partnerships. They also offer the use of their business location as the registered office in any state for an annual fee that, once again, ranges from $50 to $200. This requirement may seem costly and unreasonable, but a foreign limited partnership must comply with the limited partnership statutes of all states in which it desires to transact business.

Partners' Participation in Management

A limited partner has no right to participate in the control or management of the business of a limited partnership. A limited partner who does participate in management will be in danger of losing his or her limited liability status and may be held personally liable for the debts and liabilities of the limited partnership. Control over the management of a limited partnership lies solely with the general partners. Section 302 of the 1985 RULPA does, however, provide that the partnership agreement may grant the limited partners the right to vote on certain matters. In addition, there are certain activities a general partner may *not* conduct without the consent of the limited partners, including the admission or removal of a general partner, the sale of substantially all of the assets of the limited partnership, and any activities specifically spelled out in the partnership agreement.

Limited partners always have the right to inspect and copy certain partnership records. That right is given to them by Section 305 of the 1985 RULPA. In addition, the limited partners have the right to obtain from the general partners, upon reasonable demand, information regarding the state of the business and the financial condition of the limited partnership; copies of the partnership's federal, state, and local income tax returns; and any other information regarding the affairs of the partnership that is determined to be reasonable and just. A limited partner's participation in any of these activities will not constitute participation in management and thus will not affect that partner's limited liability status.

3–3 Liability of the Partners

The distinguishing characteristic of the limited partnership is that the limited partner is protected from the obligations and liabilities of the limited partnership. The amount of a limited partner's investment in the partnership is the limit of that partner's potential loss. A limited partner will be personally liable only if (1) he or she is also a general partner of the partnership or (2) he or she participates in or exercises control of the business. Section 303(a) of the 1985 RULPA provides in part that "A limited partner is not liable for the obligations of a limited partnership unless he [or she] is also a general partner or, in addition to the exercise of his [or her] rights and powers as a limited partner, he [or she] participates in the control of the business."

A limited partner should take great care in preserving limited liability status. It was probably the reason the limited partner found the limited partnership an attractive investment. If, however, the limited partner does participate in the management of the business, his or her liability extends only to creditors who believe him or her to be a general partner. Section 303(a) of the 1985 RULPA provides in part that "If the limited partner participates in the control of the business, he is liable only to persons who transact business with the limited partnership reasonably believing . . . that the limited partner is a general partner."

In addition, the 1985 RULPA enumerates many situations and actions that do *not* constitute participation or control *by* a limited partner in a limited partnership. Section 303(b) specifically provides that:

> (b) A limited partner does not participate in the control of the business within the meaning of subsection (a) solely by doing one or more of the following:
>
> (1) being a contractor for or an agent or employee of the limited partnership or of a general partner or being an officer, director, or shareholder of a general partner that is a corporation;
>
> (2) consulting with and advising a general partner with respect to the business of the limited partnership;
>
> (3) acting as surety for the limited partnership or guaranteeing or assuming one or more specific obligations of the limited partnership;
>
> (4) taking any action required or permitted by law to bring or pursue a derivative action in the right of the limited partnership;
>
> (5) requesting or attending a meeting of the partners;
>
> (6) proposing, approving, or disapproving, by voting or otherwise, one or more of the following matters:
>
> (i) the dissolution and winding up of the limited partnership;
>
> (ii) the sale, exchange, lease, mortgage, pledge, or other transfer of all or substantially all of the assets of the limited partnership;
>
> (iii) the incurrence of indebtedness by the limited partnership other than in the ordinary course of its business;
>
> (iv) a change in the nature of the business;
>
> (v) the admission or removal of a general partner;
>
> (vi) the admission or removal of a limited partner;

PARALEGALERT!

A limited partner will be liable for the obligations of the limited partnership if he or she is also a general partner of the partnership or if he or she participates in or exercises control over the business.

      (vii)   a transaction involving an actual or potential conflict of interest between a general partner and the limited partnership or the limited partners;

      (viii) an amendment to the partnership agreement or certificate of limited partnership; or

      (ix)   matters related to the business of the limited partnership not otherwise enumerated in this subsection (b), which the partnership agreement states in writing may be subject to the approval or disapproval of limited partners;

    (7) winding up the limited partnership . . .; or

    (8) exercising any right or power permitted to limited partners under this Act and not specifically enumerated in this subsection (b).

A general partner is personally liable for all debts, obligations, claims, and other liabilities of the limited partnership. The extent of this liability was discussed in greater detail in Section 2–4 of Chapter 2. Generally, however, the liability goes beyond the extent of any financial contribution or investment made by the general partner to the limited partnership.

3–4   Taxation of the Partners

One advantage of a limited partnership is that, like a general partnership, it is not a taxable entity for federal income tax purposes. It pays no organization, franchise, or income tax. The exception is that a limited partnership is liable for property taxes on any property held in the partnership's name, once again the same as for a general partnership.

The limited partnership itself is not taxed, but its partners are taxed on their proportionate shares of the limited partnership's income. The partnership is only an avenue for passing its income, deductions, and credits through to its partners. The tax advantage of reducing personal income by the partnership losses incurred is one reason the limited partnership is used by business organizations set up to conduct real estate activities.

Nevertheless, the partnership must file a partnership return on **Form 1065, U.S. Partnership Return of Income.** Form 1065 is an annual tax information return on which the limited partnership reports every item of partnership income, gain, loss, deduction, and credit and the names and addresses of the partners entitled to receive a distributive share of the income. A general partner must sign the return on behalf of the partnership.

In addition to filing Form 1065 with the IRS, the partnership is required to provide each partner with a **Schedule K-1, Partner's Share of Income, Credits, Deductions, etc.** On this form the partnership reports the partner's distributive share of the partnership's income, gain, loss, deduction, and credit to use in calculating his or her individual taxable income. Each partner then reports the items from the Schedule K-1 on his or her personal income tax return and pays tax at the individual income tax rate.

Copies of Form 1065 and Schedule K-1 were reproduced in Figure 2–5 (Form 1065) and Figure 2–6 (Schedule K-1) in Chapter 2.

Even though the partnership is not a taxpaying entity, it is required to apply for an employer identification number (EIN) on Form SS-4, Application for Employer Identification Number. This form is the same application used by the

---

PARALEGALERT!

The limited partnership is a nontaxpaying entity. It must, however, file an information return with the IRS, and its partners pay tax based on the partnership's income, deductions, and credits.

sole proprietorship and the general partnership to apply for the EIN. An EIN is assigned to all limited partnerships for filing and reporting purposes and must be used on any return, statement, or other document filed with the IRS. The form of application was shown in Figure 1–4 in Chapter 1.

3–5   Changes in Partnership Interests

The most common changes made to limited partnerships involve the addition and withdrawal of general and limited partners.

Addition and Withdrawal of General Partners

Generally, a limited partnership may admit a general partner only by the unanimous written consent of all the partners or by consent of all the general partners and ratification by all the limited partners, unless the partnership agreement specifically provides otherwise.

A general partner may voluntarily withdraw from the limited partnership, or a specific event may cause a general partner's withdrawal. Section 602 of the 1985 RULPA provides that "a general partner may withdraw from a limited partnership at any time by giving written notice to the other partners, but if the withdrawal violates the partnership agreement, the limited partnership may recover from the withdrawing general partner damages for breach of the partnership agreement." In addition, numerous events spelled out in Section 402 of the 1985 RULPA may cause the withdrawal of a general partner, but generally the death or bankruptcy of a general partner is cause for that partner's withdrawal from the partnership.

Addition or withdrawal of a general partner requires the filing of an amendment to the certificate of limited partnership.

Addition and Withdrawal of Limited Partners

In contrast to the rules governing general partners, very few restrictions are placed on limited partners who wish to be admitted to a partnership or to withdraw from it. A partnership agreement usually requires only the consent of the general partners for the addition or withdrawal of a limited partner. The partnership agreement may also provide that the consent of the general partners may not be unreasonably withheld.

Unless otherwise provided in the limited partnership agreement, a person may be admitted as a limited partner upon the written consent of all general and limited partners.

Generally a limited partner may withdraw from the limited partnership anytime he or she desires to do so, with certain exceptions. Section 603 of the 1985 RULPA states that "a limited partner may withdraw from a limited partnership at the time or upon the occurrence of events specified in writing in the partnership agreement. If the agreement does not specify in writing the time or the events . . . , a limited partner may withdraw upon not less than six months' prior written notice to each general partner."

The addition or withdrawal of a limited partner does *not* require the filing of an amendment to the certificate of limited partnership.

3–6 Termination of the Limited Partnership

A limited partnership may be dissolved for any number of reasons, some of which may have been contemplated by the partners and set forth in the partnership agreement. If dissolution does not occur for reasons set forth in the partnership agreement, it may occur by operation of law or as an unintended consequence of other events. A limited partnership governed by the 1985 RULPA is dissolved only upon the occurrence of specific events; Section 801 of the 1985 RULPA provides that a limited partnership is dissolved the first time one of the following events occurs:

1. The arrival of the time specified in the certificate of limited partnership.
2. An event specified in the partnership agreement.
3. Written consent of all the partners to dissolve the partnership.
4. Withdrawal of a general partner, unless the partnership agreement provides for continuation of the partnership.
5. Application by or for a partner for a court decree of dissolution.

Most limited partnerships have a fixed term of existence, and a specified date of dissolution is stated in the limited partnership agreement. The 1985 RULPA does not require that a limited partnership be formed for a specified term, but in practice, most limited partnerships are. If a date of dissolution is not established by the limited partnership agreement, any limited partner has the right to withdraw and receive a return of his or her capital on six months' written notice to the general partner.

As noted above, Section 801(2) of the 1985 RULPA authorizes the dissolution of a limited partnership upon the occurrence of an event specified in the partnership agreement. In many cases the partnership agreement will call for the dissolution of the partnership at the conclusion of the business purpose for which the partnership was formed. For example, a limited partnership formed for the sole purpose of purchasing and developing a parcel of real estate will dissolve when the development of that real estate is complete.

The dissolution and termination of the limited partnership is somewhat similar to that of a general partnership, discussed in detail in Section 2–7 of Chapter 2. There are two main differences:

1. A certificate of limited partnership is filed upon the formation of the limited partnership; therefore, a **certificate of cancellation of limited partnership** must be filed with the secretary of state upon the termination of the limited partnership. All the general partners are required to execute the cancellation certificate. A certificate of limited partnership is cancelled after the dissolution and winding up of the business affairs of the partnership or at any other time when there are no limited partners. Figure 3–5 is an example of a certificate of cancellation of limited partnership prepared in accordance with the provisions of the 1985 RULPA.
2. The limited partner plays virtually no role in the causes or events leading to the dissolution and termination of the partnership.

PARALEGALERT!

The limited partnership must file a certificate of cancellation of limited partnership upon its termination. Remember that the general partnership has no papers to file when terminating its business since its creation did not require the filing of documents with any governmental agency.

Figure 3–5   Certificate of Cancellation of Limited Partnership

Certificate of Cancellation of Limited Partnership

ABC Limited Partnership, a limited partnership organized under the Revised Uniform Limited Partnership Act of [State] (the "Act"), for the purpose of canceling its Certificate of Limited Partnership pursuant to Section 203 of the Act, hereby certifies that:

1. The name of the limited partnership is ABC LIMITED PARTNERSHIP.
2. The date of filing of the certificate of limited partnership is:

_____.

3. This certificate of cancellation of limited partnership is being filed for the

    following reason:_____.
4. The effective date of cancellation of the limited partnership is:

    ☐ Upon filing of this certificate of cancellation of limited partnership;

    or

    ☐ Specify date: _____

IN WITNESS WHEREOF, this Certificate of Cancellation of Limited Partnership has been duly executed by each general partner this ____ day of _____, 199__.

GENERAL PARTNER(S):

_____

_____

_____

LEGAL*LINKS*LEGAL*LINKS*LEGAL*LINKS*LEGAL*LINKS*

Roeschlein v. Watkins

May the general partners dissolve a limited partnership without the consent of the limited partners? Section 403(a) of the 1985 RULPA provides that "a general partner of a limited partnership has the rights and powers and is subject to the restrictions of a partner in a partnership without limited partners." One such restriction, provided in Section 9(3) of the Uniform Partnership Act, denies the general partners the authority to "do any act which would make it impossible to carry on the ordinary business of the partnership." Consider the following case, in which the court decided that the general partner had no duty to disclose to the limited partners its intention to dissolve the limited partnership.

In *Roeschlein v. Watkins*, 686 P.2d 1347 (Colo. Ct. App. 1983), the court held that Section 20 of the ULPA conferred on a sole general partner the power to dissolve a limited partnership without actually withdrawing, dying, or becoming insane. The applicable partnership agreement in that case required the approval of the limited partners "to sell, lease, transfer, dispose of, hypothecate, convey in trust, mortgage or otherwise assign the lease rights of the Partnership." The court concluded that that provision, "while applicable to conducting the business of the partnership, is not applicable to dissolution and winding up." The court found this true even though the dissolution eventually led to the sale of the partnership's assets.

The court further held that the sole general partner had no fiduciary duty to disclose in advance to the limited partners his intent to dissolve and wind up the limited partnership. Such a disclosure would have permitted the limited partners a chance to elect a replacement general partner and thereby prevent the dissolution of the partnership.

Upon dissolution, the assets of the limited partnership are distributed. In accordance with Section 804 of the 1985 RULPA, the assets are distributed in the following order:

1. To creditors, including partners who are creditors.
2. To partners and former partners in satisfaction of liabilities other than claims as partners.
3. To partners, first, for the return of their contributions and, second, for their respective partnership interests.

An interesting case is reported in the *Legal Links* on the facing page. It illustrates a general partner's ability to dissolve a limited partnership without consent of the limited partners.

3–7   Practical Considerations

Your involvement in the organization or formation of a limited partnership can be as extensive as you and the attorney for whom you are working want it to be. The attorney may ask you to meet with the client to obtain the preliminary information, or he may gather it himself and pass it along to you. Always have prepared well ahead of time a checklist of the information you will need from the client. Being prepared to ask all the appropriate questions during the first meeting with the client will give the client confidence that you can serve his or her needs.

Many of the initial tasks can be performed by the paralegal: gathering information, reviewing the state statutes, and drafting the limited partnership agreement and the certificate of limited partnership. Specific tasks the paralegal can perform include:

- Reviewing the limited partnership law of the state and recommending the procedures for organizing the partnership.
- Checking the availability of the name to be used by the partnership.
- Drafting the limited partnership agreement.
- Arranging for the execution of the partnership agreement by all the partners.
- Preparing the certificate of limited partnership and arranging for its execution.
- Determining the appropriate filing fees for the certificate and arranging for its filing.
- Filing Form SS-4 with the IRS to obtain an employer identification number for the partnership.
- Preparing and filing amendments to and cancellations of certificates of limited partnership.
- Determining the form and procedure for filing a certificate of foreign limited partnership.

SUMMARY

3-1

The limited partnership must have at least one general partner and at least one limited partner. Most states have adopted the 1985 version of the Revised Uniform Limited Partnership Act, which governs the formation and operation of limited partnerships. Any natural person, partnership, limited partnership, trust, estate, association, or corporation is permitted to act as a general or limited partner.

3-2

The filing of a certificate of limited partnership and the entering into of an agreement among the general and limited partners constitutes the proper forming of a limited partnership. The partnership agreement is the foundation; it defines all aspects of the organization, operation, and management of the limited partnership. After its initial formation, a limited partnership is permitted to amend or cancel its certificate of limited partnership. State statutes also permit the merger and consolidation of limited partnerships and their registration in states other than the state in which they initially were formed and registered. If a limited partnership registers to do business in a state in which it does not maintain an office, a service company may act as a registered agent for the limited partnership in that state. Only the general partner has the right to participate in the management of the business; a limited partner's limitation of liability will be adversely affected if he or she participates in the control of the business.

3-3

The general partner is personally liable for all the debts and obligations of the limited partnership and all the claims against it. The limited partner's liability is limited to his or her investment in the partnership. Therefore, the limited partnership is an attractive investment vehicle for many investors.

3-4

The limited partnership is not a taxpaying entity; it pays no organization, franchise, or income tax. All income, losses, deductions, and credits are passed through to the partners.

3-5

The addition or withdrawal of a general partner generally requires the consent of all the partners and an amendment to the certificate of limited partnership. Very few restrictions are placed on the addition or withdrawal of a limited partner, and no amendment to the certificate of limited partnership is required.

3-6

The 1985 RULPA prescribes events on which a limited partnership is dissolved. Additional events may be spelled out in the partnership agreement. Upon the dissolution and termination of a limited partnership, a certificate of cancellation of limited partnership is filed with the secretary of state, and the assets of the partnership are distributed in the following order: (1) creditors, (2) partners in satisfaction of liabilities, and (3) partners for the return of their contributions.

3-7

Many of the tasks to be performed in creating a limited partnership can be performed by the paralegal. The paralegal and the attorney for whom he or she is working will determine the extent of the paralegal's involvement.

REVIEW GUIDE

Key Terms

Before proceeding, review the key terms listed below to be sure you understand each one. If necessary, read over the corresponding section of the chapter. When you are ready to test your understanding, answer the review questions.

limited partnership (p. 38)
general partner (p. 38)
limited partner (p. 38)
National Conference of Commissioners on Uniform State Laws (p. 39)
Uniform Limited Partnership Act (p. 39)
ULPA (p. 39)
Revised Uniform Limited Partnership Act (p. 39)
RULPA (p. 39)
certificate of limited partnership (p. 40)
agent for service of process (p. 41)
limited partnership name (p. 41)
service companies (p. 42)
registered agent (p. 42)
amendment to certificate of limited partnership (p. 42)
certificate of cancellation of limited partnership (p. 42)
limited partnership agreement (p. 43)
merger (p. 45)
consolidation (p. 45)
foreign limited partnership (p. 45)
foreign state (p. 45)
certificate of foreign limited partnership (p. 45)
Form 1065, U.S. Partnership Return of Income (p. 47)
Schedule K-1, Partner's Share of Income, Credits, Deductions, etc. (p. 47)

Questions for Review and Discussion

1. Explain why two or more persons would want to operate a business as a limited partnership.
2. What are the differences between a general partner and a limited partner?
3. What acts constitute the proper forming of a limited partnership?
4. What must a limited partnership do so that it can do business in a state other than the state of its initial formation and registration?
5. What must be included in the name of the limited partnership?
6. Why would a limited partner not want to participate in the management of the business?
7. What is the extent of liability assumed by the limited partner for the debts and liabilities of the business?
8. Who pays tax on the income of a limited partnership?
9. What must be done if a general partner wants to withdraw from the partnership?
10. Describe some of the events that would lead to the dissolution of a limited partnership.
11. How are the assets distributed upon the dissolution of a limited partnership?

Activities

1. Go to your local law library and locate both the Revised Uniform Limited Partnership Act with the 1985 amendments and the limited partnership statutes adopted by your state. Review the provisions of both versions concerning the formation of limited partnerships and the sections of both versions covering the limited partners and the general partners. Prepare a report identifying the similarities and differences between the two versions.
2. Call the secretary of state of your state to determine the filing requirements for registering a limited partnership.
3. Using the filing requirements you identified in Activity 2, draft a certificate of limited partnership for Wacky Widgets L.P., whose general partners will be America Widgets Corporation, William Widget, and his brother, Walter Widget. Obviously, you have not been provided with all the information necessary, but provide any missing information yourself.

CHAPTER 4   Corporations and Other Forms of Business Organizations

OUTLINE

4–1   The Corporation
        Characteristics
        Advantages and Disadvantages
        Statutory Creation and Powers
4–2   Types of Corporations
        Business Corporation
        Professional Corporation
        Nonprofit Corporation
        Close Corporation
4–3   Other Forms of Business Organizations
        Limited Liability Company
        Business Trust
4–4   Practical Considerations

APPLICATIONS

Kevin Kleaner, who wants to own and operate a dry cleaning business, consults an attorney in your office. He is seeking advice on the form of business organization to choose for his business. After determining the needs and wants of the client, the attorney considers the various types of organizations: the sole proprietorship, general and limited partnerships, and the corporation. She discusses the characteristics of each with her client. She advises Kevin Kleaner to consult his accountant for expertise on the tax aspects to be considered.

For liability, tax, and various personal reasons, Kevin Kleaner decides to operate his business as a corporation. At this point the attorney asks you, the paralegal, for assistance in forming the corporation.

OBJECTIVES

This chapter will help you understand the rationale behind the decision to incorporate a business, rather than to operate a sole proprietorship or a partnership. The paralegal will have very little to do with the decision whether or not to incorporate, but an understanding of the basis for selecting the corporate form will prove helpful. After completing this chapter, you will be able to:

1. Define *corporation.*
2. Identify the characteristics of a corporation.
3. Understand the advantages and disadvantages of the corporate form of business organization.
4. Explain how a corporation is created (or formed).
5. Describe the role of the Model Business Corporation Act (1984) in governing the operation of corporations.
6. Identify the rights and powers granted to a corporation.

7. Recognize the differences among the various types of corporations and other business organizations, including the:
   - Business corporation.
   - Professional corporation.
   - Nonprofit corporation.
   - Close corporation.
   - Limited liability company.
   - Business trust.
8. Understand how the various states' statutes govern the operation of the different types of corporations and organizations.

4–1   The Corporation

Characteristics

The **corporation** is a form of business organization whose distinguishing characteristic is that it is a separate legal entity, or a *separate person*, from the shareholders, or owners, the board of directors, the officers, and the employees of the corporation. As a separate legal entity, the corporation is liable for its own obligations and debts, it can sue and be sued, and it can be fined for violating the law. Its authority to act and the liability incurred for its actions are separate from those of its shareholders, directors, and officers. For example, when a corporation enters into a contract, the corporation itself is the party to the contract. An officer of the corporation (e.g., the president or vice president) who executes the agreement or contract on behalf of the corporation does so only in his or her capacity as an officer of the corporation. There are certain circumstances in which liability may be imposed on the shareholders or the board of directors; this issue will be discussed in greater detail in Section 5–2 in Chapter 5. As you will see in this and in subsequent chapters, the corporation is more complex in its formation, structure, and operation than the sole proprietorship and the general and limited partnerships.

In general, responsibility for the overall management of the corporation lies with the board of directors, who are elected by the shareholders of the corporation. The board of directors, in turn, appoints the officers of the corporation, who are responsible for the day-to-day operations of the business. The officers will hire employees to assist in the daily operations. See Figure 4–1 for an overview of the management structure of a corporation. Chapter 5 will cover in greater detail the responsibilities and obligations of the shareholders, directors, and officers of a corporation.

The following section of this chapter will cover some of the various types of corporations with which you may deal as a corporate paralegal. The more common types of corporations include the business corporation, the professional corporation, the nonprofit corporation, and the close corporation. We will also include in our discussion the limited liability company, a new type of business organization that not all states currently recognize, and the business trust. The S corporation (previously called the Subchapter S corporation), discussed in greater detail in Chapter 5, and the publicly held corporation are business corporations, but each has special characteristics of its own. For example, the S corporation is treated differently for tax purposes only, and the **publicly held corporation** sells it shares to the general public and therefore must comply with the Securities Act of 1933, the Securities and Exchange Act of 1934, and various securities statutes of the states in which the shares are sold. The S corporation and the publicly held corporation must still comply with the general corporate statutes and regulations of their state of incorporation and of the other states in which they may be doing business.

Figure 4–1   Management Structure of a Corporation

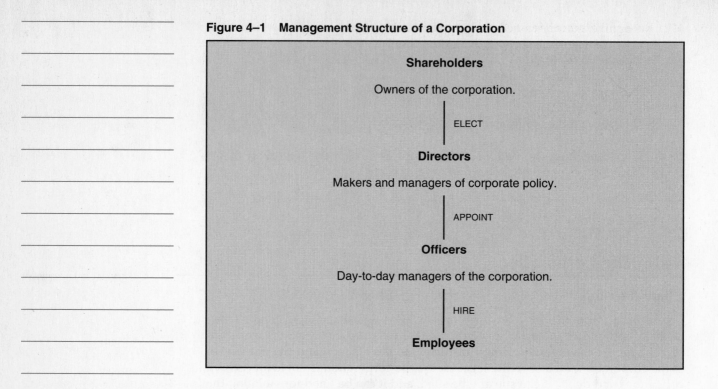

The major portion of this textbook focuses on the formation, operation, and maintenance of the business corporation. Understanding how the business corporation is formed or organized, who owns and manages it, and what procedures must be followed to maintain its existence will help you appreciate the role you play in all these activities. First, it is important that you understand why the corporate form of business organization has been selected and why a particular type of corporation is to be used. The advantages and disadvantages of the corporation form are discussed in the next section.

If you understand the procedures and rationale of forming and maintaining a business corporation, you will have an excellent basis for understanding how the professional, nonprofit, and close corporations; the limited liability company; and the business trust are formed and maintained.

Advantages and Disadvantages

As with any business decision, the advantages and disadvantages are weighed against each other, and an intelligent and well-informed decision is made. Both the advantages and the disadvantages of operating a business as a corporation are numerous, and they must be weighed against the advantages and disadvantages of operating as a sole proprietorship or as a general partnership or limited partnership. See Figure 4–2 for a summary of the advantages and disadvantages of the corporate form, all of which are discussed in this section. Of course, neither the discussion that follows nor the summary in Figure 4–2 includes *all* the potential or possible reasons for a person to incorporate his or her business or to operate it under some other form of business organization, but they include the most commonly cited reasons.

The advantages of the corporate form of business organization include: perpetual existence, limited liability, ease of raising capital, and centralized management.

Figure 4–2 Advantages and Disadvantages of the Corporate Form

---

Advantages of the Corporation

- Perpetual existence.
- Limited liability of the shareholders.
- Ease of raising capital.
- Central management by directors and officers.

Disadvantages of the Corporation

- Double taxation.
- Complex operation and maintenance.
- Cost of formation and organization.

Perpetual Existence   One of the most attractive characteristics of the corporation is its ability to exist perpetually, a right granted to corporations by state statute. This allows corporations to be unaffected by the death of a shareholder or by the transfer of his or her ownership interest in the corporation. As you remember, a sole proprietorship ends upon the death of the owner, and a partnership ends when a general partner dies or withdraws from the partnership.

Limited Liability   The greatest and most-often-cited advantage of the corporate form is that the shareholders of a corporation are generally not liable for the debts or other liabilities of the corporation. The potential risk to shareholders is limited to the amount of their investment in shares of stock of the corporation. But certain corporation formalities must be observed to maintain this limited liability status. The concept of limited liability is discussed in greater detail in Section 5–2.

PARALEGALERT!

The limited liability feature of the corporate form is usually the leading factor in deciding whether to incorporate or to operate as a partnership or sole proprietorship.

Ease of Raising Capital   Remember, the sole proprietorship has one investor, and the general and limited partnerships have at least two investors. Because the corporation generally has a greater number of investors than the sole proprietorship or the general or limited partnership, it has a greater ability to raise capital to finance projects or expand its business. It can attract hundreds or even thousands of persons interested in investing in the business. In addition, the limited liability and some of the advantageous tax aspects offered by the corporate form help the corporation attract investors.

Centralized Management   A corporation may, and generally does, have many owners, or shareholders, and therefore finds it impractical to allow all of the shareholders to participate in the management of the corporation. Instead, a board of directors is elected by the shareholders to manage the corporation, and the board of directors appoints officers to operate the day-to-day business of the corporation, usually with *little interference* from the board of directors and *no* *interference* from the shareholders. You will see the exception to this rule in our discussion of close corporations in Section 4–2; the shareholders act as the board of directors of a close corporation.

The disadvantages of the corporate form include: double taxation, complex operation and maintenance, and cost of organization.

Double Taxation   The greatest disadvantage of a corporation is the double taxation. The corporation pays tax on the income it earns because it is a separate legal entity, unlike the sole proprietorship and the general and limited partnerships. The shareholders then pay taxes on their shares of the corporation's income, distributed to them in the form of dividends. Dividends distributed to shareholders must be treated as personal income by the shareholders and must be reported on the shareholders' personal income tax returns. The net result is that the corporation and the shareholder pay tax on the same dollars. The concept of double taxation and the subject of taxation in general will be discussed in greater detail in Section 5–3.

Overall, the taxation of a corporation has certain advantages *and* disadvantages. Note that taxation is one aspect of the corporation that distinguishes it from the sole proprietorship and the general and limited partnerships, in which income and expenses are passed through to the individuals owning the businesses, who then report such income and expenses on their personal tax returns.

PARALEGALERT!

A corporation may elect to be treated as an S corporation for federal and state tax purposes. In an S corporation the shareholders report their proportionate share of the corporation's profit or loss on their personal income tax returns. In Section 5–3 we will discuss the S corporation in greater detail.

Complex Operation and Maintenance   Because the corporation is a separate legal entity and its authority to form and to operate is granted by state statute, it must comply with numerous formalities and requirements, all of which are time-consuming. For example, articles of incorporation must be prepared and filed in the state in which the corporation desires to incorporate prior to beginning its corporate existence. Also, after a corporation has been formed, it must comply with the state statutes by holding annual meetings of the shareholders and the board of directors, filing annual reports as required by many states, and filing state and federal income tax returns. Generally, the corporate paralegal will play a major role in a corporation's compliance with the state statutes.

Cost of Organization   Filing fees for organizing or forming a corporation in any one state range from $35 to $300, and in some cases an additional franchise fee or a fee based on authorized shares is added to this base fee. In addition to the initial fee charged by the state to incorporate, the cost of the services of the attorney and the paralegal in preparing and filing the proper documentation to incorporate the corporation and the expenses incurred for the purchase of the corporate seal, stock book, and minute book are also borne by the corporation. Also, a few states require that the corporation advertise in newspapers or legal journals in the state of incorporation the fact that the corporation has been formed. Annual franchise taxes and special annual report fees are imposed by many states both on corporations incorporated in that state and on other corporations doing business in that state.

Statutory Creation and Powers

A corporation is created and governed by state law. To put it another way, the **state statutes** of the state in which the corporation was incorporated—its **home state** or **state of domicile**—dictate how the corporation is formed, operated, and maintained. The home state considers the corporation a **domestic corporation.** A corporation that does business in a state other than its home state will also be subject to the statutes of that state under certain circumstances. Such a corporation is known as a **foreign corporation.** Foreign corporations will be discussed in greater detail in Chapter 9. *Domestic corporation* and *foreign corporation* are terms that further categorize all types or classes of corporations; they are not different types of corporations, like the professional, nonprofit, and close corporations we will discuss later in this chapter. For example, Crocker Cookery Corporation is incorporated in Delaware as a business corporation and is registered to do business in New York. Crocker Cookery Corporation is a domestic corporation in Delaware because it was incorporated in Delaware and is a foreign corporation in New York because it registered to do business in New York. The proper way to describe Crocker Cookery Corporation is that it is a Delaware business corporation registered as a foreign corporation in New York.

Corporations must comply with all laws, including federal, common, and case law, just as do individuals, partnerships, trusts, and other organizations or associations. For instance, in addition to the statutes of its state of incorporation, a publicly held corporation is subject to federal and state securities laws and regulations. And all forms of business organizations, including the corporation, are subject to federal and state tax laws. To reiterate, state statutes create and govern a corporation's formation, operation, and maintenance.

Every state has adopted statutes governing corporations formed in that state. These statutes even govern the internal affairs of such corporations. Most have modeled their statutes after the **Model Business Corporation Act (1984),** first adopted in 1950. The Model Business Corporation Act (1984) is continually being revised by the Committee on Corporate Laws (Section of Business Law) of the American Bar Association, and the most current version is included in this text as Appendix A. No state has adopted the Model Business Corporation Act (1984) verbatim. Throughout this and subsequent chapters, we will refer to the Model Business Corporation Act (1984) as the **Model Act.** We will use the Model Act in our discussion and examination of a corporation's formation and operation. Where appropriate—usually where a state's corporate statutes have important distinctions from the Model Act—we will refer to various states' specific statutes. If you understand the provisions of the Model Act, you will find that comprehending and interpreting any state's corporate statutes is relatively simple.

As already noted, rights and powers are expressly granted to a corporation by state statute. Section 3.02 of the Model Act, which appears in Figure 4–3, spells out the specific rights and powers given to corporations by statute. The corporate rights and powers enumerated in Section 3.02 of the Model Act are typical of the rights and powers contained in most state statutes.

PARALEGALERT!

Any business, professional, nonprofit, or close corporation is considered a *domestic corporation* in its state of incorporation. When that same corporation registers to do business in another state, it is considered a *foreign corporation* in that state.

PARALEGALERT!

What is meant by "formation, operation, and maintenance" of corporations? After a corporation is incorporated (or *formed*), it must *operate*, or do business, in accordance with the state statutes and must legally *maintain* its corporate status by properly holding shareholder and director meetings, filing timely annual corporate and tax reports, and correctly documenting all actions taken by the corporation. A paralegal is routinely involved in *all* these aspects of the corporation.

Figure 4–3 Section 3.02 of the Model Act

> **§ 3.02. General Powers.**—Unless its articles of incorporation provide otherwise, every corporation has perpetual duration and succession in its corporate name and has the same powers as an individual to do all things necessary or convenient to carry out its business and affairs, including, without limitation, power:
>
> (1) to sue and be sued, complain and defend in its corporate name;
>
> (2) to have a corporate seal, which may be altered at will, and to use it, or a facsimile of it, by impressing or affixing it or in any other manner reproducing it;
>
> (3) to make and amend bylaws, not inconsistent with its articles of incorporation or with the laws of this state, for managing the business and regulating the affairs of the corporation;
>
> (4) to purchase, receive, lease, or otherwise acquire, and own, hold, improve, use, and otherwise deal with real or personal property, or any legal or equitable interest in property, wherever located;
>
> (5) to sell, convey, mortgage, pledge, lease, exchange, and otherwise dispose of all or any part of its property;
>
> (6) to purchase, receive, subscribe for, or otherwise acquire; own, hold, vote, use, sell, mortgage, lend, pledge, or otherwise dispose of; and deal in and with shares or other interests in, or obligations of, any other entity;
>
> (7) to make contracts and guarantees, incur liabilities, borrow money, issue its notes, bonds, and other obligations (which may be convertible into or include the option to purchase other securities of the corporation), and secure any of its obligations by mortgage or pledge of any of its property, franchises, or income;
>
> (8) to lend money, invest and reinvest its funds, and receive and hold real and personal property as security for repayment;
>
> (9) to be a promoter, partner, member, associate, or manager of any partnership, joint venture, trust, or other entity;
>
> (10) to conduct its business, locate offices, and exercise the powers granted by this Act within or without this state;
>
> (11) to elect directors and appoint officers, employees, and agents of the corporation, define their duties, fix their compensation, and lend them money and credit;
>
> (12) to pay pensions and establish pension plans, pension trusts, profit sharing plans, share bonus plans, share option plans, and benefit or incentive plans for any or all of its current or former directors, officers, employees, and agents;
>
> (13) to make donations for the public welfare or for charitable, scientific, or educational purposes;
>
> (14) to transact any lawful business that will aid governmental policy;
>
> (15) to make payments or donations, or do any other act, not inconsistent with law, that furthers the business and affairs of the corporation.

In addition to the rights and powers given to corporations by state statute, a corporation's articles of incorporation or certificate of incorporation and its bylaws provide guidance in governing a corporation's activities. A corporation's articles of incorporation and bylaws are more directly related to the corporation's business and to its owners and managers than the state statutes, because they are prepared specifically for that particular corporation. The articles of incorporation must include the information required by the state statute, but may include other provisions specific to the corporation.

The bylaws provide even more specific details than the articles of incorporation on the operation of the corporation. But in any case, the state statute, the articles of incorporation, and the bylaws should all *complement* each other, and there should be *no conflict* among these documents. The content and form of articles of incorporation and bylaws will be discussed in greater detail in Sections 6–3 and 6–6, respectively, in Chapter 6.

4–2   Types of Corporations

Business Corporation

The **business corporation,** or general business corporation, is the most common type of corporate form today, and it is the main focus of this textbook. Business corporations include publicly held corporations and smaller, privately held (or family-owned) corporations.

The Model Act, previously discussed, deals with the formation and operation of a business corporation. Section 3.01 of the Model Act states that "every corporation incorporated under this Act has the purpose of engaging in any lawful business unless a more limited purpose is set forth in the articles of incorporation."

Professional Corporation

Only in recent years have lawyers, physicians, dentists, architects, accountants, engineers, and other members of the professions been permitted to operate their businesses as corporations. In the past, they could operate only as sole proprietors or partners, a limitation that kept them from taking advantage of the favorable corporate tax rates. Professional persons are now permitted to incorporate, and their corporations are called **professional corporations.** Which professions may be incorporated as professional corporations depends on the terms of the state statute.

States have adopted the Model Act's **Model Professional Corporation Supplement** or other statutes governing the operation of professional corporations. Statutes governing professional corporations vary greatly from state to state. Most states provide that professional corporations are governed by the state's business corporation law unless specific provisions of the state's professional corporation law apply. It is important that you review the statutes of the state of incorporation to determine the statutes applicable to the professional corporation.

Distinguishing characteristics of the professional corporation include the following:

1. The name of the professional corporation must usually contain a designator indicating that it is a professional corporation. For example, it must include the words *professional corporation* or *professional association* or the abbreviation *P.C.* or *P.A.*
2. Ownership of a professional corporation is limited to individuals licensed to practice the particular profession for which it was incorporated.
3. Only under certain circumstances do the shareholders of a professional corporation enjoy limited liability. Most state statutes governing professional corporations make professional persons liable for their acts and for the professional acts performed under their supervision.

4. Shareholders of a professional corporation will generally not be held liable for acts unrelated to the practice of the profession.

Refer to Section 6–7 for an example of articles of incorporation for a professional corporation.

Nonprofit Corporation

The **nonprofit corporation** is formed for the purpose of conducting a charitable, athletic, political, educational, religious, fraternal, or social service organization that does not contemplate pecuniary gain, or profit. *None* of the net earnings of the nonprofit corporation are permitted to benefit any individual, and the members, directors, officers, and employees of the corporation shall receive only reasonable compensation for the services they provide the corporation. The nonprofit corporation is a legal entity—that is, a separate person—and its organization is similar to the organization of the other types of corporations. One exception is that the nonprofit corporation can be organized on a stock basis or a nonstock basis. Most nonprofit corporations are nonstock.

If the corporation is to be a **nonprofit stock corporation,** the articles of incorporation must specify the number of shares authorized. The shares of a nonprofit corporation must be evidenced by share certificates on which is conspicuously noted that the corporation is a nonprofit corporation. Dividends are not permitted to be paid on these shares, and the shareholders are not entitled to any share of the earnings of the corporation. Figure 4–4 is a specimen form of share certificate of a nonprofit corporation, on which is indicated that it is a nonprofit corporation.

If the nonprofit corporation is organized as a **nonprofit nonstock corporation,** no shares or share certificates are issued. But certificates may be issued evidencing membership in the corporation. On those certificates also, it must be conspicuously noted that the corporation is a nonprofit corporation.

State statutes based on the **Model Non-Profit Corporation Law** govern the formation and operation of nonprofit corporations. The incorporation and general corporate maintenance of a nonprofit corporation are similar in many respects to those of the other types of corporations. These similarities include the following:

1. Articles of incorporation are filed with the secretary of state to form the nonprofit corporation.
2. The affairs of a nonprofit corporation are managed by a board of directors.
3. The directors are elected by the members or shareholders of the nonprofit corporation.
4. The use of a corporate name deceptively similar to the name of another corporation is prohibited.

The nonprofit corporation is not always assured that it will be exempt from state and federal income taxation. The IRS and the appropriate state taxing authority must approve tax-exempt status for an organization, even if it was formed as a nonprofit corporation. Section 501(c) of the Internal Revenue Code lists the activities that qualify a nonprofit corporation as a federally tax-exempt entity. The state tax code must also be reviewed to determine the activities that qualify a corporation as a tax-exempt entity in that particular state.

Refer to Section 6–7 for an example of articles of incorporation for a nonprofit corporation.

PARALEGALERT!

Generally, nonprofit corporations are organized as nonstock corporations. Often they issue "stock certificates" that evidence only membership in the corporation.

Figure 4–4   Specimen Share Certificate of a Nonprofit Organization

Close Corporation

The close corporation, or closely held corporation, is a special form of corporation in which the shares are held by a small number of shareholders, who are often relatives or friends. The distinguishing characteristic of the close corporation is that the shareholders take an active role in the management of the corporation. In addition, the transfer of stock in a close corporation is restricted, and the corporation is not permitted to make any public offering of its stock. For practical purposes, the close corporation is managed like a partnership, but the owners have selected the corporate form to take advantage of a corporation's limited liability.

The Committee on Corporate Laws of the Section of Corporation, Banking, and Business Law of the American Bar Association has adopted a Statutory Close Corporation Supplement, which, like the Model Act and the Model Non-Profit Corporation Law, is a suggested model for use by the states. Some states have adopted their own statutes governing close corporations, but many states have no separate close corporation statute. In such a state, the close corporation is formed and maintained under the state's general corporation law. Delaware is one of the few states that has adopted close corporation statutes separate from the general corporation law.

Figure 4–5   Legend on Share Certificate of Close Corporation

> The securities represented by this certificate are held subject to and may be transferred only in accordance with the certain restrictions contained within the Shareholders Agreement between the corporation and certain parties thereto. Copies of the articles of incorporation, the bylaws, the Shareholders Agreement, and other documents affecting the transfer of these securities and other rights of the shareholders may be obtained by any shareholder upon written request to the corporation.

A corporation can still operate as a close corporation in states where no separate statutes have been adopted, by complying with the appropriate sections of the Model Act. For example, one of the characteristics of the close corporation is that the business is managed by the shareholders, not by a board of directors. Section 7.32 of the Model Act authorizes the elimination of the board of directors if an agreement among the shareholders and the corporation specifically states that the board of directors shall be eliminated.

PARALEGALERT!

You will need to research the statutes of the state in which the close corporation is to be formed to determine whether separate close corporation statutes have been adopted in that state.

A restriction on the transfer of shares in a close corporation must generally be spelled out in the articles of incorporation, in a separate shareholders' agreement, or in the bylaws of the corporation. The statutes of the states vary on the placement of the restriction. Such a restriction prohibits a shareholder from transferring his or her shares to a third party with whom the remaining shareholders of the close corporation have no desire to do business. Usually the articles of incorporation or a shareholders' agreement provide that the shareholder desiring to sell his shares must first offer to sell them to the remaining shareholders or the corporation. If the remaining shareholders and the corporation decline the offer, the selling shareholder will then be free to sell his shares to the third party interested in purchasing his shares.

In addition to restricting the sale of shares, the shareholders' agreement will also define how the corporation is to be operated (e.g., management by the shareholders rather than directors, or management by a board of directors) and will specify the duties of the officers of the corporation.

Figure 4–5 contains the language that generally must be placed as a legend on share certificates of close corporations. This legend puts shareholders on notice that their shares are subject to certain restrictions and that their rights may be different from those of shareholders in other types of corporations. We will cover share transfer restrictions and shareholders' agreements in more depth in Chapter 15. Refer to Section 6–7 for an example of articles of incorporation for a close corporation.

4–3   Other Forms of Business Organizations

Limited Liability Company

A majority of the states have enacted legislation allowing the organization of the limited liability company. The first was Wyoming, in 1977. Florida adopted such legislation in 1982. Several additional states have proposed legislation, and it seems as if states are gradually adopting statutes governing the limited liability company. The limited liability company is much less popular than other forms of business entities only because of its relative newness to the business world. It is important to understand that a limited liability company is not a type of corporation, but a potential alternative to incorporation. The major disadvantage of operation as a limited liability company is that it is restricted to those states that recognize the form.

The **limited liability company** is a noncorporate form of business entity, but it is also a separate legal entity created by state statute. The limited liability company is managed similarly to the general partnership, and its owners enjoy both limited personal liability and favorable federal tax treatment.

An owner's participation in the management and operation of the limited liability company does not cause the loss of his or her limited liability status, as it could in the limited partnership, where a limited partner may lose limited liability status for participating in the management of the limited partnership. In addition, the managers and officers of the limited liability company, just like directors and officers of the corporation, are insulated from liability for their actions performed on behalf of the limited liability company. Of course, managers and officers will be held personally liable for violations of federal tax laws and environmental laws and for participation in criminal activities, just as directors and officers of the corporation would be held liable for these same violations.

Usually the limited liability company is taxed similarly to the partnership. That is, its members pay tax on the limited liability company's income proportionally to their interest in the limited liability company. However, this favorable federal income tax treatment is not automatic. The IRS uses the characteristics of the corporation set forth in Section 7701 of the Internal Revenue Code of 1986, as amended (hereafter referred to as the IRC), in determining when an organization is taxed as a corporation rather than as a partnership. An organization that possesses a majority of the characteristics spelled out in Section 7701 will be taxed as a corporation. Therefore, the articles of organization of a limited liability company must be carefully prepared to preserve favorable federal tax treatment as a partnership. The characteristics provided in Section 7701 of the IRC include the following:

- Continuity of life.
- Centralization of management.
- Free transferability of ownership interest.
- Limited liability.

The IRS also identifies two additional characteristics: that the organization is an association and that it carries on business for profit. These characteristics are met by most business organizations; therefore, the IRS does not use them in calculating whether a majority of the characteristics set forth in Section 7701 are met.

Specific provisions should be included in the articles of organization to establish the limited liability company's eligibility for taxation as a partnership rather than as a corporation. First, the duration of the limited liability company should be limited to a specified period, which can be changed only upon the unanimous consent of its members. Second, it may be advisable that the limited liability company be managed by its members (owners), rather than by a separate and distinct group of managers (directors). This is often unrealistic in a limited liability company with a large number of members. Third, a third party to whom shares of the limited liability company are transferred should become a member only upon the unanimous consent of the other members; this requirement makes the transferability of an owner's interest contingent on the approval of the other members. The fourth characteristic the IRS considers—limited liability—is impossible to dodge, since all limited liability companies possess this characteristic.

Distinguishing characteristics of the limited liability company include the following:

1. Articles of organization, rather than articles of incorporation, are filed with the secretary of state.

2. The name of the limited liability company must include a designation such as *Limited, Ltd.,* or *L.C.*

3. The name of the limited liability company must not be the same as or deceptively similar to that of a corporation (domestic or foreign), a limited partnership, or another limited liability company organized within the state of formation.

4. The limited liability company's existence is generally limited to a specific period, depending on the requirements of the state statutes.

5. Shareholders or owners are referred to as "members," and directors are referred to as "managers."

6. An operating agreement serves the same function as the bylaws of a business corporation.

Refer to Section 6–7 for an example of articles of organization for a limited liability company.

Business Trust

The **business trust,** sometimes called the "Massachusetts trust" or "common law trust," is another type of business organization. It is less popular than the other forms of organizations and is relatively uncommon in states other than Massachusetts. The Supreme Court, in *Hecht v. Malley*, 265 U.S. 144 (1924), defined the business trust as "a form of business organization . . . consisting essentially of an arrangement whereby property is conveyed to trustees, in accordance with the terms of an instrument of trust, to be held and managed for the benefit of such persons as may, from time to time, be the holders of transferable certificates issued by the trustees, showing the shares into which the beneficial interest in the property is divided."

The business trust shares some features of the corporation and some features of the partnership. Because of the increasing statutory regulation of corporations, the number of business trusts has increased over the years. The foremost characteristic of the business trust is that it may be organized without incorporating. However, the business trust has several characteristics similar to those of the corporation, including the following:

1. The trustee of the business trust has the authority to manage the overall policies of and conduct the business of the trust. The trustee's function is similar to that of the board of directors of the corporation.

2. The beneficiaries of the business trust generally may not participate in the day-to-day management of the business. Their role is analogous to the role of the shareholders in the corporation.

3. The business trust issues certificates to its beneficiaries, just as the corporation issues share certificates to its shareholders.

4. Generally, the beneficiaries of the business trust may transfer their interests without the consent of the other beneficiaries, just as the shareholders of the corporation are free to transfer their shares.

5. The business trust is liable for its debts. Neither the trustee nor the beneficiaries are personally liable. This protection from liability is identical to the limitation of liability of shareholders of the corporation.

6. The purpose of the business trust is to carry on a business and divide the profits earned—the same as the purpose of the corporation.

7. The death, bankruptcy, or withdrawal of a beneficiary does not terminate the business trust, just as the same events would not dissolve the corporation.

The issue covered in the *Legal Links* at the end of this section is a contention by a plaintiff that the business trust is governed by the Uniform Partnership Act. Refer to that feature to discover why the court disagreed.

The business trust is an unincorporated organization. It is formed by a written **agreement of trust,** often called the *articles of agreement,* the general purpose of which is to set forth (1) the responsibilities, duties, and powers of the trustee and (2) the interests of the beneficiaries. In particular, an agreement of trust will include the following provisions:

1. Name, place of business, and purpose of the business trust.
2. Designation of trustee or trustees.
3. Frequency of and requirements for holding meetings of the trustees.
4. Responsibilities, duties, and powers of the trustee(s).
5. Duration or term of the business trust.
6. Procedure for issuing certificates to beneficiaries.
7. Rights of beneficiaries of the business trust.
8. Procedure for amending the agreement of trust.

The business trust may be an unattractive form of business organization because it is unfamiliar. This unfamiliarity may hinder the trust in obtaining needed capital to finance the business. In addition, business trusts are illegal in some states, and many states provide no statutes specifically governing them. Many states treat the business trust as a partnership, since it is neither formed under limited partnership statutes nor incorporated under corporate statutes. Some states, however, do recognize business trusts and regulate them to the same extent as they regulate corporations. Other states have adopted specific statutes governing the business trust, for example:

1. In Massachusetts, where the business trust originated, the statute governing the business trust requires that copies of the agreement of trust (and all amendments thereto) be filed with the Commission of Corporations and Taxation. Copies must also be filed with the clerk of every town where the trust conducts business. The name of a business trust formed in Massachusetts must not be similar to the name of another business organization formed in that state.

2. New York requires the business trust to file in the office of the secretary of state a certificate designating: (i) the secretary of state as an agent for the receipt of process, (ii) the names of the trustees, (iii) the principal place of business, and (iv) location of its office in the state of New York. The failure of the business trust to file this certificate prevents it from enforcing a contract in the courts of New York.

3. Wisconsin regulates business trusts and requires more detailed information than Massachusetts and New York. An annual report is required, which must include, among other information, the purpose and nature of the business conducted and the total number of certificates issued to beneficiaries. In addition, restrictions are imposed on the issuance of certificates, similar to the restrictions on corporations.

Because the statutes of the states vary greatly as to the legality, the formation, and the organization of business trusts, it is critical that the statutes of the state of formation be carefully researched.

State Street Trust Co. v. Hall

State Street Trust Co. v. Hall, 311 Mass. 299, 41 N.E.2d 30 (1942), has been a leading case on the legality and limitations of the business trust. In *State Street* the plaintiff sought to terminate a trust before its term had expired and argued that this right existed pursuant to the Uniform Partnership Act. They claimed that the Uniform Partnership Act was the underlying statute governing business trusts. The court rejected this claim. It reviewed the characteristics of the typical business trust and found them inconsistent with those of the partnership, which is regulated by the Uniform Partnership Act. In support of its contention, the court said, in part:

> Not only does this trust differ in its essential features from an ordinary partnership, but it possesses many of the attributes that are characteristic of a corporation. Title to property in one case is held by the corporation and in the other by trustees; centralized management is effected in one by a board of directors and in the other by trustees; the continuity of both the corporation and the trust is uninterrupted by the death of a stockholder or shareholder; the transfer of beneficial interests in both is readily and easily accomplished by the transfer of the shares and the shareholders in each seek limited personal liability. The sum total of these distinctive features of a business trust has brought trusts into such close resemblance to corporations that they have been frequently considered as corporations, sometimes by virtue of constitutional or statutory provisions and sometimes without such provision.

The court determined that "this type of trust does not come within the act" and stated that its decision "rested upon the common law and not upon the Uniform Partnership Act."

4–4   Practical Considerations

A paralegal performs most of the activities necessary for forming and maintaining a corporation, but in most cases has very little to do with the selection of the form of business organization or the type of corporation. The principal role of the paralegal in the decision-making process is to research the statutes of the state in which the organization is to be formed. For example, suppose the attorney has decided that the best form of business organization for the client is an Ohio close corporation. He or she will ask you to research the statutes of Ohio governing close corporations. Specifically, your research should determine the following:

- The Ohio statutes that govern close corporations, whether they are the general corporate statutes or specific statutes relating to close corporations.
- The information necessary for filing articles of incorporation.
- The filing fee or fees.
- Any additional filing requirements.

In most cases, you will be asked to gather the appropriate information from the client for filing the articles of incorporation. You will also prepare and file the articles of incorporation and will draft all the necessary organizational documents. The formation of a corporation will be discussed in greater detail in Chapter 6, where we will cover the specific procedures for incorporation and will discuss the paralegal's role in that process.

SUMMARY

4-1

The corporation is a separate legal entity, distinct from its shareholders, directors, officers, and employees, and it is liable for its own obligations and debts. Responsibility for the overall management of the corporation lies with the board of directors. The shareholders elect the board of directors, the board of directors appoints the officers, and the officers hire employees to assist in the day-to-day operations of the corporation. The advantages of incorporating include perpetual existence, limited liability, ease of raising capital, and centralized management; the disadvantages include double taxation, complex operation and maintenance, and cost of organization. The corporation is created and governed by state statute. Every state has adopted statutes governing corporations, most of them modeled after the Model Business Corporation Act (1984). The full text of the Model Act is reproduced as Appendix A to this book. The state statutes also expressly grant specific rights and powers to corporations. A corporation's articles of incorporation and bylaws also provide guidance in governing the corporation's activities.

4-2

The business corporation is the most common type of corporate form and includes the publicly held corporation and the smaller, privately held corporation.

Professional corporations are organized by lawyers, dentists, architects, accountants, engineers, and other members of the professions to operate their businesses. Ownership of the professional corporation is limited to individuals licensed to practice the profession for which it was incorporated.

The nonprofit corporation is formed to conduct a charitable, athletic, political, educational, religious, fraternal, or social service organization and does not operate its business for gain or profit. Most nonprofit corporations are formed as nonstock corporations, in which no share certificates are issued. Many similarities exist between the formation and maintenance of the nonprofit corporation, and those of the business corporation. Formation of a nonprofit corporation does not ensure exemption from federal or state income taxation.

The close corporation is a form of corporation whose shares are held by a small number of shareholders. The shareholders, rather than a board of directors, manage the business of a close corporation, and transfer of shares is restricted, usually by provisions in the articles of incorporation or in a separate shareholders' agreement.

4-3

The limited liability company, relatively new to the business world, is a noncorporate form of business entity. It is created by state statute, and its owners (called "members") enjoy both limited liability status and the favorable federal tax treatment of the partnership. A majority of the states now recognize this form of business organization, as they have adopted statutes governing the formation and operation of a limited liability company.

The business trust is an unincorporated organization often referred to as the "Massachusetts trust." It is less popular and less common than other forms of business organizations. It is an arrangement whereby property of the trust is conveyed to trustees, who hold and manage the property for the benefit of holders of certificates issued by the business trust. The business trust shares many characteristics of the corporation and many of the partnership. It is formed by a written agreement of trust, the general purpose of which is to set forth (1) the responsibilities, duties, and powers of the trustees and (2) the interests of the beneficiaries.

4-4

Selecting the form of business organization or the type of corporation under which to operate a business is generally left to the attorney. The paralegal performs the research needed to determine the specific requirements of the state statutes for properly forming and maintaining the corporation. The paralegal then implements the procedures required.

REVIEW GUIDE

Key Terms

Before proceeding, review the key terms listed below to be sure you understand each one. If necessary, read over the corresponding section of the chapter. When you are ready to test your understanding, answer the review questions.

corporation (p. 55)
publicly held corporation (p. 55)
state statutes (p. 59)
home state (p. 59)
state of domicile (p. 59)
domestic corporation (p. 59)
foreign corporation (p. 59)
Model Business Corporation
   Act (1984) (p. 59)
Model Act (p. 59)
business corporation (p. 61)
professional corporation (p. 61)
Model Professional Corporation
   Supplement (p. 61)
nonprofit corporation (p. 62)
nonprofit stock corporation (p. 62)
nonprofit nonstock corporation (p. 62)
Model Non-Profit Corporation
   Law (p. 62)
close corporation (p. 63)
Statutory Close Corporation
   Supplement (p. 63)
limited liability company (p. 65)
business trust (p. 66)
agreement of trust (p. 67)

Questions for Review and Discussion

1. Why is a corporation liable for its own obligations and debts?
2. Explain what laws govern the formation, operation, and maintenance of corporations in general.
3. What are some advantages and disadvantages of operating a business as a corporation?
4. Explain the difference between a domestic corporation and a foreign corporation.
5. Who elects the directors of a corporation? Who appoints the officers? Who hires the employees?
6. What is the most common type of corporation?
7. What group of individuals might want to form a professional corporation?
8. What type of corporation will generally not issue stock to its members or shareholders?
9. What distinguishes the close corporation from all other types of corporations?
10. What are the advantages of organizing a limited liability company?
11. Give examples of tasks a paralegal might perform before a client has decided which type of corporation to form.

Activities

1. Richard Rogow, a client of the firm in which you work, wants to start a contracting and construction business. The lawyer in your office asks you to prepare a memorandum outlining the advantages and disadvantages to Mr. Rogow of operating as a sole proprietorship, a general partnership, or a corporation. Prepare this memorandum.
2. Review your state's statutes regarding corporations. Does your state have separate statutes governing professional, nonprofit, and close corporations, or are these types of corporations formed under the general business corporation law of your state?
3. Determine whether your state has adopted statutes governing the limited liability company.

CHAPTER 5   Business Corporation

OUTLINE

5–1   Ownership and Management Structure
     Shareholders
     Directors
     Officers
5–2   Liability
     Limited Liability of Shareholders
     Liability of Directors and Officers
     Indemnification of Directors and Officers
5–3   Taxation of Corporations
     Federal Income Taxation
     Double Taxation
     Subchapter S Election
     State Income Taxation
5–4   Dissolution of Corporations
5–5   Practical Considerations

APPLICATIONS

Your supervising attorney has recommended to Kevin Kleaner that he incorporate his dry cleaning business, for a variety of liability and tax reasons. The attorney now comes to you and solicits your assistance in forming the corporation. She provides you with some details, but there are gaps in her information.

Without understanding how corporations are structured, who owns them, and who operates and manages them, your assistance will be slight. Start with one basic question to your supervising attorney: In what state will the business be incorporated? The answer to that question will lead you to a review of the corporate statutes of that state, the state of incorporation.

OBJECTIVES

Before we proceed into the how-to of forming the corporation, in Chapter 6, this chapter will give you background for understanding the structure of the corporation and its management and operation. Since the corporation is a separate entity—an artificial being, created and existing under state statute—it operates its business through the individuals who own it (shareholders), manage it (board of directors), and operate it (officers). After completing this chapter, you will be able to:

1. Explain the relationships among the shareholders, the directors, and the officers of the corporation.
2. Describe the rights and powers enjoyed by the shareholders, the owners of the corporation.

3. Describe the authority granted to the directors to act on behalf of the shareholders and the corporation.
4. Describe the responsibilities of the officers of the corporation.
5. Determine when the shareholders may lose their limited-liability status.
6. Determine when the directors and officers can be held liable for their actions when acting on behalf of the corporation.
7. Explain how corporations are taxed.
8. Distinguish between the C corporation and the S corporation.
9. Explain the concept of double taxation.
10. Explain the difference between dissolution and liquidation of a corporation.

5–1 Ownership and Management Structure

The ownership and management structure of the corporation is more complex than the structures of the sole proprietorship and the general and limited partnerships. There are additional characters involved in the corporation: the shareholders, the directors, and the officers. Each of these groups has different rights, powers, and characteristics in relation to each other and to the corporation itself. In smaller, closely held corporations, the shareholders, the directors, and the officers are usually the same individuals, but understanding the functions of each position is still very important.

The following paragraphs are a brief outline of the relationship among the shareholders, directors, officers, and employees. Later in this section, we will discuss in more detail the specific rights, powers, and characteristics of each group. Also refer to Figure 4–1 in Chapter 4 for an overview of the ownership and management structure of the corporation.

In short, the shareholders are the owners of the corporation. They generally have no responsibility for its operation or management, although they are ultimately responsible for (1) deciding matters that will have a major impact on the business and (2) selecting a board of directors. The board of directors, which does manage the business, is responsible for (1) determining corporate policy and (2) appointing and overseeing the officers. The officers of the corporation carry out the directions of the board of directors and are responsible for (1) handling the day-to-day operations of the business and (2) hiring and firing employees of the corporation. As you can see, the shareholders have indirect control over the activities of the corporation because they elect the directors, who in turn appoint the officers, who in turn hire the employees.

PARALEGALERT!

Shareholders, the owners of the corporation, elect the directors. The directors are responsible for setting corporate policy and appointing officers of the corporation. The officers are responsible for carrying out the day-to-day operations of the corporation.

Generally, state statutes permit a shareholder to hold the positions of director, officer, and employee simultaneously. The rights and responsibilities of an individual acting in all of these capacities will be different for each capacity (shareholder, director, officer, or employee). For example, Jane Slade is a shareholder, a director, the treasurer, and an employee of Fancy Fabric Corporation. As a shareholder, Jane Slade is entitled to receive a distribution of the corporation's profits or, in other words, to receive a dividend in proportion to her ownership of the corporation. But in her capacity as a shareholder, Jane Slade cannot authorize the payment of a dividend. It is only upon the authorization of the corporation's board of directors that a dividend is paid to the shareholders of a corporation.

The board of directors then authorizes the appropriate officer of the corporation, usually the treasurer, to pay the dividend. In other words, Jane Slade, shareholder, is entitled to receive a dividend; Jane Slade, director, can authorize the payment of the dividend; and Jane Slade, treasurer of the corporation, issues the check for the payment of the dividend. As you can see, the duties and responsibilities of Jane Slade differ according to her role—as shareholder, director, or treasurer.

Shareholders

The owners of the corporation are the **shareholders,** and the acquisition of a share of the stock of a corporation makes a person an owner. Shareholders are owners of the corporation, but they *do not* have legal title to any of the corporation's property, such as vehicles, equipment, or real estate. They do, however, have an equitable interest in the corporation. In other words, owning a share of stock does not give the shareholder ownership of any specific asset of the corporation; it represents shared ownership of the totality of *all* assets owned by the corporation.

Section 1.40(22) of the Model Act defines a shareholder as "the person in whose name shares are registered in the records of a corporation or the beneficial owner of shares to the extent of the rights granted by a nominee certificate on file with the corporation." A shareholder's ownership in a corporation is evidenced by the possession of a **share certificate** or **stock certificate,** which is issued to the shareholder upon payment to the corporation for the shares represented by the share certificate. The payment, referred to as **consideration,** need not be cash but must be something of sufficient value to the corporation. Most states permit the payment of cash, property, services performed, or contracts for services to be performed as sufficient consideration in payment for shares of a corporation. Under Section 6.21(b) of the Model Act, shares may be issued for consideration consisting of "cash, promissory notes, services performed, contracts for services to be performed, or other securities of the corporation." The board of directors has the power to determine the amount of consideration to be paid to the corporation in exchange for the shares. This authority is given to the board of directors in Section 6.21(c) of the Model Act, which states that "the board of directors must determine that the consideration received or to be received for shares to be issued is adequate."

The rights and powers enjoyed by a shareholder are granted to the shareholder by the statutes of the corporation's state of incorporation and by the corporation's articles of incorporation. Additional responsibilities and characteristics of the shareholder are further defined in the corporation's bylaws. In general, ownership of stock in a corporation entitles the shareholder to:

1. Vote.
2. Receive a return on his or her investment (dividends).
3. Share in the assets upon dissolution or liquidation.

Several of the rights, powers, and characteristics of a shareholder will be discussed in the following paragraphs. This discussion will help you better understand the shareholder's relationship with the directors, officers, and employees of the corporation and with the corporation itself.

> **PARALEGALERT!**
>
> The consideration paid for shares is determined by the board of directors. Consideration may be in the form of cash, notes, services or contracts to be performed, or other securities of the corporation itself.

Voting Right   Every owner of stock in a corporation has a **voting right**—that is, the right to vote his or her stock at all meetings of the shareholders. It is through the power of voting that the shareholder exercises control of the corporation. Generally, a shareholder is entitled to one vote for each share of stock that he or she owns, unless the state statute or the corporation's articles of incorporation or bylaws provide otherwise. A corporation's articles of incorporation can limit or eliminate the voting rights for certain classes of shares. For example:

1. A corporation has the authority to issue voting and nonvoting common stock.
2. Owners of preferred stock are usually denied the right to vote.
3. Treasury shares—shares repurchased by the corporation from shareholders—cannot be voted until they are resold by the corporation.

Special voting techniques that can enhance the voting privileges of a shareholder include cumulative voting, voting trusts and voting agreements.

1. **Cumulative voting** is a special procedure used only in the election of directors. Under cumulative voting, each shareholder is entitled to a number of votes equal to the number of shares he or she owns multiplied by the number of directors to be elected. The shareholder may cast all the votes for one candidate for director or may distribute his or her votes among all or any number of the candidates.

    The purpose of cumulative voting is to offer minority shareholders a greater voice in the operation of the corporation by allowing them to elect at least one director to the board of directors. When cumulative voting is not used for the election of directors, **straight voting** is used. With straight voting, each shareholder is entitled to cast the number of votes equal to the number of shares that shareholder owns. If this method of voting is used, the shareholders owning a majority of the stock may elect all the directors of the corporation. Figure 5–1 provides examples of the operation of cumulative voting in the election of directors.

    Some state statutes permit cumulative voting unless it is specifically denied in the corporation's articles of incorporation, and other state statutes require that the articles of incorporation must specifically authorize it. The Model Act provides both alternatives and leaves it to each state to determine the procedure for implementing cumulative voting. It is important to review the statutes of the state of incorporation to determine how that state treats cumulative voting.

2. A **voting trust** is an agreement, between the shareholders of the corporation and a trustee, in which the shareholders confer their right to vote on the trustee by transferring their shares to the trustee. Only voting rights are conferred on the trustee; all other rights are retained by the shareholders. For example, the shareholders, not the trustee, will receive any dividends paid by the corporation. Most state statutes permit voting trust. The Model Act provides for the formation of voting trusts in Section 7.30(a), which states in part, "One or more shareholders may create a voting trust, conferring on a trustee the right to vote or otherwise act for them, by signing an agreement setting out the provisions of the trust (which may include anything consistent with its purpose) and transferring their shares to the trustee."

PARALEGALERT!

Cumulative voting applies only to the election of directors. Under cumulative voting a shareholder may vote a number equal to the number of his or her shares multiplied by the number of directorships to be filled.

Figure 5–1 Examples of Cumulative Voting for Election of Directors

> **Example 1:**
>
> The ABC Company has four directors to be elected and has issued 100 shares of stock, 51 shares owned by the majority shareholder and 49 shares owned by the minority shareholder. Under cumulative voting, the majority is entitled to 204 votes (51 shares × 4 directors), and the minority is entitled to 196 votes (49 shares × 4 directors). The minority shareholder can cast all 196 votes for a single director's seat, which guarantees his or her having at least one director on the board. The downside to voting all 196 votes for one director is that the minority shareholder has no remaining votes to cast for any of the other directors.
>
> **Example 2:**
>
> The XYZ Company has five directors to be elected and has issued 100 shares of stock, 51 shares owned by the majority and 49 shares owned by the minority. Under cumulative voting, the majority is entitled to 255 votes (51 shares × 5 directors), and the minority is entitled to 245 votes (49 shares × 5 directors). If the majority casts 85 votes for each of three directors, he or she is assured of control of the board by electing three out of the five directors. But if the majority casts equal votes for four of the directors, the minority can divide his or her votes among only three directors, and the minority will gain control of the board.

3. In a **voting agreement,** two or more shareholders agree to combine their shares and vote as a unit to maximize the effect of their combined votes. Section 7.31 of the Model Act provides that "two or more shareholders may provide for the manner in which they will vote their shares by signing an agreement for that purpose." By using a voting agreement, shareholders seek to gain voting control of the corporation.

Voting trusts and voting agreements are used to control large blocks of stock in a corporation. Under a voting trust or voting agreement, the trustee or the designated shareholder has the power to vote the shares held by other shareholders of the corporation. Dividends, however, are passed through to the owners of record of the shares.

Dividend Right   A shareholder's **dividend right** is the right to receive a return on his or her investment in the corporation. A dividend is a distribution of the profits of the corporation to the shareholders. The distribution is made only at the discretion and direction of the board of directors. Section 6.40(a) of the Model Act states that "a board of directors may authorize and the corporation may make distributions to its shareholders subject to restriction by the articles of incorporation."

In the absence of any agreement that states otherwise, only those who are shareholders of record on the day the dividend is declared by the board of directors are entitled to receive the dividend. That is, the dividend is paid only to persons whose names appear on the stock register of the corporation on the day the dividend is declared by the board of directors. Once a dividend is declared by the board of directors, it cannot be rescinded. It becomes a liability of the corporation as soon as it is declared.

Shareholders have a right to receive dividends, but dividends are distributed to the shareholders only upon the approval and at the direction of the board of directors.

Dividends can be paid to the shareholders of a corporation in any one of the following forms:

1. Cash dividend: a dividend paid in cash, usually by check.
2. Property dividend: a dividend paid in a distributable form of property.
3. Share dividend (of the corporation issuing the dividend): a distribution of additional shares of the stock of the corporation to the shareholders in proportion to their ownership. Section 6.23 of the Model Act provides that "shares may be issued pro rata and without consideration to the corporation's shareholders. . . . An issuance of shares under this subsection is a share dividend."
4. Share dividend (of another corporation): a distribution of shares of the stock of a corporation other than the corporation issuing the dividend.

State statutes vary, but most states specify the circumstances under which a cash, property, or stock dividend may be paid to shareholders. The source of the revenues used to pay the dividend is generally restricted to the retained earnings, net profit, or surplus of the corporation. Most state statutes are very explicit in describing the sources legally available for the payment of dividends.

Section 6.40(c) of the Model Act states that "no distribution may be made if, after giving it . . . , (1) the corporation would not be able to pay its debts as they become due in the usual course of business; or (2) the corporation's total assets would be less than the sum of its total liabilities plus . . . the amount that would be needed to satisfy the preferential rights upon dissolution of shareholders whose preferential rights are superior to those receiving the distribution."

In addition, a statement restricting the payment of dividends may be placed in the corporation's articles of incorporation.

In other words, a corporation is not permitted to pay a dividend to shareholders if: (1) the articles of incorporation contain a restriction on the payment of dividends, (2) the payment of the dividend would make the corporation insolvent (unable to pay its debts as they become due), or (3) there are no legally available funds out of which to pay the dividend.

The declaration of a dividend should be made by formal resolution at a directors' meeting or by unanimous written consent of the board of directors. See Figure 5–2, which is an example of a resolution of the board of directors declaring and approving the payment of a cash dividend to the shareholders of the common stock of a corporation. In Chapter 7 we will discuss in greater detail the ways in which resolutions are adopted by a board of directors and will look at more examples of resolutions. In Chapter 11 we will conduct a more exhaustive discussion of corporate distributions and the funds from which such distributions may be made.

Right to Assets When a corporation is liquidated, the shareholders have the right to receive any assets of the corporation remaining after payment has been made to satisfy all liabilities of the corporation. During the liquidation of a corporation, the assets of the corporation are converted to cash, creditors are

PARALEGALERT!

Most states restrict the source of a dividend to specified funds of the corporation. If the payment of a dividend would cause the corporation to be insolvent or, generally, if the corporation's assets are less than its liabilities, the payment of a dividend is prohibited.

PARALEGALERT!

The resolution of the board of directors to approve the payment of a dividend is adopted at a meeting of the board or by unanimous written consent.

Figure 5–2   Resolution of Board of Directors Approving the Payment of a Cash Dividend on the Common Stock

> RESOLVED, that there is hereby declared out of surplus profits of the corporation a cash dividend of Two Dollars ($2.00) per share on the common stock of the corporation, payable on March 15, 1995, to holders of record of said stock at the close of business on January 30, 1995, and the Treasurer of the corporation is hereby directed and authorized to cause the same to be paid to the shareholders of the corporation.

satisfied and paid in full, owners of preferred shares having a preference in liquidation over other shareholders are paid, and any remaining cash (or assets) is distributed to the remaining shareholders in proportion to their ownership in the corporation.

Preemptive Right   A shareholder's **preemptive right** is the right to purchase newly issued shares of the corporation before outsiders are allowed to purchase them. A shareholder exercising a preemptive right may purchase new shares in the same proportion as his or her current ownership. Thus the shareholder maintains the same proportionate control and voting power in the corporation. For example, ABC Company has four shareholders, each of whom owns 200 shares of stock. The corporation plans to issue an additional 1,000 shares of stock. Each shareholder has the right to purchase one-fourth, or 250 shares, of the 1,000 shares being sold by the corporation. If any shareholder fails to purchase his or her proportionate number of shares, the shares may then be sold to outsiders or to the other current shareholders of the corporation.

Preemptive rights are generally provided to the shareholders only of small or closely held corporations. Imagine what would happen if a corporation the size of the General Electric Company, which has millions of shareholders, had to offer its present shareholders the right to purchase newly issued shares prior to issuing shares to persons who did not already own shares of General Electric. It would be a procedural nightmare and an administrative headache for the corporation, in addition to being tremendously costly. You can see why preemptive rights are provided only in corporations with very few shareholders.

State statutes treat preemptive rights in one of the following ways:

PARALEGALERT!

The corporate statutes of most states provide that shareholders do not have a preemptive right to acquire newly issued shares unless the right is specifically provided by a corporation's articles of incorporation. A preemptive right, if exercised by a shareholder, prevents dilution of the shareholder's voting power in the corporation.

1. They are granted to the shareholders unless specifically denied in the articles of incorporation.
2. They are denied to the shareholders unless specifically granted in the articles of incorporation.

Section 6.30(a) of the Model Act provides that "the shareholders of a corporation do not have a preemptive right to acquire the corporation's unissued shares except to the extent the articles of incorporation so provide." In other words, the Model Act provides that a corporation's articles of incorporation must specifically state that the shareholders have preemptive rights. If the articles say nothing about preemptive rights, the shareholders do not have preemptive rights. See Figure 5–3, which is an example of a statement that can be included in the

Figure 5–3 Preemptive Rights Language to Be Included in the Corporation's Articles of Incorporation

> ARTICLE VI. The Corporation elects to have preemptive rights.

corporation's articles of incorporation to grant the shareholders preemptive rights. Section 6.30(b) of the Model Act suggests that the language in Figure 5–3 is appropriate for inclusion in the corporation's articles of incorporation when the shareholders are to have preemptive rights.

The shareholders usually conduct their business at a meeting. However, actions of the shareholders may also be taken by written consent. The requirements for holding meetings, taking actions, and other procedures of the shareholders will be discussed more fully in Chapter 7.

Directors

The authority of the **directors** to act on behalf of the corporation is granted by the statutes of the state of incorporation, the corporation's articles of incorporation and bylaws, and the shareholders. Section 8.01(b) of the Model Act states that "all corporate powers shall be exercised by or under the authority of, and the business and affairs of the corporation managed under the direction of, its board of directors, subject to any limitation set forth in the articles of incorporation or in an agreement authorized under Section 7.32." Section 7.32 of the Model Act authorizes agreements by the shareholders to eliminate the board of directors, establish who may be a director, or limit the directors' authority.

In general, the function of the board of directors is to manage the corporation. Management includes setting policy and overseeing the execution of the policy. The directors have the authority to delegate the management of the corporation to officers and committees of the board of directors. Because the Model Act, as do most state statutes, authorizes the corporation to be "managed under the direction of" the board of directors, the directors appoint officers to perform certain duties. The responsibilities and duties of the officers are more fully discussed in the next subsection, entitled "Officers."

Very often directors are employed by other businesses, and other obligations and interests do not permit them to participate in the day-to-day operations of the business. For example, many directors who serve on the boards of directors of such large corporations as the General Electric Company, the Ford Motor Company, and USX Corporation do so in addition to full-time employment elsewhere. Of course, they are compensated for sitting on those boards.

Even though the directors delegate certain powers to the officers to manage the business, they retain ultimate responsibility for the activities performed by the officers. The directors are responsible for all the acts of the officers because they have delegated the authority and have appointed the officers to carry out the activities.

PARALEGALERT!

Chapter 8 of the Model Act includes provisions regarding qualification, number, election, terms, resignation, removal, voting, compensation, meetings, actions, standards of conduct, and indemnification of the directors of a corporation. The state statutes, most of which are modeled after the Model Act, should be consulted first when determining the actions permitted by the directors. In addition, the articles of incorporation, the bylaws, and any resolutions of the shareholders *must* be reviewed.

Section 8.25(a) of the Model Act gives the board of directors the authority to "create one or more committees and appoint members of the board of directors to serve on them. Each committee may have two or more members, who serve at the pleasure of the board of directors." For example, most state statutes permit the board to elect an executive committee, to whom the board may delegate the power to handle interim management decisions between meetings of the board of directors. The only power the executive committee has is the authority given to it by the board of directors or, in most cases, by the corporation's bylaws. Generally, the only authority that a committee has is that delegated to it by the board of directors or given to it in the bylaws. In some cases, authority is given in the articles of incorporation.

Section 8.25(e) enumerates the actions *not* permitted to be taken by a committee designated by the board of directors. Those actions include:

1. Authorizing distributions to the shareholders.
2. Approving or proposing to shareholders any action that requires approval by shareholders.
3. Filling vacancies on the board of directors or on any of its committees.
4. Amending articles of incorporation.
5. Adopting, amending, or repealing the bylaws.
6. Approving a plan of merger that does not require shareholder approval.
7. Authorizing or approving reacquisition of shares, except under certain circumstances.
8. Authorizing or approving the issuance of shares or determining the relative rights, preferences, and limitations of a class of stock.

With the exception of the close corporation, which we covered in Section 4–5, corporations are required to have a board of directors. Section 8.01(a) of the Model Act states that "each corporation must have a board of directors," but it excepts corporations whose shareholders unanimously agree to eliminate the board of directors. Such an agreement is most likely in a close corporation.

The first board of directors is usually appointed by the incorporators immediately after the creation of the corporation (or after the filing of the articles of incorporation). In an alternative permitted by state statute, the first directors may be named in the articles of incorporation. This first board of directors serves until the first annual meeting of the shareholders. Directors elected then or at subsequent annual meetings generally serve one-year terms. Directors are reelected or new directors elected at each annual meeting of the shareholders. The only time a director is not elected by the shareholders is when a vacancy is created by the death, resignation, or removal of a director. In that case, a majority of the remaining directors will fill the vacancy. However, the shareholders still retain the power to fill the vacancy if they so desire.

To provide greater management continuity, most state statutes permit directors to be given **staggered terms**—that is, terms that expire in different years. Staggered terms for directors are explained more fully in Section 8.06 of the Model Act, the full text of which is set out in Figure 5–4.

PARALEGALERT!

Management of the corporation is vested in the board of directors as a body, not in the individuals acting as directors.

PARALEGALERT!

After a committee has been created by the board of directors, it may exercise the same authority as the board. Such authority will be limited, however, by specific board desires and by the provisions of the articles of incorporation and the bylaws of the corporation.

PARALEGALERT!

The first board of directors is either named in the articles of incorporation or elected by the incorporators immediately after creation of the corporation. In either case, the first board serves until the first annual meeting of the shareholders.

Figure 5–4   Section 8.06 of the Model Act

> **§ 8.06. Staggered Terms for Directors.** If there are nine or more directors, the articles of incorporation may provide for staggering their terms by dividing the total number of directors into two or three groups, with each group containing one-half or one-third of the total, as near as may be. In that event, the terms of directors in the first group expire at the first annual shareholders' meeting after their election, the terms of the second group expire at the second annual shareholders' meeting after their election, and the terms of the third group, if any, expire at the third annual shareholders' meeting after their election. At each annual shareholders' meeting held thereafter, directors shall be chosen for a term of two years or three years, as the case may be, to succeed those whose terms expire.

Most states set no statutory qualifications for directors; that is, most states do not require the directors to be either residents of the state of incorporation or shareholders of the corporation. However, the articles of incorporation or the bylaws of the corporation are permitted to contain qualifications for directors. For example, the articles of incorporation may require that a majority of the directors of the corporation be residents of the state of incorporation or that directors be shareholders of the corporation. The articles of incorporation or the bylaws may also impose restrictions on the minimum or maximum age of directors, and a few states require that a director be of "full age," which under the statutes that impose this restriction means 18 years old.

The number of directors who serve on a board is regulated by statute; many state statutes require that a board consist of at least three members. There is no limit to the number of directors. The exact number is usually fixed in the articles of incorporation or the bylaws. Naturally, the more directors a corporation has on the board, the more difficult it is to conduct business efficiently and productively. In any case, the number of directors can never be less than the minimum required by the statute of the state of incorporation. More and more states are relaxing their requirements and modeling their statutes more closely on the Model Act, which states in Section 8.03(a) that "a board of directors must consist of one or more individuals, with the number specified in or fixed in accordance with the articles of incorporation or bylaws."

Most states have statutes that cover the removal of directors, and the trend is moving away from requiring a showing of fraud, breach of trust, or dishonest conduct for removal of directors. These statutes, as well as the Model Act, reflect a recognition that the shareholders own the business and should have complete control over the authority to manage the business (the board of directors). Typically, state statutes provide that directors may be removed with or without cause; Section 8.08(a) of the Model Act states that "the shareholders may remove one or more directors with or without cause unless the articles of incorporation provide that directors may be removed only for cause." However, any director elected by cumulative voting is protected from removal without the consent of the shareholders that elected him or her.

As we have already discussed, the board of directors is given broad power to manage the corporation.

PARALEGALERT!

When determining the number and qualifications of the directors of a particular corporation, you must review (1) the statutes of the state of incorporation, (2) the articles of incorporation, and (3) the bylaws.

PARALEGALERT!

Most state statutes permit shareholders to remove a director without cause unless the articles of incorporation provide otherwise. Of course, a director may be removed for cause, such as fraud or breach of duty.

This power is granted to the board of directors by state statute, the articles of incorporation, the bylaws, and the shareholders. More specifically, the areas of responsibility of the board of directors include the following:

1. Determination of the consideration to be paid for shares of stock of the corporation and the issuance of shares in exchange for such consideration.
2. Declaration and payment of corporate distributions or dividends to shareholders.
3. Appointment, supervision, and removal of officers and other managerial employees of the corporation, including determination of compensation for these individuals.
4. Creation and supervision of committees of the board of directors.
5. Initiation of corporate transactions and other corporate matters, including amendment of articles of incorporation; merger, liquidation, or dissolution of the corporation; and sale or lease of substantially all the assets of the corporation.

Like the shareholders, the board of directors usually conducts its business at a meeting, but actions of the board of directors may also be approved by written consent. The requirements for holding meetings, approving actions, and other procedures of the board of directors are discussed more fully in Chapter 7.

Officers

The **officers** are agents of the corporation who are appointed by the board of directors. Their authority to act on behalf of the corporation is granted by the statutes of the state of incorporation, the articles of incorporation, the bylaws, and the board of directors. The officers' principal responsibility is the day-to-day operation and administration of the corporation. State statutes give corporations great freedom to assign specific duties to their officers. In particular, Section 8.41 of the Model Act states that "each officer has the authority and shall perform the duties set forth in the bylaws or, to the extent consistent with the bylaws, the duties prescribed by the board of directors." Therefore, an officer has the authority to perform any duties delineated in the bylaws or prescribed by the board of directors. In rare instances, an officer may prescribe the duties of other officers, if the authority to do so has been conferred by the board of directors. Usually only general duties of the officers are set forth in the bylaws. Figure 5–5 contains sample excerpts from the bylaws of a corporation, delineating the duties typically assigned to the president, vice president, secretary, and treasurer of a corporation.

One specific duty of the officers of a corporation—one that deserves particular attention—is the execution of contracts on behalf of a corporation. For a contract or other instrument to be binding on the corporation, it must be executed in the name of the corporation by the officer or officers authorized to execute that document. The officers must take great care in executing documents so that they do not find themselves personally liable under the terms of the contract. Refer to Figure 5–6 for an example of the proper way for an officer of the corporation to execute a document so that only the corporation is liable under the contract.

Most state statutes require that the board of directors appoint specific officers, usually a president, a secretary, and a treasurer, and some states require that a corporation have a chief executive officer and a

PARALEGALERT!

The authority to execute a contract on behalf of the corporation is usually given to an officer by a resolution of the board of directors that authorizes the transaction.

chief financial officer. The authority to create other offices as deemed necessary is given to the board of directors or the shareholders. For example, the board of directors may feel it is necessary to appoint a vice president of sales and a vice president of administration because of the magnitude of the responsibilities to be handled by each of these positions.

Figure 5–5 Duties Typically Assigned to the Officers by a Corporation's Bylaws

President   The president shall be the chief executive officer of the corporation, shall preside at all meetings of the shareholders and the board of directors, shall have general and active management of the business of the corporation, and shall see that all orders and resolutions of the board of directors are carried into effect. He or she shall execute bonds, mortgages, and other contracts requiring a seal under the seal of the corporation, except where required or permitted by law to be otherwise signed and executed and except where the signing and execution thereof shall be expressly delegated by the board of directors to some other officer or agent of the corporation.

Vice President   The vice president or, if there shall be more than one, the vice presidents in the order determined by the board of directors, shall, in the absence or disability of the president, perform the duties and exercise the powers of the president and shall perform such other duties and have such other powers as the board of directors may from time to time prescribe.

Secretary   The secretary shall attend all meetings of the board of directors and all meetings of the shareholders and record all the proceedings of the meetings of the corporation and of the board of directors in a book to be kept for that purpose and shall perform like duties for the standing committees when required. He or she shall give, or cause to be given, notice of all meetings of the shareholders and special meetings of the board of directors, and shall perform such other duties as may be prescribed by the board of directors or president, under whose supervision he or she shall be. The secretary shall have custody of the corporate seal of the corporation and he or she, or an assistant secretary, shall have authority to affix the same to any instrument requiring it, and when so affixed, it may be attested by his or her signature or by the signature of such assistant secretary. The board of directors may give general authority to any other officer to affix the seal of the corporation and to attest the affixing by his or her signature.

Treasurer   The treasurer shall have the custody of the corporate funds and securities and shall keep full and accurate accounts of receipts and disbursements in books belonging to the corporation and shall deposit all moneys and other valuable effects in the name and to the credit of the corporation in such depositories as may be designated by the board of directors. He or she shall disburse the funds of the corporation as may be ordered by the board of directors, taking proper vouchers for such disbursements, and shall render to the president and the board of directors at its regular meetings, or when the board of directors so requires, an account of all his or her transactions as treasurer and of the financial condition of the corporation.

Figure 5–6 Execution of Document by an Officer

RESOURCE COAL COMPANY

By _____
   John Smith, President

The number and type of offices is generally specified in the bylaws of the corporation or, less often, in the articles of incorporation. Almost every state requires that at least a president and a secretary be appointed, and some states prohibit the same individual from holding these positions. But many states are following the lead of Section 8.41 of the Model Act, which includes no statutory requirement that particular officers be appointed. That section provides that the bylaws or the board of directors shall prescribe the officers' positions and duties. No state statute restricts a person from acting as a director and an officer of the same corporation. In fact, as we discussed earlier, one person can be a shareholder, a director, and an officer simultaneously for the same corporation.

The board of directors generally appoints officers for a term of one year, and the officers are either reappointed or replaced at each annual meeting of the board of directors. However, the term of office of officers is generally fixed by the state statute, the articles of incorporation, or the bylaws. If no term of office is specified, an officer will hold office until he or she resigns or a successor is elected, unless an employment contract sets a definite period of employment. An officer may be removed from office by the party authorized to appoint that officer in the first instance, usually the board of directors. The board of directors, however, may have to justify the removal of the officer as being in the best interests of the corporation. Because many officers enter into employment agreements with the corporation, directors need to take great care that the corporation will not be in breach of the employment contract if the officer is removed. If there is a potential for liability if the officer is removed in breach of the employment contract, the directors' removal of the officer must be substantiated as being in the best interests of the corporation.

The standard of conduct required of officers is defined in Section 8.42 of the Model Act, which states that an officer shall perform his or her duties in good faith, with the care of an ordinarily prudent person, and in a manner he or she reasonably believes to be in the best interests of the corporation.

PARALEGALERT!

The duties to be performed by officers of the corporation are generally specified in the corporation's bylaws. The board of directors may, however, authorize the officers to perform specific duties as it deems necessary and appropriate.

PARALEGALERT!

An officer has a strict duty to act honestly, in good faith, and only in the best interests of the corporation. Therefore, an officer should avoid involvement in transactions in which the officer has a personal interest.

5–2 Liability

Limited Liability of Shareholders

As we have already discussed, one of the advantages of the corporate form is the limited personal liability enjoyed by the shareholders. Shareholders are usually insulated from personal liability for the debts and obligations of the corporation and for the acts of the employees of the corporation. Generally, shareholders' liability or loss is limited to the consideration they paid for their shares of stock of the corporation—that is, their investment in the corporation. But in exceptional circumstances, when a corporation is used by the shareholders for illegal purposes, the shareholders are held personally liable. Imposing liability on the shareholders is called **piercing the corporate veil.** Its purpose is to prevent a corporation from being used as an avenue to perpetrate a fraud, commit a crime, or avoid the law. The factors a court of law examines in determining whether to pierce the corporate veil and hold the shareholders of the corporation liable include:

1. Disregard for compliance with corporate formalities, including failure to hold shareholder and director meetings.
2. Commingling of corporate and personal funds.
3. Payment of a dividend when the corporation is deemed insolvent.
4. Deception of a third party by an individual who fails to disclose that he or she is acting on behalf of a corporation.
5. Underfunding or undercapitalization of the corporation.

In an interesting case, reported as Case I in the *Legal Links* on page 86, the president of a corporation was held individually liable for a corporate debt.

One way in which a court may pierce the corporate veil is by applying the **alter ego doctrine.** Under this doctrine the shareholders will be denied the protection of limited liability if the court determines that the corporation is merely the alter ego of the shareholder or shareholders of the corporation. The closely held or one-owner corporation is more susceptible to this doctrine, and great care must be taken to preserve such a corporation's autonomy. However, the mere fact that the stock of a corporation is held by one person or by members of one family does not permit a court to pierce the corporate veil. The court must demonstrate that the corporation is the alter ego of the individual shareholder and that the corporation and the shareholder are no longer separate, before it may pierce the corporate veil.

PARALEGALERT!

A court may pierce the corporate veil and impose personal liability upon a shareholder who used the corporation to perpetrate a fraud, commit a crime, or avoid the law.

Liability of Directors and Officers

Because the relationship of the directors and officers to the corporation is one of trust and confidence, they are deemed to be **fiduciaries** of the corporation. When they fail to comply with their fiduciary responsibilities, including a duty of care and a duty of loyalty, most state statutes impose liability and penalties for losses incurred by the corporation for their failures. Directors are expected to use their best judgment in managing the corporate business, but they cannot guarantee the success of the business. The **business judgment rule** immunizes the directors and officers from any losses resulting from poor judgment or honest mistakes. In the following paragraphs, we will discuss the duties of care and loyalty and the business judgment rule.

The **duty of care** owed to the corporation is the obligation of the directors and officers to be assiduous in conducting the corporate affairs and to use prudent business judgment. In other words, directors and officers should carry out their duties in an informed, professional, and businesslike manner. Section 8.30(a)(2) of the Model Act defines the degree of care required as that which "an ordinarily prudent person in a like position would

PARALEGALERT!

Because the directors and officers are fiduciaries of the corporation, they have a duty of care and a duty of loyalty to the corporation. Failure to abide by these duties can result in the imposition of fines and penalties.

exercise under similar circumstances." In fulfilling their duty of care, directors are expected to attend meetings of the board of directors, to be informed on all corporate matters, to make independent inquiries when deemed necessary, and to understand the legal and professional advice rendered to the board of directors. In addition, a director is expected to provide supervision to any officer or employee to whom he or she has delegated responsibilities. Even though directors and officers are expected to act in accordance with their own knowledge and experience, most states, as well as Section 8.30 of the Model Act, allow a director to rely on information prepared or provided by reliable and competent officers or employees of the corporation; by legal counsel, public accountants, and other professionals or experts; and by committees designated by the board of directors without being charged with violating his or her duty of care to the corporation and its shareholders.

The **duty of loyalty** is a director's or officer's faithfulness to his or her obligations and duties to the corporation; in essence, it requires that the director or officer serve the best interests of the corporation, not his or her personal interests. Section 8.30(a)(3) of the Model Act, as well as many state statutes, requires that a director discharge his (or her) duties "in a manner he reasonably believes to be in the best interests of the corporation." Therefore, a director should avoid any decision making as a director that would appear to create a conflict of interest with any personal interests. Section 8.31(a) defines "a conflict of interest transaction" as "a transaction with the corporation in which a director of the corporation has a direct or indirect interest." That same section goes on to explain that a conflict of interest transaction is not voidable, or disallowed, solely because of the director's interest in the transaction, as long as one of the following three conditions is met:

(1) the material facts of the transaction and the director's interest were disclosed or known to the board of directors or a committee of the board of directors and the board of directors or committee authorized, approved, or ratified the transaction;

(2) the material facts of the transaction and the director's interest were disclosed or known to the shareholders entitled to vote and they authorized, approved, or ratified the transaction; or

(3) the transaction was fair to the corporation.

Directors and officers are also prohibited from using confidential corporate information for personal advantage. For example, information not publicly available may not be used by a director or an officer, an insider, to make a profit on the purchase or sale of the corporation's stock.

The business judgment rule protects the directors and officers from liability for their decisions as long as they do not violate their fiduciary duties of care and loyalty and as long as the corporation has the authority to make such decisions. Even if the business suffers a loss from the poor business judgment or decision of a director or an officer, the director or officer will generally not be found liable for the loss. Under the business judgment rule, a court will not interfere with the directors' management of the corporation as long as the directors fulfill their fiduciary duties of care and loyalty. For the directors and officers to benefit from this rule, they must meet all the following requirements:

1. They must act in good faith.
2. They must act as ordinarily prudent persons in a like position would under similar circumstances.
3. They must act in a manner they reasonably believe to be in the best interests of the corporation.

You will note that we discussed these same requirements in our discussion of the duties of care and loyalty. These duties are further spelled out in Section 8.30 of the Model Act. For the directors and officers to fulfill these duties, they must make informed decisions, using logical and sound justification for making such decisions, and must allow no conflict of interest to exist between the corporation's best interest and their personal interest. Only if these duties are fulfilled will the directors and officers be absolved from liability.

Much litigation has arisen from the business judgment rule. You will see an example in Case II of the *Legal Links* below.

LEGAL *LINKS* LEGAL *LINKS* LEGAL *LINKS* LEGAL *LINKS*

DeWitt Truck Brokers, Inc. v. W. Ray Flemming Fruit Company
AmeriFirst Bank v. Bomar

CASE I

It is clearly recognized that a corporation is an entity separate and distinct from its shareholders, directors, and officers, and that its debts are not the personal indebtedness of those individuals. However, circumstances arise in which the corporate form, as separate and distinct, is disregarded and liability may be incurred by the shareholders, directors, or officers. Courts are generally reluctant to pierce the corporate veil. However, consider the findings of the lower and appeals courts in the following case.

In *DeWitt Truck Brokers, Inc. v. W. Ray Flemming Fruit Company*, 540 F.2d 681 (4th Cir. 1976), the plaintiff sought to pierce the corporate veil under the law of South Carolina and impose individual liability on the president of the corporation. The Fourth Circuit of the United States Court of Appeals upheld the District Court's findings that "there was evidence to sustain the findings, that there was here a complete disregard of 'corporate formalities' in the operation of the corporation, which functioned, not for the benefit of all stockholders, but only for the financial advantage of Flemming, who was the sole stockholder to receive one penny of profit from the corporation in the decade or more that it operated, and who made during that period all the corporate decisions and dominated the corporation's existence."

The court, in *DeWitt*, emphasized other factors to be considered in applying the doctrine of piercing of the corporate veil. Those factors include "failure to observe corporate formalities, non-payment of dividends, the insolvency of the debtor corporation at the time, siphoning of funds of the corporation by the dominant stockholder, non-functioning of other officers or directors, absence of corporate records, and the fact that the corporation is merely a facade for the operations of the dominant stockholder or stockholders. The conclusion to disregard the corporate entity may not, however, rest on a single factor, whether undercapitalization, disregard of corporation's formalities, or what-not, but must involve a number of such factors; in addition, it must present an element of injustice or fundamental unfairness."

CASE II

As we learned from the discussion of the business judgment rule, officers and directors of a corporation are free from liability if they have acted in good faith, acted as an ordinarily prudent person, and acted in a manner the officer or director believes to be in the best interests of the corporation.

In *AmeriFirst Bank v. Bomar*, 757 F. Supp. 1365 (S.D. Fla. 1991), Hattler, the bank's senior lending officer, and Cole, the chief financial officer of the bank's service corporation subsidiary, were sued, along with other defendants, for breach of fiduciary duty. Hattler and his codefendants argued against the claims of breach of fiduciary duty, negligence, breach of duty of loyalty, fraud, fraudulent misrepresentation, and negligent misrepresentation because, as officers and directors of AmeriFirst, they were shielded by the business judgment rule from liability for their actions and decisions.

The court expressly recited the business judgment rule as applying to both officers and directors and held that "unless there is a showing of an abuse of discretion, fraud, bad faith or illegality, a court will not substitute its own judgment for that of corporate management."

Indemnification of Directors and Officers

Often lawsuits or criminal charges are filed against a director or an officer for corporate actions he or she authorized. The legal fees incurred to defend the suit or charges can be substantial. Therefore, corporations will generally indemnify the directors and officers for the costs they incur, provided they acted in good faith, they reasonably believed that their conduct was in the best interests of the corporation, and—in criminal proceedings—they had no reason to believe their conduct was unlawful. **Indemnification** is a corporation's reimbursement of directors and officers of the corporation for any expenses incurred by them in defending any threatened or pending suits or criminal proceedings stemming from actions they took in their capacities as directors and officers of the corporation.

Most state statutes authorize corporations to indemnify their directors and officers. Those states either have enacted all of the Model Act's provisions on indemnification or have modeled their statutes after them. Selected provisions of Sections 8.51 and 8.56 of the Model Act are included in Figure 5–7. These sections provide for indemnification of directors (Section 8.51) and officers, employees, and agents (Section 8.56). Refer to Appendix A, the full text of the Model Act, to examine all the provisions of these sections.

Section 8.56 provides mandatory indemnification to an officer, unless the corporation's articles of incorporation provide otherwise, if the officer was successful in defending the proceeding. Mandatory indemnification also applies to a director who is successful in defending an action.

Most state statutes provide that a corporation is not required to indemnify directors if, in the actions against them, the court adjudged them liable to the corporation or if they were found to have improperly received a personal benefit. In other words, a director will not be indemnified for any expenses incurred in defending an action involving wrongdoing on his or her part.

Figure 5–7 Indemnification Provisions

> **§ 8.51. Authority to Indemnify.—**
>
> (a) Except as provided in subsection (d), a corporation may indemnify an individual made a party to a proceeding because he is or was a director against liability incurred in the proceeding, if:
>
>   (1) he conducted himself in good faith; and
>
>   (2) he reasonably believed:
>
>   (i) in the case of conduct in his official capacity with the corporation, that his conduct was in its best interest; and
>
>   (ii) in all other cases, that his conduct was at least not opposed to its best interests; and
>
>   (3) in the case of any criminal proceeding, he had no reasonable cause to believe his conduct was unlawful.
>
> **§ 8.56. Indemnification of Officers, Employees, and Agents.**—Unless a corporation's articles of incorporation provide otherwise:
>
> (a) an officer of the corporation who is not a director is entitled to mandatory indemnification under section 8.52, and is entitled to apply for court-ordered indemnification under section 8.54, in each case to the same extent as a director.

In the few states that do not have statutes granting indemnification, the corporation may still provide indemnification to the directors and officers in the articles of incorporation or the bylaws. A court of law will generally uphold indemnification of directors and officers in the articles of incorporation or the bylaws provided that a sound corporate purpose can be shown for providing the indemnification. A corporation usually finds it difficult to fill director and officer positions unless the corporation offers indemnification to directors and officers. Individuals are hesitant to serve as directors or officers when they are not guaranteed that they will be reimbursed for the expense of costly litigation arising from actions they take on behalf of the corporation. Overcoming that hesitancy is usually considered a sound reason for the corporation to offer indemnification in the articles of incorporation or the bylaws if the state statutes do not address the issue.

5–3 Taxation of Corporations

The corporation is subject to taxation by the federal, state, and local governments, just as individuals are, on the income the corporation earns. The corporation is a separate taxpaying entity; it pays income tax at corporate tax rates. In general, a corporation is treated for tax purposes as a separate and distinct entity from its shareholders or owners. Because it is a separate taxpaying entity, not just a tax-reporting entity like the partnership, its taxation is very different from the taxation of the sole proprietorship and the general and limited partnerships. The sole proprietor and the partners pay tax on their personal tax returns on the income earned by the sole proprietorship and the general and limited partnerships.

The taxation of the corporation has its advantages and disadvantages, all of which must be examined carefully before a decision is made to operate the business as a corporation. Generally, it is the client's tax lawyer or accountant who offers advice on the tax ramifications of operating as a corporation. Your involvement, as a paralegal, with the corporation will generally not begin until the tax considerations have been examined by the accountant or tax lawyer and the decision has been made to incorporate the business.

PARALEGALERT!

The client's accountant or tax lawyer will take responsibility for advising the client on the form of business organization under which the business should operate for tax purposes. It is generally not until after this decision is made that the paralegal becomes involved—usually with the formation of the business organization.

Federal Income Taxation

There are two kinds of corporations for federal income tax purposes: the C corporation and the S corporation. The **C corporation,** so named because the taxation of corporations is covered by subchapter C of subtitle A of the Internal Revenue Code, is taxed on its own income and realizes its own losses as a separate entity from the shareholders of the corporation. The **S Corporation,** covered by subchapter S, is not a taxable entity. The shareholders of the S corporation personally report the income and losses of the S corporation on their personal income tax returns in the proportions of their ownership in the corporation, much as in a partnership. The following discussion of federal income taxation applies only to C corporations; S corporations will be covered in detail in a later subsection.

If an organization incorporates under state statute, it will usually be taxed as a corporation. However, a business does not need to be incorporated to be subject to taxation as a corporation. For tax purposes, a partnership, trust, or other form of business organization may be taxed as a corporation if certain characteristics are met in accordance with Section 7701(a)(3) of the Internal Revenue Code of 1986, as amended (hereafter referred to as the IRC). Section 7701 of the IRC provides that an organization is taxed as a corporation if that organization possesses a majority of the characteristics spelled out in that section. These characteristics are:

- Existence of an association.
- Conduct of business with an intention of profit making.
- Continuity of life.
- Centralization of management.
- Free transferability of ownership interest.
- Limited liability.

The sole proprietorship is never treated as a corporation for tax purposes.

Any business organization qualifying as a corporation for tax purposes, as well as any corporation incorporated under state statutes, is required to file an annual return with the Internal Revenue Service on **Form 1120, U.S. Corporation Income Tax Return,** or **Form 1120-A, U.S. Corporation Short-Form Income Tax Return.** These forms are used by corporations to report income, gains, losses, deductions, and credits and to figure their income tax liability. Reproduced as Figure 5–8, pp. 90–91, is Form 1120-A, the short-form income tax return. The short form is permitted when both the corporation's gross receipts and its total assets are under $500,000, it does not have any ownership in a foreign corporation, it is not undergoing a dissolution or liquidation, and certain other requirements are met.

PARALEGALERT!

Business organizations taxed as "corporations" under the Internal Revenue Code are not only those that meet the definition of *corporation* under state statutes. The definition of *corporation* for tax purposes differs from the definition in the state corporate statutes.

Double Taxation

Double taxation is a particularly significant disadvantage of the corporate form, especially if a large portion of the corporation's income is being distributed to the shareholders in the form of dividends. As we have already discussed, distributions to the shareholders of a corporation are paid out of the corporation's profits, and the board of directors has the power to decide the amount of profits that will be distributed to the shareholders. The profits that remain after taxes have been paid are eligible to be distributed to the shareholders. When those profits are distributed to the shareholders as a cash dividend, the cash dividend is treated as income to the individual shareholder. The shareholder must then pay personal income tax on the cash dividend received from the corporation. That cash dividend has been paid out of profits on which the corporation has already paid tax.

To illustrate the concept of double taxation, consider the following example. A corporation pays income tax on its profits at a rate of 34%; that is, on each $100 of income, it pays $34 income tax. The $66 that remains may be paid to the shareholder of the corporation in the form of a cash dividend. If the entire $66 is paid to the shareholder, the shareholder must

PARALEGALERT!

Double taxation, in which both the corporation and the shareholder are taxed on the same dollars, is one of the disadvantages of the corporate form of business organization.

Figure 5–8   Form 1120-A, U.S. Corporation Short-Form Income Tax Return

Form **1120-A**
Department of the Treasury
Internal Revenue Service

U.S. Corporation Short-Form Income Tax Return
See separate instructions to make sure the corporation qualifies to file Form 1120-A.
For calendar year 1993 or tax year beginning .... , 1993, ending .... , 19 .....

OMB No. 1545-0890

1993

A Check this box if the corp. is a personal service corp. (as defined in Temporary Regs. section 1.441-4T—see instructions) ▶ ☐

Use IRS label. Otherwise, please print or type.

Name

Number, street, and room or suite no. (If a P.O. box, see page 7 of instructions.)

City or town, state, and ZIP code

B Employer identification number

C Date incorporated

D Total assets (see Specific Instructions)
$

E Check applicable boxes: (1) ☐ Initial return   (2) ☐ Change of address
F Check method of accounting: (1) ☐ Cash   (2) ☐ Accrual   (3) ☐ Other (specify) · · ▶

Income

1a	Gross receipts or sales [ ] **b** Less returns and allowances [ ] **c** Balance ▶	1c
2	Cost of goods sold (see instructions)	2
3	Gross profit. Subtract line 2 from line 1c	3
4	Domestic corporation dividends subject to the 70% deduction	4
5	Interest	5
6	Gross rents	6
7	Gross royalties	7
8	Capital gain net income (attach Schedule D (Form 1120))	8
9	Net gain or (loss) from Form 4797, Part II, line 20 (attach Form 4797)	9
10	Other income (see instructions)	10
11	**Total income.** Add lines 3 through 10 ▶	11

Deductions (See instructions for limitations on deductions.)

12	Compensation of officers (see instructions)	12
13a	Salaries and wages [ ] **b** Less employment credits [ ] **c** Bal ▶	13c
14	Repairs and maintenance	14
15	Bad debts	15
16	Rents	16
17	Taxes and licenses	17
18	Interest	18
19	Charitable contributions (see instructions for 10% limitation)	19
20	Depreciation (attach Form 4562) 20	
21	Less depreciation claimed elsewhere on return . . . 21a	21b
22	Other deductions (attach schedule)	22
23	**Total deductions.** Add lines 12 through 22 ▶	23
24	Taxable income before net operating loss deduction and special deductions. Subtract line 23 from line 11	24
25	**Less: a** Net operating loss deduction (see instructions) 25a	
	b Special deductions (see instructions) 25b	25c

Tax and Payments

26	**Taxable income.** Subtract line 25c from line 24	26
27	**Total tax** (from page 2, Part I, line 7)	27
28	**Payments:**	
a	1992 overpayment credited to 1993 28a	
b	1993 estimated tax payments 28b	
c	Less 1993 refund applied for on Form 4466 28c ( ) Bal ▶	28d
e	Tax deposited with Form 7004	28e
f	Credit from regulated investment companies (attach Form 2439) .	28f
g	Credit for Federal tax on fuels (attach Form 4136). See instructions .	28g
h	**Total payments.** Add lines 28d through 28g	28h
29	Estimated tax penalty (see instructions). Check if Form 2220 is attached . . . . . ▶☐	29
30	**Tax due.** If line 28h is smaller than the total of lines 27 and 29, enter amount owed	30
31	**Overpayment.** If line 28h is larger than the total of lines 27 and 29, enter amount overpaid . .	31
32	Enter amount of line 31 you want: **Credited to 1994 estimated tax ▶** Refunded ▶	32

Please Sign Here

Under penalties of perjury, I declare that I have examined this return, including accompanying schedules and statements, and to the best of my knowledge and belief, it is true, correct, and complete. Declaration of preparer (other than taxpayer) is based on all information of which preparer has any knowledge.

▶ Signature of officer   Date   ▶ Title

Paid Preparer's Use Only

Preparer's signature ▶	Date	Check if self-employed ▶ ☐	Preparer's social security number
Firm's name (or yours if self-employed) and address		E.I. No. ▶	
		ZIP code ▶	

For Paperwork Reduction Act Notice, see page 1 of the instructions.   Cat. No. 11456E   Form **1120-A** (1993)

---

include the $66 as dividend income on his personal tax return. The shareholder, then, will pay income tax on the $66, on which the corporation has already paid income tax. Double taxation can be an important disadvantage, especially if a large portion of the corporation's profits are distributed to the shareholders.

Smaller, closely held corporations can take advantage of a couple of options to help alleviate double taxation. First, because in smaller corporations shareholders are also employees of the corporation, the corporation can pay each shareholder a salary. The salary paid to the shareholder is deductible as a corporate expense from the profit on which corporate tax is paid. Obviously, the shareholder employee must pay income tax on the salary, but double taxation is avoided.

Figure 5–8, continued

Part I Tax Computation (See instructions.)

1	Income tax. Check this box if the corporation is a qualified personal service corporation as defined in section 448(d)(2) (see instructions on page 15) . . . . ▶ ☐	1
2a	General business credit. Check if from: ☐ Form 3800 ☐ Form 3468 ☐ Form 5884 ☐ Form 6478 ☐ Form 6765 ☐ Form 8586 ☐ Form 8830 ☐ Form 8826 ☐ Form 8835 **2a**	
b	Credit for prior year minimum tax (attach Form 8827) **2b**	
3	**Total credits.** Add lines 2a and 2b	3
4	Subtract line 3 from line 1	4
5	Recapture taxes. Check if from: ☐ Form 4255 ☐ Form 8611	5
6	Alternative minimum tax (attach Form 4626)	6
7	**Total tax.** Add lines 4 through 6. Enter here and on line 27, page 1	7

Part II Other Information (See instructions.)

1 Refer to page 19 of the instructions and state the principal:

  a Business activity code no. ▶ ....

  b Business activity ▶ ....

  c Product or service ▶ ....

2 Did any individual, partnership, estate, or trust at the end of the tax year own, directly or indirectly, 50% or more of the corporation's voting stock? (For rules of attribution, see section 267(c).) . . . . ☐ Yes ☐ No

If "Yes," attach a schedule showing name and identifying number.

3 Enter the amount of tax-exempt interest received or accrued during the tax year . . . . . . ▶ | $

4 Enter amount of cash distributions and the book value of property (other than cash) distributions made in this tax year . . . . ▶ | $

5a If an amount is entered on line 2, page 1, see the worksheet on page 13 for amounts to enter below:

  (1) Purchases . . . .

  (2) Additional sec. 263A costs (see instructions—attach schedule) .

  (3) Other costs (attach schedule) .

b Do the rules of section 263A (for property produced or acquired for resale) apply to the corporation? . . . . ☐ Yes ☐ No

6 At any time during the 1993 calendar year, did the corporation have an interest in or a signature or other authority over a financial account in a foreign country (such as a bank account, securities account, or other financial account)? If "Yes," the corporation may have to file Form TD F 90-22.1 . . . . ☐ Yes ☐ No

If "Yes," enter the name of the foreign country ▶ ....

Part III Balance Sheets

Assets		(a) Beginning of tax year		(b) End of tax year	
1	Cash				
2a	Trade notes and accounts receivable				
b	Less allowance for bad debts	(	)	(	)
3	Inventories				
4	U.S. government obligations				
5	Tax-exempt securities (see instructions) . . .				
6	Other current assets (attach schedule)				
7	Loans to stockholders				
8	Mortgage and real estate loans				
9a	Depreciable, depletable, and intangible assets . .				
b	Less accumulated depreciation, depletion, and amortization	(	)	(	)
10	Land (net of any amortization)				
11	Other assets (attach schedule)				
12	Total assets				

Liabilities and Stockholders' Equity					
13	Accounts payable				
14	Other current liabilities (attach schedule) . . .				
15	Loans from stockholders				
16	Mortgages, notes, bonds payable				
17	Other liabilities (attach schedule)				
18	Capital stock (preferred and common stock) . . .				
19	Paid-in or capital surplus				
20	Retained earnings				
21	Less cost of treasury stock	(	)	(	)
22	Total liabilities and stockholders' equity				

Part IV Reconciliation of Income (Loss) per Books With Income per Return *(You are not required to complete Part IV if the total assets on line 12, column (b), Part III are less than $25,000.)*

1	Net income (loss) per books	6	Income recorded on books this year not included on this return (itemize)..................
2	Federal income tax		
3	Excess of capital losses over capital gains . .	7	Deductions on this return not charged against book income this year (itemize).................
4	Income subject to tax not recorded on books this year (itemize)		
5	Expenses recorded on books this year not deducted on this return (itemize)	8	Income (line 24, page 1). Enter the sum of lines 1 through 5 less the sum of lines 6 and 7 . . ..

♻ *Printed on recycled paper*

Second, the corporation can be financed through loans from shareholders rather than investments, or capital contributions, from the shareholders. The interest on these loans will be paid to the shareholders who made the loans, and interest paid by a corporation is a deductible corporate expense. As with salary, the interest paid to shareholders is taxable income to them, but double taxation of the earnings of the corporation is eliminated. In other words, as long as the earnings paid to the shareholders are in a form that is deductible for the corporation (salaries or other compensation or interest paid on debts owed to the shareholders), double taxation is avoided. Third, the corporation and the shareholders can avoid double taxation by electing S corporation status.

Subchapter S Election

A corporation can elect to be taxed as an **S corporation** (also called a Subchapter S corporation) and thereby avoid paying income tax at the corporate income tax level while still enjoying the advantages of the corporation, especially limited liability. Any corporation that qualifies as a **small business corporation,** as defined by the Internal Revenue Service, may take advantage of the benefits of being an S corporation. The following are the more important of the numerous qualifications a corporation must meet to be classified as an S corporation:

1. There can be no more than 35 shareholders.
2. All shareholders must be natural persons, estates, or certain trusts. Corporations and partnerships cannot be shareholders.
3. No shareholder can be a nonresident alien.
4. The corporation must be a domestic corporation.
5. The corporation may have only one class of stock.

PARALEGALERT!

An S corporation is a corporation in all respects, except that it is treated as a partnership for federal income tax purposes. In effect, the S corporation itself is exempted from all federal income taxes in that all profits and losses are distributed proportionately to the shareholders of the corporation.

In many respects the S corporation is taxed like the partnership: All profits and losses incurred by the corporation are proportionately distributed to the shareholders of the S corporation. The shareholders then report their portions of the corporation's profit and loss on their personal income tax returns.

The S corporation election is usually made by the shareholders for several reasons. First, personal income tax rates are currently lower than the corporate tax rate. Several years ago, the corporate tax rates exceeded the individual tax rates for the first time. Second, the losses incurred by the corporation can be passed through to the individual shareholders, who can use them to offset their personal incomes and reduce their taxes. Third, if the corporation expects to distribute most of its profits to the shareholders, in the form of dividends, S corporation status will avoid the double taxation of the profits. In other words, the three greatest advantages of the S corporation are that:

1. Personal income tax rates are usually lower than corporate tax rates.
2. Corporate losses can be used to reduce the personal income of the shareholder.
3. Profits distributed to the shareholders are not "double-taxed."

Disadvantages of the S corporation include the many limitations or requirements for qualification as an S corporation. In addition, an important disadvantage of the S corporation is that the corporation's fringe benefit payments (for health insurance, life insurance, etc.) on behalf of employee-shareholders who own more than 2 percent of the stock are nondeductible by the corporation as an expense.

For the corporation to be an S corporation, all the shareholders must elect S corporation status. To do so, each shareholder must execute a statement acknowledging the treatment as an S corporation and must file this statement with the corporation. In addition, Form 2553, Election by a Small Business Corporation, must be completed, executed by all shareholders, and filed with the Internal Revenue Service. A copy of this form is reprinted in Figure 5–9, pp. 93–94. The election, Form 2553, is filed with the Internal Revenue Service office where the corporation will file its income tax return, Form 1120S. Form 2553 is executed by an officer of the corporation who is authorized to execute the corporation's tax return. A copy should also be retained in the permanent files of the corporation.

Figure 5–9   Form 2553, Election by a Small Business Corporation

Form **2553**
(Rev. September 1993)
Department of the Treasury
Internal Revenue Service

Election by a Small Business Corporation
(Under section 1362 of the Internal Revenue Code)
► For Paperwork Reduction Act Notice, see page 1 of instructions.
► See separate instructions.

OMB No. 1545-0146
Expires 8-31-96

Notes: 1. This election, to be an "S corporation," can be accepted only if all the tests are met under **Who May Elect** on page 1 of the instructions; all signatures in Parts I and III are originals (no photocopies); and the exact name and address of the corporation and other required form information are provided.
2. Do not file **Form 1120S**, U.S. Income Tax Return for an S Corporation, until you are notified that your election is accepted.

Part I   Election Information

Please Type or Print

Name of corporation (see instructions)
Number, street, and room or suite no. (If a P.O. box, see instructions.)
City or town, state, and ZIP code

A Employer identification number (EIN)
B Date incorporated
C State of incorporation

D Election is to be effective for tax year beginning (month, day, year) . . . . ► / /

E Name and title of officer or legal representative who the IRS may call for more information
F Telephone number of officer or legal representative ( )

G If the corporation changed its name or address after applying for the EIN shown in **A**, check this box . . . . ► ☐

H If this election takes effect for the first tax year the corporation exists, enter month, day, and year of the **earliest** of the following: (1) date the corporation first had shareholders, (2) date the corporation first had assets, or (3) date the corporation began doing business . . . . ► / /

I Selected tax year: Annual return will be filed for tax year ending (month and day) ► . . . .
If the tax year ends on any date other than December 31, except for an automatic 52-53-week tax year ending with reference to the month of December, you **must** complete Part II on the back. If the date you enter is the ending date of an automatic 52-53-week tax year, write "52-53-week year" to the right of the date. See Temporary Regulations section 1.441-2T(e)(3).

J Name and address of each shareholder, shareholder's spouse having a community property interest in the corporation's stock, and each tenant in common, joint tenant, and tenant by the entirety. (A husband and wife (and their estates) are counted as one shareholder in determining the number of shareholders without regard to the manner in which the stock is owned.)	K Shareholders' Consent Statement. Under penalties of perjury, we declare that we consent to the election of the above-named corporation to be an "S corporation" under section 1362(a) and that we have examined this consent statement, including accompanying schedules and statements, and to the best of our knowledge and belief, it is true, correct, and complete. (Shareholders sign and date below.)*		L Stock owned		M Social security number or employer identification number (see instructions)	N Share-holder's tax year ends (month and day)
	Signature	Date	Number of shares	Dates acquired		

*For this election to be valid, the consent of each shareholder, shareholder's spouse having a community property interest in the corporation's stock, and each tenant in common, joint tenant, and tenant by the entirety must either appear above or be attached to this form. (See instructions for Column K if a continuation sheet or a separate consent statement is needed.)

Under penalties of perjury, I declare that I have examined this election, including accompanying schedules and statements, and to the best of my knowledge and belief, it is true, correct, and complete.

Signature of officer ►   Title ►   Date ►

See Parts II and III on back.   Cat. No. 18629R   Form **2553** (Rev. 9-93)

continued

A corporation and its shareholders will not always find it advantageous to be treated as an S corporation; therefore, the election to be treated as an S corporation can be terminated in any one of the following ways:

1. By revoking the election.
2. By ceasing to qualify as an S corporation.
3. By violating any of the restrictions placed on S corporations.

If the S corporation status is terminated, the corporation must generally wait five years before again electing to be treated as an S corporation, unless the Internal Revenue Service consents to the election at an earlier time. In other words, a corporation cannot elect to be an S corporation this year, elect not to be one in years 2 and 3, and then decide to be an S corporation again in years 4 and 5.

Figure 5–9, continued

Form 2553 (Rev. 9-93)
Page **2**

Part II **Selection of Fiscal Tax Year (All corporations using this part must complete item O and one of items P, Q, or R.)**

O Check the applicable box below to indicate whether the corporation is:
1. ☐ A new corporation adopting the tax year entered in item I, Part I.
2. ☐ An existing corporation retaining the tax year entered in item I, Part I.
3. ☐ An existing corporation changing to the tax year entered in item I, Part I.

P Complete item P if the corporation is using the expeditious approval provisions of Revenue Procedure 87-32, 1987-2 C.B. 396, to request: **(1)** a natural business year (as defined in section 4.01(1) of Rev. Proc. 87-32), or **(2)** a year that satisfies the ownership tax year test in section 4.01(2) of Rev. Proc. 87-32. Check the applicable box below to indicate the representation statement the corporation is making as required under section 4 of Rev. Proc. 87-32.

1. **Natural Business Year** ▶ ☐ I represent that the corporation is retaining or changing to a tax year that coincides with its natural business year as defined in section 4.01(1) of Rev. Proc. 87-32 and as verified by its satisfaction of the requirements of section 4.02(1) of Rev. Proc. 87-32. In addition, if the corporation is changing to a natural business year as defined in section 4.01(1), I further represent that such tax year results in less deferral of income to the owners than the corporation's present tax year. I also represent that the corporation is not described in section 3.01(2) of Rev. Proc. 87-32. (See instructions for additional information that must be attached.)

2. **Ownership Tax Year** ▶ ☐ I represent that shareholders holding more than half of the shares of the stock (as of the first day of the tax year to which the request relates) of the corporation have the same tax year or are concurrently changing to the tax year that the corporation adopts, retains, or changes to per item I, Part I. I also represent that the corporation is not described in section 3.01(2) of Rev. Proc. 87-32.

Note: If you do not use item P and the corporation wants a fiscal tax year, complete either item Q or R below. Item Q is used to request a fiscal tax year based on a business purpose and to make a back-up section 444 election. Item R is used to make a regular section 444 election.

Q Business Purpose—To request a fiscal tax year based on a business purpose, you must check box Q1 and pay a user fee. See instructions for details. You may also check box Q2 and/or box Q3.
1. Check here ▶ ☐ if the fiscal year entered in item I, Part I, is requested under the provisions of section 6.03 of Rev. Proc. 87-32. Attach to Form 2553 a statement showing the business purpose for the requested fiscal year. See instructions for additional information that must be attached.

2. Check here ▶ ☐ to show that the corporation intends to make a back-up section 444 election in the event the corporation's business purpose request is not approved by the IRS. (See instructions for more information.)

3. Check here ▶ ☐ to show that the corporation agrees to adopt or change to a tax year ending December 31 if necessary for the IRS to accept this election for S corporation status in the event: (1) the corporation's business purpose request is not approved and the corporation makes a back-up section 444 election, but is ultimately not qualified to make a section 444 election, or (2) the corporation's business purpose request is not approved and the corporation did not make a back-up section 444 election.

R Section 444 Election—To make a section 444 election, you must check box R1 and you may also check box R2.
1. Check here ▶ ☐ to show the corporation will make, if qualified, a section 444 election to have the fiscal tax year shown in item I, Part I. To make the election, you must complete **Form 8716**, Election To Have a Tax Year Other Than a Required Tax Year, and either attach it to Form 2553 or file it separately.

2. Check here ▶ ☐ to show that the corporation agrees to adopt or change to a tax year ending December 31 if necessary for the IRS to accept this election for S corporation status in the event the corporation is ultimately not qualified to make a section 444 election.

Part III **Qualified Subchapter S Trust (QSST) Election Under Section 1361(d)(2)****

Income beneficiary's name and address	Social security number
Trust's name and address	Employer identification number

Date on which stock of the corporation was transferred to the trust (month, day, year) . . . . ▶ / /

In order for the trust named above to be a QSST and thus a qualifying shareholder of the S corporation for which this Form 2553 is filed, I hereby make the election under section 1361(d)(2). Under penalties of perjury, I certify that the trust meets the definitional requirements of section 1361(d)(3) and that all other information provided in Part III is true, correct, and complete.

Signature of income beneficiary or signature and title of legal representative or other qualified person making the election	Date

**Use of Part III to make the QSST election may be made only if stock of the corporation has been transferred to the trust on or before the date on which the corporation makes its election to be an S corporation. The QSST election must be made and filed separately if stock of the corporation is transferred to the trust after the date on which the corporation makes the S election.

Printed on recycled paper   *U.S. Government Printing Office: 1993 — 301-628/80271

Many states also recognize the S corporation. They allow corporations to be taxed as S corporations if the proper forms have been filed with the particular state's department of revenue.

State Income Taxation

Generally, a corporation's liability for state taxes depends on whether it is doing business in the state. If a corporation was incorporated in a state or does business there, the corporation will most likely be subject to state income tax in that state.

For instance, a corporation formed in Pennsylvania will be subject to taxation in that state because it was incorporated there. If it is deriving income from business conducted in Ohio and West Virginia, it may also have to pay tax on the income from its activities in those states.

The major taxes to which corporations may be subjected by states include:

1. Franchise tax—a tax on the privilege of doing business in a state.
2. Net income tax—a tax on the net income of the business.
3. Sales and use tax—a tax imposed directly on sales or measured by the sales of the business.
4. Gross receipts tax—a tax on the gross income, or gross receipts, of the business.
5. Property tax—a tax imposed on any property owned in the state.

Not included in this list are specialized taxes imposed by a state or local government, such as commodity taxes on gasoline, cigarettes, and alcohol; specialized taxes imposed on the utilities and insurance industries; and fees for qualifying to do business in a state.

States' revenue or taxation laws vary greatly in the ways in which tax is imposed on corporations. For instance, most states impose a tax measured by the corporation's net income, but Michigan imposes a single business tax on the privilege of doing business, not on the corporation's income. Several states impose both a franchise tax and a net income tax. A careful evaluation of the tax laws of the state where the corporation will be incorporated and of the states where it might do business is critical. This analysis is generally performed by the corporation's accountant or tax lawyer.

PARALEGALERT!

Whenever you, the corporate paralegal, are assisting in the completion and filing of Form 2553, Election by a Small Business Corporation, you should carefully review the filing requirements of the Internal Revenue Code. There are specific filing deadlines and requirements that must be met for a corporation to be treated as an S corporation in certain tax years. You will also need to determine the appropriate state's requirements, if any, with respect to S corporations, including the proper forms to file and the deadlines for filing them.

5–4 Dissolution of Corporations

A sole proprietorship or partnership automatically dissolves upon the death or withdrawal of the owner or a partner. In contrast, a corporation's existence does not end when any shareholder, director, officer, or employee of the corporation dies or withdraws from the business; therefore, the corporation is said to have **perpetual existence.** Most state statutes allow corporations to have perpetual existence unless the articles of incorporation specifically state otherwise. Only upon the vote of the shareholders to dissolve the corporation, usually on the recommendation of the board of directors, can the dissolution process begin.

Two terms that are often incorrectly used as synonyms are *dissolution* and *liquidation*. These are *not* synonymous terms—they are two distinct processes for a corporation, even though they often go hand in hand. It is possible for a corporation to liquidate the business, continue to exist as a corporation, and resume business activities at a later date, when economic conditions improve. That is, a corporation can liquidate its business without dissolving the corporation.

PARALEGALERT!

One of the advantages of the corporate form of business organization is its perpetual existence. The corporation will not terminate upon the death of any shareholder, director, officer, or employee. Generally, the shareholders must agree to terminate the corporation's existence.

Dissolution is the formal termination of the corporation's existence, in accordance with state statutes. Remember that the corporation is a separate legal entity created under state statute upon incorporation. Therefore, to be terminated as a separate legal entity, it must be dissolved under state statute. After the shareholders of a corporation approve the dissolution of the corporation, designated officers of the corporation proceed with the winding up of the corporation's business. The winding-up process, or **liquidation,** consists of the following actions by the officers of the corporation:

1. Conversion of the corporation's assets to cash.
2. Completion and termination of all corporate contracts.
3. Paying of creditors.
4. Distribution of the remaining cash to the shareholders.

We will discuss the dissolution of the corporation and the process of liquidation in much greater detail in Chapter 14.

5–5 Practical Considerations

The issues that must be considered before a business is incorporated may seem overwhelming to you: Should the shareholders have preemptive rights? Should they vote cumulatively in the election of directors? Should the corporation be a C corporation or an S corporation? How many directors should there be? Should they have staggered terms? Will indemnification be provided to the directors and officers? These and many other questions will be examined by your supervising attorney, who will provide you, the corporate paralegal, with the answers so that you can prepare the necessary paperwork to incorporate the business. You may or may not be asked to gather the information you need from the client. It will depend on the amount of responsibility the supervising attorney is willing to delegate.

However, as a practical matter, understanding these issues yourself will better equip you to prepare the necessary incorporation and organizational documents. You will be an invaluable asset to the attorney and an essential part of the team when you master these concepts. As soon as the supervising attorney is convinced that you are able to play a significant role in the incorporation process, your skills will be put to the test.

Here's one example of the role you can play: The attorney has provided you with the necessary information to incorporate a business. You know that the statutes of the state in which the business is to be incorporated provide that preemptive rights will be denied unless specifically authorized in the articles of incorporation. But the attorney has mentioned nothing to you about preemptive rights. You know that the corporation is to be a closely held corporation (one with few shareholders), and you know that such corporations often have preemptive rights. Therefore, you ask the attorney whether preemptive rights are to be authorized for this corporation. (Don't be afraid to ask questions or raise issues. They may be things the attorney has not focused on—until you cite them.) Without your general knowledge of the issue of preemptive rights (what they are and when they are usually given), this important right may not have been included in the corporation's articles of incorporation.

SUMMARY

5–1

The shareholders are the owners of the corporation and are ultimately responsible for deciding matters that will have a major impact upon the business and for selecting a board of directors. The board of directors is responsible for determining corporate policy and appointing and supervising the officers. The officers carry out the directions of the board of directors and handle the day-to-day operations of the business. All of the rights and powers enjoyed by the shareholders, the powers and authority granted to the directors, and the responsibilities conferred on the officers of the corporation are granted by the statutes of the state of incorporation and by the corporation's articles of incorporation and bylaws. Ownership of stock entitles a shareholder to vote, to receive a return on his or her investment (dividends), and to share in the assets upon liquidation. Directors may delegate authority to officers or to committees of the board, but are ultimately responsible for their acts. Specific duties to be performed by the officers are usually set out in the corporation's bylaws. No state statute precludes an individual from being a shareholder and simultaneously acting as a director and officer of the corporation.

5–2

Shareholders are usually insulated from personal liability for the debts and obligations of the corporation and for the acts of the employees. But in some exceptional circumstances, the shareholders may be held personally liable if the corporation is used by the shareholders for illegal purposes. In this situation, the corporate veil is pierced, and the shareholders are held liable. Under the alter ego doctrine, shareholders are denied the protection of limited liability if a court determines that the corporation is merely the alter ego of the shareholders. Directors and officers are fiduciaries of the corporation, and they must fulfill their fiduciary responsibilities by adhering to a duty of care and a duty of loyalty. The business judgment rule protects the directors and officers from liability as long as they do not violate their fiduciary duties and their business decisions are made within the powers of the corporation. The corporation may indemnify the directors and officers by reimbursing them for any expenses they incur in defending any threatened or pending suit or proceeding stemming from actions they take on behalf of the corporation.

5–3

Corporations are subject to taxation by federal, state, and local governments—generally on the income the corporation earns. There are two kinds of corporations for federal income tax purposes: the C corporation and the S corporation. The C corporation is taxed on its own income and realizes its own losses as a separate entity from the shareholders of the corporation. The S corporation is not a taxable entity, and the shareholders report the income and losses of the S corporation on their personal income tax returns. One of the greatest disadvantages of the corporate form is double taxation, in which both the corporation and the shareholders pay tax on the same dollars. Closely held corporations, therefore, try to take advantage of some of the options available to avoid double taxation. One of those options is the election to be treated as an S corporation. A corporation's liability for state tax varies greatly, depending on the state in which the corporation is doing business and from which it derives its income.

5–4

Dissolution and liquidation of the corporation are two different and distinct processes. The terms are not synonymous. The dissolution of a corporation is the formal termination of the corporation's existence, accomplished in accordance with state statute. Liquidation is the conversion of the corporation's assets to cash, the completion and termination of all corporate contracts, the paying of creditors, and the distribution of the remaining cash to the shareholders.

5–5

Once you have mastered a basic understanding of the issues involved in incorporating a business, you will be an indispensable asset to the attorney. Understanding and identifying the issues involved in the incorporation and organization of a corporation will prove to your supervising attorney just how much you can contribute to his or her practice of law. When given a task, feel free to ask questions and raise issues to the attorney, since the attorney is often unable to focus on all aspects of a client's circumstances.

REVIEW GUIDE

Key Terms

Before proceeding, review the key terms listed below to be sure you understand each one. If necessary, read over the corresponding section of the chapter. When you are ready to test your understanding, answer the review questions.

shareholders (p. 73)
share certificate (p. 73)
stock certificate (p. 73)
consideration (p. 73)
voting right (p. 74)
cumulative voting (p. 74)
straight voting (p. 74)
voting trust (p. 74)
voting agreement (p. 75)
dividend right (p. 75)
preemptive right (p. 77)
directors (p. 78)
staggered terms (p. 79)
officers (p. 81)
piercing the corporate veil (p. 84)
alter ego doctrine (p. 84)
fiduciaries (p. 84)
business judgment rule (p. 84)
duty of care (p. 84)
duty of loyalty (p. 85)
indemnification (p. 87)
C corporation (p. 88)
Form 1120, U.S. Corporation Income Tax
    Return (p. 89)
Form 1120-A, U.S. Corporation
    Short-Form Income Tax Return (p. 89)
double taxation (p. 89)
S corporation (p. 92)
small business corporation (p. 92)
perpetual existence (p. 95)
dissolution (p. 96)
liquidation (p. 96)

Questions for Review and Discussion

1. What evidence does a shareholder have that he or she is a shareholder of a corporation?
2. Explain the difference between cumulative voting and straight voting in the election of directors.
3. When may a dividend legally be declared by the board of directors?
4. List the different forms in which dividends can be paid to shareholders.
5. Explain why preemptive rights are generally provided to shareholders of smaller, closely held corporations.
6. List the areas of responsibility assigned to directors.
7. How are officers' positions created?
8. Under what circumstances might the shareholders be held personally liable for the corporation's obligations?
9. Explain the directors' and officers' fiduciary responsibilities, specifically the duty of care and the duty of loyalty.
10. How are the directors and officers protected from liability for corporate losses resulting from their poor business judgment?
11. Why would a corporation agree to indemnify a director or officer against liability?
12. How does the taxation of the C corporation differ from the taxation of the S corporation?
13. Explain the concept of double taxation.
14. Could a corporation liquidate its business without dissolving it? Explain.

Activities

1. Review the corporate statutes of your state to determine what a corporation must do to provide a director or officer indemnification against liability for his or her actions. Also determine the circumstances under which a director's liability may not be limited.
2. Using the Model Act, the full text of which is reproduced in Appendix A of this text, answer the following questions. Cite the section of the Model Act where you found the answer.
   a. How many directors must be appointed?
   b. What officers must be appointed?
   c. How are preemptive rights granted to the shareholders?
   d. Who is authorized to make distributions (pay dividends) to the shareholders?
   (Hint: Use the index at the beginning of the Model Act to help you identify the section in which you will locate the answer.)
3. Your supervising attorney has asked you to prepare a draft of a letter to Barry Moore, a shareholder of World Travel, Inc., explaining the special voting procedures that shareholders of a corporation may elect to use. Use this textbook and the appropriate provisions of the Model Act to prepare your response.

CHAPTER 6   Formation of Corporations

OUTLINE

6–1   Statutory Requirements for Incorporation
    Statutory Filing Documents
    Filing Procedures
6–2   Preincorporation Activities and Considerations
    Subscription for Shares
    State of Incorporation
    Corporate Name
    Fictitious Name
6–3   Articles of Incorporation: Statutory Provisions
    Corporate Name
    Capital Structure
    Registered Agent and Address
    Incorporator
6–4   Articles of Incorporation: Optional Provisions
    Initial Directors
    Corporate Purposes and Powers
    Period of Existence
    Preemptive Rights
    Cumulative Voting for Directors
    Quorum and Vote of Shareholders
    Indemnification of Directors and Officers
6–5   Postincorporation Activities
    Organizational Meeting
    Payment of Capital
    Minute Book, Stock Book, and Corporate Seal
    Legal Advertisement
    Securities Law Considerations
    Subchapter S Election
6–6   Bylaws
6–7   Incorporating Other Forms of Business Organizations
    Professional Corporation
    Nonprofit Corporation
    Close Corporation
    Limited-Liability Company
6–8   Practical Considerations

APPLICATIONS

On any given day, the attorneys for whom you work will interrupt your work with instructions and assignments requiring your immediate attention. Not only must you handle the interruptions amiably, but you must be prepared to act quickly if necessary.

This is often the case when the attorney has recommended that a client incorporate a business in a particular state. Generally, the client follows the recommendation and wants the business incorporated as soon as possible. You'll probably be called into the conference room on a moment's notice, with the instruction, "Mr. Smith is in the conference room and wants to incorporate his business."

A checklist of the information to gather before incorporating and a basic understanding of the procedures for incorporating will prove invaluable. (Keep copies of the checklist, in a file folder marked "Incorporation Checklist," at your fingertips at all times.) Gather your checklist, a notepad, and a pencil, and head to the conference room with the confidence that your incorporation fundamentals and your checklist will help you begin the process.

OBJECTIVES

This chapter will provide you with the basic concepts and procedures of incorporation. Don't be daunted by the length and content of this chapter because, as you will quickly discover, the procedures for incorporating are specific and provided for in each state's statutes. After completing this chapter, you will be able to:

1. Draft a subscription agreement.
2. Evaluate the factors that will influence the selection of the state of incorporation.
3. Collect the information necessary to incorporate a business.
4. Determine if the corporate name selected by the client meets statutory requirements.
5. Determine the availability of the corporate name desired and reserve the name.
6. Prepare articles of incorporation in accordance with statutory requirements.
7. Draft optional provisions of the articles of incorporation, including:
   - Naming initial directors.
   - Providing for specific corporate purposes.
   - Limiting a corporation's existence.
   - Granting or denying preemptive rights.
   - Granting or denying cumulative voting.
   - Defining voting procedures of the shareholders.
   - Providing indemnification of directors and officers.
8. File articles of incorporation.
9. Hold the organizational meeting of the incorporators or the board of directors.
10. Order the corporate minute book, stock book, and seal.
11. Arrange for advertisement of the legal notice, if required.
12. Prepare and file Form 2553, Election by a Small Business Corporation.
13. Understand the need for and prepare a draft of bylaws.
14. Prepare and file articles of incorporation for professional, nonprofit, and close corporations and articles of organization for a limited-liability company.

6–1 Statutory Requirements for Incorporation

As you will recall from previous discussions, a corporation does not exist until it has been properly incorporated. The procedures and requirements for incorporating differ among the states, but the basic requirements are comparable. **Articles of incorporation** (or, in some states, a **certificate of incorporation**) must be filed with the secretary of state of the state in which the client has chosen to incorporate the business. The paralegal is generally responsible for gathering all the necessary information for the preparation and filing of articles of incorporation. Figure 6–1 is a checklist of the information to be gathered from the client to incorporate a business. The items included in this checklist are broad in nature, but the checklist will assist you in assembling and organizing the information needed to prepare the incorporation documents and the postincorporation organizational documents. As you incorporate businesses in various states, you will obviously amend this checklist to meet specific requirements of state statutes and to suit your style and needs.

The articles of incorporation *must* contain certain provisions required by the statute of the state of incorporation. Such provisions will be discussed in Section 6–3. The articles of incorporation *may* also contain provisions that meet the specific desires of the shareholders of the corporation. Some of these provisions will be discussed in Section 6–4.

The **organization** of a corporation generally means the performance of all the tasks or "the execution of all the requirements" necessary to bring the corporation into legal existence and to permit it to conduct business. During the corporation's period of organization—until the first board of directors and officers of the corporation are elected—the incorporators are usually responsible for managing the corporation. When the initial directors have been elected (if they were not already named in the articles of incorporation), the incorporators' responsibilities end.

PARALEGALERT!

The corporate paralegal usually acts as the incorporator. When the incorporator's responsibilities end, the responsibilities of the paralegal terminate only in the role as the incorporator. Many other tasks will be required of the paralegal to complete the organization of the corporation.

Figure 6–1   Checklist of Information to Gather to Set Up and Organize a Corporation

_____ Type of corporation (such as business, professional, nonprofit, close)

_____ Corporate name (availability and reservation)
      Fictitious name registration

_____ Registered agent

_____ Registered office

_____ Period of existence

_____ Capital structure
      Common stock (par value); Preferred stock (rights and preferences)

_____ Business to be conducted (purpose)

_____ Directors (names and addresses)

_____ Shareholders (names and addresses)

_____ Share ownership by shareholders

_____ Officers (names and positions)

_____ Subchapter S election

_____ Optional provisions
      Preemptive rights; Cumulative voting; Quorum; Indemnification of directors and officers

Following are the steps for organizing a corporation:

1. Select the state of incorporation.
2. Prepare and execute the articles of incorporation.
3. File the articles of incorporation.
4. Prepare the bylaws.
5. Hold the organizational meeting of the incorporators.
6. Hold the first meeting of the board of directors.

These steps are broad and general. We will discuss each one in greater detail in this chapter and in Chapter 7.

Statutory Filing Documents

The form for articles of incorporation and the procedures for incorporation are very specific. If the proper forms and procedures are not followed exactly, third parties may challenge the existence of the corporation. For example, on the basis that the incorporation was improper, a third party bringing an action could seek to make the shareholders personally liable. Therefore, it is important to follow all the applicable procedures of the state statutes.

Sections 2.03(a) and (b) of the Model Act state that "unless a delayed effective date is specified, the corporate existence begins when the articles of incorporation are filed" and that "the secretary of state's filing of the articles of incorporation is conclusive proof that the incorporators satisfied all conditions precedent to incorporation." After the secretary of state has determined that all conditions of incorporation have been met, his or her office will, depending on the statutory requirements, (1) issue a certificate to the incorporator, which is evidence of the incorporation; (2) stamp "filed" on the duplicate copy of the articles and return the copy to the incorporator; or (3) return to the incorporator some form of documentation of the filing of the articles of incorporation. For example, Figure 6–2 is a copy of the certificate issued by the Delaware Secretary of State after that office has determined that the Certificate of Incorporation filed by the incorporator meets all conditions of incorporation.

Filing Procedures

Established filing procedures for incorporating differ among the states, but the basic requirements are generally the same. After the articles of incorporation have been prepared and properly executed, they are delivered to the secretary of state or another designated public official, sometimes the state corporation commissioner, for filing. Several states require that the articles of incorporation be filed with the designated public official of the county in which the registered office of the corporation is located. In addition, some states (e.g., New York, Rhode Island, and West Virginia) require notarization of the articles. Some states require that two originals be filed, and other states require an original and a photocopy. Almost every state has set a different fee for filing articles of incorporation, ranging from $35 to $300. In short, you need to consult the statutes of the state of incorporation to be able to answer the following questions concerning proper filing procedures:

1. How many originals or copies must be filed?
2. What constitutes proper execution? Is notarization required?
3. Must articles be filed with the county?
4. What is the state filing fee? The county filing fee?

Figure 6–2   Certificate Issued by the Secretary of State of Delaware

State of Delaware

Office of the Secretary of State

I, MICHAEL RATCHFORD, SECRETARY OF STATE OF THE STATE OF DELAWARE, DO HEREBY CERTIFY THE ATTACHED IS A TRUE AND CORRECT COPY OF THE CERTIFICATE OF INCORPORATION OF "WILMINGTON INVESTMENTS, INC." FILED IN THIS OFFICE ON THE NINTH DAY OF DECEMBER, A.D. 1992, AT 9 O'CLOCK A.M.

A CERTIFIED COPY OF THIS CERTIFICATE HAS BEEN FORWARDED TO NEW CASTLE COUNTY RECORDER OF DEEDS ON THE FOURTEENTH DAY OF DECEMBER, A.D. 1992 FOR RECORDING.

* * * * * * * * * *

Michael Ratchford, Secretary of State

AUTHENTICATION: *3698782

DATE: 12/14/1992

923445488

Depending on the urgency of filing the articles of incorporation, you must consider whether to deliver the articles by mail, by courier, or through an agent who will personally file the articles on your behalf. Several states, including Delaware, Iowa, New York, Pennsylvania, and Maryland, do not require original signatures on documents and will accept a faxed copy of the document. Also, several states will expedite the filing of articles of incorporation and other corporate documents for a fee, which ranges from $5 to $100. Some states require the payment of a franchise tax, ranging from $10 to $800, when articles of incorporation are filed. As you can see, you must research the statutory requirements and consult the secretary of state to determine filing requirements, fees, and other information each time you file articles of incorporation, or any other corporate document.

Paralegalert!

It is imperative that you consult the secretary of state and research the statutes of the state of incorporation each time you incorporate a business. Every state's requirements are different, and the states are continually amending their statutes, increasing fees, and making other changes.

6–2 Preincorporation Activities and Considerations

The formation of a corporation can be divided into two steps:

1. Preincorporation and preliminary organizational activities.
2. Statutory procedures and postincorporation activities.

In this chapter we will discuss both steps. This section will cover the preincorporation and organizational factors to be considered by individuals desiring to incorporate a business. Your role in these activities could include drafting the subscription agreement (if it is determined that one must exist); conducting a state-by-state comparison of the possible states of incorporation; determining the availability of the corporate name selected and reserving that name; determining the availability of a fictitious name (if the corporation will conduct business under a fictitious name); and researching the statutes of the state of incorporation for various provisions related to subscription agreements, name availability and reservation, and fictitious name registrations.

Subscription for Shares

Depending on the state of incorporation, persons interested in investing in the corporation may agree in writing to purchase shares of the corporation prior to its formation. They *may*, but unless the statutes of the state of incorporation require a written agreement, no agreement—written or oral—is required.

The person agreeing to purchase shares is the **subscriber,** and the written agreement is called the **subscription agreement.** Until the corporation is formed, the subscription is a continuing offer to purchase shares by the subscriber. Generally, the subscription may not be withdrawn by the subscriber, without liability, at any time prior to the filing of articles of incorporation by the incorporator. Most states' statutes and Section 6.20(a) of the Model Act provide that "a subscription for shares entered into before incorporation is irrevocable for six months unless the subscription agreement provides a longer or shorter period or all the subscribers agree to revocation."

The provisions of a subscription agreement include the subscriber's offer to purchase shares; the method and time by which the subscriptions will be paid;

and the form in which payment is to be made to the corporation, for example, cash, property, or services. If payment is to be made in a form other than cash, a value must be placed on the payment or services.

The subscriber delivers the executed subscription agreement to the incorporator. When the agreement is accepted by the corporation, the subscriber is then usually required to pay the consideration due in accordance with the subscription agreement. In most states, acceptance of a subscription agreement occurs when the board of directors takes an action formally accepting the subscription or, in some cases, when the articles of incorporation are filed. If the subscriber defaults on the promise to pay the amount due under the subscription agreement, the corporation may either (a) proceed to collect the amount owed it just as it would any other debt of the corporation or (b) sell the shares to another investor if the debt remains unpaid more than 20 days after the corporation sends written demand for payment to the subscriber. These alternatives are spelled out in Section 6.20(d) of the Model Act, and most state statutes allow for similar remedies.

According to Section 6.20(c) of the Model Act, all shares issued pursuant to the subscription agreement are considered to be **fully paid and nonassessable** when the corporation receives payment for the shares as specified in the subscription agreement. In addition, the Model Act defines fully paid and nonassessable similarly to many of the states' statutes. Specifically, Section 6.21(d) of the Model Act states as follows: "When the corporation receives the consideration for which the board of directors authorized the issuance of shares, the shares issued therefor are fully paid and nonassessable." In order for shares to be fully paid and nonassessable, a determination must be made as to whether the corporation *did receive* the consideration set by the board of directors and whether the consideration was acceptable in accordance with the appropriate state's statutes.

Figure 6–3 is a form of subscription agreement between a subscriber and a proposed corporation, in which payment for the shares is to be made in cash. This agreement could be modified to provide for payment on demand by the corporation or for payment in installments over a period of time.

Figure 6–3   Subscription Agreement Showing Payment to Be Made in Cash

Subscription Agreement

The undersigned, John Smith (the "Subscriber"), hereby subscribes to and agrees to purchase 1,000 shares of the capital stock of ABC Widget Company, a corporation to be incorporated and organized under the laws of the State of _____ (the "Corporation"). The Subscriber agrees to pay $10,000 cash for said stock to be paid to the Treasurer of the Corporation immediately upon the filing of the Articles of Incorporation with the Secretary of State of _____.

Dated: January _____, 199___.

_____
John Smith, Subscriber

Accepted by:
ABC Widget Company

By _____

Date _____

State of Incorporation

Generally, corporations will incorporate, or **domesticate,** in the state where they intend to operate their business. The state in which a corporation incorporates is the **home state** or **state of domestication.** The state of incorporation or state of domestication recognizes the corporation formed in that state as a **domestic corporation.** A state recognizes a corporation doing business in that state, but formed in another state, as a **foreign corporation.** We will discuss the qualification and operation of foreign corporations in greater detail in Chapter 9.

No state statutes prevent a corporation from incorporating in one state and conducting its business in another. The state in which the corporation will conduct a major portion of its business and locate its principal place of business is usually chosen as the state of incorporation, unless there are clear disadvantages to doing so. For example, a dry cleaning business operating in California should not consider incorporating in another jurisdiction unless the other jurisdiction offers an attractive incentive for doing so. The potential for incurring tax in both states, the cost of organizing in two states, and the additional corporate maintenance of incorporating in one state and qualifying to do business in another will, in most cases, outweigh any benefits. Usually, taxation will be the primary reason for selecting one state over another in which to incorporate the business.

On the other hand, a business organization that plans to conduct business in several states should perform a state-by-state comparison of the advantages and disadvantages of all the jurisdictions involved. Using this comparison, the client, upon the advice of the attorney, chooses the state of incorporation. Here is an area in which the paralegal can provide invaluable and cost-effective assistance. Your supervising attorney will provide you with the necessary facts, after which you can proceed to conduct the state-by-state comparison.

The issues or factors that should be considered when selecting the state of incorporation include the following:

- Cost and ease of formation.
- Flexibility of operation and management.
- Availability of corporate name.
- Treatment of director and shareholder liability.
- Accessibility and efficiency of the state judicial system.
- Taxation of domestic and foreign corporations.
- Annual reporting requirements.

Many corporations elect to incorporate in Delaware because of Delaware's permissive and flexible corporate statutes. For example, ABC Sign Corporation chose to incorporate in Delaware despite the fact that its headquarters, its manufacturing plant, and most of its customers are located in Maryland. ABC Sign Corporation probably chose to incorporate in Delaware for one or more of many reasons, including any of the following aspects of the Delaware corporate statutes:

- No corporate state income tax is imposed on corporations that do not do business in the state.
- Corporate law cases are handled efficiently and expeditiously through the judicial system.
- Maximum protection against hostile takeovers is provided to corporations.
- Directors and shareholders enjoy limited personal liability.

PARALEGALERT!

The corporate paralegal will often be asked to research the statutes of several states and provide a comparison of the advantages and disadvantages of incorporating and doing business in those states.

- Shareholders' and directors' meetings may be held outside the state.
- Directors need not be residents of the state.
- Most corporate documents require no notarization or witness and may be submitted by facsimile to the Division of Corporations.
- The Division of Corporations will provide free of charge (1) corporate forms, (2) name availability and reservation by phone, and (3) a list of professional registered agents that may be retained to serve as the corporation's agent in Delaware.

Many states in recent years have revised their corporate statutes to conform to the Model Act or to Delaware's corporate statutes. These states have realized that incorporation can generate tremendous revenue for the state. Therefore, the competition with Delaware in attracting corporations is increasing. Delaware, however, has maintained the lead as the state of incorporation most often chosen.

Corporate Name

Selecting the **corporate name** is the client's decision, but he or she should be advised of several factors before selecting and settling on a particular name. The client should be made aware that the corporate name must comply with the statutes of the state of incorporation.

First, the corporate name must contain certain words and may not contain certain other words. Section 4.01(a)(1) of the Model Act requires that a corporate name "must contain the word 'corporation,' 'incorporated,' 'company,' or 'limited,' or the abbreviation 'corp.,' 'inc.,' 'co.,' or 'ltd.,' or words or abbreviations of like import in another language." These words, or **corporate designators,** identify the business organization as a corporation. This identification notifies the general public that they are doing business with a corporation, not an individual or partnership. For example, no state would accept articles of incorporation for filing if the name of the corporation was stated as Computer Business Products. One of the corporate designators required by Section 4.01(a)(1) of the Model Act *must be contained* in the name of the corporation. Computer Business Products, Inc., would be acceptable, as would any other variation containing one of the other corporate designators, *as long as the name was available for use.* We will discuss name availability later in this section.

There are other words that are prohibited from use. The Model Act contains no prohibitions, other than those discussed in the next paragraph, but some states prohibit the following words in the corporate name:

1. Words of blasphemy or profanity.
2. Words implying that the corporation is a governmental agency of that state or of the United States.
3. Words implying that the corporation is a bank, insurance company, or public utility, unless the corporation engages in one of these businesses and is permitted to use such words under the banking, insurance, or public utility statutes of that state.

The statutes of the state in which the corporation desires to incorporate must be reviewed to determine whether the corporate name selected complies with that state's requirements. For example, the corporate statutes of Pennsylvania permit the use of the corporate designators *fund, association,* and *syndicate,* but

PARALEGALERT!

You will find that most clients are very particular about the corporate name. Generally, they are unaware of the requirement to include a corporate designator in the name of the corporation.

many other states do *not* recognize these terms as corporate designators. The corporate name American Securities Association would be permitted for use in Pennsylvania (of course, assuming the name was available for use), but most other states would not accept it without the addition of one of the corporate designators listed in Section 4.01(a)(1) of the Model Act.

Second, Section 4.01(a)(2) of the Model Act and many states require that the corporate name "may not contain language stating or implying that the corporation is organized for a purpose other than that permitted by . . . its articles of incorporation." For example, suppose a corporation's articles of incorporation include the following provision: "The corporation has been organized to buy and sell, and otherwise deal in, all types of jewelry." If this corporation desires to use the corporate name Doctor Professional Services Inc., which clearly implies that it is an organization of practicing doctors, not a company engaged in the purchase and sale of jewelry, many states will not permit the use of that name. Be aware that not all states' statutes contain this restriction, and some states do not require that the purpose of the corporation be stated in the articles of incorporation at all.

Third, the corporate name may not be the same as or deceptively similar to the name of an existing domestic corporation, the name of a foreign corporation authorized to do business in that particular state, or a name that has been reserved in that particular state. Section 4.01(b) of the Model Act and all states' statutes require that a corporate name must be distinguishable from other names registered in that particular state. For example, if an existing corporation is named Bond Travel Inc., the state will not allow any other domestic or foreign corporation to use that name and it will allow no one to reserve that name. This requirement was designed to avoid the use by one corporation of another's goodwill and reputation. A frequently cited example was the case in which the Great Atlantic and Pacific Tea Company, which operates the A & P Food Stores, prevented another corporation from using the name A & P Trucking Corporation. They believed the public would think the two companies were either related or the same corporation.

Unfortunately, complying with a state's statutes does not necessarily prevent the potential legal complications of selecting a corporate name. The acceptance and filing of the articles of incorporation by the state does not give the corporation the absolute right to use the name under which it was formed. In addition, the state's decision is not binding on a court. Courts apply the rules of unfair trade and competition in deciding whether one corporation's name is deceptively similar to that of another.

The corporate name selection process becomes more complicated when a corporation intends to do business in several states, because its corporate name cannot be deceptively similar to *any* name in *any* of the states in which the corporation wants to do business. A state will not restrict a corporation from qualifying or registering to do business in that state for the mere reason that its corporate name is similar to another. Generally, the state allows the corporation to register under its corporate name, but allows it to conduct business in that state only under a fictitious name. In addition, the fictitious name selected must not be deceptively similar to another corporate name in that state.

Even though the selection of a corporate name is left to the client, the client must be provided with the proper guidance and assistance so that the statutes of the state of incorporation will not be violated.

Determining the availability of and reserving the corporate name is usually the paralegal's responsibility. After the corporate name has been selected, the

PARALEGALERT!

The filing of articles of incorporation does not provide a corporation with an absolute right to use the name under which it was incorporated.

PARALEGALERT!

It is important to realize that the information provided by the state as to the availability of corporate names is supplied by humans, who make mistakes. In addition, the day after you check the availability of a corporate name, another paralegal may file articles of incorporation in that state for a corporation with the same name. In both instances the information you provide to the client will be wrong.

PARALEGALERT!

Upon receiving confirmation from the state that the name has been reserved, make a note in your tickler system of the date on which the name reservation is due to expire.

paralegal will be asked to determine the availability of the name with the secretary of state in the state in which the corporation desires to incorporate. You should ask the corporation division of the secretary of state's office to review the records of the state and determine if the corporate name is available for use. The state will use its discretion in determining whether the name is deceptively similar to that of another domestic or foreign corporation or to a name that has been reserved. Many secretaries of state will accept telephone requests for determining name availability and will usually provide the information immediately over the telephone. But each state has its own procedures for providing this information. For example, New Jersey will provide the information only after a credit card number is provided, to which a fee is charged; Arizona will accept a request by facsimile and will respond with a facsimile that includes an invoice for the service; Hawaii will respond in writing to a telephone request, usually within 10 business days; and California, Colorado, Hawaii, Maine, and several other states will provide the information only to service companies whose business is to check name availability for clients. The information provided by the secretary of state about the availability of a corporate name is not a guarantee that the name will be available when articles of incorporation are filed or that an error was not made when providing the information.

The discretion used in determining availability also varies from state to state. For example, the following two corporate names may be found deceptively similar by one state and not by another state: Technology Center, Inc. and Technologies Center, Inc. Most states would find these two names deceptively similar, but a few states would allow both corporations to exist. In addition, most states will not permit a mere change in the corporate designator to influence their determination of availability. For example, the only difference between Technology Center Inc. and Technology Center Corp. is the corporate designator. These two names are, in effect, the same name and would not both be permitted in the same state.

Some states will permit the use of a name similar to the name of a corporation already incorporated, or qualified or similar to a reserved name only if written consent is given by the original user of the name. The written consent must be filed with the incorporation or reservation documents. No corporation is under any obligation to allow another person to use its name, but some corporations have sold the right to use their names. Not all states permit the use of similar names even if consent is provided.

After it has been determined that a corporate name is available, the decision must be made whether to reserve the name. If articles of incorporation will be filed immediately after determining the availability of the name, it is not necessary to reserve the name. But in some cases many weeks or months may pass before articles of incorporation are filed. You will find it quite embarrassing to explain to the client that the name is no longer available and has been used by another corporation. Reserving the name will prevent the release of the name to another person until the specified period of reservation has expired. Reservation of a name is not a prerequisite to incorporation. In other words, there is no requirement that a name must be reserved before articles of incorporation are filed. The decision to reserve a name depends on the likelihood that the name will not be available when the articles of incorporation are eventually filed.

Most states have statutory provisions permitting the reservation of a name for a specified period of time. Reservation will hold the name pending the filing of articles of incorporation. Section 4.02 of the Model Act provides that "a person may reserve the exclusive use of a corporate name . . . by delivering an application to the secretary of state for filing." An application or letter, accompanied by a check for a nominal fee, will reserve a name for a specified period. The period of reservation varies considerably and may be as short as 30 days or as long as 12 months, and some states allow an extension of the reservation for an additional specified period.

Fictitious Name

As you recall from our discussion of the sole proprietorship and the general and limited partnerships, any business organization that desires to conduct business under a name other than its own name must file a **fictitious name** registration or assumed name affidavit with the secretary of state and in some cases with the county in which the business is conducted. This requirement is the same for corporations. A corporation desiring to conduct business under a name other than its corporate name (the name under which it was incorporated) may do so by registering the fictitious name. For example, World Travel Corporation desires to do business under the name Travel Around the World. Most states will require World Travel Corporation to file a fictitious name registration, assumed name affidavit, or statement in accordance with that state's statutes, registering Travel Around the World as a fictitious name. World Travel Corporation is then considered to be doing business under the fictitious or assumed name Travel Around the World. Its corporate name does not change.

Statutes governing filing for a fictitious or assumed name vary greatly from state to state. Some states require that the corporation file with the secretary of state only; other states require filing only with the county in which the entity is doing business; still other states require filing at both the state and county levels. In addition, some statutes specify that the fictitious name to be used by a corporation must contain the word *company, corporation, incorporated,* or *limited.* And, usually, fictitious or assumed names may not be the same as or deceptively similar to other corporate names, fictitious names, or reserved corporate names in a particular state. The statutes of the state will specify the requirements that must be met for the corporation to conduct business under a fictitious name in that state.

A corporation that fails to register its fictitious name is taking an unnecessary risk. It may be barred from bringing an action in court to enforce provisions of a contract made in the fictitious name of the corporation. Some courts have held that a suit will not be permitted under a fictitious name unless a fictitious name registration or assumed name affidavit is properly filed. This restriction would prevent enforcement of a contract the officers of the corporation entered into on behalf of the corporation under the corporation's fictitious name. A far greater problem arises when the officers of a corporation execute an agreement without indicating their corporate capacity or mentioning the corporation's existence. In that case, the officers may be personally liable if the other parties to the

PARALEGALERT!

Not all states protect a fictitious name from use by another corporation. Researching the statutes is critical to determining all the requirements.

agreement were unaware that they were entering into an agreement with a corporation. In short, the corporation should comply with all statutory requirements when doing business under a fictitious or assumed name.

It is usually the paralegal's responsibility to research the statutes to determine the requirements for registering to do business under a fictitious name. You can never assume that the statutes of one state are the same as or similar to those of another. Each state's statutes *must* be separately researched.

6–3   Articles of Incorporation: Statutory Provisions

In this book we use the term *articles of incorporation* to refer to the document filed to incorporate a business. The Model Act uses the term *articles of incorporation*. However, some states refer to this document as the "certificate of incorporation," the "charter," or the "articles of association."

The articles of incorporation *must* contain the information specifically required by state statute. For example, Section 2.02(a) of the Model Act states:

> The articles of incorporation must set forth:
> (1) a corporate name for the corporation that satisfies the requirements of section 4.01;
> (2) the number of shares the corporation is authorized to issue;
> (3) the street address of the corporation's initial registered office and the name of its initial registered agent at that office; and
> (4) the name and address of each incorporator.

Provisions required by statute to be contained in the articles of incorporation are called **statutory provisions**. The four items listed in Section 2.02(a) are the statutory provisions required by the Model Act. You must research the statutes of the state in which you intend to incorporate to determine that state's requirements. You will find that all state statutes require at least the four elements found in Section 2.02(a) of the Model Act, and we will discuss in greater detail each of these four elements. In Figure 6–4 are articles of incorporation prepared in accordance with the Model Act, and they contain all four elements discussed in this section.

Corporate Name

As we discussed earlier in this chapter, the corporate name selected must meet the requirements of the statutes of the state of incorporation. In the case of the Model Act, it must comply with the provisions of Section 4.01.

After it has been determined that the name selected meets the statutory requirements and is available for use in a particular state, that corporate name is usually included in the first provision of the articles of incorporation (see Figure 6–4). This name will appear in the official records of the secretary of state exactly as it is spelled and punctuated in the articles.

The corporate name set out in the articles of incorporation is the name the corporation should use in all documents. If the corporation wants to use a name other than its corporate name, that is, a fictitious name, it may do so by filing the proper registration with the state in which the corporation wants to use the fictitious name. See the discussion in Section 6–2 of the use of fictitious names.

PARALEGALERT!

In preparing the articles of incorporation, take great care to use the exact name selected by the client. Sometimes the mere inclusion of an *s*, making a word plural, will change the meaning of the name or make it different from what your client wanted. Be careful!

Figure 6–4 Articles of Incorporation Prepared in Accordance with the Model Act

---

**Articles of Incorporation
of**

_____

     The undersigned, in order to form a corporation for the purposes hereinafter stated, under and pursuant to the provisions of Section _____ of the Corporation Law of _____ , does hereby certify that:

     Article One: The name of the Corporation is _____..

     Article Two: The total number of shares of stock which the Corporation shall have the authority to issue is 1,000 shares of Common Stock.

     Article Three: The registered office of the Corporation is located at 123 America Street, Bigtown, New York 12345. The name and address of the Corporation's registered agent at such address is Service Provider Company.

     Article Four: The incorporator of the Corporation is _____ , whose mailing address is _____ .

     In Witness Whereof, the incorporator has executed and sealed these Articles of Incorporation on this _____ day of _____ , 199 ___..

_____
(Incorporator)

Capital Structure

The articles of incorporation must include the number of **authorized shares,** or the total number of shares that the corporation has the authority to issue to shareholders. The corporation may not issue a greater number of shares of stock than are authorized in the articles of incorporation. Therefore, if the corporation desires to issue more shares than it has the authority to issue, the articles of incorporation must be amended to increase the number of authorized shares. The authority to issue shares is given to the corporation by state statute, but the articles of incorporation must establish how many shares will be authorized, whether the shares will have par value or no par value, and whether preferred stock will be authorized. In this section we will discuss only the information that must be included in the articles of incorporation. Chapter 10 of this book is devoted to the financial structure and capitalization of the corporation. There we will discuss in greater detail the specifics of a corporation's capital structure.

The capital structure of the corporation can be simple or complex. In a simple capital structure, the corporation has the authority to issue one type of stock, called **common stock.** In a complex capital structure, the corporation has the authority to issue multiple classes of stock, usually referred to as **preferred stock,** with different preferences, limitations, and rights assigned to each class. In either case, Section 6.01(a) of the Model Act provides that "the articles of incorporation must prescribe the classes of shares and the number of shares of each class that the corporation is authorized to issue." If more than one class of stock is authorized, the articles of incorporation must describe each class of stock and the preferences, limitations, and rights associated with it. Classes of stock may vary in a number of ways. Different classes of stock may have different voting, dividend, liquidation, redemption, and conversion rights.

The sample articles of incorporation in Figure 6–4 include a provision authorizing the corporation to issue 1,000 shares of common stock, and they do not provide a par value for the shares. This is an example of a simple capital structure. It is commonly used when the corporation will have only a few shareholders. Figure 6–5 is an example of more complex provisions, in which the corporation is authorized to issue additional classes of stock, with different preferences, limitations, and rights associated with each class.

The **par value** assigned to stock is the minimum amount of consideration that can be paid for the stock. For example, a share of $10 par value stock can be issued only for cash, services, or property valued at no less than $10. Stock that has no par value may be sold for any amount determined by the board of directors of the corporation. The Model Act does not require that a corporation distinguish between par-value and no-par-value shares, even though many states' statutes still require the assignment of par value to a corporation's stock. If the statutes require a par value to be assigned to stock, the corporation's articles of incorporation must state the par value or must state that the shares have no par value.

Some states do not permit a corporation to begin doing business until its authorized capital has been subscribed for or paid. In addition, the fee charged by some states to incorporate the business is determined by the corporation's authorized capital, and annual franchise fees are often based on the corporation's authorized capital. The amount of filing, organization, or franchise tax fees may have some effect on the determination of the amount of capital to authorize in the articles of incorporation.

PARALEGALERT!

The par value of stock is purely an arbitrary value set in the articles of incorporation. The par value of stock is in no way related to the market value.

Registered Agent and Address

Most states require that a corporation maintain a registered office *and* a registered agent in the state of incorporation. A few states, including Pennsylvania and Minnesota, do not require that a registered agent be named in the articles. Section 5.01 of the Model Act provides, in part, that "each corporation must continuously maintain . . . (1) a registered office that may be the same as any of its places of business; and (2) a registered agent." A review of the statutes of the state of incorporation will provide you with the requirements of that state.

The **registered office** of the corporation is the address designated by the corporation in its articles of incorporation as the place where service of process may be effected. The **registered agent** is the individual or entity appointed by a corporation in its articles of incorporation to accept service of process on behalf of the corporation. Under the Model Act a registered agent may be an individual residing in the state, a domestic corporation of that state, or a foreign corporation, but the business address of the registered agent must be the same as the registered office of the corporation. Section 5.04(a) of the Model Act defines the registered agent as the "corporation's agent for service of process, notice, or demand required or permitted by law to be served on the corporation."

When a corporation incorporates in one state but has its principal place of business in another, the corporation hires a service company to represent it in the

PARALEGALERT!

For an annual fee (ranging from $75 to $175), a service company will act as registered agent and will provide its address as the registered address of the corporation. A corporation hires a service company to provide this benefit when the corporation has no office address or location in that state. The paralegal usually makes the arrangements with the service company.

Figure 6–5   Capital Stock Provisions to Be Included in Articles of Incorporation

The total number of shares which the Corporation is authorized to issue is 1,000,000 shares, of which 500,000 shares shall be Common Stock and 500,000 shares shall be Preferred Stock. The Board of Directors is expressly authorized to issue the shares of Preferred Stock in such series or classes and to fix from time to time the designations, preferences, rights and qualifications, limitations, or restrictions of the shares of each series or class. The authority of the Board of Directors shall include, but not be limited to, determining the following aspects of each series or class: (a) the number of shares constituting such series or class; (b) voting rights, if any; (c) the annual dividend rate on the shares; (d) the redemption price, if any; (e) the right of conversion of such shares into shares of other series or classes; (f) preference in the event of a dissolution or liquidation of the corporation; and (g) any other designation, preference, right and qualification, limitation, or restriction.

state of incorporation. For example, Widget Manufacturing Company incorporated in the state of Delaware because of Delaware's attractive tax laws, but Widget has no office (or address) in the state of Delaware. A service company offers its address in the state and acts as the registered agent for Widget for an annual representative fee. Figure 6–4 includes a provision naming Service Provider Company as the registered agent and includes Service Provider Company's business address as the registered address for the corporation.

Incorporator

The **incorporator** is the person who, on behalf of the corporation, executes the articles of incorporation and delivers them to the secretary of state for filing. The number of incorporators and their qualifications depend on the requirements of the statutes of the state of incorporation. Section 2.01 of the Model Act, which is entitled "Incorporators," states that "one or more persons may act as the incorporator or incorporators of a corporation by delivering articles of incorporation to the secretary of state for filing."

PARALEGALERT!

In actuality, the paralegal usually acts as the incorporator of the corporation. The paralegal's responsibilities as the incorporator will end upon the election of the directors, if the directors were not named in the articles. But the paralegal will continue the organizational activities—drafting meeting minutes, ordering the minute and stock books, and so on—all in the capacity of corporate paralegal.

As examples, some states require that an incorporator must be a natural person 18 years of age or older but need not be a citizen or resident of that particular state; other states allow a corporation to act as an incorporator. Most states require only one incorporator. Remember, you must research the statutes of the state of incorporation to determine who may act as the incorporator and who may not.

Whether the incorporator has any duties after the articles of incorporation have been filed depends on whether the initial directors are named in the articles of incorporation. If the initial directors are named in the articles, they are responsible for holding the organizational meeting, the first meeting held after incorporation. Otherwise, the incorporator must hold a meeting to elect the directors, who then hold the organizational meeting. We will discuss the procedures for the organizational meeting in greater detail in Chapter 7.

The common practice is for the attorney or paralegal who prepares the articles of incorporation to act as the incorporator, even when the attorney or paralegal has no intention of becoming a shareholder, director, or officer of the corporation.

6–4   Articles of Incorporation: Optional Provisions

In addition to the information required by the state statutes to be contained in the articles of incorporation, other provisions are permitted to be included in the articles. For example, Section 2.02(b) of the Model Act provides that articles of incorporation may contain the following:

1. Names and addresses of the initial directors.
2. The purpose or purposes for which the corporation is organized.
3. Provisions for the management and regulation of the affairs of the corporation.
4. Provisions defining, limiting, and regulating the powers of the corporation, the board of directors, and the shareholders.
5. Par value for authorized shares or classes of shares.
6. Imposition of personal liability on shareholders for debts of the corporation.
7. Any provision required or permitted to be set forth in the bylaws.
8. Elimination or limitation of liability of a director to the corporation or the shareholders.

Some of these provisions will be discussed in greater detail in the following subsections.

Initial Directors

The individuals who are to serve as the first directors, or **initial directors,** of the corporation may or may not be named in the articles of incorporation. Section 2.02(b) of the Model Act states that "the articles of incorporation may set forth: (1) the names and addresses of the individuals who are to serve as the initial directors." If the initial directors are named in the articles of incorporation, they will hold office until the shareholders elect their successors. If the initial directors are not named in the articles, the incorporators will name them at the incorporators' organizational meeting. A review of the statutes of the state of incorporation must be made to determine whether directors must be named in the original articles of incorporation.

Corporate Purposes and Powers

The purpose or purposes for which a corporation is organized and the powers granted to the corporation are distinguishable concepts. The **purposes** of the corporation are its business goals and pursuits. The **powers** granted by state statute enable the corporation to carry out the purposes for which it was formed. In short, statutory corporate powers give the corporation the authority to pursue its purposes.

Purposes may be included in the articles of incorporation. Section 3.01(a) of the Model Act provides that "every corporation . . . has the purpose of engaging in any lawful business unless a more limited purpose is set forth in the articles of incorporation." In states that have adopted statutes similar to the Model Act, the articles of incorporation are not required to contain any provision with respect to the purposes of the corporation. The corporation may engage in any lawful business. There are some states that still require that the purposes of the corporation be specifically spelled out in the articles of incorporation. Other states allow a general statement, such as "to engage in any lawful activity or business," and a few states require no statement as to the purposes of the corporation.

If a provision in the articles of incorporation states that "the corporation shall engage in the business of purchasing and selling real estate," the corporation is only permitted to purchase and sell real estate. It is usually desirable to describe the corporation's purposes broadly to include all activities the corporation currently carries on and any it intends to carry on in the future.

It is not necessary to set out in the articles of incorporation the powers that are granted to the corporation by state statute. Express powers are usually spelled out in the state statutes, and every corporation is granted the same powers as an individual to carry out its business and affairs. Section 3.02 of the Model Act enumerates those powers, which include the power "to sue and be sued, complain and defend in its corporate name"; "to sell, convey, mortgage, pledge, lease, exchange, and otherwise dispose of all or any part of its property"; "to lend money, invest, and reinvest its funds"; and "to elect directors and appoint officers, employees and agents." This is not a complete list of the powers granted the corporation. You should review Section 3.02 of the Model Act in Appendix A for the full text of this section.

Period of Existence

Almost every state provides that a corporation has the power to exist perpetually. Because this is a power granted to the corporation by state statute, it is not necessary to include a statement in the articles of incorporation regarding **perpetual existence.** The inclusion or exclusion of a statement depends on the requirements of the state statutes.

Section 3.02 of the Model Act states that "unless its articles of incorporation provide otherwise, every corporation has perpetual duration," and most state statutes provide that a corporation has perpetual existence unless a lesser period of time is specified in the articles of incorporation. The following is an example of a provision that might be included in the articles of incorporation if a lesser period of time was desired for the corporation's existence: "The Corporation's existence shall terminate on _____, 199__, unless dissolved according to law prior thereto." Because perpetual existence is one of the advantages of incorporating, it is customary to allow the corporation to exist perpetually, as opposed to stating a date on which the corporation will terminate its existence.

Preemptive Rights

Almost every state grants the shareholders of a corporation the right to purchase newly issued shares of the corporation's stock before any shares are sold to persons who are not already shareholders of the corporation. This is a shareholder's **preemptive right.** Shareholders can exercise their preemptive right to purchase the newly issued shares in the same proportionate ownership as their current stock ownership. Reasonable notice must be given to shareholders who have preemptive rights, and a shareholder must be given the opportunity to purchase his or her proportionate share on the same terms and conditions as the other shareholders. For example, if a shareholder is unable to pay for or does not desire to purchase the shares to which he or she is entitled, the shares cannot be offered to outsiders on more favorable terms than those offered to the shareholder. In addition, the shareholder may sell his or her right to anyone who is able to pay for the shares being offered.

The corporation must first offer newly issued shares to the current shareholders before offering them to outside persons if the shareholders of the corporation have preemptive rights.

Here is an example of the exercise of preemptive rights: ABC Company is authorized to issue 1,000 shares of common stock, and preemptive rights have been granted to the shareholders in the articles of incorporation. Immediately after its incorporation, ABC Company issued 300 shares to Mr. Smith, 100 shares to Mr. Jones, and 100 shares to Mr. Baxter. It now wants to issue the remaining 500 shares at a price of $10 per share. Mr. Smith must be given the opportunity to purchase 300 shares at that price, and Mr. Jones and Mr. Baxter must be given the opportunity to purchase 100 shares each at that price before the shares are offered to anyone else.

Preemptive rights are based on the principle that existing shareholders must be given the opportunity to maintain their proportionate control of the corporation. Generally, it protects the minority shareholder against directors of the corporation who arbitrarily purchase and issue stock to themselves to gain control of the corporation. If the shareholders have preemptive rights, the directors cannot issue any shares without first offering them to the current shareholders. But even then, the minority shareholder can be "frozen out" of his ownership position in the corporation if he cannot afford to buy the shares.

Most state statutes handle preemptive rights in one of two ways: (1) preemptive rights exist unless the corporation's articles of incorporation specifically deny them, or (2) preemptive rights do not exist unless the corporation's articles of incorporation specifically grant them. Section 6.30 of the Model Act provides that shareholders do not have a preemptive right to purchase shares of the corporation unless such right is granted in the corporation's articles of incorporation. Specifically, that section states that "the shareholders of a corporation do not have a preemptive right to acquire the corporation's unissued shares except to the extent the articles of incorporation so provide."

The safest route when drafting articles of incorporation is to either specifically deny or grant preemptive rights, depending on the desires of the incorporators. Figure 6–6 is an example of a provision that can be included in the articles of incorporation to deny preemptive rights to the shareholders.

Cumulative Voting for Directors

Generally, each shareholder is entitled to one vote for each share of stock that he or she owns, unless the state statute, the articles of incorporation, or the bylaws provide otherwise. This is known as **straight voting,** and it makes it possible for the owners of a majority of the stock of a corporation to elect all the directors. To give the minority shareholders the opportunity to have at least one representative on the board of directors, cumulative voting has been developed. **Cumulative voting** is the right of the shareholder to cast all his or her votes for one candidate or to divide them among several candidates in whatever way he

Figure 6–6   Provision of the Articles of Incorporation Denying Preemptive Rights

No holder of any shares of stock of the Corporation shall have any preemptive right to purchase, subscribe for, or otherwise acquire any shares of stock of the Corporation now or hereafter authorized.

or she desires. If shareholders are permitted to cumulate their shares in voting for directors, each shareholder is entitled to a total number of votes calculated by the following formula:

Number of directors to be elected × number of his or her shares of stock

Of the total number of votes derived from this formula, the shareholder may cast all of them for one candidate for director or may divide them among any number of the directors.

The effect of cumulating votes is to give the minority shareholder an opportunity to have representation on the board of directors. The following example will illustrate how this is possible: ABC Company has two shareholders: Mr. Smith, who owns 70 shares of voting stock, and Mr. Jones, who owns 30 shares of voting stock. With cumulative voting, and 3 directors being elected, Mr. Jones can vote his 90 shares (30 shares × 3 directors) for one candidate and thus control the election of at least one director. Mr. Smith cannot divide his 210 votes (70 shares × 3 directors) among his 3 candidates in such a way that each will get at least 90 votes. If Mr. Smith divides his shares between the first 2 candidates, Mr. Jones will still outvote him for the third director.

As with preemptive rights, state statutes treat cumulative voting in one of two ways: (1) cumulative voting exists unless the corporation's articles of incorporation specifically deny it, or (2) cumulative voting does not exist unless the corporation's articles of incorporation specifically grant it. Regardless of any statutory provisions, most states allow the articles of incorporation to either deny or grant cumulative voting. As with preemptive rights, the safest route when drafting articles of incorporation is to either specifically deny or grant cumulative voting, depending on the desires of the incorporators. Figure 6–7 is an example of a provision that can be included in the articles of incorporation to grant cumulative voting rights to the shareholders.

Quorum and Vote of Shareholders

Generally, all matters voted on by the shareholders require a vote of a majority of the shares entitled to vote. A majority of the shares entitled to vote constitutes a **quorum** for all matters on which the shareholders of the corporation are entitled to take action. A quorum is a majority of the shares, *not* a majority of the shareholders or persons. For an action to be properly voted upon, a quorum of the shares must be represented in person or by proxy. When it has been determined that a quorum of the shares is present, an affirmative vote of a majority of the shares present will carry any action on which a vote is taken. For example, suppose 1,000 shares are owned by four different shareholders, and these 1,000 shares constitute the total number of shares issued by the corporation. Shareholder A owns 700 shares, and Shareholders B, C, and D each own 100 shares. If only Shareholder A (representing the ownership of 700 shares) is present at a meeting of the shareholders, a quorum is present. If Shareholders B, C, and D are all present (representing the ownership of 300 shares), a quorum is not present.

Figure 6–7   Provision of the Articles of Incorporation Granting Cumulative Voting

> At all elections of directors, the shareholders shall be entitled to cumulate their votes, and they may cast all such votes for a single director or may distribute them among the number of candidate directors. The total number of votes to which a shareholder shall be entitled shall equal the number of his shares of stock multiplied by the number of candidate directors to be elected.

Most state statutes provide that the articles of incorporation may alter the definition of a quorum for voting purposes. A common provision allows the articles of incorporation to set the quorum at "any number greater than a majority, but not less than" a certain percentage, usually, one-third. Under such a provision, the articles of incorporation may provide that a quorum shall be 40 percent of the shares entitled to vote or that a quorum shall be 60 percent of the shares entitled to vote. But a quorum may never be less than one-third of the shares entitled to vote. Section 7.27(a) of the Model Act provides that "the articles of incorporation may provide for a greater quorum or voting requirement for shareholders . . . than is provided for by this Act."

Quorum and voting requirements of shareholders' and directors' meetings will be discussed in greater detail in the next chapter.

Indemnification of Directors and Officers

Very often individuals will decline to serve as directors, officers, or employees unless the corporation provides **indemnification** for any liability, penalties, or expenses incurred as a result of their actions on behalf of the corporation. Indemnification may include the reimbursement or payment of expenses actually incurred by the individual in connection with his or her defense or settlement of an action, suit, or proceeding to which the individual is a party by reason of his or her relationship with the corporation.

State statutes differ in their treatment of indemnification of directors, officers, and employees of the corporation. The Model Act grants the corporation the right to indemnify its directors, officers, and employees if the "individual . . . conducted himself in good faith and he reasonably believed . . . that his conduct was in its best interests." In states that have adopted this provision, it is not necessary to give the corporation the power of indemnification in the articles of incorporation. But many states permit indemnification only if specifically provided for in the articles of incorporation. Other states permit reimbursement only to an individual who is successful in defending litigation concerning his or her acts performed on behalf of the corporation.

To ensure that corporate personnel are indemnified for their actions, it is best to establish the scope of indemnification desired by the corporation in the articles of incorporation. Figure 6–8 is an example of language that may be included in the articles of incorporation to provide indemnification of corporate personnel.

Figure 6–8 Provision of the Articles of Incorporation for Indemnification of Corporate Personnel

> The Corporation shall indemnify the directors, officers, and employees of the Corporation against any expenses, penalties, and fines incurred by them in the connection with their defense of any threatened, pending, or completed action, suit, or proceeding, whether civil, criminal, administrative, or investigative and whether formal or informal, except for any actions by them where they have been held to be liable for negligence or misconduct in the performance of their duties.

6–5   Postincorporation Activities

After articles of incorporation have been filed and the corporation has come into existence, several steps must be taken to complete its organization and begin business. The first order of business after beginning corporate existence is to hold a meeting of the incorporators, or of the board of directors if they were named in the articles of incorporation. This meeting is conducted in the same manner as any other meeting of the directors or shareholders of the corporation. Chapter 7 will cover in greater detail the procedures for properly conducting the incorporators', directors', and shareholders' meetings.

Organizational Meeting

As we discussed earlier in this chapter, if the initial directors are named in the articles, the directors are responsible for holding the **organizational meeting,** the first meeting held after incorporation. If the directors are not named in the articles, the incorporator must hold a meeting to elect the directors, who then hold the organizational meeting.

If the incorporator holds the organizational meeting, he or she will authorize two acts: (1) the appointment of the first board of directors and (2) the adoption of the bylaws of the corporation. If the initial directors were named in the articles of incorporation, they will hold the organizational meeting, at which the following items will be discussed and approved:

1. Election of officers.
2. Adoption of the form of the share certificate.
3. Issuance of shares to the shareholders.
4. Adoption of bylaws.
5. Adoption of the corporate seal.
6. Selection of the corporation's fiscal year.
7. Authorization of the officers to perform certain acts, including preparing and filing the Subchapter S election form, entering into agreements on behalf of the corporation, and opening the corporation's bank accounts.
8. Provision for the payment of the expenses incurred to incorporate the business.

PARALEGALERT!

The organizational meeting is generally held on the date of incorporation or within several days after that. No statute or regulation requires that the meeting be held within a specified time of the date of incorporation.

Statutory requirements and provisions often included in the corporation's articles of incorporation dictate how, when, and where the organizational meeting is held. We will defer a more detailed analysis of the organizational meeting to Section 7–4.

Payment of Capital

Many states still require that a certain amount of capital be collected before the corporation can commence or transact business and before it can incur indebtedness. In the states that follow this rule, the payment of all preincorporation subscriptions must be made before the corporation commences business. Corporations in those states are required to include a provision in their articles of incorporation that states, "The minimum amount of capital with which the Corporation will commence business is _____ Dollars ($_____)."
This requirement has been eliminated from the Model Act. One by one, states are

following suit, because corporations have selected minimum amounts of capital as low as $100 and the states realize that this requirement is ineffective.

Minute Book, Stock Book, and Corporate Seal

One of the paralegal's responsibilities in the incorporation of a business is the purchase, organization, and maintenance of the corporation's minute book, stock book, and corporate seal. The **minute book** is the depository of all corporate organizational documents, including the articles of incorporation, all amendments to the articles, and the minutes of meetings of the board of directors and shareholders. Information with respect to the issuance of shares, including the number of shares issued, the type of shares issued, the date of issuance, and the shareholders' names, is maintained in the corporation's **stock book.** The corporate statutes of most states confer on the corporation the power to make and use a **corporate seal,** and the corporation generally uses its corporate seal when entering into contracts and agreements.

All these corporate supplies can be purchased from your local legal supply or stationery store. Many suppliers sell a corporate supply kit, which includes minute book, stock book, and corporate seal in one neat package. Alternatively, the books and the seal can be purchased separately. Generally, the cost the client is willing to incur will dictate where these items are purchased. In recent years many corporations have retreated from using the traditional red minute book and have begun using a three-ring binder because of its low cost and the ease of filing documents in it.

When you order the corporate seal, the supplier will need to know the exact name of the corporation, the state in which it was incorporated, and the year in which it was incorporated, all of which will appear in the impression of the corporate seal. A corporation's seal can be as informal and simple as the single word *SEAL*, or it can be a round seal similar to a notary public's seal. The trend in recent years has been to do away with corporate seals. Therefore, you may be instructed to forgo purchasing a corporate seal for the corporation you have just incorporated.

Stock books can be ordered with the name of the corporation, the state of incorporation, and the number of authorized shares preprinted on each stock certificate. Of course, such stock certificate books are costly. The alternative is to purchase a stock book in blank; the certificates can be completed as shares are sold. In this age of computerization, many corporations no longer issue stock certificates to their shareholders. However, you will find that smaller, closely held corporations continue to issue paper certificates. The article in the *Legal Links* in this chapter (next page) highlights the advantages and disadvantages of computerizing a corporation's stock records.

We will discuss the organization and maintenance of the minute book and the stock book in greater detail in Chapter 7.

Legal Advertisement

A few states, including Arizona, Georgia, Nebraska, and Pennsylvania, require the publication of a **legal notice** that the corporation was organized in that state. Usually, publication of this notice is required to be made in the legal journal or a newspaper or both in the county in which the registered office of the corporation is located. For example, Pennsylvania statutes require the notice to be published in two publications, one the legal journal and one a publication of general circulation in the county in which the registered office of the corporation is located.

The Stock Certificate: Is It Obsolete?

In today's world of computerization, many people who purchase stocks and other types of securities actually never receive a paper certificate. And now, Wall Street appears to be discouraging their use even further. For instance, Merrill Lynch, the largest stock broker-age firm, is charging for each certificate request. Experts believe that even more broker-age firms will begin charging for security certificates.

In the past, paper certificates were used to prove ownership of securities. However, since computerized records are now used to show ownership, the only paper evidence may be your monthly account statement; stocks are held for you in the brokerage's street name.

The book-entry system of ownership offers two advantages. First, no time is lost send-ing certificates to the broker when you're selling. Also, if your stocks are held in the broker's street name, the certificates cannot be stolen from your home or vault. However, street-name ownership does expose you to the brokerage's financial problems and/or fraud.

On the other hand, if you wish to put securities up as collateral, a bank or lending institution may want to hold the paper certificate. It is also easier to transfer securities from one broker to another if you have a certificate in hand.

The American Association of Individual Investors says that certificates are falling out of favor with investors. A survey by the group shows that more than two-thirds of their members favor paperless trading for stocks and other securities. However, bank trust officers prefer the certificate form of ownership for security purposes.

So, should you ask your broker for an actual certificate when you purchase stocks, bonds or other types of securities? Each investor will have to consider these pros and cons before reaching their own individual decision. (Provided with permission by D. G. Sisterson & Co., Pittsburgh, Pennsylvania.)

Figure 6–9 is an example of the notice required to be published for a corporation formed in Pennsylvania. It is generally the paralegal's responsibility to arrange for the publication of this notice.

Securities Law Considerations

Most states regulate the offer and sale of securities (shares) to shareholders in that state. State securities laws, also referred to as **blue sky laws,** vary consider-ably from state to state. They usually have a complex set of requirements that must be met before any shares are issued. However, many state securities laws provide exemptions for the issuance of stock to a small number of subscribers or in conjunction with the organization of the corporation.

In addition to blue sky laws, federal securities laws also govern the offer and sale of securities. Regulation of the offer and sale of securities is covered in greater detail in Chapter 12.

Figure 6–9   Legal Advertisement Required by Pennsylvania Statutes

Legal Notice

Notice is hereby given that Articles of Incorporation were filed with the Secretary of the Commonwealth of Pennsylvania by ABC CORPORATION, a corporation incor-porated under the provisions of the Business Corporation Law of 1988.

Subchapter S Election

If the corporation's shareholders have consented to the corporation's treatment as a **Subchapter S corporation** (also referred to as an "S Corporation"), the officers of the corporation should prepare and file the proper documentation with the Internal Revenue Service and, where required, with the department of revenue of the state of incorporation. The board of directors, at its organizational meeting, will authorize the officers of the corporation to prepare and file the required documentation. Figure 5–9 is a sample of **Form 2553,** Election by a Small Business Corporation, which is the form required to be filed with the Internal Revenue Service. Form 2553 must be filed within 75 days of the date the corporation first had assets, issued stock, or conducted business. If Form 2553 is not filed with the IRS within that time limit, the corporation will be unable to be treated as a Subchapter S corporation until the following tax year. You should carefully review the Internal Revenue Code section relating to Subchapter S corporations and consult the accountant or tax lawyer with whom you are working to verify the filing requirements. Also, refer to Section 5–3 of this book, in which we discussed the advantages and disadvantages of operating as a Subchapter S corporation.

PARALEGALERT!

It is critical that Form 2553 be filed within the time limit in order for the corporation to be treated as an S corporation. Therefore, Form 2553 should be sent to the IRS by certified mail. Copies of the form and your transmittal letter should be enclosed, along with a self-addressed stamped envelope. Ask the IRS filing clerk to date-stamp the copies of the transmittal letter and the form and return it to you as evidence of the timely filing of Form 2553.

6–6   Bylaws

The **bylaws** are the rules and regulations that govern the internal affairs of the corporation. Specifically, they define the rights, powers, and duties of the shareholders with respect to each other and the corporation, and they define the rights, powers, and duties of the directors and officers of the corporation. The bylaws may contain any valid and legal provision that is necessary to regulate the internal affairs of the corporation and to define the rights, powers, and duties of the shareholders, directors, and officers.

Section 2.06(b) of the Model Act states that "the bylaws of a corporation may contain any provision for managing the business and regulating the affairs of the corporation that is not inconsistent with law or the articles of incorporation." For example, a bylaw provision that states, "There shall be five directors" would be inconsistent with articles of incorporation that state, "There shall be six directors." In this case, two options are available to the corporation. The bylaws can be amended to provide for six directors, making them consistent with the articles of incorporation, or the articles of incorporation can be amended to provide for five directors, making them consistent with the bylaws. Generally, a corporation would amend the bylaws to conform to the articles of incorporation because of the relative ease with which the bylaws can be amended and the expense and administrative burden of amending the articles of incorporation. Although the bylaws may contain any provisions consistent with the law and the articles of incorporation, they cannot provide for the performance of an illegal act by the shareholders, directors, or officers.

PARALEGALERT!

Any provision regarding the management and business affairs of the corporation may be included in the bylaws as long as the provision is not inconsistent with the statutes of the state of incorporation or with the articles of incorporation.

Bylaws are not a public record; that is, they are not filed or recorded with the secretary of state like the articles of incorporation. Bylaws are a private document and are not open for inspection by anyone except the shareholders, directors, and officers.

Bylaws are usually adopted by the incorporator or incorporators at the organizational meeting, but they may be adopted by the directors at their initial meeting. Section 2.06(a) of the Model Act provides that "the incorporators or board of directors of a corporation shall adopt initial bylaws for the corporation." After the initial bylaws are adopted, they may be amended in any respect, they may be repealed, or new bylaws may be adopted, provided the change is legal, is consistent with the articles of incorporation, and does not violate any rights of the shareholder. Any amendment to the bylaws must be adopted and approved by either the shareholders or the board of directors, depending on the authorization required by either the articles of corporation or the state statute of the corporation's home state. The action of the shareholders or the board of directors to amend the bylaws is taken by adopting a resolution authorizing the amendment. This resolution is approved at a meeting or by written consent of the shareholders or directors. Approval of actions taken by the shareholders and directors, including the amendment of bylaws, is covered in greater detail in Chapter 7.

Provisions usually found in bylaws include the time and place for holding annual and special meetings of the shareholders and directors; the number of days' notice that must be given prior to meetings of the shareholders and directors; the number of directors to serve on the board; the procedure for election and appointment of committees and officers; the duties of the officers; the procedure for replacing lost, destroyed, or stolen certificates; the qualifications for payment of dividends; and the procedure for amending the bylaws. Of course, these are just some of the provisions that can appear in bylaws. Following is an outline of standard provisions found in most corporate bylaws:

1. Corporate offices
    a. Principal office
    b. Registered office
2. Shareholders
    a. Annual and special meetings
    b. Notice and purpose of meetings
    c. Waiver of notice of meetings
    d. Quorum
    e. Proxies
    f. Record date and closing of transfer books
    g. Voting
3. Directors
    a. Number, qualification, and term
    b. Annual and special meetings
    c. Notice and purpose of meetings
    d. Waiver of notice of meetings
    e. Quorum
    f. Vacancies
    g. Removal
    h. Compensation
4. Officers
    a. Number and term of office
    b. Vacancies
    c. Removal
    d. Duties
    e. Salaries

5. Committees
   a. Authority
   b. Meetings
   c. Vacancies
6. Indemnification
7. Certificates and ownership of stock
   a. Form of certificates
   b. Transfer of shares
   c. Transfer agent
   d. Lost, destroyed, or stolen certificates
8. Dividends
9. Corporate actions
10. Fiscal year
11. Corporate seal
12. Amendment of bylaws

Additional provisions may be included in the bylaws as long as they are not inconsistent with the state statute or the articles of incorporation. For example, bylaws may contain additional provisions regarding the issuance of stock rights or options, certain voting rights, or certain contract rights of the corporation, to name a few.

An examination of the state statute is a necessary part of drafting bylaws. The important point to remember when drafting bylaws is that they should be a practical, but thorough and comprehensive, guide for use by the directors and officers in managing the internal affairs of the corporation.

6–7 Incorporating Other Forms of Business Organizations

Professional Corporation

As we discussed in Section 4–2, most states provide that **professional corporations** are governed by the state's business corporation law unless specific provisions have been adopted governing professional corporations. Most of the filing and organization requirements of the business corporation, the main focus of this chapter, also apply to professional corporations. State statutes governing the operation of professional corporations vary greatly from state to state; therefore, a review of the individual state statutes is always necessary once the decision has been made about the state in which to incorporate. The Model Professional Corporation Supplement (1984) was developed by the American Bar Association's Committee on Corporate Laws to be used as a guide for states enacting or revising their professional corporation statutes. Not all states have adopted this supplement nor have they adopted separate professional corporation statutes.

Most statutes require that professional corporations be limited to the practice of one profession. Also, Section 14(a) of the Model Professional Corporation Supplement (1984) states that "a professional corporation may not render any professional service or engage in any business other than the professional service and business authorized by its articles of incorporation." Therefore, when the articles of incorporation are drafted, the purpose clause must specifically state the business activity in which the corporation will engage.

Some professions that are regulated by a governmental body or agency may be required by that agency to include special provisions in the articles of incorporation. Therefore, it is important that the applicable agency be contacted to identify any additional restrictions or requirements for incorporating the professional corporation. Section 15(a)(3) of the Model Professional Corporation Supplement (1984) reinforces this guideline and states that the name of a professional corporation "must conform with any rule promulgated by the licensing authority having jurisdiction over a professional service described in the corporation's articles of incorporation."

There are several aspects of the organization and formation of the professional corporation that differ from the business corporation. First, the name of the professional corporation must usually contain a designator indicating that it is a professional corporation. For example, it must use *professional corporation, P.C., professional association,* or *P.A.* to distinguish that it is a professional corporation. Second, the purpose clause of the articles of incorporation must specifically state the type of business activity to be conducted and must state that the corporation is a professional corporation. Third, a statement must appear conspicuously on each share certificate issued by the professional corporation. An example of the statement, required by Section 21(a) of the Model Professional Corporation Supplement (1984), is shown in Figure 6–10. This statement may be printed anywhere on the share certificate but is usually printed on the back of the certificate. When preparing share certificates for the professional corporation, the name of the statute that governs professional corporations in the state of incorporation would replace the reference to the Model Professional Corporation Supplement used in Figure 6–10. Fourth, at least one-half of the directors and all of the officers must be individuals who are authorized by law to render the professional service described in the articles of incorporation. And fifth, the shareholders of the professional corporation are limited to those individuals licensed to practice the particular profession for which it was incorporated.

The organizational procedures discussed in Section 6–5 and the bylaws discussed in Section 6–6 are generally appropriate for use by the professional corporation. However, these organizational procedures and bylaws should be reviewed carefully before they are used for the professional corporation. State statutes differ, and some place other restrictions or requirements on the professional corporation. However, most states' statutes governing business corporations apply to the professional corporation, to the extent those statutes are not inconsistent with the provisions of any professional corporation statutes adopted in that state.

Provided in Figure 6–11 are articles of incorporation for use by a professional corporation. These articles have been prepared to comply with the Model Professional Corporation Supplement (1984).

You will have many opportunities to sharpen your investigative and analytical skills because of the inability of this textbook to cover all state statutes regarding the formation of all types of corporations. The professional corporation will offer some of those opportunities.

Figure 6–10   Statement for Inclusion on Share Certificate of Professional Corporation, Required by Section 21(a)

The transfer of shares of a professional corporation is restricted by the [Model Professional Corporation Supplement] and is subject to further restriction imposed from time to time by the licensing authority. Shares of a professional corporation are also subject to a statutory compulsory repurchase obligation.

Figure 6–11   Articles of Incorporation of a Professional Corporation

**Articles of Incorporation
of**

_____, P.C.
(A Professional Corporation)

The undersigned, in order to form a corporation for the purposes hereinafter stated, under and pursuant to the provisions of Section _____ of the Professional Corporation Law of _____, does hereby certify that:

Article One: The name of the Corporation is _____, P.C.

Article Two: The registered office of the Corporation is located at _____ _____. The name and address of the Corporation's registered agent at such address is _____.

Article Three: The purpose for which the Corporation is organized is to engage in the specific business of the practice of the profession of _____.

Article Four: The total number of shares of stock which the Corporation shall have the authority to issue is _____ shares of Common Stock, such shares having a par value of $_____.

Article Five: The shares of stock of the Corporation shall be issued and transferred (other than by operation of law or court decree) only to individuals who are authorized to practice the profession of _____ in the State of _____. No transferee of shares of stock of the Corporation by operation of law or court decree may vote such shares for any purpose whatsoever.

Article Six: The names, residences, and license or certificate numbers permitting the practice of the profession of _____ in the State of _____ of the individuals who are to be the original shareholders, directors, and officers of the Corporation are as follows:

Name	Residence	License or Certificate No.
_____	_____	_____
_____	_____	_____
_____	_____	_____

All the aforementioned individuals are licensed by the State of _____ to practice the profession of _____.

Article Seven: The incorporator of the Corporation is _____, whose mailing address is _____. The powers of the incorporator are to terminate upon the filing of these Articles of Incorporation.

In Witness Whereof, the incorporator has executed and sealed these Articles of Incorporation on this _____ day of _____, 199_.

_____
(Incorporator)

Nonprofit Corporation

As we discussed in Section 4–2, the **nonprofit corporation** is formed for the purpose of providing a charitable, athletic, political, educational, religious, fraternal, or social service, and it does not anticipate showing a gain or profit from the organization's activities. Although a nonprofit corporation is prohibited from distributing to its members, directors, or officers any incidental income earned in its activities, it is not prohibited from making a profit.

Many nonprofit organizations do not feel compelled to incorporate the business because the organizers, officers, and directors are generally serving the organization in a charitable capacity. They mistakenly believe either that they cannot be held liable for their actions performed on behalf of the organization or that they will not be held liable because they are performing a charitable deed. But nonprofit organizations should seek corporate status to provide the benefits of limiting potential liability of the officers and directors acting on behalf of the organization.

The Model Nonprofit Corporation Act was originally drafted in 1952, and was revised in 1964, by the Committee on Corporate Laws of the Section of Corporation, Banking, and Business Law of the American Bar Association. In 1987 the Revised Model Nonprofit Corporation Act was adapted to be compatible with the Model Act adopted in 1984. Each state has chosen to govern nonprofit corporations in one of three ways: (1) some states have adopted, either in whole or in part, the Model Nonprofit Corporation Act; (2) some states have used the Model Nonprofit Corporation Act as a pattern and have adopted their own statutes; and (3) other states have general corporation statutes that govern both nonprofit and profit corporations.

After the state of incorporation for the nonprofit corporation has been determined, you, the corporate paralegal, will usually be responsible for researching the statutes of that state to ensure that the incorporation and organizational documents are prepared in accordance with those statutes. Your investigative and analytical skills will once again be put to the test. The supervising attorney relies greatly on the accuracy and thoroughness of a paralegal's research.

There is one point worth mentioning about the drafting of articles of incorporation for a nonprofit corporation. A nonprofit corporation must limit the activities in which it may engage to one of the exempt purposes set out in Section 501(c)(3) of the Internal Revenue Code of 1986, as amended, if the corporation seeks federal tax-exempt status under that section. Therefore, the articles of incorporation must limit the purposes of the corporation to one or more of those exempt purposes. In addition, the articles of incorporation must provide that upon dissolution or liquidation, the corporation will distribute its assets to one or more exempt purposes or to the federal, state, or local government. The articles of incorporation may not provide that the assets will be distributed to the members upon dissolution or liquidation.

In Figure 6–12 are articles of incorporation for use by a nonprofit corporation. They have been prepared in accordance with the provisions of the Model Nonprofit Corporation Act. Articles of incorporation prepared under the Revised Model Nonprofit Corporation Act would differ slightly, as would articles prepared in accordance with any of the various states' statutes governing nonprofit corporations. Unfortunately, space does not permit us to cover the statutes of every state. The articles of incorporation in Figure 6–12 were prepared under the Model Nonprofit Corporation Act, as opposed to the Revised Model Nonprofit Corporation Act, because most states have followed or patterned their statutes after the earlier act.

Close Corporation

Many states have not adopted separate statutes governing the **close corporation,** even though more and more corporations are choosing to be characterized as close corporations. The Model Statutory Close Corporation Supplement (hereafter referred to as the Close Corporation Supplement) was developed for use by states that find it advisable to govern close corporations under a separate statute from that state's general corporation statute. Some states have chosen to

Figure 6–12   Articles of Incorporation of a Nonprofit Corporation

---

**Articles of Incorporation
of**

_____

The undersigned, in order to form a nonprofit corporation for the purposes hereinafter stated, under and pursuant to the provisions of Section _____ of the Nonprofit Corporation Act of _____, does hereby certify that:

Article One: The name of the Corporation is _____.

Article Two: The initial registered office of the Corporation is located at _____. The name and address of the Corporation's initial registered agent at such address is _____.

Article Three: The purpose for which the Corporation is organized is _____
_____.
_____.

Article Four: The period of its duration is _____ .

Article Five: Provisions for the regulation of the internal affairs of the Corporation, including provisions for the distribution of assets on dissolution or liquidation, are as follows: _____

Article Six: The number of directors constituting the initial Board of Directors of the Corporation is _____, and the names and addresses of the persons who are to serve as the initial directors are:

Name   Address

_____   _____

_____   _____

_____   _____

Article Eight: The incorporator of the Corporation is _____,
whose mailing address is _____.

In Witness Whereof, the incorporator has executed and sealed these Articles of Incorporation on this _____ day of _____, 199_.

_____
(Incorporator)

---

govern close corporations through their general corporation statutes, others have adopted provisions similar to the Close Corporation Supplement, and others have provided for no special provisions relating to close corporations. Because of the variety of different provisions adopted by the states, we will refer to the provisions of the Close Corporation Supplement in our discussion of close corporations.

Because of the size of closely held corporations, there are some practical differences between them and other corporations. The Close Corporation Supplement permits certain actions that would not otherwise be permitted and imposes restrictions not applicable to ordinary business corporations. For example, the close corporation may dispense with the board of directors and may delegate to the shareholders the power to manage the corporation. Section 21(a) of the Close Corporation Supplement states that "a statutory close corporation may operate without a board of directors if its articles of incorporation contain a statement to that effect." A concern for a close corporation operating without a board of directors is that the shareholders will have legal liability imposed on them as directors because they are acting in a managerial capacity.

For a corporation to be accorded close-corporation status, it generally must comply with certain provisions. First, the articles of incorporation must specifically refer to the corporation as a close corporation. Section 3(a) of the Close Corporation Supplement states that "a statutory close corporation is a corporation whose articles of incorporation contain a statement that the corporation is a statutory close corporation." Second, a corporation electing to become a close corporation by amending its articles of incorporation to include the required statement mentioned above must have no more than 50 shareholders. However, under the Close Corporation Supplement, a new corporation electing close corporation status at the time of its initial incorporation is not required to meet this 50-shareholder requirement. And third, share certificates issued by a close corporation must contain a statement, or stock legend, that puts shareholders on notice that their shares are subject to certain transfer restrictions. Refer to Figure 4–5 in Chapter 4, which is an example of the statement that must appear on all share certificates issued by a close corporation. This statement may be printed anywhere on the share certificate but is usually printed on the back of the certificate. Figure 6–13 is an example of a share certificate that shows the placement of the statement required to be printed on share certificates issued by close corporations.

Once a close corporation is formed, it retains its status as a close corporation until it files articles of amendment deleting from its articles of incorporation the statement required under Section 3(a) of the Close Corporation Supplement. An increase in the number of shareholders to more than 50 will cause a termination of close-corporation status only if neither the corporation nor its shareholders take any action to cure the violation within a reasonable period of time. If a corporation does terminate its close-corporation status, it will thereafter be subject to the provisions of the general corporation statute of the state.

In Figure 6–14 are articles of incorporation for use by a close corporation. These articles have been prepared to comply with the Close Corporation Supplement.

Limited-Liability Company

As we discussed in Section 4–3, the **limited-liability company** (hereafter referred to as *LLC*) is a relatively new form of business organization created by state statutes. A majority of the states have adopted statutes governing the creation and maintenance of LLCs, and most of the remaining states have either considered legislation or legislation is pending.

All current statutes governing LLCs require the filing of articles of organization before an LLC may be formed. This is much the same as the requirement for corporations governed by state statutes. The state statutes governing LLCs have requirements for the content of the articles of organization that are similar to the requirements for articles of incorporation. Some states require such information as the total amount of cash and the agreed value of any property contributed to the LLC; the names of the members, unless the LLC is to be managed by managers; whether the LLC may continue the business after the retirement or death of a member; and the identification of the person who maintains the business information. Only minimal information is required in other states.

In particular, the following are some differences in the statutes of the states that provide for the creation of the LLC:

Figure 6–13   Share Certificate of a Close Corporation

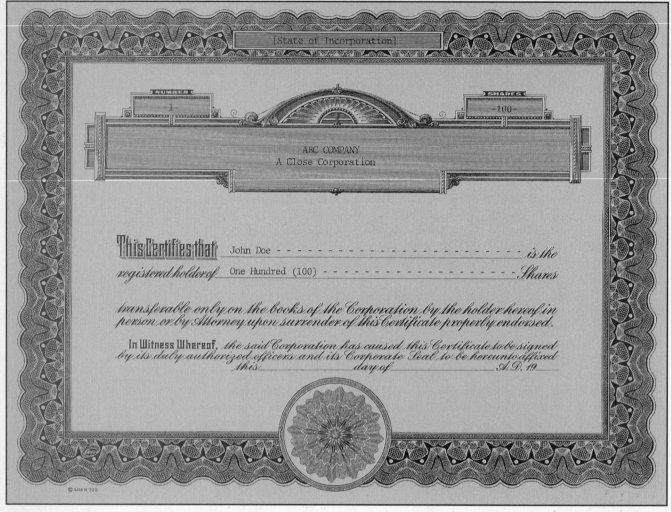

[State of Incorporation]

NUMBER
1

SHARES
-100-

ABC COMPANY
A Close Corporation

This Certifies that   John Doe - is the

registered holder of   One Hundred (100) - - - - - - - - - - - - - - - - - - Shares

transferable only on the books of the Corporation by the holder hereof in person or by Attorney upon surrender of this Certificate properly endorsed.

In Witness Whereof, the said Corporation has caused this Certificate to be signed by its duly authorized officers and its Corporate Seal to be hereunto affixed this _____ day of _____ A.D. 19____

FRONT (continued on next page)

1. Wyoming and Florida are two of the states that require the names of the members to be reported in the articles of organization. Very often members of LLCs want to keep their identity confidential; the need for confidentiality may dictate the type of entity organized.

2. Most of the states require an official action by the secretary of state before the LLC is considered organized. For example, upon the issuance of a certificate of organization, the LLC is organized under state statute.

3. Many of the states differ on the number of persons needed to form an LLC. Some statutes state that "two or more persons may form a limited liability company," Wyoming permits "any person" to form an LLC, and Colorado provides that "one or more natural persons eighteen years of age or older may organize a limited liability company."

There is one requirement of formation on which all the states agree: they all collect a fee for the organization of the LLC. In addition, all states require that most management activities of the LLC be governed by the articles of organization and an operating agreement. These documents are similar to the articles of incorporation and the bylaws of the corporation and the limited partnership agreement of the limited partnership. These examples should reinforce the importance of carefully researching the individual state LLC statutes so that key differences are

Figure 6–13, continued

NOTICE

The securities represented by this certificate are held subject to and may be transferred only in accordance with the certain restrictions contained within the Shareholders Agreement between the corporation and certain parties thereto. Copies of the articles of incorporation, the by-laws, the Shareholders Agreement and other documents affecting the transfer of these securities and other rights of the shareholders may be obtained by any shareholder upon written request to the corporation.

For Value Received, _____ hereby sell, assign and transfer unto _____ Shares represented by the within Certificate, and do hereby irrevocably constitute and appoint _____ Attorney to transfer the said Shares on the books of the within named Corporation with full power of substitution in the premises. Dated _____ 19___

In presence of

_____

_____

NOTICE THE SIGNATURE OF THIS ASSIGNMENT MUST CORRESPOND WITH THE NAME AS WRITTEN UPON THE FACE OF THE CERTIFICATE, IN EVERY PARTICULAR, WITHOUT ALTERATION OR ENLARGEMENT OR ANY CHANGE WHATEVER.

BACK

identified and the articles of organization and the operating agreement are properly prepared.

Provided in Figure 6–15 are articles of organization that have been prepared to comply with the Texas Limited Liability Company Act. These articles do not include several optional provisions that may be included in the articles, because they are not required to be included in the articles of organization of a Texas LLC. These optional provisions include actions of the members taken without a meeting, preemptive rights, cumulative voting, and indemnification of directors. Any of these provisions may be included in the articles of organization, depending on the desires of the members.

Figure 6–14 Articles of Incorporation of a Close Corporation

**Articles of Incorporation
of**

_____

(A Close Corporation)

The undersigned, in order to form a corporation for the purposes hereinafter stated, under and pursuant to the provisions of Section _____ of the Corporation Law of _____, does hereby certify that:

Article One: The name of the Corporation is _____.

Article Two: The registered office of the Corporation is located at _____ _____. The name and address of the Corporation's registered agent at such address is _____.

Article Three: The purpose for which the Corporation is organized is to engage in any lawful act or activity for which corporations may be organized under the Corporate Law of _____.

Article Four: The total number of shares of stock which the Corporation shall have the authority to issue is _____ shares of Common Stock, such shares having a par value of $_____.

Article Five: The Corporation shall make no public offering of any of its stock of any class which would constitute a "public offering" within the meaning of the Securities Act of 1933, as it may be amended from time to time. All of the issued stock of all classes may be subject to such restrictions on transfer as shall be permitted by law and as shall be provided in a written agreement among all the shareholders of each class of stock or among such holders and the Corporation; provided that no stock of any class may be issued until such agreement shall be in effect providing for at least one of the restrictions on transfer permitted by Section _____ of the Corporation Law of _____; and provided further that at least one of such restrictions must remain in effect as to each class at all times while the Corporation is a close corporation.

Article Six: The business of the Corporation shall be managed by the shareholders of the Corporation, rather than a board of directors, such shareholders being deemed to be directors for purposes of applying the provisions of the Corporation Law of _____. The shareholders may enter into any written agreement concerning the conduct of the business and affairs of the Corporation as shall be permitted by the Corporation Law of _____ and which shall not be inconsistent with these Articles of Incorporation.

Article Seven: Any amendment of the Articles of Incorporation to terminate its status as a close corporation shall require unanimous consent of all shareholders.

Article Eight: The incorporator of the Corporation is _____, whose mailing address is _____. The powers of the incorporator are to terminate upon the filing of these Articles of Incorporation.

In Witness Whereof, the incorporator has executed and sealed these Articles of Incorporation on this _____ day of _____, 199_ .

_____
(Incorporator)

6–8   Practical Considerations

Two common assumptions made in drafting articles of incorporation can lead to mistakes. These incorrect assumptions are (1) that _only_ the statutory provisions are to be included in the articles and (2) that one state's statutes are the same as

Figure 6–15 Articles of Organization of a Texas Limited-Liability Company

---

**Articles of Organization
for**

_____

The undersigned, acting as the sole organizer of a limited-liability company under the Texas Limited Liability Company Act (the "Act"), does hereby adopt the following Articles of Organization for _____ (the "Company").

Article One: The name of the Company is _____.

Article Two: The period of duration of the Company is until the close of Company business on _____ or until the earlier dissolution of the Company in accordance with the provisions of its regulations.

Article Three: The purpose for which the Company is organized is the transaction of any or all lawful business for which limited-liability companies may be organized under the Act.

Article Four: The principal place of business of the Company in the State of Texas is _____, _____, Texas _____.

Article Five: The name of the initial registered agent of the Company in the State of Texas is _____, and the address of such initial registered agent is _____, _____, Texas _____.

Article Six: The Company is to be managed by one or more managers. Three initial managers shall serve as managers until the first annual meeting of members of the Company or until their successors are duly elected. The names and addresses of such initial managers shall be as follows:

_____   _____
                     _____

_____   _____
                     _____

_____   _____

In Witness Whereof, these Articles of Organization have been executed on this _____ day of _____, 199_, by the undersigned.

_____
(Name of Sole Organizer)

---

another state's statutes. As you have learned in this chapter, the corporate statutes vary greatly from state to state. Some states have adopted the Model Act almost verbatim, others have modeled some sections of their statutes after the Model Act, and others have used the Model Act only as a guide in drafting their corporate statutes. Therefore, you have only one option available to ensure that the corporate documents you prepare for the client (articles of incorporation, name reservation, fictitious name registration, bylaws, organizational meeting minutes, etc.) comply with the statutes of the state of incorporation. That is, you must research the statutes of the particular state in which your client intends to incorporate.

Form books, looseleaf services, and computer research services provide quick and easy access to the statutes of all the states. These kinds of reference materials can generally be found in the county or city law library, in law school libraries, and in privately maintained libraries at law firms and corporations. For example, Prentice-Hall offers a looseleaf service that includes the corporate statutes of all the states in a several-volume set. The advantage of a looseleaf service is that pages within the volumes can be replaced easily as the state statutes are amended; hence comes the term **looseleaf service.** Similar services are provided by Commerce Clearing House (CCH), Clark Boardman Callaghan, West Publishing Company, and Warren Gorham Lamont, in addition to many others.

Form books, looseleaf services, and computer research services also provide model forms of the following types of documents and agreements: articles of incorporation for the business, professional, nonprofit, and close corporation and articles of organization for the limited-liability company, including an extensive array of optional provisions that incorporators often desire to include in articles of incorporation; subscription agreements; minutes of the organizational meeting of the incorporators or the board of directors; a legal notice for advertising; and bylaws for all types of corporations. Of course, this is not an exhaustive list of the forms available, but it is a short compilation of models available relating to the formation of the corporation.

It is unrealistic to think that you will ever become familiar with the corporate statutes of every state (or even of several of them). You should take comfort in the knowledge that the information is readily available. Don't memorize the statutes of any state. You should strive to become *acquainted* with the use of the corporate statutes of one or more states, *familiar* with the use of the looseleaf services and form books, and *secure* in your knowledge of the basic concepts and procedures of incorporation in your particular state.

SUMMARY

6–1

Basic requirements are comparable, but the procedures and requirements for incorporating differ among the states. Generally, articles of incorporation must be filed with the secretary of state, who will issue a certificate after determining that the articles were properly filed. The number of copies to be filed, the filing fees, and the form of the articles of incorporation to be filed differ from state to state; therefore, a review of the statutes of the state of incorporation is always necessary.

6–2

Before the articles of incorporation are filed, several issues must be resolved, including the following: (1) Will the individuals agreeing to purchase shares of the corporation enter into a subscription agreement? (2) In which state will the corporation be incorporated? (3) Is the corporate name selected by the client available for use in the state of incorporation? (4) Should the corporate name be reserved for a specified period of time? (5) Will the corporation operate under a fictitious name? The paralegal's major responsibility is researching the statutes of the state of incorporation to determine the requirements for entering into a subscription agreement, to ensure use of a proper corporate name, to reserve and determine the availability of the corporate name, and to determine whether the corporation must file a fictitious name registration.

6–3

The articles of incorporation *must* contain the information specifically required by the statutes of the state of incorporation. Generally, the articles must set forth the corporate name, number of shares the corporation is authorized to issue (the capital structure), the initial registered office and registered agent, and the name and address of the incorporator. Some states require additional provisions. Only a review of the statutes of the state of incorporation will inform you of the statutory, or mandatory, provisions of that state.

6–4

Additional provisions are permitted to be included in the articles of incorporation, depending on the desires of the incorporators and the organizers. The provisions that may be incorporated in the articles include, but are not limited to, naming initial directors, specifying a business purpose of the corporation (such a provision is required in some states), stating a period of existence (generally, the corporation will exist perpetually unless otherwise stated), granting or denying shareholders' preemptive rights and cumulating voting in the election of directors, requiring a quorum for shareholder voting purposes that is greater than or less than majority, and providing indemnification for the directors and officers.

Other provisions may be contained in the articles of incorporation, provided they are not inconsistent with the statutes of the state of incorporation.

6–5

After articles of incorporation are filed, the organization of the corporation continues with the holding of the organizational meeting by either the incorporators or the initial directors, if they were named in the articles of incorporation. Many states still require that a specified amount of capital be contributed to the corporation by the subscribers of the corporation's stock before the corporation commences business. The purchase, organization, and maintenance of the corporation's minute book, stock book, and corporate seal are generally the paralegal's responsibility. Only a few states require the publication of a legal notice, but the paralegal must research the state statutes to determine whether this requirement must be met. State securities laws, or blue sky laws, and federal securities laws regulate the offer and sale of securities (shares), and a determination must be made whether these laws apply. Within a specified time period, the Subchapter S election forms must be filed with the IRS and the state's department of revenue, if applicable.

6–6

The corporation's bylaws are the rules and regulations that govern the internal affairs of the corporation. Bylaws are not a public record and are, therefore, not required to be filed with the secretary of state or any other governmental agency. Because they are a private document, they are open for inspection and review only by the shareholders, directors, and officers of the corporation.

Typical provisions that may be found in the bylaws include, but are not limited to, the time and place of holding meetings of the shareholders and the board of directors; the number of days' notice that must be given prior to holding a meeting; the number of directors to serve on the board; the procedure for the election of committees and officers; the officers' duties; the procedure for replacing lost, destroyed, or stolen certificates; the qualification of the funds out of which dividends may be paid to the shareholders; and the procedure for amending the bylaws.

6–7

Incorporating the professional, nonprofit, and close corporations and organizing the limited-liability company are similar to incorporating the general business corporation. You will need to review the statutes of the state of incorporation to determine requirements specific to organizing these other types of entities.

6–8

Becoming acquainted with the use of the corporate statutes of various states, becoming familiar with the looseleaf services and form books available to use as a reference, and becoming secure in your knowledge of the basic concepts and procedures of incorporation is critical to your practice as a paralegal. When you have been given a task with which you are not familiar, refer to the state statutes and the form books available to you. Someone has always done the task before you.

REVIEW GUIDE

Key Terms

Before proceeding, review the key terms listed below to be sure you understand each one. If necessary, read over the corresponding section of the chapter. When you are ready to test your understanding, answer the review questions.

articles of incorporation (p. 101)
certificate of incorporation (p. 101)
organization (p. 102)
subscriber (p. 105)
subscription agreement (p. 105)
fully paid and nonassessable (p. 106)
domesticate (p. 107)
home state (p. 107)
state of domestication (p. 107)
domestic corporation (p. 107)
foreign corporation (p. 107)
corporate name (p. 108)
corporate designators (p. 108)
fictitious name (p. 111)
statutory provisions (p. 112)

authorized shares (p. 113)
common stock (p. 113)
preferred stock (p. 113)
par value (p. 114)
registered office (p. 114)
registered agent (p. 114)
incorporator (p. 115)
initial directors (p. 116)
purposes (p. 116)
powers (p. 116)
perpetual existence (p. 117)
preemptive right (p. 117)
straight voting (p. 118)
cumulative voting (p. 118)
quorum (p. 119)
indemnification (p. 120)
organizational meeting (p. 121)
minute book (p. 122)
stock book (p. 122)
corporate seal (p. 122)
legal notice (p. 122)
blue sky laws (p. 123)
Subchapter S corporation (p. 124)

Form 2553 (p. 124)
bylaws (p. 124)
professional corporation (p. 126)
nonprofit corporation (p. 128)
close corporation (p. 129)
limited-liability company (p. 131)
looseleaf service (p. 136)

Questions for Review and Discussion

1. Who executes and files the articles of incorporation?

2. Explain why a corporation may want to incorporate in a state other than the state in which its principal place of business is to be located.

3. Would the name Floral Design Limited be permitted as a corporate name in a state whose statutes were identical to the Model Act (assuming the name is available for use)?

4. If a corporation has not designated a registered agent, how is service of process made on a corporation according to the Model Act provisions?

5. Explain how the availability of a corporate name is determined. Who is generally responsible for obtaining this information?

6. Identify the provisions that must be included in articles of incorporation.

7. Name two optional provisions that *may* be included in articles of incorporation, and explain why the corporation or its shareholders would want to include those provisions in the articles.

8. Explain the difference between the powers and the purposes of a corporation. Where will you find the powers and purposes of a corporation?

9. Explain how the state statutes handle the granting and denying of preemptive rights and cumulative voting.

10. Why would a corporation want to provide indemnification to its directors, officers, and employees for their actions performed on behalf of the corporation?

11. When is the organizational meeting of the incorporators or the initial board of directors held?

12. What is the minimum amount of consideration that must be paid for 100 shares of common stock whose par value is $5 per share?

13. Who is authorized to amend a corporation's bylaws?

14. Name several provisions generally found in the corporation's bylaws.

15. Identify one important distinguishing characteristic for each of the following types of organizations: professional, nonprofit, and close corporations and the limited-liability company.

Activities

1. Select a corporate name that you would like to use, and determine whether it is available for use in your state. Also, outline the procedures for reserving a corporate name in your state.

2. Draft a provision, to be included in ABC Company's articles of incorporation, that grants preemptive rights to the shareholders.

3. Research the corporate statutes of your state and determine the following: (1) the provisions that *must* be contained in articles of incorporation, and (2) the provisions that *may* be included in articles of incorporation. Then prepare articles of incorporation for Pencil Point Company that comply with the statutes of your state. Select all the necessary information required by the statute, and explain why you selected such information.

4. Under the corporate statutes of your state, would the following corporate names be permitted for use by a corporation operating a gift and craft shop?

   Engineering Crafts for Gifts, Inc.
   Craft Shop USA Company
   Crafts Unlimited
   Gifts for the Crafty
   Gifts Galore and More Corporation

CHAPTER 7   Corporate Meetings and Actions

OUTLINE

7–1   Types of Meetings
   Organizational Meetings
   Directors' Meetings
   Shareholders' Meetings
7–2   Organizational Meetings
   Business Transacted at Meetings
   Incorporators' Organizational Meeting
   Directors' Organizational Meeting
   Location of the Meeting
   Calling the Meeting and Satisfying Quorum Requirements
7–3   Requirements of Directors' Meetings
   Annual, Special, and Regular Meetings
   Location of Meetings
   Notice
   Waiver of Notice
   Quorum and Voting
7–4   Requirements of Shareholders' Meetings
   Annual and Special Meetings
   Location of Meetings
   Setting the Record Date
   Notice and Waiver of Notice
   Proxy
   Quorum
   Voting of Shares
7–5   Other Procedures and Types of Meetings
   Distinction Between Call and Notice of Meetings
   Meetings by Conference Telephone
   Meetings of Committees of the Board
7–6   Documenting Business Conducted at Meetings
   Resolutions
   Meeting Minutes
   Action Without a Meeting
7–7   Organization of the Corporate Minute Book
7–8   Practical Considerations

APPLICATIONS

Peter Paralegal is a corporate paralegal with the law firm of Ruff & Reddy, P.C. Peter has been asked to prepare the proper corporate documentation for the merger of Book Distributing Company, a Florida corporation, into Publishers, Inc., a Delaware corporation. He knows that the approval of the boards of directors and the shareholders of both corporations must be obtained. Those approvals may be obtained either at meetings held by the boards of directors and the shareholders or by written consent of both the boards and the shareholders.

Before Peter begins preparing the corporate documentation for this transaction, he knows that he must research the appropriate provisions of the Florida and Delaware corporate statutes and determine the requirements for approving and effecting the merger of these two corporations. He will also need to obtain copies of the articles of incorporation and the bylaws of both corporations.

OBJECTIVES

This chapter will provide guidelines (statutory and practical) and examples for preparing all documentation required for (1) holding meetings and (2) preparing written consent of the incorporators, the shareholders, and the board of directors. After completing Chapter 7, you will be able to:

1. Determine when the existence of a corporation begins.
2. Define the different types of meetings of the corporation: organizational, annual, and special or regular.
3. Determine the business activities and corporate actions that require the approval of the incorporators, the shareholders, and the board of directors.
4. Understand the requirements for holding a valid and proper organizational meeting of the corporation.
5. Understand the requirements for holding a valid and proper directors' meeting.
6. Understand the requirements for holding a valid and proper shareholders' meeting
7. Prepare a notice of meeting and a waiver of notice for shareholders', directors', and incorporators' meetings.
8. Determine when a quorum is present for the conducting of business for shareholders' and directors' meetings.
9. Prepare resolutions documenting business activities approved by the incorporators, the shareholders, and the directors.
10. Prepare minutes of meetings.
11. Prepare written consent of the incorporators, the shareholders, and the board of directors.
12. Organize the corporation's minute book.

7–1   Types of Meetings

The moment a corporation's existence begins as a separate legal entity depends on the statutes of the state of incorporation. Generally **corporate existence** begins upon the filing of articles of incorporation. Section 2.03 of the Model Act states that "the corporate existence begins when the articles of incorporation are filed." But in some states corporate existence begins when a certificate of incorporation is issued by the secretary of state. Others require the filing of a copy of the articles with a county office. Some require the subscription or payment of capital stock or the holding of the organizational meeting, at which bylaws are adopted and directors and officers are elected.

After a corporation's existence begins, it is considered a separate legal entity. From that point all **corporate actions** taken by the corporation must be approved at, and business conducted through, meetings of the incorporators (until the board of directors is appointed), the shareholders, and the board of directors. The three categories of meetings at which these internal corporate persons may approve corporate actions and conduct business are (1) organizational meetings, (2) annual meetings, and (3) special or regular meetings.

Actions of the corporation are approved by *one* of the following groups of corporate persons: (1) the incorporators, (2) the shareholders, or (3) the board of directors. Each of these groups of persons performs a distinct, separate, and well-defined function in the corporation. Therefore, each of these groups of persons is responsible for approving *different* actions of the corporation. For example, the incorporators elect the first board of directors (if directors were not named in the articles of incorporation), the directors appoint officers of the corporation, and the shareholders approve the dissolution of the corporation. Figure 7–1 is a list of the types of actions of the corporation for which approval must be obtained from the incorporators, the shareholders, or the board of directors.

Generally, a corporate action is discussed at a meeting, and then a vote is taken at the meeting to approve the action. As an alternative to holding a meeting to approve an action, the incorporators, shareholders, or directors may approve an action by written consent. In this case, no meeting is held, but a written consent (written document) is executed by the group of persons who must approve the action. We will discuss procedures for holding meetings and procedures for approving actions by written consent in greater detail later in this chapter.

The preparation of meeting minutes and written consent and the organization of the corporation are often the responsibility of the corporate paralegal. After the paralegal has gathered the necessary information and

PARALEGALERT!

Corporate actions of the incorporators, shareholders, or directors are adopted in one of two ways: (1) at meetings held by these corporate groups or (2) by unanimous consent in writing.

Figure 7–1   Corporate Actions Requiring Approval by the Incorporators, Shareholders, or Board of Directors

Actions for Approval by Incorporators

- Election of directors.
- Adoption of bylaws.

Actions for Approval by Shareholders

- Election of directors.
- Removal of directors.
- Merger or consolidation.
- Amendment of articles of incorporation.
- Dissolution of corporation.
- Sale of corporation's assets.

Actions for Approval by Board of Directors

- Election of officers.
- Issuance of stock.
- Recommendation to shareholders of a merger, consolidation, dissolution, or sale of assets.
- Designation of committees of the board.
- Adoption of corporate seal and form of stock certificate.
- Opening of bank accounts.
- Qualification of corporation to do business in a foreign jurisdiction.
- Application for use of a fictitious or assumed name.
- Borrowing by corporation.
- Amendment of articles of incorporation (in certain circumstances).
- Adoption of bylaws.

has prepared and filed the articles of incorporation, he or she is usually responsible for preparing the proper documentation necessary to substantiate the corporate actions taken by the incorporators, shareholders, or board of directors. Also, at a meeting, the paralegal will verify that a quorum (discussed later in this chapter) is present for the conducting of business.

Organizational Meetings

After the corporation has been formed, usually upon the filing of the articles of incorporation with the secretary of state in the state of incorporation, an organizational meeting must be held. Some state statutes require the holding of the organizational meeting before the corporation commences business operations. The statute of the state of incorporation prescribes the business that must be conducted at the organizational meeting.

Most state statutes require either the initial directors named in the articles of incorporation or the incorporators (if directors were not named in the articles of incorporation) to hold the organizational meeting. Some states *require* that directors be named in the articles of incorporation, and other states *allow* the directors to be named in the articles. If directors have been named in the articles, they are the corporate group to hold the organizational meeting. If directors have not been named in the articles, the incorporators hold the organizational meeting. Section 2.05 of the Model Act states that "after incorporation . . . the initial directors shall hold an organizational meeting" and that section goes on to state that, if initial directors are not named in the articles, "the incorporator or incorporators shall hold an organizational meeting."

PARALEGALERT!

The organizational meeting is held by either the incorporators or the initial directors. Who holds the meeting depends on whether or not directors were named in the articles of incorporation.

Requirements for holding the organizational meeting vary greatly from state to state. You must review the statutes of the state of incorporation to determine the proper procedures for holding the meeting, and the business that must be conducted at it. The requirements for holding, and the business to be conducted at, the organizational meeting are discussed more fully in Section 7–2 of this chapter.

Upon the election of directors by the incorporators (if directors were not named in the articles), the incorporators' responsibility with respect to the formation and organization of the corporation is concluded. After either the incorporators or the board of directors hold the organizational meeting, all other meetings of the corporation will be either shareholders' meetings or directors' meetings.

Directors' Meetings

Directors' meetings may be held annually, quarterly, monthly, or even weekly to conduct business and approve corporate actions—as often as the business of the corporation dictates. Because of the impracticality of requiring the directors to approve *every* business transaction of the corporation, the directors elect officers to oversee the daily business affairs. The directors oversee and supervise the actions of the officers. It is for this reason that most state statutes do not require that the directors hold meetings at any regular intervals; they will only hold a meeting when it is necessary to approve certain corporate actions. Figure 7–1 lists specific actions that require approval by the board of directors.

Section 8.20(a) of the Model Act and many of the states' statutes direct that the board of directors *may* hold regular or special meetings. In fact, there is generally no requirement that even annual meetings of the directors be held. In practice, though, an annual meeting of the directors is held immediately following the annual meeting of the shareholders. The annual meeting of the directors is held to appoint officers of the corporation. However, the bylaws should be reviewed prior to the annual directors' meeting to determine whether appointment of officers is required annually.

Typically, the bylaws of the corporation address the issues of calling, providing notice of, and conducting business at directors' meetings. Therefore, bylaws must be carefully drafted to include specific procedures for holding directors' meetings.

Shareholders' Meetings

Shareholders' meetings are the vehicles for shareholders to participate in the operation and management of the corporation, even though shareholders have little or no control over the day-to-day operations of the corporation. Remember that the shareholders elect a board of directors to manage the overall business and set corporate policy. Therefore, through the election of directors, the shareholders have indirect control over the management of the corporation. An exception exists in the close corporation, where the shareholders act in the capacity of a board of directors.

There are, however, certain corporate actions that are reserved for approval by the shareholders. These actions generally fall into two categories:

1. Those that significantly affect the structure of the corporation (for example, merger, consolidation, dissolution, or sale of substantially all of the assets).
2. Those that affect the ownership rights of the shareholders (for example, an increase in the number of authorized shares or the creation of stock with senior rights).

Refer to Figure 7–1 for additional specific actions that require shareholders' approval.

The state statute and the corporation's articles of incorporation and bylaws establish the procedures for calling, providing notice of, and conducting meetings and for recording the actions taken at shareholders' meetings. The officers of the corporation must be particularly familiar with these procedures because it is generally their responsibility to hold valid meetings of the shareholders.

7–2   Organizational Meetings

The **organizational meeting** is held to **organize** the corporation, and it usually includes the election of directors (if they were not named in the articles of incorporation), the appointment of officers, the adoption of bylaws, the acceptance of stock subscriptions, the receipt of payment for and the issuance of stock, and any other business necessary to enable the corporation to transact the business for which it was incorporated.

The organizational meeting is held by either (1) the incorporators or (2) the directors named in the articles of incorporation. Typically, if the meeting is held by the incorporators, a meeting of the board of directors immediately follows. If the meeting is held by the directors, no meeting of the incorporators is required. Only a few states require the shareholders to hold an organizational meeting.

The procedure for holding the organizational meeting depends on statutory requirements of the state of incorporation and on the general procedures followed by corporations organized in that state.

A few states require that the organizational meeting be held within a specified period after the filing of articles of incorporation. Generally, however, the organizational meeting should be held within a reasonable time, but most state statutes do not specify a time within which a meeting is to be held.

PARALEGALERT!

The organizational meeting is held to complete the organization of the corporation's structure. For example, at the organizational meeting, directors are elected, bylaws are adopted, and generally, stock is authorized to be issued.

Business Transacted at Meetings

The business transacted at an organizational meeting depends on whether it is a meeting of the incorporators or of the initial board of directors. The business transacted by the incorporators will differ from that transacted by the initial board of directors.

Incorporators' Organizational Meeting

At an organizational meeting held by the incorporators, called the **incorporators' organizational meeting,** the business conducted is the election of the directors. Some state statutes allow the incorporators to adopt the bylaws, although this power is often reserved for the directors or shareholders. Section 2.05(a)(2) of the Model Act states that "if initial directors are not named in the articles, the incorporator or incorporators shall hold an organizational meeting . . . (1) to elect directors and complete the organization of the corporation . . . or (2) to elect a board of directors who shall complete the organization of the corporation." This section gives the incorporators the option to complete the organization of the corporation or to elect the directors who will complete the organization.

Once again, a review of the statutes of the state of incorporation is necessary to determine what powers the incorporators have in the organization of the corporation. Figure 7–2 is an example of the minutes of an incorporators' organizational meeting at which directors are elected. You should also refer to Figure 7–3, an example of a written consent that documents the election of directors by the incorporators. Written consents, prepared in lieu of holding meetings, are discussed in Section 7–6.

Directors' Organizational Meeting

At an organizational meeting held by the initial board of directors, called the **directors' organizational meeting,** the business to be transacted includes the following:

1. Accept and approve the filed articles of incorporation.
2. Adopt bylaws.
3. Authorize the placing of legal advertising (if required).
4. Adopt the form for share certificates.
5. Adopt the accounting year.
6. Adopt the corporate seal.
7. Accept subscriptions for stock.

Figure 7–2   Minutes of Organizational Meeting of the Incorporators

Organizational Meeting of the Incorporators

The organizational meeting of the incorporators of Bird Baths, Inc., a _____ corporation (the "Corporation"), was held on Monday, June 12, 1995, at 10:00 a.m.

The following incorporators were present: John Cardinal and Rita Finch. A quorum of the incorporators was present for the conducting of business. John Cardinal acted as Chairman of the meeting, and Rita Finch recorded the minutes of the meeting.

After discussion, upon motion duly made, seconded, and unanimously carried, the following resolutions were approved:

RESOLVED, that Sandra Sparrow and Rebecca Robin are hereby elected directors of the Corporation to hold office, subject to the provisions of the Bylaws, until their successors shall be elected and shall qualify; and

FURTHER RESOLVED, that the form of Bylaws attached hereto be and hereby is adopted as the Bylaws of the Corporation.

There being no further business to come before the meeting, it was, upon motion duly made, seconded, and unanimously carried, adjourned.

_____
Rita Finch, Recording Secretary

Figure 7–3   Written Consent of Incorporators

Written Consent of the Incorporators

The undersigned, John Cardinal and Rita Finch, being the incorporators of Bird Baths, Inc., a _____ corporation (the "Corporation"), hereby adopt the following resolutions in accordance with Section _____ of the Business Corporation Law of (State):

WHEREAS, the Articles of Incorporation were filed in the Office of the Secretary of State of the State of _____ on June 9, 1995, be it:

RESOLVED, that Sandra Sparrow and Rebecca Robin are hereby elected directors of the corporation to hold office, subject to the provisions of the Bylaws, until their successors shall be elected and shall qualify; and

FURTHER RESOLVED, that the form of Bylaws attached hereto be and hereby is adopted as the Bylaws of the corporation.

WITNESS the due execution as of this 12th day of June, 1995.

_____
John Cardinal

_____
Rita Finch

8. Issue stock.
9. Approve the opening of bank accounts.
10. Elect officers.
11. Fix the number of directors.
12. Approve the S Corporation election (if appropriate).
13. Ratify and approve all acts of the incorporator taken on behalf of the corporation.

Section 2.05(a)(1) of the Model Act states that "if initial directors are named in the articles of incorporation, the initial directors shall hold an organizational meeting, at the call of a majority of the directors, to complete the organization of the corporation by appointing officers, adopting bylaws, and carrying on any other business brought before the meeting."

Location of the Meeting

As we have already stated, the incorporators or the board of directors (if named in the articles of incorporation), whichever the case may be, are required to hold the organizational meeting. The statutes of the state of incorporation provide where the meeting must take place. Some states require that the meeting be held within the state, and other states do not. Section 2.05(c) of the Model Act provides that the "organizational meeting may be held in or out of this state." If the meeting is held outside the state, but the statute requires that the meeting be held within the state, the meeting may be invalid and may result in the defective organization of the corporation. By subsequently meeting within the state, the organizers (incorporators or board of directors) can cure the problem.

Calling the Meeting and Satisfying Quorum Requirements

The statutes of the state of incorporation designate who is to call the organizational meeting, what notice must be provided, how notice is to be transmitted to the holders of the meeting (incorporators or board of directors), and what constitutes a quorum for conducting business.

Generally, incorporators holding the organizational meeting must comply with notice-of-meeting and quorum requirements prescribed by the statutes of the state of incorporation. The Model Act does not make provision for sending notice of the meeting to the incorporators specifically, but it does provide general notice provisions in Section 1.41. Incorporators should be guided by this section, or if a particular state does not provide for giving notice, the incorporators should be guided by the rules governing shareholders' meetings (discussed in Section 7–4 of this chapter).

If the directors are to hold the organizational meeting, the requirements for holding directors' meetings (discussed in Section 7–3 of this chapter) should be observed. These requirements include (1) calling the meeting upon giving proper notice and (2) ensuring that a quorum of the directors (the minimum number of directors required for the transacting of business) is present at the meeting.

PARALEGALERT!

One particular item of business to be conducted by the directors is the adoption of the corporate seal. Most states no longer require the use of corporate seals, so the use of corporate seals by corporations is becoming passé.

PARALEGALERT!

Whoever holds the organizational meeting, the incorporators or the initial directors, the requirements for holding a valid and proper meeting—providing notice and determining whether a quorum is present—must be met.

Figure 7–4 Call of Organizational Meeting of the Directors by a Majority of the Directors

---

**Call of Organizational Meeting
of the Directors**

June 12, 1995

To the Directors of Bird Baths, Inc.:

The undersigned, being a majority of the initial directors of Bird Baths, Inc. (the "Corporation"), hereby calls the organizational meeting of the directors of the Corporation, to be held at the office of the Corporation at 123 America Street, Montgomery, Alabama, on Friday, June 23, 1995, at 10:00 AM.

_____
Director

_____
Director

Sections 2.05(a)(1) and (2) of the Model Act provide that the directors or incorporators shall hold an organizational meeting "at the call of a majority of the directors" or "at the call of a majority of the incorporators," respectively. Figure 7–4 is an example of a call of the organizational meeting by the directors. The call of the incorporators would obviously be similar to this example, except that the word *incorporators* would be substituted for *directors.*

7–3 Requirements of Directors' Meetings

Requirements for holding valid and proper directors' meetings (annual, special, and regular) are found in the statutes of the corporation's state of incorporation and the corporation's bylaws and, in less often cases, in the corporation's articles of incorporation. Two requirements for holding valid and proper (legal) meetings are the following:

1. Proper and timely notice of the meeting must be provided to the directors.
2. A quorum must be present at the meeting for business to be conducted.

These requirements are discussed in greater detail in this section.

At directors' meetings resolutions are adopted. By means of these resolutions, the directors document and approve the activities of the corporation, its directors, and its officers.

PARALEGALERT!

For a directors' meeting to be valid and proper, proper and timely notice must be provided to the directors, and a quorum must be present at the meeting.

Annual, Special, and Regular Meetings

Although shareholders are required to hold annual meetings, the board of directors is not. Most state statutes require only that the directors hold regular or special meetings whenever necessary to conduct business on behalf of the corporation. Section 8.20(a) of the Model Act states that "the board of directors may hold regular or special meetings." Several states still do require the directors to meet annually, but the current tendency of states is to allow annual meetings of the board of directors to be optional. The statutes of the state of incorporation and, more particularly, the corporation's bylaws should be reviewed for requirements regarding the frequency of holding, the calling and providing notice of, determination of the location of, and the procedures for conducting directors' meetings.

If an annual meeting is required by statute or bylaws, the directors usually hold their meeting immediately after the annual meeting of the shareholders. The customary business to be transacted at a directors' **annual meeting** is the election of officers. Other business may also be transacted including ratification of actions taken by the officers during the previous year and approval of the corporation's financial statements.

Meetings other than the annual meeting of the directors are either special or regular. All meetings of the directors—whether annual, special, or regular—must be conducted in accordance with the state statute and the bylaws of the corporation. That is, you need to review the statute and the bylaws to determine who has the authority to call meetings, how and when notice of the meeting is provided, and the procedures for conducting business at the meeting.

Special meetings may be held by the directors whenever the corporation's activities require that actions be approved by the board of directors. Provision for holding special meetings will be found in the corporation's bylaws. The following is an example of a provision that might be included in the bylaws regarding special meetings:

> Special meetings of the Board of Directors may be called by the President on one day's notice to each director, either personally or by mail, telegram, or telecopy or may be called by the President or Secretary in like manner and on like notice on the written request of two directors.

Regular meetings are those held on a specified day each week or month, with the day designated in the corporation's bylaws, or they may be held at a time and place from time to time designated by the board of directors. For example, the bylaws might include a provision that "regular meetings of the Board of Directors shall be held on the third Wednesday of each month, and no notice is required to be provided to the directors for regular meetings." Or the bylaws might include a provision such as, "Regular meetings of the Board of Directors may be held upon such notice and at such time and at such place as shall from time to time be determined by the Board."

Location of Meetings

Almost all states, as well as the Model Act, authorize the holding of directors' meetings either within or outside the state of incorporation. Generally, the bylaws include a provision similar to the following regarding the location of meetings:

PARALEGALERT!

If the bylaws or the state statute requires that directors' meetings be held within the state, any actions taken by the directors at a meeting outside the state will be valid if the actions are subsequently approved by the directors at a meeting within the state or by unanimous written consent (to be discussed later in this chapter).

Meetings of the Board of Directors, including the annual meeting and special or regular meetings, may be held either within or outside the State of _____ and at such place as shall be determined from time to time by the Board of Directors.

Notice

The state corporate statutes may specify the procedures for calling and providing notice of the annual, special, or regular meetings of the directors, but usually the corporation's bylaws specify these procedures. Provisions may also be found in the corporation's articles of incorporation. Corporate statutes covering notice provisions often begin with the phrase "unless the articles of incorporation or the bylaws provide otherwise," which allows the corporation to adopt procedures different from the corporate statutes as long as provision is made in the articles of incorporation or the bylaws.

Special meetings usually *do* require notice to members of the board, but regular meetings usually do *not* require notice. Section 8.22(a) of the Model Act states that "regular meetings of the board of directors may be held without notice of the date, time, place, or purpose of the meeting." On the other hand, Section 8.22(b) requires that "special meetings of the board of directors must be preceded by at least two days' notice of the date, time, and place of the meeting. The notice need not describe the purpose of the special meeting."

Providing notice of annual meetings of directors is not covered by the Model Act, and many states follow the Model Act in this respect. However, the corporation's articles of incorporation and bylaws should be reviewed when the statute makes no provision for such procedure.

Figure 7–5 is a sample notice of a special meeting of the board of directors. Observe that this notice includes the purpose for which the special meeting was called. Many state statutes, unlike the Model Act, require that the purpose be stated in the notice of the meeting.

Figure 7–5   Notice of Special Meeting of the Board of Directors

> **Notice of Special Meeting
> of the Board of Directors**
>
> August 25, 1995
>
> To the Directors of XYZ Corporation:
>
> Notice is hereby given that, in accordance with Section _____ of the Bylaws of the XYZ Corporation (the "Corporation") and in accordance with the requirements of the laws of the State of _____ , a special meeting of the Board of Directors of the Corporation will be held at the Corporation's principal place of business, 123 America Street, Anytown, Anystate, on Tuesday, September 26, 1995, at 12:00 Noon, for the purpose of:
>
> 1. Recommending to the shareholders of the Corporation that the Corporation be liquidated and dissolved; and
> 2. Transacting such other business as may lawfully come before the meeting.
>
> Dated this 25th day of August, 1995.
>
> _____
> Secretary

Waiver of Notice

The object of providing notice to directors is to afford them the opportunity to be present at a meeting, participate in discussions, and vote on matters that require action by the directors. However, the requirements to provide notice to directors, which are set forth in either the statutes, the articles of incorporation, or the bylaws, may be waived by a director. A director waives notice by (1) executing a **waiver of notice** or (2) attending the meeting.

A director may waive notice by executing and delivering to the corporation a waiver of notice. Most state statutes, like Section 8.23(a) of the Model Act, provide that when any notice is required to be given, a written waiver of notice, signed by the director entitled to the notice and filed with the minutes or corporate records, is the equivalent of providing the notice.

For example, the bylaws of Office Products Corporation require that directors be provided five days' written notice prior to the holding of a meeting. If notice was not provided five days prior to the meeting date or if no notice was provided, those directors not receiving timely notice may execute a statement waiving their right to be provided notice of the meeting. The waiver of notice acts as a cure to the failure to provide the proper notice required by the state statutes, the articles of incorporation, or the bylaws. A form for a waiver of notice of directors is provided in Figure 7–6.

In addition, attendance by a director at a meeting will also act as a waiver of the notice requirement, unless he or she attends the meeting and objects to the calling of the meeting. Section 8.23(b) states that "a director's attendance at or participation in a meeting waives any required notice to him of the meeting unless the director at the beginning of the meeting . . . objects to holding the meeting or transacting business at the meeting."

Any business transacted at a meeting for which proper notice was not given may be ratified at a future meeting, provided that proper notice is given for the subsequent meeting.

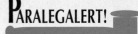

PARALEGALERT!

The Model Act provides that a director may waive notice of a meeting prior to or after the date and time of the meeting. Many states concur with this provision.

Figure 7–6 Waiver of Notice by Directors

> **Waiver of Notice**
>
> We, James Bond and Donald Smith, directors of XYZ Corporation (the "Corporation"), a corporation organized under the laws of the State of _____, hereby waive notice of the time, place, and purpose of a special meeting of the Board of Directors of the Corporation, to be held at the office of the Corporation on Tuesday, September 26, 1995, at 12:00 Noon, for the purpose of:
>
> 1. Recommending to the shareholders of the Corporation that the Corporation be liquidated and dissolved; and
> 2. Transacting such other business as may lawfully come before the meeting.
>
> _____
> James Bond
>
> _____
> Donald Smith

Quorum and Voting

A **quorum** is the minimum number of directors who must be present at a meeting for business to be properly transacted at the meeting. If a quorum of the directors is not present at a meeting, any action taken by the directors at that meeting will be invalid. Therefore, when a quorum is not present, no business should be transacted. The directors may continue their meeting for discussion only, but they should take no corporate actions requiring a vote. To cover directors' meetings, at which quorum is not present, the corporation's bylaws might include the following provision:

> If a quorum shall not be present at any meeting of directors, the directors present may adjourn the meeting from time to time, without notice other than announcement at the meeting, until a quorum shall be present.

Generally, a **majority** of the directors—that is, any number greater than half—constitutes a quorum at a directors' meeting, unless the articles of incorporation or bylaws of the corporation provide otherwise. For example, the bylaws might provide that:

> At least two-thirds of the directors shall constitute a quorum for the transaction of business unless a greater or lesser number is required by law or by the articles of incorporation.

The Model Act does, in Section 8.24(b), however, provide that "the articles of incorporation or bylaws may authorize a quorum of a board of directors to consist of no fewer than one-third of the fixed . . . number of directors."

Unless otherwise provided in the state statutes or in the corporation's articles of incorporation or bylaws, a vote of a majority of the directors present at a meeting *at which a quorum is present* is sufficient for the approving or adopting of actions. For example, if the total number of directors is nine, a quorum (the number required for a meeting) is five. If five directors are at the meeting, at least three of them must vote in favor of a resolution to pass it. In this case, only three directors of the nine total directors are needed to carry the resolution. The examples in Figure 7–7 provide further illustration of quorum and voting requirements.

PARALEGALERT!

A majority of the directors entitled to vote at a meeting constitutes a quorum at a directors' meeting, unless, of course, the corporation's articles of incorporation or bylaws provide otherwise.

Figure 7–7   Examples of Voting and Quorum Requirements

The following table provides three examples of quorum and voting requirements. For each example assume that a majority (more than 50 percent) will satisfy both quorum and voting requirements. Thus, in the first example, in which the board of directors of the corporation has six members, four of the six directors must be present to meet quorum requirements, and three of the four present must vote affirmatively for a proposal to be adopted. Note the relationship of the total number of directors to the number required to meet the quorum requirement and the number required to meet the voting requirement.

Total Number of Directors	Quorum	Minimum Votes to Approve Proposals
6	4	3
11	6	4
15	8	5

Directors have a fiduciary duty to the shareholders. The shareholders have the right to expect the directors, whom the shareholders elected, to act in their best interests and to give careful consideration to the matters voted on by the board of directors. Therefore, directors are required to vote in person; directors *may not* authorize anyone to vote for them. If they did so, they would not be fulfilling their duty to the shareholders.

The following provision dealing with voting and quorum requirements might be found in the bylaws of a corporation:

> The vote of a majority of the directors present at any meeting at which a quorum is present shall be the act of the board of directors, unless the vote of a greater number is required by law or by the articles of incorporation.

Quorum and voting requirements, like many other provisions, vary from state to state. Therefore, the state statutes and the corporation's articles of incorporation and bylaws must *always* be reviewed to determine that all quorum and voting requirements have been met.

PARALEGALERT!

If a provision of the statute, the articles of incorporation, or the bylaws is not met, any action taken by the directors will be invalid. It could prove embarrassing to your supervising attorney and detrimental to your employment if a client had to be told that a directors' meeting was invalid because a provision of the corporation's bylaws or articles was violated.

7–4 Requirements of Shareholders' Meetings

Major decisions involving a change in the structure of the corporation (e.g., merger, consolidation, liquidation, dissolution, and sale of substantially all the assets), require the approval of the shareholders. But the most important business conducted by the shareholders is the election of directors, because it is through the directors that the shareholders maintain indirect control over the corporation's management, policies, and procedures. These corporate actions of the shareholders are documented and approved through resolutions adopted by the shareholders at their meetings.

Requirements for holding valid and proper shareholders' meetings (both annual and special) are found in the statutes of the corporation's state of incorporation, the corporation's bylaws, and in fewer cases, in the corporation's articles of incorporation. Two requirements for holding valid and proper (i.e., legal) meetings are (1) proper and timely notice of the meeting and (2) a quorum for the conducting of business. These requirements will be discussed in greater detail in this section.

PARALEGALERT!

For a meeting of the shareholders to be valid and proper, proper and timely notice must be provided to the shareholders entitled to receive notice and vote, and a quorum must be present, in person or by proxy, at the meeting.

Annual and Special Meetings

Most states require the corporation to hold an annual meeting of the shareholders. The annual meeting of the shareholders is generally held to elect directors of the corporation, but any other appropriate business of the shareholders is permitted to be conducted. Section 7.01(a) of the Model Act provides that "a corporation shall hold annually at a time stated in or fixed in accordance with the bylaws a meeting of shareholders."

While almost all states require annual meetings of shareholders, the failure to hold an annual meeting at the time and place specified in a corporation's bylaws will not affect the validity of any corporate action taken at a shareholders' meeting, nor will it cause a dissolution of the corporation. The Model Act provides for this situation in Section 7.01(c), which states that "failure to hold an annual meeting . . . does not affect the validity of any corporate action." Many state statutes do, however, provide a shareholder the right to obtain a court order compelling the corporation to hold an annual shareholders' meeting.

A special meeting of the shareholders is held either when the board of directors calls one, or when holders of at least 10 percent of the voting stock of the corporation demand one. It is sometimes necessary to obtain shareholder approval of a corporate action prior to the holding of the next annual meeting. In such cases, the corporation holds a special shareholders' meeting.

Location of Meetings

Most states, as well as the Model Act, authorize the holding of shareholders' meetings either within or outside the state of incorporation. Some states require the meetings to be held within the state of incorporation, and others require the bylaws to designate the place for holding shareholders' meetings. In any case, the state statute must be followed as to the location of shareholders' meetings.

The bylaws, whether required to or not, usually include a provision regarding the location of meetings. The following is an example of a provision that might be included in the bylaws:

> Meetings of the shareholders, including the annual meeting and special meetings, may be held either within or outside the State of _____ and at such place as shall be determined from time to time by the board of directors.

Sections 7.01(b) and 7.02(c) of the Model Act provide that annual and special meetings of the shareholders "may be held in or out of this state at the place stated in or fixed in accordance with the bylaws." Both sections also provide that "if no place is fixed in accordance with the bylaws," meetings shall be held at the corporation's principal office.

Setting the Record Date

Most state statutes permit the corporation to select a **record date,** prior to the meeting date, on which the stock transfer records of the corporation will be reviewed to determine who is entitled to vote as a record owner of shares of the corporation. Setting a record date prior to the meeting date provides the time necessary for the corporation to prepare a list of the shareholders, or **holders of record**. Those shareholders listed in the stock records on the record date are those entitled to receive notice and to vote at the meeting.

The procedure of setting a record date was established to allow for the orderly process of sending notices to shareholders and determining those entitled to vote on the day of the meeting. A requirement of most states and the Model Act is the preparation and availability of a list of the names, addresses, and numbers of shares held for all shareholders prior to the meeting date. Setting a record date, or cutoff date, assists the persons responsible for preparing and making the list available for inspection.

State statutes place restrictions on the number of days prior to the meeting date that the record date may occur. The Model Act allows the record date to be no more than 70 days before the meeting. Many states require that the record date be no less than 10 days, but no more than 50 days, before the meeting date.

The alternative to setting a record date is to close the transfer records for a specified number of days before the meeting, during which time no stock transfers are recorded. This also allows time for the preparation and completion of the list of shareholders, or holders of record. The closing of the transfer records does *not*, of course, preclude a shareholder from selling his or her shares. It merely means that a shareholder who sells his or her shares during that period will still be entitled to receive notice of the meeting and to vote.

The board of directors may determine the record date, or the date may be fixed in the bylaws. Section 7.07(a) of the Model Act provides that "the bylaws may fix or provide the manner of fixing the record date . . . in order to determine the shareholders entitled to notice of a shareholders' meeting, to demand a special meeting, to vote, or to take any other action. If the bylaws do not fix . . . a record date, the board of directors . . . may fix . . . the record date." Following is an example of a provision of the bylaws fixing the record date:

Fixing the Record Date

For the purpose of determining shareholders entitled to notice of or to vote at any meeting of shareholders or any adjournment thereof, the board of directors may fix a date as the record date. Such date shall be not more than fifty nor less than ten days before the date of any meeting.

Case I, discussed in the *Legal Links* in this chapter, deals with a statute that prohibits the board of directors from closing the stock transfer books for a period longer than fifty days before any meeting of stockholders. In the reported case, the court found that a shareholders' meeting scheduled for December 28 was invalid because the stock transfer books had been closed since April 29—clearly exceeding the fifty-day limit.

The list of shareholders, prepared as of the record date, must be made available for inspection by any shareholder, beginning two business days after notice of the meeting is given. The Model Act, in Sections 7.20(b) and 7.20(c), states that "the shareholders' list must be available for inspection by any shareholder, beginning two business days after notice of the meeting is given" and "the corporation shall make the shareholders' list available at the meeting, and any shareholder, his agent, or attorney is entitled to inspect the list." Many states provide similar requirements.

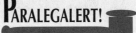

PARALEGALERT!

The general rule is that only those shareholders entitled to vote have the right to be present at a shareholders' meeting. Nonvoting shareholders may be permitted to be present at the meeting, but they may not vote.

Notice and Waiver of Notice

After the list of shareholders has been prepared, the secretary or other person designated in the corporation's bylaws must provide notice to all shareholders entitled to receive notification that a meeting will be held.

Bryan v. Western Pac. R. Corporation
Goldboss v. Reimann

CASE I

In *Bryan v. Western Pac. R. Corporation*, 35 A.2d 909 (Del. Ch., 1944), Thomas H. Bryan, on behalf of himself and others, asked the court to enjoin the holding of a stockholders' meeting of Western Pacific Railroad Corporation, a Delaware corporation, based on the following facts: In November 1943, a special meeting of the stockholders was called for December 28, 1943. A notice of the meeting was prepared, by order of the board of directors, and the notice set forth the purposes for which the meeting was to be held. The shareholders were to consider and vote on a resolution approving the directors' execution of an agreement, to elect directors, and to transact such other business as might come before the meeting. Copies of the notice, dated November 24, were sent to the persons appearing on the corporation's list of registered shareholders. Because the corporation had failed to register any transfers of shares of the corporation after April 29, 1943, the persons thus notified of the meeting were the stockholders of record on April 29. In effect, the stock transfer books of the corporation had been continuously closed since April 29.

The court cited Section 17 of the Delaware Corporation Law, which provides the board of directors the power "to close the stock transfer books of the corporation for a period not exceeding fifty days preceding the date of any meeting of stockholders." The court found that the corporation owes a duty to register transfers of shares of its stock and that the board of directors may properly close the transfer books only for limited purposes and for a limited period. Therefore, the court issued the preliminary injunction to prevent the corporation from recognizing the stockholders' meeting as valid.

CASE II

In *Goldboss v. Reimann*, 55 F.Supp. 811 (S.D.N.Y., 1943), the plaintiff had signed a proxy for a meeting, appointing Ross Beason, Cedric H. Smith, Bernard E. Lawson, Harold F. Dugan, and Wallace A. Bond as her proxies to vote in favor of an amendment to the corporation's charter and bylaws. The plaintiff's shares were voted by proxy, and the court held that "her stock was so voted, and its use was as effective as if she had voted in person."

A **notice of meeting,** which should state the date, time, and place of the meeting proposed to be held, is required to be given only to shareholders entitled to vote at the meeting. Many states and, in particular, Section 7.05(a) of the Model Act require that "a corporation shall notify shareholders of the date, time, and place of each annual and special shareholders' meeting no fewer than 10 nor more than 60 days before the meeting date. Unless this Act or the articles of incorporation require otherwise, the corporation is required to give notice only to shareholders entitled to vote at the meeting." Some states, however, do not specify when notice must be given.

The Model Act provides that notice of a special meeting of the shareholders must include the purpose or purposes for which the meeting was called. Only the business described in the notice of the meeting may be conducted at a special meeting of the

PARALEGALERT!

Do not confuse the period established for the record date with the period during which the notice of meeting must be sent. First, the shareholders entitled to receive notice are determined. Second, notice is provided to those shareholders within a specified time.

Figure 7–8   Notice of Annual Meeting of the Shareholders

> **Notice of Annual Meeting**
> **of the Shareholders**
>
> August 25, 1995
>
> To the Shareholders of XYZ Corporation:
>
> Notice is hereby given that, in accordance with Section _____ of the Bylaws of the XYZ Corporation (the "Corporation") and in accordance with the requirements of the laws of the State of _____, the annual meeting of the shareholders of the Corporation will be held at the Corporation's principal place of business, 123 America Street, Anytown, Anystate, on Wednesday, September 27, 1995, at 11:00 a.m., for the purpose of:
>
> 1. Electing directors;
> 2. Voting on the recommendation of the board of directors that the corporation be liquidated and dissolved; and
> 3. Transacting such other business as may lawfully come before the meeting.
>
> Dated this 25th day of August, 1995.
>
> _____
> Secretary

shareholders. The notice of an annual meeting, however, need not include a description of the purpose for which the meeting was called.

In Figure 7–8 is an example of a notice of meeting for an annual meeting of the shareholders. This notice of meeting was prepared in accordance with the provisions of the Model Act.

The period within which notice must be given varies from state to state. Some state statutes require longer notice periods when the shareholders are to consider certain matters. For example, several states require a minimum of twenty days' notice when the shareholders' meeting is being held to consider a plan of merger or consolidation or the sale of the corporation's assets outside the ordinary course of business.

The purpose of providing notice to shareholders is to afford them the opportunity to be present at the meeting and to vote on matters requiring action by the shareholders. However, the requirements for providing notice to the shareholders, which are set forth in the statutes, the articles of incorporation, or the bylaws, may be waived by a shareholder. The shareholder waives notice by (1) executing a waiver of notice, (2) attending the meeting, or (3) authorizing another person to attend the meeting and vote on his or her behalf.

PARALEGALERT!

A waiver may be either in writing or by action. That is, a shareholder can (1) execute and deliver a waiver of notice (writing) or (2) attend the meeting in person or by proxy (action).

A waiver of notice, executed and delivered to the corporation, waives any objection by that shareholder to a lack of notice (notice not sent) or a defective notice (notice not sent within the statutory period). For example, the bylaws of Office Products Corporation require that shareholders be provided ten days' written notice of a meeting. If notice is not provided ten days before the meeting date or if no notice is provided, the shareholders may execute a statement waiving their right to be provided notice of the meeting. The waiver of notice acts as a

Figure 7–9   Waiver of Notice by Shareholders

Waiver of Notice

   We, the undersigned shareholders of XYZ Corporation (the "Corporation"), a corporation organized under the laws of the State of _____, hereby waive notice of the time, place, and purpose of the annual meeting of the shareholders of the Corporation, to be held at the office of the Corporation on Wednesday, September 27, 1995, at 11:00 a.m. for the purpose of:

1. Electing directors;
2. Voting on the recommendation of the Board of Directors that the Corporation be liquidated and dissolved; and
3. Transacting such other business as may lawfully come before the meeting.

_____

_____

---

cure for the failure to provide the proper notice required by the state statutes, the articles of incorporation, or the bylaws. A sample waiver of notice by shareholders is provided in Figure 7–9.

In addition, a shareholder's attendance at a meeting, either in person or by proxy, also acts as a waiver of the notice requirement, unless he or she attends the meeting only for the purpose of objecting to the holding of the meeting or to the transaction of business at the meeting. Most state statutes, like Section 7.06(b) of the Model Act, provide that "a shareholder's attendance at a meeting . . . waives objection to lack of notice or defective notice of the meeting, unless the shareholder at the beginning of the meeting objects to holding the meeting or transacting business at the meeting."

Proxy

Generally, the term **proxy** refers to the written document given by the holder of stock to another person to authorize that person to exercise the shareholder's voting rights. The term *proxy* is applied, however, both to the written document and to the person authorized to vote on behalf of the shareholder, also called the **proxyholder.** Unlike a director, who *may not* direct another person to vote on his or her behalf, shareholders are permitted to vote by proxy. All states, and the Model Act, permit shareholders to vote by proxy. The Model Act, in Section 7.22(a), states that "a shareholder may vote his shares in person or by proxy." A form for the proxy of a shareholder is provided in Figure 7–10.

A shareholder's vote by proxy is as effective as if the shareholder had voted in person. (See Case II of the *Legal Links* in this chapter.)

A proxy is permitted to be given only by the registered owner of the stock of the corporation. The form of the proxy depends on the desires of the shareholder. For example, the proxy may be **general**, granting the proxyholder the authority to vote on behalf of the shareholder as the proxyholder deems appropriate. Or the proxy may be **limited**, specifying

PARALEGALERT!

All states allow shareholders to vote by proxy. But some states restrict voting by proxy for directors, and others restrict a shareholder's choice of the person to act as proxy.

Figure 7–10 Proxy of Shareholder

Proxy

KNOW ALL MEN BY THESE PRESENTS, that the undersigned, Joseph Smith, does hereby constitute and appoint Victoria Leone his true and lawful attorney, agent, and proxy, with full power of substitution and revocation for and in his name, to vote all shares of stock of ABC Company standing in his name, at a Special Meeting of Shareholders of ABC Company to be held on Monday, March 6, 1995, 123 America Street, Anytown, Anystate, and at any adjournment of such meeting for such business as may properly come before the meeting.

IN WITNESS WHEREOF, Joseph Smith has executed this Proxy as of this _____ day of _____, 199 ___ .

_____
Joseph Smith

---

the manner in which the proxyholder may vote on behalf of the shareholder. A limited proxy binds the proxyholder to vote in the manner directed by the shareholder.

Unless required by state statute or the articles of incorporation or bylaws of the corporation, a proxy may be executed in blank, need not be witnessed or notarized, and need not specify the meeting date. The Model Act requires that the shareholder sign "an appointment form" and is not specific about the information to be contained in the proxy. Generally, the management of the corporation provides a proxy form acceptable to the corporation.

The appointment of a proxy to vote on behalf of a shareholder is not effective until the form of proxy is received by the secretary or another officer of the corporation who is authorized to tabulate the votes at a meeting. The corporation must be in possession of the proxy prior to the meeting.

The period of duration of a proxy varies among the states, but in states that follow the Model Act, a proxy automatically expires eleven months from its date of execution unless a longer period is expressly provided in the proxy. In addition, a proxy is revocable by the shareholder unless the proxy specifically states that it is irrevocable. An irrevocable proxy must be coupled with an interest. For example, when stock is pledged to a bank as collateral for a loan, an irrevocable proxy is given to the bank until the loan has been repaid. During this period the bank is authorized to vote the shares. When the interest with which the proxy is coupled is extinguished, the irrevocable proxy is revoked.

Quorum

We already know that when consent of the shareholders is required, the shareholders may approve the action (e.g., amending the articles of incorporation) at a meeting. It is necessary, however, that the appropriate percentage of the stock of the corporation be represented at the meeting for the meeting to be valid and proper. A proposal cannot be adopted unless the meeting is valid and proper.

A quorum is the minimum percentage of the stock of the corporation that must be represented at a meeting (in person or by proxy) for the meeting to be valid and proper. If a quorum is not present at a meeting of the shareholders, any actions taken by the shareholders will not be valid. Therefore, it is important to determine whether a quorum is present at the meeting before any business is conducted.

PARALEGALERT!

It should be determined at the outset of a shareholders' meeting whether a quorum is present for the conducting of business. If a quorum is not present, no business should be conducted.

The corporate statute of the corporation's state of incorporation and a corporation's articles of incorporation and bylaws must be reviewed to determine what constitutes a quorum for voting purposes. Quorum may be any of the following:

- majority (at least 51 percent)
- greater than a majority (greater than 51 percent)
- unanimous (no less than 100 percent)

However, a quorum is usually a majority unless a greater percentage is required by the articles of incorporation. For example, the articles of incorporation might include a provision that "seventy percent (70%) of the votes entitled to be cast shall constitute a quorum." In this case, shareholders holding at least 70 percent of the shares entitled to vote must be present in person or by proxy for the meeting to be valid and proper.

Section 7.25 of the Model Act defines a quorum as "a majority of the votes entitled to be cast on the matter," and generally similar provisions will be found in the states' corporate statutes. However, the language of some state statutes is ambiguous and fails to specify whether a quorum is based on the number of shareholders or on the number of shares. The general rule is that the number of shares, *not* the number of shareholders, is used for determining a quorum.

Voting of Shares

We will discuss in greater detail in Chapter 10 the rights and privileges associated with the ownership of common and preferred stock. Therefore, the discussion in this section will be limited to procedures for voting at shareholders' meetings.

When a quorum is present at a meeting, an affirmative vote of a majority of the shares represented at the meeting is sufficient for approving and adopting any proposal (unless, of course, the articles of incorporation require a greater-than-majority vote for the approval of a proposal). For example, if a corporation has 100 shares of voting stock issued and outstanding, 51 shares must be represented at a meeting to constitute a quorum. Of 51 shares represented, 26 shares would have to be voted affirmatively for a proposal to be adopted. In this case, which is permitted by the Model Act and most states, a proposal could be adopted with the approval of the holders of only 26 percent (26 shares) of the stock.

All states' statutes provide that one share of stock is entitled to one vote. Section 7.21 of the Model Act provides that "each outstanding share . . . is entitled to one vote on each matter voted on at a shareholders' meeting." For example, a shareholder owning 25 shares of XYZ Corporation is entitled to 25 votes.

However, some corporations may have issued shares that give the holders more than one vote per share or limited voting rights. In any case, all shareholders have the right to vote their stock at all meetings of the shareholders, unless that right is denied by either the state statute, the corporation's articles of incorporation or bylaws, or an agreement among the shareholders.

Specific procedures for conducting a vote at a shareholders' meeting are not usually prescribed by the statutes. Either a voice vote (or a show of hands) or a written ballot is acceptable as a method of voting. At more formal meetings, the

PARALEGALERT!

The state statutes must always be reviewed. They may require a greater-than-majority vote on certain matters on which the shareholders must vote.

written ballot is appropriate, but voting at meetings of smaller corporations is generally done by a voice vote. A voice vote at some meetings may cause disagreement, and shareholders may request a ballot vote. Remember that the *number of shares* (not the number of shareholders) voting in favor of a proposal determines whether the proposal is approved.

Even though the business transacted at a meeting need not follow a particular order, a logical order will help keep the meeting orderly. Following is a logical order of business to be followed at a meeting of the shareholders:

1. Call to order.
2. Appointment of chairman and secretary of the meeting.
3. Presentation of list of shareholders.
4. Presentation of call and notice of meeting.
5. Inspection and presentation of proxies.
6. Announcement that quorum is present.
7. Reading and approval of last meeting's minutes.
8. Reports by officers, committees, and board members.
9. Approval of proposals before the shareholders.
10. Election of directors (if this is the annual meeting).
11. Declaration of directors elected (if this is the annual meeting).
12. Ratification of previous actions taken by the directors.
13. Discussion of new business.
14. Adjournment of the meeting.

PARALEGALERT!

A show of hands or a voice vote may cause disagreement at a meeting, because it is usually not the number of shareholders voting for a proposal that determines whether the proposal is approved. The shares are counted in determining whether an action is approved, and one shareholder may hold most of the outstanding shares of the corporation.

7–5 Other Procedures and Types of Meetings

Distinction Between Call and Notice of Meetings

The call of a meeting and the notice of a meeting—whether of the incorporators, the shareholders, or the directors—are often confused, and they are usually not the same.

The **call of a meeting** is the procedure for bringing the meeting into existence, accomplished by the person or persons of the corporation who have the power to call a meeting. For example, the call might be a written document addressed to the secretary of the corporation, requesting that the appropriate group of corporate persons (incorporators, shareholders, or directors) be notified of a meeting. Refer to Figure 7–4, which is a form for the call of the organizational meeting of the initial directors.

On the other hand, the notice of a meeting is the written document advising the incorporators, the shareholders, or the directors that a meeting has been scheduled. Refer to Figure 7–5, which is a form for a notice of a special meeting of the board of directors.

The common practice is to provide only the notice of meeting, which may begin with the words "By order of," followed by the names or offices of the person or persons empowered to call the meeting. A corporation's bylaws generally specify who is authorized to call a meeting and who is authorized to send a notice that a meeting has been called and scheduled.

States vary in the terms they use for call and notice. For example, certain states refer to a notice as a "Call and Waiver of Notice," and others use the term

"Notice and Waiver of Notice." Only upon review of the state statutes can you be sure of the terminology utilized in that state.

Meetings by Conference Telephone

The availability of special telephone equipment has influenced many states, as well as the drafters of the Model Act, to permit the use of conference telephones to hold and conduct meetings of the board of directors. These meetings are called **conference telephone meetings.** Generally, state statutes permit the use of any communication equipment as long as all directors participating in the meeting can simultaneously hear each other. Thus the directors can hold meetings without having to travel long distances and incur the resultant loss of time.

Specifically, Section 8.20(b) of the Model Act states:

PARALEGALERT!

The director participating in a meeting by conference telephone must be provided timely notice of the meeting, even if the person providing notice knows that the director will not be present in person.

Unless the articles of incorporation or bylaws provide otherwise, the board of directors may permit any or all directors to participate in a regular or special meeting by, or conduct the meeting through the use of, any means of communication by which all directors participating may simultaneously hear each other during the meeting. A director participating in a meeting by this means is deemed to be present in person at the meeting.

The holding of a directors' meeting by conference telephone or other communication does *not* negate the notice, waiver of notice, and quorum and voting requirements of the statutes.

Meetings of Committees of the Board

As we have already discussed in Chapter 5, the board of directors is permitted to create one or more committees and appoint members of the board of directors to serve on such committees. Any committee established by the board is required to comply with the same provisions governing the board of directors, including provisions governing meetings, notice and waiver of notice, quorum and voting requirements, and adoption actions by written consent.

Section 8.25(c) of the Model Act states that "Sections 8.20 through 8.24, which govern meetings, action without meetings, notice and waiver of notice, and quorum and voting requirements of the board of directors, apply to committees and their members as well."

Figure 7–11 is an example of the minutes of a meeting of the executive committee of a corporation. These minutes were drafted in accordance with the provisions of the Model Act.

7–6 Documenting Business Conducted at Meetings

It is important that the corporation maintain and preserve a permanent record of the corporate actions taken by the incorporators, shareholders, and directors. The secretary of the corporation is usually responsible for maintaining this permanent record, but the corporation's articles of incorporation or bylaws or the state statutes may impose this responsibility on another officer or agent of the

Figure 7–11   Minutes of Meeting of Executive Committee

Special Meeting of the Executive Committee
Held on Friday, August 18, 1995

A Special Meeting of the Executive Committee (the "Committee") of ABC Company (the "Corporation"), a _____ corporation, was held on Friday, August 18, 1995, at 9:30 a.m. EST at the principal office of the Corporation at 123 America Street, Anytown, Anystate.

Michael Kramer acted as Chairman of the meeting, and Kevin Tobin acted as Secretary and recorded the minutes.

The following members of the Committee were present: Michael Kramer and Kevin Tobin.

A quorum of the Committee members being present, Mr. Kramer called the meeting to order. Mr. Kramer stated that the Committee was considering the recommendation to the Board of Directors of the Corporation that directors' compensation should be set at $250 per meeting attended by each director.

Upon motion duly made and seconded, the following resolution was unanimously approved by all the members of the Committee:

RESOLVED, that the Committee deems it advisable that each director of the Corporation shall receive $250 for each meeting of the Board of Directors that such director attends.

There being no further business to come before the meeting, it was, upon motion duly made, seconded, and unanimously carried, adjourned.

_____
Kevin Tobin, Secretary

---

corporation. The documentation or permanent record of the corporate actions taken by the incorporators, the shareholders, and the board of directors is kept in the corporation's **minute book**.

Accurate documentation of corporate actions is important. For example, in future litigation, accurate documentation may be useful as legal evidence of action taken by the shareholders or the board of directors. Clear records can protect the corporation and the persons who own and operate it, but unfortunately, such records can also be used against them. Clear and concise records also serve as reminders to the shareholders or directors of their intent or reasoning in reaching a decision on a particular issue.

The corporate paralegal is often assigned the task of documenting the corporate actions taken on behalf of the corporation, even though this is ultimately the responsibility of the secretary of the corporation. These corporate actions are documented in the form of resolutions, which are then adopted and incorporated into either (1) meeting minutes or (2) written consents. The corporate actions of the incorporators, shareholders, or directors, all of which are required to be documented, are listed in Figure 7–1. That list obviously does not include all actions that are possible, but it provides a basis for determining which actions must be documented.

Resolutions

A **resolution** is a statement documenting an action taken or the authorization of an action to be taken. Documenting an action in the form of a resolution lessens the chance of any misinterpretation within the corporation or by any outside persons dealing with the corporation. A resolution usually names the corporate person authorized to take the action and identifies the action to be taken. However, some resolutions merely state the intention of the persons taking the action. For example, in the election of directors, the shareholders adopt a resolution stating that certain individuals are elected as directors of the corporation. See Figure 7–12 for an example of a resolution of the shareholders electing directors.

A resolution is not valid if it violates state statute or conflicts with the articles of incorporation or bylaws of the corporation. Provisions of the state statute, the articles of incorporation, and the bylaws prevail over any action authorized by resolution. For example, suppose the articles of incorporation contain a provision that there shall be five directors of the corporation. At the organizational meeting of the corporation, the directors adopt a resolution setting the number of directors at seven. The articles prevail; the corporation may have only five directors serving on the board.

Resolutions are an essential part of conducting business, even though there is no hard and fast rule for when they must be used. However, a formal resolution is not necessary to bind the corporation. For example, the president of Acme Trucking Corporation executes an agreement to borrow $5,000,000 from First National Bank. The provisions of the loan agreement are binding on the corporation even if the president has not received authorization from the board of directors to enter into the loan agreement. With that in mind, consider the following circumstances, in which the use of a resolution is appropriate and, in some cases, required:

1. The state statute, the articles of incorporation, or the bylaws require the action to be approved by resolution.
2. The action taken must be certified by an officer of the corporation to third parties as an action authorized by the shareholders or the board of directors.
3. The action establishes or amends corporate policy.
4. The action changes the corporate structure, as in a merger, consolidation, or dissolution.
5. The action is one of importance to the corporation.

Resolutions relating to a particular matter to be discussed and voted on at an upcoming meeting are often drafted prior to the meeting and distributed to the directors or shareholders for review. Discussion on the subject can then be expedited at the meeting. Depending on the complexity of the resolution, either the secretary of the corporation or the legal counsel to the corporation will prepare resolutions.

PARALEGALERT!

Generally, it is a task assigned to the corporate paralegal to prepare a draft of resolutions to be adopted by the incorporators, shareholders, or directors.

Figure 7–12 Resolution of the Shareholders Electing Directors

> RESOLVED, that Donald Smith, James Bond, and Elizabeth Williams be, and they hereby are, elected directors of the corporation, to serve until the next annual meeting of the shareholders.

In Figure 7–13, pages 166–168, are forms of resolutions for the actions listed in Figure 7–1. Remember that these are only forms, or examples, of resolutions. The person drafting a resolution has his or her own preferred style. Therefore, do not be dismayed if the attorney for whom you are working redrafts your resolutions or finds their form unacceptable.

Figure 7–13 Forms of Resolutions

Election of directors (by shareholders)

RESOLVED, that John Smith, Harry Jones, and Joseph Adams be and hereby are elected directors of the Corporation, to serve as such until the next annual meeting of the shareholders.

Removal of directors (by shareholders)

RESOLVED, that John Smith, Harry Jones, and Joseph Adams be and hereby are removed, without cause, as directors of the Corporation.

Merger or consolidation (by shareholders)

RESOLVED, that the Agreement of Merger, dated _____ _____ , 199____ , for the merger of the Corporation with XYZ Corporation, in the form attached hereto, is hereby approved, and the directors and officers of the Corporation are hereby authorized to take all necessary action and to execute and deliver all documents and instruments that may be necessary to consummate and carry out the intent of the Agreement of Merger.

Amendment of Articles of Incorporation (by shareholders)

WHEREAS, the Board of Directors of the Corporation deems it advisable that Article _____ of the Articles of Incorporation of the Corporation be amended and changed, and the shareholders of the Corporation do hereby approve the proposed amendment; be it

RESOLVED, that Article _____ of the Articles of Incorporation of the Corporation be amended and changed so that Article _____ shall read as follows:

[Insert new article or provision to be amended.]

FURTHER RESOLVED, that the Board of Directors is authorized to cause to be prepared, executed, and filed with the Secretary of State of _____ all necessary and proper documentation for amending the Articles of Incorporation of the Corporation.

Dissolution of corporation (by shareholders)

RESOLVED, that the Plan of Complete Liquidation and Dissolution be and hereby is adopted and approved and that the Corporation be completely liquidated at the earliest practicable date, that all debts and liabilities of the Corporation be paid, and that the remaining assets be distributed to the shareholders in accordance with the Corporation's Articles of Incorporation.

continued on pages 166–168

Figure 7–13, continued

Sale of corporation's assets (by shareholders)

RESOLVED, that the Board of Directors is hereby authorized to sell, lease, or dispose of all the real estate, machinery, fixtures, and other assets of the Corporation, in whole or in parcels, for such consideration and upon such terms as it may in its discretion and judgment deem the most advantageous for the shareholders of the Corporation; and

FURTHER RESOLVED, that all actions of the Board of Directors in carrying out the intent of the shareholders are hereby ratified and approved, and it is unnecessary for the Board of Directors to obtain further confirmation of the intent of the shareholders of the Corporation.

Amendment of Articles of Incorporation (by directors)

RESOLVED, that the Board of Directors of the Corporation deems it advisable that Article _____ of the Articles of Incorporation of the Corporation be amended and changed so that Article _____ shall read as follows:

[Insert new article or provision to be amended.]

FURTHER RESOLVED, that this proposal for amending Article _____ of the Articles of Incorporation be submitted to the shareholders of the Corporation for their consideration; and

FURTHER RESOLVED, that upon the shareholders' approving the amendment to Article _____ of the Articles of Incorporation, the officers of the Corporation are hereby authorized to prepare, execute, and deliver to the Secretary of State of _____ all necessary and proper documentation for amending the Articles of Incorporation of the Corporation.

Adoption of bylaws (by directors)

RESOLVED, that the form of Bylaws of the Corporation submitted to the Board of Directors be, and the same hereby are, adopted as and for the Bylaws of the Corporation, and the Secretary is instructed to cause the same to be inserted in the minute book of the Corporation.

Election of officers (by directors)

RESOLVED, that the following individuals be and hereby are elected to the offices of the Corporation to serve in accordance with the Bylaws of the Corporation and at the discretion of the Board of Directors until their successors shall be elected and qualified:

President	Michael Kramer
Vice President	James Bond
Secretary	Kevin Tobin
Treasurer	Mary Banker

Issuance of stock (by directors)

RESOLVED, that the officers of the Corporation be and hereby are authorized to issue to each of the following persons a stock certificate registered in the name listed, representing the following number of shares, and in consideration for the following amount in cash:

Name	No. of Shares	Consideration
Michael Kramer	100	$100
Kevin Tobin	100	$100
Genesis Corporation	200	$200

Figure 7–13, continued

Recommendation to the shareholders of the dissolution and liquidation of the corporation (by directors)

RESOLVED, that the Board of Directors of the Corporation deems it in the best interests of the Corporation and the shareholders of the Corporation that the Corporation be voluntarily dissolved and liquidated; and

FURTHER RESOLVED, that the Board of Directors hereby recommends to the shareholders of the Corporation that the Corporation be dissolved; and

FURTHER RESOLVED, that the Plan of Liquidation and Dissolution (the "Plan"), a copy of which is attached hereto, be and hereby is adopted and approved; and

FURTHER RESOLVED, that the officers of the Corporation be and hereby are authorized to convey and transfer the assets of the Corporation to the shareholders of the Corporation upon the agreement of the shareholders to be liable for any and all debts, taxes, fees, and expenses of the Corporation; and to cancel all issued and outstanding shares of the Corporation that shall be surrendered by the shareholders of the Corporation; and to take any other actions that may be necessary in accordance with the Plan.

Recommendation to the shareholders of a merger of the corporation (by directors)

RESOLVED, that the Board of Directors of the Corporation deems it in the best interests of the Corporation and the shareholders of the Corporation that the Corporation be merged with XYZ Corporation; and

FURTHER RESOLVED, that the Board of Directors hereby recommends to the shareholders of the Corporation that the Corporation be merged with XYZ Corporation; and

FURTHER RESOLVED, that the officers of the Corporation be, and they hereby are, authorized to execute, deliver, and file with the Secretary of State of _____ Articles of Merger for the merger of the Corporation and XYZ Corporation, pursuant to which XYZ Corporation shall be merged with and into the Corporation, the separate existence of XYZ Corporation shall cease, and the Corporation shall continue in existence as the surviving corporation; and

FURTHER RESOLVED, that the officers of the Corporation be, and they hereby are, authorized to execute and deliver such other documents and to take such other actions necessary to carry into effect the merger of the Corporation and XYZ Corporation.

Designation of a committee of the board (by directors)

RESOLVED, that a Finance Committee is hereby appointed to consist of James Bond and Mary Banker, with power in such Committee to increase its number by naming another member of the Board of Directors; and

FURTHER RESOLVED, that the Finance Committee shall have the power to supervise the financial affairs of the Corporation, and that it shall report to the Board of Directors from time to time, or whenever called upon to do so by the Board of Directors.

Opening of bank accounts (by directors)

RESOLVED, that Mary Banker, Treasurer of the Corporation, be, and she hereby is, authorized to designate from time to time such banks and trust companies as depositories for the funds of the Corporation as she shall determine to be necessary or desirable, which determination shall be conclusively evidenced by her execution and delivery to such bank of written instructions appointing it such depository; and

Figure 7–13, continued

FURTHER RESOLVED, that Mary Banker, Treasurer of the Corporation, be, and she hereby is, authorized to terminate from time to time by written instructions any such bank or trust company as a depository of the funds of the Corporation; and

FURTHER RESOLVED, that Mary Banker, Treasurer of the Corporation, be, and she hereby is, authorized and empowered to determine from time to time the procedure for the issuance of checks, drafts, or other orders for the payment of money drawn in the name of the Corporation on funds now or hereafter held in any depository and to designate in addition to herself the persons authorized to sign such checks, drafts, or orders (including instructions for wire transfer or other transfers by electronic means).

Adoption of corporate seal and form of stock certificate (by directors)

RESOLVED, that the corporate seal, an impression of which is hereby affixed, be, and the same hereby is, adopted as the corporate seal of the Corporation; and

FURTHER RESOLVED, that the specimen form of stock certificate attached hereto as Exhibit A, be, and the same hereby is, approved, adopted, and prescribed as the form of stock certificate for the shares of stock to be issued by the Corporation.

Qualification to do business in a foreign jurisdiction (by directors)

RESOLVED, that the officers of the Corporation be, and they hereby are, authorized to execute and file all documents and perform all acts that may be necessary to qualify the Corporation to do business in the State of _____ .

Use of a fictitious or assumed name (by directors)

RESOLVED, that the Corporation is authorized to do business using the fictitious name "_____" and that the officers of the Corporation are hereby authorized to execute and file all documents and perform all acts that may be necessary to register the fictitious name with the Secretary of State of _____ .

Borrowing by the corporation (by directors)

RESOLVED, that the officers of the Corporation are hereby authorized to borrow, on behalf of the Corporation, from such banks or trust companies as they may determine appropriate, an amount not to exceed _____ Dollars ($_____), for such period of time and upon such terms and conditions as may to them in their discretion seem advisable; and

FURTHER RESOLVED, that the officers of the Corporation are hereby authorized to execute and deliver notes in the name of the Corporation for the payment of the amounts borrowed from said banks or trust companies.

Meeting Minutes

Although there is no mandatory procedure for conducting business at a meeting, state statutes require that the corporation maintain a permanent record of its meetings. Section 16.01(a) of the Model Act requires the corporation to keep permanent records but does not specify the manner in which they are to be kept. That section states that "a corporation shall keep as permanent records minutes of all meetings of its shareholders and board of directors, a record of all actions taken by the shareholders or board of directors without a meeting, and a record of all actions taken by a committee of the board of directors in place of the board of directors of the corporation."

The record of minutes kept of meetings is called **meeting minutes.** Items that become part of the meeting minutes include motions, resolutions, votes, statements explaining a motion or resolution, and any information that a shareholder or director specifically requests be made part of the record. A good practice to follow when preparing meeting minutes is to be as clear, concise, and simple as possible. Every tiny detail of the meeting need not be made part of the meeting minutes, but the secretary or the other person recording the minutes should not hesitate to provide some details.

Figure 7–14 is an example of the minutes of a meeting of the board of directors. Pay particular attention to the elements covered in these minutes:

1. Date, time, and place of meeting.
2. Confirmation that proper notice was given or waived.
3. Names of the chairman and the secretary of the meeting.
4. Confirmation that a quorum was present for the conducting of business (possibly including the names of persons present).
5. A clear, concise, and simple report of all business transacted at the meeting.

Figure 7–14   Minutes of Meeting of Board of Directors

Special Meeting of the Board of Directors
Held on Friday, February 3, 1995

A Special Meeting of the Board of Directors of ABC Company (the "Corporation"), a _____ corporation, was held on Friday, February 3, 1995, at 10:00 a.m. EST at the principal office of the Corporation at 123 America Street, Anytown, Anystate.

Michael Kramer acted as Chairman of the meeting, and Kevin Tobin acted as Secretary and recorded the minutes.

The following directors were present: Michael Kramer, Brian Benjamin, Samuel Adams, and Rebecca Finch.

A quorum being present, Mr. Kramer called the meeting to order. Mr. Kramer stated that the Board of Directors of the Corporation should consider recommending to the shareholders that the Corporation be liquidated. He distributed a draft of a Plan of Complete Liquidation and Dissolution (the "Plan"), a copy of which is attached to these meeting minutes.

Upon motion duly made and seconded, the following resolutions were approved unanimously by all the directors present:

RESOLVED, that the Board of Directors of the Corporation deems it in the best interests of the Corporation and the shareholders of the Corporation that the Corporation be voluntarily dissolved and liquidated; and

FURTHER RESOLVED, that the Board of Directors hereby recommends to the shareholders of the Corporation that the Corporation be dissolved; and

FURTHER RESOLVED, that the Plan, a copy of which is attached hereto, be and hereby is adopted and approved; and

---

continued on next page

Figure 7–14, continued

FURTHER RESOLVED, that the officers of the Corporation be and hereby are authorized to convey and transfer the assets of the Corporation to the shareholders of the Corporation upon the agreement of the shareholders to be liable for any and all debts, taxes, fees, and expenses of the Corporation; and to cancel all issued and outstanding shares of the Corporation, which shall be surrendered by the shareholders of the Corporation; and to take any other actions that may be necessary in accordance with the Plan.

There being no further business to come before the meeting, it was, upon motion duly made, seconded, and unanimously carried, adjourned.

Kevin Tobin, Secretary

Action Without a Meeting

You have already learned that corporate actions are approved and business is conducted at meetings of the incorporators, the shareholders, and the board of directors. When there is no disagreement on the matters on which a vote must be taken, a corporation may dispense with a meeting. Most state statutes permit approval of corporate actions and the conducting of business by written consent in lieu of a meeting. A **written consent** documents the actions taken without the formality of holding a meeting.

Section 7.04(a) of the Model Act provides that "action required or permitted . . . to be taken at a shareholders' meeting may be taken without a meeting if the action is taken by all the shareholders entitled to vote on the action." The Model Act also requires that "the action must be evidenced by one or more written consents describing the action taken, signed by all the shareholders entitled to vote on the action." Section 8.21 of the Model Act is similar to Section 7.04, but Section 8.21 provides that "unless the articles of incorporation or bylaws provide otherwise, action required or permitted . . . to be taken at a board of directors' meeting may be taken without a meeting if the action is taken by all members of the board." Note that the Model Act permits the articles of incorporation or the bylaws to deny the use of written consents for the directors, but it does not permit such denial for the shareholders.

An obstacle to the adoption of corporate actions by written consent is that the consent must be *unanimous*. That is, *all shareholders* or *all directors* must approve the action. Sections 7.04 and 8.21 of the Model Act provide that consents must be "signed by all the shareholders" or "signed by each director." If even *one* shareholder or *one* director opposes a corporate action, a meeting must be held. And as we already know, if a meeting is to be held, notice must be properly delivered, a quorum must be present, and a vote must be taken on the corporate action. Only a few states permit less-than-unanimous approval by shareholder written consent, and those states generally require that the articles of incorporation or the bylaws authorize such approval. In Figure 7–15 are two examples of provisions of the articles of incorporation allowing less-than-unanimous written consent by the shareholders.

PARALEGALERT!

Smaller corporations often use the written consent in lieu of holding meetings of the shareholders and directors. They do so to avoid the requirements of providing notice, making sure a quorum is present, and actually holding the meeting.

Figure 7–15   Sample Provisions Allowing Less-Than-Unanimous Written Consent of the Shareholders

> ### Example 1: Requiring not less than 75 percent vote.
>
> Any action required or permitted to be taken at a meeting of the shareholders or of a class of shareholders may be taken without a meeting upon the written consent of not less than 75 percent of the shareholders who would have been entitled to cast their votes to authorize the action at a meeting at which all shareholders entitled to vote thereon were present and voting.
>
> ### Example 2: Requiring the minimum number of votes.
>
> Any action required or permitted to be taken at a meeting of the shareholders or of a class of shareholders may be taken without a meeting upon the written consent of shareholders who would have been entitled to cast the minimum number of votes that would be necessary to authorize the action at a meeting at which all shareholders entitled to vote thereon were present and voting.

Obviously the use of the written consent is impractical for large corporations with numerous shareholders, but it provides an advantage for corporations with a smaller number of directors or shareholders. The use of a written consent can eliminate the need for directors or shareholders to incur expenses and travel long distances to attend a meeting. For example, when the directors are to reelect the same officers of a corporation, the use of a written consent could provide a savings to the corporation and the directors.

Provided in Figures 7–16 and 7–17 are examples of consents of the shareholders and the board of directors, prepared in accordance with the relevant provisions of the Model Act.

Figure 7–16   Consent of the Shareholders

> **ABC Company**
> **Consent of the Shareholders**
>
> The undersigned, being all of the shareholders of ABC Company, a _____ corporation (the "Corporation"), acting under the provisions of Section _____ of the Model Business Corporation Act, as amended and supplemented, and under the Bylaws of the Corporation, hereby adopt the following resolution by unanimous written consent:
>
> RESOLVED, that Deborah Alexander and Brian Benjamin be and hereby are elected directors of the Corporation, to serve as such until the next annual meeting of the shareholders.
>
> IN WITNESS WHEREOF, the shareholders of the Corporation have executed this Consent this 27th day of November, 1994.
>
> _____
> Andrew Aaron
>
> _____
> Brian Brubaker
>
> _____
> Cynthia Carter

Figure 7–17 Consent of the Board of Directors

> ABC Company
> Consent of the Directors
>
> We, the undersigned, being all the members of the Board of Directors of ABC Company, a _____ corporation (the "Corporation"), acting under the provisions of Section ____ of the Model Business Corporation Act, as amended and supplemented, and under the Bylaws of the Corporation, hereby adopt the following resolution by unanimous written consent:
>
> RESOLVED, that the following individuals be and hereby are elected to the offices set forth after their names:
>
> | | |
> |---|---|
> | Samuel Adams | President |
> | Abraham Lincoln | Vice President |
> | George Washington | Secretary |
> | Brian Benjamin | Treasurer |
>
> IN WITNESS WHEREOF, the Directors of the Corporation have executed this Consent this 27th day of November, 1994.
>
> _____
> Deborah Alexander
>
> _____
> Brian Benjamin

7–7 Organization of the Corporate Minute Book

The corporation's minute book is usually kept in the corporate attorney's office. If there is litigation involving the corporation or if a governmental authority requests information, a warrant or subpoena must be obtained to gain access to the minute book and its contents. In any case, because the minute book is retained by the attorney, the organization and maintenance of the minute book is usually the responsibility of the corporate paralegal.

State statutes generally require the corporation to keep copies of its corporate records, but they generally do *not* dictate the manner or method of organizing the minute book or the types of documents to be included in the minute book. Use logic and common sense as guidelines for organizing a minute book.

The minute book should be organized chronologically and should contain all the corporate records of the corporation. When the secretary of state returns the articles of incorporation to the incorporator (usually the corporate paralegal), they will be stamped "Filed" to indicate that they were accepted for filing. These original articles of incorporation should be the first document filed in the minute book and should be followed, chronologically, by all other corporate documents, many of which are listed next.

PARALEGALERT!

The best advice to anyone who is given responsibility for organizing and maintaining minute books is to use logic and common sense. Obviously, you will not include every corporate document in the minute book.

Documents that should be filed in a corporation's minute book include the following:

1. Articles of incorporation, certificate of incorporation, or other documents filed by the incorporators.
2. Certificate issued by the secretary of state to evidence filing of the articles.
3. Subscription agreements (if any).
4. Proofs of publication (if the state of incorporation required publication).
5. Corporate bylaws.
6. Notice or waiver of notice of organizational meeting.
7. Minutes of the organizational meeting (either by the incorporator or the board of directors).
8. Specimen form of share certificate.
9. Notices or waivers of notice of meetings of the shareholders and the board of directors.
10. Minutes of meetings of the shareholders and the board of directors.
11. Written consents of the shareholders and the board of directors.
12. Resignations of the directors and officers.
13. Proxies of the shareholders.

In addition to the documents listed, other important corporate documents should be included in the minute book. For example, when a corporation amends its articles of incorporation, it is required to file articles of amendment with the secretary of state in the state of incorporation. After these articles of amendment have been filed, the copy stamped "Filed" and returned by the secretary of state should be placed in the minute book. The same is true for all other corporate filings made with the secretary of state: all should be kept in the corporation's minute book.

Some corporations keep copies of all resolutions adopted by the shareholders and the board of directors in a file or in a book that is separate from the minute book. This practice helps reduce the sometimes tedious task of leafing through numerous pages of unrelated materials in the minute book. Active corporations may produce hundreds of pages each year that could be included in the minute book; keeping and indexing resolutions in separate files or books is more practical in such circumstances. The corporate paralegal will, in most cases, be responsible for organizing and maintaining those files or books as well as the minute book.

Many of the reports and financial documents discussed and reviewed at meetings of the shareholders or the board of directors are lengthy and too cumbersome to be included in the corporation's minute book. Therefore, many corporations will bind or file these reports separately and make reference to them in the minute book. As with the practice of maintaining a separate file or book for resolutions of the corporation, this practice eliminates the need to file bulky reports and other documents within the minute book. Whether these reports or other documents are separately filed or bound, it is important that a record or index be kept of the documents referred to in the minutes of meetings.

7–8 Practical Considerations

The issues covered in this chapter include (1) determining which business activities must be approved by the incorporators, which by the shareholders, and which by the board of directors; (2) interpreting and complying with the procedures required for holding meetings; and (3) documenting the actions taken at meetings. The corporate paralegal usually performs all these tasks; therefore, it is important to understand the statutory and practical requirements of corporate meetings and actions.

When given an assignment similar to Peter Paralegal's task discussed at the beginning of this chapter, it is practical and advisable to follow this procedure:

1. Determine the state of incorporation of each corporation whose incorporators, shareholders, or directors must take some action. Obtain a copy of the corporate statutes of each state involved. Corporate statutes are usually printed in book form. They can be found at the law firm or corporation law department for which you work, at the local law school library, or at the county law library, or they can be requested directly from the secretary of state. Prentice-Hall and other legal publishers have produced multiple-volume looseleaf services, which include the corporate statutes of all the states, plus other related statutes. A few states print simplified, shortened versions of their corporate statutes, but a short version may omit important details. Be sure to obtain a full and complete copy of the statutes. Having incomplete or partial information is dangerous.

2. Obtain copies of each corporation's articles of incorporation and bylaws. Remember, these corporate documents should be kept in the corporation's minute book. You may have to contact an individual at the corporation to obtain copies. Or, if your office has previously performed legal services for the corporation, you may already have copies in your office files, or you may have the actual minute book.

3. Maintain access to form books and materials previously prepared by colleagues and other legal professionals, as well as your own previous work. Several legal publishers—including Prentice-Hall Information Services, West Publishing Company, Clark Boardman Callaghan, and Matthew Bender & Co.—offer manuals, guidebooks, and other legal publications that contain examples of minutes of meetings, notices and waivers of notice, proxies, and written consents and resolutions authorizing all types of corporate actions. In addition, you should maintain your own file of sample documents and materials produced in your work or gathered from other sources.

7–1

After the corporation's existence begins, usually upon the filing of the articles of incorporation, the corporation is considered a separate legal entity. The corporation is then required to approve all corporate actions of the incorporators, shareholders, and directors through meetings held by each of these corporate groups. Corporate actions are approved by these corporate groups at one of the following types of meetings: organizational, annual, and special or regular. The organizational meeting is held either immediately before or after the corporation's existence begins. It is held by either the incorporators or the initial board of directors (if they are named in the articles of incorporation). Shareholders' meetings allow the shareholders to participate in the operation and management of the corporation, even though they have no control over the day-to-day management of the business. The directors, through their meetings, oversee the daily affairs of the corporation by electing officers.

7–2

The organizational meeting is held by either the incorporators or the initial board of directors, if they were named in the articles of incorporation. The business transacted at the organizational meeting depends on whether the incorporators or the initial directors hold the meeting. If the incorporators hold the meeting, generally, they will elect directors and adopt the corporation's bylaws, and the first meeting of the directors, often called the directors' organizational meeting, will immediately follow. At the directors' first meeting, officers are elected, stock subscriptions are accepted, stock is issued, bank accounts are authorized to be opened, the corporate seal and the form of stock certificate are adopted, and so on. As with shareholder and directors' meetings, the organizational meeting may be required to be held within the state of incorporation. Also, notice must be provided, and a quorum must be present for the conducting of business.

7–3

Most state statutes require only that the directors hold regular meetings or special meetings as needed, not annual meetings like the shareholders. Valid and proper meetings of the directors are held only when (1) proper and timely notice of the meeting has been sent or delivered to the directors (or the directors execute and deliver waivers of notice to the corporation or attend the meeting) and (2) a quorum is present at the meeting. Directors are not permitted to authorize anyone to vote in their place, because they have a fiduciary duty to represent the shareholders and act in the shareholders' best interests. Meetings of the directors may be held within or outside the state of incorporation. Unless a quorum is present at the meeting, no business should be transacted. A majority of the directors entitled to vote constitutes a quorum at directors' meetings, unless the articles of incorporation or the bylaws provide otherwise. Provisions for holding and conducting directors' meetings vary from state to state, and the statutes of the state of incorporation must always be reviewed before a meeting is held.

7–4

Changes in the corporate structure (e.g., merger, consolidation, liquidation, dissolution, or sale of substantially all the assets of the corporation) require the approval of the shareholders. But the most important matter decided by the shareholders is the election of directors, through which the shareholders maintain control of the corporation. Shareholders hold at least an annual meeting, and they may hold special meetings as the need for approval by the shareholders arises. Meetings of the shareholders may be held within or outside the state of incorporation. The holders of record on the record date are the shareholders entitled to receive notice of the meeting and to vote at the meeting. For a valid and proper meeting to be held, (1) notice of the meeting must be sent or delivered to all shareholders (unless a waiver of notice is executed and delivered to the corporation or the shareholder attends the meeting personally or sends a proxy), *and* (2) a quorum must be present. When a quorum is present at a meeting, the affirmative vote of a majority of the shares (*not* the shareholders) represented at the meeting is sufficient for approving and adopting proposals submitted for shareholder consideration. Provisions for holding and conducting shareholders' meetings vary from state to state, and the statutes of the state of incorporation must always be reviewed before a meeting is held.

7–5

The call and the notice of a meeting are not the same. The call of a meeting is the procedure followed by the person authorized in the corporation's bylaws to request that a meeting be held. The notice of a meeting is the written document sent by the person authorized in the corporation's bylaws to advise that a meeting has been scheduled.

Most state statutes permit the use of any means of communication (e.g., a conference telephone) to hold and conduct meetings of the board of directors, as long as all directors participating in the meeting can hear each other during the meeting.

Committees established by the board of directors must comply with the provisions (notice and waiver of notice, quorum and voting requirements, and actions without meeting) governing board of directors' meetings.

7–6

Documenting corporate actions taken at meetings of the incorporators, shareholders, or directors is often the responsibility of the corporate paralegal. Actions taken by these corporate groups are documented in the form of resolutions, which are adopted either at meetings or by written consent. Meeting minutes are a record of the procedures conducted and the resolutions adopted at meetings of the incorporators, shareholders, or directors. Most state statutes permit the approval of corporate actions by written consent, which is a written document evidencing the actions taken without the formality of holding a meeting. The obstacle to the adoption of corporate actions by written consent is that the consent must be unanimous; therefore, unless all shareholders or directors approve the corporate action, a meeting will have to be held.

7–7

The organization and maintenance of the corporation's minute book is generally the responsibility of the corporate paralegal. State statutes require that the corporation maintain corporate records, but they do not dictate the manner in which the records are to be kept. Logic and common sense should be your guidelines in organizing the minute book. Minute books are generally organized chronologically. The types of documents filed in the minute book include articles of incorporation; certificate of incorporation; subscription agreements; proofs of publication (if required by the statute); bylaws; notices and waivers of notice of meetings; minutes of the organizational, shareholders, and directors meetings; written consents of the incorporators, shareholders, and directors; resignations of directors and officers; proxies of the shareholders; and corporate filings made with the secretary of state.

7–8

An understanding of the statutory (state statutes) and practical requirements of the following activities is important: (1) determining which business activities require the approval of the incorporators, the shareholders, or the directors; (2) analyzing the procedures for holding meetings; and (3) documenting the actions taken at meetings. To perform these tasks, you need to have copies of the statutes of the corporation's state of incorporation, and the corporation's articles of incorporation and bylaws. You also need access to form books and other sample materials, which include examples and forms of minutes of meetings, notices and waivers of notice, proxies, and written consents and resolutions authorizing various corporate actions.

REVIEW GUIDE

Key Terms

Before proceeding, review the key terms listed below to be sure you understand each one. If necessary, read over the corresponding section of the chapter. When you are ready to test your understanding, answer the review questions.

corporate existence (p. 141)

corporate actions (p. 141)

directors' meetings (p. 143)

shareholders' meetings (p. 144)

organizational meetings (p. 144)

organize (p. 144)

incorporators' organizational meeting (p. 145)

directors' organizational meeting (p. 145)

annual meeting (p. 149)

special meetings (p. 149)

regular meetings (p. 149)

waiver of notice (p. 151)

quorum (p. 152)

majority (p. 152)

record date (p. 154)

holders of record (p. 154)

notice of meeting (p. 156)

proxy (p. 158)

proxyholder (p. 158)

general proxy (p. 158)

limited proxy (p. 158)

call of a meeting (p. 161)

conference telephone meetings (p. 162)

minute book (p. 163)

resolution (p. 164)

meeting minutes (p. 169)

written consent (p. 170)

Questions for Review and Discussion

1. How do you determine when the corporate existence begins for a corporation incorporated in your state?

2. What type of meeting is held by the incorporators?

3. If directors are not named in the articles of incorporation, when is the first meeting of the directors held?

4. Describe the types of corporate actions that require the approval of the shareholders.

5. Describe the types of corporate actions that require the approval of the directors.

6. What are the requirements for holding valid and proper meetings of the shareholders and directors of the corporation?

7. Who is entitled to receive notice of and vote at meetings of the shareholders?

8. What is the cure for not providing proper notice to the shareholders prior to a meeting?

9. How would you determine whether a greater-than-majority vote is required by the directors?

10. Why are directors not permitted to vote by proxy?

11. Describe the difference between a call of a meeting and notice of a meeting.

12. Under what circumstances may a directors' meeting be held by conference telephone?

13. In what form are the actions taken at a meeting adopted by the incorporators, shareholders, or directors?

14. How are resolutions adopted?

15. Describe the types of corporate documents that are included in a corporation's minute book.

Activities

1. Book Distributing Company is merging into Publishers, Inc. Assume that both these corporations were incorporated in your state. Using the corporate statutes of your state, prepare the proper documentation for the shareholders' and board of directors' meetings at which approval will be given for the merger of these two corporations. (*Hint:* Include in your documentation notices of both the shareholders' and the directors' meetings and the minutes of both meetings.)

2. Prepare a written consent of the board of directors electing George Washington, James Madison, and Abraham Lincoln as President, Secretary, and Treasurer, respectively, of President Club Corporation. Use provisions of the Model Act to prepare this consent.

3. Research the statutes of your state to find the requirements for holding meetings of the shareholders. You should determine the requirements for choosing the meeting location, setting the record date, providing notice, accepting proxies, determining whether a quorum is present to conduct business, and counting votes.

CHAPTER 8 Amendments to Articles of Incorporation and Bylaws

OUTLINE

8–1   Amendment to the Articles of Incorporation
       Board of Directors' Approval
       Limited Power of Board of Directors to Authorize Amendments
       Shareholders' Approval
       Preparation and Filing of Articles of Amendment
       Amendment Prior to Issuance of Shares
8–2   Postamendment Formalities
       Effectiveness of Amendment
       Postamendment Procedures
8–3   Restated Articles of Incorporation
8–4   Amendment to the Bylaws
8–5   Practical Considerations
       Articles of Amendment
       Restated Articles of Incorporation
       Amendment to the Bylaws

APPLICATIONS

While reviewing the corporation's articles of incorporation and all the amendments made to the articles over the past 35 years, the secretary of the corporation discovers that its articles of incorporation require that the corporation name six directors and its bylaws require that it name eight directors. It took the secretary several hours to review the articles because they had been amended nine times since its incorporation. Your supervising attorney asks you to recommend a way to cure the inconsistency between the corporation's articles of incorporation and its bylaws and to suggest an alternative to having the secretary perform the tedious task of reviewing the articles and all the amendments when a question arises in the future.

OBJECTIVES

Chapter 6 covered the activities and formalities necessary for filing the original articles of incorporation. After completing this chapter and the related questions and activities, you will understand the procedures involved in amending the articles of incorporation and bylaws of the corporation and will be able to:

1. Determine when an amendment to the articles of incorporation must be filed.
2. Decide whether the board of directors or the shareholders must approve an amendment to the articles of incorporation.
3. Draft resolutions approving an amendment to the articles of incorporation.
4. Gather all the information you need to file articles of amendment.
5. Learn when filed articles of amendment become effective.
6. Prepare restated articles of incorporation.

7. Draft resolutions approving a restatement to the articles of incorporation.
8. Decide whether the board of directors or the shareholders have authority to amend the bylaws.
9. Draft resolutions approving an amendment to the bylaws.

8–1   Amendment to the Articles of Incorporation

A corporation has the right, within statutory guidelines, to amend its articles of incorporation by adding a new provision, deleting a current provision, or modifying an existing provision.

Before the articles of incorporation are amended, the tax and legal aspects should be considered carefully, and the corporation's articles of incorporation and the state's corporate law should be reviewed to ensure that all proper steps are taken and that the corporation has the authority to make the amendment. Also, you should check the corporation's bylaws before the articles are amended to avoid any inconsistencies between these two corporate documents.

Some states' corporate laws specifically list some of the amendments that can be made to the articles of incorporation. These lists are partial and are not intended to be the only ways in which the articles may be amended. Any provision may be amended in the articles of incorporation as long as that provision could have been included in the original articles of incorporation.

Specifically, a corporation may want to amend its articles of incorporation for any of the following purposes (keep in mind that this list is *not* all-inclusive):

- Changing its corporate name.
- Changing its period of duration.
- Changing its corporate purposes.
- Increasing or decreasing its number of authorized shares or their par value.
- Changing par-value shares to shares without par value (and vice versa).
- Creating new classes of shares.
- Dividing classes of shares.
- Granting or denying preemptive rights to shareholders.
- Granting or denying cumulative voting for the election of directors.
- Creating or changing designations, preferences, limitations, or rights of its shares.

The reasons why a corporation would amend its articles vary greatly, as the business environment is a dynamic one in which new opportunities and new problems continually arise. The existing articles may expressly restrict the type of business in which the corporation may engage. For example, the articles may state that "X Corporation is formed to engage only in the manufacture of roller skates." Or the articles may restrict the corporation's ability to raise new capital through the issue and sale of corporate stock. For example, the articles may state "X Corporation has the authority to issue 100 shares of stock." Because the business environment is not static, X Corporation may find that it is no longer able to operate profitably in the roller skate business or that it needs to finance the modernization of its roller skate factory by selling additional stock. In both of these situations, X Corporation would want to amend its articles of incorporation. Otherwise, it might soon find

PARALEGALERT!

A careful review of the state's corporate statutes and the corporation's articles of incorporation and bylaws must be made before the corporation's articles of incorporation are amended.

itself at a significant disadvantage relative to its competitors.

Corporations are creatures of the states in which they are incorporated. The method of amending the articles is therefore dictated by the state statutes. If a Florida corporation, Josephine's Poodle Parlor, Inc., desires to amend its articles, it must comply with Florida's state statutes governing corporations. What about a Florida corporation named Penny's Poodle Emporium, Inc., which is also registered to do business as a foreign corporation in ten other states? Would the amendment process be hopelessly complicated by the need to comply with the laws of all ten states? Not at all. The corporation is required to comply with the laws of the state in which it was incorporated. The topic of foreign corporations is discussed in much greater detail in Chapter 9.

For our purposes here, we will refer to the corporation's charter or incorporation document as the "articles of incorporation." Some states refer to this document as the "articles of incorporation," and others call it the "certificate of incorporation."

Board of Directors' Approval

The corporate laws of several states permit the corporation's board of directors to adopt certain amendments without obtaining shareholder approval. These amendments are usually considered routine—part of corporate housekeeping—and include amendments accomplishing the following:

- Extending a corporation's duration.
- Deleting the names and addresses of initial directors.
- Deleting the names and addresses of the initial registered agent and office (as long as a current agent and office are on file).
- Increasing, reducing, or eliminating the par value of the stock (discussed in Chapter 10).
- Canceling the authorization for a class of stock that has not yet been issued.
- Substituting one corporate designator for another in the corporation's name.
- Adding, deleting, or changing a geographical reference in the corporation's name.
- Any other changes specifically authorized by the articles of incorporation.

To approve an amendment to the articles of incorporation, the board of directors adopts a resolution approving such amendment at a duly called and convened *meeting* of the board of directors or by *written consent* of all members of the board, as permitted by the state's corporate laws. In Figure 8–1 is an example of resolutions of a board of directors approving an amendment to the articles of incorporation.

Figure 8–1   Resolutions of the Board of Directors

RESOLVED, that Article I of the Articles of Incorporation of World Travel Corporation be amended to read as follows:

"The name of the Corporation is World Travel Limited."

FURTHER RESOLVED, that the officers of the Corporation are hereby authorized to prepare, execute, and file Articles of Amendment with the Corporation Division of the State of Ohio.

PARALEGALERT!

When a corporation has decided to change its name, you must verify that the new name is available for use in the state. The procedure for verifying the availability of the new corporation name is the same as for checking availability prior to incorporation, as discussed in Chapter 6. A few states would allow World Travel Corporation and World Travel Limited to be used by two separate corporations, but most states would find the names deceptively similar and would not allow two separate corporations to use them.

Limited Power of Board of Directors to Authorize Amendments

Although the board of directors appears to wield extensive powers, most of these powers relate to the day-to-day management of the corporation. The board of directors serves at the pleasure of the shareholders. Remember that the shareholders—not the directors—are the owners of the corporation. Because the directors are elected to oversee the management of the corporation, they cannot authorize measures that would substantially alter the nature of the corporation itself. For instance, they cannot decide to shut down the corporation's factory or sell all of its assets without the express consent of the shareholders. The situation is somewhat different in small, privately held companies in which the shareholders also serve as directors. But even in such companies, the shareholders must formally approve board action and must do so in their capacity as shareholders.

The powers of the board of directors are ultimately limited by state law, regardless of how much discretion is given them by the shareholders. For example, the articles of incorporation may give authority to the directors to sell all the corporation's assets without the consent of the shareholders. If this authority contradicts the authority given to the board by state law, the action is not permitted.

Shareholders' Approval

To approve any amendment to the articles of incorporation, most states' corporate laws require the affirmative vote of the holders of a majority of the shares entitled to vote. In other words, a **majority vote** is required to amend the articles. However, the articles may provide that a higher percentage of the shares than required by the state's corporate laws must vote in favor of any amendment. For example, a provision in the articles of incorporation might require a **greater-than-majority vote** to approve amendments.

If an amendment affects the rights of shareholders of a particular class of stock, those shareholders must approve the amendment even if they would not otherwise have been entitled to vote on such matters.

The shareholders entitled to vote on any amendment do so by adopting a resolution approving such amendment at a duly called and convened *meeting* or by *written consent*, as permitted by the state's corporate laws. In Figure 8–2 is a resolution of shareholders approving an amendment to the articles of incorporation.

Figure 8–2 Resolution of the Shareholders

RESOLVED, that the number of authorized shares of the Corporation shall be increased and that Article IV of the Articles of Incorporation of the Corporation shall be amended to read as follows:

> "The number and class of shares that the Corporation shall have the authority to issue is 100,000 shares of Common Stock."

To reiterate, the shareholders' approval is required for major decisions affecting the operation of the business, such as the sale of all the corporation's assets. But what if the corporation decided to discontinue its business altogether? Suppose that the Wizard Toy Corporation decides that it wants to stop producing toys and instead shift to a more profitable business, such as recycling aluminum cans. Even though the prospects for this business are promising, the directors could not authorize such a change in business without the consent of the shareholders. As the owners of the corporation, the shareholders will be affected by the change. Their financial stake in the corporation is at risk; the new business may turn out not to be profitable.

Preparation and Filing of Articles of Amendment

After the amendment has been approved by either the board of directors or the shareholders, **articles of amendment** must be prepared, executed, and filed with the secretary of state of the state of incorporation. The information required to be contained in the articles of amendment is spelled out in the state's corporate laws. It generally includes:

- Name and registered office of the corporation.
- Text of amendment adopted by the corporation.
- Manner in which the amendment was adopted:
  - Whether by the board of directors or the shareholders.
  - Whether at a meeting or by written consent.

Before you begin to draft the amendment, you will need to obtain the information to be included in the amendment itself. You should attempt to ascertain what the corporation expects to gain from the amendment. You should also determine when the corporation wants the amendment to become effective. By insisting that the corporation specify the effective date, you can avoid potentially embarrassing and costly problems. Suppose that the Zippo Gadget Corporation wishes to amend its articles to secure a certain tax benefit that will no longer be available at the end of the current fiscal year. The Zippo officers would not be pleased to learn that you had failed to file the amendment before the end of the year. Their failure to tell you when the amendment should be filed would be irrelevant; they would focus on the tax benefit they had lost and on your failure to secure it. Consequently, you must take the initiative and contact the Zippo officers as soon as you receive the assignment. You must ask the appropriate questions, because the Zippo officers may not know what information you need to file the articles of amendment.

When drafting the amendment, you should include the corporation's name, the text of the amendment itself, the effective date of the amendment, and a statement that the amendment was approved by the shareholders. The amendment will also have to be executed by an officer of the corporation, such as the president or vice president. See Figure 8–3, which shows the form in which articles of amendment would be prepared for a Pennsylvania corporation.

PARALEGALERT!

After the shareholders of a corporation have approved an amendment to the articles of incorporation, the board of directors will authorize the appropriate officers of the corporation to prepare, execute, and file the articles of amendment with the secretary of state.

PARALEGALERT!

Most state corporation divisions offer preprinted forms of articles of amendment, which contain all the information required by that state's corporate laws. The forms are generally provided free of charge and can be ordered by telephone or by written request. Also, independent stationery suppliers or printers provide preprinted forms for a nominal fee. Most states accept articles of amendment that are not on preprinted forms (see Figure 8–3), as long as all required information is included.

Figure 8–3   Articles of Amendment, Pennsylvania Corporation

**Articles of Amendment
Domestic Business Corporation**

In compliance with the requirements of 15 Pa.C.S. §1915, the undersigned business corporation desires to amend its articles of incorporation and hereby states:

1. The name of the Corporation is Grant Foundation, Inc.
2. The address of the Corporation's registered office in the Commonwealth of Pennsylvania is 135 America Street, Pittsburgh, Pennsylvania, 15230, Allegheny County.
3. The statute under which the Corporation was incorporated is the Business Corporation Law of 1988.
4. The original date of its incorporation is June 14, 1990.
5. The amendment shall be effective upon the filing of these Articles of Amendment.
6. The amendment was adopted by the shareholders pursuant to 15 Pa.C.S. §1914(a) and (b).
7. The amendment adopted by the Corporation is set forth in full as follows:

RESOLVED, that the number of authorized shares of the Corporation shall be increased and that Article IV of the Articles of Incorporation of the Corporation shall be amended to read as follows:

"The number and class of shares that the Corporation shall have the authority to issue is 100,000 shares of Common Stock."

IN WITNESS WHEREOF, the undersigned Corporation has caused these Articles of Amendment to be signed by a duly authorized officer this 11th day of May, 1995.

GRANT FOUNDATION, INC.

By _____
President

PARALEGALERT!

Besides shares not having been issued before articles of amendment are filed, officers of the corporation may not have been elected. In this case, the incorporators or a member of the initial board of directors can prepare, execute, and file the articles of amendment.

Amendment Prior to Issuance of Shares

Most state's corporate laws have established a special procedure for amending the articles of incorporation before shares have been issued. These provisions usually state that an amendment to the articles may be adopted by the incorporators or by the initial board of directors named in the articles of incorporation.

8–2   Postamendment Formalities

When the articles of amendment are filed with the state's corporation division, they become a **document of public record,** just as the articles of incorporation are. For a fee (set, for corporation documents, by the state's corporation division), any person may obtain a copy of any document of public record. This accessibility can be useful to persons who wish to purchase shares of stock in the corporation or to do business with the corporation. Because the articles represent the "constitution" of the corporation, a prospective investor can assess whether the structure of the corporation's decision-making process is to his or her liking. The articles can also provide clues to the extent of influence an outside investor can expect to have on corporation decisions.

Alley v. Miramon
Goodwyne v. Moore

As mentioned in this chapter, a corporation may change its name upon the approval of the shareholders and the board of directors. The corporation accomplishes a name change by amending its articles of incorporation. A change in a corporation's name does *not*, however, change anything about the corporation except its name. The identity, property, rights, and liabilities remain unchanged when a corporation changes its name. If Pamela Jones changes her name to Pamela Smith, she is not transformed into another person merely because she changes her name. She continues to own the same property, her liabilities remain due and payable, and her social security number does not change. She is the same person before and after she changes her name. *Alley v. Miramon*, 614 F.2d 1372 (5th Cir. 1980), emphasizes that this is also true for the corporation.

In *Alley v. Miramon* the shareholders and directors amended the articles of incorporation and changed the corporation's name from Maison Miramon to Greenbriar Nursing Home, Inc. The court held in this case that "the change of a corporation's name is not a change of the identity of a corporation and has no effect on the corporation's property, rights, or liabilities." In addition, the court determined that any equity interest in a successor corporation is not divested merely upon the change of a corporation's name.

In another case, *Goodwyne v. Moore*, 316 S.E.2d 601 (Ga. App. 1984), the court held that the procedure of changing a corporation's name "does not cause a new corporation to come into 'existence'."

Effectiveness of Amendment

In most states, the amendment to the articles of incorporation is effective upon the issuance of a **certificate of amendment** by the state's corporation division. In some states, the amendment is effective upon the filing of the amendment, and in a very few states, the amendment is effective at a later date specified in the articles of amendment.

Postamendment Procedures

All documents relating to the amendment should be filed in the corporation's minute book. These documents include the actions of the board of directors and the shareholders approving the amendment and the certificate of amendment received from the state's corporation division showing evidence that articles of amendment were filed.

Only a few states require publication of the filing of articles of amendment to notify the public and the legal community of the action taken by the corporation. The publication is in the form of an advertisement setting forth the corporation's name and the reason for filing articles of amendment. It is the same type of advertisement that is required when articles of incorporation are filed, as discussed in Chapter 6. After the advertising has been completed, a **proof of publication** will be issued by the publisher of the legal journal or other publication, which will evidence that the advertisement or legal notice was placed by the corporation. This proof of publication should be filed in the corporation's minute book.

Once the articles have been amended, the corporation may be required to notify certain organizations of the amendment. First, a letter and a copy of the amendment should be sent to the Internal Revenue Service, especially if the corporation is a special type of corporation (e.g., a Subchapter S corporation). Second, if the corporation's stock is publicly traded on a major stock exchange (e.g., New York Stock Exchange, American Stock Exchange), you may have to file a notification with that exchange. Third, it may be necessary to contact state or local licensing agencies. Fourth, copies of the articles of amendment must be filed with the secretaries of state of the states in which the corporation does business.

8–3   Restated Articles of Incorporation

Over a period of years the original articles of incorporation may be amended several times. Determining the current provisions requires a careful examination of all amendments to the articles of incorporation, which could be an enormous task. In addition, having several amendments can add considerably to the expense of retrieving certified copies of the articles—used for corporate financings and for registering to do business in other states—from the state's corporation division. The alternative is to consolidate the original articles of incorporation with all amendments into one new document, which replaces the original articles and all amendments. This new document is called the **restated articles of incorporation.**

The state's corporate laws must be examined to see whether the statute authorizes a restatement of the articles of incorporation. Some states leave the task of preparing a restatement to the state's corporation division, and other states give the responsibility to the corporation itself.

Either the board of directors or the shareholders must approve the restatement of the articles of incorporation, by adopting a resolution approving such action at a duly called and convened meeting or by written consent, as permitted by the state's corporate laws. In Figure 8–4 is an example of a resolution of the shareholders of a corporation when the articles are being amended *and* restated. Shareholder approval is required only when an amendment to the articles of incorporation is being made at the same time as the restatement of the articles of incorporation and all amendments thereto.

The restated articles must include the name of the corporation, the date of adoption, and the text of the restated articles. See Figure 8–4. The directors can approve the restated articles only if there are no substantive changes that could be considered actual amendments. The person drafting the restated articles must be careful not to alter the articles themselves. Otherwise, the approval of the shareholders will have to be obtained. Suppose that the Pyramid Sales Corporation wishes to restate its articles because no one really knows what the articles say after the numerous amendments. The paralegal will, in most cases, be given the task of sifting through the amendments and determining what changes have been made to the original articles. It would not be surprising to find that some articles had been amended several times. Once the cumulative effects of the amendments have been assessed, however, the job of drafting the restated articles is much easier.

8–4   Amendment to the Bylaws

As we already discussed in Chapter 6, the **bylaws** of a corporation are the rules and regulations by which the corporation governs its internal affairs and operations. Bylaws are not a matter of public record; that is, they are not filed with any

Figure 8–4   Resolution of the Shareholders to Amend and Restate the Articles of Incorporation

RESOLVED, that the Articles of Incorporation of the Corporation are hereby amended and restated in their entirety and shall read in full as set forth below:

**Amended and Restated
Articles of Incorporation**

1.   The name of the Corporation is Grant Foundation, Inc. (the "Corporation").
2.   The address of the Corporation's registered office in the Commonwealth of Pennsylvania is 135 America Street, Pittsburgh, Pennsylvania, 15230, Allegheny County.
3.   There shall be no cumulative voting in the election of directors.
4.   The number and class of shares that the Corporation shall have the authority to issue is 100,000 shares of Common Stock.
5.   The name and address of the incorporator is:

Sylvia Kramer   1000 Public Street
                           Pittsburgh, Pennsylvania 15219

IN WITNESS WHEREOF, the undersigned Corporation has caused these Amended and Restated Articles of Incorporation to be signed by a duly authorized officer this 8th day of September, 1994.

GRANT FOUNDATION, INC.

By _____
   President

governmental agency. They are therefore generally easy to amend because no filing must be made, such as the filing of articles of amendment that is required when a change is made to the articles of incorporation.

The authority to alter, amend, repeal, or adopt a new set of bylaws is provided in the corporation's articles of incorporation or in the bylaws themselves. You should examine the articles of incorporation and the appropriate provision of the bylaws to determine whether the authority to alter, amend, repeal, or adopt new bylaws has been given to the board of directors or the shareholders of the corporation.

If the board of directors has been given the authority to amend the bylaws, it should adopt a resolution setting forth the amendment to be made to the bylaws. This resolution may be adopted at a duly called and convened meeting of the board of directors or by written consent, as permitted by the state's corporate laws. If the shareholders have been given the authority to amend the bylaws, the same procedure for adopting a resolution setting forth the amendment should be followed. See Figure 8–5 for an example of a resolution that might be adopted by either the board of directors or the shareholders.

More than one provision may be amended at one time, any number of provisions may be repealed or altered, or an entirely new set of bylaws may be adopted. In general, anything may be added to the bylaws by amendment that could have been included in the bylaws originally, provided the provision does not conflict with the articles of incorporation or the state's corporate laws.

PARALEGALERT!

After any provision of the bylaws has been amended, you should indicate on the copy of the bylaws the amendment and the date it was approved. This will help prevent mistakes when the bylaws are referred to in the future. The bylaws are kept in the corporation's minute book.

Figure 8–5   Resolution of the Board of Directors or the Shareholders to Amend the Bylaws

> RESOLVED, that Section 3.4 of the Bylaws of the Corporation be amended to read as follows:
>
> > "Section 3.4. The number of directors shall be not less than three nor more than ten. The first Board shall consist of three directors. Thereafter, within the limits above specified, the number of directors shall be determined by resolution by the Board of Directors or by the shareholders at the annual meeting."

8–5   Practical Considerations

Amending and restating the articles of incorporation and amending the bylaws of a corporation are relatively simple procedures. But be aware of the important distinction between these two documents: the articles of incorporation are a public document on file with the secretary of the state, and the bylaws are an internal company document used by the officers and directors for guidance in operating and managing the corporation.

Outlined in this section are some of the specific responsibilities that the paralegal might be called on to handle when a corporation amends articles, restates articles, or amends bylaws. For drafting tips, see Figure 8–6.

Articles of Amendment

- Review the corporation's articles of incorporation and bylaws and the state's corporate law to determine the legal aspects of amending the corporation's articles of incorporation.

Figure 8–6   Drafting Tips for Amendments

Amending the Articles of Incorporation

- Draft the amendment so that it is clear that it is changing the existing articles. Include a statement that the shareholders wish to change, for example, Article IV of the articles of incorporation. Then insert the language of the article as it will read when amended. (See Figure 8–3.)

- Make clear the effective date of the amendment.

- Be sure that the article as amended does not violate the state statute.

Amending the Bylaws

- Draft the amendment so that it is clear that it is changing the existing bylaws. Include a statement that the directors (or shareholders) of the corporation wish to change, for example, Section 3.4 of the bylaws. Then insert the language of the section as it will be after the desired amendment. (See Figure 8–5.)

- Make sure that the amendment is consistent with the articles of incorporation of the corporation.

- Be sure that the bylaw as amended does not violate the state statute.

- Determine whether board of directors' or shareholders' approval is required for amending the articles of incorporation.
- If shareholders' approval is required, determine whether a majority or greater-than-majority vote is required for approving the amendment.
- Gather from your client all necessary information for completing the articles of amendment.
- Draft the appropriate board of directors' or shareholders' resolutions for approving the amendment.
- Prepare the articles of amendment for filing with the state's corporation division.
- Determine the fee for filing the articles of amendment.
- Ascertain whether any other documents, besides the articles of amendment, must be filed with the state's corporation division.
- Transmit all appropriate documents and the filing fee to the state's corporation division.
- Determine whether your state requires publication of the filing of the articles of amendment.
- File in the corporation's minute book all board of directors' or shareholders' actions approving the amendment, the articles of amendment, the certificate of amendment, and proofs of publication (if required).

Restated Articles of Incorporation

- Obtain a copy of the original articles of incorporation and all amendments filed to date.
- Ascertain whether the articles are being amended as well as restated.
- Review your state's corporate law and determine the procedure for restating the articles of incorporation.
- Draft the appropriate board of directors' or shareholders' resolutions approving the restatement of the articles of incorporation.
- Draft restated articles of incorporation.
- Determine the fee for filing restated articles of incorporation.
- Ascertain whether any other documents, besides the restated articles of incorporation, must be filed with the state's corporation division.
- Transmit all appropriate documents and the filing fee to the state's corporation division.
- Determine whether your state requires publication of the filing of the restated articles of incorporation.
- File in the corporation's minute book all board of directors' or shareholders' actions approving the restatement, the restated articles of incorporation, the certificate of restatement, and proofs of publication (if required).

Amendment to the Bylaws

- Review the articles of incorporation and the bylaws of the corporation to determine if the board of directors or the shareholders have the authority to amend the bylaws.
- Draft the appropriate board of directors' or shareholders' resolutions approving the amendment to the bylaws.
- Physically indicate the amendment to the bylaws on the copy of the bylaws that is in the corporation's minute book.

SUMMARY

8–1

Tax and legal aspects must be carefully considered prior to amending a corporation's articles of incorporation. The statutes of the state of incorporation must be reviewed to ensure that all steps for amending the articles of incorporation are properly taken. Either the board of directors or the shareholders must approve the amendment. Articles of amendment are prepared and executed by an appropriate officer (usually the president or vice president) of the corporation and then are filed with the state's corporation division.

8–2

Generally, an amendment to the articles of incorporation is effective upon the filing of the articles of amendment with the state's corporation division. The board of directors' or shareholders' approval and all documents prepared and filed in connection with the amendment are filed in the corporation's minute book. Some states require the advertisement of the amendment; proofs of publication provided by the publisher are also filed in the corporation's minute book.

8–3

When, over time, several amendments have been made to the articles of incorpo-

ration, the corporation may restate its articles of incorporation, consolidating the original articles of incorporation and all amendments into one new document. The corporation may decide to amend the articles at the same time the articles are being restated. If no amendment is being made to the articles, only the board of directors' approval is required for the restatement of the articles.

8–4

Since a corporation's bylaws are not a public document, it is less time-consuming and less costly to amend. Either the board of directors or the shareholders must approve an amendment to the bylaws. Anything may be added to the bylaws by amendment that could have been included in the original bylaws.

8–5

The paralegal's role in amending or restating the articles of incorporation or amending the bylaws of the corporation can be quite extensive. It is important to be sure that all proper steps are taken by the corporation to effect any amendments.

REVIEW GUIDE

Key Terms

Before proceeding, review the key terms listed below to be sure you understand each one. If necessary, read over the corresponding section of the chapter. When you are ready to test your understanding, answer the review questions.

majority vote (p. 182)
greater-than-majority vote (p. 182)
articles of amendment (p. 183)
document of public record (p. 184)
certificate of amendment (p. 185)
proof of publication (p. 185)
restated articles of incorporation (p. 186)
bylaws (p. 186)

Questions for Review and Discussion

1. What should you review before drafting an amendment to a corporation's articles of incorporation?

2. List some of the reasons for a corporation to file articles of amendment.

3. Describe the instances in which shareholder approval would *not* be required to amend the articles of incorporation.

4. Where would you find a provision requiring a greater-than-majority vote of the shareholders to amend the articles of incorporation?

5. Who generally executes and arranges for the filing of articles of amendment?
6. What role might the incorporators or the initial board of directors play in amending the articles of incorporation?
7. Name the documents that should be filed in a corporation's minute book after articles of amendment are filed.
8. When should the articles of incorporation be restated?
9. Explain the difference between amending and restating the articles of incorporation.
10. Why is it relatively easy to amend a corporation's bylaws?
11. Explain who has the authority to amend a corporation's bylaws.

Activities

1. Review your state's corporation law and determine what amendments to a corporation's articles of incorporation would not require approval by the shareholders.
2. Following the requirements of your state's corporate law, draft articles of amendment for Bond Travel, Inc., which desires to grant preemptive rights to its shareholders.
3. Draft resolutions for Genesis Book Corporation, which desires to change its name to Perrigo Books Limited and to restate its articles of incorporation. Explain who should adopt these resolutions.

CHAPTER 9 Qualification of Corporations in Foreign Jurisdictions

OUTLINE

9–1   Foreign Corporations
       Qualifying to Do Business
       What Constitutes Doing Business

9–2   Certificate of Authority
       Application for Certificate of Authority
       Filing Requirements
       Board of Directors' Approval
       Corporate Name
       Registered Address and Agent

9–3   Postqualification Requirements
       Taxes and Annual Reports
       Amendment to the Certificate of Authority
       Merger of the Foreign Corporation
       Legal Advertising

9–4   Penalties for Failure to Qualify

9–5   Withdrawal of Authority

9–6   Revocation of Authority

9–7   Practical Considerations

APPLICATIONS

You incorporated Trucking Service Corporation in the state of Delaware in 1985. At that time your research concluded that it was advantageous for Trucking Service Corporation to incorporate in Delaware because of certain tax aspects, provisions of the statute governing directors' and officers' liability, and the ease of filing corporate documents in that state. And, most important, the company would operate its business from a building it owned in Wilmington, Delaware, where more than 25 employees would work.

Trucking Service Corporation now desires to purchase a building and trucks and to employ several employees in Florida. Your supervising attorney has asked you to research the corporate statutes of Florida to determine whether the business to be conducted by Trucking Service Corporation would require it to register or qualify in that state and, if so, to summarize the requirements (including filing and postfiling requirements) of the Florida corporate statutes.

The president and secretary of Trucking Service Corporation will be visiting your office next week seeking advice and recommendations on the process of registering to do business in Florida and the requirements the company may be subject to if it does register to do business in Florida.

OBJECTIVES

This chapter will present the factors to be considered by a corporation when deciding whether to qualify to do business in a foreign jurisdiction. It will also cover the statutory requirements imposed upon foreign corporations. After completing Chapter 9, you will be able to:

1. Distinguish between a domestic corporation and a foreign corporation.
2. Understand what constitutes doing business, or transacting business, by a corporation.
3. Prepare and file an application for certificate of authority.
4. Determine whether a corporate name is appropriate for use by a foreign corporation.
5. Understand the role of service companies in representing a foreign corporation.
6. Understand the state requirements that must be fulfilled by foreign corporations, including the following:
   - Preparing and filing annual reports.
   - Paying franchise and income taxes.
   - Amending the certificate of authority.
   - Notifying the foreign state of a merger of the corporation.
   - Arranging for legal advertisement upon qualifying to do business.
7. Prepare and file an amended certificate of authority.
8. Understand that penalties are imposed on corporations that fail to qualify.
9. Prepare and file an application for certificate of withdrawal.
10. Understand why a state revokes a foreign corporation's certificate of authority.

9–1   Foreign Corporations

As we have previously discussed, the moment a corporation's existence begins (usually upon the filing of articles of incorporation), the corporation becomes a separate legal entity and is authorized to transact business within the state of incorporation. The state of incorporation is called the **home state** or the **state of domestication,** and a corporation is considered a **domestic corporation** by the state of incorporation. For example, if ABC Trucking Corporation were incorporated in Montana, the State of Montana would consider ABC Trucking a domestic corporation. And Montana would be ABC Trucking's home state or state of domestication.

Qualifying to Do Business

Although the corporation does not legally exist beyond the boundaries of its state of incorporation, not every corporation restricts its business to its home state. Therefore, the corporation must register or **qualify** in states other than its home state if it desires to transact business beyond its home state boundaries. States other than the home state, usually called **foreign jurisdictions,** consider the corporation a **foreign corporation.** In other words, a corporation is a foreign corporation in every state except its home state, or state of incorporation.

The Model Act, in Section 15.01(a), like most state statutes, provides that "a foreign corporation may not transact business in this state until it obtains a certificate of authority from the secretary of state." Most state statutes have similar provisions. Every state has adopted statutes regarding the qualification of corporations to transact business within that state's boundaries. The corporation is required to obtain a certificate of authority from the secretary of state or to comply with a similar registration procedure. No state restricts corporations from entering and doing business in the state, except under circumstances in which domestic corporations in that state are similarly restricted. For example, a Mississippi corporation that was organized to conduct riverboat gambling on the Mississippi River may be precluded from doing business in a state that does not allow riverboat gambling.

When a corporation is qualified to do business in a particular state, that state then has the authority to regulate and tax that corporation (now considered a foreign corporation), just as the state has the power to regulate and tax domestic corporations.

A professional corporation may have to qualify in a foreign jurisdiction, just as a business corporation may. In addition, certain shareholders, directors, officers, or employees of the professional corporation may be required to register or obtain a license to practice in a foreign state. For example, a lawyer, doctor, or other professional generally must obtain a license to practice his or her profession in that state. This requirement applies whether the professional is operating as a professional corporation, in a partnership, or as a sole proprietor.

Prior to qualifying or registering to do business in any state, the corporation should consider certain factors. The attorney and the paralegal assisting the attorney will research the statutes of the state or states in which the corporation desires to do business and will evaluate the necessity and the requisites for qualifying to do business. The factors that a corporation should define and consider before qualifying to do business in a state include:

1. The nature of the corporation's business conducted in the state.
2. The foreign jurisdiction's definition of what constitutes doing business.
3. The cost of qualifying to do business, including the tax implications.
4. Penalties for transacting business within the state without having obtained the authority to do so.

The difficult decision to be made by the corporation is whether or not to qualify in a state. If the corporation is doing business in a state, it *must* register (or qualify) in that state. However, the definition of "doing business" is difficult and has been the cause of much litigation. Many states have defined "doing business" differently. Many questions about what constitutes doing business can be answered by researching and reviewing state judicial decisions.

The failure to qualify can lead to the imposition of penalties and sanctions, which we will discuss later in this chapter. Generally, any penalty imposed on a corporation must be revealed in applications that are filed in other states. This information may prejudice the corporation's attempt to register to do business in other states.

What Constitutes Doing Business

As we have already discussed, a corporation doing business in any state other than its state of incorporation must register or qualify to do business in that state. Determining whether a corporation is doing business in a particular state

PARALEGALERT!

A corporation does not necessarily have to have been incorporated abroad (e.g., in England, Germany, or Mexico) to be a foreign corporation. A corporation is considered a foreign corporation in *every state* except its home state.

PARALEGALERT!

Determining whether a corporation is doing business in a particular state can be difficult. Many would advise the following: When in doubt, qualify. But qualifying in any state should come only after careful research of the statutes and case law regarding the qualification of corporations.

requires research of the statutes of the state in which the corporation desires to do business. First, the corporation must decide the nature and extent of its activities in a particular state, and second, the corporation must determine whether those activities constitute doing business in the state.

Whether a corporation is considered to be doing business in a state is dictated by the nature and extent of the business being transacted. A corporation doing business in a state is (1) subject to taxation in that state, (2) subject to service of process and suit in that state, and (3) required to qualify or register to do business in that state. The business activities that would require the corporation to qualify would also subject it to taxation and service of process and suit.

States vary in specifying what they consider transacting business by corporations. Defining the activities that constitute transacting business is not as simple as it sounds. Some state statutes provide a list of the activities that constitute transacting business within that state. But Section 15.01(b) of the Model Act, which is set forth in Figure 9–1, lists those activities that do *not* constitute transacting business. Most states have adopted provisions similar to this section of the Model Act.

The courts often must determine whether a corporation is doing business in a particular state. *Legal Links*, p. 202, focuses on a case in which the court determined that a corporation's activities were insufficient to require the corporation to obtain a certificate of authority.

Figure 9–1   Section 15.01(b) of the Model Act

§15.01(b)   The following activities, among others, do not constitute transacting business within the meaning of subsection (a):

(1)   maintaining, defending, or settling any proceeding;

(2)   holding meetings of the board of directors or shareholders or carrying on other activities concerning internal corporate affairs;

(3)   maintaining bank accounts;

(4)   maintaining officers or agencies for the transfer, exchange, and registration of the corporation's own securities or maintaining trustees or depositories with respect to those securities;

(5)   selling through independent contractors;

(6)   soliciting or obtaining orders, whether by mail or through employees or agents or otherwise, if the orders require acceptance outside this state before they become contracts;

(7)   creating or acquiring indebtedness, mortgages, and security interests in real or personal property;

(8)   securing or collecting debts or enforcing mortgages and security interests in property securing debts;

(9)   owning, without more, real or personal property;

(10)   conducting an isolated transaction that is completed within 30 days and that is not in the course of repeated transactions of a like nature;

(11)   transacting business in interstate commerce.

9–2 Certificate of Authority

Application for Certificate of Authority

After a corporation decides that it must register or qualify to do business in a particular state, it is required to file an **application for certificate of authority** with the secretary of state in that state. Section 15.03(a) of the Model Act provides that "a foreign corporation may apply for a certificate of authority to transact business in this state by delivering an application to the secretary of state for filing."

States vary in the information they require to be provided in an application for certificate of authority. Section 15.03(a) of the Model Act provides that:

The application must set forth:

(1) the name of the foreign corporation or, if its name is unavailable for use in this state, a corporate name that satisfies the requirements of section 15.06;
(2) the name of the state or country under whose law it is incorporated;
(3) its date of incorporation and period of duration;
(4) the street address of its principal office;
(5) the address of its registered office in this state and the name of its registered agent at that office; and
(6) the names and usual business addresses of its current directors and officers.

Figure 9–2 is an example of an application for a certificate of authority. It has been prepared in accordance with the provisions of the Model Act. In this section we will discuss in greater detail the requirements for qualifying to do business in a foreign jurisdiction. Remember that you must always review the statutes of the foreign state to determine the requirements of that foreign state.

Filing Requirements

The most important task in evaluating the requirements for applying as a foreign corporation is the careful review of the applicable state statutes. The statutes covering corporations qualifying to do business as foreign corporations are usually included in the state's corporate statutes. You must be sure that all the provisions of the state statutes covering foreign corporations are met. For example, Travel Incorporated is a Delaware corporation; that is, it is incorporated in Delaware. Because of the nature of its business activities, it must now register to do business in New Jersey. The corporate statutes of New Jersey should be researched to determine what must be done to prepare and file the application to register to do business in New Jersey.

Many states require the submission of additional documents with the application for certificate of authority. For example, many states require evidence that the corporation is in **good standing** in the state of incorporation. Usually, a corporation in good standing is one that has not filed an application to merge, liquidate, or dissolve the corporation or one that has paid all taxes due to the state, or both. Upon written or telephone request to the secretary of state and payment of a fee, the secretary of state will issue a certificate evidencing that the corporation is in good standing. The certificate is usually called a **good standing certificate** or a **certificate of existence**. Section 15.03(b) of the Model Act requires that "the foreign corporation shall deliver with the completed application a certificate of existence (or a document of similar import) duly authenticated by the secretary of state or other official having custody of corporate records in the state or country under whose law it is incorporated." Only a few states do not require the submission of a good standing certificate (or certificate of existence) with an application for certificate of authority.

Figure 9–2 Application for Certificate of Authority

**Application for Certificate
of Authority of
Trucking Service Corporation**

The undersigned corporation, in order to transact business in the State of _____, under and pursuant to the provisions of Chapter 15 of the Model Business Corporation Act, does hereby certify that:

1. The name of the Corporation is TRUCKING SERVICE CORPORATION.

2. The Corporation was incorporated in Delaware.

3. The Corporation was incorporated on July 17, 1985, and its period of duration is perpetual.

4. The Corporation's principal office is 123 Fifth Avenue, Wilmington, Delaware 19888.

5. The Corporation's registered agent and office in the State of _____ is ABC Service Corporation, 456 Sixth Avenue, Anytown, _____ 19002.

6. The names and addresses of the Corporation's directors and officers are as follows:

        James Bond   President and Director
        123 Fifth Avenue
        Wilmington, Delaware 19888

        Steven Ford   Secretary, Treasurer, and Director
        123 Fifth Avenue
        Wilmington, Delaware 19888

        Charles Jones   Director
        123 Fifth Avenue
        Wilmington, Delaware 19888

    IN WITNESS WHEREOF, a duly authorized officer of the Corporation has executed this Application for Certificate of Authority this 12th day of June, 1995.

                    TRUCKING SERVICE CORPORATION

                    By _____
                            President

Good standing certificates are also required to be obtained in other circumstances. For example, when a corporation's stock or assets are sold, the buyer usually requires the corporation or the seller of the corporation's stock to obtain good standing certificates from the secretaries of state of the state of incorporation and all states in which the corporation is qualified to do business. This provides evidence to the buyer that the corporation has not elected to merge, liquidate, or dissolve the corporation. In addition, a good standing certificate evidences that the corporation's certificate of authority has not been revoked by a foreign state in which it is qualified to do business.

In addition, many states require the submission of a certified copy of the corporation's articles of incorporation with the application for certificate of authority. Upon written or telephone request to the secretary of state and payment of a fee, the secretary of state will send a certified copy of a corporation's articles of incorporation.

PARALEGALERT!

If a good standing certificate is required to be submitted with the application for certificate of authority and you fail to submit it, the application will be returned. You must then refile the application with all the proper documentation. Your omission will thus cause a delay in the filing of the qualification documents.

Generally, the state will first send an invoice for the photocopying and certification of the articles of incorporation. Upon receipt of payment, the secretary of state will forward the certified articles of incorporation to you. These certified articles are then filed with the application for certificate of authority in the foreign jurisdiction.

Typically, in an application for qualification as a foreign corporation, the items to be included in the filing package include the following: the application for certificate of authority, a good standing certificate (or certificate of existence), a check for the filing fee, and a cover letter that lists all the items being sent to the state. In some instances, certified articles of incorporation are required in lieu of the good standing certificate.

Upon receipt of the application for certificate of authority, with all the proper documentation and the filing fee required to be submitted with the application, the secretary of the foreign state will issue a **certificate of authority.** The corporation is then authorized to transact business within the foreign state. Section 15.05(a) of the Model Act provides that "a certificate of authority authorizes the foreign corporation to which it is issued to transact business in this state." Figure 9–3 is an example of a certificate of authority issued by the Office of the Secretary of State of the State of Illinois.

Board of Directors' Approval

The qualification of a corporation in a foreign jurisdiction imposes certain obligations on the corporation. For example, some states require that a foreign corporation file an annual report, pay tax based on income derived in that state, and amend its certificate of authority whenever it amends its articles of incorporation. Because of the obligations imposed on the corporation, approval by the corporation's board of directors should be obtained before the corporation qualifies to do business in any state.

The board of directors must adopt resolutions approving the preparation, execution, and filing of an application for certificate of authority in a particular state. Figure 9–4 is an example of such resolutions of the board of directors. The resolutions should authorize the corporation to qualify to do business in the foreign jurisdiction and should authorize the officers of the corporation to prepare, execute, and file the necessary documents to complete the qualification process.

Remember from our discussion in Chapter 7 that the board of directors would adopt these resolutions in one of the following two ways: (1) at a meeting of the board of directors, for which proper notice was sent and a quorum was present for the conducting of business, or (2) by unanimous written consent, executed by all directors of the corporation.

Figure 9–3 Certificate of Authority Issued by the State of Illinois

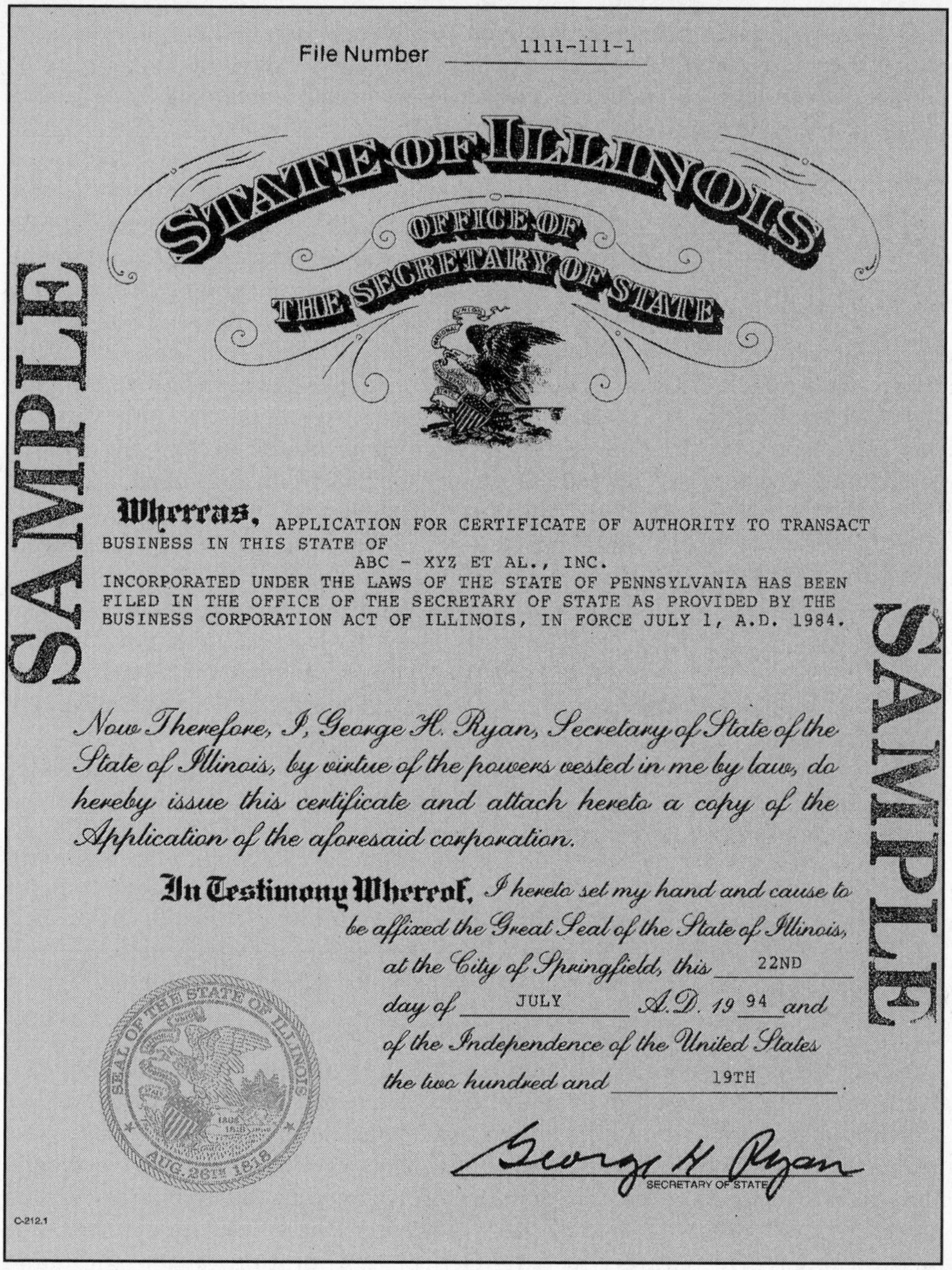

File Number 1111-111-1

STATE OF ILLINOIS

OFFICE OF

THE SECRETARY OF STATE

SAMPLE

Whereas, APPLICATION FOR CERTIFICATE OF AUTHORITY TO TRANSACT BUSINESS IN THIS STATE OF

ABC - XYZ ET AL., INC.

INCORPORATED UNDER THE LAWS OF THE STATE OF PENNSYLVANIA HAS BEEN FILED IN THE OFFICE OF THE SECRETARY OF STATE AS PROVIDED BY THE BUSINESS CORPORATION ACT OF ILLINOIS, IN FORCE JULY 1, A.D. 1984.

Now Therefore, I, George H. Ryan, Secretary of State of the State of Illinois, by virtue of the powers vested in me by law, do hereby issue this certificate and attach hereto a copy of the Application of the aforesaid corporation.

In Testimony Whereof, *I hereto set my hand and cause to be affixed the Great Seal of the State of Illinois, at the City of Springfield, this* 22ND *day of* JULY *A.D. 19*94 *and of the Independence of the United States the two hundred and* 19TH.

SEAL OF THE STATE OF ILLINOIS AUG. 26TH 1818

George H Ryan

SECRETARY OF STATE

SAMPLE

C-212.1

Figure 9–4 Resolutions of the Board of Directors Approving Qualification in Another State

RESOLVED, that the Corporation is authorized to qualify to do business as a foreign corporation under the laws of the State of ________________ ; and

FURTHER RESOLVED, that the proper officers of the Corporation be, and they hereby are, authorized to prepare, execute, and deliver to the Secretary of State of ________________ an application for certificate of authority and to prepare and file any and all other documents and to pay any fees and expenses charged in connection with the qualification of the corporation as a foreign corporation in the State of ________________ .

Corporate Name

A foreign corporation must comply with the foreign jurisdiction's statutes governing corporate names permitted to be used in that state. Essentially, most states require that foreign corporations meet the same requirements as corporations incorporated in that state (domestic corporations).

Generally, the requirements governing the use of corporate names by domestic corporations (those incorporated in the state) must be met by foreign corporations. First, the foreign corporation's name must include the word *corporation, incorporated, company,* or *limited* or an abbreviation of any of these words and may not imply that the corporation is organized for a purpose other than those permitted. And second, the corporate name of the foreign corporation may not be deceptively similar to that of a corporation incorporated or qualified to do business in that state. Section 4.01(b)(1) of the Model Act provides that "a corporate name must be distinguishable upon the records of the secretary of state from . . . a corporation incorporated or authorized to transact business in this state." Therefore, you must check the availability of the corporate name in the foreign state prior to submitting the application for certificate of authority.

If a corporate name is not available for use by a foreign corporation, the states have adopted a variety of provisions to resolve the conflict. A state will allow the foreign corporation to do one of the following:

1. Add a distinguishing word or words to the name of the foreign corporation, thus making it different from the name with which it conflicts.
2. Use a fictitious name when doing business within the foreign state.
3. Obtain approval from the corporation with the same or deceptively similar name.

Under the first option, the foreign corporation would be permitted to add a distinguishing word or words to make its corporate name different from another corporation incorporated or qualified in a state. For example, Creative Crafts, Inc. is a Georgia corporation that desires to qualify to do business in Pennsylvania. However, a corporation has already been incorporated in Pennsylvania with the name Creative Crafts, Inc. The secretary of state of Pennsylvania may grant permission to Creative Crafts, Inc. (the Georgia corporation) to use the name Creative Crafts of Pennsylvania, Inc. within Pennsylvania. The name under which it was incorporated in Georgia—Creative Crafts, Inc.—will not change, but it will be required to do business in Pennsylvania as "Creative Crafts of Pennsylvania."

A second alternative is for the foreign corporation to adopt a fictitious or assumed name under which it may transact business in that state. In this case, the corporation *must* use the fictitious name when transacting business in the foreign state. This option may not be so attractive when a corporation has built its reputation and business on its corporate name and now is restricted from using that name in the foreign state. Figure 9–5 is an example of a certificate of authority to transact business issued by the secretary of state of Illinois. In this case, the corporation's name, Medical Services, Inc., was unavailable for use in Illinois. Therefore, the corporation agreed to transact all business in Illinois under the assumed name of Medical Services Provider, Inc.

PARALEGALERT!

One of the first responsibilities of the paralegal is to verify that the corporate name is available for use in the foreign state. This is accomplished by calling the corporate division of the secretary of state's office in the foreign state and asking whether the name is available for use by a foreign corporation. Remember that most information provided by telephone is not guaranteed to be accurate or correct.

File Number _____23-456-7890_____

STATE OF ILLINOIS
OFFICE OF
THE SECRETARY OF STATE

Whereas, APPLICATION FOR CERTIFICATE OF AUTHORITY TO TRANSACT BUSINESS IN THIS STATE OF MEDICAL SERVICES, INC.

INCORPORATED UNDER THE LAWS OF THE STATE OF PENNSYLVANIA HAS BEEN FILED IN THE OFFICE OF THE SECRETARY OF THE STATE TO TRANSACT ALL BUSINESS IN ILLINOIS UNDER THE ASSUMED NAME OF
            MEDICAL SERVICES PROVIDER, INC.
AS PROVIDED BY THE "BUSINESS CORPORATION ACT" OF ILLINOIS, IN FORCE JULY 1, A.D. 1984.

Now Therefore, I, George H. Ryan, Secretary of State of the State of Illinois, by virtue of the powers vested in me by law, do hereby issue this certificate and attach hereto a copy of the Application of the aforesaid corporation.

In Testimony Whereof, *I hereto set my hand and cause to be affixed the Great Seal of the State of Illinois, at the City of Springfield, this* _____21ST_____ *day of* _____JULY_____ *A.D. 19* _92_ *and of the Independence of the United States the two hundred and* _____17TH_____.

_____
SECRETARY OF STATE

The third option is for the foreign corporation to obtain the approval of the corporation that has the same or a deceptively similar corporate name. The foreign corporation is required to submit documentation to the secretary of the foreign state, evidencing approval by the domestic or other foreign corporation of the use of their corporate name. Such documentation would consist of a letter from the corporation already incorporated or doing business in the foreign state, authorizing the foreign corporation to use the corporate name in that state.

Rock-Ola Manufacturing Corporation v. Wertz

Rock-Ola Manufacturing Corporation appealed a decision of the lower court, which had determined that Rock-Ola had failed to obtain a certificate of authority to transact business in Virginia. This decision precluded Rock-Ola from recovering a balance that it claimed was due for merchandise purchased by defendant Wertz.

Wertz contended that he was an agent of Rock-Ola. He repaired all Rock-Ola machines in Virginia, and he maintained servicemen in Virginia for that purpose. His contention that he was an agent of Rock-Ola was based on Rock-Ola's requirement of him to maintain a "clean, properly arranged and attractive showroom and office facilities at [Rock-Ola's] own expense." However, Rock-Ola had none of its money invested in Wertz's repair business, it shared none of Wertz's losses or profits, and it dictated none of the details of the repair operation.

Based on these and other facts of the case, the appeals court in *Rock-Ola Manufacturing Corporation v. Wertz*, 249 F.2d 813 (4th Cir., 1957), reversed the lower court's decision and held that all of Rock-Ola's activities in their totality "were not sufficient to subject the corporation to the qualification statute, and so, failure to qualify will not bar the corporation from maintaining this suit."

Registered Address and Agent

Every state requires that a foreign corporation maintain a **registered office** and, in most cases, a **registered agent** in the foreign state. Remember, as we discussed in Section 6–3 in Chapter 6, states require a corporation to maintain a registered office and registered agent to accept service of process or notice served upon the corporation. This requirement is the same for the foreign corporation. Section 15.07 of the Model Act provides that "each foreign corporation authorized to transact business in this state must continuously maintain in this state: (1) a registered office that may be the same as any of its places of business; and (2) a registered agent."

The registered office may be any physical location within the foreign state where the individual or entity named as registered agent may accept service of process or notice on behalf of the foreign corporation. If a registered office and a registered agent are not appointed by the foreign corporation in the application for certificate of authority, the foreign state will deny the application and return it until they are appointed. In some cases, after a registered address and agent have been appointed but have failed to serve in that capacity, the secretary of state of the foreign state will accept service of process on behalf of the corporation. The secretary of state will then send any service to the corporation at its principal place of business in the corporation's state of incorporation.

Like domestic corporations, foreign corporations are required to notify the secretary of the foreign state of any changes in the registered address or registered agent. According to the Model Act, Section 15.08, any foreign corporation may change its registered address and agent "by delivering to the secretary of state for filing a statement of change."

Even though a corporation may be required to qualify to do business in a particular state because of the nature of its business activities, it may have no office or personnel located within the state. Nevertheless, it must maintain a registered office and registered agent in the foreign state. To assist foreign corporations in this situation, **service companies**—CorpAmerica; Corporation Service Company; CT Corporation; Parasec, Incorporated; Prentice-Hall; and many other corporations and individuals—will serve as registered agent and provide a registered office in the foreign state. Of course, these service companies charge a fee for providing this service. Fees range from $75 to $175 a year for each corporation for which they provide the service.

9–3 Postqualification Requirements

After a foreign corporation has received the authority to transact business in the foreign state, it is entitled to the same rights and privileges as domestic corporations. On the other hand, it has also subjected itself to the regulations, reporting requirements, tax implications, duties, and responsibilities imposed on domestic corporations. In addition, the foreign corporation is also subject to the laws of its home state.

The numerous responsibilities of the foreign corporation in a foreign state may include preparing and filing annual reports, paying franchise and income taxes, amending the certificate of authority under certain circumstances, notifying the foreign state of a merger of the corporation, and arranging for legal advertisement upon qualifying to do business.

Because fees vary to a great degree among the states and are continually being increased, you must always confirm all filing fees with the secretary of state.

Taxes and Annual Reports

When a corporation qualifies to do business within a state, it thereby subjects itself to the laws of that state and agrees to pay taxes to and file annual or other reports in the foreign state.

Because of complexity of the state, city, and county tax laws with which a corporation may be required to comply, the following discussion will be general, providing only a basis for understanding the intricacies of the tax laws. The decision to qualify to do business in any state greatly depends on the tax laws or provisions of the state. Therefore, a tax lawyer or accountant is generally consulted before a corporation qualifies to do business in any state.

A foreign corporation *may* be subject to any one or all of the following types of taxes:

1. An **initial franchise tax** is imposed on the foreign corporation at the time of filing of the application for certificate of authority. This tax is generally calculated on the number of authorized shares of the corporation and may vary according to the par value of the authorized shares. Any amount of initial franchise tax due is in addition to the fee required for filing the application for certificate of authority. (Note: Many states have eliminated this calculation based on the par value of the shares. However, some states have not.)
2. An **annual franchise tax** imposed on the foreign corporation, like the initial franchise tax, is generally calculated on the authorized capital of the corporation. The amount of franchise tax due is usually calculated by a formula adopted by the state taxing authorities.
3. An **income tax** imposed on the corporation may be calculated on the dollar amount of revenues generated by sales or business conducted within the state, the value of property located in the state, the number of employees working in the state, or the type of business activities conducted within the state. You can assume that the states will impose on corporations the taxes that will generate the greatest amount of revenue for the state.

Section 16.22(a) of the Model Act provides that "each domestic corporation, and each foreign corporation authorized to transact business in this state,

Do not be concerned because you are not familiar with the statutes of every state regarding the qualification of corporations. Even if you work day in and day out with the statutes of a particular state, you should always rely on current research.

shall deliver to the secretary of state for filing an annual report." An **annual report** usually contains the name of the corporation, the state of incorporation, addresses of the registered and principal offices, names and business addresses of the directors and officers, a description of the corporation's business, and the total number of authorized and issued shares of the corporation. Most, but not all, states require corporations, including foreign corporations, to file annual reports with the state. Failure to file in states requiring an annual report may result in the revocation of that corporation's certificate of authority or loss of corporate status. In Section 9–6 we will discuss in greater detail the events that cause a revocation of certificate of authority.

Remember that when a corporation qualifies to do business in a foreign state, it is treated the same as any domestic corporation in that state. That is, both domestic and foreign corporations enjoy the same rights and privileges, and both must comply with the same statutes and regulations.

Amendment to the Certificate of Authority

When any change occurs to any of the information provided in the application for certificate of authority filed with the foreign state, the foreign corporation is required to amend its certificate of authority. An **application for amended certificate of authority** must be filed with the secretary of the foreign state. Upon the filing of an application for amended certificate of authority, the secretary of state will issue an **amended certificate of authority.** Figure 9–6 is an application for an amended certificate of authority. The application was prepared in accordance with the provisions of the Model Act. Figure 9–7 is a sample of a certificate of qualification (or amended certificate of authority) issued by the Secretary of State of California after a corporation changed its name. Note that this corporation was incorporated in Delaware and qualified to do business in California.

An amendment to a corporation's articles of incorporation will generally require the filing of an application for amended certificate of authority. For example, if Ambulatory Care Corporation, a Florida corporation, changes its name to Ambulance Service Corporation, it must file an amendment to its

Figure 9–6   Application for Amended Certificate of Authority

**Application for Amended Certificate
of Authority of
Trucking Service Corporation**

The undersigned corporation, in order to amend its authority to transact business in the State of _____, under and pursuant to the provisions of Chapter 15 of the Model Business Corporation Act, does hereby certify that:

1.   The name of the Corporation is TRUCKING SERVICE CORPORATION. The Corporation was incorporated in Delaware on July 17, 1985.
2.   The Corporation wishes to amend its certificate of authority to change its name to BIG RIG TRUCKING CORPORATION.

IN WITNESS WHEREOF, a duly authorized officer of the Corporation has executed this Application for Amended Certificate of Authority this 15th day of December, 1994.

TRUCKING SERVICE CORPORATION

By _____
President

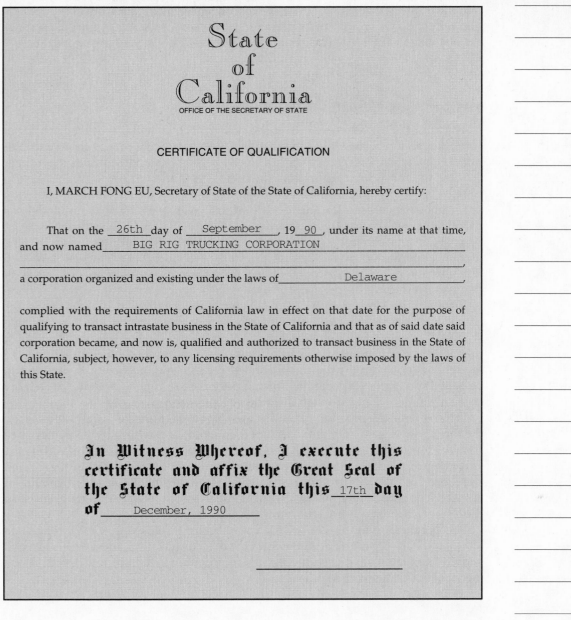

State
of
California

OFFICE OF THE SECRETARY OF STATE

CERTIFICATE OF QUALIFICATION

I, MARCH FONG EU, Secretary of State of the State of California, hereby certify:

That on the __26th__ day of ___September___, 19_90_, under its name at that time, and now named_____BIG RIG TRUCKING CORPORATION_____

_____,

a corporation organized and existing under the laws of_____Delaware_____,

complied with the requirements of California law in effect on that date for the purpose of qualifying to transact intrastate business in the State of California and that as of said date said corporation became, and now is, qualified and authorized to transact business in the State of California, subject, however, to any licensing requirements otherwise imposed by the laws of this State.

In Witness Whereof, I execute this certificate and affix the Great Seal of the State of California this _17th_ **day of** ___December, 1990___

articles of incorporation with the secretary of state in Florida. If this same corporation is qualified to do business in any other state, that state will require the filing of an application for amended certificate of authority. Before changing its name, the corporation should verify that the new name is available for use in all the states in which it is qualified to do business. Failure to do so is a common oversight and can cause obvious problems.

Section 15.04(a) of the Model Act provides that "a foreign corporation authorized to transact business in this state must obtain an amended certificate of authority from the secretary of state if it changes: (1) its corporate name; (2) the period of its duration; or (3) the state or country of its incorporation."

PARALEGALERT!

When a corporation is amending its articles of incorporation, it is important for the paralegal to ask whether the corporation is qualified to do business in any state. A determination must then be made as to the document, if any, that must be prepared and filed in the foreign state.

However, an amended certificate of authority should be obtained when a change occurs in any pertinent information supplied in the original application for certificate of authority. States vary in their requirements for filing an amended application for certificate of authority. Therefore, a review of the statutes of the state or states involved is a must. This responsibility is usually given to the paralegal.

Merger of the Foreign Corporation

State statutes allow the merger of corporations, and we will discuss the merger of corporations in greater detail in Chapter 13. In a merger, two or more corporations combine into one corporation. The one corporation that survives the merger is called the **surviving corporation;** the other corporation or corporations cease to exist. When a foreign corporation is involved, it can be the surviving corporation or it can be the corporation that ceases to exist. Section 11.07(a) of the Model Act permits the merger of a foreign corporation and states that "one or more foreign corporations may merge . . . with one or more domestic corporations if . . . the merger is permitted by the law of the state or country under whose law each foreign corporation is incorporated and each foreign corporation complies with that law in effecting the merger."

If the foreign corporation is the surviving corporation, it is required to file a copy of the articles of merger with the secretary of state of the foreign state within 30 days of the filing of the articles of merger in the home state. The foreign corporation will then continue to be authorized to transact business within the foreign state. An application for amended certificate of authority is required to be filed only if the corporation's name, period of duration, or state or country of incorporation changed when the merger took place.

If the foreign corporation ceases to exist upon the filing of articles of merger, the foreign state generally requires that the corporation withdraw its authority to transact business in the state. If the foreign corporation ceases to exist but the surviving corporation desires to continue to transact business within the foreign state, the surviving corporation must file its own application for certificate of authority. It cannot rely on the certificate of authority that had been granted to the foreign corporation not surviving the merger.

The paralegal may have to work many hours researching the various state statutes for a corporation that is qualified to transact business in numerous states. The states vary greatly in their requirements for foreign corporations merging with other corporations.

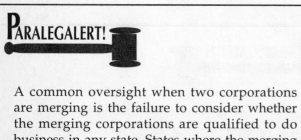

A common oversight when two corporations are merging is the failure to consider whether the merging corporations are qualified to do business in any state. States where the merging corporations are qualified to do business may impose penalties when they are not notified or the proper documentation is not filed.

Legal Advertising

Just as some states require a corporation to advertise its intention to file or its filing of articles of incorporation, as we discussed in Section 6–5 of Chapter 6, the foreign corporation is sometimes required to advertise its intention to file or its filing of an application for certificate of authority. Figure 9–8 is a sample form for legal advertising required to be placed in a legal publication or newspaper. This form meets the requirements of Section 4124(b) of the Business Corporation Law of 1988 of the Commonwealth of Pennsylvania, which states that "a foreign corporation shall officially publish notice of its intention to apply or its application for a certificate of authority.

Figure 9–8   Form of Legal Advertisement

Legal Advertisement

TRUCKING SERVICE CORPORATION, a corporation incorporated under the laws of the State of Delaware, has applied for a certificate of authority under the provisions of the Business Corporation Law of 1988. The address of its principal office in the State of Delaware is 123 Fifth Avenue, Wilmington, Delaware 19888. The Corporation's registered agent and office in the Commonwealth of Pennsylvania is CorpAmerica, Inc., 456 First Street, Bradford, Pennsylvania 16767.

The notice may appear prior to or after the day on which application is made to the Department of State." The Model Act, like many states, does not require that a foreign corporation advertise.

After the legal advertisement has been placed, the legal publication or newspaper will send a proof of publication to the paralegal who requested that the ad be run. The **proof of publication** evidences that the advertisement was placed and should be filed in the corporation's minute book. Generally, the paralegal is responsible for placing of the advertisement and filing the proof of publication in the corporation's minute book.

9–4   Penalties for Failure to Qualify

The risks and penalties to the corporation for failing to qualify when required are great and vary from state to state. Factors to consider when determining whether a corporation should or should not qualify are the penalties and fines imposed on unqualified corporations. The penalties are prescribed by the state statutes and usually include (1) denial of access to the state courts for any action, suit, or proceeding and (2) imposition of fines and penalties on the corporation and often on the directors, officers, or agents of the corporation.

Almost every state bars an unqualified corporation from maintaining an action in state court. The Model Act concurs in this and in Section 15.02(a) states that "a foreign corporation transacting business in this state without a certificate of authority may not maintain a proceeding in any court in this state until it obtains a certificate of authority." The effect of this sanction is that an unqualified corporation is unable to enforce its contracts in that state. In other words, it cannot sue another party for breach of contract, failure to perform or make payment under a contract, and so on.

Two states, Alabama and Vermont, do not permit subsequent qualification by a corporation in order to enforce a contract. In these states, if a contract was entered into prior to the corporation's qualifying in the state, the contract is not enforceable in court. All other states permit the subsequent qualification of the corporation at any time before a lawsuit is brought, and some permit qualification during the suit. Specifically, Section 450.2051 of Michigan Compiled Laws Annotated provides that "an action commenced by a foreign corporation having no certificate of authority shall not be dismissed if a certificate of authority has been obtained before the order of dismissal."

Even though unqualified corporations are denied access to the state courts to enforce contracts and sue, they *are* permitted the right to defend themselves in court. The Model Act, in Section 15.02(e), concurs with the states and provides

that "the failure of a foreign corporation to obtain a certificate of authority does not . . . prevent it from defending any proceeding in this state."

Many states impose monetary penalties on an unqualified corporation. Section 15.02(d) of the Model Act provides, in part, that "a foreign corporation is liable for a civil penalty of $___ for each day, but not to exceed a total of $____ for each year, it transacts business in this state without a certificate of authority." Note that no dollar amounts are stated in the Model Act, but states' penalties vary from $5 per day to $10,000.

In addition, the directors, officers, and agents of the corporation may also be held personally liable for the unqualified corporation. The individuals on whom the liability falls vary greatly from state to state. A few states impose criminal penalties for failure to qualify. For example, in Virginia (Section 13.1-613 of the Virginia Stock Corporation Act) it is a misdemeanor "for any person to transact business in this Commonwealth as a corporation unless the alleged corporation is . . . a foreign corporation authorized to transact business in this Commonwealth." Louisiana imposes a fine, and in the event that the offender fails to pay the fine, he or she may be imprisoned for 3 days to 4 months.

9–5   Withdrawal of Authority

When a corporation ceases doing business in a foreign state, it must withdraw its authority to transact business in that state. In addition, any corporation that dissolves in its state of incorporation must also withdraw its authority to transact business in any foreign state. The withdrawal from any foreign state will terminate the foreign corporation's responsibility to file annual reports, pay annual franchise or income taxes, and comply with that state's statutes. Therefore, it is to the advantage of the foreign corporation that it withdraw its authority as soon as it ceases doing business in that state or dissolves in its state of incorporation.

The procedure for withdrawing from doing business is prescribed in the states' statutes. It usually requires obtaining a **certificate of withdrawal** from the secretary of state of the foreign state. Until the foreign corporation obtains a certificate of withdrawal, it will not be relieved of the requirements of filing annual reports, paying tax, and so on. Section 15.20(a) of the Model Act provides that "a foreign corporation authorized to transact business in this state may not withdraw from this state until it obtains a certificate of withdrawal from the secretary of state."

A certificate of withdrawal is obtained by filing an **application for certificate of withdrawal** and complying with any other provisions of the statute. Many states have statutes similar to the Model Act, which in Section 15.20(b) states that:

> (b)   A foreign corporation authorized to transact business in this state may apply for a certificate of withdrawal by delivering an application to the secretary of state for filing. The application must set forth:
> (1) the name of the foreign corporation and the name of the state or country under whose law it is incorporated;
> (2) that it is not transacting business in this state and that it surrenders its authority to transact business in this state;

(3) that it revokes the authority of its registered agent to accept service on its behalf and appoints the secretary of state as its agent for service of process in any proceeding based on a cause of action arising during the time it was authorized to transact business in this state;

(4) a mailing address to which the secretary of state may mail a copy of any process served on him under subdivision (3); and

(5) a commitment to notify the secretary of state in the future of any change in its mailing address.

Figure 9–9 is an application for certificate of withdrawal, prepared in accordance with the provisions of the Model Act. Be aware that some states require that the application be completed and filed on the state's preprinted form, which you can generally obtain by calling the secretary of state and asking that a copy be sent to you. Other states require only that all information be provided and do not dictate the form in which the information is to be presented for filing.

While reviewing the foreign state's statute for the requirements for filing the application for certificate of withdrawal, you should also determine whether the state requires that other documents accompany the application or that other procedures be followed. For example, in some states, a corporation must file its final tax returns before the state will issue the certificate of withdrawal. Others require the foreign corporation to advertise that it intends to withdraw from doing business in that state, just as some states require advertising when a corporation applies to do business in the state. Other states require that the application for certificate of withdrawal be filed or recorded with the appropriate county in which the corporation has transacted business. And some states require that the corporation obtain certificates from the taxing and employment authorities of the state, which evidence that all taxes (corporate income tax and employment taxes) have been paid. These types of certificates are often called **clearance certificates.**

Figure 9–9 Application for Certificate of Withdrawal

**Application for Certificate
of Withdrawal of
Big Rig Trucking Corporation**

The undersigned corporation, in order to withdraw from transacting business in the State of _____, under and pursuant to the provisions of Chapter 15 of the Model Business Corporation Act, does hereby certify that:

1. The name of the Corporation is BIG RIG TRUCKING CORPORATION, and the Corporation was incorporated in Delaware.

2. The Corporation is not transacting business in the State of _____, and it hereby surrenders its authority to transact business in the State of _____.

3. The Corporation revokes its registered agent and appoints the Secretary of State of _____ as the Corporation's agent for service of process in any proceeding based on a cause of action arising during the time the Corporation was authorized to transact business in the State of _____.

4. The Corporation's mailing address to which the Secretary of State of _____ may mail a copy of any process is 123 Fifth Avenue, Wilmington, Delaware 19888.

5. The Corporation commits to notifying the Secretary of State of _____ in the future of any change in the Corporation's mailing address.

IN WITNESS WHEREOF, a duly authorized officer of the Corporation has executed this Application for Certificate of Withdrawal this 10th day of September, 1994.

BIG RIG TRUCKING CORPORATION

By _____
          President

You will be able to determine these requirements only by reviewing the statutes of the foreign state.

When a corporation decides that it no longer desires to transact business in a state, it must withdraw in accordance with the procedures set out in the statute. A corporation cannot merely terminate transacting business. To relieve itself of such requirements as filing tax returns, paying tax, and filing annual reports, the corporation must follow the statutory procedures for withdrawing its certificate of authority.

9–6 Revocation of Authority

The authority granted to a corporation to transact business within a state may be revoked by that state under certain circumstances. A corporation's certificate of authority may be revoked, or taken away, when the foreign corporation fails to comply with requirements of the state law. For example, Section 15.30 of the Model Act provides that "the secretary of state may commence a proceeding . . . to revoke the certificate of authority of a foreign corporation authorized to transact business in this state" if the foreign corporation:

1. Does not file its annual report on time.
2. Does not pay on time any franchise tax due.
3. Is without a registered agent or registered office for 60 days or more.
4. Does not inform the secretary of state that its registered agent or registered office has changed.
5. Has submitted a document to the secretary of state for filing that it knew was false in any material respect.
6. Has dissolved or disappeared as a result of a merger and failed to notify the secretary of state.

Upon determination by the secretary of state that the foreign corporation failed to comply with any requirement of the state's laws, the secretary of state will commence revocation proceedings against the corporation. Such proceedings begin when the state serves notice on the corporation that the state intends to revoke the certificate of authority. The notice states the grounds for revocation of the corporation's certificate of authority. The corporation then has the right to cure the violation within a specified time. If the corporation does not cure its default, the secretary of state will issue a certificate, usually called a **certificate of revocation**, revoking the corporation's certificate of authority.

The corporation, under most state statutes, is provided an opportunity to appeal the revocation. But if the corporation fails to exercise its right to appeal and still desires to transact business within the foreign state, it must file a new application for certificate of authority.

Recall our discussion in Section 9–2 regarding the good standing certificate (or certificate of existence). When the secretary of state has revoked a corporation's certificate of authority, the corporation is no longer in good standing and the secretary of state will not issue a good standing certificate. The state will issue a good standing certificate *only* after the corporation has cured the violation and complied with the state statutes.

PARALEGALERT!

A violation can usually be cured by performing the action whose omission caused the foreign corporation to be in violation. For example, if an annual franchise tax was not paid, the corporation should arrange to pay the tax and any penalties imposed by the foreign state.

9–7 Practical Considerations

Most of this chapter has dealt with the statutory procedures for qualifying to do business in foreign states. The corporate paralegal is generally responsible for complying with these requirements and procedures, so it is important to become familiar with the process of researching states' corporate statutes. Do not hesitate to contact a representative of the secretary of state's office, call an agent of one of the service companies, meet with the librarian at the local law school or county law library, contact another corporate paralegal working in the area, or pull the corporate statutes off the library shelf to get acquainted with the states' statutes.

The statutory procedures governing the qualification of corporations in foreign jurisdictions include the following:

1. Determining whether the corporate name is available for use in the foreign state.
2. Obtaining approval of the board of directors.
3. Preparing and filing the application for certificate of authority.
4. Maintaining a registered agent and a registered office in the foreign state.
5. Complying with postqualification requirements, including paying franchise and income tax, filing annual reports, amending the certificate of authority, notifying the foreign state of a merger of the foreign corporation, and in some states, advertising the qualification of the foreign corporation.
6. Accepting the risks and penalties for failing to qualify.
7. Preparing and filing an application for certificate of withdrawal.
8. Curing violations by the foreign corporation of any requirements of the state's laws, thereby avoiding revocation of authority.

The most critical consideration for the corporation is determining whether the business activity it is conducting in the foreign state requires it to qualify to do business in that state. Determining whether a corporation is doing business in a state is not simple and has caused considerable problems for corporations and states over the years. In obvious situations, where there is no doubt that the corporation is doing business in a foreign state, qualification is mandatory. But doubt is raised when the business activity is questionable.

Ultimately and practically the decision whether to qualify is left to the corporation (your firm's client). It will be your supervising attorney's responsibility to advise the corporation of the ramifications, costs, and requirements of qualifying, and it will be your supervising attorney's decision to determine your involvement in this process. After the decision has been made to qualify, you can perform most, if not all, of the statutory requirements for qualifying a corporation in a foreign jurisdiction.

SUMMARY

9–1

As corporations expand their businesses, they will often transact business in other states in addition to their state of incorporation. If a corporation is doing business in states other than its state of incorporation (often called its home state), it must register or qualify to do business in those other states. States other than the home state are called *foreign jurisdictions*, and these foreign jurisdictions consider corporations incorporated in other states to be foreign corporations. Determining whether a corporation is doing business in a particular state requires research of the statutes of the foreign jurisdiction. Most states, like the Model Act, have adopted provisions that list the activities that, when engaged in by corporations, do *not* constitute transacting business.

9–2

When a corporation decides that it must qualify to do business in a foreign state, it must file an application for certificate of authority with the secretary of state of the foreign state. The application, with other documents required by state statute, must be filed with the secretary of state, who will then issue a certificate of authority. Because the qualification of a corporation imposes certain responsibilities and liabilities on the corporation, the board of directors of the corporation must approve the qualification. The corporate name must comply with the statutes of the foreign state, and the foreign corporation must maintain a registered office and a registered agent in the foreign state. In general, the foreign corporation is subjected to the same rules and regulations as the domestic corporation in any state.

9–3

By qualifying to do business in a state, the foreign corporation subjects itself to numerous requirements of the foreign state. These responsibilities include preparing and filing annual reports, paying franchise and income taxes, amending the certificate of authority under certain circumstances, notifying the foreign state upon the merger of the cor-

poration, and arranging for legal advertisement upon qualifying to do business.

9–4

If a corporation fails to qualify to do business in a state in which it is transacting business, it may suffer consequences, which vary greatly from state to state. Most states bar an unqualified corporation from maintaining an action in state court. That is, an unqualified corporation cannot bring suit against another party for breach of contract, failure to perform or make payment under a contract, and so on. However, most states permit an unqualified corporation to defend itself in court. Monetary penalties may be imposed on the corporation and its directors, officers, or agents for failure to qualify, and some states will hold directors, officers, and agents of the corporation personally liable.

9–5

A foreign corporation must withdraw its authority to transact business in a state when it ceases doing business in that state or when the corporation dissolves. The corporation must file an application for certificate of withdrawal, after which the secretary of state will issue a certificate of withdrawal. The corporation is then relieved of filing annual reports, paying tax, and complying with the foreign state's statutes. Some states require the filing of final tax returns, the advertising of the corporation's intention to withdraw from doing business, and the obtaining of clearance certificates from various state agencies before the secretary of state will issue a certificate of withdrawal.

9–6

The secretary of state may revoke a foreign corporation's certificate of authority if it fails to file annual reports, fails to pay income or franchise taxes, is without a registered agent or office, fails to inform the secretary of state of a change in registered agent or office, knowingly submits false documents to the secretary of state, or fails to notify the secretary of state of a merger or dissolution of the corporation in the home state. If the corporation fails to cure the violation, after receiving notice from the secretary of state, the secretary of state will issue a certificate of revocation.

9–7

Most of this chapter has dealt with the statutory requirements and procedures for qualifying corporations in foreign jurisdictions, because the corporate paralegal will generally be responsible for complying with these requirements and procedures. Therefore, the paralegal should, most important, become familiar with researching states' corporate statutes and should feel comfortable about contacting state representatives, service company agents, librarians, and colleagues to help guide him or her and answer questions. The ultimate decision to qualify is left to the corporation, and your supervising attorney will advise the corporation of the ramifications, costs, and requirements of qualifying. Your supervising attorney will determine your involvement in this process.

REVIEW GUIDE

Key Terms

Before proceeding, review the key terms listed below to be sure you understand each one. If necessary, read over the corresponding section of the chapter. When you are ready to test your understanding, answer the review questions.

home state (p. 193)
state of domestication (p. 193)
domestic corporation (p. 193)
qualify (p. 193)
foreign jurisdictions (p. 193)
foreign corporation (p. 193)
application for certificate of authority
   (p. 196)
good standing (p. 196)
good standing certificate (p. 196)
certificate of existence (p. 196)
certificate of authority (p. 198)
registered office (p. 202)
registered agent (p. 202)
service companies (p. 202)
initial franchise tax (p. 203)
annual franchise tax (p. 203)
income tax (p. 203)
annual report (p. 204)
application for amended certificate
   of authority (p. 204)
amended certificate of authority (p. 204)
surviving corporation (p. 206)
proof of publication (p. 207)
certificate of withdrawal (p. 208)
application for certificate of withdrawal
   (p. 208)
clearance certificates (p. 209)
certificate of revocation (p. 210)

Questions for Review and Discussion

1. What is the difference between a domestic corporation and a foreign corporation?
2. According to the Model Act, when is a corporation "doing business" in a foreign state?
3. What must a corporation do to register or qualify to do business in a foreign state?
4. What is a good standing certificate?
5. Why must the board of directors approve the qualification of a corporation in a foreign jurisdiction?
6. Under what circumstance might a foreign corporation be required to use a fictitious name in a foreign state?
7. Explain the role of a service company.
8. What might a corporation subject itself to by qualifying to do business in a foreign state?
9. Under what circumstances must a certificate of authority be amended?
10. Identify the penalties imposed on a corporation that fails to qualify to do business when its business activities in a state require it to. (Use the Model Act to answer this question.)
11. When must a corporation apply for a certificate of withdrawal?
12. Why would the secretary of state revoke a foreign corporation's certificate of authority?

Activities

1. Determine what constitutes doing business in your state and the penalties, if any, for failing to qualify to do business.

2. Using the statutes of your state, prepare an application for certificate of authority for Travel Incorporated, a South Carolina corporation. Determine whether your state requires a preprinted form, what the fee for filing the application is, and what other documents, if any, are required to be submitted with the application.

3. Call the secretary of state of your state and request a copy of an application for amended certificate of authority.

CHAPTER 10   Financing the Corporation

OUTLINE

10–1   Capitalization of the Corporation
10–2   Types of Corporate Securities
     Equity Securities
     Debt Securities
     Variations Between Equity and Debt
10–3   Equity Securities
     Authorized, Issued, and Outstanding Shares
     Treasury Shares
     Class and Series of Shares
     Par Value and Market Value of Shares
     Issuance of Share Certificates
     Consideration Paid for Shares
10–4   Common Stock
     Voting Rights
     Liquidation Rights
     Dividend Rights
     Preemptive Rights
10–5   Preferred Stock
     Voting Rights
     Liquidation Rights
     Dividend Rights
     Redemption Rights and Sinking Fund
     Conversion Rights
     Creation of Preferred Stock
10–6   Debt Securities
     Secured and Unsecured Debt
     Short-Term and Long-Term Debt
10–7   Types of Debt Securities
     Promissory Note
     Bond
     Debenture
     Provisions of Debt Securities
        Redemption
        Conversion
        Subordination
10–8   Practical Considerations

APPLICATIONS

Susan Minahan has gathered all the pertinent information and has drafted articles of incorporation for Water Bottle Company, with the exception of the capitalization provisions, which are required to be included in the articles. She has already verified that the name is available for use in the state of incorporation. She has been waiting for instructions from the lawyer responsible for this client as to the capitalization of the corporation. She receives the following memorandum from Larry Lawyer:

TO: Susan Minahan
FROM: Larry Lawyer
RE: Capitalization of Water Bottle Company

In lieu of the minimum capitalization provisions we generally use for our clients desiring to incorporate, Water Bottle Company will be capitalized as follows:

50,000 shares of capital stock, which shall include the following:
10,000 shares Common Stock, $1.00 par value per share, which shall consist of Class A Common Stock, the holders of which shall be entitled to vote on all matters presented to the shareholders, and Class B Common Stock, the holders of which shall not be entitled to vote on any matters presented to the shareholders, including the election of directors; and
40,000 shares of Preferred Stock, without par value. The board of directors of the corporation is authorized to create and fix the designation, preferences, and special or relative rights, and the qualifications, limitations, or restrictions of those rights, of one or more series of the Preferred Stock.

This provision should be included in the articles of incorporation. Please see me before filing the articles if you have any questions regarding this matter.

OBJECTIVES

The corporate paralegal will have little involvement in advising the client on the capitalization of the corporation. However, the paralegal should have a basic understanding of the way a corporation is financed and the characteristics of the vehicles for financing the corporation—namely, equity and debt securities. After completing Chapter 10, you will be able to:

1. Understand what constitutes the corporate financial structure or capitalization of the corporation.
2. Distinguish between equity securities and debt securities.
3. Understand the corporation's reasons for issuing equity or debt securities.
4. Understand the differences among authorized, issued, outstanding, and treasury shares.
5. Prepare capitalization provisions of the articles of incorporation.
6. Understand the difference between par value and market value.
7. Prepare resolutions of the board of directors that authorize the issuance of shares and set the consideration to be paid for those shares.
8. Prepare share certificates for issuance to shareholders.
9. Understand the different rights associated with common shares.
10. Understand the different rights associated with preferred shares.
11. Prepare the documents necessary to create a series of preferred shares.
12. Distinguish among the various types of debt securities.
13. Draft a promissory note and understand the other forms of debt securities.
14. Understand the different provisions of debt securities.

10–1   Capitalization of the Corporation

All business organizations, including sole proprietorships, partnerships, and corporations, require a source of funds to operate their businesses. A corporation must have available to it a source of funds, or **capital,** sufficient to enable it to operate the business successfully. (Obviously, the availability of capital is not the only factor in the profitability of a corporation. A corporation may have funds available but be unable to operate profitably.)

A corporation's operations must be adequately financed if it desires to continue the business and return a portion of the profits to the shareholders. Corporations, like other business organizations, reinvest all or a part of their earnings from their operations back into the business. Newly formed corporations, which have no earnings to reinvest, raise capital through the issuance of securities in exchange for cash, property, or services payable to the corporation. These securities are called equity securities. And corporations with a history of successful business practices may raise capital through the issuance of securities accompanied by the corporation's promise to repay an obligation. These securities are called debt securities. Reinvestment of profits, issuance of equity securities, and issuance of debt securities are all methods used by a corporation to finance its operations.

The **capitalization,** or the financial structure, of a corporation may typically include a combination of any or all of the three methods of financing mentioned in the preceding paragraph. That is, capitalization may include one or more of the following elements: (1) reinvestment of profits, (2) issuance of equity securities, (3) issuance of debt securities. The focus of this chapter is the issuance of equity securities and debt securities to finance the corporation.

The power to issue equity and debt securities is conferred on the corporation by the statute under which the corporation was incorporated. As examples of the authority provided by the Model Act, Section 6.03(a) states that "a corporation may issue the number of shares of each class or series authorized by the articles of incorporation," and Section 3.02(7) of the Model Act provides that every corporation has the power to "borrow money, issue its notes, bonds, and other obligations." In turn, the board of directors is authorized to determine the corporation's capitalization, which may take on a diverse mixture of equity and debt. The authority to issue securities to equity holders or debt holders is granted to the board of directors of the corporation.

PARALEGALERT!

Any combination of reinvestment of profits, equity securities, and debt securities may compose the capitalization of the corporation.

10–2 Types of Corporate Securities

A corporation raises capital, or finances the corporation, through the issuance of securities. When a corporation issues a security, the investor, or holder of the security, expects to profit from the purchase of the security in exchange for providing the corporation with money, property, or other capital. A **security** is evidence of (1) an ownership interest in the property of the corporation (equity security) or (2) an obligation of the corporation to repay a loan or debt (debt security). For example, one type of equity security is common stock. Common stock is evidence of a shareholder's ownership interest in a corporation. A promissory note is one type of debt security; a person holding a promissory note issued by a corporation will be repaid by the corporation at a future date, as promised under the terms of the note.

Equity Securities

Equity securities are those that evidence an ownership interest in, and represent an investment in, the corporation. An owner of equity securities is called a **shareholder**. The ownership of equity securities is evidenced by a **share**, which is defined in Section 1.40(21) of the Model Act as the "unit into which the proprietary interests in a corporation are divided." The tangible evidence of a shareholder's ownership in the corporation is a **share certificate**, an example of which is provided in Figure 10–1. We will discuss the specific characteristics of a share certificate in greater detail in the next section.

You should be aware that state statutes vary in identifying the unit into which interests of the corporation are divided (a share) and the tangible evidence of owning shares (a share certificate). Some states use the terms *share* and *share certificate* and others use *stock* and *stock certificate*. We will follow the Model Act in the use of the terms *share* and *share certificate*.

Ownership of equity securities entitles a shareholder to certain rights, and these rights may be altered only by an agreement between the corporation and the holder of the equity securities. The rights conferred on a shareholder, by virtue of being an owner of equity securities, include: (1) the right to receive a proportionate share of the earnings of the corporation (earnings of the corporation are usually distributed to shareholders in the form of dividends), (2) the right to receive a proportionate share of the assets upon dissolution and liquidation of the corporation, and (3) the right to vote on certain corporate matters of concern to the owners, or shareholders, of the corporation. In short, a shareholder is entitled to receive the corporation's profits, to receive the corporation's assets upon liquidation, and to vote.

Debt Securities

Debt securities are those that evidence a corporation's obligation to repay money borrowed from a creditor, or lender. The corporation executes and delivers to the creditor a document that evidences the corporation's promise to repay the funds that were borrowed. Examples of types of documents that evidence debt securities are promissory notes, bonds, and debentures. Figure 10–2 is an example of a promissory note. We will refer to it again in a later section when we discuss debt securities more specifically.

Ownership of debt securities entitles the holder, or creditor, to certain rights, which are provided in the promissory note, bond, or debenture issued by the corporation. In particular, a holder of debt securities is entitled to (1) repayment of the principal, the amount loaned to the corporation, and (2) interest that accrues on the principal. The holder of debt securities does not, however, obtain an ownership interest in the corporation.

Figure 10–1 Form of Share Certificate (front)

FLORIDA

NUMBER   1

SHARES   -100-

WATER BOTTLE COMPANY

This Certifies that James Drink - *is the*
registered holder of One Hundred (100) - - - - - - - - - - - - - - - - - *Shares*
Class A Common Stock

transferable only on the books of the Corporation by the holder hereof in person or by Attorney upon surrender of this Certificate properly endorsed.

In Witness Whereof, the said Corporation has caused this Certificate to be signed by its duly authorized officers and its Corporate Seal to be hereunto affixed this_____ day of_____ A.D. 19____

Secretary   President

© GOES 722

Variations Between Equity and Debt

Whether a corporation issues equity or debt securities or both to raise capital is an important and often difficult decision. The cost of, benefits derived from, and consequences of issuing equity or debt securities are considerable, and all these factors determine the decision of the board of directors. Generally, the board of directors of the corporation considers the current market conditions and interest rates, the amount of capital required by the corporation, and the tax consequences before determining the corporation's mix of equity and debt securities.

More specifically, a corporation's board of directors considers the following factors, among others, before issuing equity or debt securities:

1. Dividends, or return to the shareholders (holders of equity securities) of a corporation's profits, are *not* a tax-deductible expense for the corporation, but the interest required to be paid to lenders or creditors holding debt securities is deductible by the corporation.

PARALEGALERT!

Because of the legal and tax issues involved in determining the corporation's mix of equity and debt, the corporation's accountant and corporate lawyer will generally be involved to a great extent in the corporation's consideration of its equity and debt mixture.

Figure 10–1, continued (back)

The Corporation will furnish to any shareholder, upon request and without charge, a full statement of the designations, preferences, limitations, and relative rights of the shares of each class authorized to be issued and of the variations in the relative rights of the preferences between the shares of each such series, so far as the same have been fixed and determined, and the authority of the board of directors to fix and determine the relative rights and preferences of subsequent series.

For Value Received,_____ hereby sell, assign and transfer unto_____

_____ Shares represented by the within Certificate, and do hereby irrevocably constitute and appoint_____

_____ Attorney to transfer the said Shares on the books of the within named Corporation with full power of substitution in the premises.

Dated_____ 19___

In presence of

NOTICE. THE SIGNATURE OF THIS ASSIGNMENT MUST CORRESPOND WITH THE NAME AS WRITTEN UPON THE FACE OF THE CERTIFICATE, IN EVERY PARTICULAR, WITHOUT ALTERATION OR ENLARGEMENT OR ANY CHANGE WHATEVER.

2. The holders of equity securities are entitled to participate in the management of the corporation by electing directors and voting on certain corporate actions, whereas holders of debt securities are not entitled to participate in management (except under certain unusual circumstances).
3. Corporations engaging in high-risk businesses may have to rely on equity securities to finance their businesses, because lenders and holders of debt securities may be unwilling to lend capital for high-risk ventures.
4. The issuance of securities, equity or debt, may require compliance with the regulations of the Securities and Exchange Commission and the securities laws of one or more of the states.

Figure 10–2 Promissory Note (Installment)

Promissory Note

$20,000.00

April 30, 1995
Wilmington, Delaware

FOR VALUE RECEIVED, MOUNTAIN SPRING WATER COMPANY ("Payor") hereby promises to pay to WATER BOTTLE COMPANY ("Payee"), on April 30, 1996, the principal sum of Twenty Thousand Dollars and 00/100 ($20,000.00), and to pay interest monthly from the date said funds were advanced until paid in full. Interest will accrue on any unpaid principal at a rate of 10 percent per annum and shall be computed on a 365-day year.

All payments of principal and interest shall be made via bank check delivered by mail to the Payee at 100 Market Street, Wilmington, Delaware 19801, or elsewhere as the holder hereof shall direct.

MOUNTAIN SPRING WATER COMPANY

By _____
President

The relationship between the corporation and its shareholders, often called **equity holders,** is different from the relationship between the corporation and its creditors, often called **debt holders.** For example, some of the differences include:

1. Shareholders have an ownership interest in the corporation, and creditors do not.
2. Shareholders are not required to be repaid for their investment, but creditors must be repaid the capital loaned to the corporation.
3. Creditors are due to be paid interest on the loans they have made to the corporation, but shareholders are not guaranteed a return on their investment, although they may receive one through the payment of dividends.
4. Creditors are afforded greater protection for repayment of the money they have provided to the corporation, as they are repaid prior to the shareholders in the dissolution and liquidation of the corporation.

10–3   Equity Securities

As we have already discussed, equity securities represent an ownership interest in the corporation. The right of the corporation to issue shares is conferred on it by the statutes of the corporation's state of incorporation, and the statutes of every state authorize corporations to issue shares and allow corporations to divide the shares into different classes or series with different characteristics and rights associated with each class or series.

You should take the time to review Sections 6.01 through 6.31 of the Model Act. (The full text of the Model Act is included in this manual as Appendix A.) In these sections, the terms *common stock* and *preferred stock* are not used when referring to shares. The Model Act refers only to "class of shares" or "classes of shares" and authorizes the issuance of a class or classes of shares that differ in their designations, preferences, limitations, and relative rights. However, state statutes of many states refer to shares as *common* or *preferred,* and we will do so also for our discussion.

Equity securities consist of common stock and preferred stock, which are not created equal with respect to their rights. We will discuss the specific characteristics and rights of common and preferred stock in the following sections. This section is devoted to a discussion of equity securities in general and the issues related to them.

Authorized, Issued, and Outstanding Shares

The articles of incorporation must state the maximum number and the types of shares of stock that the corporation may issue, or sell. These shares are called the **authorized shares.** The following is an example of a provision of the articles of incorporation: "The authorized capital of the corporation shall consist of 1,000 shares of Common Stock, without par value." In this example, the corporation is permitted to sell up to *and no more than* 1,000 shares of common stock of the corporation. If the corporation is authorized to sell both common and preferred stock, the following provision might be found in the articles of incorporation: "The authorized capital of the corporation shall consist of 10,000 shares, which shall be divided into 5,000 shares of Common Stock, without par value, and 5,000 shares of Preferred Stock, $10.00 par value." In this example, the corporation is permitted to sell up to 10,000 shares of stock, 5,000 shares of common and 5,000 shares of preferred, *and no more.*

The state statutes provide the rules requiring that the articles of incorporation contain the number of shares that the corporation has the authority to issue. In particular, Section 6.01(a) of the Model Act states, in part, "The articles of incorporation must prescribe the classes of shares and the number of shares of each class that the corporation is authorized to issue." In addition, Section 6.01(b) requires that "the articles of incorporation must authorize (1) one or more classes of shares that together have unlimited voting rights, and (2) one or more classes of shares . . . that together are entitled to receive the net assets of the corporation upon dissolution." In other words, at least one class (or type) of shares issued by the corporation *must* (1) have voting rights and (2) be entitled to a distribution of the corporation's assets when the corporation dissolves. These two requirements guarantee that the corporation will, at all times, have voting shareholders able to approve corporate transactions and have shareholders eligible to receive a distribution of the remaining assets of the corporation after its debts have been paid upon dissolution.

It is neither mandatory nor advisable for a corporation to issue all its authorized shares. Some authorized shares should be reserved for additional future financing of the corporation. If a corporation has issued all the shares authorized in the articles of incorporation and desires to issue additional shares, the articles must be amended to increase the number of authorized shares. Remember from our discussion in Chapter 8 that a change or amendment to any provision of the articles of incorporation requires the filing of articles of amendment. Except in certain circumstances, the shareholders and the board of directors must approve an amendment to the articles of incorporation.

After the authority has been created in the articles of incorporation to issue a specified number of shares, the power to issue (or sell) the authorized shares is vested in the board of directors. After the board of directors has approved the sale of shares of the corporation and consideration has been paid to the corporation by the buyers, the shares sold then become **issued and outstanding shares.** Shares remain issued and outstanding until the corporation repurchases the shares or redeems them or converts them into another type of equity security. In other words, shares are issued and outstanding as long as a person, other than the corporation itself, owns the shares. Section 6.03(a) of the Model Act states that "shares that are issued are outstanding shares until they are reacquired, redeemed, converted, or cancelled."

Shares that have been repurchased, redeemed, or converted by the corporation are not outstanding shares. These shares are, however, considered authorized and issued shares. Consider the example in Figure 10–3, which should give you a better understanding of authorized, issued, outstanding, and treasury shares.

Treasury Shares

As already mentioned, shares that are sold are considered issued and outstanding shares as long as they are owned or held by any person other than the corporation that sold the shares. A corporation is permitted to repurchase the shares that it originally issued or sold. Shares repurchased by the corporation are called **treasury shares;** treasury shares are authorized and issued, but they are not outstanding. However, the Model Act and some states designate treasury shares as authorized but unissued. Section 6.31(a) of the Model Act states that "a corporation may acquire its own shares and shares so acquired constitute authorized but unissued shares." You must review the statutes of the state under which the corporation was incorporated to determine how that state treats treasury shares.

Figure 10–3   Example Illustrating Authorized, Issued, Outstanding, and Treasury Shares

Definitions

Authorized shares—Maximum number of each type of share the corporation has the authority to issue, according to the articles of incorporation.

Issued and outstanding shares—Shares authorized in the articles of incorporation and sold or issued to investors.

Treasury shares—Shares held by the corporation itself.

Example

The articles of incorporation of Water Bottle Company authorize the corporation to issue up to 1,000 shares of common stock, no par value. The board of directors of Water Bottle Company authorized the sale of the following shares to the following persons: 100 shares to Mr. Water and 200 shares to Ms. Bottle. Six months after Mr. Water purchased 100 shares, the corporation repurchased 50 of his shares. Thus, the following are the authorized, issued, outstanding, and treasury shares of Water Bottle Company:

- Authorized shares: 1,000
- Issued shares: 300
- Outstanding shares: 250
- Treasury shares: 50

For a shareholder to enjoy fully the rights conferred on him as an owner of shares of the corporation, the shares must be issued *and* outstanding. Therefore, treasury shares, which are not outstanding shares, are not entitled to the same rights as issued and outstanding shares. That is, treasury shares are not entitled to (1) receive dividends or a distribution of the corporation's profits, (2) receive a proportion of the assets on liquidation of the corporation, or (3) vote on corporate matters.

Class and Series of Shares

The articles of incorporation may provide for the division of shares into one or more **classes,** and any class may be further divided into one or more **series.** The financial structure of a corporation may be as simple as the authorization by the articles of incorporation of the issuance of only one class of shares—common stock. Or it may be more complicated and authorize the issuance of numerous classes and series of shares. Refer to Figure 10–4 for examples of two different financial structures for a corporation—a simple structure and a more complex structure.

Statutory authority for classifying shares is provided in practically every state, and in the Model Act. The Model Act, in Section 6.02(a), provides that "if the articles of incorporation so provide, the board of directors may determine, in whole or part, the preferences, limitations, and relative rights . . . of (1) any class of shares before the issuance of any shares of that class or (2) one or more series within a class before the issuance of any shares of that series." This permits a corporation to classify shares into classes, and each class may be further classified into series. For example, a corporation may issue Class A Common Stock and Class B Common Stock, where Class A Common Stock has voting control and Class B Common Stock has no voting control. Refer to Figure 10–5, which is an example of a provision of the articles of incorporation that authorizes the issuance of these two classes of common stock.

As we have discussed, shares of the corporation may be issued in one or more classes, and those classes may be issued in one or more series, as permitted and authorized by the articles of incorporation. When one or more classes or series of

Figure 10–4   Corporate Financial Structures

Simple Financial Structure

10,000 shares of Common Stock, $1.00 par value per share

Complex Financial Structure

50,000 shares of capital stock, which shall include the following:

10,000 shares Common Stock, $1.00 par value per share, which shall consist of Class A Common Stock, the holders of which shall be entitled to vote on all matters presented to the shareholders, and Class B Common Stock, the holders of which shall not be entitled to vote on any matters presented to the shareholders, including the election of directors; and

40,000 shares of Preferred Stock, no par value per share. The Board of Directors of the Corporation is authorized to create and fix the designations, preferences, and special or relative rights, and the qualifications, limitations, or restrictions thereof, of one or more series of the Preferred Stock.

Figure 10–5   Provision of the Articles of Incorporation, Authorizing Two Classes of Common Stock

> **Article IV.**   The authorized capital of the Corporation shall be 1,000,000 shares, divided into 200,000 shares of Class A Common Stock, par value $1.00 per share, and 800,000 shares of Class B Common Stock, par value $.50 per share. Shares of Class A Common Stock and Class B Common Stock shall be identical in all respects except that the holders of Class A Common Stock shall be entitled to vote on all matters submitted to a vote of shareholders and holders of Class B Common Stock shall not be entitled to vote on any matters submitted to a vote of shareholders.

shares are authorized, the articles of incorporation must set forth the preferences, limitations, and relative rights of each class or series. In other words, the articles of incorporation must specifically define all of the characteristics (preferences, limitations, and relative rights) of each class and series of shares authorized. The characteristics of the classes of shares may differ in any one or more of the following respects: voting rights, dividend rights, and liquidation rights upon dissolution of the corporation. For example, two classes of common stock may be authorized, of which one class grants shareholders a preferred right to dividends and another class a preferred right to the assets of the corporation on dissolution. Series within a class of shares further define the numerous characteristics of shares of a corporation. For example, holders of a particular class of preferred stock may have the right to convert the preferred shares to common shares at some future date. We have only briefly discussed this issue here and will discuss it in greater detail later in this chapter.

All the preferences, limitations, and rights of each class or series of shares authorized by the corporation must be specified in the articles of incorporation or in an amendment to the articles.

In accordance with Section 6.02(b) of the Model Act, "each series of a class must be given a distinguishing designation." You are probably familiar with the terms or designations *common stock* and *preferred stock*. As we have already noted, you will not find these terms used in the Model Act. But most states continue to use these terms, corporations use them to identify their shares, and these terms are the ones with which people are most familiar. The point here is that the classes and series of shares of a corporation may be given any name selected by the corporation. Generally, the only requirement of most state statutes and the Model Act is that the preferences, limitations, and relative rights of the shares must be fully defined in the articles of incorporation. See Figure 10–6 for an example of a capitalization provision of the articles of incorporation that authorizes different classes and series of shares and gives them all distinguishing designations.

Par Value and Market Value of Shares

Most states require that the articles of incorporation indicate a par value for the shares authorized or indicate that the shares shall be without par value. **Par value** is the minimum dollar amount for which the shares can be sold by the corporation.

The following is an example of a provision in the articles of incorporation that designates a par value for the shares: "The corporation is authorized to issue 10,000 shares of Common Stock, $1.00 par value per share." In this example, shares of this corporation could not be sold for less than $1.00 per share, because the par value of the shares is stated as $1.00. Remember, shares with a par value may not be issued for an amount less than the par value stated in the articles of

Figure 10–6   Provision of Articles of Incorporation, Authorizing Different Classes and Series of Shares

> **Article IV.**   The authorized capital of the corporation shall be 1,000,000 shares, divided into the following classes and series of shares:
>
>   (a) 200,000 shares of Class A Common Stock, par value $1.00 per share. Holders of Class A Common Stock shall be entitled to vote on all matters submitted to a vote of shareholders.
>
>   (b) 300,000 shares of Class B Common Stock, no par value per share. Holders of Class B Common Stock shall not be entitled to vote on any matters submitted to a vote of shareholders.
>
>   (c) 500,000 shares of Preferred Stock, no par value per share. The authority to create and fix the designations, preferences, and special or relative rights, and the qualifications, limitations, or restrictions thereof, of one or more series of Preferred Stock is hereby vested in the Board of Directors of the Corporation.

incorporation. For example, shares with a par value of $5.00 may be issued for $10.00 (as long as an investor is willing to pay $10.00 per share), but they may not be issued for less than $5.00 per share.

The articles of incorporation may also provide that shares shall be without par value. The following is an example of a provision in the articles of incorporation that authorizes shares to be issued without par value: "The corporation is authorized to issue 10,000 shares of Common Stock, without par value." In this example, shares of this corporation may be sold for any consideration agreed to by the board of directors. Only a few states grant the shareholders the right to issue shares and determine the consideration to be paid.

While many states still require the designation of par value or a designation that the shares shall be without par value, the Model Act and several states have eliminated this requirement. The trend is to eliminate the par value requirement. You must review the statutes of the state of incorporation to determine whether that state requires the designation of a par value. The states that have eliminated the requirement still permit a corporation to designate a par value if it desires. Only the *requirement* to designate a par value has been eliminated.

PARALEGALERT!

More and more states are following the lead of the Model Act in eliminating the requirement to designate a par value, but many states still require such a designation. It is important that you research the state's statutes before filing the articles of incorporation. Failure to designate a par value, or state that the shares shall be without par value, will result in the articles of incorporation being returned.

The designation of par value or the provision that the shares shall be without par value has tax and accounting ramifications. In some states a franchise tax is computed on the capital stated in the articles of incorporation. For example, if a corporation has authorized 1,000 shares of Common Stock, $10 par value, tax is computed on the total value of the authorized shares, or $10,000 (1,000 shares × $10/share = $10,000). However, if a corporation has authorized 1,000 shares of Common Stock, $.01 par value, tax is computed on $10 (1,000 shares × $.01/share = $10), which will result in a lower franchise tax liability. Generally, it is more advantageous for the corporation to authorize more shares, but to set a lower par value for those shares. We will discuss the accounting issues regarding par-value shares in greater detail in Chapter 11.

As we have just discussed, issuance of shares of the corporation must be for consideration equal to or greater than the par value stated in the articles of incorporation. It is important to distinguish between par value and market value.

Par value and market value are not synonymous, and they have no relationship to one another.

The **market value** of a share is the price a person is willing to pay for the share. And the **market price** is the price at which the corporation or another person offers to sell a share.

When the corporation's board of directors first determines to sell shares directly from the corporation, often called a **new issue** of shares, it considers several factors before determining the market price, or the consideration to be paid by purchasers of shares.

Par value and market value have no relationship to one another. Par value does not affect the market value of shares, and vice versa.

These factors include (1) the current financial condition of the corporation, (2) the current financial condition of the stock market, (3) an evaluation of the corporation's expected future earnings, and (4) the expected dividends to be paid on shares of the corporation. After evaluating these factors, the board of directors determines the market price at which to offer the shares to investors. This market price must be at least the par value of the shares, but the par value of the shares plays no role in the board of directors' determination of the shares' market price.

After shares have been sold by the corporation to a purchaser, that purchaser may then resell those shares in the marketplace to other investors. The price of those shares will reflect the conditions of the marketplace and the financial condition of the corporation, including earnings and dividends. The seller of the shares will ask the market price for the shares and will, in all likelihood, receive the market value of the shares—the price a purchaser is willing to pay.

The important fact to remember about this discussion is that the par value of shares and the market value of shares have no relationship. Par value is also an arbitrary dollar value placed on shares, and market value reflects the current marketplace and current and future earnings and dividends of the corporation.

Issuance of Share Certificates

Except in certain circumstances, the board of directors is authorized to issue shares of the corporation. Section 6.21(b) of the Model Act provides that "the board of directors may authorize shares to be issued." The board of directors authorizes the issuance of shares by adopting a resolution. The resolution or resolutions should contain the following information:

1. The type of shares to be issued.
2. The number of shares to be issued.
3. The consideration to be paid by the purchaser to the corporation.
4. The terms of the sale.
5. Authorization for the officers to issue share certificates to the investors when the corporation receives payment.

Figure 10–7 is an example of a board of directors' resolution authorizing the issuance of shares of a corporation. Remember from our discussion in Chapter 7 that the board of directors would adopt this resolution in one of the following two ways: (1) at a meeting of the board of directors, for which proper notice was sent and a quorum was present at the meeting for the conducting of business, or (2) by unanimous written consent, executed by *all* directors of the corporation.

No specific form of share certificate is required, but the Model Act and most state statutes require the share certificate to contain certain information. Section 6.25(b) of the Model Act provides that "at a minimum each share certificate must state on its face: (1) the name of the issuing corporation and that it is organized under the law of this state; (2) the name of the person to whom issued; and

Figure 10–7   Resolution of the Board of Directors Approving the Issuance of Shares

> RESOLVED, that the officers of the Corporation are hereby authorized to issue each of the following individuals a share certificate registered in his or her name representing the following number of shares and in consideration of the following amount in cash, upon receiving payment in full from that individual:
>
> | Name | No. & Class of Shares | Consideration |
> | --- | --- | --- |
> | James Drink | 100, Class A Common Stock | $14,000 |
> | Kathleen Water | 200, Class B Common Stock | $12,000 |

PARALEGALERT!

The corporate paralegal will, in most cases, be assigned the task of drafting the resolutions of the board of directors approving the issuance of shares and the task of preparing the share certificates themselves.

(3) the number and class of shares and the designation of the series, if any, the certificate represents." Refer to Figure 10–1, which is an example of a share certificate. This share certificate was prepared in accordance with the provisions of the Model Act, but for purposes of providing this example, we have assumed that Water Bottle Company is a Florida corporation.

In addition, share certificates must be signed by two officers of the corporation. Section 6.25(d) of the Model Act requires that "each share certificate (1) must be signed (either manually or in facsimile) by two officers designated in the bylaws or by the board of directors and (2) may bear the corporate seal or its facsimile."

A corporation may choose to issue shares in various classes or in various series. In this case, each share certificate must describe the particular elements of each class or series by imprinting on the share certificates a full statement of the designations, preferences, limitations, and relative rights of the shares of each class authorized to be issued. The Model Act requires that the different classes of shares or different series within a class must be summarized on either the front or back of the share certificate. This summary or statement required to be printed on share certificates is called a **share legend** (or stock legend). The text of the share legend should summarize the capitalization provisions included in the articles of incorporation, which can be very lengthy.

As an alternative to printing the full text of *all the rights* associated with all the classes and series of shares authorized by the corporation, share certificates may include a statement that describes the corporation's obligation to furnish to any shareholder on request and without charge a description of the corporation's capital structure. Figure 10–8 is an example of the language that may be printed on share certificates in lieu of a full description of the shares authorized by the corporation. Using this statement requires less space on the share certificate and avoids the expense of having certificates reprinted if the different rights change for various classes and series of shares. The Model Act permits this alternative, as it provides in Section 6.25(c) that "each certificate may state conspicuously on its front or back that the corporation will furnish the shareholder this information on request in writing and without charge." Refer to Figure 10–1 and note the placement of the share legend on the back of the certificate. The share legend was printed where it could fit appropriately and be conspicuously seen.

Shareholders often lose or unintentionally destroy share certificates, and in some cases share certificates are stolen. The procedure for replacing lost, stolen, or destroyed share certificates is usually spelled out in the corporation's bylaws. Figure 10–9 is an example of a provision of the bylaws for the replacement of share certificates. Note that this provision provides that the board of directors "may require such indemnities as it deems adequate, to protect the corporation

Figure 10–8   Legend to Be Printed on Share Certificate (in Lieu of Full Description)

> The Corporation will furnish to any shareholder, upon request and without charge, a full statement of the designations, preferences, limitations, and relative rights of the shares of each class authorized to be issued and of the variations in the relative rights of the preferences between the shares of each such series, so far as the same have been fixed and determined, and the authority of the board of directors to fix and determine the relative rights and preferences of subsequent series.

from any claim that may be made against it with respect to any such certificate alleged to have been lost or destroyed." The corporation may require the shareholder to execute and deliver to the corporation an **affidavit of lost certificate.** Figure 10–10 is a form of affidavit of lost certificate. This affidavit provides (1) certification to the corporation that the shareholder was, in fact, the owner of the shares represented by the lost certificate and (2) indemnity against any loss the corporation incurs because of the lost, stolen, or destroyed share certificate.

The corporate paralegal is generally responsible for issuing share certificates of small, closely held corporations. However, this responsibility may fall on the secretary of the corporation. Larger corporations usually hire outside professional assistance, a **transfer agent,** for the issuance of shares. A transfer agent maintains the corporation's stock ledger, which contains the names and addresses of all the shareholders, the date on which the shares were acquired, and the amount of consideration paid to the corporation. In addition, the transfer agent issues share certificates; replaces lost, stolen, or destroyed certificates; and may be given other responsibilities relating to the issuance of share certificates and the maintenance of share records or other tasks as the board of directors of the corporation may determine. In any case, the issuing of shares should not be viewed as an unimportant task, nor should it be done carelessly.

PARALEGALERT!

If the corporate paralegal is assigned the task of issuing the corporation's share certificates, the paralegal will, in all likelihood, be responsible for purchasing the share certificate book. Such books may be purchased from most legal stationery stores or from businesses that offer other legal supplies, such as minute books and corporate seals.

Consideration Paid for Shares

State statutes usually regulate the *type* of consideration that a corporation may accept as payment for shares. Section 6.21(b) of the Model Act provides that the board of directors is authorized to issue shares only in exchange for certain types

Figure 10–9   Provision of Bylaws Regarding Replacement of Lost Share Certificates

> The Board of Directors may direct a new share certificate to be issued in place of any share certificate theretofore issued by the Corporation alleged to have been lost or destroyed. When authorizing such issue of a new share certificate, the Board of Directors, in its discretion and as a condition precedent to the issuance thereof, may prescribe such terms and conditions as it deems expedient, and may require such indemnities as it deems adequate, to protect the Corporation from any claim that may be made against it with respect to any such share certificate alleged to have been lost or destroyed.

Figure 10–10   Lost-Certificate Affidavit

Lost-Certificate Affidavit

STATE OF _____   )
)
COUNTY OF _____   )

      BEFORE ME, the undersigned authority, personally appeared Kathleen Water on this _____ day of January, 199__, and certified that:

1. She is the owner of _____(____) shares of Common Stock of Water Bottle Company, a _____ corporation (the "Company"), represented by share certificate no. _____.

2. The share certificate representing the _____ shares of Common Stock of the Company owned by her has been lost, stolen, or destroyed; and

3. She agrees to indemnify and hold the Company harmless with respect to the issuance of a replacement share certificate.

                           By _____
                               Kathleen Water

Sworn to and subscribed before me
this _____ day of January, 199___.

_____
            Notary Public

---

of consideration. In particular, that section says that shares may be issued "for consideration consisting of any tangible or intangible property or benefit to the corporation, including cash, promissory notes, services performed, contracts for services to be performed, or other securities of the corporation." In addition, the articles of incorporation may also limit the types of consideration a corporation may accept. For example, the articles of incorporation may include the following provision: "The common stock of the corporation may be issued for cash or for property, but no share of the common stock shall be issued for labor done or services rendered, unless two-thirds of the board of directors shall approve the sale."

The Model Act and most state statutes provide that the amount of consideration to be paid for shares shall be determined by the board of directors, unless this power is reserved for the shareholders by the corporation's articles of incorporation. Section 6.21(c) of the Model Act states that "before the corporation issues shares, the board of directors must determine that the consideration received or to be received for shares to be issued is adequate." However, par value stock must be sold for at least the par value of the shares. In addition, the articles of incorporation may restrict the sale of shares unless a stated dollar amount is paid for the shares. For example, the articles of incorporation could provide the following: "The common stock of the corporation may be issued for cash, property, or labor done or services rendered, but no shares of the common stock shall be issued for less than Ten Dollars ($10.00) in cash."

When a corporation receives the consideration determined by the board of directors, the shares issued in exchange for such consideration are considered to be **fully paid and nonassessable shares.** Shares are fully paid and nonassessable upon the corporation's receipt of the consideration set by the board of directors if such consideration is acceptable in accordance with the appropriate state's statutes.

As already stated, the board of directors generally has complete discretion to determine the consideration to be paid for shares of the corporation, and the board approves the issuance of such shares by adopting a resolution. Refer to Figure 10–7, which is an example of a resolution of the board of directors approving the issuance of shares.

10–4   Common Stock

When the capitalization of the corporation includes only one class of stock, that class is **common stock.** The exceptional characteristic of common stock is that the holders of shares of common stock share identical interests in the corporation's assets on dissolution and in profits distributed in the form of dividends. In other words, when no other class of shares has been issued, the holders of the common shares are entitled to vote on *all matters* and to share in *all profits* of the corporation. For example, the following is a provision of the articles of incorporation: "The corporation is authorized to issue 1,000 shares of stock, without par value." In this case, where the authorized shares are not identified as common or preferred, the shares are deemed to be common shares.

Generally, shares of common stock have no special features. However, state statutes permit the creation of various classes of common shares, with each permitted to possess different characteristics and rights. The articles of incorporation must authorize common shares and, if the shares are to possess different rights, must also specifically define those rights. If the articles of incorporation do not specifically define special rights, common shares will enjoy unlimited voting rights, receive all net assets of the corporation on dissolution, and participate in distribution of the corporation's profits.

PARALEGALERT!

Unless the articles of incorporation specifically provide otherwise, common shares will have unlimited voting rights, receive all net assets on dissolution, and enjoy full dividend rights. The articles may, however, provide for special voting and dividend rights. The common shareholders will always receive any remaining assets after creditors have been satisfied and any required distribution has been made to holders of shares having a preference over the common shareholders.

Under most state statutes, common shares may possess different voting, liquidation, and dividend rights. In addition, common shares may possess preemptive rights. Each of these varying rights is discussed in greater detail below.

Voting Rights

Unless the articles of incorporation state otherwise, every share is entitled to one vote. For example, a shareholder owning 25 shares of common stock is entitled to cast 25 votes on a matter to be voted on by the shareholders. Section 7.21(a) of the Model Act provides that "unless the articles of incorporation provide otherwise, each outstanding share, regardless of class, is entitled to one vote on each matter voted on at a shareholders' meeting." The articles of incorporation may, however, permit a class of shares more than one vote per share. For example, one share may carry two, three, or any other number of votes, provided this variance is authorized by the articles of incorporation.

The right of shareholders to vote cumulatively for the directors is an exception to the one-vote-for-one-share rule. As you will remember from our discussion of cumulative voting in Chapter 6, shareholders may cumulate their shares in voting for directors if permitted by the state statute and authorized by the articles of incorporation. When cumulative voting is permitted, the total number of votes a shareholder may cast is derived by multiplying the number of directors to be elected by the number of shares of stock owned by the shareholder. In that way, a shareholder is permitted to cast more than one vote for each share of stock he or she owns.

Additionally, exceptions may be made in the articles of incorporation to provide for greater voting rights, limited voting rights, or no voting rights. If the corporation has only one class of stock, that class must have full voting rights. But if there is more than one class, a class or series of shares may have greater, limited, or no voting rights, as long as at least one class has full voting rights. For example, consider the example in Figure 10–5, where two classes of common stock are authorized in the articles of incorporation. In this example, Class A Common Stock has full voting rights and Class B Common Stock has no voting rights. The only exception in which the Class B shareholders are entitled to vote is any action that will affect any right of the Class B shareholders. For example, suppose the Class B shareholders are entitled to receive dividends, and the shareholders are now voting to deprive the Class B shareholders of the right to receive dividends. In this case, the Class B shareholders are entitled to vote.

Liquidation Rights

When the shareholders of the corporation agree that the corporation is to be dissolved, any corporate assets remaining after all obligations and liabilities have been satisfied are distributed to the shareholders of the corporation. Usually the common shareholders receive the remaining assets in proportion to their ownership of the corporation. There may, however, be a class of shares with preferential rights to the assets on dissolution. The class with preferential rights will receive their shares of the assets first, in accordance with the provisions of the articles of incorporation, and then the common shareholders will receive the remaining assets, if any exist.

The state statutes and the Model Act require that the articles of incorporation authorize at least one class of shares, whose holders are entitled to receive the assets of the corporation on dissolution. Unless the articles of incorporation state otherwise, the shareholders of the common stock of the corporation are entitled to receive the net assets of the corporation upon dissolution of the corporation. Section 6.01(b) of the Model Act states that "the articles of incorporation must authorize . . . one or more classes of shares . . . that together are entitled to receive the net assets of the corporation upon dissolution." Consider the situation in which no class of shares were entitled to receive the assets. To whom would the corporation distribute any assets remaining after all debts and obligations of the corporation were paid?

Dividend Rights

A corporation may distribute its profits to the shareholders, but such distribution may be made only on the authority of the board of directors. Prior to giving such authority, the board of directors must consider whether any restrictions against making a distribution exist in the articles of incorporation and whether making a distribution would impede the corporation's ability to pay its debts as they become due. If such conditions do not prohibit the distribution of the

Wood v. Coastal States Gas Corporation

The issues of *Wood v. Coastal States Gas Corporation*, 401 A.2d 932 (Del. 1979), were part of a complex controversy. However, the core of the case involved a contention by the plaintiffs that their rights as preferred shareholders had been violated.

Coastal States Gas had entered into a settlement arrangement whereby the common shareholders of Coastal would receive a distribution of shares of Valero Energy Corporation, a spinoff of a subsidiary of Coastal, and the preferred shareholders would receive nothing. Among other counts, plaintiffs contended that (1) the settlement plan breached the Certificate of the Designations, Preferences and Relative, Participating Optional or Other Special Rights of the preferred stock (the Certificate), (2) the settlement plan should have been put to a special two-thirds vote of the preferred shareholders as a class, and (3) the settlement plan unjustly enriched the common shareholders at the expense of the preferred shareholders.

The court found that "shares are not to be issued under the settlement plan which would rank superior to plaintiffs' shares, either as to payment of dividends or distribution of assets. And the settlement plan will not change the preferences, rights or powers of the preferred. As we have said, the special features of the preferred stock are those fixed by the share contract and the settlement plan comports with that contract, as we have construed it. It follows that Coastal has not 'change[d] the preferences, rights or powers' of the preferred shareholders and, so, the latter are not entitled to vote on the plan as a class."

In addition, the court found that the holders of the preferred stock were not entitled to vote as a class on the settlement plan because the requirements of the Certificate for such a vote had not been met.

Finally, the court concluded that the rights of the preferred shareholders were found solely in the Certificate.

corporation's profits—in other words, the issuance of dividends—the board of directors is free to issue dividends at its discretion. The corporation is never obligated to pay dividends to shareholders. Dividends are paid only after the board of directors has determined that funds are available out of which to pay the dividend.

The articles of incorporation may restrict the payment of dividends to the common shareholders if they authorized another class of shares that have preferential rights to dividends. In this case, dividends are paid first to the class of shares with preferential rights and then to the common shareholders, as long as a sufficient amount of profits remain to do so.

Chapter 11 of this text is devoted to the distribution of the corporation's profits in the form of cash, property, or other shares of the corporation. Therefore, our discussion of dividend rights in this section is limited.

Preemptive Rights

If the shareholders of the corporation have **preemptive rights,** they possess the right to purchase newly issued shares of the corporation's stock before any shares are sold to persons who are not then shareholders of the corporation. This right may be granted or denied in the articles of incorporation, depending on the approach taken by the state statute. Refer to Section 6–4 of Chapter 6 for additional discussion of preemptive rights.

10–5   Preferred Stock

Preferred stock is a class of stock that has preference over other classes of stock of the corporation. Preference over one or more other classes of stock may be with respect to the right to vote, the right to the assets on dissolution of the corporation, the right to dividends or distribution of profits, or some other rights, including the right to cumulate dividends. Preferred stock does have special features, unlike common stock, but none of these features are typical of all types of preferred stock. For example, preferred stock generally does not have voting rights. But you cannot be sure that it does not unless you review the articles of incorporation.

In addition to the preferred rights afforded the holder of preferred shares, these shares may have other characteristics and rights, including redemption rights, conversion rights, and provisions for a sinking fund.

The corporation's articles of incorporation must explicitly set forth the rights, privileges, and limitations of the preferred stock. The rights of the preferred shareholders (voting and dividend rights, liquidation preferences, redemption and conversion rights, etc.) are contractual and are agreed on when the preferred stock is created. The Supreme Court of Delaware confirmed this contractual right in *Wood v. Coastal States Gas Corp.*, which is discussed further in the *Legal Links* in this chapter.

The rights identified in the articles of incorporation must also be printed on the front or back of the corporation's share certificates. Often the rights are too lengthy for the space provided on a share certificate. Therefore, share certificates may include a share legend, on either the front or the back of the certificate, indicating that the corporation will provide a description of all the rights of all classes of shares of the corporation upon the request of a shareholder. Remember that the share legend is used in lieu of providing the full description of the designations, preferences, limitations, and relative rights of the shares of each class authorized to be issued by the corporation. Refer to Figure 10–8, which is an example of a share legend. Also refer to Figure 10–1, which indicates an appropriate placement of the share legend on the certificate.

As you study the various characteristics and rights of preferred shares, which are discussed in greater detail in the following paragraphs, refer to Figure 10–11. The example there illustrates the different characteristics and rights of preferred shares.

Voting Rights

Remember that at least one class of shares must have full voting rights, and that class of shares is generally the common shares. As long as this requirement is met, the corporation is permitted to have any other classes of shares with full, limited, or no voting rights. The articles of incorporation must identify any shares that have anything less than full voting rights. When the articles do not specifically provide that shares of any particular class or series are to have limited or no voting rights, the presumption is that those shares are voting shares. For example, if the articles authorize the issuance of 10,000 shares of Series B Preferred Stock, and the articles provide no other identifying characteristics of this stock, you can assume that these shares have full voting rights.

Figure 10–11   Designation, Preferences, and Special Rights of A Series of Preferred Stock

(A) The distinctive designation of the Series A shall be "Series A Preferred Stock," and the number of shares which shall constitute the Series A shall be 40,000 shares.

(B) Holders of shares of the Series A shall not be entitled to vote in any matters submitted to the shareholders of the Corporation.

(C) In the event of any consolidation, liquidation, whether voluntary or involuntary, dissolution, or winding up of the affairs of the Corporation, the amount payable on shares of the Series A shall be $50.00 per share, plus dividends accrued and unpaid.

(D) The amount hereby fixed as the annual rate of dividends payable on shares of the Series A is $4.00 per share, and no more, which shall be payable in equal quarterly installments on the first day of January, April, June, and December, beginning on the next installment date following the creation of the Series A. Dividends on the Series A shall be cumulative.

(E) The shares of the Series A shall be redeemable in whole or in part at the option of the Board of Directors at any time or from time to time. The amount payable upon the exercise of the right to redeem such shares shall be $35.00 per share, plus dividends accrued and unpaid thereon to the date fixed for redemption. The Corporation shall provide not less than 30 days prior written notice to the record owners of the Series A, and such notice shall provide the procedures for surrendering the share certificates of the Series A and shall provide a time and place where payment for such shares shall be made, all as determined by the Board of Directors.

(F) The Corporation shall set aside in a sinking fund a sum or sums sufficient to redeem shares of the Series A at $35.00 per share plus an amount equal to all accrued and unpaid dividends. The sinking fund shall be funded out of legally available funds of the Corporation after cumulative dividends have been paid and before any dividends are paid in respect of any Common Shares of the corporation. Any sums set aside shall never exceed the amount sufficient to redeem the shares of the Series A then issued and outstanding, and all sums set aside for the sinking fund shall be applied only to the redemption of the Series A.

(G) Shares of the Series A shall be convertible, at the option of the holder of Series A shares, into shares of Common Stock at a rate of one share of Common Stock for each share of the Series A. Such conversion rate shall be adjusted, and notice provided within 10 days of such adjustment to the holders of the Series A, upon a change in the capitalization of the Corporation, including a stock dividend, stock split, or reverse stock split. Upon providing the Corporation 30 days' written notice, the holder of the Series A shall surrender to the Corporation share certificates of the Series A, and shall thereupon be entitled to receive share certificates of the Common Stock. No fractional shares of the Common Stock shall be issued, and the Series A shareholder shall receive the appropriate cash value for such fractional share, as shall be determined by the Board of Directors. Forty thousand shares of Common Stock of the Corporation shall be reserved and set aside and issued only for the conversion of the Series A as provided for herein.

A corporation gives certain shares full voting rights and other shares no voting rights because it wants voting control to remain with only one class of shares. For example, a corporation that needs to finance a project may decide to issue additional shares to raise the required capital. The original shareholders, however, desire to maintain voting control of the corporation and are unwilling to dilute their voting control by selling additional shares. In this case, the corporation will sell nonvoting shares to raise the capital needed. Remember from our previous discussion that common shares are permitted to be nonvoting. As long as one class of shares has full voting rights, the corporation is permitted to give any other class limited or no voting rights.

Even though voting privileges may be denied to any class or series of shares, those nonvoting shares will be entitled to vote in circumstances where any rights or privileges of that class or series of shares are being amended or taken away. Consider the example where Series A Preferred Stock has no voting rights, but does have a preference as to the assets upon dissolution of the corporation. The class of shares permitted to vote could, in effect, arbitrarily vote to change the rights of the Series A Preferred Stock and eliminate the Series A preference with respect to the assets of the corporation. Therefore, state statutes provide for class voting on matters that affect the rights of that particular class. Section 10.04(d) of the Model Act provides that "a class or series of shares is entitled to the voting rights granted by this section, although the articles of incorporation provide that the shares are nonvoting shares."

The Model Act specifically sets out, in Section 10.04, the instances in which voting on amendments may be done by voting groups. In short, that section provides that any class of shares is entitled to vote as a voting group on a proposed amendment to the articles (even if that class or any series of the class is not generally entitled to vote) if the amendment:

1. Increases or decreases the number of authorized shares.
2. Allows an exchange or reclassification of the nonvoting class of shares into another.
3. Changes the designation, rights, preferences, or limitations of the nonvoting class of shares.
4. Creates a new class of shares having preferences that are equal or superior to the nonvoting class of shares.
5. Increases the rights, preferences, or number of authorized shares of any class of shares, making another class equal or superior to the nonvoting class of shares.
6. Limits or denies any existing preemptive rights.
7. Cancels or affects rights to dividends that have accumulated but have not yet been paid to the nonvoting class of shares.

Refer to paragraph B of Figure 10–11, which includes a provision describing the voting rights of the Series A Preferred Stock.

Liquidation Rights

Generally, the holders of preferred shares have a preference over other classes of shares upon the dissolution and liquidation of the corporation. Remember that the common shares will receive the assets of the corporation remaining after *all debts and obligations* of the corporation are satisfied. Therefore, the obligation to the preferred shareholders must be satisfied before the common shareholders receive their distribution.

Even though the preferred shareholders have a preference over the common shareholders, they are subordinate to any creditors of the corporation. For example, all debts and obligations for employee wages, income tax and other forms of tax, loans from banks and other lenders, utilities, rent, and the like, must be satisfied before the preferred shareholders receive a distribution. But the preferred shareholders will receive a distribution prior to the common shareholders. Often no assets remain for distribution to the common shareholders after debts and obligations have been satisfied. Sometimes no assets remain for distribution to the preferred shareholders.

The preference that may be enjoyed by the preferred shareholder upon liquidation may be determined in one of the following two ways: (1) a fixed amount, plus any accrued and unpaid dividends, or (2) a fixed percentage of the par value of the shares, plus any accrued and unpaid dividends. Paragraph C of Figure 10–11 is an example of a provision that sets a fixed amount to be paid upon liquidation of the corporation.

Dividend Rights

As we mentioned in our discussion of dividend rights for common shareholders, a corporation may distribute its profits to the shareholders, but the authority to do so must be given by the board of directors. The corporation is never obligated to pay dividends to shareholders, including preferred shareholders. But preferred shareholders may have the right to require the corporation to pay a dividend to them prior to paying a dividend to the common shareholders or to the holders of other shares that are subordinate with respect to the payment of dividends. The right to a preference in the payment of dividends is the most common privilege afforded the preferred shareholder. Of course, dividends may be paid only after the board of directors has determined that funds are available out of which to pay the dividend.

The dividend preference enjoyed by preferred shareholders may be cumulative or noncumulative. Preferred shareholders with rights to **cumulative dividends** are entitled to dividends each year. If a dividend is not paid during any particular year, dividends cumulate until the board of directors determines that dividends may be paid. For example, suppose that the terms of the preferred stock entitle the shareholders to a cumulative dividend of $10 per share per year, and that Abe Smith, the only preferred shareholder, owns 25 shares. This entitles Abe Smith to a dividend of $250 per year, and this amount will accumulate each year until dividends are paid by the corporation. During the first year, the corporation is not profitable and pays no dividends. During the second year, the board of directors declares that dividends totaling $500 are to be distributed. Abe Smith will receive the entire $500 because the corporation must first pay him $250 for the previous year, in which dividends were not paid. He then receives another $250 in dividends for the second year, which leaves no amount for distribution to any other class of shareholders.

Preferred shareholders with rights to **noncumulative dividends** are entitled to receive dividends only when dividends are declared by the board of directors. If dividends are not paid in any particular year, the preferred shareholders lose their right to receive dividends for that year. These rights are the same as those of the common shareholder, to whom dividends are distributed only when declared by the board of directors. Suppose that Abe Smith's 25 shares of preferred stock have noncumulative dividend rights. If no dividends are paid in the first year, Abe Smith loses his right to receive dividends for that year. If dividends totaling $500 are declared in the second year, he will receive $250 in dividends, as his right to receive dividends is noncumulative.

Preferred stock is usually given preference over the common stock as to the issuance of dividends. Authorization of this preference is given in the articles of incorporation. The following terms and conditions will be found in the articles when a dividend preference is given to the preferred stock: (1) the annual rate at which dividends are to be paid, (2) the frequency at which dividends are to be paid (annually, semiannually, quarterly, etc.), and (3) whether dividends are cumulative or noncumulative. You will find these terms in the dividend preference provisions in the example in Figure 10–11. Paragraph D of Figure 10–11 provides for cumulative dividends to be paid on the preferred shares authorized.

Chapter 11 of this book will be devoted to the distribution of the corporation's profits in the form of cash, property, or other shares of the corporation. Therefore, our discussion of dividend rights in this section is limited.

Redemption Rights and Sinking Fund

Preferred stock provisions often provide the corporation the right to redeem shares on the terms and conditions set forth in the articles of incorporation. The corporation's **right of redemption** is the agreement of the corporation and the preferred shareholder that permits the corporation to redeem, or repurchase, the shares held by the preferred shareholder at some point in the future. Unless redemption provisions are spelled out in the articles of incorporation, the corporation does *not* have the right of redemption.

You can determine whether redemption rights exist by examining the articles of incorporation. If no provision is found, then the corporation does not have the right of redemption.

A corporation might desire to exercise its right of redemption if it had issued the preferred shares at an attractively high rate of return for the holders of the shares. The corporation may have been desperate for capital at the time of issuing the shares and may have offered a dividend rate of 25 percent on the shares. In a market where interest rates are 10 percent, this is attractive for the holders of the shares. But the corporation may be unable to continue paying the 25 percent dividend rate. Therefore, the corporation will redeem those shares if it has redemption rights.

A problem may arise, however, for the corporation with redemption rights. Even though the corporation is unable to pay the high dividend rate, it may not have funds available to redeem the shares from the shareholders. The corporation should plan for this situation and provide a **sinking fund.** A sinking fund, similar to a savings account, is an account in which regular amounts are saved for eventual use by the corporation in redeeming shares. Therefore, in the future, when a large sum is required to redeem shares, the corporation will have the funds available. Very often prospective purchasers of redeemable preferred shares will require that the corporation create a sinking fund as a condition of their purchasing the shares. They want to be assured that the funds will be available for the corporation to repurchase their shares.

The terms of the redemption *must be included* in the description of the class of shares to which it relates. They will be found in the articles of incorporation and printed on the share certificates of the corporation (unless a share legend is used). Refer to paragraph E of Figure 10–11, which includes a provision granting the corporation the right of redemption. The example also includes, in paragraph F, a provision by the corporation of a sinking fund.

Redemption provisions should include the following terms, all of which you will find in the example in paragraph E of Figure 10–11:

1. The future date or dates on which the shares will be redeemable by the corporation.
2. The price or prices at which the shares will be redeemable.
3. The persons to whom notice of the redemption must be provided and the number of days prior to the redemption that notice must be provided.
4. The method, the time, and the place for the payment for shares to be made.
5. Procedures for surrender of share certificates.

The board of directors of the corporation is vested with the authority to approve the redemption of stock by adopting a resolution or resolutions. Figure 10–12 is an example of resolutions of the board of directors approving the redemption of stock by a corporation.

Figure 10–12   Resolutions of Board of Directors Approving Redemption of Stock

WHEREAS, in accordance with Article IV of the Articles of Incorporation of the Corporation, the Corporation may redeem all of its Series A Preferred Stock at any time; and

WHEREAS, the Board of Directors deems it advisable to redeem all outstanding shares of the Series A Preferred Stock; therefore, be it

RESOLVED, that all outstanding shares of the Series A Preferred Stock, totaling forty thousand (40,000) shares, be redeemed by the Corporation on June 1, 1995; and

FURTHER RESOLVED, that if any shareholder of the Series A Preferred Stock fails to surrender his or her certificate(s) by July 1, 1995, such shareholder shall not be entitled to receive dividends thereon or to exercise any rights with respect thereto, except to receive from the Corporation the amount set aside for the redemption of said shares without interest; and

FURTHER RESOLVED, that the Secretary of the Corporation is authorized to send to each shareholder of the Series A Preferred Stock a written notice advising the shareholders of the redemption of such shares.

Conversion Rights

A class of shares may be entitled to **conversion rights,** which give the holder of the shares the option to convert his or her shares to shares of another class. Conversion rights provide the holder of these shares the advantages of owning preferred stock, with such preferences as dividend and liquidation rights, and of having the option to convert the shares to common shares when such a conversion would prove profitable. For example, the holder of shares of preferred stock with conversion rights may desire to convert the shares to common shares when the market value of the common shares exceeds the market value of the preferred shares.

Terms of the conversion, which must be included in the description of the class of shares to which they relate, are found in the articles of incorporation and printed on the share certificates issued by the corporation (unless a share legend is used on the certificates). In particular, the conversion provisions should include the following terms:

1. The conversion rate—the number of common shares into which each preferred share is convertible.
2. The method of conversion—the number of days prior to the conversion that the shareholder must provide written notice to the corporation of the shareholder's intention to convert, the effective date of the conversion, and the method of treating fractional shares.
3. The conversion rate adjustment—an adjustment to the conversion rate due to a change in the capitalization of the corporation (stock dividend, stock split, or reverse stock split).
4. Notice of conversion rate adjustment—the method by which the board of directors will notify shareholders of an adjustment in the conversion rate.
5. Reservation of common shares—authorization of the board of directors to set aside an adequate number of common shares for the exercise of conversion rights.

Conversion provisions can be very complicated, and drafting such provisions often requires expert skills. Paragraph G of Figure 10–11 provides an example of simplified conversion provisions for the conversion of preferred shares into common shares. The following list describes the provisions included in paragraph G of Figure 10–11 and, in some cases, goes on to explain some of the pitfalls of more complicated conversion provisions:

1. The example provides that one share of preferred stock may be converted into one share of common stock. But conversion rates not as simple as the one in our example may cause problems when fractional shares are involved. For example, suppose a shareholder is to receive two shares of common stock for every three shares of preferred stock upon conversion. In this case, 20 shares of preferred would convert to 13⅓ shares of common stock. A procedure must be established to allow payment in cash in lieu of issuing a fractional share of common stock. Usually the board of directors is given the authority to determine the fair market value of a share of common stock, and cash is paid to the preferred shareholder for the fractional share.

2. The example provides that the conversion rate will be adjusted when a change occurs in the capitalization of the corporation. For example, when additional common shares are issued in a stock dividend or stock split or when common shares are canceled in a reverse stock split, the preferred shareholder's rights to convert at the originally agreed-upon conversion rate must be preserved. Therefore, an adjustment must be made to the conversion rate and notice must be provided to the preferred shareholder. The notice must include an explanation of the cause in the adjustment.

3. At all times the corporation must have available a sufficient number of common shares to permit the conversion of preferred shares to common shares. The board of directors will adopt a resolution authorizing the reservation of a specific number of shares to be used for conversion privileges of the preferred stock.

Creation of Preferred Stock

Under statutory authority, the corporation is permitted to issue preferred shares as authorized in the articles of incorporation. The board of directors has the authority to issue those shares at its discretion. When the articles of incorporation are initially drafted or subsequently amended, they generally give the corporation authority to have one or more classes of shares. However, classes of shares may be divided into series, and these series may have different rights and characteristics. A corporation may not specifically define the rights of the series when they are initially authorized in the articles, because it does not always know the future desires of the corporation and its board of directors. To eliminate the necessity of amending the articles of incorporation whenever the board of directors decides to issue a new series of preferred shares, the articles may vest authority in the board to determine the rights and characteristics of any series of preferred shares without obtaining shareholder approval and amending the articles. In carrying out this procedure, the board of directors is creating a series of preferred shares.

PARALEGALERT!

The articles of incorporation usually vest authority in the board of directors to create a series of preferred shares and to determine its preferences, limitations, and relative rights. If so, shareholder approval and amendment of the articles are not required.

To gain a better understanding of the procedure for creating a series of preferred shares, examine Figures 10–4 and 10–6. In these examples, the articles of incorporation vest authority in the board of directors to create any one or more series of preferred shares. Therefore, when the board of directors determines at some future date to create a particular series of the preferred stock, it may do so without obtaining shareholder approval and amending the articles. The board of directors will be required, however, to adopt a resolution authorizing the creation of a series of preferred stock. Figure 10–13 is an example of a resolution of the board of directors authorizing the creation of a series of preferred stock.

Figure 10–13 **Resolution of the Board of Directors Creating a Series of Preferred Stock**

> RESOLVED, that pursuant to the authority vested in the Board of Directors of the Corporation by the provisions of the Articles of Incorporation, the Board of Directors hereby creates and authorizes the issuance of a series of 40,000 shares of Preferred Stock of the Corporation (such series being hereinafter called the "Series A"), and hereby fixes the designation, preferences, and special or relative rights of the shares of such series and the qualifications, limitations, or restrictions thereof (in addition to the preferences and relative or special rights and the qualifications, limitations, or restrictions thereof set forth in the Articles of Incorporation, which are applicable to the Preferred Stock of all series) as follows:
>
> [The designation, preferences, and special or relative rights provided in Figure 10–11 should be repeated and included here.]

After the board of directors has approved the resolutions that authorize the creation of a series of preferred shares, the corporation must file a document with the secretary of state in the state of incorporation. This document, sometimes called a **designation statement,** spells out all the preferences and rights of the newly created series of shares. The designation statement acts as an amendment to the articles of incorporation because it affects the capitalization provisions in the articles. Figure 10–14 is an example of a designation statement.

Generally, it is the responsibility of the corporate paralegal to determine the state's requirements for preparing and filing a designation statement. Not all states refer to this type of document as a designation statement, and the procedures vary from state to state.

10–6   Debt Securities

As we have already discussed, debt securities evidence a corporation's obligation to repay money loaned to the corporation by a person (lender) or any number of persons. When capital is loaned to the corporation, a debt of the corporation is created. At this point the corporation is considered the **debtor,** and the lender of the funds is the **creditor.** The tangible evidence that the creditor has loaned funds to the debtor is called a debt security. The issuance of debt securities is the second method discussed in this chapter that is used by the corporation to finance its operations.

The creditor or debt holder of a corporation's debt securities is entitled to specific rights. These rights include (1) payment of interest as a return on the amount loaned to the corporation and (2) repayment of the principal loaned to the corporation. However, debt holders are generally *not* entitled to vote at meetings of the shareholders, unless the debt instrument, or debt security, provides for such right to vote. In addition, because the principal amount loaned to the corporation must be repaid, a debt security constitutes a temporary, not permanent, investment in the corporation.

The right of the corporation to borrow money to finance its operations or repay its debts is conferred on it by the statutes of the corporation's state of incorporation. Section 3.02(7) of the Model Act permits the corporation "to make contracts and guarantees, incur liabilities, borrow money, issue its notes, bonds, and other obligations (which may be convertible into or include the option to purchase other securities of the corporation), and secure any of its obligations by mortgage or pledge of any of its property, franchises, or income." The board of directors is vested with the authority to issue debt securities at its discretion. After the board of directors approves their

Figure 10–14 Designation Statement

DESIGNATION STATEMENT

Pursuant to the provisions of Section _____ of the Business Corporation Law of the State of _____, the undersigned corporation hereby submits the following statement for the purpose of establishing a series of shares and fixing the preferences, limitations, and relative rights thereof:

1. The name of the Corporation is Water Bottle Company.

2. The resolution establishing a series of shares and fixing the preferences, limitations, and relative rights was adopted by the Board of Directors of the Corporation.

    (a) At a meeting duly called and held on _____, 199__; or
    (b) By unanimous written consent of the Board of Directors.

3. Following is the resolution adopted by the Board of Directors:

[INSERT RESOLUTION ADOPTED, AN EXAMPLE OF
WHICH APPEARS IN FIGURE 10–13.]

IN WITNESS WHEREOF, a duly authorized officer of the Corporation has executed this Designation Statement this 10th day of February, 1995.

WATER BOTTLE COMPANY

By _____
        President

---

issuance, the officers of the corporation are free to prepare the notes, bonds, or debentures and sell them to debt holders. Generally, corporate and tax counsel are hired by the corporation to handle all aspects of the sale of the various types of debt securities.

Debt securities may be secured or unsecured, and debt securities may represent short-term debt or long-term debt of the corporation. The types of instruments or documents that evidence debt of the corporation include promissory notes, bonds, and debentures. Debt securities may contain redemption and conversion provisions similar to those for preferred stock. In addition, debt securities may contain provisions giving them priority over or subordination to other securities issued by the corporation. All of these characteristics and types of debt securities will be discussed in greater detail in the following subsections.

Secured and Unsecured Debt

Certain bonds—namely, the mortgage bond and the collateral trust bond—are secured by property or assets of the corporation. **Secured debt** is debt that requires a pledge of real property, personal property, equipment, inventory, or other property of the corporation to ensure the repayment of the principal loaned to the corporation. As examples, a mortgage bond is secured by a mortgage on specified real property of the corporation, and a collateral trust bond is secured by other securities or bonds owned by the corporation. When personal property, equipment, or inventory is pledged to secure repayment of principal, a security agreement must be executed and delivered by the corporation to the debt holder.

On the other hand, the promissory note, certain bonds, and debentures are debt securities that are generally unsecured. **Unsecured debt** requires no pledge of any property of the corporation as security to ensure the repayment of the debt. Unsecured loans are based on the creditworthiness of the corporation, and the debt holders are not entitled to any specific assets of the corporation if the corporation defaults on the loan.

Short-Term and Long-Term Debt

Any debt instrument of the corporation may evidence short-term or long-term debt of the corporation. **Short-term debt** consists of any loan by a creditor for which the corporation will repay the principal within one year or less from the date the loan was originally made to the corporation. For example, when Water Bottle Company loaned Mountain Spring Water Company $20,000 on April 30, 1995, as shown in the example in Figure 10–2, Mountain Spring Water Company agreed to repay the principal on or before April 30, 1996. This promissory note evidences short-term debt of the corporation.

Long-term debt consists of any loan by a creditor for which the corporation will repay the principal more than one year after such funds were loaned to the corporation. A debenture is an example of a long-term debt instrument, since the principal to be repaid by the corporation on a debenture is often not due for 10, 20, or even 30 years after the debenture was originally issued by the corporation.

10–7   Types of Debt Securities

Promissory Note

A **promissory note,** or note, the simplest form of debt of the corporation, provides for the repayment of the principal in accordance with the terms and conditions of the note in one of the following two ways: (1) in one or more installments paid at stated intervals or on specific dates or (2) on demand made by the holder of the note. The sample form of note in Figure 10–2 is an example of an installment note. Note that this example provides that Mountain Spring Water Company promises to repay to Water Bottle Company the principal sum of $20,000 on April 30, 1996, and to pay interest each month at a rate of 10 percent per annum. An installment note could also provide for the repayment of principal monthly, quarterly, semiannually, or at some other intervals, but in this example one installment of $20,000 will be repaid on April 30, 1996.

Figure 10–15 is an example of a demand note. The difference between the installment note in Figure 10–2 and the demand note in Figure 10–15 is that the principal and any accrued interest due under the demand note must be repaid by Mountain Spring Water Company at the demand of Water Bottle Company, that is, on whatever date Water Bottle Company designates as the date when they desire to be repaid.

At a minimum a note should contain the following elements:

PARALEGALERT!

A promissory note provides for the repayment of the principal sum of the note either (1) in installments at stated intervals of time or (2) on demand made by the holder of the note. The corporate paralegal is often assigned the task of preparing installment and demand notes.

1. The amount of principal borrowed by the corporation.
2. A promise by the corporation to repay the principal in one or more installments or on the demand of the lender.
3. A promise by the corporation to pay interest, or a statement that no interest is to be paid.
4. The signature of the person issuing the note.
5. The date on which the note was issued.

Upon reviewing Figures 10–2 and 10–15, you will find that these elements are present in both sample notes.

Bond

A **bond,** which may be secured or unsecured, is a long-term debt instrument of the corporation. The bond is similar to the promissory note in that the bond evidences the corporation's promise to repay the owner of the bond, or bondholder, a set amount of principal and interest at a specified date in the future. The bond, however, is generally a more lengthy and complex instrument. A bond evidences a contract or agreement between the corporation and the bondholder whereby the corporation promises to pay a sum plus interest at stated intervals to the bondholder.

Unsecured bonds include coupon bonds and registered bonds, both of which evidence the corporation's promise to repay the bondholder but do not involve the corporation's pledge of its property or assets. Coupon bonds have interest coupons attached to them, which may be presented at a bank designated by the corporation or at the corporation's office for payment of the sum of money designated on the coupon. Registered bonds are registered on the books of the corporation in the name of the holder of the bonds and may be transferred or redeemed only upon endorsement by the owner of the bonds.

Secured bonds, which include the mortgage bond and the collateral trust bond, involve the corporation's pledge of certain of its property and stocks and bonds that it holds from other companies to ensure repayment of the loan by the bondholder. Both the mortgage bond and the collateral trust bond evidence the

Figure 10–15   Promissory Note (Demand)

Promissory Note

$20,000.00

April 30, 1995
Wilmington, Delaware

FOR VALUE RECEIVED, MOUNTAIN SPRING WATER COMPANY ("Payor") hereby promises to pay to WATER BOTTLE COMPANY ("Payee"), on demand, the principal sum of Twenty Thousand Dollars and 00/100 ($20,000.00), and to pay interest monthly from the date said funds were advanced until paid in full. Interest will accrue on any unpaid principal at a rate of 10 percent per annum and shall be computed on a 365-day year.

All payments of principal and interest shall be made via bank check delivered by mail to the Payee at 100 Market Street, Wilmington, Delaware 19801, or elsewhere as the holder hereof shall direct.

MOUNTAIN SPRING WATER COMPANY

By _____
President

corporation's promise to pay the bondholder a stated sum plus interest, but the mortgage bond is secured by a mortgage on the property owned by the corporation, and the collateral trust bond is secured by the stocks and bonds of other corporations, which are owned by the creditor corporation.

Debenture

A **debenture** is a long-term, unsecured bond that is issued without the pledge of any of the corporation's property or assets. The debenture is issued solely on the good credit and the good-faith promise of the corporation issuing the debenture. The debenture evidences the corporation's promise to pay the holder of the debenture a specified sum of money at a certain time with the payment of interest at specified intervals (monthly, quarterly, etc.) until the entire principal of the debenture is repaid.

Debentures are issued pursuant to a **trust indenture,** which is an agreement between the corporation and a trustee. A bank or other lending institution acts as trustee under the trust indenture. The trustee is responsible for acting on behalf of the holders of the debentures in case the corporation defaults on the payment of any principal or interest due to be paid to the holders. This arrangement saves the corporation from having to deal with numerous individual creditors in the event that the corporation does default on the loan. The trust indenture includes the terms and conditions under which the debentures are issued, including—among others— provisions for making payments of interest, remedies in the case of default in the payment of interest or principal, the trustee's duties, redemption procedures, and the form of debenture to be issued.

PARALEGALERT!

Both the bond and the debenture are generally very complex documents that are prepared by the attorney. However, the corporate paralegal should be familiar with the provisions of both. Examples of corporate bonds and debentures can be found in form books and manuals.

Provisions of Debt Securities

Debt securities may contain many of the same provisions that are found in designations of preferred stock. For example, debt securities may contain redemption provisions whereby the corporation may repurchase the debt at a future date. And debt securities may contain conversion privileges whereby the holder of the debt security has the option to convert such debt to a form of equity security, usually common stock. In addition, debt securities may be subordinate to other debt of the corporation. Subordination provides that other debt holders of the corporation will be repaid prior to the holder of the subordinated debt.

Redemption   Bonds and debentures usually include the right of the corporation to redeem the bonds or debentures at the discretion of the board of directors. The **right of redemption,** which allows the corporation to repurchase the security at a specified date and price, is spelled out in the provisions of the debt security (bond or debenture) itself. When the board approves the redemption of the bonds or debentures issued by the corporation, the corporation must send all holders of the security a notice of the decision of the board to redeem such bonds or debentures.

When an investor purchases a bond or debenture, it is generally with the expectation that the investment will provide a return. Therefore, the right of the corporation to redeem such bond or debenture prior to its maturity may require

Figure 10–16 Redemption Provisions

The bonds shall be redeemable in whole or in part at the option of the Board of Directors at any time after July 1, 1997, and from time to time thereafter at the following redemption prices (expressed in percentages of the principal amount of the bonds), together with all accrued and unpaid interest to the date fixed for redemption:

July 1, 1997 to June 30, 2001	110%
July 1, 2001 to June 30, 2005	105%
July 1, 2005 to maturity	100%

The Corporation shall provide not less than 30 days prior written notice to the record owners of the bonds, and such notice shall provide the procedures for surrendering the bonds and shall provide a time and place where payment for such bonds shall be made, all as determined by the Board of Directors. The bonds shall be deemed to have been redeemed on the date specified for redemption, and all liability of the Corporation shall cease on such redemption date, as shall all rights with respect to such bonds called for redemption. The Corporation shall set aside in a sinking fund the sum or sums sufficient to redeem the bonds, plus accrued and unpaid interest on the bonds. Any sums set aside shall never exceed the amount sufficient to redeem the bonds then outstanding, and all sums set aside for the sinking fund shall be applied only to the redemption of the bonds.

that the corporation pay additional principal, or a premium, to the debt holder. The promise of such a premium provides the debt holder assurance of receiving the anticipated return on investment and enhances the value of the bond or debenture so as to entice an investor to purchase it. The amount of the premium declines as the maturity date of the security becomes closer.

To ensure that the corporation has the funds available to exercise its right of redemption when it desires or to repay the debt holders upon maturity of the bonds or debentures, the corporation may set up a sinking fund. This fund is similar to the one we discussed for redemption of preferred stock. Provisions setting up a sinking fund require the corporation to set aside funds for the specific purpose of redeeming debt securities of the corporation, either as the corporation desires to do so or at maturity.

Figure 10–16 is an example of redemption provisions, which permit the corporation the right to redeem its bonds. These provisions would be included within the terms and conditions of the bond and may also be included in the terms and conditions of the corporation's debentures.

Figure 10–17 Conversion Provisions

This bond is convertible at the option of the holder of such bond, at any time prior to maturity (or at any time prior to the date fixed for redemption by the corporation) into shares of Common Stock of the Corporation at the rate of one share for each $100 of principal sum of the bond. Such conversion rate shall be adjusted, and notice provided within 10 days of such adjustment to the holder of this bond, upon a change in the capitalization of the Corporation, including a stock dividend, stock split, or reverse stock split. Upon providing the Corporation 30 days' written notice, the holder of this bond shall surrender to the Corporation this bond, and shall thereupon be entitled to receive share certificates of the Common Stock. No fractional shares of the Common Stock shall be issued, and the holder of this bond shall receive the appropriate cash value for such fractional share, as shall be determined by the Board of Directors. One hundred shares of Common Stock of the Corporation shall be reserved and set aside and issued only for the conversion of the bonds as provided for herein.

Figure 10–18   Subordination Provisions

> The rights of the holder of this bond as to the principal sum and the interest thereon shall be subject to and remain subordinate to the claims to principal and interest of the holders of the Corporation's debentures, and upon dissolution and liquidation of the Corporation no payment shall be payable on this bond until all claims of the holders of the debentures of the Corporation have been paid in full.

Conversion   Debt securities will often provide a **conversion privilege,** which gives the holder of the debt security the right to convert it to equity securities. This privilege is designed to make the debt security more attractive to potential investors and is similar to the conversion right provided to the holders of equity securities, which we discussed earlier in this chapter.

Terms of the conversion must be included in the terms and conditions of the debt security being issued. Generally a bond or debenture, but not a promissory note, includes provisions for the conversion of the bond or debenture to a particular class of equity security.

Figure 10–17 is an example of the provisions of a conversion privilege. These provisions would be included within the terms and conditions of a bond. Similar provisions could also be used in the provisions of a corporation's debenture. Note that these provisions include the following elements: (1) the number of shares into which the debt security is convertible, (2) the procedure for converting the debt security to common stock, (3) the reservation of a sufficient number of common shares to be available upon conversion, and (4) a provision for adjusting the conversion rate upon recapitalization of the corporation.

Subordination   The corporation may provide that any of its debt securities will be subordinate to other debt securities issued by the corporation. By purchasing debt securities that are subordinate to other securities, or **subordinated debt,** investors agree to permit the repayment of one debt security over the one that has been subordinated. This allows the corporation to maximize its borrowing capacity. For example, a bank or other lender hesitant to lend a corporation capital to finance its operations may be more willing to do so if that bank's debt will be senior, or superior, to other debt issued by the corporation. In the case where debt (note, bond, or debenture) has already been issued, the corporation must obtain the agreement of the debt holders to subordinate their debt.

Subordinated debt will be attractive to investors only if other features of the debt instrument compensate for the disadvantage. For example, a bond that is subordinated to all other debt of the corporation may pay the debt holder a higher rate of interest, may include conversion privileges, or may offer favorable redemption rights.

Figure 10–18 is an example of provisions that would be included in the terms and conditions of a bond to permit certain debt to be subordinated. Similar provisions could also be provided in any debenture issued by the corporation.

10–8   Practical Considerations

The role of the corporate paralegal in determining the capitalization of the corporation is generally minimal. However, many tasks that are assigned to a paralegal require an understanding of the types of equity and debt securities that a corporation may issue. We will discuss in this section some of the corporate paralegal's responsibilities, areas with which the paralegal should be most familiar, and pitfalls to avoid.

Responsibilities of the paralegal relating to the financing of the corporation, which were discussed in this chapter, include the following:

1. Drafting articles of incorporation, which include the capitalization provisions required by all state statutes.
2. Preparing resolutions for adoption by the board of directors to approve the following actions by the corporation:
   - Issuance of share certificates evidencing ownership of equity securities, including the consideration to be paid for those shares.
   - Issuance of notes, bonds, or debentures evidencing outstanding debt of the corporation.
   - Creation of series of preferred stock, spelling out the preferences, limitations, and relative rights of each series.
3. Purchasing share certificate books from a legal supplier.
4. Preparing share certificates after determining whether a share legend is required to be imprinted on such certificates.
5. Drafting a lost-certificate affidavit.
6. Determining the state's requirements for preparation and filing of a designation statement, which creates a series of preferred stock.
7. Drafting promissory notes and, to a lesser extent, bonds and debentures.
8. Drafting specific provisions for all types of equity and debt securities, including rights relating to voting, dividends, liquidation, redemption, sinking funds, conversion, and subordination.

These duties, in addition to other specific tasks too numerous to list, should all be ones with which a practicing corporate paralegal is familiar.

A common mistake is assuming that the capitalization of a corporation will be "1,000 shares of Common Stock, $1.00 par value." You have already learned in this chapter the extent to which the articles of incorporation may vary with respect to the capitalization of the corporation. Always confirm with your supervising attorney exactly how the corporation will be capitalized. After articles of incorporation have been filed, they may be amended to reflect the proper capitalization. But remember that amending the articles requires, at a minimum, shareholder and board approval and the filing of articles of amendment with the secretary of state. In addition, an explanation must be given to the client for not properly preparing the capitalization provisions of the articles the first time.

SUMMARY

10–1

The corporation, like any other business organization, must have a source of funds, or capital, available to it to be able to operate its business successfully. The capitalization, or financial structure, of the corporation can consist of any combination of the following ways of financing a corporation: reinvestment of the corporation's profits, sale of equity securities, and issuance of debt securities.

10–2

A corporation raises capital or finances its business through the issuance of equity securities and debt securities. Equity securities evidence an ownership interest in the corporation, and the owner of equity securities is called a shareholder. A share certificate is the tangible evidence of a shareholder's ownership interest in the corporation. Debt securities evidence the corporation's obligation to repay a debt to a creditor, or lender. Such documents as promissory notes, bonds, or debentures are the tangible evidence of a creditor's ownership of a corporation's debt security. The board of directors determines the mix of debt and equity securities that the corporation should issue, and several factors play a role in the board's decision, including current market conditions and interest rates, the amount of capital required by the corporation, and the tax consequences of issuing equity or debt securities.

10–3

Equity securities consist of common and preferred shares, but there are features found in both common and preferred shares. Authorized shares are the maximum number of shares (common and preferred) that a corporation has the authority to sell. Those sold by the corporation are called issued and outstanding shares, and those repurchased by the corporation are considered treasury shares. Treasury shares are authorized and issued, but are not outstanding. Shares may be divided into any number of classes or series as authorized in the articles of incorporation. The par value of shares, or the minimum dollar amount for which shares may be sold, has no relationship to the market value of shares, or the dollar amount that a person is willing to pay for a share. The issuance of shares requires approval of the board of directors. The information to be contained on a share certificate is prescribed by the appropriate state statute. If a share certificate is lost, destroyed, or stolen, the shareholder may execute and deliver an affidavit of lost certificate to the corporation or the transfer agent, who will then reissue the share certificate. State statutes or the articles of incorporation regulate the type of consideration to be paid for shares, but the board of directors is given the discretion to determine the amount of consideration to be paid. Shares are considered to be fully paid and nonassessable when the corporation has received the type and amount of consideration approved by the board of directors.

10–4

When a corporation is capitalized with only one class of stock, that class is common stock. If no other class of shares exists, the holders of the common shares are entitled to vote on all matters and to share in all profits of the corporation. Generally, shares of common stock have no special features, but state statutes permit the creation of any number of classes of common shares, with each permitted to possess different characteristics and rights. Common shares may possess different voting, liquidation, dividend, and preemptive rights. However, if the articles of incorporation do not specifically define special rights, common shares enjoy unlimited voting rights (one vote for one share, except in the case of cumulative voting), receive all net assets of the corporation on dissolution, and participate in distribution of the corporation's profits. One class of common stock may have preference over another class of common stock, and these preferred rights must be defined in the articles of incorporation.

10–5

Preferred stock generally has preference over other classes of stock with respect to the right to receive assets on dissolution of the corporation and the right to receive dividends. In addition to these preferences, provisions for preferred stock may also include the following: full, limited, or no voting rights; the right of the corporation to redeem shares; the option of shareholders to convert shares of the preferred stock to another class of shares; and provision for a sinking fund. All preferences, limitations, and rights of preferred stock must be specifically spelled out in the articles of incorporation and must be printed on share certificates issued by the corporation. Any series of preferred stock may be created by the board of directors, at its discretion, provided the authority to do so was vested in it in the articles of incorporation. The corporation must file a designation statement with the secretary of state upon the creation of a series of preferred stock. The designation statement acts as an amendment to the articles.

10–6

Capital or funds loaned to the corporation are considered debt of the corporation, and the tangible evidence that a lender, or creditor, has loaned funds to the corporation, or debtor, is called a debt security. The statutes of the corporation's state of incorporation confer on the corporation the right to borrow money to finance its operations or repay its debts, and the board of directors is vested with the authority to issue debt securities at its discretion. Debt securities may be secured or unsecured, may represent short-term debt or long-term debt of the corporation, may contain redemption and conversion provisions, and may contain provisions giving them priority over or subordination to other securities issued by the corporation.

10–7

Examples of debt securities include promissory notes, bonds, and debentures. The promissory note, the simplest form of debt security of the corporation, provides for the repayment of the principal loaned to the corporation and usually provides for the payment of interest on the outstanding principal. The bond, which may be secured or unsecured and which is long-term debt of the corporation, is a more complex debt instrument than the note. The bond does, however, also provide for the repayment of a sum plus interest at stated intervals to the holder of the bond. The debenture, which is a long-term, unsecured bond, will be issued without the pledge of any corporate property or assets. Debt securities may contain many of the same features as preferred stock, such as redemption provisions and conversion privileges. In addition, debt securities may be subordinate to other forms of debt of the corporation in their priority of repayment.

10–8

The role of the corporate paralegal in determining the capitalization of the corporation is generally minimal, but the paralegal must have an understanding of the types of equity and debt securities that a corporation may issue. The paralegal is usually responsible for drafting several documents related to a corporation's financing, including the articles of incorporation, provisions relating to the specific series of preferred stock, the designation statement, the affidavit of lost certificate, promissory notes, and resolutions of the board of directors approving corporate actions related to corporate financing. The paralegal should avoid making the common mistake of assuming that the capitalization of a corporation will be simple and failing to ask the supervising attorney for the capitalization provisions.

REVIEW GUIDE

Key Terms

Before proceeding, review the key terms listed below to be sure you understand each one. If necessary, read over the corresponding section of the chapter. When you are ready to test your understanding, answer the review questions.

capital (p. 216)
capitalization (p. 217)
security (p. 217)
equity securities (p. 218)
shareholder (p. 218)
share (p. 218)
share certificate (p. 218)
debt securities (p. 218)
equity holders (p. 221)
debt holders (p. 221)
authorized shares (p. 222)
issued and outstanding shares (p. 223)
treasury shares (p. 223)
classes (p. 224)
series (p. 224)
par value (p. 225)
market value (p. 227)
market price (p. 227)
new issue (p. 227)
share legend (p. 228)
affidavit of lost certificate (p. 229)
transfer agent (p. 229)
fully paid and nonassessable shares (p. 230)
common stock (p. 231)
preemptive rights (p. 233)
preferred stock (p. 234)
cumulative dividends (p. 237)
noncumulative dividends (p. 237)
right of redemption (preferred shares) (p. 238)
sinking fund (p. 238)
conversion rights (preferred shares) (p. 239)
designation statement (p. 241)
debtor (p. 241)
creditor (p. 241)
secured debt (p. 242)
unsecured debt (p. 243)
short-term debt (p. 243)
long-term debt (p. 243)
promissory note (p. 243)
bond (p. 244)
debenture (p. 245)
trust indenture (p. 245)
right of redemption (debt security) (p. 245)
conversion privilege (debt security) (p. 247)
subordinated debt (p. 247)

Questions for Review and Discussion

1. Identify the ways in which the corporation is financed or capitalized.
2. What tangible evidence would a person have in his or her possession to show that he or she has an ownership interest in a corporation?
3. Explain the differences between equity securities and debt securities and the reasons for the board of directors of a corporation to decide to issue one over the other.
4. Where would you find the number of shares that the corporation has the authority to issue?
5. How would you determine what differences exist between Class A Common Stock and Class B Common Stock issued by ABC Company?
6. How does the par value and the market value of shares differ?
7. In the liquidation of the corporation, will a fixed amount ever be set for common shareholders to receive? Why or why not?
8. Identify the ways in which preferred stock has a preference over other classes of stock of the corporation.
9. Why would a corporation issue both voting and nonvoting shares?
10. Of the various characteristics associated with preferred shares, which characteristic do you think a shareholder would find least attractive. Why?
11. How would you determine whether the board of directors had the authority to create a series of preferred stock?
12. What is the difference between debt of the corporation that is secured and debt that is unsecured? Give examples.
13. How does a promissory note differ from a bond or a debenture?
14. Who has the right to redeem bonds or debentures?
15. Explain subordination provisions and tell why an investor would purchase debt securities that are subordinated to other debt of the corporation.

Activities

1. Your supervising attorney, Larry Lawyer, has been asked by his client to advise him on the types of securities that can be issued by a corporation. Larry Lawyer asks you to prepare a memorandum that outlines the attributes of the various types of corporate securities. Prepare such a memorandum, outlining the types of corporate securities, their particular attributes, and suggestions as to the desirability of those securities in any given situation.

2. Draft a promissory note using the following information. Determine whether this note should be an installment or demand note.

   Jeffrey Davis loaned Seminar Specialists Inc. the sum of $150,000 on February 15, 1996. Mr. Davis expects to be repaid the principal on February 15, 1998, and to be paid interest quarterly at a rate of 9.5 percent per annum. Seminar Specialists Inc. is a Wyoming corporation, and Mr. Davis lives in Cheyenne, Wyoming.

3. Visit the local law library and locate form books or manuals that contain examples of provisions of equity securities and forms of debt securities. Find examples of the following: (a) provisions of preferred stock with conversion privileges, (b) form of a demand promissory note, and (c) form of a debenture that includes redemption provisions.

CHAPTER 11 Corporate Dividends and Distributions

OUTLINE

11–1 Dividends and Distributions
> Authorization to Make Distributions
> Corporation's Repurchase of Shares

11–2 Sources of Funds for Distribution as Dividends
> Corporation's Balance Sheet
> Sources from Which Dividends May Be Declared
> Restrictions on Payment

11–3 Cash and Property Dividends
> Right to Receive Dividends
> Procedure for Payment
> Accounting Procedures
> Tax Implications

11–4 Share Dividends
> Procedure for Issuance
> Accounting Procedures
> Reasons for Paying Share Dividends
> Tax Implications

11–5 Stock Split
> Procedure for Issuance
> Accounting Procedures
> Reasons for Effecting Stock Splits
> Tax Implications

11–6 Reverse Stock Split
> Procedures
> Accounting Procedures
> Reasons for Effecting Reverse Stock Splits

11–7 Practical Considerations

APPLICATIONS

Susan Minahan has been working as the sole corporate paralegal for the law firm of Barney & Rubble, P.C., for a little over a year. Therefore, her experience and knowledge of the firm's corporate practice is limited. She has been asked to accompany her supervising attorney, Larry Lawyer, to a meeting with the president and the secretary of Bicycle Manufacturing Company. These officers must report back to their board of directors with recommendations for effecting a split of the common stock of the corporation. Larry Lawyer has asked Susan Minahan to be present because he knows some of the work involved in the split of a corporation's stock is most efficiently accomplished by a paralegal.

Unfortunately, Susan Minahan has never worked in this area. She does, however, have a basic understanding of the requirements for and the mechanics of the stock split.

OBJECTIVES

This chapter introduces issues and concepts usually found in accounting textbooks, but your understanding of these principles is important. After completing Chapter 11, you will be able to:

1. Understand investors' reasons for purchasing shares of a corporation.
2. Define *treasury shares.*
3. Understand the components of the balance sheet—in particular, the components of the net worth section.
4. Define the sources from which distributions may be made.
5. Distinguish the differences between cash and property dividends.
6. Understand the reasons for the board of directors to issue share dividends and effect stock splits.
7. Prepare board of directors' resolutions approving the issuance of cash, property, and share dividends and effecting stock splits and reverse stock splits.
8. Determine the necessity of amending the articles of incorporation when the corporation issues additional shares.
9. Understand the basic accounting principles involved in the various types of corporate dividends and distributions.

11–1 Dividends and Distributions

Persons usually acquire shares of a corporation with the goal of deriving economic benefit from ownership of those shares. This economic benefit can be realized in one or both of two ways: (1) through the distribution of the corporation's profits, in the form of dividends, property, or shares of the corporation, and (2) by the sale of the shares at a price higher than the price paid for the shares, that is, through a capital gain on the sale of the shares. In this chapter we will examine the first of these two methods. In particular, we will study the authority under which profits may be distributed, the funds out of which profits may legally be distributed, and the procedures for distributing corporate profits to the shareholders.

In general, a **dividend** is a distribution of the corporation's earnings to its shareholders. A corporation's earnings or profits may be distributed in one or more of the following forms: cash, property, or shares of the corporation itself. Hence, we have the terms *cash dividend, property dividend,* and *share dividend.* Unless the articles of incorporation specify the form in which dividends are to be paid, the decision is left to the board of directors. We will also discuss in this chapter the two other types of corporate distributions, the stock split and the reverse stock split.

PARALEGALERT!

A dividend is the form in which the corporation will distribute its profits to the shareholders. Dividends may be issued in the form of cash, property, or shares of the corporation itself.

Authorization to Make Distributions

As you remember from discussions in previous chapters, the ownership of shares in a corporation carries with it the right to share in the profits of the corporation. Shareholders do not have the right to make withdrawals of the corporation's assets, as the owner of a sole proprietorship is permitted to do, but they do have the right to receive dividends when dividends are declared by the board of directors. Section 6.40(a) of the Model Act permits that "a board of directors may authorize and the corporation may make distributions to its shareholders subject to restriction by the articles of incorporation." The statutes of *all states* permit corporations to make distributions or pay dividends to their shareholders.

The board of directors of the corporation has the authority to declare and pay dividends to the shareholders. The shareholders have the right to receive such dividends or distributions, but they cannot declare that a dividend shall be paid to them even if they unanimously agree at a validly called and held shareholders' meeting. The power lies solely with the board of directors. This power is limited only by (1) a statutory restriction; (2) a restriction in the articles of incorporation, the bylaws, or an agreement between the corporation and its shareholders; or (3) a court order compelling the payment of a dividend when the directors have not acted in good faith. For example, the articles may provide that dividends may be paid to the common shareholders only if funds are available after making dividend payments to the preferred shareholders.

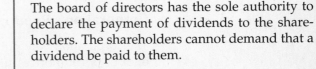

PARALEGALERT!

The board of directors has the sole authority to declare the payment of dividends to the shareholders. The shareholders cannot demand that a dividend be paid to them.

The case cited in the *Legal Links* in this chapter confirms the directors' power to declare the payment of dividends to the shareholders. However, the directors are permitted to use their discretion in the payment of dividends. Directors may apply the profits of a corporation, out of which dividends may be distributed to shareholders, to some other corporate purpose. For example, the directors may use the profits of a corporation to purchase real estate or invest in additional inventory instead of paying a dividend to the shareholders.

As we have stated, dividends are declared by the board of directors, and the board of directors carries out the declaration in the form of a resolution. The resolution should include the following:

1. The amount and type of the dividend to be paid.
2. The date on which the dividend is to be paid.
3. The class of stock on which the dividend is to be paid.
4. The record date for determining which shareholders will receive the dividend.
5. The corporate officer authorized to pay the dividend.

Figure 11–1 is an example of a board of directors' resolution declaring the payment of a cash dividend to the common shareholders. Remember from our discussion in Chapter 7 that the board of directors would adopt this resolution in one of the following two ways: (1) at a meeting of the board of directors, for which proper notice was sent and at which a quorum was present for the conducting of business, or (2) by unanimous written consent, executed by all the directors of the corporation. This same procedure for adopting resolutions of the board of directors applies to all resolutions discussed in this chapter.

Figure 11–1 Resolution of Directors Declaring the Payment of a Cash Dividend

RESOLVED, that a dividend of $.55 per share is declared to be paid on the Common Stock of the Corporation out of the earned surplus of the Corporation to the holders of stock as shown by the records of the Corporation on March 10, 1995, distributable on April 1, 1995, and that the Treasurer is directed to pay the dividend declared by mailing checks for the same to the shareholders of record.

Unless the articles of incorporation provide otherwise, dividends are permitted to be paid to the shareholders of common stock. In the case of preferred shareholders, the articles of incorporation must state what preferences and limitations are placed on dividend payments, whether dividends are cumulative or noncumulative, and whether the payment of dividends to common shareholders is dependent on the payment of dividends to preferred shareholders. In short, the articles of incorporation must clearly spell out the dividend rights of the preferred shareholder, and dividends may be paid to common shareholders unless the articles provide otherwise.

Corporation's Repurchase of Shares

The corporation may purchase its own shares from its shareholders if the board of directors authorizes such purchase and the statute of the corporation's state of incorporation allows such repurchase. Section 6.31(a) of the Model Act provides that "a corporation may acquire its own shares and shares so acquired constitute authorized but unissued shares." A corporation's own shares that it repurchases are called **treasury shares.**

According to the Model Act, treasury shares are authorized but unissued shares of the corporation. You must, however, review the statutes of a particular state to determine how treasury shares in that state are treated. Not all states consider treasury shares unissued shares.

The corporation may desire to repurchase its own shares for one or more of several reasons. First, the corporation may wish to reduce the payment of dividends on issued and outstanding shares. As you remember from a previous discussion, treasury shares are not outstanding and dividends are not paid on them. So the corporation would not pay itself a dividend. Second, the corporation may believe that the corporation itself is a good investment. As stated earlier, shares of a corporation are usually purchased with a favorable economic goal in mind. Third, the corporation desires to reduce the number of persons holding shares of the corporation. Another way in which the corporation can accomplish a reduction in the number of persons holding its shares is through a reverse stock split, which we will discuss later in this chapter.

The funds used to purchase treasury shares must come from certain corporate accounts of the corporation. The repurchase of shares is treated as a distribution to the shareholders and must therefore comply with the same restrictions imposed on the distribution of dividends. In general, most states provide that dividends may be paid only from the following sources: (1) earned surplus or retained earnings, (2) capital surplus, and (3) the amount received as consideration for shares without par value that is treated as surplus rather than stated capital. You will gain a better understanding of these sources of funds and accounts from Section 11–2.

11–2 Sources of Funds for Distribution as Dividends

The Model Act and all states' statutes prescribe the circumstances under which dividends or corporate distributions may be paid. Section 6.40(c) of the Model Act provides that

No distribution may be made if, after giving it effect:

(1) the corporation would not be able to pay its debts as they become due in the usual course of business; or

(2) the corporation's total assets would be less than the sum of its total liabilities plus (unless the articles of incorporation permit otherwise) the amount that would be needed, if the corporation were to be dissolved at the time of the distribution, to satisfy the preferential rights upon dissolution of shareholders whose preferential rights are superior to those receiving the distribution.

In other words, the board of directors in its discretion may direct that a distribution be made only if two criteria are met:

1. The corporation must still be able to pay its debts that regularly become due in the normal course of business. That is, a distribution should not be made if the funds used to pay such distribution should be used to pay rent, utilities, bank loans, payments for equipment and inventory, or other expenses.

2. The corporation's total assets must be greater than its total liabilities *plus* any amount that would be due to preferred shareholders if the corporation were to dissolve at the same time the distribution of profits were made.

> ## PARALEGALERT!
>
> The corporation must be able to answer yes to both of the following questions prior to distributing its profits in the form of dividends: (1) Will all debts that occur during the normal course of business be paid? (2) Are total assets greater than total liabilities plus accrued and unpaid dividends due the preferred shareholders?

Corporation's Balance Sheet

Before we discuss the sources from which dividends may be paid, we will examine the components of a corporation's balance sheet to gain a better understanding of the sources from which corporate distributions or dividends may be paid. State statutes permit the payment of dividends only out of particular corporate accounts, which are found on the corporation's balance sheet. It is the net worth section of the balance sheet in which we are particularly interested in regard to the payment of dividends.

As we discuss each section or component of the balance sheet, refer to Figure 11–2, which is the balance sheet for Bicycle Manufacturing Company. This corporation's balance sheet gives in dollar amounts the assets, liabilities, and net worth of the corporation as of a specific date. Other names that may be used for the net worth section of the balance sheet include *net assets, capital,* and *shareholder's equity.*

The balance sheet, one of the financial statements of the corporation, reports the assets, liabilities, and net worth of the corporation. The assets must equal (or balance) the total of the liabilities and the net worth of the corporation. In other words, the net worth, or capital, of the corporation is equal to the excess of the assets over the liabilities. Note that, in our example, total assets equal $50,000, liabilities equal $10,000, and net worth is $40,000. Our definition holds true in that assets exceed liabilities by $40,000, which is the net worth of the corporation as indicated on the balance sheet.

Consider the following definitions in relationship to the balance sheet in Figure 11–2:

1. **Net worth** (often referred to as net assets, capital, or shareholders' equity)— The amount by which total assets exceed total liabilities. In the example, total assets are $50,000, and total liabilities (debts) are $10,000; therefore, net worth is $40,000.

Figure 11–2   Balance Sheet of Bicycle Manufacturing Company

Bicycle Manufacturing Company

BALANCE SHEET as of December 31, 1994

ASSETS

Cash	5,000	
Marketable Securities	8,000	
Accounts Receivable	2,000	
Real Estate	20,000	
Inventory	10,000	
Equipment	5,000	
TOTAL ASSETS		**50,000**

LIABILITIES

Accounts Payable	6,000	
Note Payable	4,000	
TOTAL LIABILITIES		**10,000**

NET WORTH

Stated Capital

Common Stock, $1.00 par value; 5,000 authorized, 5,000 issued and outstanding	5,000	
Preferred Stock, 5% Cumulative; $100.00 par value; 10,000 authorized, 50 issued and outstanding	5,000	
Total Stated Capital		10,000
Capital Surplus		20,000
Earned Surplus		10,000
TOTAL NET WORTH		**40,000**
TOTAL LIABILITIES AND NET WORTH		**50,000**

2. **Stated capital** — The sum of (1) the par value of all par-value shares of the corporation that have been issued and (2) the amount of consideration received by the corporation for shares without par value that have been issued. In the example, stated capital equals the par value of the 5,000 common shares that are issued and outstanding (5,000 × $1 par value = $5,000) plus the par value of the 50 preferred shares issued and outstanding (50 × $100 par value = $5,000). Therefore, the total stated capital for this corporation is $10,000.

With respect to shares without par value, what portion of the consideration paid for shares is to be treated as stated capital and what portion is to be treated as capital surplus will be fixed in the articles of incorporation or determined by the directors or shareholders of the corporation.

Stated capital is the portion of the capital of the corporation that cannot be distributed to shareholders. The purpose of not permitting stated capital to be distributed is the protection of creditors of the corporation. Stated capital is often called **legal capital**.

3. **Capital surplus** — The total amount of consideration received by the corporation for the sale of shares minus the par value of the shares sold. Capital surplus results from the excess paid for the shares over the par value of those shares. The balance sheet shows a capital surplus of $20,000, which came from the following sales of the corporation's stock: (a) 5,000 common shares were sold for $4/share ($1/share is stated capital and $3/share is capital surplus), and (b) 50 preferred shares were sold for $200/share ($100/share is stated capital and $100/share is capital surplus).

4. **Earned surplus** or **retained earnings** — Cumulation of net profits, income, gains, and taking into account losses of the corporation from the date of incorporation minus distributions and dividends paid out of earned surplus. Earned surplus is the accumulated profits retained in the corporation since it began doing business. It has been earned by the corporation through its profitable conduct of its business operations.

5. **Surplus** — The total of earned surplus, capital surplus, and the portion of the consideration for shares without par value that is treated as surplus rather than as stated capital. In our example, surplus is $30,000, which comes from $10,000 in earned surplus and $20,000 in capital surplus. The third element that makes up surplus is not relevant in our example as the shares all have a par value.

Sources from Which Dividends May Be Declared

State statutes regulate the manner in which a corporation may distribute its assets to the shareholders, and each state statute identifies the particular corporate accounts from which a distribution may be made. You must review the statutes of the corporation's state of incorporation to determine the specific requirements for the payment of dividends. However, in general, most states provide that dividends may be paid only from the following sources: (1) earned surplus, or retained earnings; (2) capital surplus; and (3) the portion of the consideration for stock without par value that is treated as surplus rather than as stated capital. All these sources are generally referred to as *surplus,* as already defined. Be aware that what the statutes of one state regard as surplus, the statutes of another state may not. Therefore, a careful review of the statutes is important.

Refer again to our example in Figure 11–2. Bicycle Manufacturing Company has legal sources for cash dividends of up to $30,000 (the total of capital surplus and earned surplus), but it may not be able to declare such a large dividend, for the following reason: The corporation has only $5,000 in cash, and it will need some cash to continue ordinary business operations. It may, therefore, issue a cash dividend of only $3,000, leaving $2,000 in cash to pay the liabilities of the corporation as they become due. If the corporation does not have the cash available to pay such debts, it may become **insolvent**—that is, unable to meet its debts as they become due in the usual course of business. The

PARALEGALERT!

The following are the components of the net worth section of a corporation's balance sheet: stated capital, capital surplus, and earned surplus. The corporate paralegal is not responsible for preparing a balance sheet but should understand its components.

PARALEGALERT!

Most statutes provide that dividends may be paid out of earned surplus (retained earnings), capital surplus, or that portion of consideration received for stock without par value that is treated as surplus, as opposed to stated capital.

board of directors cannot legally declare a dividend if it will result in the corporation's insolvency, or inability to pay its debts. Refer again to Section 6.40(c) of the Model Act, which was cited at the beginning of Section 11–2.

Restrictions on Payment

The source of funds from which dividends may be paid may be limited by the state statute or by the articles of incorporation. For example, the articles may permit the payment of dividends only out of earned surplus, by including the following provision: "No dividends on any share or shares of stock of the corporation shall be paid at any time, except out of the earned surplus or retained earnings of the corporation." This provision is not frequently found in the articles of incorporation, as corporations generally do not want to limit their ability to issue dividends.

11–3 Cash and Property Dividends

Most dividends are payable in cash as long as the cash (an asset of the corporation found in the asset section of the balance sheet) and the surplus (the total of which is found in the net worth section of the balance sheet) are available. A dividend paid in cash, called a **cash dividend,** is generally distributed in the form of a check.

When a dividend is paid in the form of property, it is called a **property dividend.** Property dividends include real estate, equipment, inventory, and other assets owned by the corporation. A corporation that manufactures bicycles could distribute those bicycles as property dividends. The shareholders do not have to accept payment of a dividend in this form. Unless the shareholders find the property dividend acceptable, the corporation may have to hold the property in trust for the shareholders or sell the property on behalf of the shareholders.

Right to Receive Dividends

Different classes of stock may be treated differently with respect to the payment of dividends. The preferred shareholders usually have a preference with respect to the payment of dividends and are entitled to be paid dividends before the common shareholders. For example, when the board of directors declares a total cash dividend of $2,000 to be paid to the shareholders, the preferred shareholders receive their dividend first, in accordance with the preference spelled out in the articles of incorporation. The common shareholders then receive the remaining portion of the $2,000, if any remains after payment of dividends to the preferred shareholders.

In addition, all the shareholders of any particular class of stock must be treated equally in the payment of dividends. For example, all common shareholders must receive the same amount of dividends per share. One common shareholder could not receive $1.00 per share in dividends and others receive $.50 per share in dividends.

PARALEGALERT!

Preferred shareholders usually have a preference with respect to the payment of dividends. To determine whether such a preference exists, you must review the articles of incorporation. All rights of preferred shares must be spelled out in the articles.

Figure 11–3   Resolution of Directors Declaring the Payment of a Property Dividend

> RESOLVED, that the President and the Secretary of the Corporation are authorized to convey real property of the Corporation, namely, bicycles manufactured by the Corporation as listed below, with a total aggregate value of $10,000, to the following shareholders of the Corporation:
>
> | | |
> |---|---|
> | Betty Biker | Bicycle Model XT-1455 |
> | Jeremy Jumper | Bicycle Model XT-1566 |
> | Randy Rider | Bicycle Model XT-1677 |

After the board of directors declares that a dividend is to be paid, the obligation to pay such dividend becomes an obligation, or debt, of the corporation. After the declaration of payment has been made by the board of directors, the actual payment of the dividend is generally not made for several days or several weeks. In the interim between the board of directors' declaration that a dividend shall be paid and the actual payment of that dividend, the dividend to be paid is a liability of the corporation.

Procedure for Payment

For both the cash dividend and the property dividend, the board of directors must declare that such a dividend is to be paid to the shareholder. Refer to Figure 11–1, which is an example of a resolution of the directors declaring the payment of a cash dividend. Figure 11–3 is an example of a resolution of the directors declaring the payment of a property dividend. Note that both of these resolutions authorize an officer of the corporation to arrange for payment of the dividend.

Accounting Procedures

Dividends may be declared and paid, in cash or property, only out of available funds. Distributions of cash or property decrease both the total assets and the total net worth of the corporation. Therefore, the board of directors must first determine if there are sufficient funds out of which to pay a dividend. For a corporation to pay dividends, profits must have been earned (as evidenced by the amount of earned surplus or retained earnings), and cash or property (as evidenced by the cash and property accounts) must be available for distribution. For example, with respect to the payment of a cash dividend, the board of directors must take into account the amount of cash on hand. If the corporation has no cash immediately available, it may not be desirable for the corporation to liquidate or sell its property, inventory, equipment, or other assets and convert it into cash in order to pay a cash dividend.

When a cash or property dividend is paid, the following accounts on the balance sheet are affected:

1. Cash is reduced (or the amount of property, if a property dividend).
2. Earned surplus (or retained earnings) is reduced.

The balance sheet will continue to be in balance because the reduction in cash or property reduces the total assets and the reduction in the earned surplus account reduces the total net worth. Remember that total assets are equal to total liabilities and net worth.

Wabash Railway Company v. Barclay

The Supreme Court held in *Wabash Railway Company v. Barclay*, 280 U.S. 197 (1930), that it was within the directors' discretion to use profits for capital improvements instead of distributing such profits to the shareholders. The Court stated, "We believe that it has been the common understanding of lawyers and business men that in the case of non-cumulative stock entitled only to a dividend if declared out of annual profits, if those profits are justifiably applied by the directors to capital improvement and no dividend is declared within the year, the claim for that year is gone and cannot be asserted at a later date."

The Court assumed that the plaintiffs in this case believed that the directors were attempting to abuse their power and apply earnings to capital improvements rather than to make dividend payments in which they did not share. However, the Court remarked that the law "has long advised [the shareholders] that their rights depend upon the judgment of men subject to just that possible bias."

Tax Implications

Recall from discussions earlier in this book that one disadvantage of the corporate form of business organization is that the corporation and its shareholders are subject to double taxation. **Double taxation** occurs when both the corporation and the shareholders pay tax on the same dollars. The corporation pays tax on its profits. It then distributes dividends to the shareholders. The dividends are paid out of the profits on which the corporation has already paid tax. The shareholders must then pay tax on the dividends paid to them. The corporation pays corporate income tax on the profits, and the shareholder pays personal income tax on the dividends paid from those profits. The result is double taxation of the profits.

In smaller, closely held corporations, shareholders who are also employees of the corporation may take a larger salary from the corporation in lieu of receiving dividends. This practice eliminates the double taxation, since salaries paid by the corporation are a tax-deductible expense. However, corporations should consult proper accounting or tax counsel because the Internal Revenue Service keeps a close watch on these types of activities.

11–4   Share Dividends

A **share dividend** is a distribution of the corporation's own shares to the shareholders. (Less frequently, the corporation may distribute shares of another corporation to the shareholders. For example, a corporation may distribute to its shareholders shares of a subsidiary corporation. However, that does not usually occur.) The result of a share dividend is that the total number of shares owned by the shareholders increases, but the proportionate share ownership of each shareholder does not change. This type of distribution adds nothing to a shareholder's percentage ownership interest, as all shareholders receive their proportionate share ownership in the corporation. It dilutes the value of each share owned by the shareholder. Each shareholder owns more shares, but each share's value is proportionately less.

Authority to distribute shares of the corporation is provided by the state statutes. Section 6.23(a) of the Model Act provides that "unless the articles of incorporation provide otherwise, shares may be issued pro rata and without consideration to the corporation's shareholders or to the shareholders of one or more classes or series. An issuance of shares under this subsection is a share dividend."

A share dividend payable in one class of stock may not be paid to holders of another class of stock, unless the articles of incorporation or the shareholders to whom the payment is to be made authorize such issuance. In almost every instance, shares of one class will be paid to the holders of the same class of shares in a share dividend. For example, shares of preferred stock may not be issued to holders of common shares as a stock dividend unless, of course, this action has been authorized as just described. Section 6.23(b) of the Model Act states that "shares of one class or series may not be issued as a share dividend in respect of shares of another class or series unless (1) the articles of incorporation so authorize, (2) a majority of the votes entitled to be cast by the class or series to be issued approve the issue, or (3) there are no outstanding shares of the class or series to be issued." Most states have adopted provisions similar to that of the Model Act.

To summarize, a share dividend has the following results:

- Additional shares are issued.
- There is no change in the par value of the corporation's shares.
- There is no change in percentage ownership by the shareholders.
- Stated capital is increased by the amount derived by multiplying the number of shares issued by the par value of those shares.
- Earned surplus is decreased by this same amount.
- Total capital remains the same.

Procedure for Issuance

The decision to declare a share dividend is made at the sole discretion of the board of directors. The directors adopt a resolution specifying the number of shares to be distributed, the proportion of distribution, a record and payment date, the authority for the transfer of earned surplus to stated capital, and the officer of the corporation with the authority to issue the additional shares to the shareholders. Figure 11–4 is an example of a resolution of the directors declaring the issuance of a share dividend.

An officer of the corporation, usually the secretary or treasurer, arranges for the issuance of the additional shares. For smaller, closely held corporations, the corporate paralegal may be responsible for issuing the shares. The number of new share certificates that must be issued dictates who is responsible for issuing the shares. If a voluminous number of certificates must be issued, the corporation may assign the task of issuing the shares to a transfer agent.

> **PARALEGALERT!**
>
> The corporation's distribution of shares of the corporation itself is a share dividend, which results in each shareholder's owning more shares. Because every shareholder receives his or her proportionate share of all the shares being distributed, the percentage ownership does not change.

Figure 11–4   Resolution of Directors Declaring the Issuance of a Share Dividend

RESOLVED, that the officers of the Corporation are hereby authorized to issue a 10% stock dividend, represented by a total of 1,000 shares of the authorized and unissued Common Stock of the Corporation, payable on June 1, 1995, to holders of record of Common Stock at the close of business on May 15, 1995, in proportion to their holdings of Common Stock of the Corporation.

Accounting Procedures

Before declaring a share dividend, the board of directors should consider the following questions:

1. Does the corporation have sufficient treasury shares or authorized shares to issue the additional shares required for the share dividend? If adequate shares have not been authorized or are not in the treasury of the corporation, the articles of incorporation must be amended to increase the authorized shares.
2. Does the corporation have adequate earned surplus available to transfer to the stated capital account? In determining the amount to be transferred between accounts, the number of shares to be issued is multiplied by the par value per share. This amount is then transferred from the earned surplus account to the stated capital account. Note that neither the asset nor the liability section is affected. Only the net worth section of the balance sheet is affected.

In issuing a share dividend, the corporation is merely transferring funds within the net worth section of the balance sheet and is not distributing any assets of the corporation. Only the earned surplus and stated capital accounts are affected by a share dividend. To gain a better understanding of the effects a share dividend has on the accounts on the balance sheet, refer to Figure 11–5. This example is an accounting for the issuance of a 10% stock dividend. In determining a 10% stock dividend in our example, the 1,000 shares issued and outstanding is multiplied by 10% to get 100 (1,000 × .10 = 100). Add the 100 additional shares to be issued to the 1,000 shares already issued and outstanding, and the total shares issued and outstanding after the 10% stock dividend will be 1,100. Also note that total capital remains the same before and after the issuance of the share dividend.

PARALEGALERT!

Prior to the declaration of a share dividend, the board of directors must consider the following: (1) whether sufficient treasury or authorized shares exist and (2) whether adequate earned surplus is available.

Reasons for Paying Share Dividends

Corporations often prefer to issue share dividends because they do not require the distribution of any cash or property of the corporation. Suppose that a corporation has planned to use its available cash on an expansion project. It does not want to deplete its cash reserves until the project is complete. On the other hand, it wants to provide its shareholders with some evidence that the corporation is profitable. The board of directors will, in this case, issue a share dividend.

Figure 11–5   Accounting for a 10% Stock Dividend

10% Stock Dividend			
Before Dividend		**After Dividend**	
1,000 shares Common Stock par value $1.00 per share		1,100 shares Common Stock par value $1.00 per share	
Stated Capital	1,000	Stated Capital	1,100
Earned Surplus	10,000	Earned Surplus	9,900
Total Capital	11,000	Total Capital	11,000

A second reason for paying a share dividend is to increase the marketability of the shares. Investors in the stock market are accustomed to seeing stock prices at certain levels. When a share of stock rises beyond a certain level, investors may be reluctant to purchase it. For some reason, investors are more likely to buy 100 shares of $20 stock than 20 shares of $100 stock. Therefore, when the board of directors feels that the price of the corporation's stock is too high, it will declare a share dividend. This will reduce the price of each share and increase the marketability of the stock. The same result can be obtained by effecting a stock split, which we will discuss in the next section.

Consider the following example: Stock A is currently selling for $100/share. Upon the board of directors' declaration of a 100% share dividend, the value of each share of Stock A is reduced to $50/share. The reduction in value from $100 to $50 occurs because the number of outstanding shares doubles while the total value of the shares remains the same. For example, two shares with a total value of $200 before the share dividend become four shares with a total value of $200 immediately after the share dividend. In all likelihood—though there is no guarantee—the shares of Stock A will increase in value from $50 to $100 (their customary level) more quickly than they would increase from $100 to $150. Therefore, the shareholders benefit by holding 50% more shares of Stock A.

Tax Implications

Generally, the receipt of a share dividend is a nontaxable event to the shareholder. In other words, shareholders pay no federal income tax on the shares they receive in the form of share dividends. However, the tax implications of a share dividend get complicated when the shareholder decides to sell the shares. The basis of the shares, which must be calculated to determine the capital gain or loss on the sale of the shares, must be adjusted to account for the share dividend. This calculation can be complicated, and therefore a share dividend may be unpopular with shareholders. However, in most cases, the benefits of receiving a share dividend outweigh the sometimes confusing tax implications. In general, the issuance of a share dividend is looked on as favorable by the shareholders of the corporation.

11–5   Stock Split

A **stock split** is very similar to a share dividend in that it results in a distribution of the corporation's own shares to the shareholders. The result of a stock split is that the total number of shares owned by the shareholders increases, but their proportionate share ownership of the corporation does not change. For example, a 2-for-1 stock split is similar to a 100% share dividend in that, in both cases, the shareholders will own twice as many shares as they did before the stock split or share dividend. But a stock split *should be distinguished* from a share dividend.

Remember that the issuance of a share dividend requires a transfer from the earned surplus account to the stated capital account. This transfer, in effect, acts like a distribution to the shareholders because the earned surplus, or profit, account is reduced. But in a stock split, the earned surplus and stated capital accounts of the net worth section of the balance sheet remain unchanged. A second difference is that the par value of the shares is decreased and the number of issued and outstanding shares is increased by the same proportion in a stock split; thus, the stated capital account remains unaffected. And third, shareholder approval must be obtained to effect the stock split, because of the change in par value of the shares of the corporation. Remember that the designation of par value is made in the articles of incorporation, and any change to the articles requires the approval of the shareholders of the corporation. These issues will be discussed in greater detail in this section of the chapter.

Many states, as well as the Model Act, no longer require corporations to designate shares as with par value or without par value. A corporation whose articles of incorporation do not designate a par value for its shares, does not have to amend its articles of incorporation. However, to effect the stock split and issue additional shares, the corporation may have to authorize additional shares. In that case, the articles of incorporation must be amended to increase the corporation's capitalization.

The proportion of the split of the corporation's stock is determined by the board of directors. For example, shares may be split 2-for-1, which means that for every 1 share owned, 2 shares will be owned after the split. Splits may be 3-for-1, 5-for-1, 10-for-1, 100-for-1, and so on, in any denomination. In a 100-for-1 stock split, 100 shares will be owned by a shareholder for each share that was owned prior to the stock split.

To summarize, a stock split has the following results:

- Additional shares are issued.
- There is no change in percentage ownership by the shareholders.
- There is a change (decrease) in the par value of the corporation's shares.
- Stated capital and earned surplus are unaffected.
- The capital account remains the same.

Procedure for Issuance

The decision to declare a stock split is made at the sole discretion of the board of directors. The directors adopt a resolution specifying the number of shares into which each share will be split, a record and payment date, and the officer of the corporation with the authority to issue the additional shares to the shareholders. Figure 11–6 is an example of a resolution of the directors declaring a 2-for-1 stock split.

In addition to the approval of the split by the board of directors, the approval of the shareholders must be obtained for the change in par value of the shares. As we have mentioned, the designation of the par value of shares of the corporation is made in the articles of incorporation. Any change to the articles of incorporation requires approval of the shareholders. When the articles are amended to reflect the change in par value, they may also need to be amended to increase the number of authorized shares. For example, suppose the articles authorized 1,000 shares of common stock and all 1,000 shares have been issued. In order for the corporation to issue additional shares for a share dividend or a stock split, the articles must be amended to increase the number of authorized shares from 1,000 to some higher number.

PARALEGALERT!

The stock split differs from the share dividend in the following respects: (1) no accounts on the balance sheet, in particular the net worth section, are affected; (2) the par value of the shares is decreased; and (3) the articles of incorporation must be amended to reflect the change in par value.

Figure 11–6   Resolution of Directors Declaring a 2-for-1 Stock Split

> WHEREAS, there are currently 1,000 shares of Common Stock of the Corporation issued and outstanding; and
>
> WHEREAS, the Board of Directors deems it advisable to effect a 2-for-1 stock split of the issued and outstanding shares of the Corporation, after which 2,000 shares of Common Stock will be issued and outstanding; therefore, be it
>
> RESOLVED, that the officers of the Corporation are hereby authorized to issue one share of Common Stock for every one share of Common Stock held by shareholders of the Corporation, such 1,000 additional shares to be issued from the authorized and unissued shares of Common Stock of the Corporation and payable on June 1, 1995, to holders of record of Common Stock at the close of business on May 15, 1995.

Remember from our discussion in Chapter 7 that the shareholders would approve an amendment to the articles by adopting a resolution in one of the following two ways: (1) at a meeting of the shareholders, for which proper notice was sent and at which a quorum was present for the conducting of business, or (2) by unanimous written consent, executed by *all* shareholders of the corporation.

An officer of the corporation, usually the secretary or treasurer, arranges for the issuance of the additional shares. For smaller, closely held corporations, the corporate paralegal may be responsible for issuing the shares. The issuance of shares as a result of a stock split can be handled in one of two ways: (1) shareholders can be requested to return all currently held share certificates to the corporation, and the corporation, in turn, can issue new certificates for the total number of shares held by each shareholder, or (2) the corporation can issue share certificates representing only the new shares issued as a result of the stock split.

Accounting Procedures

Before declaring a stock split, the board of directors must consider whether the corporation has sufficient treasury shares or authorized shares to issue the additional shares required to effect the stock split. If adequate shares have not been authorized or are not in the treasury of the corporation, the articles of incorporation must be amended to increase the authorized shares.

In effecting the stock split, no accounts in the net worth section of the balance sheet are affected, and no assets of the corporation are distributed. To better understand the effects of a stock split, refer to Figure 11–7, which is an accounting for a 2-for-1 stock split. In this example, the split will result in the ownership of 2 shares for every 1 share already owned. Therefore, if 1,000 shares were issued and outstanding prior to the split, 2,000 shares will be issued and outstanding after the stock split. In addition, the par value of the shares will decrease in the same proportion as the issued and outstanding shares increase. Therefore, in our example the par value decreases from $1.00 per share to $.50 per share. Note that stated capital remains the same before and after the stock split.

PARALEGALERT!

The par value of shares issued by the corporation must be stated on all share certificates of the corporation. When the par value changes as a result of a stock split, the corporation will not necessarily ask the shareholders to return those certificates. To do so can be extremely costly and time-consuming.

Figure 11-7 Accounting for a 2-for-1 Stock Split

	2-for-1 Stock Split	
Before Split		**After Split**
1,000 shares Common Stock par value $1.00 per share		2,000 shares Common Stock par value $.50 per share
Stated Capital 1,000		Stated Capital 1,000

Reasons for Effecting Stock Splits

The desire of the corporation to increase the marketability of the shares of the corporation is generally the principal reason for effecting a stock split, just as it is one of the reasons for issuing a share dividend. For nothing more than psychological reasons, investors are more likely to buy 100 shares of $20 stock than 20 shares of $100 stock. Therefore, when the board of directors feels that the price of the corporation's stock is too high, it may authorize a stock split. This will reduce the price of each share and increase the marketability of the stock, resulting in broadening the supply of the corporation's stock to a wider range of investors.

Consider the following example: Stock B is selling for $100/share prior to the board's declaration of a 2-for-1 stock split. Immediately after this split, the share's value is $50/share. Shares of Stock B will return to their value of $100/share more quickly than they would have increased to a value of $150/share. In addition, at $50/share, shares are available to a broader range of investors and not only to those investors willing to purchase shares at $100/share. For these reasons, a stock split is viewed favorably by the shareholders of the corporation and is interpreted in the market as an increase in the value of the corporation.

PARALEGALERT!

The board of directors will authorize a stock split if it believes that the price of each share is too high. A stock split will result in a decrease in the price of each share and thereby increase the marketability and availability of shares to a broader segment of the market.

Tax Implications

A stock split results in no change in the capitalization of the corporation and therefore is tax-free to the corporation. In addition, a stock split is a nontaxable event to the shareholder. Shareholders pay no federal income tax on the additional shares they receive as a result of a stock split. However, just like the share dividend, the tax implications of a stock split get complicated when the shareholder decides to sell his or her shares. The basis of the shares, which must be calculated to determine the capital gain or loss on the sale of the shares, must be adjusted to account for the stock split. This can be complicated, and therefore a stock split may be unpopular with shareholders. However, the benefits of a stock split far outweigh any tax complications resulting from the split, and the stock split is usually looked on very favorably by the shareholders of the corporation.

11–6   Reverse Stock Split

A **reverse stock split** is a second type of stock split, in which the issued and outstanding shares are combined into a lesser number of shares. The result of a reverse stock split is that the total number of shares owned by the shareholders decreases, but their proportionate share ownership of the corporation does not change. For example, a shareholder owning 100 shares will own 50 shares after a 1-for-2 reverse stock split. Because the share holdings of all shareholders are reduced in the same proportion, the percentage ownership of the corporation by the shareholders does not change. Even though percentage ownership does not change, shareholders do *not* look favorably on a reverse stock split.

Just as in the stock split, the earned surplus and stated capital accounts of the net worth section of the balance sheet remain unchanged. The par value of the shares is increased, and the number of issued and outstanding shares is decreased in the same proportion; thus, the stated capital account remains unaffected. Shareholder approval must be obtained to effect the reverse stock split, just as for the stock split, because of the change in par value of the shares of the corporation. Remember that the designation of par value is made in the articles of incorporation, and any change to the articles requires the approval of the shareholders of the corporation.

Just like the stock split, the proportion in the reverse split of the corporation's stock is determined by the board of directors. For example, shares may be split 1-for-2, which means that for every two shares owned, one share will be owned after the reverse split. Splits may be 1-for-3, 1-for-5, 1-for-10, 1-for-100, and so on, in any denomination. In a 1-for-100 stock split, 1 share will be owned by a shareholder for each 100 shares that were owned prior to the reverse stock split.

To summarize, a reverse stock split has the following results:

- There is a decrease in the number of issued shares.
- There is no change in percentage ownership by the shareholders.
- There is a change (increase) in the par value of the corporation's shares.
- Stated capital remains the same.
- Earned surplus is unaffected.

Procedures

The decision to declare a reverse stock split is made at the sole discretion of the board of directors. The directors adopt a resolution specifying the numerical denomination of the reverse split and a record and effective date of the reverse split. Figure 11–8 is an example of a resolution of the directors declaring a 1-for-2 reverse stock split.

In addition to the approval of the board of directors for the reverse stock split, the approval of the shareholders must be obtained for the change in the par value of the shares. As we have mentioned, the designation of the par value of shares of the corporation is made in the articles of incorporation, and any change to the articles of incorporation requires the approval of the shareholders.

Remember from our discussion in Chapter 7 that the shareholders approve an amendment to the articles by adopting a resolution in one of the following two ways: (1) at a meeting of the shareholders, for

> **P**ARALEGALERT!
>
> The reverse stock split results in a decrease in the number of issued and outstanding shares and an increase in the par value of those shares. The shareholders' percentage ownership of the corporation does not change.

Figure 11–8   Resolution of Directors Declaring a 1-for-2 Reverse Stock Split

> WHEREAS, there are currently 1,000 shares of Common Stock of the Corporation issued and outstanding; and
>
> WHEREAS, the Board of Directors deems it advisable to effect a 1-for-2 reverse stock split of the issued and outstanding shares of the Corporation, after which 500 shares of Common Stock will be issued and outstanding; therefore, be it
>
> RESOLVED, that the officers of the Corporation are hereby authorized to (1) take any and all actions necessary to cancel share certificates of the Corporation representing the 1,000 shares of issued and outstanding shares of the Corporation and (2) reissue certificates to the shareholders of record of Common Stock at the close of business on May 15, 1995, so that upon effecting the 1-for-2 reverse stock split, a total of 500 shares of the Common Stock of the Corporation will be issued and outstanding.

which proper notice was sent and at which a quorum is present for the conducting of business, or (2) by unanimous written consent, executed by *all* the shareholders of the corporation.

Accounting Procedures

In effecting the reverse stock split, no accounts in the net worth section of the balance sheet are affected, and of course, no assets of the corporation are distributed. To better understand the effects of a reverse stock split, refer to Figure 11–9, which is an accounting for a 1-for-2 reverse stock split. In this example, the split will result in the ownership of 1 share for every 2 shares already owned. Therefore, if 1,000 shares were issued and outstanding prior to the split, 500 shares will be issued and outstanding after the reverse stock split. In addition, the par value of the shares will increase in the same proportion as the issued and outstanding shares decrease. Therefore, in our example, the par value increases from $1.00 per share to $2.00 per share. Note that stated capital remains the same before and after the reverse split.

Reasons for Effecting Reverse Stock Splits

In an attempt to reduce the number of shareholders of the corporation or to **freeze out,** or eliminate minority shareholders, the board of directors will recommend a reverse stock split.

Consider the following example: James Bond owns 50 shares of the common stock of the corporation, making him a minority shareholder and the holder of an insignificant number of shares when compared with the 1,000,000 issued and outstanding shares of the corporation. James Bond will be eliminated as a shareholder when the board of directors authorizes a 1-for-100 reverse stock split. In a 1-for-100 reverse split, for every 100 shares owned before the split, a shareholder will own 1 share after the split. The effect on James Bond will be ownership of a ¹/₂ share, for which he will receive cash from the corporation, as share certificates will not be issued for fractional shares. After receiving cash for his 50 shares, which were reduced to a ¹/₂ share by the reverse stock split, James Bond will no longer be a shareholder of the corporation.

PARALEGALERT!

A reverse split is not looked on very favorably by shareholders, as their share holdings are reduced, even though their percentage ownership does not change. Psychologically, shareholders dislike owning fewer shares.

Figure 11–9   Accounting for a 1-for-2 Reverse Stock Split

1-for-2 Reverse Stock Split	
Before Reverse Split	**After Reverse Split**
1,000 shares Common Stock par value $1.00 per share	500 shares Common Stock par value $2.00 per share
Stated Capital 1,000	Stated Capital 1,000

Figure 11–10   Summary Requirements, Mechanics, and Effects on Balance Sheet of Various Types of Corporate Dividends and Distributions

	Requirements	Mechanics	Balance Sheet
Cash or property dividend	Sufficient amounts of earned surplus and cash or property	Board of directors' resolution declaring payment of dividend	Decrease in assets (cash or property) Decrease in earned surplus
Stock dividend	Sufficient number of authorized and unissued shares Sufficient amount of earned surplus	Board of directors' resolution declaring payment of dividend Amendment to articles of incorporation if authorized shares need to be increased	Increase in stated capital Decrease in earned surplus
Stock split	Sufficient number of authorized and unissued shares	Board of directors' resolution approving stock split Shareholders' approval of amendment to articles of incorporation to change par value and to increase authorized shares if needed	Increase in issued shares Decrease in par value of those shares
Reverse stock split		Board of directors' resolution approving reverse stock split Shareholders' approval of amendment to articles of incorporation to change par value	Decrease in issued shares Increase in par value of those shares

11–7 Practical Considerations

Figure 11–10, on the previous page, is a table that summarizes the requirements, the mechanics, and the balance sheet effects of the cash or property dividend, the share dividend, the stock split, and the reverse stock split. The table represents the crux of this chapter, and you can feel confident in your study if you are able to comprehend the areas covered there.

If you have only begun to work in the corporate area or hope to some day, or even if you have been a corporate paralegal for some time, you might question the importance of understanding the concepts presented here. The following list gives just a few examples of the ways you will use the knowledge gained in this chapter:

1. One of the many responsibilities of the corporate paralegal is the completion of corporate reports or tax reports, which are usually required to be filed annually by various states. Both domestic and foreign corporations are generally required to comply with these requirements. Information that must be reported includes, among other things, the corporation's authorized capital, issued and outstanding shares, stated capital, and capital surplus. Therefore, the corporate paralegal must understand where this information can be obtained.
2. The corporate paralegal is usually responsible for preparing the resolutions of the board of directors to approve the declaration and issuance of cash, property, and share dividends.
3. When an amendment to the articles of incorporation must be filed in connection with a stock split or reverse stock split (because of the accompanying increase or decrease in par value), the paralegal is responsible for preparing the shareholders' resolutions and the articles of amendment and for properly filing such amendment.

It is important to understand the big picture of a transaction and to be able to focus on the specific details required to accomplish that transaction or corporate goal. This is usually the paralegal's function.

SUMMARY

11–1

Investors acquire shares to derive economic benefit in one or both of two ways: (1) through the distribution of the corporation's profits and (2) by the sale of the shares at a price higher than the price paid for the shares. A dividend is a distribution of the corporation's earnings to its shareholders. These profits can be distributed in the form of cash, property, or shares of the corporation itself. The form in which dividends are distributed is the decision of the board of directors.

In addition, the board of directors has the sole authority to declare and pay dividends to the shareholders. The shareholders have the right to receive such distributions, but they cannot demand that a dividend be paid to them. The corporation may purchase its own shares from its shareholders. When repurchased, these shares become treasury shares. The corporation may desire to repurchase its shares to reduce the payment of dividends, to invest in the corporation itself, or to reduce the number of persons holding shares of the corporation.

11–2

Dividends or distributions are not permitted by the corporation if the corporation would not be able to pay its debts as they become due in the usual course of business or if the corporation's total assets would be less than the sum of its total liabilities plus amounts needed to pay accrued and unpaid dividends to preferred shareholders. The corporation's balance sheet consists of three components: assets, liabilities, and net worth. Total assets must equal the total of the liabilities and the net worth of the corporation. The net worth section of the balance sheet consists of stated capital (which is often called *legal capital*), capital surplus, and earned surplus. Statutes regulate the manner in which profits may be distributed to the shareholders and identify the particular corporate accounts from which a distribution may be made. Dividends are usually permitted to be made out of earned surplus. However, the state statutes must be reviewed to determine a state's particular requirements.

11–3

Most dividends are payable in cash and generally distributed in the form of a check. Dividends payable in the form of property are called property dividends, but shareholders must find the payment of a dividend in the form of property acceptable. Different classes of stock may be treated differently with respect to the payment of dividends, but all shareholders of any particular class of stock must be treated equally in the payment of dividends. The declaration and payment of both cash and property dividends are made at the sole discretion of the board of directors. Dividends may be declared and paid in cash or property only out of available funds, and the board of directors must determine if sufficient amounts of earned surplus and cash or property are available for distribution. The effect of a cash or property dividend is that cash is reduced (or the amount of property, if a property dividend) and earned surplus (or retained earnings) is reduced. Double taxation occurs when the corporation pays corporate income tax on its profits and then distributes such profits to the shareholders, who pay personal income tax on the distribution.

11–4

A share dividend is a distribution of the corporation's own shares to the shareholders. It causes the total number of shares owned by the shareholders to increase. The shareholder's ownership interest does not change, as each shareholder receives his or her proportionate share of the distribution. A share dividend results in additional issued and outstanding shares, no change in the par value of those shares, an increase in stated capital, and a proportionate decrease in earned surplus. Therefore, total capital remains unchanged. Shares of one class are paid only to the holders of the same class of shares in a share dividend. The decision to declare a share dividend is made at the sole discretion of the board of directors, who must consider whether the corporation has sufficient treasury shares or authorized shares to issue the additional shares and whether the corporation has adequate earned surplus available to transfer to the stated capital account. A corporation may prefer to issue share dividends because it is unable to distribute cash or property of the corporation. The share dividend may also, in effect, increase the marketability of the shares on the market. The receipt of a share dividend is a nontaxable event to the shareholder. In general, the issuance of a share dividend is looked on as favorable by the shareholders of the corporation.

11–5

A stock split is very similar to a share dividend in that it results in a distribution of the corporation's own shares to the shareholders, but it is not the same as a share dividend. First, a share dividend requires a transfer from the earned surplus account to the stated capital account, and in a stock split the earned surplus and stated capital accounts of the net worth section of the balance sheet remain unchanged. Second, the par value of the shares is decreased and the number of issued and outstanding shares is increased by the same proportion in a stock split; thus, the stated capital account remains unaffected. And third, shareholder approval must be obtained to effect the stock split, because of the change in par value of the shares of the corporation. Shares may be split 2-for-1, which means that for every share owned, 2 shares will be owned after the split. Splits may be 3-for-1, 5-for-1, 10-for-1, 100-for-1, and so on, in any denomination. The decision to declare a stock split is made at the sole discretion of the board of directors, who must consider whether the corporation has sufficient treasury shares or authorized shares to issue the additional shares required to effect the stock split. The desire of the corporation to increase the marketability of the shares of the corporation is generally the principal reason for effecting a stock split. A stock split results in no change in the capitalization of the corporation and therefore is tax-free to the corporation. It is also a nontaxable event to the shareholder. The stock split is looked on very favorably by the shareholders of the corporation.

11–6

The reverse stock split results in a decrease in the number of shares issued and outstanding and an increase in the par value of those shares. Therefore, the total number of shares owned by each shareholder decreases, but each shareholder's proportionate ownership of the corporation remains the same. Earned surplus and stated capital, components of the net worth section of the balance sheet, remain unchanged. Shareholder approval must be obtained to effect the reverse stock split, because the change in par value of the shares of the corporation requires an amendment to the articles of incorporation. The decision to declare a reverse stock split lies solely with the board of directors, who approve it by resolution. The corporation's desire to reduce the number of shareholders of the corporation or to freeze out minority shareholders is the reason for effecting the reverse stock split.

11–7

A basic understanding of the requirements for, the mechanics of, and the effects on the balance sheet of the cash, property, or share dividend; the stock split; and the reverse stock split is important to a paralegal's work.

REVIEW GUIDE

Key Terms

Before proceeding, review the key terms listed below to be sure you understand each one. If necessary, read over the corresponding section of the chapter. When you are ready to test your understanding, answer the review questions.

dividend (p. 254)
treasury shares (p. 256)
net worth (p. 257)
stated capital (p. 258)
legal capital (p. 259)
capital surplus (p. 259)
earned surplus (p. 259)
retained earnings (p. 259)
surplus (p. 259)
insolvent (p. 259)
cash dividend (p. 260)
property dividend (p. 260)
double taxation (p. 262)
share dividend (p. 262)
stock split (p. 265)
reverse stock split (p. 269)
freeze out (p. 270)

Questions for Review and Discussion

1. Why do investors purchase shares of a corporation?
2. Why would a corporation want to repurchase its own shares from shareholders?
3. Name the conditions under which the corporation is not permitted to pay dividends.
4. What are the three components that make up the balance sheet? Identify some of the accounts found in each component.
5. Generally, from what sources may funds be used to make distributions of the corporation's profits?
6. Who declares that dividends may be paid to the shareholders? Are there any circumstances under which shareholders may declare the payment of a dividend?
7. How do a share dividend and a stock split differ?
8. What must the board of directors do to effect a stock split? A reverse stock split?
9. Why must the articles of incorporation be amended in conjunction with a stock split or a reverse stock split? Under what circumstance would an amendment not be necessary?
10. What type of corporate distribution is not looked on favorably by the shareholders of the corporation?

Activities

1. Obtain a copy of the financial statements for a corporation. A corporation whose shares are publicly traded in the market will send you a copy of its financial statements on request. Also, copies are usually kept in a library's business section or branch or in any college or university library. After you have obtained the financial statements, identify the balance sheet. Review it and determine the corporation's stated capital, capital surplus, and earned surplus (sometimes called *retained earnings* or *profit*). Also, attempt to determine the amount of capital that the corporation has authorized and issued.
2. Research the statutes of your state, and determine the sources from which distributions of cash and property dividends may be made. In addition, determine if these sources differ from those a corporation is permitted to use to repurchase shares of the corporation.
3. Consider the following information about XYZ Corporation and answer the questions below.

   - XYZ Corporation has the following capital structure as authorized in its articles of incorporation: 1,000 shares common stock, $1.00 par value; 500 shares series A preferred stock, $5.00 par value; and 10,000 shares series B preferred stock, $2.00 par value.
   - XYZ Corporation made the following sales of its stock: 200 shares of common stock for $1,000; 200 shares of series A preferred stock for $10,000; and 3,000 shares of series B preferred stock for $6,000. XYZ repurchased 50 shares of its common stock for $250.
   - Questions:
     a. How many shares are authorized?
     b. How many shares are issued?
     c. How many shares are issued and outstanding?
     d. What is XYZ's stated capital?
     e. What is XYZ's capital surplus?

CHAPTER 12   Securities Regulation

OUTLINE

12–1   Introduction to Securities Regulation
Laws Governing the Issuance of Securities
Uniform Securities Act
Commonly Used Definitions in the Securities Industry
What Is a Security?
Securities Markets
12–2   Securities Act of 1933
Registration Statement
Registration Process
Exemptions from 1933 Act Registration
Liability and Antifraud Provisions
12–3   Securities Exchange Act of 1934
Securities and Exchange Commission
Registration Under the 1934 Act
Reporting and Disclosure Requirements
Insider Short-Swing Profits
Liability and Antifraud Provisions
12–4   Blue-Sky Laws
Registration Process
Exemptions from Registration
Antifraud Provisions and Enforcement
12–5   Practical Considerations

APPLICATIONS

After Susan Minahan incorporated Water Bottle Company, she proceeded to prepare the organizational minutes, which included a unanimous consent of the directors authorizing the issuance of shares to the persons who had subscribed for shares prior to the incorporation. Susan has been instructed by her supervising attorney, Larry Lawyer, and the treasurer of the corporation to prepare share certificates for issuance and delivery to the shareholders. She prepares share certificates representing the following ownership: 100 shares class A common stock issued to James Drink and 200 shares of class B common stock issued to Kathleen Water. Susan knows that these share certificates represent "securities," and she must be sure that the issuance of these securities complies with federal and state securities laws or that such laws do not apply.

OBJECTIVES

Securities regulation is one of the most complex areas of the law. It is practiced today by highly specialized lawyers and paralegals. Because of the complexity of legal practice in this area, this chapter will provide only a basic understanding of the content and structure of the federal and state securities laws and regulations and the potential for paralegal involvement in this area. The corporate paralegal must be fully cognizant of the effects of the regulation of securities in the business arena today. After completing Chapter 12, you will be able to:

1. Determine the applicability of federal and state securities laws.
2. Identify the different federal securities statutes.
3. Understand the relevance of the Uniform Securities Act.
4. Define terms commonly used in the securities industry.
5. Define *security* as used in the federal and state securities laws.
6. Describe the securities markets in which securities are sold and purchased.
7. Understand the purposes of the Securities Act of 1933, the Securities Exchange Act of 1934, and the blue-sky laws.
8. Understand the registration requirements and processes promulgated under the Securities Act of 1933, the Securities Exchange Act of 1934, and the blue-sky laws.
9. Distinguish between security exemptions and transaction exemptions available under the federal and state securities laws.
10. Understand the role of the Securities and Exchange Commission.
11. Identify the circumstances in which liability is incurred under the federal and state securities laws.

12–1   Introduction to Securities Regulation

Advantages of the corporate form of business organization, which we discussed early in this textbook, include the abilities of the corporation to accumulate capital from investments made by shareholders and to secure access to funds by borrowing from banks, shareholders, and other lenders. And as we discussed in Chapter 10, the corporation accumulates capital or borrows funds to finance its operations through the issuance of equity securities and debt securities. Remember, an equity security (stock) is the evidence of an ownership interest in the property of the corporation, and a debt security (note, bond, or debenture) is the evidence of an obligation of the corporation to repay a loan or debt of the corporation.

Corporate securities, which include both equity and debt securities, merely *represent* an ownership interest in or a claim against the corporation. Unlike real and tangible property, such as real estate, equipment, and inventory, a corporate security evidences an ownership interest in the corporation or an obligation of the corporation and is tangibly represented by the share certificate, note, bond, or debenture. The tangible evidence of the corporate security (the share certificate, note, etc.) has no value itself, since anyone with access to a photocopy machine or printing equipment can duplicate a share certificate or other form of corporate security. Therefore, corporate securities have no intrinsic value. It is, therefore, difficult for an investor to determine the value of his or her ownership interest—the value of the securities he or she owns—unless the investor can determine the underlying value of the corporation that issued and sold the corporate security. In other words, the value of corporate securities lies in the ownership interest they represent.

Let's consider the example of the investor who wishes to purchase 100 shares of Kitchen Supplies, Inc. Before deciding to invest, he or she must have information about the corporation's business, the value

PARALEGALERT!

A corporate security is tangibly represented by a share certificate, a note, a bond, or a debenture, each of which represents an ownership interest in or a claim against the corporation.

of its assets, its profitability, its future business prospects, and so on, to determine the value of the shares. And, *most important*, the investor must be able to rely on the information provided by the corporation as a full and fair disclosure of this information. As you can imagine, the potential for fraud, manipulation, deceit, misinformation, or failure to disclose information is great.

To prevent such fraud and deceit and to ensure the full disclosure of information to investors, the federal government and the states have adopted comprehensive statutes regulating the offer and sale of securities to the public. In addition, federal and state statutes also regulate the securities markets through which securities are offered and traded, they control the qualifications of the persons who operate the securities markets, and they impose sanctions for violations of the statutes and permit civil recoveries by injured persons.

The offer and sale of securities are subject to *both* federal and state securities laws. Federal securities laws govern securities transactions that "make use of any means or instruments of transportation or communication in interstate commerce or of the mails to sell" (Section 5(a) of the Securities Act of 1933). In effect, this means that any use of the mails in accomplishing an offer or sale of securities is enough to require compliance with the federal securities laws. State securities laws govern all transactions accomplished intrastate—that is, transactions that are completed within the state's boundaries. Generally, *interstate* transactions are governed by both federal and state securities laws, and *intrastate* transactions are governed only by the state securities laws.

Laws Governing the Issuance of Securities

In 1911, Kansas became the first state to enact legislation prohibiting fraudulent and deceptive practices in the offer and sale of securities. However, Kansas and other states that subsequently adopted such laws could not restrict fraudulent practices in sales of securities across state lines, and the states' securities laws proved to be inadequate. When the stock market crashed in 1929 and continued to decline through the early 1930s, the Congress of the United States stepped in with the enactment of the federal securities laws.

Congress initiated the regulation of securities in 1933 and since then has enacted seven statutes, all of which together make up the **federal securities laws.** These statutes include:

1. Securities Act of 1933.
2. Securities Exchange Act of 1934.
3. Public Utility Holding Company Act of 1935.
4. Trust Indenture Act of 1939.
5. Investment Company Act of 1940.
6. Investment Advisers Act of 1940.
7. Securities Investor Protection Act of 1970.

The **Securities Act of 1933,** to which we will refer throughout this chapter as the *1933 Act,* was the first federal securities law enacted by Congress. The 1933 Act regulates the initial issuance of securities by corporations, requires broad disclosure of corporate and financial information to potential investors, prohibits fraudulent and deceptive practices in the sale of securities, and provides remedies for violations of any provisions of this statute. Generally, offers and sales of securities are prohibited unless a registration process has been completed prior to such offer and sale. There are, however, exemptions available for certain securities and for certain types of transactions.

The **Securities Exchange Act of 1934,** to which we will refer throughout this chapter as the *1934 Act,* regulates the trading of securities already issued by corporations and requires securities brokers and dealers to register. In addition, the 1934 Act created the **Securities and Exchange Commission,** commonly referred to as the **SEC,** the federal agency responsible for evaluating the sufficiency of the information disclosed to investors. The 1934 Act also governs the periodic disclosure of corporate and financial information by corporations whose securities are registered and publicly traded, and it regulates the national securities exchanges.

The **Public Utility Holding Company Act of 1935** was passed by Congress in response to manipulative practices in the public utilities industry. From the late 1930s through the 1950s, much of the SEC's time and resources were spent enforcing the Public Utility Holding Company Act and correcting the abuses in the financing of public utilities. The SEC's current involvement in enforcing this statute is minimal.

The **Trust Indenture Act of 1939** helps protect investors purchasing bonds, debentures, notes, and other debt securities by regulating the terms and conditions of the trust indenture under which debt securities are sold and the actions of the trustee of the trust indenture. Compliance with the Trust Indenture Act of 1939 is in addition to the registration of the securities under the provisions of the 1933 Act and the 1934 Act.

The **Investment Company Act of 1940** was enacted to regulate publicly owned companies, such as mutual funds, that engage in the business of investing and trading securities on behalf of others. In particular, the Investment Company Act controls the management of investment companies; approves their investment advisory contracts and general investment policies; and requires an investment company to obtain SEC approval for any transactions involving the investment company and its officers, directors, and affiliates.

The **Investment Advisers Act of 1940** requires persons or organizations who are in the business of rendering investment advice to others to register with the SEC. This is similar to the provision of the 1934 Act that requires broker-dealers to register.

The **Securities Investor Protection Act of 1970,** enacted as an amendment to the 1934 Act, created the Securities Investor Protection Corporation, commonly called the **SIPC.** The SIPC was created in response to the failures of many broker-dealers in the 1960s, and it manages a fund to protect investors against losses caused by the failures or financial difficulties of broker-dealers. The SIPC acts similarly to the Federal Deposit Insurance Corporation, which protects the customers of banks.

In addition to the federal statutes, all states have adopted securities laws, which are commonly referred to as **blue-sky laws.** Like the federal securities laws, the purpose of the blue-sky laws is to prevent fraud in the sale of securities to investors. Federal securities laws maintain that the states may regulate securities activities; therefore, the sale of or any transaction dealing in securities may be subject to one or more state securities laws in addition to the federal securities laws.

The 1933 Act and the 1934 Act remain to this day the pieces of federal legislation that protect the investors

PARALEGALERT!

The major pieces of federal legislation enacted to protect investors and participants in the securities markets are the Securities Act of 1933 and the Securities Exchange Act of 1934.

PARALEGALERT!

In addition to the federal securities laws, all states have enacted securities laws, which are called *blue-sky laws.* These laws also regulate the offer and sale of securities to investors.

and participants in the securities markets. Therefore, the major focus of this chapter will be the 1933 Act, the 1934 Act, and the blue-sky laws. The other federal securities laws discussed in this section are important aspects of the regulation of securities, but our discussion will focus on the laws with which most business corporations must comply and with which the corporate paralegal will deal more frequently. The 1933 Act, the 1934 Act, and the blue-sky laws will be discussed in greater detail in this chapter.

Uniform Securities Act

In addition to the federal securities laws, all states have adopted statutes regulating the offer and sale of securities. Most of the states' statutes differ in many respects, but many states have adopted standard provisions. In adopting standard or uniform securities laws, many states have looked to the Uniform Securities Act for guidance. The Commissioners on Uniform State Laws adopted the **Uniform Securities Act** (referred to hereafter as the *USA*) in 1956, and it was revised in 1985 and amended further in 1988.

The USA has been adopted by more than half of the states; however, many of those states adopted substantial changes to the original text of the USA. Some states—for example, New York, California, and Texas—have not adopted any portion of the USA. In addition, state courts in the states that have adopted the USA have interpreted provisions of the USA in dramatically different ways. This lack of uniformity has only complicated the offer and sale of securities in numerous states. Regardless, adoption of the USA has assisted in a much more consistent interpretation of the various states' securities laws than existed prior to its adoption. We will, in any case, refer to provisions of the USA throughout this chapter. The ability to interpret and understand the USA's provisions will enhance your proficiency in construing the sometimes complicated provisions of the states' securities laws and will assist you in understanding the federal securities laws.

The USA is divided into the following eight parts:

Part I	Definitions
Part II	Licensing of Broker-Dealer, Sales Representative, and Investment Adviser
Part III	Registration of Securities
Part IV	Exemptions from Registration
Part V	Fraudulent and Other Prohibited Practices
Part VI	Enforcement and Civil Liability
Part VII	Administration
Part VIII	Miscellaneous Provisions

Commonly Used Definitions in the Securities Industry

The terminology most commonly used by those practicing in the securities area includes the terms defined in the following list. Of course, this is not an all-inclusive list. As with this entire chapter, the purpose here is to increase your familiarity with concepts and terms by providing you with as much information as practical. Because the securities area is complex and is regulated on both the federal and the state levels, entire textbooks, manuals, and treatises have been devoted to this topic. Several of the following definitions are taken in part from the definitions provided in the federal securities laws and the USA.

- **Issuer**—An individual, corporation, partnership, association, trust, or unincorporated organization that issues or proposes to issue any security.
- **Public corporation**—A corporation whose securities are registered under the federal securities laws and traded on one or more of the securities markets.
- **Prospectus**—A document that contains information about the issuer and its business, the security being offered, the finances of the issuer, risk factors in purchasing the security, and other information required to enable the investor to make an informed decision about purchasing the security.
- **Registration statement**—A document filed with the Securities and Exchange Commission that includes the prospectus and other information and exhibits required by either the 1933 Act or the 1934 Act or by the Securities and Exchange Commission's rules and forms.
- **Public offering**—The process of registering the security with the Securities and Exchange Commission and offering such security for sale to the public. An initial public offering is the first public offering made by a corporation, as opposed to subsequent offerings of securities.
- **Security**—A share certificate, note, bond, debenture, or other evidence of the right to participate in the profits of the issuer or evidence of the indebtedness of the issuer.
- **Effective date**—The date, 20 days after the filing of a registration statement with the Securities and Exchange Commission, on which the issuer is free to sell the securities to the public.
- **Tombstone ad**—A notice that contains information about a proposed securities offering. It is called a tombstone ad because of the black borders that are typically placed around the notice. Figure 12–1 is an example of a tombstone ad that appeared in *The Wall Street Journal*.
- **Underwriter**—Any person or organization that purchases securities from an issuer with a view to offer or sell such securities to the public. Financial institutions (banks, brokers, investment bankers, etc.) generally act as underwriters.
- **Insider trading**—Sales or purchases by persons who have access to and take advantage of information about an issuer or a security when the information is not available to the public.

What Is a Security?

The fundamental issue of securities law is whether an instrument is a security. Whether an investment instrument is a security determines whether an issuer must comply with the registration procedures of the federal and state securities laws. If an investment instrument is determined to be a security, the issuer must comply with the federal and state securities laws requiring registration of the security, unless the security or transaction is exempt from registration.

Both the federal and state securities laws define *security* very broadly to include such instruments as a preorganization certificate or subscription; an investment contract; and traditional securities such as stocks, bonds, and debentures. Section 2(1) of the 1933 Act and Section 1.01(16) of the USA have virtually identical definitions of *security*. Figure 12–2 is the definition of *security* provided in Section 2(1) of the 1933 Act. Note the broad nature of the definition of *security*, which includes "any interest or instrument commonly known as a 'security'."

Section 2(1) of the 1933 Act itemizes the instruments that *do* fall under the definition of *security*.

PARALEGALERT!

Once an investment instrument is determined to meet the definition of a security under the federal and state securities laws, an issuer must decide whether the issuance of that security requires registration or is exempt from registration.

Figure 12–1 Tombstone Ad That Appeared in The Wall Street Journal

This advertisement is not an offer to sell nor a solicitation of an offer to buy these securities.
The offering is made only by the Prospectus.

April 15, 1994

1,400,000 Shares

Common Stock

Price $8 Per Share

NASDAQ Symbol–HIFI

Copies of the Prospectus may be obtained from any of the several Underwriters only
in such states in which such Underwriters are qualified to act as dealers in
securities and in which the Prospectus may be legally distributed.

HAMBRECHT & QUIST	TUCKER ANTHONY
Incorporated	Incorporated

ALEX. BROWN & SONS   CS FIRST BOSTON   COWEN & COMPANY   MONTGOMERY SECURITIES
Incorporated

MORGAN STANLEY & CO.   OPPENHEIMER & CO., INC.   ROBERTSON, STEPHENS & COMPANY

WILLIAM BLAIR & COMPANY   LADENBURG, THALMANN & CO. INC.

LEGG MASON WOOD WALKER   NEEDHAM & COMPANY, INC.   RAYMOND JAMES & ASSOCIATES, INC.
Incorporated

THE ROBINSON-HUMPHREY COMPANY, INC.   WESSELS, ARNOLD & HENDERSON

ADAMS, HARKNESS & HILL, INC.   ADVEST, INC.   FIRST ALBANY CORPORATION

RAGEN MACKENZIE   SOUNDVIEW FINANCIAL GROUP, INC.   SUTRO & CO. INCORPORATED
Incorporated

UNTERBERG HARRIS   VAN KASPER & COMPANY

Figure 12–2 Definition of Security Under Section 2(1) of the Securities Act of 1993

Section 2. . . .

(1) The term "security" means any note, stock, treasury stock, bond, debenture, evidence of indebtedness, certificate of interest or participation in any profit-sharing agreement, collateral-trust certificate, preorganization certificate or subscription, transferable share, investment contract, voting-trust certificate, certificate of deposit for a security, fractional undivided interest in oil, gas, or other mineral rights, any put, call, straddle, option, or privilege on any security, certificate of deposit, or group or index of securities (including any interest therein or based on the value thereof), or any put, call, straddle, option, or privilege entered into on a national securities exchange relating to foreign currency, or, in general, any interest or instrument commonly known as a "security," or any certificate of interest or participation in, temporary or interim certificate for, receipt for, guarantee of, or warrant or right to subscribe to or purchase, any of the foregoing.

Section 3(a) of the 1933 Act contains a list of the instruments that are securities but are exempt from the registration requirements. The most important of the exempted securities are any securities issued or guaranteed by the United States or by any state or local government. Exemptions from the registration requirements of the 1933 Act and the 1934 Act are discussed in greater detail in the following sections.

On numerous occasions the Supreme Court has interpreted the definition of *security*. In one such case, reported in the *Legal Links*, p. 287, the Supreme Court determined that the stock sold was a security within the definitions of the 1933 Act and the 1934 Act.

Securities Markets

Securities offered for sale by issuers, directly or through underwriters or broker-dealers, are first issued, sold, and traded in the securities markets. **Securities markets** are the mechanisms that allow the sellers of securities (issuers) and the investors to consummate transactions. Organized securities exchanges and the over-the-counter market are the securities markets through which issuers and investors are brought together. When a corporation decides to offer its securities to the public, it must also decide on which organized securities exchange its securities will be sold or whether its securities will be sold in the over-the-counter market.

Organized securities exchanges include the New York Stock Exchange, the American Stock Exchange, the Midwest Stock Exchange, the Pacific Stock Exchange, and the Boston Stock Exchange, among others. These exchanges are physical locations where securities are sold and purchased. For example, the New York Stock Exchange is located on Wall Street in New York, and it accounts for the greatest volume of securities transactions consummated in the United States. The second largest organized securities exchange in the United States is the American Stock Exchange. Securities traded on the organized securities exchanges are called **listed securities,** as a corporation must file an application with a stock exchange to become "listed" on that exchange.

The **over-the-counter market,** referred to as the **OTC,** does not have a specific location but, rather, is a network of over-the-counter dealers who are linked by telecommunications equipment through the National Association of Securities Dealers Automated Quotation (NASDAQ) System. Trading of securities occurs from hundreds of locations; therefore, the computer, the telephone, and the fax machine make up the OTC market. Securities traded in the OTC are called **unlisted securities.**

Federal securities laws, specifically the 1934 Act, regulate the organized securities exchanges and the OTC. Section 6 of the 1934 Act and Rule 6a-1 of the SEC provide for the registration of and the exemptions available to national securities exchanges.

> **PARALEGALERT!**
>
> The closely held corporations with which the corporate paralegal may deal do not trade their shares on any national securities exchange or in the over-the-counter market. The sale and purchase of shares of these smaller corporations is generally minimal, not requiring a market through which the trade takes place.

12–2 Securities Act of 1933

The principal purposes of the 1933 Act are (1) to assist the investor in making an informed decision about an investment by requiring the issuer to make full disclosure of certain information and (2) to prohibit manipulative, deceitful, and fraudulent activities in connection with the sale of securities. However, the act is not intended to advise an investor to purchase or not purchase securities or to assess the merits of an offering of securities. It merely requires the full disclosure of information that would allow a prudent investor to make an informed decision.

To accomplish its goals of requiring full and fair disclosure of information and prohibiting fraudulent acts in disseminating the information, the 1933 Act requires an issuer to file a registration statement with the SEC. Generally, the registration statement must be filed with and approved by the SEC prior to an issuer's offering securities to the public. The 1933 Act also protects investors from fraudulent and deceptive practices in the offer and sale of securities, even under circumstances in which securities are not required to be registered.

One of the most important provisions of the 1933 Act is Section 5, which provides the actions that may and may not be taken: Section 5(a) prohibits sales of securities *prior to the effective date* of the registration statement; Section 5(b) prohibits the use of any prospectus that does not meet the requirements of the 1933 Act and prohibits the delivery of a security unless it is accompanied by the prospectus; Section 5(c) prohibits offers to sell and offers to buy securities *prior to the filing* of the registration statement. In effect, Section 5 of the 1933 Act prohibits offers and sales of securities unless the issuer has filed and received approval of its registration statement, and it ensures that the prospectus, which is part of the registration statement, is made available to the investing public.

Registration Statement

The registration statement is a document that fully discloses all material facts about the issuer and the securities to be sold by the issuer. The registration statement consists of two parts. Part I is the prospectus, which must be delivered to all purchasers of securities. Part II includes additional financial and business information about the issuer not required to be contained in the prospectus but required to be available for public inspection at the SEC's public reference libraries. The contents of the prospectus, or Part I, are controlled by Section 10 of the 1933 Act, and the contents of the entire registration statement are controlled by Section 7 of the 1933 Act.

The rules and regulations under the 1933 Act describe the form of registration statement, prescribe the information to be provided therein, and provide general instructions for preparing and submitting a registration statement on the form that must be used. For example, the general form of registration statement under the 1933 Act is Form S-1. The cover page of a Form S-1 appears in Figure 12–3. Obviously, the entire text of this form cannot be reproduced in this book.

In addition to Form S-1, Form S-2 is for the registration of securities of certain issuers, Form S-3 is for the registration of securities of certain issuers offered pursuant to certain types of transactions, Form S-4 is for the registration of securities issued in business combination transactions (mergers), and Form S-8 is for securities to be offered to employees pursuant to employee benefit plans. Many other registration forms are provided for in the 1933 Act, varying with the type of security or the type of transaction in which the security is to be offered and sold.

The registration statement must include the information prescribed by the 1933 Act, in accordance with the rules and regulations promulgated thereunder.

PARALEGALERT!

A registration statement contains two parts: (1) the prospectus and (2) additional financial and business information. The prospectus must be delivered to all purchasers of securities of the issuer, and the additional financial and business information must be made available for public inspection at the SEC libraries.

Figure 12–3   Front Cover, or Facing Sheet, of Form S-1 Registration Statement

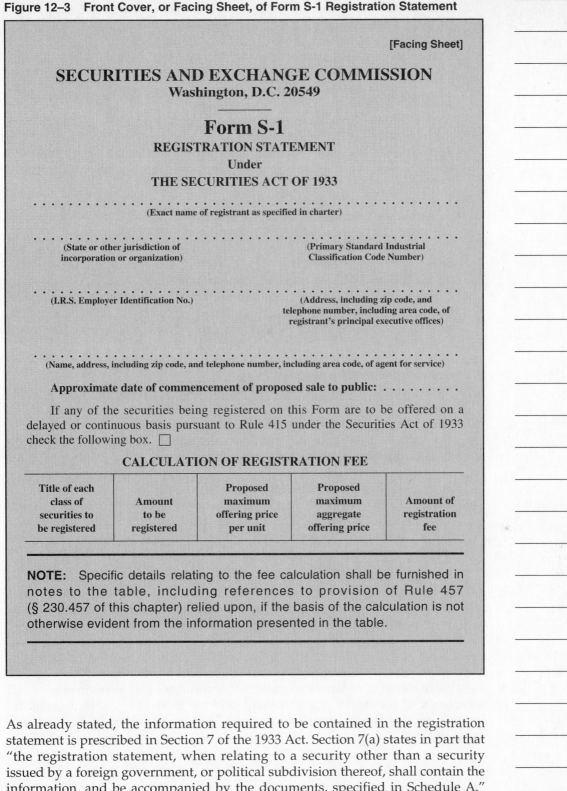

[Facing Sheet]

SECURITIES AND EXCHANGE COMMISSION
Washington, D.C. 20549

Form S-1
REGISTRATION STATEMENT
Under
THE SECURITIES ACT OF 1933

. . . .
(Exact name of registrant as specified in charter)

. . . .

| (State or other jurisdiction of incorporation or organization) | (Primary Standard Industrial Classification Code Number) |

. . . .

| (I.R.S. Employer Identification No.) | (Address, including zip code, and telephone number, including area code, of registrant's principal executive offices) |

. . . .
(Name, address, including zip code, and telephone number, including area code, of agent for service)

Approximate date of commencement of proposed sale to public: . . . .

If any of the securities being registered on this Form are to be offered on a delayed or continuous basis pursuant to Rule 415 under the Securities Act of 1933 check the following box. ☐

CALCULATION OF REGISTRATION FEE

Title of each class of securities to be registered	Amount to be registered	Proposed maximum offering price per unit	Proposed maximum aggregate offering price	Amount of registration fee

NOTE: Specific details relating to the fee calculation shall be furnished in notes to the table, including references to provision of Rule 457 (§ 230.457 of this chapter) relied upon, if the basis of the calculation is not otherwise evident from the information presented in the table.

As already stated, the information required to be contained in the registration statement is prescribed in Section 7 of the 1933 Act. Section 7(a) states in part that "the registration statement, when relating to a security other than a security issued by a foreign government, or political subdivision thereof, shall contain the information, and be accompanied by the documents, specified in Schedule A." The Schedule A referred to in this section is titled "Requirements for Registration of Securities Other Than a Security Issued by a Foreign Government or Political Subdivision Thereof." The following is a *summary* of the information and documents required by Section 7 of the 1933 Act and specifically set forth in Schedule A:

1. The name of the issuer, the location of its principal business office, the state under which it is organized, and the general character of its business.

2. Names and addresses of the directors, the chief executive officer, and the financial and accounting officers or persons performing similar functions, and the amounts, if any, of securities of the issuer they own.
3. Names and addresses of the underwriters and the amounts, if any, of securities of the issuer they own.
4. Names and addresses of all persons owning more than 10% of any class of stock and the amount of securities they own.
5. Capitalization of the issuer, including any options and the amount of stock to be offered.
6. Total amount of debt outstanding or to be created by the security offered, specific uses for such funds, and the net proceeds to be derived from the security offered.
7. The remuneration paid and to be paid to directors and officers, or persons performing similar functions, by the issuer.
8. The price at which the security will be offered to the public.
9. Commissions or discounts to be paid by the issuer to the underwriters, and other expenses, itemized in detail, to be paid for legal, engineering, accounting, and other services in connection with the offering.
10. The net proceeds derived from and the amounts paid in connection with the offering of securities, and the interest of directors, officers, and 10% shareholders of the issuer in acquired property for two years prior to the current offering.
11. Names and addresses of vendors and the purchase price of property to be purchased with the proceeds of the offering.
12. Names and addresses of legal counsel who advised on the legality of the offering.
13. Dates of and parties to every material contract entered into by the issuer.
14. The balance sheet and the profit-and-loss statement of the issuer, which must be certified by an independent public accountant.
15. The balance sheet and the profit-and-loss statement of any business to be purchased with the proceeds of the offering.
16. Copies of agreements with underwriters; opinions of legal counsel; material contracts entered into by the issuer; organization documents of the issuer; and all agreements or contracts affecting any stock, bonds, or debentures sold in the offering.

In addition, Regulation C under the 1933 Act contains rules governing the preparation and filing of a registration statement and provides general requirements, form and content, filing fees, and specific procedures to be followed in preparing and filing the registration statement. As examples, the rules under Regulation C prescribe the number of copies to be filed, including specific instructions as to the binding, the size and type of paper to be used, and the legibility of printing; the filing fee; the calculation and acceleration of the effective date; procedures for registration of additional securities and amendments to and withdrawal of the registration statement; and the method of distribution of the prospectus. This is only a partial list of the 76 rules contained in Regulation C under the 1933 Act.

Registration Process

The registration process can be broken down into three distinctive time periods: the prefiling period (the period *before* the registration statement is filed with the SEC), the waiting period (the period *between* the filing and the effective date of the registration statement), and the posteffective period (the period *after* the SEC declares the registration statement effective). The registration statement is filed with the SEC

Landreth Timber Co. v. Landreth

Samuel Dennis and John Bolten purchased the stock of a lumber mill in Tonasket, Washington, from Ivan Landreth and his sons. After they had acquired the stock, the mill did not meet their expectations, and eventually they sold the mill at a loss and went into receivership. In their suit, Dennis and Bolten sought rescission of the sale of the stock and $2,500,000 in damages. They alleged that the Landreths had widely offered and then sold their stock without registering it as required by the 1933 Act. They further alleged that Ivan Landreth and his sons had negligently and intentionally made misrepresentations and failed to state material facts about the lumber company, thus violating the federal securities laws.

Both the District Court and the United States Court of Appeals of the Ninth Circuit found that the stock purchased by Dennis and Bolten could not be considered a security unless they had entered into the transaction with the anticipation of earning profits derived from the efforts of others. In *Landreth Timber Co. v. Landreth,* 105 S.Ct. 2297 (1985), the Supreme Court, however, reversed the decision and found that the stock was a security within the meaning of the 1933 Act and the 1934 Act. Therefore, the antifraud provisions of the federal securities laws applied to the transaction.

prior to the offering of the securities for sale to the public, and upon the SEC's approval of the registration statement, the registration statement becomes effective.

Prior to the filing of the registration statement, or during the prefiling period, no sales or offers to buy or sell securities are permitted. Other than normal communications, an issuer should scrutinize all its activities with the investing public and in the securities markets. It is during the prefiling period that the registration statement is prepared by the issuer and its legal counsel and accountants.

During the waiting period, or the time between the filing of the registration statement and its effective date, the issuer is permitted the use of a preliminary, or red-herring, prospectus to provide information about the securities. The **red-herring prospectus** is preliminary and is not the final prospectus. In accordance with SEC Rule 430, the red-herring prospectus must contain a red-printed legend on its cover identifying it as preliminary and subject to change. In addition, it must state that the registration statement has not yet become effective, that no sale can be made nor can offers to buy the security be accepted during this waiting period, and that delivery of the preliminary prospectus does not constitute an offer to sell or the solicitation of an offer to buy.

Also, during the waiting period, SEC Rule 134 permits the use of a tombstone ad, a notice that contains information about a proposed securities offering. The ad may include the following limited information: (1) the identity of the security and its price, (2) the persons who may execute orders to purchase, and (3) the persons from whom a prospectus may be obtained. Refer to Figure 12–1 for an example of a tombstone ad.

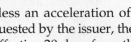

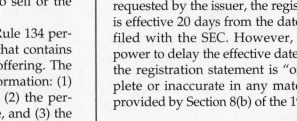

Unless an acceleration of the waiting period is requested by the issuer, the registration statement is effective 20 days from the date the statement is filed with the SEC. However, the SEC has the power to delay the effective date if it believes that the registration statement is "on its face incomplete or inaccurate in any material respect," as provided by Section 8(b) of the 1933 Act.

Sales of securities may be consummated and underwriters and dealers may make offers and sales of the registered securities after the registration statement becomes effective, or during the posteffective period. During this period any underwriter or dealer or the issuer must deliver a copy of the prospectus to any purchaser of securities. If a purchase of the securities is made more than 9 months after the effective date of the registration statement, the prospectus must be updated so that the information contained therein is not more than 16 months old. In addition, any material change occurring after the effective date and prior to the end of the 9-month period must be reported, and the prospectus must be updated to reflect the change.

When the registration statement filed under the 1933 Act becomes effective, the corporation or issuer must then comply with the reporting and disclosure requirements under the 1934 Act. Section 15(d) of the 1934 Act provides in part that the corporation must file "such supplementary and periodic information, documents, and reports as may be required pursuant to section 13 of this title [the 1934 Act]". The reporting and disclosure requirements under Section 13 of the 1934 Act are discussed in greater detail in Section 12–3.

Exemptions from 1933 Act Registration

Section 5(a) of the 1933 Act requires that all securities and transactions involving securities are subject to the registration requirements under the 1933 Act. In effect, Section 5(a) provides that every security sold by every person in any transaction must comply with the registration requirements, *unless* the security or transaction is exempt from these requirements. Sections 3 and 4 of the 1933 Act provide such exemptions. Even though exemptions from registration are available, the 1933 Act's antifraud provisions are still applicable.

Sections 3(a)(2) through 3(a)(8) and Section 3(c) of the 1933 Act specify the *securities* exempt from the registration requirements under the 1933 Act. Generally, these sections of the 1933 Act exempt from registration the securities of federal, state, and local governments; banks; savings and loans; charitable or nonprofit organizations; federally regulated common carriers; and insurance organizations. Specifically, exempt securities include (1) any security, including certificates of deposit, issued or guaranteed by the United States, a territory thereof, or any state or local government; (2) securities issued or guaranteed by banks; (3) industrial development bonds; (4) any note, draft, or bill of exchange; (5) securities issued by nonprofit organizations; (6) any security issued by a savings and loan association, building and loan association, cooperative bank, homestead association, or similar institution; (7) interests in a railroad equipment trust; (8) certificates issued in a case under title 11 of the U.S. Code (bankruptcy proceeding); and (9) insurance or endowment policies or annuity contracts issued by a corporation subject to supervision by the insurance or bank commissioners.

In addition to these specific securities, Sections 3(a)(9), (10), and (11) and Section 4 exempt securities that are sold in certain types of *transactions*. In general, these exempt transactions include (1) limited or small offerings and private placements, (2) intrastate offerings, and (3) transactions by persons other than an issuer.

The following is a brief overview of the specific transaction exemptions available under the 1933 Act:

1. Section 4(2) of the 1933 Act exempts "transactions by an issuer not involving any public offering," and includes offerings of securities in private placements. A **private placement** involves the sale of substantial amounts of a security to an institutional investor, such as an insurance company or a pension fund, or to a small group of individuals. The SEC determined that certain purchasers are sophisticated and capable of requiring from the issuer all necessary information to make the investment; therefore, they are not in need of protection under the 1933 Act.

PARALEGALERT!

Exemptions from the registration requirements of the 1933 Act are available to issuers. Certain *securities* are exempt, and certain types of *transactions* in the offer and sale of securities are exempt. Most of the research conducted of the federal securities laws is done to determine whether an exemption is available to an issuer of securities.

2. Section 3(b) of the 1933 Act gives the SEC the authority "by its rules and regulations" to exempt certain transactions "if it finds that the enforcement of this title with respect to such securities is not necessary in the public interest and for the protection by investors by reason of a small amount involved or the limited character of the public offering." But securities offerings relying on this exemption may not exceed $5,000,000. Pursuant to its authority under Section 3(b) of the 1933 Act, the SEC adopted **Regulation A** (comprising Rules 251–264 under the 1933 Act), which requires the issuer to file an "offering statement," including a "notification" and an "offering circular," at least 10 days prior to the commencement of the offering. Under Regulation A, the aggregate amount offered by the issuer may not exceed $5,000,000. Much less detail about the issuer is required under Regulation A than in a prospectus prepared in accordance with the 1933 Act.

3. Section 4(6) of the 1933 Act exempts "transactions involving offers and sales by an issuer solely to one or more accredited investors." For a transaction so exempted, advertising and public solicitation of investors are not permitted, and the resale of the securities purchased is restricted. **Accredited investor** is defined in the 1933 Act to include banks; insurance companies; investment companies; registered dealers; directors, executive officers, or general partners of the issuer; individuals with net worth exceeding $1,000,000; trusts with total assets exceeding $5,000,000; certain natural persons with income exceeding $200,000; and entities of which all the owners are accredited investors.

4. Rules 501–508, which make up **Regulation D,** were adopted under the authority of Section 3(b) of the 1933 Act. The essence of Regulation D is that the accredited investor (as defined under the 1933 Act) does not need protection in making its investment decisions. Rules 501–503 contain definitions and filing and disclosure requirements relevant to the exemptions contained in Rules 504, 505, and 506. Specifically, Rule 504 exempts securities offerings up to $1,000,000 to an unlimited number of investors in any 12-month period, Rule 505 allows an issuer to sell up to $5,000,000 of securities in any 12-month period to any number of accredited investors and up to 35 other purchasers, and Rule 506 allows an issuer to sell an unlimited amount of securities to any number of accredited investors and up to 35 other purchasers. However, under Rules 505 and 506 the issuer must reasonably believe that any nonaccredited investor has "knowledge and experience in financial and business matters" and that "he is capable of evaluating the merits and risks of the prospective investment," as specifically stated in Rule 506(b)(2)(ii).

5. Section 3(a)(11) of the 1933 Act exempts from the registration requirements "any security which is a part of an issue offered and sold only to persons resident within a single State . . . , where the issuer of such security is a person resident and doing business within, or, if a corporation, incorporated by and doing business within, such State." This exemption is available only if *all* purchasers are residents of a single state *and* the issuer is incorporated in and doing business within the same single state. It may be difficult to meet the strict requirements of this type of securities offering, sometimes called an **intrastate offering,** when the business is located near a state border.

6. The securities offerings that we have discussed so far have involved the original distribution of securities by the issuer. However, most sales and purchases of securities occur in the secondary trading market, where securities already issued and outstanding are sold and purchased. Generally, all sales by persons other than the issuer, an underwriter, or a dealer are exempt from the registration requirements under the federal securities laws. Section 4(1) of the 1933 Act exempts securities "transactions by any person other than an issuer, underwriter, or dealer," thereby exempting transactions by nonprofessionals.

Exempt Securities

- Securities of banks, savings and loans, and similar institutions.
- Federal, state, and local government securities.
- Notes, drafts, and bills of exchange.
- Securities of certain nonprofit organizations.
- Securities of federally regulated common carriers.
- Insurance or endowment policies and annuity contracts.

Exempt Transactions

- Limited or small offerings and private placements (Sections 4(2), 3(b), and 4(6); Regulation A (Rules 251–264); Regulation D (Rules 501–508).
- Intrastate offerings (Section 3(a)(11)).
- Sales by persons other than the issuer.

Figure 12–4 is an overview of the security and transaction exemptions available under the 1933 Act, as just described.

Liability and Antifraud Provisions

Numerous provisions of the 1933 Act give the SEC the power to enforce compliance with the Act. Remedies available for use by the SEC include issuance of cease-and-desist orders, administrative proceedings, court injunctions, and criminal prosecution. In particular, the following sections impose liabilities and penalties for failing to comply with the 1933 Act:

1. Section 12(1) of the 1933 Act provides that "any person who offers or sells a security in violation of section 5" is liable to the purchaser of the securities, who may sue to rescind the sale and recover the purchase price of the securities plus accrued interest after returning the security to the issuer. Under this section, the plaintiff must establish only that the defendant sold the security to the plaintiff. The defendant then must establish the exemption (if any are applicable) on which the defendant is relying.

2. Section 11(a) of the 1933 Act imposes liability if the registration statement "contained an untrue statement of a material fact or omitted to state a material fact required to be stated therein or necessary to make the statements therein not misleading."

3. Sections 12(2) and 17(a) are the 1933 Act's antifraud provisions, which impose liability for fraud and misrepresentation in the sale of securities. Section 12(2) states that "any person who offers or sells a security . . . , by means of a prospectus or oral communication, which includes an untrue statement of a material fact or omits to state a material fact necessary in order to make the statements . . . not misleading . . . shall be liable to the person purchasing such security." Section 17(a) is the general antifraud provision that applies to sales of all securities, whether they have been registered or were exempt from registration. Section 17(a) of the 1933 Act is reproduced in Figure 12–5.

PARALEGALERT!

The exemption of a security or a transaction from registration does *not* provide relief from compliance with the liability and antifraud provisions of the 1933 Act.

Figure 12–5　Section 17(a) of the Securities Act of 1933

> **Section 17. . . .**
>
> (a)　It shall be unlawful for any person in the offer or sale of any securities by the use of any means or instruments of transportation or communication in interstate commerce or by the use of the mails, directly or indirectly—
>
> （1）　to employ any device, scheme, or artifice to defraud, or
>
> （2）　to obtain money or property by means of any untrue statement of a material fact or any omission to state a material fact necessary in order to make the statements made, in the light of the circumstances under which they were made, not misleading, or
>
> （3）　to engage in any transaction, practice, or course of business which operates or would operate as a fraud or deceit upon the purchaser.

4.　Section 24 of the 1933 Act imposes criminal penalties:

> Any person who willfully violates any of the provisions of this title, or the rules and regulations promulgated by the Commission . . . , or any person who willfully, in a registration statement . . . , makes any untrue statement of a material fact or omits to state any material fact . . . , shall upon conviction be fined not more than $10,000 or imprisoned not more than five years, or both.

12–3　Securities Exchange Act of 1934

The principal purposes of the 1934 Act are relatively similar to those of the 1933 Act; the 1934 Act imposes registration requirements on issuers and prohibits manipulative, deceitful, and fraudulent activities in connection with the offer and sale of securities. In addition, the 1934 Act imposes disclosure requirements on issuers, national securities exchanges, brokers and dealers, and the self-regulating organizations. Unlike the 1933 Act, which regulates the *initial* offering of securities to the public, the 1934 Act regulates the *subsequent* trading of securities and the *continuous* disclosure of information.

Specifically, the 1934 Act regulates the markets in which securities are traded and the persons who conduct securities transactions; requires the filing of periodic reports and disclosure documents; and regulates proxy solicitation, tender offers, and short-swing transactions. In addition, the 1934 Act contains numerous antifraud provisions that affect the issuer, its officers and directors, and shareholders owning more than 10% of the issuer's stock. We will briefly discuss several of the actions regulated by the 1934 Act, but we will begin with the agency established to administer the federal securities laws.

PARALEGALERT!

The Securities Exchange Act of 1934 most directly concerns issuers by imposing disclosure and reporting requirements under Section 13(a) and concerns insiders of the corporation by imposing reporting requirements under Sections 16(a) and 16(b).

Securities and Exchange Commission

The 1934 Act established the Securities and Exchange Commission, commonly referred to as the SEC, which was given the power to administer the federal securities laws and regulate the organized securities exchanges and their members, the over-the-counter market, broker-dealers, investment advisers, investment companies, attorneys and accountants who practice before the SEC, and the securities that are traded in the securities markets. Reproduced in Figure 12–6 is Section 4(a) of the 1934 Act, which outlines the establishment and composition of the SEC.

The SEC, which has its headquarters in Washington, D.C., has nine regional and six branch offices throughout the United States. The SEC comprises five divisions: enforcement, corporate finance, market regulation, investment management, and corporate regulation. The corporate finance division is responsible for examining registration statements and other disclosure documents to ensure that full and fair disclosure has been made to the public.

The SEC promulgates rules and regulations, which are published in Volume 17 of the Code of Federal Regulations. In addition, the SEC has adopted forms that are used to comply with the disclosure and reporting requirements under the securities laws. It also publishes SEC releases, which assist in interpreting the SEC's views on certain issues, and it responds to individual inquiries on certain issues.

Registration Under the 1934 Act

The 1934 Act requires that certain issuers file a registration statement with the SEC. The filing of a registration statement under the 1934 Act is in addition to the filing of a registration statement under the 1933 Act upon the initial offering of securities. An issuer who has registered securities under the 1934 Act must still register those securities under the 1933 Act, unless a securities or transaction exemption is available. In this section, we discuss the circumstances under which an issuer must register under the 1934 Act.

Section 12 of the 1934 Act and the rules in Regulation 12b (which includes Rule 12b-1 through Rule 12h-4) provide registration requirements and exemptions from registration for securities.

Figure 12–6   Section 4(a) of the Securities Exchange Act of 1934

Section 4. Securities and Exchange Commission

(a)   There is hereby established a Securities and Exchange Commission (hereinafter referred to as the "Commission") to be composed of five commissioners to be appointed by the President by and with the advice and consent of the Senate. Not more than three of such commissioners shall be members of the same political party, and in making appointments members of different political parties shall be appointed alternately as nearly as may be practicable. No commissioner shall engage in any other business, vocation, or employment than that of serving as commissioner, nor shall any commissioner participate, directly or indirectly, in any stock-market operations or transactions of a character subject to regulation by the Commission pursuant to this title. Each Commissioner shall hold office for a term of five years and until his successor is appointed and has qualified, except that he shall not so continue to serve beyond the expiration of the next session of Congress subsequent to the expiration of said fixed term of office, and except

(1)   any Commissioner appointed to fill a vacancy occurring prior to the expiration of the term for which his predecessor was appointed shall be appointed for the remainder of such term, and

(2)   the terms of office of the Commissioners first taking office after the enactment of this title shall expire as designated by the President at the time of nomination, one at the end of one year, one at the end of two years, one at the end of three years, one at the end of four years, and one at the end of five years, after the date of the enactment of this title.

First, Section 12(g) of the 1934 Act provides that "every issuer which is engaged in interstate commerce, or in a business affecting interstate commerce, or whose securities are traded by use of the mails or any means or instrumentality of interstate commerce shall . . . register such security by filing with the Commission a registration statement." Under this section, an issuer with a class of equity securities held by 500 or more persons and with $5,000,000 or more in total assets must register under the 1934 Act. Be aware that Section 12(g) of the 1934 Act requires registration of issuers with assets exceeding $1,000,000; however, Rule 12g-1 under the 1934 Act exempts issuers with less than $5,000,000 in total assets. Section 12(g) registration requirements *do not apply* to "any security listed and registered on a national securities exchange" and other types of securities more particularly defined in Section 12(g)(2) of the 1934 Act.

Second, in addition to Section 12(g) requirements, Section 12(a) of the 1934 Act requires issuers that have securities traded on a national securities exchange to register with the SEC pursuant to the requirements of Section 12(b) of the 1934 Act. This section states, in part, that "a security may be registered on a national securities exchange by the issuer filing an application with the exchange (and filing with the Commission such duplicate originals thereof as the Commission may require)." Generally, the application, or registration statement, must contain organizational, financial structure, and business information; the capital structure; information about the directors, officers, and beneficial owners of securities of the corporation; the remuneration paid to directors, officers, and others; bonus and profit-sharing arrangements; management, service, and material contracts; and financial statements of the corporation.

Upon the filing and effectiveness of a registration statement, filed in compliance with the rules and regulations of the 1934 Act, the issuing corporation becomes an **Exchange Act company**—that is, a reporting company under the 1934 Act. This status triggers numerous reporting and disclosure requirements.

PARALEGALERT!

A corporation that has registered a security under the 1933 Act is not deemed an Exchange Act company, because it is not registered under the 1934 Act. It will, however, be subject to the reporting and disclosure requirements under Section 15 of the 1934 Act.

Reporting and Disclosure Requirements

In addition to the registration requirement, an issuer may become subject to the 1934 Act reporting and disclosure requirements. All issuers whose securities are registered under Section 12 of the 1934 Act are subject to the reporting and disclosure requirements of Section 13 of the 1934 Act. In addition, issuers with an effective registration statement filed under the 1933 Act are also subject to the reporting and disclosure requirements of Section 13 of the 1934 Act.

In particular, Section 13(a) of the 1934 Act states that

> Every issuer of a security registered pursuant to section 12 of this title shall file with the Commission, in accordance with such rules and regulations as the Commission may prescribe as necessary or appropriate for the proper protection of investors and to insure fair dealing in the security—
> (1) Such information and documents . . . as the Commission shall require to keep reasonably current the information and documents . . . filed pursuant to section 12. . . .
> (2) Such annual reports . . . , and such quarterly reports, . . . as the Commission may prescribe.

Regulation 13(a) of the 1934 Act, which is titled "Reports of Issuers of Securities Registered Pursuant to Section 12," provides rules that specify the types of annual and quarterly and other periodic reports required to be filed by issuers. These reports ensure that current information is publicly available about corporations whose shares are publicly traded. These reports include the following:

1. An annual report on **Form 10-K** must be filed with the SEC within 90 days after the end of the issuer's fiscal year. The information that must be furnished on Form 10-K is similar to that required for a registration statement and generally includes the following: the business conducted and the properties owned by the corporation; any legal proceedings against the corporation; matters submitted to a vote of the shareholders; financial information, including management's discussion and analysis of the corporation's financial condition; and identification of directors, officers, and certain shareholders, including the compensation paid and certain relationships and related transactions among these groups and the corporation.

2. A quarterly report on **Form 10-Q** must be filed with the SEC within 45 days after the end of each of the first three quarters of the issuer's fiscal year. A Form 10-Q is not required for the fourth quarter because the information otherwise required to be reported for the fourth quarter will be included in the annual report on Form 10-K. A corporation required to file Form 10-K must also file a quarterly Form 10-Q. The Form 10-Q includes financial information and management's discussion and analysis of the financial condition of the corporation, any legal proceedings in which the corporation is involved, changes in the rights of shareholders, defaults in the payment of principal and interest with respect to any indebtedness of the corporation, any matters submitted to a vote of the shareholders, and any other matters of a material nature.

3. A current report on **Form 8-K** must be filed with the SEC within 5 days after a change in the corporation's certifying accountant or the resignation of a director of the corporation. A Form 8-K must be filed within 15 days after any of the following occurrences: (1) a change in control of the corporation; (2) the acquisition or disposition of a significant amount of assets other than in the ordinary course of business; or (3) the appointment of a receiver, fiscal agent, or similar officer in a proceeding under the Bankruptcy Act.

General rules for the disclosure of information and the preparation and filing of Form 10-K, Form 10-Q, and Form 8-K are provided in the general instructions for each of those forms.

Section 16 of the 1934 Act, titled "Directors, Officers, and Principal Stockholders," governs the actions of and imposes filing requirements on (1) beneficial owners of more than 10% of the shares of any one class of securities of an issuer registered under Section 12 of the 1934 Act and (2) directors and officers of such an issuer. In part, Section 16(a) provides that

> Every person who is directly or indirectly the beneficial owner of more than 10 per centum of any class of any equity security . . . which is registered pursuant to section 12 of this title, or who is a director or an officer of the issuer of such security, shall file, at the time of the registration of such security . . . , or within ten days after he becomes such beneficial owner, director, or officer, a statement with the Commission.

Owners of more than 10% of the shares of any one class of securities of an issuer and the issuer's directors and officers are deemed the **insiders** of the corporation.

The statement required to be filed under Section 16(a) of the 1934 Act by beneficial owners, directors, and officers of the corporation is any one of the following forms:

1. **Form 3,** Initial Statement of Beneficial Ownership of Securities, must be filed within 10 days after an event that triggers the requirement to file such form. The filing requirement is triggered by a person's acquiring beneficial ownership of more than 10% of any class of equity security or by the appointment

of a director or officer (1) at any time or (2) upon the corporation's registration of any class of equity security. For example, Form 3 must be filed by a director of a corporation registered under Section 12 of the 1934 Act within 10 days of such registration. A copy of Form 3 is reproduced in Figure 12–7.

2. **Form 4,** Statement of Changes of Beneficial Ownership of Securities, is filed by the directors, officers, and beneficial owners when any change of beneficial ownership occurs or a director or officer ceases to serve in such capacity. A Form 4 must be filed on or before the tenth day of the month following the month in which the change occurred. For example, if a beneficial owner sold shares of common stock on April 3, the sale must be reported on Form 4, which must be filed with the SEC on or before May 10. A copy of Form 4 is reproduced in Figure 12–8.

3. **Form 5,** Annual Statement of Changes in Beneficial Ownership of Securities, is filed annually, by directors, officers, and persons with more than a 10% beneficial ownership of any class of equity security, before the 45th day after the end of the issuer's fiscal year. Generally, if these persons have complied with the disclosure requirements and have reported all transactions on either Form 3 or Form 4 through the year, no Form 5 need be filed. A copy of Form 5 is reproduced in Figure 12–9.

Once a director or an officer files Form 3 with the SEC, he or she must continue to file Form 4 and Form 5 until the time when he or she is no longer a director or an officer. This is also true of a beneficial owner, who upon obtaining more than 10% beneficial ownership of a class of equity security of a corporation must file a Form 3. A beneficial owner must continue to file Form 4 upon every sale or purchase of securities until his or her beneficial ownership falls below 10%.

Beneficial ownership is not specifically defined in the 1934 Act, but the SEC has determined that **beneficial ownership** includes the ability to vote or the ability to dispose of, transfer, or receive income from the security. In other words, a person is deemed the beneficial owner of an equity security when that person has the right to (1) vote or control the voting of the security, (2) dispose of or transfer or control the disposition or transfer of the security, or (3) receive income from the security. The instructions accompanying Form 5 address beneficial ownership and state in part that "a person is deemed to beneficially own securities over which that person exercises voting or investment control . . . or shares the opportunity, directly or indirectly, to profit or share in any profit derived from a transaction in the securities."

A beneficial owner of a security is not necessarily the record owner of the security. For example, the trustee of a trust may be the beneficial owner of shares held by the trust, since the trustee has the right to vote the securities on behalf of the trust. However, the trust will be the record owner of the shares. That is, the share certificate will identify the trust as being the owner of the shares.

Insider Short-Swing Profits

Section 16(a) of the 1934 Act is one response to the problem of insiders trading securities because of information about an issuer that is not readily available to the investing public. In addition to the disclosure and filing requirements imposed by Section 16(a), Section 16(b) helps to prevent the unfair use of information about an issuer or a corporation that may have been obtained by any beneficial owner, director, or officer by virtue of their relationship with the corporation. The restrictions imposed by Section 16(b) of the 1934 Act could be costly to the insider who violates the statute.

PARALEGALERT!

It is not necessary that the trading of securities in violation of Section 16(b) be based on inside information. Any trade of securities made within the six-month period is subject to the restrictions of Section 16(b), whether or not inside information was used by the insider.

Figure 12–7   Form 3, Initial Statement of Beneficial Ownership of Securities

FORM 3	**U.S. SECURITIES AND EXCHANGE COMMISSION** Washington, D.C. 20549 **INITIAL STATEMENT OF BENEFICIAL OWNERSHIP OF SECURITIES** Filed pursuant to Section 16(a) of the Securities Exchange Act of 1934, Section 17(a) of the Public Utility Holding Company Act of 1935 or Section 30(f) of the Investment Company Act of 1940	OMB APPROVAL OMB Number 3235-0104 Expires: February 1, 1994 Estimated average burden hours per response 0.5

1. Name and Address of Reporting Person	2. Date of Event Requiring Statement (Month/Day/Year)	4. Issuer Name and Ticker or Trading Symbol

(Last)   (First)   (Middle)

(Street)

(City)   (State)   (Zip)

3. IRS or Social Security Number of Reporting Person (Voluntary)

5. Relationship of Reporting Person to Issuer (Check all applicable)

_____ Director   _____ 10% Owner
_____ Officer (give   _____ Other (specify
             title below)   below)
_____

6. If Amendment, Date of Original (Month/Day/Year)

Table I — Non-Derivative Securities Beneficially Owned

1. Title of Security (Instr. 4)	2. Amount of Securities Beneficially Owned (Instr. 4)	3. Ownership Form: Direct (D) or Indirect (I) (Instr. 5)	4. Nature of Indirect Beneficial Ownership (Instr. 5)

Reminder: Report on a separate line for each class of securities beneficially owned directly or indirectly.
(Print or Type Responses)

(Over)

(BACK PAGE)

FORM 3 (continued)   **Table II — Derivative Securities Beneficially Owned** (*e.g.*, puts, calls, warrants, options, convertible securities)

1. Title of Derivative Security (Instr. 4)	2. Date Exercisable and Expiration Date (Month/Day/Year)		3. Title and Amount of Securities Underlying Derivative Security (Instr. 4)		4. Conversion or Exercise Price of Derivative Security	5. Ownership Form of Derivative Security: Direct (D) or Indirect (I) (Instr. 5)	6. Nature of Indirect Beneficial Ownership (Instr. 5)
	Date Exercisable	Expiration Date	Title	Amount or Number of Shares			

Explanation of Responses:

Signature of Reporting Person   Date

Page 2

Figure 12–8   Form 4, Statement of Changes in Beneficial Ownership of Securities

---

| FORM 4 | U.S. SECURITIES AND EXCHANGE COMMISSION
Washington, D.C. 20549

STATEMENT OF CHANGES IN BENEFICIAL OWNERSHIP | OMB APPROVAL
OMB Number   3235-0287
Expires: February 1, 1994
Estimated average burden
hours per response . . . . 0.5 |

Filed pursuant to Section 16(a) of the Securities Exchange Act of 1934, Section 17(a) of the Public Utility
Holding Company Act of 1935 or Section 30(f) of the Investment Company Act of 1940

1. Name and Address of Reporting Person	2. Issuer Name and Ticker or Trading Symbol	6. Relationship of Reporting Person to Issuer (Check all applicable)
(Last) (First) (Middle)	3. IRS or Social Security Number of Reporting Person (Voluntary)	4. Statement for Month/Year	_____ Director _____ 10% Owner _____ Officer (give title below) _____ Other (specify below)
(Street)		5. If Amendment, Date of Original (Month/Year)	_____
(City) (State) (Zip)			

Table I — Non-Derivative Securities Acquired, Disposed of, or Beneficially Owned

1. Title of Security (Instr. 3)	2. Transaction Date (Month/Day/Year)	3. Transaction Code (Instr. 8)		4. Securities Acquired (A) or Disposed of (D) (Instr. 3, 4 and 5)			5. Amount of Securities Beneficially Owned at End of Month (Instr. 3 and 4)	6. Ownership Form: Direct (D) or Indirect (I) (Instr. 4)	7. Nature of Indirect Beneficial Ownership (Instr. 4)
		Code	V	Amount	(A) or (D)	Price			

Reminder: Report on a separate line for each class of securities beneficially owned directly or indirectly.
(Print or Type Responses)   (Over)

(BACK PAGE)

FORM 4 (continued)

Table II — Derivative Securities Acquired, Disposed of, or Beneficially Owned
(e.g., puts, calls, warrants, options, convertible securities)

1. Title of Derivative Security (Instr. 3)	2. Conversion or Exercise Price of Derivative Security	3. Transaction Date (Month/Day/Year)	4. Transaction Code (Instr. 8)		5. Number of Derivative Securities Acquired (A) or Disposed of (D) (Instr. 3, 4, and 5)		6. Date Exercisable and Expiration Date (Month/Day/Year)		7. Title and Amount of Underlying Securities (Instr. 3 and 4)		8. Price of Derivative Security (Instr. 5)	9. Number of Derivative Securities Beneficially Owned at End of Month (Instr. 4)	10. Ownership Form of Derivative Security: Direct (D) or Indirect (I) (Instr. 4)	11. Nature of Indirect Beneficial Ownership (Instr. 4)
			Code	V	(A)	(D)	Date Exercisable	Expiration Date	Title	Amount or Number of Shares				

Explanation of Responses:

_____   _____
Signature of Reporting Person   Date

Page 2

Figure 12–9   Form 5, Annual Statement of Changes in Beneficial Ownership of Securities

FORM 5	U.S. SECURITIES AND EXCHANGE COMMISSION Washington, D.C. 20549 **ANNUAL STATEMENT OF CHANGES IN BENEFICIAL OWNERSHIP** Filed pursuant to Section 16(a) of the Securities Exchange Act of 1934, Section 17(a) of the Public Utility Holding Company Act of 1935 or Section 30(f) of the Investment Company Act of 1940	OMB APPROVAL OMB Number 3235-0362 Expires: February 1, 1994 Estimated average burden hours per response 1.0

1. Name and Address of Reporting Person	2. Issuer Name and Ticker or Trading Symbol	6. Relationship of Reporting Person to Issuer
		(Check all applicable)
		____ Director ____ 10% Owner
		____ Officer (give ____ Other (specify
		            title below)
		            below)

(Last) (First) (Middle)	3. IRS or Social Security Number of Reporting Person (Voluntary)	4. Statement for Month/Year	
(Street)		5. If Amendment, Date of Original (Month/Year)	
(City) (State) (Zip)	Table I — Non-Derivative Securities Acquired, Disposed of, or Beneficially Owned	

Table I — Non-Derivative Securities Acquired, Disposed of, or Beneficially Owned

1. Title of Security (Instr. 3)	2. Transaction Date (Month/Day/Year)	3. Transaction Code (Instr. 8)	4. Securities Acquired (A) or Disposed of (D) (Instr. 3, 4 and 5)			5. Amount of Securities Beneficially Owned at End of Issuer's Fiscal Year (Instr. 3 and 4)	6. Ownership Form: Direct (D) or Indirect (I) (Instr. 4)	7. Nature of Indirect Beneficial Ownership (Instr. 4)
			Amount	(A) or (D)	Price			

Reminder: Report on a separate line for each class of securities beneficially owned directly or indirectly.   (Over)
(Print or Type Responses)

(BACK PAGE)

FORM 5 (continued)   **Table II — Derivative Securities Acquired, Disposed of, or Beneficially Owned**
(e.g., puts, calls, warrants, options, convertible securities)

1. Title of Derivative Security (Instr. 3)	2. Conversion or Exercise Price of Derivative Security	3. Transaction Date (Month/Day/Year)	4. Transaction Code (Instr. 8)	5. Number of Derivative Securities Acquired (A) or Disposed of (D) (Instr. 3, 4, and 5)		6. Date Exercisable and Expiration Date (Month/Day/Year)		7. Title and Amount of Underlying Securities (Instr. 3 and 4)		8. Price of Derivative Security (Instr. 5)	9. Number of Derivative Securities Beneficially Owned at End of Year (Instr. 4)	10. Ownership of Derivative Security: Direct (D) or Indirect (I) (Instr. 4)	11. Nature of Indirect Beneficial Ownership (Instr. 4)
				(A)	(D)	Date Exercisable	Expiration Date	Title	Amount or Number of Shares				

Explanation of Responses:

_____   _____
Signature of Reporting Person   Date

Page 2

Section 16(b) of the 1934 Act provides that

> For the purpose of preventing the unfair use of information which may have been obtained by such beneficial owner, director, or officer by reason of his relationship to the issuer, any profit realized by him from any purchase and sale, or any sale and purchase, of any equity security of such issuer . . . within any period of less than six months, . . . shall inure to and be recoverable by the issuer.

The profit derived by the insider on the sale and purchase or purchase and sale of the security in any six-month period reverts to the corporation. This profit is often called a **short-swing profit.**

Remember, the sale and purchase of securities by an insider must be reported on a statement (Form 3, Form 4, or Form 5) required under Section 16(a) of the 1934 Act. Any short-swing profit derived by an insider can be identified easily on review of these forms, as long as they were filed on time with the SEC. The SEC will not enforce the restriction imposed by Section 16(b); however, the corporation or a shareholder of the corporation may sue the insider in federal court for any violation. The corporation will, of course, recover the short-swing profit enjoyed by the insider.

Liability and Antifraud Provisions

To ensure that no false or misleading statement is made in any application, report, or other document filed in accordance with any provision of the 1934 Act, Section 18(a) of the 1934 Act imposes liability on any person who violates the provisions of this section. Specifically, that section provides that

> Any person who shall make or cause to be made any statement in any application, report, or document filed pursuant to this title or any rule or regulation thereunder or any undertaking contained in a registration statement . . . , which statement was . . . false or misleading with respect to any material fact, shall be liable to any person (not knowing that such statement was false or misleading) who, in reliance upon such statement, shall have purchased or sold a security.

Under Section 18(a), a defendant may avoid liability by proving that "he acted in good faith and had no knowledge that such statement was false or misleading." Any suit brought under Section 18 must be commenced within one year after the discovery of the violation.

Section 10 of the 1934 Act and Rule 10b-5 contain the general antifraud provisions imposed on persons to prevent manipulative and deceptive practices in the offer and sale of securities. Rule 10b-5 is reproduced in Figure 12–10. Note that it prohibits the use of any device, scheme, or artifice to defraud or make any untrue or misleading statement or engage in any act, practice, or course of business that would defraud any person in connection with the purchase or sale of any security. Rule 10b-5 and the antifraud provisions of the 1934 Act are applicable to securities transactions in general, whether or not a registration statement has been filed under the 1934 Act. They apply to all private purchases and sales, including those of closely held corporations.

In addition, Section 32 of the 1934 Act imposes criminal penalties on any person who willfully violates any 1934 Act provision. Specifically, Section 32(a) of the 1934 Act states that

> Any person who willfully violates any provision of this title . . . , or any rule or regulation thereunder . . . , or any person who willfully and knowingly makes, or causes to be made, any statement in any application, report, or document required to be filed under this title or any rule or regulation thereunder . . . , shall upon conviction be fined not more than $1,000,000 or imprisoned not more than 10 years, or both.

PARALEGALERT!

Rule 10b-5 is one of the most important provisions of the 1934 Act in that it prohibits any fraudulent act, practice, or course of business in the offer and sale of securities. This prohibition extends to *all* offers and sales of securities, including those that are not registered under the 1934 Act.

Figure 12–10   Rule 10b-5

> It shall be unlawful for any person, directly or indirectly, by the use of any means or instrumentality of interstate commerce, or of the mails, or of any facility of any national securities exchange,
>
> (1) to employ any device, scheme, or artifice to defraud,
>
> (2) to make any untrue statement of a material fact or to omit to state a material fact necessary in order to make the statements made, in light of circumstances under which they were made, not misleading, or
>
> (3) to engage in any act, practice, or course of business which operates or would operate as a fraud or deceit upon any person,
>
> in connection with the purchase or sale of any security.

The SEC itself does not prosecute violators of this provision. It does, however, provide the information to the U.S. Department of Justice, which determines whether or not to prosecute for the violation.

12–4   Blue-Sky Laws

As previously mentioned, the first state to enact securities laws was Kansas, in 1911. Since then, all states have followed suit and have enacted statutes governing the offer and sale of securities. State statutes regulating securities are commonly referred to as *blue-sky laws*. The term was coined in the Supreme Court case *Hall v. Geiger-Jones Company*, 242 U.S. 539 (1917). The Court found in this case that the purpose of securities laws was the prevention of fraudulent activities carried out through "speculative schemes which have no more basis than so many feet of 'blue sky'." Blue-sky laws prevented investors from being sold nothing more than blue sky.

Blue-sky laws vary greatly among the states, but they generally (1) require registration of securities being sold within the state, (2) require registration of broker-dealers acting on behalf of investors, and (3) prohibit fraudulent and deceptive conduct. As long as provisions of the blue-sky laws do not contradict or conflict with the federal securities laws, they are deemed valid and are upheld as lawful. Because of the diversity of the states' securities laws, we will refer to provisions of the Uniform Securities Act (referred to as the USA) throughout this section.

Interpretive questions and controversy often arise in determining which states' blue-sky laws must be complied with. For example, suppose that an issuer in one state makes an offer to a buyer in another state. The important question is, Which state's statutes govern the transaction? Because of the variations among the states, the statutes of both states must be researched to determine the requirements for registration of the securities or registration of the transaction.

The USA requires registration in either one of two situations. First, registration is required when an offer to sell is made within the state. Section 801(a) of the USA states that "a person . . . sells or offers to sell a security if (1) an offer to sell

PARALEGALERT!

State blue-sky laws apply to the offer and sale of securities within a particular state. However, questions of jurisdiction arise when an issuer and purchasers of securities do not belong to the same state or when offers are made within a state but sales are not. Several other circumstances require a close examination of the securities laws of all states involved.

is made in this State; or (2) an offer to purchase is made and accepted in this State." Second, registration is required when an offer to buy is made within the state. Section 801(b) of the USA states that "a person . . . purchases or offers to purchase a security if: (1) an offer to purchase is made in this State; or (2) an offer to sell is made and accepted in this State." In summary, any offer to sell or buy made within a particular state requires some type of registration under the USA. Remember, however, that not all states have adopted the language of the USA.

A security to be issued or a transaction in which the security is to be sold may be exempt from registration under the blue-sky laws. The registration requirement of the USA (Section 301) states that "a person may not offer to sell or sell a security in this State unless it is registered under this Act or the security or transaction is exempt under this Act." In other words, the security must be registered unless the security or transaction is exempt. The USA and the blue-sky laws of most states specify the types of securities and types of transactions that do not require registration under the statute.

Registration Process

Most states require some form of registration of securities before the securities can be offered and sold in that particular state. Exemptions from registration will be discussed in the next subsection. Sections 302, 303, and 304 of the USA identify the three categories of registration—namely, registration by filing (Section 302 of the USA), registration by coordination (Section 303), and registration by qualification (Section 304). Remember, not all states have adopted the USA, and you must research the blue-sky laws of the individual states involved in an offer and sale of securities. However, the following registration procedures exemplify many states' securities statutes:

1. **Registration by filing**—In accordance with Section 302(a) of the USA, issuers desiring to offer securities for which a registration statement has been filed under the 1933 Act may register by filing if the following requirements are met: (1) the issuer is organized under the laws of the United States or a state or has appointed an agent for service of process if organized outside the United States, (2) the issuer has been actively engaged in business operations in the United States for a period of 36 months prior to the filing of the federal registration statement, (3) the issuer has a class of securities registered under the 1933 Act that is held by more than 500 persons, (4) the issuer meets specific net worth tests and has not less than 400,000 units of securities registered under the 1933 Act held by the public, (5) the issuer has been subject to the requirements of the 1934 Act for at least 36 months and has promptly filed all reports required to be filed under the 1934 Act, (6) specific requirements for offering the issuer's securities in the market with the participation of underwriters and broker-dealers have been met, (7) commissions charged by underwriters do not exceed 10%, (8) neither the issuer nor any of its subsidiaries have failed to pay a dividend on preferred stock or defaulted on any indebtedness, and (9) the price at which the security is to be offered is not less than $5. Section 302(b) of the USA provides additional requirements for registration by filing.

2. **Registration by coordination**—Registration by coordination is similar to registration by filing. Section 303(a) of the USA states that "securities for which a registration statement has been filed under the Securities Act of 1933 in connection with the offering of the securities may be registered by coordination." However, registration by coordination does not require the issuer to meet the same financial and qualification tests required under Section 302 of the USA for registration by filing. However, additional

information and documents must be filed with the registration statement required for registration by coordination. These additional documents include the articles of incorporation and the bylaws of the issuer, an agreement with or among the underwriters, an indenture or other document governing the issuance of the securities, and a specimen copy of the security to be registered. Section 303(b) of the USA identifies specifically the additional information and documents required to be filed for registration by coordination.

3. **Registration by qualification**—Registration by qualification is the procedure followed by issuers who have not met or cannot meet the requirements for registration under the other two methods. Section 304(b) of the USA requires the issuer to file a registration statement similar to the registration statement required to be filed under the 1933 Act. Issuers use registration by qualification when they are *not* required to file a registration statement under the 1933 Act but must meet the requirements of a state's securities laws. Registration by qualification is the most time-consuming and complex of the three methods available to an issuer for registering securities, because it is used when registration under the 1933 Act is not required. If the issuer had prepared a registration statement for filing in accordance with the 1933 Act, most of the information and documentation would have been gathered and provided to meet the federal securities requirements.

PARALEGALERT!

Registration by qualification is the most burdensome of the methods of registering under state securities laws. An issuer is required to prepare a registration statement, similar to that required under the 1933 Act, for filing on the state level.

Exemptions from Registration

Exemptions from registration are available under the blue-sky laws, similar to the exemptions provided under the 1933 Act. Part IV of the USA, particularly Sections 401 and 402, outlines the circumstances under which securities and transactions may be exempt from the registration procedures just discussed. Remember, not all states follow the USA. Therefore, you must research each state's specific securities laws to identify the exemptions from registration available in that state.

Section 401(b) of the USA provides a list of the securities that are exempt from the registration procedures. If a securities exemption is available, the offer and sale of those exempt securities does not require registration. The following is a list of the *types* of securities that are usually exempt from registration:

1. A security issued, insured, or guaranteed by the United States or Canada.
2. A security issued by a depository institution insured by the Federal Deposit Insurance Corporation, the Federal Savings and Loan Insurance Corporation, or the National Credit Union Share Insurance Fund.
3. Securities listed on the major securities exchanges (New York Stock Exchange, American Stock Exchange, etc.).
4. A security issued by an insurance company, railroad, or public utility company.
5. A security issued by an entity organized for a religious, educational, benevolent, fraternal, social, athletic, or reformatory purpose.
6. A promissory note payable within nine months after the date of issuance and issued in denominations of at least $50,000.
7. A security issued in connection with an employee's stock purchase, savings, or option plan.

Sections 402(1) through 402(18) of the USA provide a list of the types of transactions that are exempt from the registration procedures. In other words, certain types of transactions do not require registration. The following is a noninclusive list of the *types* of transactions that are usually exempt from registration:

1. Isolated nonissuer transactions (e.g., a sale by one person to another person, as opposed to a sale by the issuer to another person).
2. An offer to sell to a financial or institutional investor or to a broker-dealer.
3. Transactions in which there is no general solicitation or advertising and there are no more than 25 purchasers in a particular state during any 12 consecutive months.
4. Transactions in connection with the organization of the corporation, including subscriptions to stock prior to incorporation. Other exemptions are available under the USA, but those listed here are the transaction exemptions most often utilized by issuers.

PARALEGALERT!

Exemptions from registration are based on either the type of security or the specific transaction involving a security. Even when an exemption from the registration requirements is available, an issuer may still be required to comply with other provisions of a particular state's securities laws.

Antifraud Provisions and Enforcement

The USA and all state securities laws prohibit fraudulent activities in the offer to sell, the sale, the offer to purchase, and the purchase of securities. Sections 501–505 of the USA relate to the prohibition of deceptive and fraudulent activities. Specifically, these sections cover prohibitions against fraudulent activities in the offer, sale, and purchase of securities (Section 501); manipulation of the market (Section 502); fraudulent activities by investment advisers (Section 503); false and misleading information and documents (Section 504); and unlawful representations concerning licensing, registration, or exemption (Section 505).

Section 501 of the USA is similar to the antifraud provisions of Section 10b-5 of the 1933 Act, which we discussed earlier in this chapter. Section 501 of the USA is reproduced in Figure 12–11. Note the similarities to Section 17(a) of the 1933 Act (Figure 12–5) and Rule 10b-5 of the 1934 Act (Figure 12–10).

Sanctions, the consequences of violating the antifraud provisions of the USA, are provided in Sections 601–609 of the USA. In effect, the enforcement and liability provisions of the USA authorize the appropriate governmental agency to investigate, hold administrative hearings, and impose legal or equitable remedies for violations of provisions of the USA.

In addition, the USA imposes civil liability on the persons—including partners, officers, and directors of the seller of securities—who offer to sell or who

Figure 12–11 Section 501 of the Uniform Securities Act

Sec. 501. Offer, sale, and purchase. In connection with an offer to sell, sale, offer to purchase, or purchase, of a security, a person may not, directly or indirectly:

(1) employ a device, scheme, or artifice to defraud;

(2) make an untrue statement of a material fact or omit to state a material fact necessary in order to make the statements made not misleading, in the light of the circumstances under which they are made; or

(3) engage in an act, practice, or course of business that operates or would operate as a fraud or deceit upon a person.

sell securities in violation of provisions of the USA. As a remedy, the purchaser may recover the consideration paid for the security, accrued interest, costs, and reasonable attorney's fees.

12–5   Practical Considerations

Research of questions or issues regarding the federal or state securities laws may be done by the paralegal. The places to begin are the federal securities statutes and the state securities statutes, which are often vague and ambiguous. Therefore, the following additional supplemental sources should be relied on in performing your research: (1) rules and regulations adopted under the statutes; (2) forms used by issuers, broker-dealers, and others in complying with disclosure requirements; (3) releases, called **SEC releases,** which are statements distributed by the SEC that set forth the views of the SEC on certain issues; (4) **no-action letters,** or **interpretative letters,** which are responses by the SEC to individual inquiries by members of the public, attorneys, issuers, or other persons, interpreting the statutes or application of the statutes with regard to a particular transaction; and (5) court decisions reached in federal and state jurisdictions.

Commerce Clearing House, Inc., often called CCH, produces a comprehensive eight-volume looseleaf service titled *Federal Securities Law Reports.* This reporter contains a full text of the federal securities laws with all changes and amendments; the rules and regulations interpreting the laws; official forms promulgated thereunder; SEC interpretative releases, which comment on the statutes and regulations; no-action, or interpretative, letters; court decisions on federal securities law issues; and releases and materials containing rulings of the SEC. This service should provide most, if not all, of the material necessary to research federal securities issues from the simplest to the most complex. In addition, this reporter contains helpful features, such as a division titled "How to Answer Form S-1," which includes a complete editorial explanation of the information required in a Form S-1 registration statement. It also has a division containing information concerning the functions, organization, regional offices, and personnel of the SEC.

CCH also produces a five-volume looseleaf service titled *Blue Sky Law Reports,* which contains the laws and regulations of all fifty states, the District of Columbia, Guam, and Puerto Rico; the Uniform Securities Act; a survey of the blue-sky laws and a historical case digest; statements of policy, orders, and rulings; uniform forms; and materials relating to insurance securities and legal investments. Research of any state securities issue should not be undertaken without the use of this five-volume reporter.

Both the federal and state securities reporters should be available in any law library and in the libraries of all securities practitioners. You should become familiar with these reporters before embarking on any securities research project.

Paralegals are often responsible for the preparation of disclosure and compliance documents under Section 16 of the 1934 Act, including Form 3, Form 4, and Form 5. An excellent treatise authored by Peter J. Romeo and Alan L. Dye covers the insider reporting and short-swing liability provisions under Section 16 of the Securities Exchange Act of 1934. This treatise is titled *Section 16 Treatise and Reporting Guide.* Along with its companion materials, titled *Section 16 Treatise and Service, Section 16 Forms and Filings Handbook,* and *Comprehensive Section 16 Outline,* it is the most comprehensive and practical treatment of the requirements under Section 16 of the 1934 Act. Sample reporting forms, examples, and compliance documents are included in the treatise and the accompanying handbook.

SUMMARY

12–1

The offer and sale of securities are subject to both federal and state securities laws. Interstate transactions involving securities are subject to federal and state securities laws, and intrastate transactions are usually governed only by state securities laws. In response to fraudulent practices in the sales of securities, which several states had difficulty in controlling, the Congress of the United States adopted the Securities Act of 1933 and followed it with the Securities Exchange Act of 1934. Enactment of additional federal securities laws and state securities laws adopted by all 50 states followed. The Uniform Securities Act was adopted by the Commissioners on Uniform State Laws to promote uniformity in state securities laws. Whether an investment instrument is a security determines the necessity of complying with the registration requirements of the federal and state securities laws. Securities are issued, sold, and traded through the securities markets, which consist of the organized securities exchanges and the over-the-counter market.

12–2

To assist an investor in making an informed decision about an investment and to prohibit fraudulent and deceitful activities in the sale of securities, the Securities Act of 1933 requires an issuer to file a registration statement with the SEC prior to the offer and sale of securities. The registration statement must disclose all material facts about the issuer and the securities being offered. The SEC, which must approve the registration statement, reviews it for completeness and for the proper disclosure of information to enable the investor to make an informed investment decision. The prospectus is part of the registration statement; it contains the information required by the 1933 Act and by the rules and regulations promulgated thereunder. The registration process includes the prefiling period, the waiting period, and the posteffective period, all of which revolve around the filing and effectiveness of the registration statement. On the effective date, the issuer is free to offer and sell its securities. Sections 3 and 4 of the 1933 Act exempt certain securities and transactions from the registration requirements. Sanctions are imposed on those who fail to comply with the 1933 Act.

12–3

The 1934 Act regulates the trading of securities, the continuous disclosure of information to the investing public, and the persons who conduct securities transactions, including issuers, national securities exchanges, brokers and dealers, and the self-regulating organizations. The Securities and Exchange Commission was established to administer the federal securities laws and regulate the organized securities exchanges, including their members, broker-dealers, investment advisers, investment companies, attorneys and accountants who practice before the SEC, and the securities that are traded in the securities markets. Certain issuers must file a registration statement with the SEC. This requirement may be in addition to or in lieu of registration requirements under the 1933 Act. An issuer becomes an Exchange Act company on the effective date of a registration statement filed under the 1934 Act. Certain securities and specific types of transactions involving securities are exempt from the registration requirements. Directors, officers, and beneficial owners of more than 10% of any class of security of an issuer are subject to the reporting and disclosure requirements of Section 16(a), which requires an issuer to file annual, quarterly, and other periodic reports with the SEC. One of the most important provisions of the 1934 Act is Rule 10b-5, which prohibits fraud in the sale and purchase of securities.

12–4

All states have enacted statutes governing the offer and sale of securities. States' securities laws are called blue-sky laws because they have been adopted to prevent investors from being sold nothing more than "blue sky." The Uniform Securities Act, and many states, provide three categories of registration: registration by filing, registration by coordination, and registration by qualification. Specific types of securities and certain types of transactions are exempt from registration requirements under blue-sky laws. The Uniform Securities Act and all the state securities laws prohibit deceptive and fraudulent activities in the offer and sale of securities and impose sanctions for violating those provisions. Civil liabilities may also be imposed on individuals violating the securities laws.

12–5

A paralegal should not embark on the research of any federal or state securities law issue without first consulting a comprehensive securities law or blue-sky law reporter, which includes the federal and state securities laws. Commerce Clearing House, Inc. (CCH) produces *Federal Securities Law Reports* and *Blue Sky Law Reports,* both of which contain excellent and comprehensive materials on federal and state securities law issues. No reporting or compliance forms should be completed in accordance with Section 16 of the Securities Exchange Act of 1934 until the materials contained in *Section 16 Treatise and Reporting Guide* and its accompanying supplements have been reviewed.

REVIEW GUIDE

Key Terms

Before proceeding, review the key terms listed below to be sure you understand each one. If necessary, read over the corresponding section of the chapter. When you are ready to test your understanding, answer the review questions.

federal securities laws (p. 278)
Securities Act of 1933 (p. 278)
Securities Exchange Act of 1934 (p. 279)
Securities and Exchange Commission (p. 279)
SEC (p. 279)
Public Utility Holding Company Act of 1935 (p. 279)
Trust Indenture Act of 1939 (p. 279)
Investment Company Act of 1940 (p. 279)
Investment Advisers Act of 1940 (p. 279)
Securities Investor Protection Act of 1970 (p. 279)
SIPC (p. 279)
blue-sky laws (p. 279)
Uniform Securities Act (p. 280)
issuer (p. 281)
public corporation (p. 281)
prospectus (p. 281)
registration statement (p. 281)
public offering (p. 281)
security (p. 281)
effective date (p. 281)

tombstone ad (p. 281)
underwriters (p. 281)
insider trading (p. 281)
securities markets (p. 283)
organized securities exchanges (p. 283)
listed securities (p. 283)
over-the-counter market (p. 283)
OTC (p. 283)
unlisted securities (p. 283)
red-herring prospectus (p. 287) ·
private placement (p. 288)
Regulation A (p. 289)
accredited investor (p. 289)
Regulation D (p. 289)
intrastate offering (p. 289)
Exchange Act company (p. 293)
Form 10-K (p. 294)
Form 10-Q (p. 294)
Form 8-K (p. 294)
insiders (p. 294)
Form 3 (p. 294)
Form 4 (p. 295)
Form 5 (p. 295)
beneficial ownership (p. 295)
short-swing profit (p. 299)
registration by filing (p. 301)
registration by coordination (p. 301)
registration by qualification (p. 302)
SEC releases (p. 304)
no-action letters (p. 304)
interpretative letters (p. 304)

Questions for Review and Discussion

1. What precipitated the enactment of federal and state securities laws?
2. What is the Uniform Securities Act?
3. Why is the definition of *security* a central issue in securities law?
4. Describe the mechanisms in place to facilitate the consummation of sales and purchases of securities by investors.
5. How do the Securities Act of 1933 and the Securities Exchange Act of 1934 differ? How are they the same?
6. What purpose does a registration statement serve?
7. What activities are permitted by the issuer during the waiting-period phase of the registration process?
8. Explain why an issuer may not be required to file a registration statement.
9. What role does the Securities and Exchange Commission play in the regulation of the offer and sale of securities?
10. Name some of the reporting and disclosure forms and documents required to be filed by issuers under the Securities Exchange Act of 1934.
11. Who is an insider of the corporation?
12. Under what circumstances may liability be imposed on a person for failing to comply with the provisions of the Securities Act of 1933 and the Securities Exchange Act of 1934?
13. By what methods are securities registered under the blue-sky laws?
14. Why is registration by qualification, a procedure of registration under the Uniform Securities Act, the most time-consuming and complex of all the methods of registration?

Activities

1. Obtain a complete copy of Schedule A, referred to in Section 7 of the Securities Act of 1933. (Note: The list of information provided in this chapter is only a summary of Schedule A.) Obtain a copy of the prospectus from the initial public offering of a corporation. Review it for the information required to be contained in the prospectus, and compare it with the requirements of Schedule A.
2. Call the shareholders' relations department of a public corporation located in your area and ask them to send you a copy of the corporation's most recent prospectus and Form 10-Q or Form 10-K, whichever is most recently available.
3. Review the blue-sky laws of your state to determine the exemption, if any, available to a newly organized corporation incorporated in your state. Assume that the corporation desires to issue shares of common stock to six shareholders, all of whom are individuals, immediately after the incorporation date. It plans to issue additional shares to three individuals approximately one year later. If you do not have access to the securities laws of your state, use the provisions of the Uniform Securities Act.

CHAPTER 13   Merger, Share Exchange, Consolidation, and Sale and Purchase of Stock and Assets

OUTLINE

13–1 Corporate Structural Changes
13–2 Merger, Share Exchange, and Consolidation
        Merger
        Short-Form Merger
        Share Exchange
        Consolidation
13–3 Procedures for Merger, Share Exchange, and Consolidation
        Plan of Merger
        Plans of Share Exchange and Consolidation
        Directors' and Shareholders' Approval
        Statutory Filing Requirements
13–4 Sale and Purchase of Stock
        Negotiating the Transaction
        Procedures
        Stock Purchase Agreement
13–5 Sale and Purchase of Assets
        Negotiating the Transaction
        Procedures
        Bulk Transfer Law
        Asset Purchase Agreement
13–6 Dissenting Shareholders' Rights
13–7 Practical Considerations

APPLICATIONS

Coffee Beans, Inc., a client of your firm, has entered into a letter of intent for the purchase of all the outstanding stock of Tea Bags, Inc., a corporation located in Charlotte, North Carolina. Your supervising attorney provides you with a copy of the letter of intent between the parties and asks you to attend a meeting on October 22, which is the next morning. You note that the letter of intent specifies November 15 as the closing date, indicating to you that your next few weeks will be filled with the details of this transaction. You will have to make at least one trip to the offices of Tea Bags, Inc., in Charlotte to review their books and records. You know you will also be responsible for preparing board of directors' resolutions authorizing the transaction, preparing corporate certificates required under the stock purchase agreement, and assembling documents for the closing, among other things.

OBJECTIVES

While the attorneys are negotiating the details of a merger, share exchange, or consolidation, or the sale or purchase of a corporation's stock or assets, the corporate paralegal is generally busy drafting numerous agreements, documents, and resolutions of the board of directors and the shareholders necessary to close, or consummate, the transaction. Therefore, it is important for the paralegal to understand the procedures for carrying out the types of corporate structural changes discussed in this chapter. After completing Chapter 13, you will be able to:

1. Understand the differences among the merger, the share exchange, and the consolidation.
2. Draft plans of merger, share exchange, and consolidation.
3. Prepare resolutions of the board of directors and the shareholders approving a merger, share exchange, or consolidation.
4. Prepare and file articles required by statute for a merger, share exchange, or consolidation.
5. Understand the differences between a stock purchase and an asset purchase.
6. Understand the procedures for negotiating and entering into a stock transaction or an asset transaction.
7. Prepare resolutions authorizing a stock purchase and an asset purchase.
8. Identify the components of the stock and asset purchase agreements.
9. Prepare a bill of sale and an assignment for the transfer of assets.
10. Understand the requirements of the Uniform Commercial Code imposed on a selling corporation.
11. Understand the rights of dissenting shareholders.
12. Perform duties and responsibilities in connection with the due diligence process and the closing of the transaction.

13–1 Corporate Structural Changes

Up to this point we have examined the different types of business organizations—in particular, the corporation. You should now have a basic understanding of the corporation's structure, including:

1. The rights of the corporation to carry out its business and affairs.
2. The powers and responsibilities of the shareholders, directors, and officers.
3. The procedures for holding meetings, qualifying to do business in foreign jurisdictions, financing the corporation through the sale of equity and debt securities, and distributing the corporation's profits.

All these transactions generally occur in the ordinary course of business and fall within the scope of the powers delegated to the board of directors. The board of directors, in turn, authorizes the officers to carry out these procedures and transactions. Shareholder approval is usually not required.

However, the corporation may engage in transactions that change the complexion of the corporation, and therefore *do* require the approval of the shareholders of the corporation. These transactions include mergers, share exchanges, consolidations, sale of the corporation's stock, sale of the corporation's assets, amendments to the articles of incorporation and the bylaws, and dissolution and liquidation of the corporation. As you know, we devoted Chapter 8 to amending the articles of incorporation and the bylaws, and Chapter 14 will be devoted to the dissolution and liquidation of the corporation.

In this chapter we will cover the statutory and corporate procedures for mergers, share exchanges, consolidations, sale of the corporation's stock, and sale of the corporation's assets. These transactions are considered extraordinary corporate procedures and are governed by the corporate statutes of the states. However, as in previous chapters, we will refer to the provisions of the Model Act in our discussion here.

A very important point is that these corporate structural changes usually affect the ownership rights of the shareholders, and approval of the shareholders *must* be obtained before any of these changes are implemented. If a shareholder does not approve of the transaction and opposes the decision of the other shareholders, the opposing shareholder may file objections to the change and ask to be granted dissenter's rights. All these issues will be covered in greater detail in this chapter.

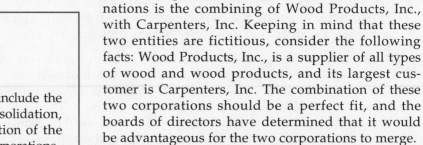

PARALEGALERT!

Extraordinary corporate transactions include merger, share exchange, consolidation, sale of the corporation's stock, and sale of the corporation's assets, all of which require approval by the shareholders of the corporation.

13–2 Merger, Share Exchange, and Consolidation

Two or more corporations may combine by using one of the following methods: merger, share exchange, or consolidation. In other sections in this chapter, we will discuss the acquisition by one corporation of the assets or stock of other corporations as a means of combining entities.

Merger, share exchange, and consolidation are governed by statutory provisions and guidelines. The Model Act addresses the merger and the share exchange, as do most state statutes. However, the consolidation is not addressed by the Model Act, and not all states provide statutes governing the procedures for consolidation. We will briefly discuss the consolidation as an option for combining two or more corporations. All three types of combinations discussed in this section and the purchase and sale of a corporation's stock or assets, discussed later, affect the rights of the shareholders and the corporations involved.

One corporation may combine with one or more other corporations as an avenue for raising capital to help finance the corporation's operations, for enhancing or expanding the corporation's business lines, and for broadening its access to markets previously unattainable. A situation we will use throughout this chapter to illustrate various forms of combinations is the combining of Wood Products, Inc., with Carpenters, Inc. Keeping in mind that these two entities are fictitious, consider the following facts: Wood Products, Inc., is a supplier of all types of wood and wood products, and its largest customer is Carpenters, Inc. The combination of these two corporations should be a perfect fit, and the boards of directors have determined that it would be advantageous for the two corporations to merge.

Also, maintaining a subsidiary corporation, which must pay separate taxes, hold its own board of directors' and shareholders' meetings, and comply with other statutory guidelines, may be a burden on the parent corporation. The parent corporation may decide that operating a segment of its business through a subsidiary corporation is not profitable and is a duplication of administrative and record-keeping functions. It may, therefore, merge that subsidiary into itself.

PARALEGALERT!

The types of corporate combinations include the merger, the share exchange, the consolidation, and the acquisition by one corporation of the assets or stock of one or more other corporations.

Merger

A **merger** is the combination of two or more corporations into one legal entity in which *only one* of the merging corporations remains after, or survives, the merger. That corporation is called the **surviving corporation**. The other corporation or corporations, which cease to exist as separate legal entities after the merger, are called the **merged corporations.** For example, consider the situation illustrated in Figure 13–1, in which Corporation A and Corporation B decide to merge. Corporation A agrees to absorb Corporation B or, in other words, permits Corporation B to merge into Corporation A. Upon the merger of these two corporations, Corporation B (the merged corporation) ceases to exist as a separate legal entity, while Corporation A continues to exist as the surviving corporation. Section 11.06(a)(1) of the Model Act states that "when a merger takes effect . . . every other corporation party to the merger merges into the surviving corporation and the separate existence of every corporation except the surviving corporation ceases."

Upon the merger of two or more corporations, the surviving corporation assumes the debts and obligations and takes over the business of the merged corporation. Ownership and title to the assets of the merged corporation are transferred to the surviving corporation. In short, all assets (cash, property, inventory, equipment, rights, etc.) and liabilities (loans and other obligations) of the merged corporation become part of the surviving corporation's assets and liabilities. Sections 11.06(a)(2) and (3) state that "when a merger takes effect . . . the title to all real estate and other property owned by each corporation party to

Figure 13–1 Graphic Illustration of Merger of Two Corporations

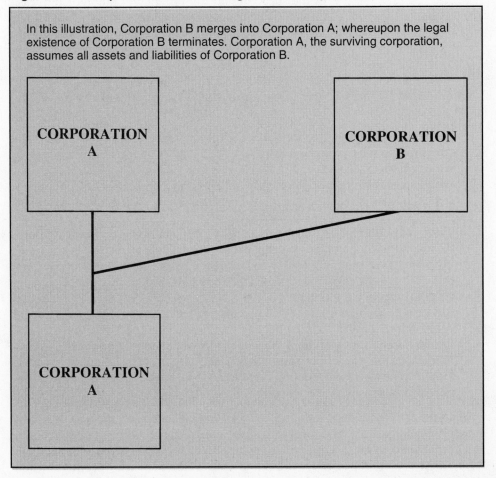

In this illustration, Corporation B merges into Corporation A; whereupon the legal existence of Corporation B terminates. Corporation A, the surviving corporation, assumes all assets and liabilities of Corporation B.

CORPORATION
A

CORPORATION
B

CORPORATION
A

the merger is vested in the surviving corporation without reversion or impairment" and "the surviving corporation has all liabilities of each corporation party to the merger."

In addition, a corporation may not avoid its contractual duties or obligations by merging into another corporation. Contracts and other agreements are not automatically terminated on the consummation of a merger. The surviving corporation will assume the duties and obligations of the merged corporation. The court in *Fitzsimmons v. Western Airlines, Inc.*, in the *Legal Links*, p. 318, held that the rights of employees of a merged corporation are not automatically terminated by the merger of the corporation.

Because the obligations of the merged corporation become the obligations of the surviving corporation, any proceedings actively pending against the merged corporation continue as if the merger had not taken place. The surviving corporation will most likely be substituted in the proceeding for the corporation whose existence has been terminated. This is permitted under Section 11.06(a)(4) of the Model Act, which states that "a proceeding pending against any corporation party to the merger may be continued as if the merger did not occur."

As the result of a merger, the surviving corporation may issue shares or pay consideration to the shareholders of the merged corporation. In many cases, the shareholders of the merged corporation receive shares of the surviving corporation and, as a result, become shareholders of the surviving corporation. Section 11.01(b)(3) of the Model Act permits, as do the statutes of most states, the conversion of shares of the merged corporation into "shares, obligations, or other securities of the surviving or any other corporation or into cash or other property in whole or part." In addition to permitting the issuance of shares of the surviving corporation, this provision authorizes the surviving corporation to issue debt securities or other property to the shareholders of the merged corporation.

PARALEGALERT!

In a merger, all assets and liabilities of the merged corporation become the assets and liabilities of the surviving corporation. In addition, all actions or proceedings pending against the merged corporation continue against the surviving corporation.

Certain relationships among the merging corporations call for various special types of mergers:

1. **Upstream merger**—The merger of a parent corporation and subsidiary corporation whereby the subsidiary corporation merges into the parent corporation.
2. **Downstream merger**—The merger of a parent corporation and a subsidiary corporation whereby the parent corporation merges into the subsidiary corporation.
3. **Triangular merger**—The merger of three corporations (a parent corporation, a subsidiary of the parent corporation, and a target corporation) whereby the target corporation is merged into the subsidiary corporation. Both the parent corporation and the subsidiary corporation are surviving corporations in the merger.
4. **Reverse triangular merger**—The merger of three corporations (a parent corporation, a subsidiary of the parent corporation, and a target corporation) whereby the subsidiary corporation is merged into the target corporation. Both the parent corporation and the target corporation survive the merger. The target corporation then becomes a subsidiary of the parent corporation as a result of the merger.

In addition to those mergers of related corporations, there are mergers of two or more unrelated parties. The Practical Considerations section of this chapter (Section 13–7) is devoted to the issues involved when two unrelated parties combine their businesses. When two or more unrelated corporations desire to combine their businesses, the corporation that will survive requests the opportunity to examine the books and records of the corporation to be merged. This examination is to assure the surviving corporation that it is not acquiring problems or liabilities that the merged corporation has hidden or failed to disclose.

Short-Form Merger

The upstream merger (discussed in the previous subsection) is also known as a **short-form merger** when the procedure for merging the subsidiary corporation into the parent corporation is simplified. In a short-form merger, it is unnecessary to obtain approval by the shareholders of the parent and subsidiary corporations. As long as the parent corporation owns at least 90% of the outstanding shares of *all classes* of stock of the subsidiary corporation, the merger may be approved by the boards of directors of both corporations, without shareholder approval. The Model Act, in Section 11.04(a), provides that "a parent corporation owning at least 90 percent of the outstanding shares of each class of a subsidiary corporation may merge the subsidiary into itself without approval of the shareholders of the parent or subsidiary."

For parent and subsidiary corporations to use the short-form merger procedure, the parent corporation must mail a copy of the plan of merger to each shareholder of the subsidiary corporation before filing articles of merger with the secretary of state. The Model Act restricts the parent corporation from delivering articles of merger to the secretary of state for filing until at least 30 days after the date the plan of merger was mailed to the subsidiary corporation shareholders.

PARALEGALERT!

The short-form merger is identical in all respects to other mergers, except that it does not require the approval of the shareholders of the parent corporation or the subsidiary corporation.

Share Exchange

A **share exchange** is the combination of two or more corporations whereby one corporation (the purchasing corporation) acquires all the outstanding shares of one or more classes or series of the stock of another corporation (the target corporation). Both corporations remain in existence, or survive, after the share exchange has been consummated. The purchasing corporation may either pay cash for the shares of the target corporation or issue shares of a class or series of its own stock in exchange for the shares of the target corporation. Section 11.02(a) of the Model Act permits the share exchange and provides that "a corporation may acquire all of the outstanding shares of one or more classes or series of another corporation if the board of directors of each corporation adopts and its shareholders . . . approve the exchange."

The effect of a share exchange is that the purchasing corporation owns at least one class or series of shares of the target corporation. For example, Corporation A could exchange some portion of its common shares for a series of preferred shares of Corporation B, or Corporation A could exchange a series or class of its preferred shares for Corporation B's common shares. The variety of share exchanges possible for corporations is limited only by the creativity of the lawyers involved and the desires of their corporate clients.

PARALEGALERT!

In a share exchange, one corporation acquires all of one or more classes or series of the outstanding shares of another corporation. Both corporations survive the share exchange.

Figure 13–2   Graphic Illustration of Consolidation of Two Corporations

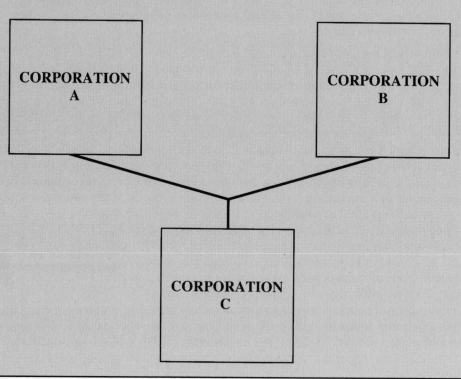

In this illustration, Corporation A and Corporation B consolidate their businesses, whereupon the legal existence of both Corporation A and Corporation B terminates. Corporation C, the new corporation that is created, assumes all assets and liabilities of Corporation A and Corporation B.

Consolidation

A **consolidation** is the combination of two or more corporations into one entirely new legal entity. None of the consolidating corporations remain after, or survive, the consolidation. The statutes of many states still provide for consolidations. The Model Act, however, has no provision for consolidations.

Consider the following example of a consolidation. In the illustration in Figure 13–2, Corporation A and Corporation B have decided to consolidate. Corporations A and B consolidate their assets and liabilities and form an entirely new entity, Corporation C. Upon the consolidation of Corporations A and B, both corporations cease to exist as separate legal entities, and Corporation C comes into existence as a new entity.

Upon the consolidation of two or more corporations, the new corporation formed in the consolidation assumes all the debts and obligations and takes over the business of all the corporations involved in the consolidation. Ownership and title to the assets of the consolidating corporations are transferred to the newly formed corporation. In short, all assets (cash, property, inventory, equipment, rights, etc.) and liabilities (loans and other obligations to pay) of the consolidating corporations become the newly formed corporation's assets and liabilities.

PARALEGALERT!

In a consolidation, all corporations combining their businesses terminate their existence, and a new corporation is formed. This new corporation assumes all the consolidating corporations' assets and liabilities.

13–3 Procedures for Merger, Share Exchange, and Consolidation

Plan of Merger

To achieve or accomplish a merger, a plan must be adopted by the board of directors and approved by the shareholders of all corporations involved in the merger. Section 11.01(a) of the Model Act provides that "one or more corporations may merge into another corporation if the board of directors of each corporation adopts and its shareholders approve a plan of merger."

The **plan of merger,** sometimes called a *merger agreement* or *agreement and plan of merger,* provides specific details of the agreement between the corporations that are parties to the merger. These details include, among others:

1. Identification of the surviving and merged corporations and a description of their capitalization before the merger.
2. The method and rate of converting or exchanging shares of one corporation for those of the other.
3. Provisions for submitting the plan to the shareholders for their approval.
4. Designation of the directors and officers of the surviving corporation.
5. Procedures for the surviving corporation to assume all the assets and liabilities of the merged corporation.
6. Amendments to the articles of incorporation and bylaws of the surviving corporation.
7. A plan for dissolving the merged corporation.
8. The effective date of the merger and the date, time, and place of the closing.
9. Provision for abandoning the merger upon the decision of the board of directors or the shareholders.

Additional terms and conditions may be included in the plan of merger, as long as they are agreed on by the boards of directors and the shareholders of both corporations.

Section 11.01(b) of the Model Act provides, as do most state statutes, requirements for the contents of the plan of merger. In particular, that section states that "the plan of merger must set forth: (1) the name of each corporation planning to merge and the name of the surviving corporation into which each other corporation plans to merge; (2) the terms and conditions of the merger; and (3) the manner and basis of converting the shares of each corporation into shares, obligations, or other securities of the surviving or any other corporation or into cash or other property in whole or part." Section 11.01(c) goes on to provide that "the plan of merger may set forth: (1) amendments to the articles of incorporation of the surviving corporation; and (2) other provisions relating to the merger."

Figure 13–3 is a sample plan of merger prepared in accordance with the provisions of the Model Act. Note that this plan of merger is titled Agreement and Plan of Merger and that it includes all the provisions identified in items 1–9 of our list of details.

PARALEGALERT!

The plan of merger is the agreement between the corporations that are parties to the merger. The plan contains the terms and conditions under which the corporations will merge.

Plans of Share Exchange and Consolidation

Just as in the merger, a plan must be adopted by the boards of directors and approved by the shareholders of all the corporations involved in a share

Figure 13–3   Plan of Merger

Agreement and Plan of Merger

This AGREEMENT AND PLAN OF MERGER is made this 10th day of February, 1995, pursuant to Section 11.01 of the Model Business Corporation Act of the State of _____, between Wood Products, Inc., a _____ corporation ("Wood Products"), and Carpenters, Inc., a _____ corporation ("Carpenters").

WHEREAS, the authorized capitalization of Wood Products consists of 10,000 shares of Common Stock, $1.00 par value; and

WHEREAS, the authorized capitalization of Carpenters consists of 500,000 shares of Common Stock, no par value, and 500,000 shares of Preferred Stock, $10.00 par value; and

WHEREAS, the Boards of Directors of Wood Products and Carpenters deem it advisable and to the advantage and welfare of the two corporate parties and their respective shareholders that Wood Products merge with and into Carpenters pursuant to the provisions of the Model Business Corporation Act of the State of _____.

NOW, THEREFORE, in consideration of the premises and of the mutual agreements herein contained and of the mutual benefits hereby provided, it is agreed by and between the parties hereto as follows:

1. MERGER. Wood Products shall be and it hereby is merged into Carpenters, the surviving corporation.

2. EFFECTIVE DATE. Following compliance with the laws of the State of _____, this Agreement of Merger shall become effective upon the filing of Articles of Merger with the Secretary of State of the State of _____ (the "Effective Date").

3. SURVIVING CORPORATION. Carpenters shall survive the merger herein contemplated and shall continue to be governed by the laws of the State of _____, and the separate corporate existence of Wood Products shall cease upon the Effective Date. The directors and officers of Carpenters, duly elected on December 15, 1994, shall continue as the directors and officers of Carpenters until the next annual meetings of the shareholders and directors of Carpenters.

4. AMENDMENT TO ARTICLES OF INCORPORATION. Article 3 of the Articles of Incorporation of Carpenters shall be amended to read as follows: "Article 3. The total number of shares that this corporation is authorized to issue is 2,000,000 shares, no par value." As so amended, the Articles of Incorporation of Carpenters shall be and will continue as the Articles of Incorporation of Carpenters, until the same are amended in accordance with the Model Business Corporation Act.

5. PROPERTY RIGHTS AND LIABILITIES OF WOOD PRODUCTS. All the property—real, personal, and mixed—all franchises, and all debts due on whatever account of Wood Products, including subscriptions for shares, shall be deemed to be transferred to and vested in Carpenters without further action. Carpenters shall be responsible for all the liabilities of Wood Products. Liens on the property of Wood Products shall not be impaired by the merger, and any claim existing or action or proceeding pending by or against Wood Products may be prosecuted to judgment as if the merger had not taken place, and Carpenters may be proceeded against and substituted in its place.

6. TAXES. Any taxes, penalties, and public accounts of the State of _____ claimed against Wood Products and not settled, assessed, or determined prior to the merger shall be settled, assessed, or determined against Carpenters and, together with interest thereon, shall be a lien against the franchises and property, both real and personal, of Carpenters.

---

exchange or consolidation before the share exchange or consolidation can be accomplished. Section 11.02(a) of the Model Act provides that "a corporation may acquire all of the outstanding shares of one or more classes or series of another corporation if the board of directors of each corporation adopts and its

Figure 13–3, continued

7. CONVERSION OF SHARES OF WOOD PRODUCTS. Upon the Effective Date, each share of the Common Stock and Preferred Stock of Wood Products presently issued and outstanding shall be converted to and exchanged for one-tenth (1/10) of a share of presently authorized and unissued Common Stock of Carpenters, provided that no fractional share of Common Stock of Carpenters shall be issued in exchange for the shares of Wood Products.

8. SERVICE OF PROCESS ON CARPENTERS. Carpenters agrees that it may be served with process in the State of _____ in any proceeding for enforcement of any obligation of Wood Products as well as for the enforcement of any obligation of Wood Products arising from the merger, including any suit or other proceeding to enforce the right of any shareholder as determined in appraisal proceedings pursuant to the Model Business Corporation Act of the State of _____.

9. AUTHORIZATION TO CONSUMMATE MERGER. Wood Products and Carpenters shall take, or cause to be taken, all actions and shall do, or cause to be done, all things necessary and proper to consummate and make effective the merger of Wood Products and Carpenters, including, but not limited to, obtaining consent of the shareholders of each corporation in accordance with the provisions of the Model Business Corporation Act.

10. TERMINATION. This Agreement and Plan of Merger may be terminated and abandoned by action of the Board of Directors of either Wood Products or Carpenters at any time prior to the Effective Date. Carpenters and Wood Products represent and warrant to each other that between the date hereof and the Effective Date, they will not enter into any employment contracts, grant any stock options or rights, or declare or pay any dividends in stock or cash with respect to their outstanding shares.

IN WITNESS WHEREOF, pursuant to the approval and authority duly granted by resolution adopted by the Boards of Directors of Wood Products and Carpenters, Wood Products and Carpenters have caused this Agreement and Plan of Merger to be executed as of the date stated above.

WOOD PRODUCTS, INC.

By _____
          Frederick Oak, President

CARPENTERS, INC.

By _____
          Joseph Hammer, President

---

shareholders . . . approve the exchange." As previously stated, the consolidation is not provided for in the Model Act.

Sections 11.02(b) and 11.02(c), which relate to the plan of share exchange, contain provisions similar to the sections that govern the plan of merger. You should refer to these sections of the Model Act, which is reproduced as Appendix A of this book. The **plan of share exchange** differs somewhat from plans of merger and consolidation because both corporations survive the share exchange. A share exchange is merely an exchange of one class or series of shares of one corporation for one class or series of shares of another corporation. Therefore, the plan of share exchange does not address such issues as the dissolution of the merged or consolidating corporations, procedures for the assumption of assets and liabilities, or designation of directors and officers.

Because of the similarities between the merger and consolidation, the plan of merger, an example of which appears in Figure 13–3, can be adapted to fit the characteristics of the consolidation. Remember, the major difference between the

Fitzsimmons v. Western Airlines, Inc., 290 A.2d 682 (Del. Ch. 1972)

The shareholders of Western Airlines and American Airlines had approved a merger of the companies, with American Airlines surviving the merger. Fitzsimmons, General Vice President of the teamsters' union, brought this action against Western Airlines and American Airlines, seeking a declaratory judgment that the bargaining agreements between the union and the airlines survived the merger of the two airlines and would be binding upon the surviving corporation.

The merger agreement between Western and American contained the following section:

"Section 7. Certain Effects of the Merger. On the effective date of the merger, all the rights, privileges, powers and franchises, as well of a public as of a private nature, of each of the Constituent Corporations shall be possessed by the Surviving Corporation (the name of which shall be American Airlines, Inc.) subject to all restrictions, disabilities and duties of each of the . . . Constituent Corporations . . . and all debts, liabilities and duties of the respective Constituent Corporations shall upon the effective date of the merger attach to the Surviving Corporation, and may be enforced against it to the same extent as if such debts, liabilities and duties had been incurred or contracted by it."

The court found that this section of the merger agreement tracked the language in the corporate statute in Delaware. Therefore, it concluded that "a Delaware corporation may not avoid its contractual obligations by merger; those duties 'attach' to the surviving corporation and may be 'enforced against it'." In short, the survivor must assume the obligations of the constituent.

The court denied the defendants' motion and found that under Delaware corporation law, the rights of Western Airlines' employees, who were covered by collective bargaining contracts between Western Airlines and the union, will not be automatically terminated on the consummation of the merger of Western Airlines and American Airlines.

merger and the consolidation is that, in a consolidation, a new corporation comes into existence when two or more corporations combine their businesses. Therefore, the **plan of consolidation** must address the characteristics of the newly formed corporation, the distribution of shares to shareholders of the combining corporations, and designation of the individuals who are to act as the directors and officers of the newly formed corporation until the first annual meeting of the shareholders.

Directors' and Shareholders' Approval

Pursuant to the statutes of all the states and in accordance with provisions of the Model Act, the board of directors and shareholders of each corporation involved in the merger, share exchange, or consolidation must approve the plan for the combinations. Although the procedures vary somewhat from state to state, the basic statutory requirements for approving a merger, share exchange, or consolidation are as follows:

First, the board of directors of each corporation involved in the combination must adopt a plan of merger, share exchange, or consolidation and must then recommend the plan to the shareholders by submitting the plan to the shareholders for approval. Refer to Figure 13–4, which is an example of resolutions of the directors authorizing the merger of Wood Products, Inc., and Carpenters, Inc. Similar resolutions could be drafted for the adoption and approval of the plan of share exchange or the plan of consolidation.

Second, the shareholders of each corporation involved in the combination must approve the plan submitted to them by the directors. Figure 13–5 is an example of resolutions of the shareholders authorizing the merger of Wood

Figure 13-4   Resolutions of the Directors Approving the Merger of Two Corporations

WHEREAS, Wood Products, Inc. ("Wood Products"), a _____ corporation, and Carpenters, Inc. ("Carpenters"), a _____ corporation, desire to merge; therefore, be it

RESOLVED, that the Board of Directors hereby recommends and adopts the Plan of Merger between Wood Products and Carpenters (the "Plan"), substantially in the form presented to the Board of Directors of this corporation; and

FURTHER RESOLVED, that the officers of this corporation be, and they hereby are, authorized to execute the Plan; and

FURTHER RESOLVED, that the Plan be submitted to the shareholders of this corporation for their consideration; and

FURTHER RESOLVED, that upon the approval of the Plan by the shareholders of this corporation, the officers shall execute, deliver, and file with the Secretary of State of the State of _____, Articles of Merger for the merger of Wood Products and Carpenters, pursuant to which Wood Products shall be merged with and into Carpenters, the separate existence of Wood Products shall cease, and Carpenters shall continue in existence as the surviving corporation; and

FURTHER RESOLVED, that the officers of this corporation be, and they hereby are, authorized to execute and deliver such other documents and to take such other actions necessary to carry into effect the merger of Wood Products and Carpenters.

Products, Inc., and Carpenters, Inc., and approving the plan submitted to them by the directors.

Remember from our discussion in Chapter 7 that both the board of directors and the shareholders may adopt resolutions in one of the following two ways: (1) at a meeting of the board of directors or shareholders, for which proper notice was sent and at which a quorum was present for the conducting of business, or (2) by unanimous written consent, executed by *all* directors or by *all* shareholders of the corporation.

However, specific procedures are provided in the Model Act regarding the notice to be provided to the shareholders if a meeting is held to consider the plan. Section 11.03(d) states that "the corporation shall notify each shareholder, whether or not entitled to vote, of the proposed shareholders' meeting. . . . The notice must also state that the purpose, or one of the purposes, of the meeting is to consider the plan of merger or share exchange and contain or be accompanied by a copy or summary of the plan." Figure 13–6 is an example of a notice of a meeting of the shareholders of Wood Products, Inc., to consider the agreement and plan of merger. Remember that the plan may instead be adopted by unanimous written consent of the shareholders of both corporations.

By the time the directors have adopted the plan for the merger, share exchange, or consolidation and are ready to submit it to the shareholders for their approval,

Figure 13-5   Resolutions of the Shareholders Approving the Merger of Two Corporations

WHEREAS, Wood Products, Inc. ("Wood Products"), a _____ corporation, and Carpenters, Inc. ("Carpenters"), a _____ corporation, desire to merge; and

WHEREAS, the Board of Directors of this corporation has recommended the merger and has adopted a Plan of Merger between Wood Products and Carpenters (the "Plan"); therefore, be it

RESOLVED, that the merger of Wood Products and Carpenters is hereby approved and that the Plan is hereby adopted and approved; and

FURTHER RESOLVED, that upon the effectiveness of the merger, the separate existence of Wood Products shall cease and Carpenters shall continue in existence as the surviving corporation.

Figure 13–6   Notice of Meeting of Shareholders to Consider and Approve Plan of Merger

---

**Notice of Special Meeting
of the Shareholders**

January 3, 1995

To the Shareholders of Wood Products Company:

Notice is hereby given that, in accordance with Section _____ of the bylaws of Wood Products, Inc. (the "Corporation"), and in accordance with the requirements of the laws of the State of _____, a special meeting of the shareholders of the Corporation will be held at the Corporation's principal place of business, 123 America Street, Anytown, Anystate, on Tuesday, February 15, 1995, at 11:00 a.m., for the following purposes:

1.   To consider the merger between the Corporation and Carpenters, Inc., under the terms and conditions contained in the Agreement and Plan of Merger between the Corporation and Carpenters, Inc., a copy of which is set forth in Exhibit A attached hereto.
[Exhibit A is omitted from this example. Refer to Figure 13–3 for an example of the Agreement and Plan of Merger.]

2.   To transact such other business as may properly come before the meeting of the shareholders.

By order of the Board of Directors.

_____
Secretary

PARALEGALERT!

The board of directors and the shareholders of each corporation involved in a merger, share exchange, or consolidation must approve the plan.

weeks or even months of negotiations have occurred between the corporations that wish to combine their businesses. Therefore, early in the negotiation stage, the board of directors of each corporation involved may adopt a resolution approving the officers' actions in negotiating the terms and conditions of the transaction on behalf of the corporation. Figure 13–7 is an example of resolutions of the board of directors authorizing actions by the officers to arrange a merger.

In the case of an upstream or short-form merger, approval by shareholders of both the parent and subsidiary corporations is not required. Remember from our discussion of the short-form merger that Section 11.04(a) of the Model Act permits the merger of a subsidiary corporation into its parent corporation without the approval of the

Figure 13–7   Resolutions of the Board of Directors Approving Actions of Officers in Negotiating the Terms and Conditions of the Transaction

---

WHEREAS, it has been proposed that Wood Products, Inc., merge into Carpenters, Inc., and the Board of Directors deems it advisable that this corporation enter into negotiations for the merger of the two corporations; therefore, be it
RESOLVED, that the officers of this corporation are hereby authorized to enter into negotiations for the merger of Wood Products, Inc., and Carpenters, Inc.; and
FURTHER RESOLVED, that the officers of this corporation are hereby authorized to prepare a plan of merger setting forth the terms and conditions under which the merger shall take effect and such other provisions as the officers may deem necessary and appropriate.

---

shareholders. However, if amendments are being made to the parent corporation's articles of incorporation in conjunction with the merger, shareholder approval *must be obtained*. Section 11.04(e) of the Model Act, which permits short-form mergers, states that "articles of merger under this section may not contain amendments to the articles of incorporation of the parent corporation."

Statutory Filing Requirements

After the plan of merger, share exchange, or consolidation has been approved by the shareholders—or adopted by the board of directors if shareholder approval is not required—the surviving corporation or the acquiring corporation must file with the secretary of state **articles of merger, articles of share exchange,** or **articles of consolidation,** whichever is appropriate for the type of combination being effected. (*Note:* The term *articles* will be used throughout this subsection to mean any of the three types of articles: articles of merger, articles of share exchange, or articles of consolidation.)

The articles that must be filed with the secretary of state usually contain the following information: (a) the plan or a summary thereof; (b) a statement that shareholder approval was not required, if such was the case; (c) the total number of votes entitled to be cast; and (d) the number of votes cast for and against the plan. In addition, the articles may state a date on which the combination is to be effective. For example, articles of merger might say, "The effective date of this merger shall be January 31, 1995." In this case, the articles may be filed and accepted any time prior to January 31, but the merger will not be effective until the date indicated in the articles. Unless the articles otherwise provide, a merger, share exchange, or consolidation will be effective in accordance with the state statutes. Figure 13–8 is an example of articles of merger for two corporations incorporated in the same state. These articles have been prepared in accordance with the provisions of Section 11.05 of the Model Act. You should refer to that section of the Model Act in Appendix A.

State statutes vary in their filing requirements. Some states do not require that separate articles be filed, but instead require that the plan be filed with the secretary of state. Some states require advertising or publication of the fact that corporations have combined their businesses. And some states refer to the articles as the *certificate.* You must review the state's statutes to determine the specific requirements before you file any document related to a combination of corporations.

Upon accepting the articles for filing, the secretary of state usually issues a **certificate of merger, certificate of share exchange,** or **certificate of consolidation,** whichever is appropriate. Unless the articles provide otherwise, the effective date of the merger, share exchange, or consolidation is usually the date on which the secretary of state issues the certificate. Other states consider the effective date the date on which the secretary of state receives the articles. You must check with the secretary of state to determine the procedures followed in that state.

The corporations involved in the types of combinations discussed in this chapter may be incorporated in different states or may be qualified to do business in any number of states. When the corporations involved have been incorporated in the same state and none of them are qualified to do business in any other state, the statutes of the state of incorporation of the corporations involved will govern

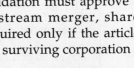

PARALEGALERT!

The short-form merger is the exception to the rule that the shareholders of all corporations involved in the merger, share exchange, or consolidation must approve the transaction. In an upstream merger, shareholder approval is required only if the articles of incorporation of the surviving corporation are being amended.

PARALEGALERT!

The corporate paralegal will be heavily involved in the preparation of articles and will be responsible for the proper filing of the articles with the secretary of state, including determining the correct filing fee. The most reliable way to do this is to call the secretary of state.

Figure 13–8   Articles of Merger

Articles of Merger

The undersigned corporations, in order to merge these corporations in the State of _____, under and pursuant to the provisions of Chapter 11 of the Model Business Corporation Act, do hereby certify that:

1.   The corporations party to the merger are Wood Products, Inc., a _____ corporation, and Carpenters, Inc., a _____ corporation.

2.   The Plan of Merger is made a part of these Articles of Merger and is attached hereto as Exhibit A.
(Exhibit A is omitted from this example. Refer to Figure 13–3.)

3.   The Plan of Merger was adopted, pursuant to Section 11.03(b) of the Model Business Corporation Act, by a unanimous vote of the shareholders of the corporations entitled to vote at a meeting of the shareholders of Wood Products, Inc., held on February 15, 1995, and a meeting of the shareholders of Carpenters, Inc., held on February 16, 1995.

IN WITNESS WHEREOF, duly authorized officers of the corporations have executed these Articles of Merger this 25th day of February, 1995.

WOOD PRODUCTS, INC.

By _____
     Frederick Oak, President

CARPENTERS, INC.

By _____
     Joseph Hammer, President

the procedures for combining the corporations. However, when the combining corporations are incorporated in different states or are qualified to do business in a number of states, the procedures become a little complicated.

Let's consider the following example. Wood Products, Inc., is incorporated in Texas and is qualified to do business in Mississippi. Carpenters, Inc., is incorporated in Oklahoma and is qualified to do business in Arkansas. If Wood Products, Inc., decides to merge into Carpenters, Inc., the statutes of all the states involved, including Texas, Mississippi, Oklahoma, and Arkansas, must be reviewed to determine the filing procedures in those states. Since Wood Products, Inc., will be the merged corporation and will cease to exist as a result of the merger, it must terminate its existence in Texas and Mississippi in accordance with the statutes of those states. Carpenters, Inc., the surviving corporation, must comply with the statutes of Oklahoma and Arkansas. In addition, Carpenters, Inc., may be required to qualify to do business in Texas and Mississippi, since it is assuming the business of Wood Products, Inc., which transacted business in those states before the merger.

Sections 11.07(a)(1) and (2) of the Model Act provide that "one or more foreign corporations may merge or enter into a share exchange with one or more domestic

PARALEGALERT!

The responsibility for reviewing the statutes of the corporations' states of incorporation and the states in which the corporations are qualified usually falls to the corporate paralegal. You should become familiar with locating and reviewing statutes, but do not be concerned with memorizing every state's particular provisions.

corporations if: (1) in a merger, the merger is permitted by the law of the state or country under whose law each foreign corporation is incorporated and each foreign corporation complies with that law in effecting the merger; (2) in a share exchange, the corporation whose shares will be acquired is a domestic corporation, whether or not a share exchange is permitted by the law of the state or country under whose law the acquiring corporation is incorporated." Note that both sections permit the merger and share exchange of foreign corporations, as long as such combination is permitted by the statutes of the state in which the corporation was incorporated. It is imperative that the statutes of the states of incorporation of all corporations involved in the combination be reviewed.

13–4   Sale and Purchase of Stock

The sale or purchase of a corporation's stock is another method used by corporations to combine their businesses. The corporation desiring to sell its shares is usually called the **selling corporation,** and the corporation desiring to purchase shares of another corporation is called the **acquiring corporation.** In a **stock transaction,** the shareholders of the selling corporation agree to sell or transfer their shares to the acquiring corporation in exchange for some form of consideration, usually cash. Unlike the merger, share exchange, and consolidation, which are governed by statute, the procedures for carrying out the sale or purchase of stock depend on the desires of the corporations involved in the transaction. However, any sale of a corporation's stock may be restricted by the articles of incorporation or the bylaws of the selling corporation or may be restricted by an agreement among the shareholders of the selling corporation. Chapter 15 is devoted to an in-depth discussion of the shareholders' agreement and the issues related thereto.

Our discussion here will focus on the mechanics of a stock sale and the procedures for carrying out such a sale between closely held corporations. Remember that a closely held corporation is one with relatively few shareholders, and its shares are not registered under the federal and state securities laws. More complicated issues and procedures are involved in the acquisition of a corporation whose shares are publicly traded, and entire texts and treatises deal with that type of transaction. We will concentrate on the sale and purchase of shares between two corporations with a small number of shareholders.

In a stock sale, the acquiring corporation is purchasing the selling corporation's stock. Therefore, it is acquiring both the selling corporation's assets *and* its liabilities. If contingent liabilities of the selling corporation are anticipated to be substantial, the acquiring corporation may operate the selling corporation's business as a subsidiary corporation. That arrangement will shield the acquiring corporation from potentially costly contingent liabilities of the selling corporation. For example, future environmental cleanup costs could destroy a corporation's ability to conduct its business profitably. As you will see in the next section, when only assets are acquired, the selling corporation remains liable for its debts because stock ownership does not change.

Negotiating the Transaction

Preliminary negotiations for the purchase and sale of stock generally involve all parties to the transaction, including the officers of the acquiring corporation, the selling shareholders or one or more representatives of the selling shareholders, and legal counsel for all parties to the transaction. In this initial stage of the transaction, the fundamental aspects of the proposed transaction are discussed and agreed on. For example, the price of the shares, any adjustment to the purchase price based on the acquiring corporation's review of the selling corporation's books and records, the terms of payment for such shares, and the possible employment of the selling shareholders by the acquiring corporation, among other things, are negotiated by the parties early in the process.

The result of the initial negotiations among the parties may be the entering into of a **letter of intent.** The letter of intent is not an agreement to sell and purchase the shares, but it is an agreement that spells out the terms and conditions under which a stock purchase agreement will be executed by all the parties. The letter also restricts the selling corporation's ability to negotiate with other parties while the acquiring corporation is conducting its review of the selling corporation's books and records. In addition, it usually prohibits either party from discussing the terms of the agreement.

The letter of intent usually covers the following aspects of the transaction:

1. The consummation or closing date of the stock transaction.
2. The proposed purchase price of the shares, allowing for increases or decreases based on certain agreed-upon adjustments.
3. Provision for employment of the selling shareholders by the acquiring corporation.
4. Conditions for the consummation of the transaction, including successful negotiation of a stock purchase agreement; receipt of all necessary governmental approvals; consents of third parties in accordance with agreements entered into by the selling corporation; and satisfactory review by the acquiring corporation of the selling corporation's books, records, and dealings.
5. Agreement of all parties to nondisclosure of all aspects of the transaction.
6. Agreement by the acquiring corporation to keep confidential any information it obtains through the due diligence process.
7. Agreement of the parties to bear their respective expenses incurred in connection with the transaction.

After the negotiation and execution of the letter of intent, the acquiring corporation is provided time in which it may examine the books, records, and dealings of the selling corporation. In this procedure, called the **due diligence process,** the acquiring corporation conducts a review of the selling corporation to uncover potential liabilities of the selling corporation, identify contracts that require a third party to approve the stock transaction, and confirm the overall accuracy and validity of the representations and statements made in the agreement. In other words, the acquiring corporation does its homework by confirming exactly what it is purchasing. The selling corporation usually requires the acquiring corporation to enter into a confidentiality agreement, whereby it agrees to keep confidential all information obtained in the due diligence process.

Procedures

The purchase of a corporation's stock is usually accomplished by negotiating with the majority shareholder or shareholders for the purchase of their shares of the selling corporation. Overall shareholder approval by the selling corporation is not required in the case of a stock sale because the individual shareholders of the selling corporation determine independently whether to sell their shares. Their approval of the sale is evidenced by their execution of the agreement by which the sale is consummated. Often, the acquiring corporation desires to purchase *all* shares of the selling corporation. If the acquiring corporation is unable to purchase all the shares, it may decide not to purchase any shares. The acquiring corporation may want to wholly own the selling corporation and may not want to deal with minority shareholders who decide not to sell their shares.

Generally, the purchase of the selling corporation's shares need not be approved by the shareholders of the acquiring corporation. The need for their approval depends on the complexity of the transaction and the extent to which their rights are affected. However, the board of directors of the acquiring corporation should approve the purchase of such shares, and it should authorize the officers to negotiate the transaction, to enter into and execute the agreement for the purchase, and to perform all other acts and execute all other documents or agreements to carry out the stock purchase. Figure 13–9 is an example of resolutions by which the board of directors of the acquiring corporation authorizes the transaction.

The board of directors of the selling corporation *may* not need to approve the transaction, as the transaction is between the acquiring corporation and the shareholders of the selling corporation. However, when the selling corporation is a party to the stock purchase agreement, in which it makes representations and warranties, it must authorize the officers of the selling corporation to enter into and execute the agreement and to perform other acts ancillary thereto.

Stock Purchase Agreement

The **stock purchase agreement,** sometimes called a *stock purchase and sale agreement*, represents the agreement between the acquiring corporation and the shareholders of the selling corporation for the purchase and sale of shares, and it sets forth all the terms, conditions, and agreements of such purchase and sale. Because the effect of the stock purchase includes the purchase of the selling

PARALEGALERT!

Board of directors' approval is generally required for both the selling corporation and the acquiring corporation. The selling shareholders' approval of the sale is evidenced by their execution of the agreement, and shareholders of the acquiring corporation generally need not approve the purchase.

Figure 13–9 Resolutions of Board of Directors of Acquiring Corporation

WHEREAS, all the shareholders of Genesis Corporation ("Genesis") desire to sell and transfer all the outstanding capital stock of Genesis to this corporation in consideration of $1,000,000, payable in cash; and

WHEREAS, the Board of Directors deems the acquisition of the stock of Genesis to be in the best interests of this corporation and recommends the acceptance of the offer by the shareholders of Genesis; therefore, be it

RESOLVED, that the officers of this corporation are hereby authorized to negotiate and execute a stock purchase agreement between this corporation and the shareholders of Genesis for the purchase of all the outstanding capital stock of Genesis in consideration of $1,000,000, payable to the shareholders of Genesis in cash; and

FURTHER RESOLVED, that the officers of this corporation are hereby authorized to execute all other documents and agreements and to perform such other acts and deeds as may be necessary and deemed appropriate by such officers in order to carry out the intent of the foregoing resolution.

corporation's assets and the assumption of the selling corporation's liabilities, the agreement should contain the terms and conditions under which the assets are being purchased and the liabilities assumed. The selling corporation must warrant that the information provided in the stock purchase agreement regarding its assets and liabilities is true and correct. This section of the agreement, including the representations and warranties of the selling shareholders and the selling corporation, is usually the most extensive portion.

Specifically, the categories or types of information and provisions generally found in a stock purchase agreement include the following:

1. Identification of the persons entering into the agreement.
2. The purchase price of the shares, including the form and method of payment and adjustments to the purchase price.
3. Representations and warranties of the selling shareholders and the selling corporation, including disclosure of information about the corporation encompassing:

   - Organization and capitalization.
   - Legal proceedings.
   - Employment and other related contracts.
   - Title to and condition of property owned (real and personal).
   - Leases.
   - Franchises and other licenses.
   - Federal, state, local, and other taxes.
   - Insurance.
   - Accounts and notes receivable.
   - Inventories.
   - Customers and suppliers.
   - Consents of governmental agencies and third parties.
   - The authority on which the selling shareholders and the corporation have acted in entering into the agreement.
   - Assurance that no changes have occurred in the corporation except in the ordinary course of business.

4. Representations and warranties of the buyer or buyers, including organization and capitalization (if buyer is a corporation).
5. Conduct of the corporation prior to the closing, including the operation of its business, engagement in contracts and agreements, and access by the buyer to its records and property.
6. Obligations of selling shareholders prior to closing, including a certification that the representations and warranties are true and correct as of the date of the closing.
7. Obligations of the buyer prior to closing, including a certification that the representations and warranties are true and correct as of the date of closing.
8. An agreement by the selling shareholders not to engage in any business in competition with the business of the buyer.
9. Indemnification of the buyer by the selling shareholders for future liabilities caused by any breach of the selling shareholders or corporation.
10. Indemnification of the selling shareholders and corporation by the buyer for any breach of the buyer.
11. An agreement to terminate the agreement upon the mutual consent of all parties to the agreement.
12. The date, time, place, and method of closing the transaction.
13. Miscellaneous provisions, including the laws under which the agreement will be construed and enforced, the nonassignability of rights under the agreement and a prohibition of amendment or modification to the agreement without the prior consent of the parties, the addresses where notices

may be sent to the parties in the future, the binding effect and benefit of the agreement on successors to the parties to the agreement, and an agreement that all expenses incurred by each party will be paid by that party.

The stock purchase agreement may include several exhibits that provide information about the selling corporation. For example, the selling shareholders and the selling corporation usually must provide the status of current and foreseeable litigation engaged in by the corporation. Because that information may be lengthy, the agreement usually includes a provision as follows: "Section ___. Legal Proceedings. There are no proceedings or investigations of any kind pending or threatened against the corporation that would materially adversely affect the corporation, except as set forth in Exhibit C to this Agreement." Exhibit C of the stock purchase agreement then lists all the legal proceedings, pending or threatened, against the corporation. This procedure would also be followed for the listing of property, contracts, leases, inventories, and other items listed in item 3 in the list of contents of a stock purchase agreement.

PARALEGALERT!

For the seasoned corporate paralegal, the first responsibility in a stock transaction may be preparing the initial draft of the stock purchase agreement. In other cases, the paralegal may be given a draft of the agreement by the supervising attorney and be asked to prepare the exhibits or other supporting documents required by the agreement.

13–5   Sale and Purchase of Assets

The sale or purchase of a corporation's assets is the last method we will discuss for the combination of two or more businesses. In an **asset transaction,** the seller, called the *selling corporation,* agrees to sell all or substantially all its assets to the buyer, called the *acquiring corporation,* which agrees to purchase the assets in exchange for some form of consideration. The assets involved in this type of transaction include real estate, inventory, equipment, accounts receivable, contracts and agreements, leases, employee benefit plans, and other types of tangible and intangible property.

As a result of purchasing the assets of the selling corporation, the acquiring corporation holds title to all the assets it purchases. In some cases, the acquiring corporation assumes specific liabilities related to certain assets purchased. For example, if equipment is purchased for which a liability has been created to pay for the equipment, the acquiring corporation may assume the debt on such equipment. Generally, the acquiring corporation is not responsible for the liabilities of the selling corporation. Therefore, the assumption of any liabilities must be specifically agreed on and set forth in the agreement between the parties.

Upon a corporation's sale of *all* of its assets, it becomes a **shell corporation**. Because it has no assets, the corporation is unable to engage in its normal business. It therefore has a couple of options available. It may distribute the proceeds from the sale of its assets, satisfy any remaining liabilities, and dissolve the corporation in accordance with the statutes of its state of incorporation. Or it may purchase the assets of another business and continue to operate under the same corporate name.

PARALEGALERT!

In an asset transaction, the acquiring corporation gains title to all the assets it purchases, but it assumes only such liabilities associated with assets as it agrees to assume under the provisions of the asset purchase agreement.

Negotiating the Transaction

Preliminary negotiations for the purchase and sale of assets are not very different from those for a stock transaction. The asset transaction differs in that specific assets are being purchased and sold, not stock as in the stock transaction. As in the stock transaction, negotiations involve all parties to the transaction, including officers of both the acquiring and the selling corporations and legal counsel for both corporations. In the initial stage of the transaction, the fundamental aspects of the proposed transaction are discussed and agreed on. The result of the initial negotiations among the parties is the entering into of a letter of intent, which spells out the terms and conditions under which an asset purchase agreement will be executed by all the parties. The contents of the letter of intent are similar to those in the stock transaction, except that the letter of intent in an asset transaction identifies the assets to be sold and the price at which they will be sold. Refer to the preceding section, where we discussed the letter of intent in greater detail.

After the negotiation and execution of the letter of intent, the acquiring corporation is provided time in which it may examine all documents, agreements, and records relating to the assets being purchased. That examination is the due diligence process, which is conducted by the acquiring corporation in an attempt to identify all the assets being purchased and any liens or debts relating to those assets and to confirm the accuracy and validity of the representations and statements made in the agreement concerning those assets.

Procedures

Most state statutes, as well as the Model Act, permit the sale of assets within the normal course of business upon approval by the board of directors only. Shareholder approval is not required. Section 12.01(b) of the Model Act provides that "approval by the shareholders of a transaction described in subsection (a) is not required," and Section 12.01(a) lists the transactions that may be approved by the directors only. It states that "a corporation may, on the terms and conditions and for the consideration determined by the board of directors: (1) sell, lease, exchange, or otherwise dispose of all, or substantially all, of its property in the usual and regular course of business."

However, any sale of *all or substantially all* the assets of the corporation that does not fall within the usual and regular course of business requires approval by the shareholders. Section 12.02(a) of the Model Act states that "a corporation may sell, lease, exchange or otherwise dispose of all, or substantially all, of its property . . . , otherwise than in the usual and regular course of business, on the terms and conditions and for the consideration determined by the corporation's board of directors, if the board of directors proposes and its shareholders approved the proposed transaction." In other words, shareholder approval is required if the sale of assets is extraordinary.

The procedures to be followed in obtaining authorization to sell a corporation's assets otherwise than in the regular course of business are similar to those for the merger, share exchange, and consolidation. The board of directors recommends the proposed transaction to the shareholders, and the shareholders vote to approve the transaction. Section 12.02(b) of the Model Act provides these procedures and states that "for a transaction to be authorized: (1) the board of directors must recommend the proposed transaction to the shareholders . . . ; and (2) the shareholders entitled to vote must approve the transaction." The board of directors may determine, however, that a conflict of interest exists in the sale of the assets, and they may decide *not* to recommend the sale to the shareholders. In this case, the board must communicate to the shareholders the terms and conditions of the proposed transaction and the basis for its decision not to recommend approval.

Remember from our discussion in Chapter 7 that both the board of directors and the shareholders may adopt resolutions in one of the following two ways: (1) at a meeting of the board of directors or the shareholders, for which proper notice was sent and at which a quorum is present for the conducting of business, or (2) by unanimous written consent, executed by *all* directors or by *all* shareholders of the corporation.

However, specific procedures are provided in the Model Act regarding the notice to be provided to the shareholders if a meeting is to be held to consider the sale of assets. Section 12.02(d) states that "the corporation shall notify each shareholder, whether or not entitled to vote, of the proposed shareholders' meeting. . . . The notice must also state that the purpose, or one of the purposes, of the meeting is to consider the sale, lease, exchange, or other disposition of all, or substantially all, the property of the corporation and contain or be accompanied by a description of the transaction." Refer to Figure 13–6, which is an example of a notice of meeting of the shareholders for approval of a merger. The notice required for the sale of assets would not differ much from that notice. In addition, state statutes permit shareholders to approve transactions by unanimous written consent executed by *all shareholders*. Figures 13–10 and 13–11 are resolutions of the board of directors and the shareholders, respectively, approving the sale of all assets.

Bulk Transfer Law

The **Uniform Commercial Code,** some form of which has been adopted in every state, generally protects buyers in any commercial transaction. It therefore protects creditors of the selling corporation. When the selling corporation sells its assets outside the normal and regular course of business, the creditors have the right to protection of the interests they have in the assets of that business. The Uniform Commercial Code does not cover sales of assets in the normal course of business, such as the sale of baseball bats by a corporation whose business purpose was to manufacture and

Figure 13–10   Resolutions of Board of Directors Approving Sale of Assets

WHEREAS, an offer has been made to this corporation by Genesis Corporation to purchase all this corporation's property and assets for the consideration and upon the terms and conditions set forth in the proposed form of asset purchase agreement, a copy of which is attached hereto; and
WHEREAS, the Board of Directors deems it in the best interests of this corporation that its property and assets be sold to Genesis Corporation for the consideration and upon the terms and conditions set forth in the asset purchase agreement; therefore, be it
RESOLVED, that the offer of Genesis Corporation be and hereby is accepted, such acceptance subject to the approval of the shareholders of this corporation; and
FURTHER RESOLVED, that the officers of this corporation be and hereby are authorized to execute the asset purchase agreement, upon such terms and conditions as the officers executing the same may agree on, subject to the approval of the shareholders of this corporation; and
FURTHER RESOLVED, that the offer by Genesis Corporation for the purchase of the property and assets of this corporation be submitted to the shareholders of this corporation for their consideration and approval.

Figure 13–11   Resolution of Shareholders Approving Sale of Assets

WHEREAS, the Board of Directors of this corporation has recommended the sale of this corporation's property and assets to Genesis Corporation; therefore, be it
RESOLVED, that the sale of this corporation's property and assets to Genesis Corporation is hereby approved and that the asset purchase agreement, in the form and under the terms and conditions approved by the directors of this corporation, be and hereby is approved.

sell baseball bats. But imagine what would happen if that corporation sold off its inventory, the machinery and equipment used in manufacturing the bats, the real estate on which its manufacturing plant was located, and the trucks it used to transfer the bats, all without providing notice to its creditors. The creditors' chances of being paid would be greatly reduced. Therefore, the Uniform Commercial Code contains provisions protecting the rights of creditors. Specific provisions of the Uniform Commercial Code designed to protect creditors are often referred to as the **bulk transfer law.**

The Uniform Commercial Code provides that creditors who have claims against the selling corporation as of the date of the sale of the assets should receive notice of the sale. The selling corporation is required to furnish a list of its existing creditors to the acquiring corporation, and that list must contain the names and business addresses of all creditors of the selling corporation, indicating the amount owed to each creditor. In addition, the selling corporation must prepare a schedule of all property being transferred, maintain such schedule for six months following the transfer of the property, and make a copy available for inspection and copying by any creditor of the selling corporation.

If the selling corporation fails to prepare and maintain the schedule of property transferred or fails to provide notice to its creditors of the transfer of property, the transfer of the assets to the acquiring corporation will be deemed invalid for the purpose of claims by the creditors. In that case, creditors may disregard the transfer of the property and make claims against that property as if the transfer had not occurred. Therefore, it is important that the acquiring corporation, which assumes it has clear title to the assets transferred to it, takes great care in assuring that the selling corporation has complied with all provisions of the Uniform Commercial Code.

Asset Purchase Agreement

The **asset purchase agreement,** sometimes called the *asset purchase and sale agreement,* represents the agreement between the acquiring corporation and the selling corporation for the purchase and sale of certain assets of the selling corporation. The agreement sets forth all the terms, conditions, and agreements of such purchase and sale of the assets and provides for the disposition of any obligations or debts relating to the assets.

The actual transfer of ownership of the assets is accomplished through the execution and delivery by the selling corporation of documents transferring specific assets. These documents are the assignment, the bill of sale, and the deed. In particular, intangible personal property, such as accounts receivable, leases, and contracts, is transferred by the **assignment.** Tangible property, such as inventory, equipment, motor vehicles, and machinery, is transferred by the **bill of sale.** Real estate is transferred by the **deed.** Figures 13–12 and 13–13 are examples of an assignment and a bill of sale, respectively. Pay particular attention to the types of assets being transferred in the assignment and the bill of sale. The form of the deed is similar to the form of deed you receive when you purchase a home.

Specifically, the categories or types of information and provisions generally found in an asset purchase agreement include:

1. Identification of the persons entering into the agreement.
2. A description of and the purchase price of the assets.
3. The form and method of payment and any adjustments to the purchase price.
4. The terms and conditions for assuming any debts and obligations related to the assets.
5. Representations and warranties of the selling corporation, including disclosure of information about the corporation encompassing:

Figure 13–12 Assignment

Assignment

For and in consideration of One Dollar ($1.00), receipt of which is hereby acknowledged, and other good and valuable consideration, the undersigned, Baseball Bat Company (the "Assignor"), does hereby bargain, sell, convey, transfer, and assign to Hank Aaronsen, his heirs, and his personal representatives all of its right, title, and interest in the following assets:

1. Promissory Note, dated December 10, 1989, of Beaver Baseball Club;
2. Lease, dated January 1, 1990, between Assignor and Store-It Warehouse, Inc.; and
3. All accounts and notes receivable relating to Assignor's business.

IN WITNESS WHEREOF, the duly authorized officer of Baseball Bat Company has executed this Assignment this 15th day of September, 1994.

BASEBALL BAT COMPANY

By _____
Wayne Winner, President

Figure 13–13 Bill of Sale

Bill of Sale

KNOW ALL MEN BY THESE PRESENTS that Baseball Bat Company ("Seller"), a _____ corporation, for and in consideration of One Hundred Thousand Dollars ($100,000), does hereby grant, bargain, sell, transfer, assign, and deliver to Hank Aaronsen ("Purchaser"), his heirs, and his personal representatives all of the following assets:

1. The fixtures, furniture, equipment, and other items of personal property owned by Seller that comprise the personal property heretofore used in the operation of the Seller's business;

2. All inventory, stock in trade, merchandise, goods, supplies, and other products owned by Seller or otherwise under the control of Seller that are a part of Seller's business;

3. All business records, files, books of account, customer and supplier lists, and other books and records of Seller relating to the assets transferred hereunder and the liabilities assumed by Purchaser; and

4. Six Model XT-1466 18-wheel trucks, including the attached trailers, used in the Seller's business.

Seller does hereby covenant and warrant to the Purchaser, his heirs, and his personal representatives that Seller is the lawful owner of the Assets, that said Assets are free from all claims, liens, and encumbrances, that Seller has good and marketable title to the Assets, and that Seller, for itself, its successors, and its assignees, covenants and agrees to and with the Purchaser to warrant and defend the title to the Assets unto the Purchaser, his heirs, and his personal representatives against all claims and demands of all and every person or persons whosoever.

IN WITNESS WHEREOF, the duly authorized officer of Baseball Bat Company has executed this Bill of Sale this 15th day of September, 1994.

BASEBALL BAT COMPANY

By _____
Wayne Winner, President

- Organization and capitalization.
- Legal proceedings.
- Agreements and contracts with customers and suppliers.
- Intangible property.
- Liens and encumbrances.
- Liabilities.
- Business operations of the selling corporation.
- Federal, state, local, and other taxes.
- Financial statements.
- Accounts receivable.
- Inventory valuations.
- Consents of third parties to the transfer.
- The authority on which the selling corporation has acted in entering into the agreement.
- Assurance that no changes have occurred in the corporation except in the ordinary course of business.

6. Representation of ownership of and title to assets being sold.
7. Representations and warranties of the buyer, including its organization and capitalization (if the buyer is a corporation).
8. Conduct of the selling corporation prior to the closing, including the care to be taken of the assets being sold and access by the buyer to its records and property.
9. Obligations of the selling shareholders prior to closing, including a certification that the representations and warranties are true and correct as of the date of the closing.
10. Obligations of the buyer prior to closing, including a certification that the representations and warranties are true and correct as of the date of closing.
11. Delivery by the selling corporation of bills of sale, assignments, and deeds for transfer of assets.
12. Indemnification of the buyer by the selling corporation for any breach by the selling corporation.
13. Indemnification of the selling corporation for any breach by the buyer.
14. An agreement to terminate the agreement upon the mutual consent of all parties to the agreement.
15. The date, time, place, and method of closing the transaction.
16. Miscellaneous provisions, including the laws under which the agreement will be construed and enforced, the nonassignability of rights under the agreement and a prohibition of amendment or modification to the agreement without the prior consent of the parties, the addresses where notices may be sent to the parties in the future, the binding effect and benefit of the agreement on successors to the parties to the agreement, and an agreement that all expenses incurred by each party will be paid by that party.

The asset purchase agreement may cover the sale of all the corporation's assets or only part of the assets. In either case, the agreement will cover the same core elements. In addition, every asset transaction is unique, and the asset purchase agreement must be drafted to meet the desires of the parties involved. Consider the following examples of the ways in which asset purchase agreements may differ. First, the type of assets being sold dictates which transfer document or documents (assignment, bill of sale, or deed) must be prepared. Second, the buyer's intention to maintain or continue valuable relationships with the selling corporation's customers and suppliers determines whether the buyer will ask the selling corporation's shareholders to enter into noncompetition agreements with the buyer. Such agreements prohibit the selling corporation's shareholders or employees from working for a business in competition with the business purchased by the buyer. Third, if the buyer intends to continue the selling corporation's business, the selling corporation should provide additional warranties to the buyer pertaining to future tax liabilities and pending litigation.

13–6   Dissenting Shareholders' Rights

The extraordinary corporate transactions and corporate combinations that we have discussed in this chapter may not always be agreed to by *all* shareholders of the corporation. Certain shareholders may feel that a merger, share exchange, consolidation, or sale of the corporation's assets outside the normal course of business are not in their best economic interests. But they must live with the decision of the majority even if the transaction adversely affects their rights as shareholders. To remedy this situation, state statutes and the Model Act provide shareholders the right to *dissent* from a transaction under certain circumstances and have their shares appraised and purchased by the corporation. This right afforded the dissenting shareholder is often called **dissenters' rights** or *appraisal rights.* It awards the dissenting shareholder the fair value of his or her shares.

Actions from which a shareholder may dissent include merger, share exchange, consolidation, sale of all or substantially all the assets of the corporation, amendment of the articles of incorporation, and any other corporate action from which shareholders have been given the right to dissent. Section 13.02(a) of the Model Act provides that "a shareholder is entitled to dissent from, and obtain payment of the fair value of his shares in the event of, any of the following corporate actions: (1) consummation of a plan of merger . . . ; (2) consummation of a plan of share exchange . . . ; (3) consummation of a sale or exchange of all, or substantially all, of the property of the corporation . . . ; (4) an amendment of the articles of incorporation that materially and adversely affect rights in respect of a dissenter's shares . . . ; or (5) any corporate action taken pursuant to a shareholder vote to the extent the articles of incorporation, bylaws, or a resolution of the board of directors provides that . . . shareholders are entitled to dissent."

The procedures for dissenting from a transaction are complicated, and the statutes vary greatly from state to state. Generally, a shareholder desiring to dissent from a transaction that was agreed to by a majority of the voting shares must follow specific procedures. An important concern is the time limit imposed on the institution of actions by the dissenting shareholder and on the response of the corporation to the dissent. Statutory procedures and time limits must be strictly observed. You should conduct a careful review of the state statutes governing dissenters' rights. The procedures summarized in the following paragraphs are those provided in the Model Act.

First, the shareholders' meeting notice must state that shareholders of the corporation may be entitled to assert dissenters' rights, and a copy of the chapter of the state statute providing for dissenters' rights must be provided with the meeting notice. The meeting notice includes a dissenters' rights statement only when the corporate action to be considered at the meeting is an action that creates dissenters' rights, such as a merger, a share exchange, or a sale of assets outside the normal course of business.

Second, shareholders who desire to assert dissenters' rights must deliver a notice to the corporation of their intent to demand payment for their shares if the corporate action is approved and effectuated, *and* they must not vote their shares in favor of the proposed corporate action. A shareholder who fails to provide notice to the corporation or votes his or her shares in favor of the action is not entitled to payment for the shares under dissenters' rights.

Third, if the corporate action creating the dissenters' rights is approved by the shareholders at their meeting, the corporation must deliver a written notice to the shareholders who dissented from such action. Such notice must be sent no later than 10 days after the corporate action was taken. The notice provided by the corporation must include (1) the address where the demand for payment and the share certificates of the corporation are to be sent, (2) a form of certification on which the dissenting shareholder must certify that he or she is the beneficial owner of the shares and that the shares were acquired prior to the date of the corporation's dissenters' notice, (3) the date by which the corporation must receive the demand for payment from the dissenting shareholder, and (4) a copy of the chapter of the state statute providing for dissenters' rights.

Fourth, the dissenting shareholder must (1) demand payment, (2) certify that he or she acquired beneficial ownership of the shares prior to the date of the corporation's dissenters' notice, and (3) deposit his or her share certificates in accordance with the terms of the corporation's dissenters' notice. A dissenting shareholder who fails to comply with these requirements is not entitled to receive payment for his or her shares.

And fifth, the corporation must pay the dissenting shareholder the amount the corporation estimates to be the fair value of the dissenting shareholder's shares, plus accrued interest, as soon as the corporate action is taken or upon receipt of the payment demand from the dissenting shareholder.

The dissenting shareholder does not always agree with the corporation as to the fair value of the shares and may be dissatisfied with the payment or offer of payment. Therefore, the dissenting shareholder has the right to provide the corporation with his or her own estimate of the fair value of the shares and the amount of interest due. The shareholder may believe that the corporation incorrectly calculated the amount or the corporation may have failed to make payment (after receiving the demand for payment) within 60 days of the date set for demanding payment. In either case, the dissenting shareholder must notify the corporation, within 30 days after the corporation made or offered payment for the shares, of his or her dissatisfaction with the payment or offer. When the demand for payment remains unsettled, the corporation must commence a judicial proceeding, within 60 days after receiving the payment demand, petitioning the court to determine the fair value of the shares.

The filing of numerous dissents against a particular corporate transaction may delay or even block the transaction. Even though the intent of the dissenting shareholder is to block a transaction, the procedures for dissenting are an unpopular route for the dissenting shareholder to take. The judicial determination of fair value in a dissent procedure creates expenses and delays, which can be detrimental to both the corporation and the dissenting shareholder.

13–7   Practical Considerations

When two businesses that wish to combine by one of the methods discussed in this chapter are related parties, the due diligence process is virtually nonexistent. Related parties, such as a parent corporation and a subsidiary or two sister (subsidiary) corporations, usually have documents and records readily available in the normal course of business. Therefore, it is generally not necessary to conduct a review of a related corporation's books and records. However, when two or more unrelated parties decide to combine their businesses, the due diligence process can be quite extensive and time-consuming.

The due diligence process is generally conducted by the surviving corporation in a merger, by the purchasing corporation in a share exchange, by the consolidating corporations in a consolidation, and by the acquiring corporation in a stock or asset transaction. In each case, the corporation continuing its existence after consummation of the transaction should be provided an opportunity to review the books and records and confirm the validity of the statements, representations, and warranties made in the agreement by the organization whose existence will terminate or whose shares or assets are being purchased. In particular, in a merger, share exchange, or consolidation, the surviving corporation will be interested in examining the other corporation's operations, usually in an on-site inspection, and its books and records in their entirety. In a stock purchase, the purchasing entity will want to examine the selling corporation's books and records and, more particularly, the specific shares being purchased and any future potential liabilities of the corporation. In an asset purchase, the purchasing corporation is particularly interested in the assets being purchased and any liens or liabilities on those assets. As you can see, the types of documents or information to be reviewed depend on the type of business combination to be consummated by the parties.

The following is a fairly inclusive list of (1) the types of documents to be reviewed and (2) the procedures to be followed by the acquiring corporation in the acquisition of stock of another corporation. Of course, the list will be slightly different for other types of business combinations.

1. The minute book, which includes the articles of incorporation, all amendments thereto, minutes of meetings or written consents of the shareholders and the board of directors, and the bylaws.
2. Stock books and stock ledgers.
3. Share certificates evidencing the stock to be purchased.
4. Shareholders' agreements, which may restrict the sale of shares.
5. Evidence of existence and of good standing. A good standing certificate, which may be obtained from the secretary of state of the state of incorporation, evidences that a corporation exists in that state and that it is in good standing.
6. Documents relating to any pending or threatened litigation.
7. Contracts or agreements for employment, consulting, and noncompetition of employees or consultants.
8. Title to or leases for real property owned or leased.
9. A list of personal property, inventory, and equipment owned or leased.
10. Licenses and franchises issued by local, state, and federal governmental agencies and other third parties.
11. Local, state, and federal tax returns.
12. Evidence of insurance on real and personal property and of all other insurance policies maintained.
13. A list of accounts receivable.
14. A list of loans and notes payable, plus copies of all loan documents.
15. Financial statements.
16. Agreements requiring third-party or governmental consent to the transaction.
17. A review of the local and state records to identify liens on real and personal property.
18. A list of customers and suppliers.
19. A list of employees and the benefits provided to those employees.

Attorneys representing all parties to the transaction will agree on the arrangements for the due diligence process, the review of documents just outlined. Most often the corporate paralegal is responsible for (1) conducting the review, (2) identifying issues to be raised with the supervising attorney, and (3) providing photocopies of relevant documents to other experts for identification of potential problems. Following are examples of issues with which the paralegal may have to deal:

1. While conducting the review, the paralegal discovers a shareholders' agreement, which states that no shareholder may sell or transfer his or her shares without first offering them for sale to the corporation itself. The paralegal should immediately notify the supervising attorney and provide him or her with a copy of that shareholders' agreement.

2. The paralegal locates copies of the financial statements and tax returns for the past five years. Photocopies should be made and forwarded immediately to the supervising attorney and the tax counsel for the client corporation, who will review the financial statements and tax returns for potential problems.

3. While reviewing the bylaws, the paralegal finds a provision that requires the corporation to have at least five directors. However, minutes of the last annual shareholders' meeting indicate that only three directors were elected. The paralegal should immediately provide this information to the supervising attorney. Before closing the transaction, the corporation whose bylaws are inconsistent must either amend the bylaws to provide for only three directors or have the shareholders elect two additional directors.

4. The secretary of state indicates by letter that the corporation for which the paralegal requested a good standing certificate is not in good standing in its state of incorporation. The letter from the secretary of state indicates that the corporation failed to pay its annual franchise fee for the two previous years. The paralegal should immediately notify the supervising attorney; arrangements must be made to cure this obstacle to closing the transaction.

The potential issues that the paralegal could identify in the due diligence process are endless. The paralegal who understands the types of corporate structural changes and the issues involved with each, which are discussed in this chapter, will have an advantage and will play a vital part in the due diligence process.

SUMMARY

13–1

Corporate transactions in which the corporation's complexion and the rights of the shareholders are affected include mergers, share exchanges, consolidations, sale of the corporation's stock, sale of the corporation's assets, amendments to the articles of incorporation and the bylaws, and dissolution and liquidation of the corporation. All these transactions require the approval of the shareholders of each corporation involved in such transactions.

13–2

Two or more corporations may combine by merger, share exchange, or consolidation, and these combinations are governed by statutory guidelines. A merger is the combination of two or more corporations into one legal entity whereby one corporation, the surviving corporation, remains after, or survives, the merger and the merged corporations cease to exist as separate legal entities after the merger. The procedure for merging a subsidiary corporation into the parent corporation is simplified and is called a short-form merger. A share exchange is the combination of two or more corporations whereby one corporation acquires all the outstanding shares of one or more classes or series of another corporation and both corporations survive after the share exchange has been consummated. A consolidation is the combination of two or more corporations into one entirely new legal entity. None of the consolidating corporations survive the consolidation.

13–3

Pursuant to the statutes of all the states and in accordance with provisions of the Model Act, the board of directors and shareholders of each corporation involved in the merger, share exchange, or consolidation must approve the plan. The plan represents the agreement between the corporations that are parties to the merger, share exchange, or consolidation, and it contains the terms and conditions under which the corporations have agreed to combine their businesses.

The board of directors of each corporation involved in the combination must adopt the plan and then recommend the plan to the shareholders. The shareholders of each corporation involved must approve the plan for the combination to be effective. In the case of an upstream or short-form merger, shareholder approval of the parent and subsidiary corporations is not required. After the plan has been approved, the surviving or acquiring corporation must file with the secretary of state articles of merger, articles of share exchange, or articles of consolidation, whichever are appropriate for the type of combination being effected.

13–4

The sale or purchase of a corporation's stock may be used by corporations to combine their businesses. The corporation selling its shares is the selling corporation, and the corporation desiring to purchase shares is the acquiring corporation. Procedures for carrying out a sale or purchase of stock depend on the desires of the corporations involved in the transaction. Such sale may be restricted by the articles of incorporation or the bylaws of the selling corporation or may be restricted by an agreement among the shareholders of the selling corporation. In a stock sale, the acquiring corporation is purchasing the selling corporation's assets *and* liabilities. A letter of intent, which spells out the terms and conditions under which the stock purchase agreement will be executed, may be entered into by the parties to the stock purchase and sale. The acquiring corporation is provided the opportunity to examine the books, records, and dealings of the selling corporation. This procedure is the due diligence process. The boards of directors of both the selling and the acquiring corporations must approve the stock transactions. The stock purchase agreement is the agreement between the acquiring corporation and the shareholders of the selling corporation for the purchase and sale of shares. It sets forth all the terms, conditions, and agreements of such purchase and sale.

13–5

In an asset transaction the seller, or the selling corporation, agrees to sell all or substantially all of the assets of the corporation to the buyer, or the acquiring corporation, who agrees to purchase the assets in exchange for some form of consideration. Assets usually sold include real estate, inventory, equipment, accounts receivable, contracts and agreements, leases, employee benefit plans, and other tangible and intangible property. As a result of the asset transaction, the buyer holds title to all the assets it purchases and may assume, in rare instances, the liabilities related to the assets purchased. The letter of intent identifies the assets to be sold and their price. The sale of all or substantially all the assets of a corporation outside the usual and regular course of business requires approval by the shareholders. The Uniform Commercial Code protects the interest of creditors of the selling corporation by requiring that notice be provided to the creditors prior to the sale of the assets. Such protection is given only in the sale of assets outside the normal and regular course of business. The asset purchase agreement is the agreement between the acquiring corporation and the selling corporation for the purchase and sale of the assets. The assignment, the bill of sale, and the deed are the documents that evidence the actual transfer of the assets.

13–6

Shareholders may feel that a merger, share exchange, consolidation, or sale of the corporation's assets outside the normal course of business is not in their best economic interests. Therefore, in a situation where they may be forced to live with the decision of the majority of voting shares, they have the right to dissent from the transaction. Generally, dissenters' rights provide the shareholders the statutory power to have their shares appraised and purchased by the corporation at fair value. Actions from which a shareholder may dissent include merger, share exchange, consolidation, sale of all or substantially all the assets of the corporation, amendment of the articles of incorporation, and any other corporate action from which shareholders have been given the right to dissent. The procedures for dissenting from a transaction are complicated, and the statutes vary greatly from state to state.

13–7

When two or more unrelated parties decide to combine their businesses, the due diligence process can be quite extensive and time-consuming. Attorneys representing all parties to the transaction will agree on the arrangements for the due diligence process. The corporate paralegal is generally responsible for (1) conducting the review, (2) identifying issues to be raised with the supervising attorney, and (3) providing photocopies of relevant documents to other experts for identification of potential problems. The paralegal who understands the types of corporate structural changes and the issues involved with each will have an advantage and will play a vital part in the due diligence process.

REVIEW GUIDE

Key Terms

Before proceeding, review the key terms listed below to be sure you understand each one. If necessary, read over the corresponding section of the chapter. When you are ready to test your understanding, answer the review questions.

merger (p. 311)
surviving corporation (p. 311)
merged corporations (p. 311)
upstream merger (p. 312)
downstream merger (p. 312)
triangular merger (p. 312)
reverse triangular merger (p. 312)

short-form merger (p. 313)
share exchange (p. 313)
consolidation (p. 314)
plan of merger (p. 315)
plan of share exchange (p. 317)
plan of consolidation (p. 318)
articles of merger (p. 321)
articles of share exchange (p. 321)
articles of consolidation (p. 321)
certificate of merger (p. 321)
certificate of share exchange (p. 321)
certificate of consolidation (p. 321)
selling corporation (p. 323)
acquiring corporation (p. 323)
stock transaction (p. 323)
letter of intent (p. 324)
due diligence process (p. 324)
stock purchase agreement (p. 325)
asset transaction (p. 327)
shell corporation (p. 327)
Uniform Commercial Code (p. 329)
bulk transfer law (p. 330)
asset purchase agreement (p. 330)
assignment (p. 330)
bill of sale (p. 330)
deed (p. 330)
dissenters' rights (p. 333)

Questions for Review and Discussion

1. Explain why the shareholders must approve such transactions as a merger, a share exchange, a consolidation, or a sale of the corporation's stock or assets.
2. What is a merger?
3. How does the short-form merger differ from other mergers?
4. For each of the following types of mergers, explain the relationship between the merged corporation and the surviving corporation: upstream, downstream, triangular, and reverse triangular.
5. What events occur in a share exchange?
6. What is a consolidation?
7. What procedures must be taken to approve a plan of merger, share exchange, or consolidation?
8. When does a merger become effective?
9. What is a letter of intent?
10. Is approval by the board of directors of a selling corporation required for the purchase of its shares by the acquiring corporation? Why or why not?
11. What is the due diligence process? Who is involved in this process?
12. How do the assignment, the bill of sale, and the deed differ? What is the purpose of these documents?
13. Explain how creditors are protected in commercial transactions. What requirements must be met by a selling corporation under the Uniform Commercial Code?
14. What corporate transactions create dissenters' rights?
15. Why would a shareholder want dissenters' rights?

Activities

1. Prepare a plan of merger that meets the statutory requirements of your state. Assume that the two corporations involved are both domestic corporations of your state. You select all the additional information that must be provided in the plan of merger. In addition, draft the necessary board of directors' and shareholders' resolutions approving the transaction.
2. Draft a notice of a shareholders' meeting to approve the sale of all the assets of Bond Computer Company, a corporation incorporated in accordance with the Model Act. Also prepare the resolutions that will be adopted by the shareholders at their meeting.
3. Go to the law library and obtain forms of a letter of intent for a stock transaction. Using those models and the information provided in this chapter, draft a letter of intent for the purchase of all the outstanding stock of Tea Bags, Inc., by Coffee Beans, Inc. Assume that both corporations were incorporated in North Carolina, and assume the corporate statutes of North Carolina mirror those of the Model Act. Use your imagination to provide all additional information required in the letter of intent.
4. Assume that the shareholders of XYZ Corporation have approved the sale of substantially all the assets of the XYZ Corporation to ABC Company. James Bond, a dissenting shareholder, provided a notice to the corporation

of his intent to dissent from such corporate action and did not vote his shares in favor of the action. Using the provisions of the Model Act, draft the notice required to be provided by XYZ Corporation to James Bond after the action was approved by the shareholders. Within how many days after such action was taken must the notice be sent to James Bond?

CHAPTER 14 Dissolution and Liquidation

OUTLINE

14–1 Dissolution and Liquidation
14–2 Voluntary Dissolution
    Prior to Commencement of Business
    After Commencement of Business
14–3 Articles of Dissolution
    Board of Directors' Approval
    Shareholders' Approval
    Filing Requirements
14–4 Postdissolution Procedures and Requirements
    Winding Up and Liquidating
    Tax Considerations
    Revocation of Dissolution
14–5 Involuntary Dissolution
    Administrative Dissolution
    Judicial Dissolution
14–6 Practical Considerations

APPLICATIONS

Office Equipment Corporation operates a small warehouse on the south side of town and can no longer compete with the larger office supply companies. The board of directors plans to seek a buyer, possibly a competitor, to purchase the corporation's inventory and take over its lease at the warehouse. At the direction of the board of directors, Alexander Desktop, president of Office Equipment Corporation, has consulted the corporation's accountant and attorney. They advised Mr. Desktop of the most advantageous strategies for liquidating and dissolving the corporation. Based on this advice, the directors will recommend to the shareholders of the corporation that they liquidate the business and dissolve the corporation, as the directors believe this plan to be in the best interests of the shareholders.

OBJECTIVES

A common misconception is that *dissolution* and *liquidation* are synonymous terms, but they are not. A corporation that no longer desires to transact business, or is unable to conduct business, may liquidate *and* dissolve its business or it may merely liquidate its business. You will understand the distinction between the dissolution and the liquidation of a corporation and will know the procedures that must be followed to dissolve and to liquidate a corporation after reviewing this chapter. After completing Chapter 14, you will be able to:

1. Distinguish between dissolution and liquidation.
2. Understand the two situations in which a corporation may voluntarily dissolve.

3. Prepare and file articles of dissolution.
4. Prepare resolutions of the board of directors and the shareholders for approving the dissolution of a corporation.
5. Prepare a plan of liquidation and dissolution.
6. Understand the variations in the filing requirements of the states.
7. Understand the procedures for winding up and liquidating the affairs and business of the corporation.
8. Arrange for the timely filing of Form 966, Corporate Dissolution or Liquidation.
9. Prepare articles of revocation of dissolution.
10. Understand the circumstances in which the corporation may be involuntarily dissolved.
11. Distinguish between administrative and judicial involuntary dissolutions.

14–1   Dissolution and Liquidation

Just as the legal existence of the corporation begins when articles of incorporation are filed, the corporation's existence terminates upon the filing of articles of dissolution. In rare circumstances, the articles of incorporation provide for termination of the corporation's existence at some specified date. For example, the articles of incorporation may include a provision that states, "The corporation's existence shall terminate on December 31, 2025." In that case, the corporation will automatically dissolve on December 31, 2025. However, you will rarely find this type of provision in the articles of incorporation, as most corporations exist perpetually. That is, they exist until formally dissolved in accordance with the state statutes.

The **dissolution** of a corporation is the cessation or termination of a corporation's legal existence. The procedure for dissolving a corporation is dictated by the statutes of the state in which the corporation was incorporated, and these statutes vary greatly among the states. There are two types of dissolution: voluntary dissolution and involuntary dissolution. In the following sections, we will discuss both.

Liquidation is the process of selling off and converting the corporation's assets to cash, completing and terminating all contracts and agreements to which the corporation was a party or was obligated, paying creditors and expenses, and distributing the remainder to the shareholders of the corporation.

A corporation may liquidate its business without legally terminating or dissolving the corporation. Sometimes a corporation desires to continue its legal existence after it liquidates, in the hope that at some future point it will resume business activities. To accomplish this, the corporation will liquidate (sell its assets, pay off its liabilities, and distribute any remainder to the shareholders) but will not dissolve. Nonetheless, most liquidated corporations dissolve as soon as the liquidation process is completed, and the activities involved in the liquidation (the process) of a corporation generally precede the dissolution (legal termination) of a corporation. The state statute should always be consulted to determine whether the corporation is to be liquidated before or after the dissolution.

A corporation's existence continues after dissolution for the purpose of winding up and liquidating the business and affairs of the corporation. The only business a

---

PARALEGALERT!

Dissolution, the legal termination of the business, is effective at a moment in time. Liquidation is the ongoing process, which may take months and sometimes years, of winding down the business and the affairs of the corporation.

dissolved corporation is permitted to carry on is the winding up of business, which includes the fulfilling of previously executed contracts. Refer to Section 14–4 for further discussion on the corporation's process of winding up and liquidating.

In summary, dissolution is the legal termination of a corporation's existence, and liquidation is the process of winding up and concluding the business and affairs of the corporation.

14–2   Voluntary Dissolution

Upon the approval of a corporation's shareholders and board of directors, a corporation may elect a **voluntary dissolution** of the corporation. In a voluntary dissolution, the board of directors approves the dissolution of the corporation and proposes to the shareholders that it is in the corporation's and the shareholders' best interests that the corporation be dissolved. The shareholders entitled to vote must then approve the dissolution; thereupon the corporation begins the dissolution process.

The board of directors may propose dissolution of a corporation for numerous reasons. For example, the corporation may have sold all or substantially all of its assets, the corporation may have been declared bankrupt or insolvent, or the corporation may merely desire to cease transacting business. Whatever the reason for dissolving the corporation, the statutes of the corporation's state of incorporation must be followed when dissolving a corporation. The states' statutes and procedures for dissolving a corporation differ significantly; therefore, it is important to research the statutes carefully.

A corporation may voluntarily dissolve either (1) prior to the corporation's commencement of business or (2) after the corporation's commencement of business.

PARALEGALERT!

In reality, the corporate paralegal prepares the board of directors' and shareholders' resolutions approving the dissolution and then, at the direction of the supervising attorney, begins the procedures to dissolve the corporation.

Prior to Commencement of Business

For a variety of reasons, the incorporators or initial directors may dissolve a corporation prior to the corporation's commencement of business or prior to its issuance of shares. Generally, a corporation does not commence business unless it has issued shares. If the corporation has not commenced business, it should have no liabilities to satisfy or debts to pay, and it will have no assets to distribute to the shareholders. For these reasons the procedures for dissolving the corporation are relatively simple.

Section 14.01 of the Model Act provides that "a majority of the incorporators or initial directors of a corporation that has not issued shares or has not commenced business may dissolve the corporation." States provide similar provisions; most require only the filing with the secretary of state of a document requesting that the corporation be dissolved. This document is called the articles of dissolution. The Model Act, in Section 14.01, spells out the information that should be included in articles of dissolution when a corporation is dissolving prior to the commencement of business or the issuance of shares. That section states that the corporation may dissolve by delivering to the secretary of state for filing articles of dissolution that set forth:

(1) the name of the corporation;

(2) the date of its incorporation;

(3) either (i) that none of the corporation's shares has been issued or (ii) that the corporation has not commenced business;

(4) that no debt of the corporation remains unpaid;

(5) that the net assets of the corporation remaining after winding up have been distributed to the shareholders, if shares were issued; and

(6) that a majority of the incorporators or initial directors authorized the dissolution.

Figure 14–1 is an example of articles of dissolution for use prior to commencement of business. They were prepared in accordance with Section 14.01 of the Model Act. Note that these articles of dissolution have been prepared for execution and filing by the incorporators. If initial directors were named in the articles of incorporation, the initial directors should execute and file the articles of dissolution. Remember that this form of articles of dissolution is used by corporations that have not commenced business or have not issued shares.

After Commencement of Business

The procedures for dissolving the corporation differ when a corporation has commenced business or has issued shares. The most important difference is that the corporation now must obtain the approval of its shareholders before dissolving the corporation. In addition, some states require that final tax returns be filed and

Figure 14–1   Articles of Dissolution (Prior to Commencement of Business or Issuance of Shares)

Articles of Dissolution
Prior to Commencement of Business

The undersigned, being a majority of the incorporators, in order to dissolve this corporation in the State of _____ , under and pursuant to the provisions of Chapter 14 of the Model Business Corporation Act, do hereby certify that:

1. The name of the Corporation is OFFICE EQUIPMENT CORPORATION.

2. The Corporation was incorporated on September 1, 1975.

3. The Corporation has not commenced business, and no shares of the Corporation have been issued.

4. No debts of the Corporation remain unpaid.

5. A majority of the incorporators of the Corporation have authorized the dissolution of the Corporation.

IN WITNESS WHEREOF, the incorporators of the Corporation have executed these Articles of Dissolution Prior to Commencement of Business this 1st day of December, 1994.

By _____
James Bond, Incorporator

By _____
Anthony Moore, Incorporator

By _____
Gail Webster, Incorporator

finalized, that the corporation obtain a clearance certificate evidencing that no taxes are due to the state, that all annual reports have been filed, and that the corporation advertise its intention to dissolve after receiving approval from its shareholders.

State statutes governing dissolution of corporations are very specific and vary greatly. It is important that a careful review of the statutes be undertaken and that the procedures be followed exactly. However, an important provision that does not vary in the states' statutes is that a dissolution must be approved by the shareholders of the corporation.

Section 14.02 of the Model Act provides for the dissolution of a corporation by the board of directors and the shareholders. The full text of Section 14.02 of the Model Act is provided in Figure 14–2. The following list summarizes the procedures outlined in this section of the Model Act:

1. The board of directors submits a proposal to the shareholders that the corporation be dissolved.
2. Notice is provided to the shareholders of a meeting at which the shareholders will consider the proposal of the board of directors.
3. The shareholders approve the proposal of dissolution.
4. Unless otherwise provided in the articles of incorporation, a majority of all the votes entitled to be cast must approve the proposal for dissolution.

The Model Act, in Section 14.03(a), spells out the information to be included in articles of dissolution when a corporation dissolves after the commencement of business and the issuance of shares. Note that these articles of dissolution have the same name but are different from the articles of dissolution prepared and filed prior to a corporation's commencement of business. Section 14.03(a) states that

> At any time after dissolution is authorized, the corporation may dissolve by delivering to the secretary of state for filing articles of dissolution setting forth:

Figure 14–2   Section 14.02 of the Model Act

---

§14.02.   Dissolution by Board of Directors and Shareholders.—

(a) A corporation's board of directors may propose dissolution for submission to the shareholders.

(b) For a proposal to dissolve to be adopted:

   (1) the board of directors must recommend dissolution to the shareholders unless the board of directors determines that because of conflict of interest or other special circumstances it should make no recommendation and communicates the basis for its determination to the shareholders; and

   (2) the shareholders entitled to vote must approve the proposal to dissolve as provided in subsection (e).

(c) The board of directors may condition its submission of the proposal for dissolution on any basis.

(d) The corporation shall notify each shareholder, whether or not entitled to vote, of the proposed shareholders' meeting in accordance with section 7.05. The notice must also state that the purpose, or one of the purposes, of the meeting is to consider dissolving the corporation.

(e) Unless the articles of incorporation or the board of directors [acting pursuant to subsection (c)] require a greater vote or a vote by voting groups, the proposal to dissolve to be adopted must be approved by a majority of all the votes entitled to be cast on the proposal.

Figure 14–3 Articles of Dissolution (After Commencement of Business or Issuance of Shares)

Articles of Dissolution

The undersigned corporation, in order to dissolve this corporation in the State of _____ , under and pursuant to the provisions of Chapter 14 of the Model Business Corporation Act, does hereby certify that:

1. The name of the Corporation is OFFICE EQUIPMENT CORPORATION.

2. Dissolution of the Corporation was authorized on March 4, 1995.

3. Dissolution of the Corporation was approved by the shareholders of the Corporation. The number of votes cast on the proposal to dissolve the Corporation was 10,000, of which 9,500 shares voted "FOR" the proposal and 500 shares voted "AGAINST" the proposal.

4. The number of votes cast "FOR" the proposal was sufficient for approval of the proposal to dissolve the Corporation.

IN WITNESS WHEREOF, a duly authorized officer of the Corporation has executed these Articles of Dissolution on this 10th day of March, 1995.

OFFICE EQUIPMENT CORPORATION

By _____
      Alexander Desktop, President

(1) the name of the corporation;
(2) the date dissolution was authorized;
(3) if dissolution was approved by the shareholders:
   (i) the number of votes entitled to be cast on the proposal to dissolve; and
   (ii) either the total number of votes cast for and against dissolution or the total number of undisputed votes cast for dissolution and a statement that the number cast for dissolution was sufficient for approval.
(4) If voting by voting groups was required, the information required by subparagraph (3) must be separately provided for each voting group entitled to vote separately on the plan to dissolve.

Figure 14–3 is an example of articles of dissolution prepared in accordance with Section 14.03 of the Model Act. These articles of dissolution have been prepared for execution and filing by an officer of the corporation. Remember, they are the form used by the corporation after it has commenced business or has issued shares.

14–3 Articles of Dissolution

As we discussed in Section 14–2, articles of dissolution are filed by either (1) the incorporators or the initial directors when the corporation has not commenced business or has not issued shares or (2) the officers of the corporation, at the direction and authorization of the board of directors after the shareholders have approved the dissolution. In other words, the method by which a corporation voluntarily dissolves depends on whether the corporation has commenced business.

Board of Directors' Approval

As already mentioned, the board of directors must submit to the shareholders a proposal recommending that the corporation be dissolved. They do so by adopting a resolution or resolutions recommending to the shareholders that the corporation be dissolved. In particular, the resolutions should (1) recommend that the corporation be dissolved, (2) direct that the matter be submitted to a vote of the shareholders, and (3) authorize the officers of the corporation to prepare and file articles of dissolution and all other documents necessary to complete the dissolution of the corporation.

Figure 14–4 is an example of the resolutions that should be adopted by the board of directors. Note that these resolutions also approve a plan of liquidation and dissolution. A **plan of liquidation and dissolution** is an outline of the procedures for the board of directors and the officers to follow in the winding up and liquidating of the business and affairs of the corporation. The provisions found in the plan could have been included and approved in the resolutions, and in that case, there would have been no need for a separate plan of liquidation and dissolution. Figure 14–5 is a sample plan of liquidation and dissolution.

Remember from our discussion in Chapter 7 that the board of directors can adopt these resolutions in one of the following two ways: (1) at a meeting of the board of directors, for which proper notice was sent and at which a quorum is present for the conducting of business, or (2) by unanimous written consent, executed by all directors of the corporation.

PARALEGALERT!

The corporate paralegal is responsible for meeting all the requirements for the proper filing of articles of dissolution. It is important that all procedures be followed precisely. The secretary of state will return any filing that does not meet that state's requirements.

PARALEGALERT!

If the corporation has not commenced business, the incorporators or the initial directors may dissolve the corporation. If the corporation has commenced business, the corporation may be dissolved only upon the approval of the shareholders. In either case, articles of dissolution must be filed with the secretary of state.

Figure 14–4   Resolutions of Board of Directors Recommending and Approving Dissolution

RESOLVED, that the Board of Directors of the Corporation deems it in the best interests of the Corporation and the shareholders of the Corporation that the Corporation be voluntarily dissolved and liquidated; and

FURTHER RESOLVED, that the Board of Directors hereby recommends to and hereby submits a proposal to the shareholders of the Corporation that the Corporation be dissolved and liquidated; and

FURTHER RESOLVED, that the Plan of Liquidation and Dissolution (the "Plan"), a copy of which is attached hereto, be and hereby is adopted and approved; and

FURTHER RESOLVED, that the officers of the Corporation be and hereby are authorized to convey and transfer the assets of the Corporation to the shareholders of the Corporation upon the agreement of the shareholders to be liable for any and all debts, taxes, fees, and expenses of the Corporation; and to cancel all issued and outstanding shares of the Corporation, which shall be surrendered by the shareholders of the Corporation; and to take any other actions that may be necessary in accordance with the Plan and may be required to effectuate the dissolution of the Corporation and wind up its business affairs; and

FURTHER RESOLVED, that the officers of the Corporation are hereby authorized to execute and deliver to the Secretary of State of the State of _____ all documents necessary to dissolve the Corporation.

Figure 14–5   Plan of Liquidation and Dissolution

Plan of Liquidation and Dissolution

This is a Plan of Liquidation and Dissolution (the "Plan") of Office Equipment Corporation, a _____ corporation (the "Corporation"), pursuant to Section 332 of the Internal Revenue Code of 1986, as amended (the "Code").

1. The Plan shall become effective upon its adoption by the shareholders of the Corporation.

2. As soon as practicable after the adoption of the Plan, the Corporation shall (i) collect all sums due the Corporation, (ii) pay, to the extent that it is possible to do so, all of the liabilities and obligations of the Corporation, including its liquidating expenses, accounts payable, and any other indebtedness, and (iii) distribute any remaining property to the shareholders of the Corporation in accordance with the Corporation's Articles of Incorporation and in complete liquidation and cancellation of all the outstanding shares of the Corporation's capital stock.

3. The officers of the Corporation shall take such action as may be appropriate or desirable to carry out the Plan, to liquidate the Corporation completely pursuant to the requirements of the Code, and to dissolve the Corporation pursuant to the Model Business Corporation Act.

4. When adopted according to its terms by the Board of Directors and shareholders of the Corporation, this Plan shall constitute the consent to dissolve the Corporation required under Section _____ of the Model Business Corporation Act.

Shareholders' Approval

Section 14.02(e) of the Model Act provides that "the proposal to dissolve to be adopted must be approved by a majority of all the votes entitled to be cast on that proposal." However, many state statutes require a greater-than-majority vote to approve the dissolution of the corporation. Very often states require a two-thirds vote. The reason for this greater-than-majority (more than 51 percent) vote is that the dissolution of the corporation is the corporate action with the greatest impact on the shareholders of the corporation.

Approval by the shareholders is accomplished by the adoption of a resolution or resolutions accepting the recommendation of the board of directors to dissolve the corporation and authorizing that the corporation be dissolved in accordance with the state statutes. In particular, the resolutions should (1) accept the recommendation made by the board of directors to dissolve the corporation, (2) approve the dissolution of the corporation, and (3) authorize the board of directors to wind up and liquidate the business and affairs of the corporation. Figure 14–6 is an example of the resolutions that should be adopted by the shareholders.

If a plan of liquidation and dissolution has been approved by the board of directors, the shareholders should also approve the plan. Refer to Figure 14–5, which is an example of a plan of liquidation and dissolution.

Remember from our discussion in Chapter 7 that the shareholders can adopt these resolutions in one of the following two ways: (1) at a meeting of the shareholders, for which proper notice was sent and at which a quorum is present for the conducting of business, or (2) by unanimous written consent, executed by *all* shareholders of the corporation.

Figure 14–6   Resolutions of Shareholders

> RESOLVED, that the Plan of Liquidation and Dissolution be and hereby is adopted and approved and that the Corporation be completely liquidated at the earliest practicable date, that all debts and liabilities of the Corporation be paid, and that the remaining assets be distributed to the shareholders in accordance with the Corporation's Articles of Incorporation; and
>
> FURTHER RESOLVED, that the Corporation cease all business except as may be necessary to wind up the business affairs of the Corporation; and
>
> FURTHER RESOLVED, that the officers of the Corporation are hereby authorized to execute and deliver to the Secretary of State of the State of _____ all documents necessary to dissolve the Corporation.

Filing Requirements

As already mentioned several times in this chapter, the states' statutes differ in many respects in their requirements for preparing and filing articles of dissolution. The following are just some of the ways in which the requirements of the states' statutes differ:

1. Some states require that the corporation file final income or franchise tax returns and obtain a **tax clearance certificate** before the state issues the certificate of dissolution.
2. Some states require that the corporation apply for a **clearance certificate,** which evidences that the corporation has filed all annual reports.
3. Some states require the corporation to advertise its intention to dissolve the corporation by filing a **legal advertisement.** Pennsylvania is one state that requires corporations to advertise their intention to dissolve. Figure 14–7 is an example of a legal advertisement required in Pennsylvania.
4. Other states require the corporation to mail all creditors and taxing authorities notification of the corporation's intention to dissolve. Section 14.06(b) of the Model Act provides that "the dissolved corporation shall notify its known claimants in writing of the dissolution at any time after its effective date." That section of the Model Act goes on to specify the information that must be provided in the notice to creditors, or **notice to claimants.** Figure 14–8 is an example of a notice to claimants prepared in accordance with Section 14.06(b) of the Model Act.
5. And yet other states require that a **notice of intent to dissolve** be filed with the secretary of state before the articles of dissolution are submitted. The notice of intent to dissolve puts the state on notice that the corporation has dissolved and is about to begin the process of winding up the business and other affairs of the corporation. Figure 14–9 is an example of a notice of intent to dissolve. In jurisdictions that require such notice, the articles of dissolution are filed only after all liabilities have been satisfied and all assets have been distributed to the shareholders.

Figure 14–7   Form of Legal Advertisement

> ### Legal Advertisement
>
> NOTICE IS HEREBY GIVEN THAT the shareholders and directors of OFFICE EQUIPMENT CORPORATION, a Pennsylvania corporation, with an address at 123 America Street, Anytown, Pennsylvania, have approved a proposal that the Corporation voluntarily dissolve, and that the Board of Directors has now engaged in winding up and settling the affairs of the Corporation under the provisions of Section 1975 of the Pennsylvania Business Corporation Law of 1988, as amended.

Figure 14–8   Notice to Claimants

Notice to the Claimants of
Office Equipment Corporation

The shareholders and directors of Office Equipment Corporation, a Corporation incorporated under the laws of the State of _____ , have approved the voluntary dissolution of the Corporation. You are hereby notified that:

1. A claim against the Corporation must be made in writing and must include the amount of the claim, the basis for the claim, and the date on which the claim originated.

2. A claim may be sent to the Corporation's registered office at 123 America Street, Anytown, Anystate 12345.

3. The deadline for submitting a claim to the Corporation is October 31, 1995, which is no sooner than 120 days from the date of this notice.

4. A claim will be barred if not received on or before the deadline, which is October 31, 1995.

Date: April 1, 1995.

_____
Henrietta Binderclip, Secretary

Figure 14–9   Notice of Intent to Dissolve

Notice of Intent to Dissolve

The undersigned Corporation, in order to provide notice to the Secretary of State of the Corporation's intent to dissolve, hereby provides the following Notice of Intent to Dissolve and certifies that:

1. The name of the Corporation is OFFICE EQUIPMENT CORPORATION.

2. A meeting of the shareholders of the Corporation was held on March 4, 1995, and at such meeting resolutions were adopted by the shareholders to begin the voluntary dissolution of the Corporation.

3. The Board of Directors of the Corporation is authorized to take any and all actions necessary to wind up the business and affairs of the Corporation, which includes the collection of the Corporation's assets, the payment of all debts and liabilities of the Corporation, and the distribution of all remaining assets to the shareholders of the Corporation.

IN WITNESS WHEREOF, a duly authorized officer of the Corporation has executed this Notice of Intent to Dissolve this 5th day of March, 1995.

OFFICE EQUIPMENT CORPORATION

By _____
Alexander Desktop, President

In addition, all states require a fee to be paid when articles of dissolution are filed. And, of course, that fee varies from state to state.

If all provisions have been met and the procedures have been properly completed, the secretary of state issues a **certificate of dissolution** to the individual who filed the articles of dissolution. That individual is usually the corporate paralegal.

14–4   Postdissolution Procedures and Requirements

Upon the filing of the articles of dissolution, the corporation's legal existence is terminated. At that time the corporation is effectively dissolved. In some states, the corporation is not dissolved until it receives the certificate of dissolution. Section 14.03(b) of the Model Act states that "a corporation is dissolved upon the effective date of its articles of dissolution." Generally, the **effective date** is the date of the filing of the articles of dissolution. However, the corporation's existence will continue for the purpose of complying with postdissolution procedures and requirements.

An important consideration in the liquidation and dissolution process is whether the corporation is qualified to do business in any state. In other words, is it a foreign corporation in any foreign state? If so, the statutes of the foreign state must be reviewed to determine the procedures for withdrawing the corporation from doing business in that state. You should refer to Section 9–6 in Chapter 9, in which we discussed the withdrawal of foreign corporations.

Winding Up and Liquidating

The dissolved corporation continues its existence for the purpose of winding up and liquidating the business and affairs of the corporation. The only business a dissolved corporation may carry on is the liquidation process—the winding up of business and affairs and the fulfilling of previously executed contracts. For example, after Office Equipment Corporation dissolves, it still must fulfill any obligations to deliver office equipment that a customer ordered and paid for prior to the dissolution. Section 14.05(a) of the Model Act states that "a dissolved corporation continues its corporate existence but may not carry on any business except that appropriate to wind up and liquidate its business and affairs." The acts of the corporation in winding up and liquidating the business include the following:

PARALEGALERT!

One of the first questions the paralegal should ask is whether the corporation being liquidated or dissolved is qualified to do business in any foreign state. You must comply with the foreign state's statutes for withdrawing the corporation from doing business in the foreign state.

1. Collecting all of the corporation's assets.
2. Disposing of or selling all of the corporation's assets, except those that will be distributed to the shareholders after all liabilities of the corporation have been satisfied.
3. Discharging or paying all debts and liabilities of the corporation.
4. Distributing all remaining assets, including cash and property, to the shareholders according to their percentage interests in the corporation.

Generally, the shareholders give the board of directors the authority to wind up the business and affairs of the corporation. But the directors then authorize the officers to carry out the intent of the shareholders. Therefore, in reality, the officers of the

First National Bank of Boston v. Nichols

The winding up and liquidating of a corporation is a process that may take months and possibly years. During this process, however, the corporation may continue its corporate existence, as permitted by the state statute, to carry on any business appropriate to the winding up and liquidation of its business and affairs. As part of this process, the corporation must perform its obligations under contracts entered into prior to the vote of the shareholders to liquidate the corporation. This reqirement was supported by the court in the following case.

In *First National Bank of Boston v. Nichols*, 294 Mass. 173, 200 N.E. 869 (1936), the court held that "the vote for voluntary liquidation did not put an end to the corporate existence of the bank or render performance of the contract impossible according to its terms, though such vote imposed limitations on the bank's doing any new business not incidental to liquidation."

corporation collect the corporation's assets, pay the corporation's debts, and distribute the remaining assets to the shareholders. The ultimate responsibility for accomplishing the desires of the shareholders, however, lies with the board of directors.

In the process of discharging and paying the corporation's debts and liabilities and distributing any remaining assets to the shareholders, the officers of the corporation may be unable to locate a creditor or a shareholder. The statutes provide a remedy for this problem. Section 14.40 of the Model Act states that "assets of a dissolved corporation that should be transferred to a creditor, claimant, or shareholder of the corporation who cannot be found or who is not competent to receive them shall be reduced to cash and deposited with the state treasurer or other appropriate state official for safekeeping."

After a corporation has been dissolved, it may continue to defend or maintain an action in court that began prior to the dissolution. Usually, the corporation may not commence any litigation on its own behalf after dissolution. But Section 14.05(b)(5) of the Model Act provides that "dissolution of a corporation does not . . . prevent commencement of a proceeding by or against the corporation in its corporate name." Some states agree with the Model Act and allow the corporation to commence a court action, and other states do not.

The *Legal Links* in this chapter focuses on a court's determination that the voluntary liquidation of a corporation did *not* put an end to that corporation's existence. That decision supports what has been stated here: that a corporation continues to exist for the purpose of winding up and liquidating the business and affairs of the corporation.

PARALEGALERT!

Usually, the corporate paralegal has little responsibility for the actions of liquidating the corporation. An officer of the corporation sells off the assets and pays the corporation's debts.

Tax Considerations

The corporation's tax counsel or accountant may play a significant role in the dissolution of the corporation because of regulations imposed by the Internal Revenue Service. An obvious objective in the dissolution of a corporation is that it be accomplished in a manner most advantageous to the shareholders of the corporation. And that generally requires the expertise of a tax lawyer or accountant.

Section 6043(a) of the Internal Revenue Code of 1986, as amended, requires the filing of **Form 966, Corporate Dissolution or Liquidation.** Form 966 is reproduced in Figure 14–10. This form must be filed within 30 days of the adoption or approval of the resolutions or plan by the shareholders of the corporation.

Figure 14–10   Form 966, Corporate Dissolution or Liquidation

Form **966** (Rev. January 1993) Department of the Treasury Internal Revenue Service	**Corporate Dissolution or Liquidation** (Required under section 6043(a) of the Internal Revenue Code)	OMB No. 1545-0041 Expires 1-31-96

Please type or print

Name of corporation	Employer identification number
Number, street, and room or suite no. (If a P.O. box number, see instructions below.)	Check type of return ☐ 1120 ☐ 1120L
City or town, state, and ZIP code	☐ 1120-IC-DISC ☐ 1120S ☐ Other ▶

1 Date incorporated	2 Place incorporated	3 Type of liquidation ☐ Complete ☐ Partial	4 Date resolution or plan of complete or partial liquidation was adopted

5 Service Center where corporation filed its immediately preceding tax return	6 Last month, day, and year of immediately preceding tax year	7a Last month, day, and year of final tax year	7b Was corporation's final tax return filed as part of a consolidated income tax return? If "Yes," complete 7c, 7d, and 7e. ☐ Yes ☐ No

7c Name of common parent	7d Employer Identification Number of Common Parent	7e Service Center where consolidated return was filed

		Common	Preferred
8	Total number of shares outstanding at time of adoption of plan or liquidation		
9	Date(s) of any amendments to plan of dissolution		
10	Section of the Code under which the corporation is to be dissolved or liquidated . . .		
11	If this return concerns an amendment or supplement to a resolution or plan, enter the date the previous Form 966 was filed		

Attach a certified copy of the resolution or plan and all amendments or supplements not previously filed.

Under penalties of perjury, I declare that I have examined this return, including accompanying schedules and statements, and to the best of my knowledge and belief it is true, correct, and complete.

▶ _____   _____   _____
   Signature of officer   Title   Date

Instructions

Paperwork Reduction Act Notice.—We ask for the information on this form to carry out the Internal Revenue laws of the United States. You are required to give us the information. We need it to ensure that you are complying with these laws and to allow us to figure and collect the right amount of tax.

The time needed to complete and file this form will vary depending on individual circumstances. The estimated average time is:

Recordkeeping	5 hr., 1 min.
Learning about the law or the form	6 min.
Preparing and sending the form to the IRS	11 min.

If you have comments concerning the accuracy of these time estimates or suggestions for making this form more simple, we would be happy to hear from you. You can write to both the **Internal Revenue Service,** Washington, DC 20224, Attention: IRS Reports Clearance Officer, T:FP; and the **Office of Management and Budget,** Paperwork Reduction Project (1545-0041), Washington, DC 20503. **DO NOT** send the tax form to either of these offices. Instead, see **When and Where To File** below.

Who Must File.—A corporation must file Form 966 if its adopts a resolution or plan to dissolve the corporation or liquidate any of its stock. Exempt organizations are not required to file Form 966. These organizations should see the Instructions for Form 990 or 990-PF.

When and Where To File.—File Form 966 within 30 days after the resolution or plan is adopted to dissolve the corporation or liquidate any of its stock. If the resolution or plan is amended or supplemented after Form 966 is filed, file another Form 966 within 30 days after the amendment or supplement is adopted. The additional form will be sufficient if the date the earlier form was filed is entered on line 11 and a certified copy of the amendment or supplement is attached. Include all information required by Form 966 that was not given in the earlier form.

File Form 966 with the Internal Revenue Service Center where the corporation is required to file its income tax return.

Distribution of Property.—A corporation must recognize gain or loss on the distribution of its assets in the complete liquidation of its stock. For purposes of determining gain or loss, the distributed assets are valued at fair market value. Exceptions to this rule apply to liquidation of a subsidiary and to a distribution that is made pursuant to a plan of reorganization.

Address.—Include the suite, room, or other unit number after the street address. If mail is not delivered to the street address and the corporation has a P.O. box, enter the box number instead of the street address.

Signature.—The return must be signed and dated by the president, vice president, treasurer, assistant treasurer, chief accounting officer, or any other corporate officer (such as tax officer) authorized to sign. A receiver, trustee, or assignee must sign and date any return required to be filed on behalf of a corporation.

*U.S. Government Printing Office: 1993 — 343-034/80074   Cat. No. 17053B   Form **966** (Rev. 1-93)

In addition, a copy of the resolutions or plan adopted by the shareholders must be attached to Form 966. Generally, the corporation's tax counsel or accountant takes responsibility for timely preparation and filing of this form. The paralegal may be requested to provide a copy of the resolutions or plan that was adopted, which must be attached to Form 966.

Revocation of Dissolution

At any time prior to the issuance of the certificate of dissolution by the secretary of state, the corporation may revoke its voluntary dissolution proceedings.

PARALEGALERT!

The only case in which the board of directors may approve the revocation of dissolution is one in which authorization to do so was given them in the articles of dissolution.

Figure 14–11 Articles of Revocation of Dissolution

Articles of Revocation of Dissolution of Office Equipment Corporation

The undersigned Corporation, in order to revoke the dissolution of this Corporation in the State of _____ , under and pursuant to the provisions of Chapter 14 of the Model Business Corporation Act, does hereby certify that:

1. The name of the Corporation is OFFICE EQUIPMENT CORPORATION.

2. The effective date of the dissolution, which is revoked, was April 1, 1995.

3. The revocation of the dissolution of the Corporation was approved by the shareholders of the Corporation on December 26, 1994. The number of votes cast to revoke the dissolution of the Corporation was 10,000, of which 9,900 shares voted "FOR" the revocation and 100 shares voted "AGAINST" the revocation.

IN WITNESS WHEREOF, a duly authorized officer of the Corporation has executed these Articles of Revocation of Dissolution this 31st day of December, 1994.

OFFICE EQUIPMENT CORPORATION

By _____
Alexander Desktop, President

The Model Act also provides, in Section 14.04(a), that a "corporation may revoke its dissolution within 120 days of its effective date." States following the provisions of the Model Act, therefore, allow the corporation to revoke a dissolution within 120 days of the effective date of the articles of dissolution.

A corporation's **revocation of dissolution** is authorized and approved in the same manner as the dissolution was authorized and approved. That is, if the dissolution was accomplished by shareholder approval, the revocation of dissolution must also be approved by the shareholders. A revocation of dissolution without shareholder approval would not be permitted unless authorization had been given to the board of directors in the articles of dissolution filed with the secretary of state.

After the revocation has been approved, the officers of the corporation are generally responsible for preparing **articles of revocation of dissolution** and filing them with the secretary of state. This responsibility will, in most cases, fall to the paralegal who was involved in the dissolution of the corporation. A copy of the articles of dissolution should accompany the articles of revocation of dissolution. The Model Act specifies the information that should be included in the revocation articles. Figure 14–11 is an example of articles of revocation of dissolution. These articles were prepared in accordance with Section 14.04(c) of the Model Act.

A revocation of dissolution generally becomes effective on the original effective date of the dissolution. When the secretary of state has accepted the articles of revocation of dissolution for filing, the corporation carries on its business as if the dissolution had never occurred.

14–5 Involuntary Dissolution

Most of the dissolutions in which a paralegal is involved are voluntary dissolutions, in which the corporation voluntarily elects to dissolve the corporation. However, in some circumstances, a corporation may be *forced* to dissolve by (1) the state of incorporation, (2) the shareholders of the corporation, or (3) the creditors or claimants of the corporation. An **involuntary dissolution** is the cessation or termination of a corporation imposed on the corporation and accomplished without the approval of the corporation's shareholders and board of directors.

Administrative Dissolution

An **administrative dissolution** is one in which the state of incorporation dissolves the corporation. Many state statutes provide an array of grounds for an administrative dissolution, and many states have patterned their statutes after the Model Act. Section 14.20 of the Model Act provides grounds (or reasons) for the state to dissolve a corporation. That section states that

> The secretary of state may commence a proceeding . . . to administratively dissolve a corporation if:
> (1)   the corporation does not pay within 60 days after they are due any franchise taxes or penalties imposed by this Act or other law;
> (2)   the corporation does not deliver its annual report to the secretary of state within 60 days after it is due;
> (3)   the corporation is without a registered agent or registered office in this state for 60 days or more;
> (4)   the corporation does not notify the secretary of state within 60 days that its registered agent or registered office has been changed, that its registered agent has resigned, or that its registered office has been discontinued; or
> (5)   the corporation's period of duration stated in its articles of incorporation expires.

In other words, the Model Act very clearly states that grounds for revocation include:

1. Failure to pay franchise tax.
2. Failure to file an annual report.
3. Failure to maintain a registered office and registered agent.
4. Failure to notify the state of a change in registered office or registered agent.
5. Failure to comply with the expiration of the corporation's period of duration.

Some states include such grounds as insolvency (the corporation's inability to pay its debts as they become due) and a consistent violation of the state's laws.

A corporation may *inadvertently* fail to file its annual report, fail to pay a franchise tax, or violate other provisions of the statute. Therefore, most state statutes and the Model Act offer the corporation an opportunity to cure the violation. Before the secretary of state formally dissolves the corporation, the secretary of state's office must serve the corporation a written notice of its violation and must give the corporation a specified amount of time to cure the violation. Under the Model Act, the secretary of state must give the corporation 60 days to correct the violation after notice is served on the corporation. If the corporation fails to correct the violation within the specified time, the secretary of state may administratively dissolve the corporation. The secretary of state issues a certificate of dissolution upon dissolving the corporation. The certificate of dissolution recites the ground or grounds for dissolution and states the effective date of the dissolution. As with a voluntary dissolution, the corporation may continue its existence only for the purpose of liquidating and winding up its business and affairs.

A corporation may apply to the secretary of state for reinstatement within two years after the effective date of the administrative dissolution. The application must conform to the requirements of the state statute. If the secretary of state accepts the application for reinstatement, he or she cancels the certificate of dissolution and issues a certificate of reinstatement. A **certificate of reinstatement** cites the secretary of state's determination that the corporation should be reinstated and gives the effective date of the reinstatement. When the reinstatement is effective, it will have effect from the effective date of the administrative dissolution. The corporation may then resume carrying on business as if the administrative dissolution had never occurred.

Judicial Dissolution

A **judicial dissolution** is initiated by (1) the state of incorporation, (2) shareholders of the corporation, or (3) creditors of the corporation, and it is accomplished through the court system. When grounds for an involuntary judicial dissolution exist, the attorney general of the state brings an action against the corporation and seeks a decree ordering the dissolution and liquidation of the corporation.

Section 14.30 of the Model Act provides the grounds for a judicial dissolution initiated by (1) the state, (2) the shareholders, or (3) the creditors. Refer to Figure 14–12, which is the full text of Section 14.30. Parts of it have been highlighted by boldface type to emphasize the identity of the entities that may bring an action against the corporation for a judicial dissolution.

Judicial dissolutions instituted by the three types of entities named in the statutes are discussed in the following paragraphs.

State or Attorney General: State-initiated judicial dissolution is probable if the corporation obtained its articles of incorporation through fraudulent means or

Figure 14–12   Section 14.30 of the Model Act

§14.30. **Grounds for Judicial Dissolution.**—The [name or describe court or courts] may dissolve a corporation:

   (1) **in a proceeding by the attorney general** if it is established that:

   (i) the corporation obtained its articles of incorporation through fraud;

   or

   (ii) the corporation has continued to exceed or abuse the authority conferred upon it by law;

   (2) **in a proceeding by a shareholder** if it is established that:

   (i) the directors are deadlocked in the management of the corporate affairs, the shareholders are unable to break the deadlock, and irreparable injury to the corporation is threatened or being suffered, or the business and affairs of the corporation can no longer be conducted to the advantage of the shareholders generally, because of the deadlock;

   (ii) the directors or those in control of the corporation have acted, are acting, or will act in a manner that is illegal, oppressive, or fraudulent;

   (iii) the shareholders are deadlocked in voting power and have failed, for a period that includes at least two consecutive annual meeting dates, to elect successors to directors whose terms have expired; or

   (iv) the corporate assets are being misapplied or wasted;

   (3) **in a proceeding by a creditor** if it is established that:

   (i) the creditor's claim has been reduced to judgment, the execution on the judgment returned unsatisfied, and the corporation is insolvent; or

   (ii) the corporation has admitted in writing that the creditor's claim is due and owing and the corporation is insolvent; or

   (4) **in a proceeding by the corporation** to have its voluntary dissolution continued under court supervision.

the corporation has a history of continually abusing the rights conferred on it by the state.

Shareholders: Under certain circumstances, a corporation may be dissolved by minority shareholders, even though a dissolution generally requires a vote of at least a majority of the shareholders. Minority shareholders may initiate an involuntary judicial dissolution of the corporation in the following cases: (1) the directors are deadlocked, and the effects of that deadlock will cause irreparable harm to the corporation; (2) the directors have acted in an illegal, oppressive, or fraudulent manner; (3) for two consecutive annual meetings, the shareholders are deadlocked in voting to elect directors; or (4) corporate assets have been misapplied or wasted.

Creditors: A corporation may attempt to continue to transact business, although it has many judgments entered against it. Creditors are in an unfortunate position because the corporation is insolvent and unable to satisfy the judgments. The courts, however, can provide creditors some relief. A creditor may force an involuntary dissolution if (1) the creditor's claim has been reduced to a judgment and the corporation is unable to pay on the judgment because it is insolvent or (2) the corporation has admitted in writing that the creditor's claim is due but the corporation is unable to pay because it is insolvent.

The Model Act provides that if the court determines that one or more of the grounds for judicial dissolution exist, the court must issue a decree ordering the dissolution of the corporation. The decree will specify the effective date of the dissolution. After entering the decree of dissolution, the court will order the winding up and liquidation of the corporation's business and affairs.

14–6   Practical Considerations

A corporation's management (the officers and directors) and the corporation's attorneys and accountants generally work closely to determine the procedure for dissolving and liquidating the corporation. The procedure selected is the one most advantageous to the shareholders of the corporation. The paralegal's role in this process can be quite extensive in that the procedures dictated by state statute are often arduous and time-consuming.

The paralegal's role consists primarily of complying with the state statutes. That work includes drafting and preparing all appropriate documents and filing necessary applications and documents. The paralegal may also be responsible for the review and update of the corporation's records to limit any future liability of the corporation.

The following is a list of specific activities for which a paralegal may be responsible:

1. Researching the statutes of the state to determine all document and filing requirements for dissolving a corporation. This research may include a telephone call to the secretary of state to gather additional information and confirm relevant aspects of the statute. It may also include consultation with other paralegals about dissolution and liquidation procedures.
2. Preparing shareholders' and board of directors' resolutions for adoption. This work will include either (1) sending notice of and preparing minutes of the meeting or (2) preparing a written consent.
3. Drafting the plan of liquidation and dissolution.
4. Preparing articles of dissolution for the corporation. Whether the dissolution is before or after the commencement of business determines the exact procedures.

5. Determining if any of the following documents or procedures are required and preparing the proper documentation for each that is required:
   - Tax clearance certificate
   - Clearance certificate
   - Legal advertising
   - Notice to claimants
   - Notice of intention to dissolve
6. Assisting the officers of the corporation in winding up the business and affairs of the corporation.
7. Preparing Form 966, Form of Dissolution and Liquidation, arranging for its execution by an officer of the corporation, and filing it with the Internal Revenue Service.
8. Filing shareholders' and board of directors' meeting minutes or written consents, the articles of incorporation, the certificate of dissolution, and any other corporate documents in the corporation's minute book.
9. Preparing articles of revocation of dissolution and arranging for the execution and filing of those articles. This work will include preparing the necessary shareholder and board of director approvals for the revocation of the dissolution.
10. Calling the secretary of state to determine the procedures for curing a corporation's violation of the state statute. This call will be made after the corporation receives a notice from the secretary of state that the corporation may be administratively dissolved by the state.

SUMMARY

14–1

Dissolution is the cessation or termination of a corporation's legal existence. A dissolution may be either voluntary or involuntary. Liquidating a corporation is the process of selling off the corporation's assets for cash, completing and terminating all corporate contracts and agreements, paying creditors and expenses, and distributing the remaining assets to the shareholders of the corporation. A corporation may liquidate its business without legally dissolving it. As a practical matter, most liquidated corporations dissolve as soon as the liquidation process is complete. The state statutes dictate the procedures for liquidation and dissolution and the order in which they take place.

14–2

A voluntary dissolution is proposed by the board of directors to the shareholders of the corporation, who must approve the dissolution. A corporation may voluntarily dissolve either (1) prior to the corporation's commencement of business or (2) after the corporation's commencement of business. The incorporators or the initial directors approve the dissolution prior to the commencement of business. In both cases, articles of dissolution are filed with the secretary of state of the state of incorporation, and the dissolution is generally effective upon the filing of the articles of dissolution.

14–3

In a voluntary dissolution after the commencement of business, the board of directors submits a proposal for the dissolution of the corporation to the shareholders, who must then approve the dissolution. The shareholders and the board of directors may adopt and approve a plan of liquidation and dissolution, which is an outline of the procedures for winding up and liquidating the business and affairs of the corporation. States differ in many respects in their requirements for dissolving a corporation. They may require any or all of the following: tax clearance or clearance certificates, legal advertisement, notification to creditors of the corporation, and filing of a notice of intent to dissolve.

14–4

The only business that a dissolved corporation may carry on is the liquidation process, which includes the winding up of business and affairs and the fulfilling of previously executed contracts. If the corporation is unable to locate a creditor or shareholder while paying the corporation's debts and distributing the remaining assets to the shareholders, the corporation can deposit cash with the state treasurer for safekeeping until the creditor or shareholder appears or is found. The corporation must file IRS Form 966, Corporate Dissolution or Liquidation, within 30 days of the approval of the dissolution or liquidation by the shareholders. A copy of the resolutions or plan adopted by the shareholders must be attached to that form. At any time prior to the issuance of the certificate of dissolution by the secretary of state, a corporation may revoke the dissolution proceedings. Of course, the shareholders must approve such revocation.

14–5

In an involuntary dissolution, a corporation may be forced to dissolve by the state of incorporation, the shareholders of the corporation, or the creditors of the corporation. Shareholders' and board of directors' approval is not obtained in an involuntary dissolution. There are two types of involuntary dissolutions: administrative dissolution (initiated by the secretary of state) and judicial dissolution (initiated by the state, the shareholders, or the creditors through the court system). In an administrative dissolution, the state may issue a certificate of dissolution on the grounds that the corporation failed to do any of the following: pay franchise tax, file an annual report, maintain a registered office and registered agent, notify the state of a change in registered office or registered agent, or comply with the expiration of the corporation's period of duration. Judicial dissolution may be initiated by one of the following parties: (1) the state, (2) shareholders, or (3) creditors. Grounds for judicial dissolution generally include the corporation's having obtained its articles of incorporation through fraud, the corporation's continued abuse of its authority, shareholder or director deadlock in the control and management of the corporation, misapplication or waste of corporate assets, and a creditor's judgment against the corporation that results in the corporation's insolvency.

14–6

Corporate management and the corporation's attorney and accountant generally work closely in determining the strategy for dissolving and liquidating the corporation. The procedure will be the most advantageous to the shareholders of the corporation. The paralegal's role in this process can be quite extensive in that the procedures are dictated by state statute and vary greatly from state to state.

REVIEW GUIDE

Key Terms

Before proceeding, review the key terms listed below to be sure you understand each one. If necessary, read over the corresponding section of the chapter. When you are ready to test your understanding, answer the review questions.

dissolution (p. 342)
liquidation (p. 342)
voluntary dissolution (p. 343)
articles of dissolution (p. 344)
plan of liquidation and dissolution (p. 347)
tax clearance certificate (p. 349)
clearance certificate (p. 349)
legal advertisement (p. 349)
notice to claimants (p. 349)
notice of intent to dissolve (p. 349)
certificate of dissolution (p. 351)
effective date (p. 351)
Form 966, Corporate Dissolution or Liquidation (p. 352)
revocation of dissolution (p. 354)
articles of revocation of dissolution (p. 354)
involuntary dissolution (p. 355)
administrative dissolution (p. 355)
certificate of reinstatement (p. 355)
judicial dissolution (p. 356)

Questions for Review and Discussion

1. Explain the difference between liquidation and dissolution of a corporation.

2. What are the two types of dissolutions?
3. Under what circumstances may the incorporators or the initial directors approve the dissolution of a corporation?
4. Except in a dissolution prior to the commencement of business, who must *always* approve the dissolution of the corporation?
5. What is the purpose of a plan of liquidation and dissolution?
6. Name three of the many ways in which the filing requirements can differ among the states.
7. What acts of the corporation are involved in the winding up and liquidating of its business?
8. If a corporation is qualified to do business in another state, what is required of the corporation by the foreign state after the shareholders have approved the dissolution of the corporation?
9. What is Form 966 and when must it be filed?
10. Who must approve the corporation's revocation of dissolution?
11. Who may force the corporation to dissolve?
12. Explain the difference between an administrative dissolution and a judicial dissolution, and give examples of each type.

Activities

1. Prepare articles of dissolution for Graham Books, Inc., which was incorporated under the provisions of the Model Act. This corporation has not commenced business and has not issued shares, because its organizers were unsuccessful in obtaining a contract to print books.

2. Visit the law library and locate a book or manual that contains forms and examples of corporate and other legal documents. Locate one or more examples of a plan of liquidation and dissolution. (Examples may be called Plan of Liquidation or Plan of Dissolution.) Compare the examples you find with the sample plan in Figure 14–5 of this chapter, and identify some of the differences, if any.

3. Prepare a checklist of the procedures for dissolving a corporation that has commenced business and has issued shares. Try to be as specific and detailed as possible.

CHAPTER 15 Shareholders' Agreements

OUTLINE

15–1   Closely Held Corporations
15–2   Characteristics of a Shareholders' Agreement
15–3   Share Transfer Restrictions
          Protection of Shareholders' Interests
          Share Certificate Legend
15–4   Procedures for Selling Shares Under a Shareholders' Agreement
          Mandatory Obligation to Purchase and Sell
          Option to Purchase
15–5   Mechanisms for Pricing Shares
15–6   Practical Considerations

APPLICATIONS

Diane and Doug Hastings and Sue and Tom Southwick purchased a landscape and garden center. The Hastings had previously owned a small garden shop and had expertise in landscaping and gardening. The Southwicks provided most of the capital and handled the financial management of the business. To limit their potential liability as owners of the center, the two couples incorporated Genesis Garden Corporation to operate the business.

The Hastings and the Southwicks had successfully operated Genesis Garden Corporation for four years when, on the advice of their respective attorneys, they entered into a shareholders' agreement. The agreement imposed a restriction on the disposition of the shares held by each shareholder, to promote continuity in the management and operation of the corporation. Specifically, a provision of the agreement stated that "the shareholders may not sell, exchange, pledge, encumber, give, devise, or otherwise dispose of, either voluntarily or by operation of law, any of the Stock, whether now owned or hereafter acquired, except as permitted by this Agreement."

After several years of successfully operating the lawn and garden center, the Hastings have decided to sell their shares and retire. You originally assisted in preparing the shareholders agreement for the Hastings and the Southwicks. Your supervising attorney has asked you to evaluate the procedures the Hastings must follow so that they may properly sell their shares. You must report to the attorney before the end of the day.

OBJECTIVES

Drafting a shareholders' agreement is a task likely to be assigned to the corporate paralegal. This chapter is organized to give an overview of the events or reasons that motivate shareholders to enter into an agreement. The components of a shareholders' agreement, illustrated by a sample agreement, are provided and discussed in detail. The requirements for competently drafting a shareholders' agreement are (1) understanding of the goals of the shareholders and the corporation in entering into an agreement and (2) comprehension of the components that make up the agreement. After completing Chapter 15, you will be able to:

1. Distinguish between the publicly held corporation and the closely held corporation.
2. Identify the goals of the shareholders and the corporation in entering into a shareholders' agreement.
3. Explain the major characteristics of a shareholders' agreement.
4. Explain the right of first refusal.
5. Describe the procedures to be followed by a shareholder who receives a bona fide offer.
6. Understand whose interests are to be protected by the shareholders' agreement.
7. Prepare a share certificate that includes the share certificate legend required to be imprinted on it.
8. Distinguish between the option of the corporation and the nonselling shareholders and the mandatory obligation to purchase shares by a selling shareholder.
9. Understand the various mechanisms used to determine the price at which shares may be purchased.
10. Draft a simple shareholders' agreement.

15–1 Closely Held Corporations

Remember from discussions earlier in this book that the corporation is a legal entity separate from its owners (shareholders), managers (directors), and day-to-day personnel (officers and employees). The corporate statutes of the state in which the corporation was incorporated govern its creation, operation, and activities. They also provide for and regulate the rights, duties, and functions of the shareholders, directors, and officers. These statutes, however, have been designed to regulate *all* corporations, including the publicly held corporation and the closely held corporation. Most corporations in the United States are closely held corporations.

The **publicly held corporation** usually conducts a large amount of business and has numerous—sometimes hundreds, thousands, or tens of thousands—shareholders. Its shares are easily transferable in that they are traded on a national securities exchange or over the counter, facilitating a shareholder's ability to purchase and sell shares. Publicly held corporations strictly adhere to the corporate formalities set out in the corporate statutes.

On the other hand, the **closely held corporation** has relatively few shareholders, and many of its shareholders are also directors or officers of the corporation. The shareholders, directors, and officers often work very closely and conduct business without corporate formalities, the shareholders are often related, and profits from the business generally provide a shareholder's only income. Because shares of a closely held corporation are not readily available for purchase or sale publicly—that is, they are not **publicly traded**—it is difficult for the shareholders to purchase and sell shares.

Consider the example of the Hastings and Southwicks, shareholders of Genesis Garden Corporation. The Hastings will have a difficult time selling their shares because there is no public market for shares of this corporation. The benefits of owning shares of a corporation like Genesis Garden Corporation are indirect. Any profit or benefit derived from this corporation is realized in the form of salaries distributed to its officers and employees. In addition, the Southwicks may find it undesirable to operate the business with the persons to whom the Hastings sell their shares.

A corporation that is closely held *may or may not* be incorporated under a state's corporate statutes as a **close corporation.** Remember from the discussion in Chapters 4 and 6 that not all states have adopted statutes that specifically regulate the close corporation. The close corporation enjoys the advantage of a corporation's limited liability status, but its distinguishing characteristic is that the shareholders take an active role in its management. For practical purposes, the close corporation is managed like a partnership, and it may operate without a board of directors. Generally, in all other respects, it is treated as a corporation.

We have begun this chapter about shareholders' agreements with a discussion of the closely held corporation because the shareholders of the closely held corporation are those who most often desire to enter into an agreement among themselves and between themselves and the corporation. In fact, once a corporation becomes publicly held, a shareholders' agreement ceases to be effective. Section 7.32(d) of the Model Act provides that "an agreement authorized by this section shall cease to be effective when shares of the corporation are listed on a national securities exchange or regularly traded in a market maintained by one or more members of a national or affiliated securities association."

The shareholders' agreement addresses the problem of having no public market for the purchase and sale of the shares of the closely held corporation. In addition, the agreement may offer guidance in the management of the corporation, since corporate formalities are often not observed. This chapter examines the characteristics and some examples of a shareholders' agreement that is often entered into by the shareholders of a closely held corporation.

15–2 Characteristics of a Shareholders' Agreement

A **shareholders' agreement**—sometimes referred to as a *stock purchase agreement, restrictive transfer agreement, buy-sell agreement,* or *stock redemption agreement*—is a written agreement entered into by two or more shareholders and, typically, the corporation itself. In most cases, all shareholders and the corporation are parties to the agreement. However, this is not always the case. The corporation *must* be a party to the agreement if it is to be bound by any obligations under the agreement or to be granted certain rights. For example, to preserve the rights of the then-current shareholders, the corporation is usually restricted from selling additional shares of the corporation. If the corporation were free to sell additional shares whenever it desired, the percentage ownership of the shareholders would be diluted.

In certain instances, the shareholders' agreement requires the corporation to repurchase shares of the deceased, insane, bankrupt, or retired shareholder. In addition, the corporation may be required to purchase life insurance on the lives of the shareholders. The insurance proceeds would provide the corporation with the funds to repurchase the shares from the deceased shareholder's estate.

Without the corporation's written agreement to be bound by the shareholders' agreement, the corporation would be free to sell additional shares and would not be bound to fulfill its obligations. The board of directors must approve the corporation's becoming a party to the agreement. Figure 15–1 is an example of resolutions of the board of directors authorizing the corporation to enter into a

**Figure 15–1   Resolutions of Board of Directors Authorizing
                 Shareholders' Agreement**

> RESOLVED, that the officers of the Corporation be, and they hereby are, authorized to execute and deliver the Shareholders' Agreement dated as of November 27, 1994, by and among the Corporation and the shareholders of the Corporation; and FURTHER RESOLVED, that the officers of the Corporation be, and they hereby are, authorized to execute and deliver such other documents and to take such other actions necessary in connection with the Shareholders' Agreement, including, but not limited to, the preparation and delivery of share certificates to the shareholders.

shareholders' agreement and authorizing the officers to execute the agreement on behalf of the corporation.

Most shareholders' agreements restrict (1) the disposition of shares by the shareholders, both during their lifetimes and upon their deaths, and (2) the sale of shares by the corporation. In addition, a shareholders' agreement may also govern certain management aspects of the corporation that deviate from or are inconsistent with statutory requirements. Courts have upheld a closely held corporation's right to flexibility in the management of the corporation. For example, a shareholder of a closely held corporation usually has no readily available market for the sale of his or her shares. Therefore, that shareholder believes that he or she should be able to participate more actively in the management of the corporation. This more active participation can be accomplished by eliminating the board of directors and having the shareholders perform the duties traditionally performed by the directors. This permits the shareholder to protect his or her investment through active participation in the corporation's management. The opinion of the Illinois Supreme Court, discussed in the *Legal Links* in this chapter, p. 371, supports the desires of the shareholders of a closely held corporation.

PARALEGALERT!

Typically, shareholders and the corporation enter into a shareholders' agreement to restrict the sale or transfer of shares of the corporation.

The Model Act identifies instances in which the closely held corporation may operate inconsistently with a state's corporate statutes. Those instances of inconsistency may be covered in a shareholders' agreement. For example, a shareholders' agreement may provide the terms of office of the officers and directors, instead of allowing the terms to be set at the annual meetings of the shareholders and directors.

Section 7.32(a) of the Model Act specifically provides:

   (a) An agreement among the shareholders of a corporation that complies with this section is effective among the shareholders and the corporation even though it is inconsistent with one or more other provisions of this Act in that it:

      (1) eliminates the board of directors or restricts the discretion or powers of the board of directors;

      (2) governs the authorization or making of distributions . . . ;

      (3) establishes who shall be directors or officers of the corporation, or their terms of office or manner of selection or removal;

      (4) governs, in general or in regard to specific matters, the exercise or division of voting power by or between the shareholders and directors . . . ;

      (5) establishes the terms and conditions of any agreement for the transfer or use of property or the provision of services between the corporation and any shareholder, director, officer or employee . . . ;

      (6) transfers to one or more shareholders or other persons all or part of the authority to exercise the corporate powers or to manage the business and affairs of the corporation . . . ;

      (7) requires dissolution of the corporation at the request of one or more of the shareholders or upon the occurrence of a specified event . . . ; or

(8)   otherwise governs the exercise of the corporate powers or the management of the business and affairs of the corporation or the relationship among the shareholders, the directors and the corporation . . . and is not contrary to public policy.

The shareholders of the closely held corporation and the corporation itself may enter into a shareholders' agreement at any time agreed on by those parties. Most frequently, shareholders' agreements are entered into when any one of the following events occurs:

1. Incorporation.
2. Issuance of shares to one or more shareholders subsequent to the date of incorporation.
3. A dispute among the shareholders, which is resolved by the shareholders' agreement.

PARALEGALERT!

A shareholders' agreement may restrict the sale or other disposition of shares by the shareholders. However, the shareholders must be provided a mechanism, or set of procedures, to follow so that they *may* dispose of their shares.

The function of a shareholders' agreement is much like that of a partnership agreement. The partners of a partnership must approve the addition and withdrawal of partners in the partnership. That requirement prevents the partners from doing business with an undesirable or competitive partner. The same holds true for the shareholders of a closely held corporation. As already stated, one purpose of the shareholders' agreement is to restrict the sale or other disposition of shares. However, the agreement may *not* impose an *absolute* prohibition against the sale of shares. A court will not uphold an agreement that contains an absolute restriction on the sale or transfer of shares. In light of this fact, a shareholders' agreement outlines the procedures that must be followed by a shareholder desiring to sell his or her shares. After the selling shareholder has complied with the procedures set forth in the agreement, the selling shareholder is then free to sell the shares to anyone he or she chooses.

Procedures are included in a shareholders' agreement that provide the mechanism for the disposition of shares by a shareholder (1) upon the receipt of an offer from an outside third party or (2) upon the death, insanity, bankruptcy, or retirement of the shareholder. The general restriction in shareholders' agreements prohibits a shareholder from selling or transferring his or her shares without first providing the corporation, the other shareholders, or both with the **option** to purchase the shares—that is, with a chance to purchase them before anyone else is given the opportunity. After this option has been given to the corporation or the other shareholders or both, the selling shareholder is free to sell the shares. Upon the death, insanity, bankruptcy, or retirement of a shareholder, the corporation or the other shareholders usually have a **mandatory obligation** to purchase the shares from the selling shareholder or from the deceased shareholder's estate; that is, they must purchase them.

The shareholders' agreement may contain both the option to purchase shares and the mandatory obligation to purchase the shares, or it may contain only the option or only the mandatory obligation. The desires and needs of the shareholders and the corporation determine when an option is provided and when a mandatory obligation is imposed. We will cover the options and mandatory obligations imposed on the corporation and the shareholders in greater detail in a later section of this chapter.

Figure 15–2 lists the major components of a shareholders' agreement. Note that both the option and the mandatory obligation are included in this list.

Figure 15–2   Components of a Shareholders' Agreement

1. Recitals.
   a. Identification of parties to the agreement.
   b. Reasons the agreement is being entered into.
2. Restrictions on disposition of shares.
   a. Description of the restrictions on the transfer of shares.
   b. Identification of the persons restricted from selling their shares.
   c. Notice (or legend) of the restrictions to be placed on share certificates.
3. Right of first refusal (option) on shares of a shareholder (one of the following).
   a. Granting of first option to the corporation.
   b. Granting of first option to the nonselling shareholders.
4. Purchase and sale of shares upon certain events (mandatory purchase and mandatory sale).
   a. Death of a shareholder.
   b. Bankruptcy or insolvency of a shareholder.
   c. Total disability or insanity of a shareholder.
   d. Termination of shareholder's employment (retirement or dismissal).
5. Procedure for exercise of option, including scheduling of closing.
6. Formula for determining price to be paid per share upon exercise of option or upon mandatory purchase or sale, and method of payment (cash, promissory note, etc.).
7. Miscellaneous.
   a. Insurance.
   b. Notice provisions.
   c. Term of agreement.

Provided in Figure 15–3, pp. 367-370, is an example of a simple shareholders' agreement, which we will refer to throughout the remainder of this chapter.

Figure 15–3   Shareholders' Agreement (through page 370)

Shareholders' Agreement

THIS AGREEMENT is made and dated as of November 27, 1994, by and among Diane Hastings, Douglas Hastings, Suzanne Southwick, and Thomas Southwick, individuals (individually called the "Shareholder" and collectively called the "Shareholders"), and Genesis Garden Corporation, a _____ corporation (the "Corporation").

Recitals

WHEREAS, the Shareholders are the owners of all the issued and outstanding shares of the Corporation's stock (the "Stock"), each Shareholder owning 250 shares of Stock; and

WHEREAS, the Corporation and the Shareholders desire to provide for continuity of harmonious management of the Corporation and to restrict the sale and other disposition of Stock previously or hereafter issued;

NOW, THEREFORE, in consideration of the mutual promises contained herein and for other good and valuable consideration, the parties hereto agree as follows:

Section 1.   *Share Transfer Restrictions*

(a)   The Shareholders may not sell, exchange, pledge, encumber, give, devise, or otherwise dispose of ("transfer"), either voluntarily or by operation of law, any of the Stock, whether now owned or hereafter acquired, except as permitted by this Agreement.

continued

Figure 15–3, continued

(b)   The Corporation shall not cause or permit the sale of any shares of Stock or the transfer of any shares of Stock to be made on its stock books, unless such transfer is permitted in accordance with the provisions of this Agreement.

Section 2.   *Right of First Refusal.* If any Shareholder (the "Selling Shareholder") receives a bona fide offer, whether or not solicited, for the purchase of any Stock, which he or she proposes to accept, the Corporation and then the other Shareholders (the "Nonselling Shareholders") shall have the right to purchase all, but not less than all, shares of the Stock proposed to be sold by the Selling Shareholder, upon and subject to the terms and conditions set forth in this Agreement.

Section 3.   *Price.* The price at which such shares of Stock may be purchased under Section 2 shall be the price contained in such offer. If the price contained in such offer shall consist of consideration other than cash, the cash-equivalent fair market value of such consideration shall be the price at which such shares may be so purchased.

Section 4.   *Notice to the Company and Other Shareholders.* The Selling Shareholder shall furnish to the Corporation and the Nonselling Shareholders written notice of his or her receipt of the offer, together with a copy or summary of the terms of said offer and a statement of the identity of each real party in interest making the offer. In this case, the Corporation, and then the Nonselling Shareholders, shall have the option to purchase all, but not less than all, the Stock proposed to be sold.

Section 5.   *Exercise of Right.* Upon receipt of the offer from the Selling Shareholder, the Corporation shall have 15 days in which to exercise its right of first refusal. If the Corporation fails to exercise its option within 15 days, its right of first refusal terminates. The Nonselling Shareholders shall then have 15 days in which to exercise their first refusal rights, and such rights shall terminate upon the failure of the Nonselling Shareholders to notify the Selling Shareholder of their intention to exercise such rights. A written notice must be delivered to the Selling Shareholder by the Corporation or the Nonselling Shareholders prior to the expiration of the 15-day period in which either party has the right to exercise their first refusal rights.

Section 6.   *Failure to Exercise.* If the Corporation and the Nonselling Shareholders do not exercise their first refusal rights or if there shall be any default in making payment in full for all the Stock to be sold, in accordance with the applicable requirements of this Agreement, the Selling Shareholder may accept the offer referred to in Section 2 hereof and, pursuant thereto, may sell the shares of Stock, so offered to the Corporation and the Nonselling Shareholders, free and clear of all the restrictions, terms, and conditions of this Agreement. If the Selling Shareholder does not accept the bona fide offer within 30 days of the termination of the first refusal rights of the Corporation and the Nonselling Shareholder, the Selling Shareholder may not thereafter transfer any shares without again complying with the provisions of this Agreement.

Section 7.   *Duty to Sell.* The Shareholder shall be obligated to sell his or her Stock under the following circumstances:

(a)   In the event of the death of a Shareholder, the Corporation and then the other Shareholders shall have the right and obligation to purchase all of the deceased Shareholder's shares of Stock at the Stipulated Value, as defined in Section 8 of this Agreement.

(b)   In the event that (i) a proceeding shall have been instituted in a court seeking a decree or order for relief in respect of any Shareholder in any voluntary or involuntary proceeding under any applicable bankruptcy, insolvency, or other similar law now or hereafter in effect, or for the appointment of a receiver, liquidator, assignee, trustee, custodian, or sequestrator (or similar official) for any substantial part of his or her property; (ii) any Shareholder shall fail generally to pay his or her debts as they become due; (iii) the Stock of any Shareholder is attached or garnished; or (iv) any formal action in furtherance of any of the foregoing is commenced or pending; then, the Corporation and then the other Shareholders shall have the right to purchase the shares of Stock from such Shareholder at the Stipulated Value, as defined in Section 8 of this Agreement.

continued

Figure 15–3, continued

(c)   In the event of the total disability of any Shareholder, the Company and then the other Shareholders shall have the right to purchase the shares of Stock from such Shareholder at the Stipulated Value, as defined in Section 8 of this Agreement.

(d)   If any Shareholder separates or is separated from the Corporation's employment for any reason other than death, total disability, or retirement, the Corporation and then the other Shareholders shall have the right to purchase the shares of Stock from such Shareholder at the Stipulated Value, as defined in Section 8 of this Agreement.

To exercise the rights to purchase pursuant to the provisions of this Section 7, the Corporation or the other Shareholders shall deliver written notice of the election not later than the first business day after the expiration of 30 days after the right of purchase shall have accrued, specifying in such notice the number of shares to be purchased and the purchase price of such shares.

Section 8.   *Stipulated Value.* The Stipulated Value shall be determined from time to time by the Board of Directors of the Corporation, taking into consideration whatever factors it deems in good faith to be relevant, in its sole discretion. The Stipulated Value so determined by the Board of Directors shall apply in all circumstances arising under Section 7 of this Agreement, except that in the case of dismissal of the Shareholder from employment by the Corporation on account of his or her infidelity with respect to the Corporation's interests, or willful failure or refusal to perform his or her duties, or gross negligence or recklessness in performance of his or her duties, the price at which the shares of Stock may be purchased shall be 50 percent of the Stipulated Value.

Section 9.   *Share Certificates.* The Shareholders and the Corporation agree that the share certificate or certificates issued from time to time by the Corporation shall bear the following conspicuous legend, such legend to give notice that the shares represented thereby are subject to legal restrictions against transfer and are held under and subject to the terms and provisions of this Agreement:

Notice is hereby given that the shares of stock represented by this certificate are held subject to, and may not be transferred except in accordance with, the provisions of that certain Shareholders' Agreement, dated as of November 27, 1994, between the Corporation and the Shareholders, a copy of which is on file at the registered office of the Corporation, where it may be inspected.

Section 10.   *Insurance.* To fund the purchase of shares of Stock upon the death of a Shareholder pursuant to Section 7(a), the Corporation shall purchase and maintain insurance on the lives of the Shareholders in amounts that, together with the amount of its available cash and resources, will be adequate in the opinion of the Board of Directors of the Corporation to fund its obligations under Section 7(a) of this Agreement. Each Shareholder shall cooperate fully in performing all reasonable requirements of the insurer that are necessary to the issuance of an insurance policy on such Shareholder's life.

Section 11.   *Closings.* The Stock purchase transaction between the parties hereto pursuant to this Agreement shall be consummated at a closing to be held at the principal executive offices of the Corporation on the first business day after the expiration of 30 days after the right of purchase shall have accrued. At the closing, the Corporation or the Nonselling Shareholders shall deliver to the Selling Shareholder the full purchase price, in cash or by certified or bank check, against delivery of the appropriate share certificate(s) endorsed in blank.

Section 12.   *Miscellaneous.*

(a)   This Agreement constitutes the entire agreement of the parties hereto and supersedes all prior agreements, whether oral or written. This Agreement shall be binding upon and shall inure to the benefit of the parties hereto, their heirs, personal representatives, successors, and assignees.

(b)   All notices required to be given or made under this Agreement shall be in writing and shall be deemed given when delivered in person or when mailed by

continued

Figure 15–3, continued

first-class mail, with postage or other charges prepaid, to the parties at the addresses set forth below their signatures to this Agreement, or to such other addresses as the parties hereto may from time to time designate by notice hereunder.

(c)   This Agreement shall not be changed, waived, terminated, or assigned, except by written agreement signed by all parties hereto.

(d)   The term of this Agreement shall expire on November 26, 2004.

(e)   This Agreement has been prepared, negotiated, and delivered in, and shall be construed and enforced in accordance with, the laws of the State of _____.

(f)   This Agreement may be executed in counterparts, in which case all such counterparts shall constitute one and the same agreement.

IN WITNESS WHEREOF, the parties hereto have executed this Shareholders' Agreement this 27th day of November, 1994.

GENESIS GARDEN CORPORATION

By _____
     President

_____
Diane Hastings

_____
Douglas Hastings

_____
Suzanne Southwick

_____
Thomas Southwick

15–3   Share Transfer Restrictions

Limits on the sale, transfer, or other disposition of shares by shareholders of the corporation are called **share transfer restrictions.** These restrictions may be imposed on the shareholders and may be included in any one or all of the following corporate documents: (1) the articles of incorporation, (2) the bylaws, or (3) a shareholders' agreement. For example, Sections 1 through 10 of the shareholders' agreement in Figure 15–3 could also be included within the articles of incorporation or the bylaws of the corporation.

The Model Act permits an agreement among the shareholders to be included in any of these documents. In particular, Section 7.32(b) of the Model Act provides that "an agreement authorized by this section shall be: (1) set forth (A) in the articles of incorporation or bylaws and approved by all persons who are shareholders at the time of the agreement or (B) in a written agreement that is signed by all persons who are shareholders at the time of the agreement."

If share transfer restrictions and the procedures for properly disposing of shares are included in the articles of incorporation or the bylaws, the articles or bylaws must be amended upon any changes in those restrictions or procedures. Any amendment in a shareholders' agreement would require the approval of the shareholders, but an amendment to the articles would require the effort and expense of filing articles of amendment with the secretary of state.

Share transfer restrictions prohibit a shareholder from selling or transferring his or her shares unless certain procedures are followed. Refer to Section 1 of the shareholders' agreement in Figure 15–3. This section is an example of a typical provision restricting the transfer of shares. Note that this section also restricts the corporation from selling additional shares of the corporation.

The share transfer restrictions in Section 1 in Figure 15–3 seem, at first, to be unconditional and absolute. As we have already discussed, share transfer restrictions that are unconditional and absolute would probably not be enforceable in a court of law. Therefore, the shareholders' agreement provides a mechanism whereby any shareholder desiring to sell his or her shares must first offer the shares to the corporation and then to any or all of the other shareholders of the corporation. The right of the corporation or the other shareholders to buy or refuse to buy the shares being offered by the selling shareholder is called the **right of first refusal.**

The right of first refusal may be offered (1) to the corporation only, (2) to the other shareholders only, (3) to the corporation and then to the other shareholders, or (4) to the other shareholders and then to the corporation. Typically, shareholders' agreements provide that if a shareholder receives a **bona fide offer** for the purchase of his or her shares—that is, a legitimate offer made in good faith by a third party—that offer can be accepted only after the shares have first been offered to the corporation. If the corporation declines the offer to purchase the shares, they can then be sold to the person who made the bona fide offer. Refer to Section 2 of the shareholders' agreement in Figure 15–3, which requires the selling shareholder to offer the shares, at the bona fide offer price, first to the corporation and then to the other shareholders. If a shareholder receives a bona fide offer from a purchaser, the **bona fide offer price,** the price in the bona fide offer, is the price at which the corporation or the other shareholders may exercise the right of first refusal.

LEGAL*LINKS*LEGAL*LINKS*LEGAL*LINKS*LEGAL*LINKS*

Galler v. Galler

The shareholders of a closely held corporation believe they have the right to participate in the management of the corporation to a greater degree than the shareholders of a publicly held corporation. The Illinois Supreme Court agreed in *Galler v. Galler*, 32 Ill.2d 16, 203 N.E.2d 577 (1964), in which it stated in part that:

> [S]hareholder agreements . . . are often, as a practical consideration, quite necessary for the protection of those financially interested in the close corporation. While the shareholder of a public-issue corporation may readily sell his shares on the open market should management fail to use, in his opinion, sound business judgment, his counterpart of the close corporation often has a large total of his entire capital invested in the business and has no ready market for his shares should he desire to sell. He feels, understandably, that he is more than a mere investor and that his voice should be heard concerning all corporate activity. Without a shareholder agreement, specifically enforceable by the courts, insuring him a modicum of control, a large minority shareholder might find himself at the mercy of an oppressive or unknowledgeable majority. . . . [T]he shareholders of a close corporation are often also the directors and officers thereof. With substantial shareholding interests abiding in each member of the board of directors, it is often quite impossible to secure, as in the large public-issue corporation, independent board judgment free from personal motivations concerning corporate policy. For these and other reasons . . . , the only sound basis for protection is afforded by a lengthy, detailed shareholder agreement.

The shareholder may or may not have solicited the offer from the outside party. Often a bona fide offer is difficult to obtain. An outside party who knows that a shareholders' agreement exists generally does not want to wait to purchase the shares while the selling shareholder complies with the terms and conditions of the shareholders' agreement.

Protection of Shareholders' Interests

Share transfer restrictions are intended to discourage the sale of a corporation's shares to outsiders, thereby protecting the interests of the shareholders remaining after the sale of shares. Let's use the example of the Hastings and Southwicks. When those parties incorporated their business and subsequently entered into a shareholders' agreement, their intention was, in all likelihood, to continue to do business with each other until they all mutually agreed to terminate the business. However, the Hastings now want to sell their shares and retire. The Southwicks are left with the choice of exercising their right of first refusal or allowing the Hastings to sell their shares to whomever the Hastings find as a buyer.

Although in the Hastings-Southwick example all the shareholders hold equal interests in the corporation, share transfer restrictions are also intended to protect the interests of both majority and minority shareholders in corporations in which the shares are not equally distributed.

Shareholders owning a majority of the shares of a corporation essentially control all decisions concerning the management and operation of the corporation. That control could prove unfavorable to the minority shareholders. Because control of the corporation generally rests with the majority shareholders, they are more likely to find purchasers for their shares. In addition, the sale of the majority shareholders' interests could also result in the dismissal of any minority shareholder who is also an officer or employee of the corporation. The majority shareholders may also decide to eliminate or curtail the issuance of dividends, upon which the minority shareholder may have relied heavily for income. The cumulative effect of these possibilities could make the shares of the minority shareholders worthless. Therefore, the share transfer restrictions imposed on all shareholders, majority and minority, can be a valuable asset.

The majority shareholders also have an interest to protect, so they welcome the imposition of share transfer restrictions. Minority shareholders must also be restricted from selling their shares to an unfriendly buyer, possibly a competitor of the majority shareholders and the corporation. Share transfer restrictions require the minority shareholders to offer their shares first to the corporation or the other shareholders or both before selling them to outside third parties. The restrictions provide the majority shareholders some comfort in that the minority shareholders cannot sell their shares to a competitor or adversary of the corporation.

PARALEGALERT!

Both the majority shareholders and the minority shareholders have interests to protect by imposing share transfer restrictions on all shareholders.

Share Certificate Legend

The shareholders' agreement generally includes a provision that requires the corporation to imprint a legend (or statement) on each share certificate issued by the corporation. The purpose of the legend is to notify any potential purchaser of the shares that an agreement is in effect and that such agreement imposes certain restrictions on the transfer of the shares. The legend is usually called a **share certificate legend.**

The Model Act requires the share certificate to be imprinted with a legend. Section 7.32(c) of the Model Act requires that "the existence of an agreement authorized by this section shall be noted conspicuously on the front or back of each certificate for outstanding shares."

Figure 15–4 is a share certificate on which is imprinted the legend required under Section 9 of the shareholders' agreement in Figure 15–3. Compare the language imprinted on the share certificate with the provisions of Section 9 of the shareholders' agreement in Figure 15–3, p. 369.

If the corporation fails to imprint the share certificate with the legend that identifies the existence of a shareholders' agreement, the agreement and any action taken pursuant to the agreement will still be held to be valid. However, a purchaser of shares who, at the time of purchase of the shares, did not know of the existence of the shareholders' agreement may rescind the purchase of the shares. According to Section 7.32(c) of the Model Act, a purchaser who desires to rescind a purchase, based on the corporation's failure to imprint the legend, must commence the action "within the earlier of 90 days after discovery of the existence of the agreement or two years after the time of purchase of the shares."

15–4 Procedures for Selling Shares Under a Shareholders' Agreement

The mandatory obligation and option provisions in a shareholders' agreement can vary greatly, depending on the desires of the parties to the agreement. Generally, agreements may provide that:

1. The corporation or the shareholders or both have a *mandatory obligation to purchase* from a shareholder.
2. A shareholder has a *mandatory obligation to sell* to the corporation or to the other shareholders.
3. The corporation or the shareholders or both have an *option to purchase* from a shareholder.

Mandatory Obligation to Purchase and Sell

A mandatory obligation to purchase or sell shares is usually imposed only upon the happening of specific events. Those events include the death, total disability, bankruptcy or insolvency, or termination from employment of the shareholder. For example, upon the termination of an employee who is also a shareholder of the corporation, the corporation or the other shareholders or both may be *obligated* to purchase shares held by the terminated employee. In the same circumstances, the terminated employee would be obligated to sell his or her shares to the corporation. This mandatory obligation is also imposed when the shareholder dies, becomes totally disabled, or becomes bankrupt or insolvent.

A minority shareholder of a corporation should insist that the corporation be obligated to purchase the shares upon his or her death. That obligation provides the deceased shareholder's beneficiaries some comfort because they receive a cash distribution from the ownership of the shares. The beneficiaries would not want to be left owning shares of stock that were not marketable or tradeable. In addition, often a salary is paid in lieu of dividends to a shareholder who is an employee. In this case, a deceased shareholder's beneficiaries could not enjoy the benefit of the issuance of dividends if they continued to hold the shares. It is for these reasons that the corporation is usually obligated to purchase shares from a deceased shareholder's estate.

Figure 15–4 Share Certificate with Legend

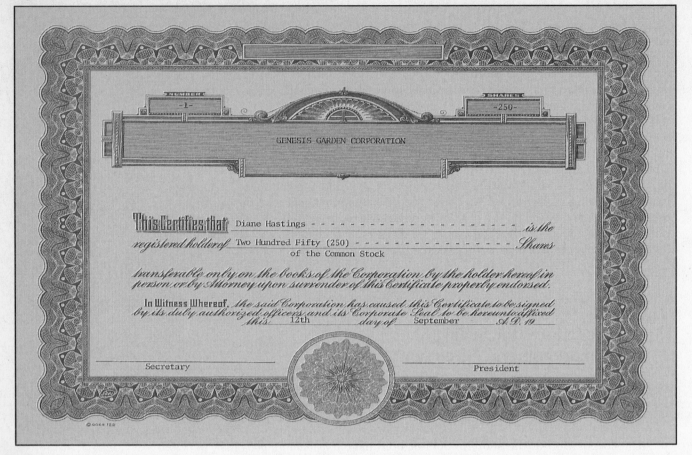

Figure 15–4 used with permission of Goes Lithographing Company of Chicago. All rights reserved.

Shareholders' agreements frequently treat the death of a shareholder in a separate provision as follows: (1) the corporation is obligated to purchase the shares from the deceased shareholders' estate, and (2) the deceased shareholder's estate is obligated to sell the shares to the corporation. Note that this provision places the mandatory obligation on both the deceased shareholder's estate and the corporation. The agreement may also obligate the other shareholders to purchase the deceased shareholder's shares in the event that the corporation does not desire or is unable to purchase the shares. As previously discussed, when the corporation has the obligation to purchase the deceased shareholder's shares, the corporation purchases life insurance on the lives of the shareholders. The insurance provides the cash necessary to purchase the shares. As an example, refer to Section 7(a) of the agreement in Figure 15–3. This provides that the corporation *and then* the other shareholders have the *obligation* to purchase all of the deceased shareholder's shares.

The price at which shares are purchased in the circumstances discussed in this section—mandatory obligation and option—are predetermined and set in the shareholders' agreement.

Option to Purchase

The *option* to purchase shares is usually provided to the corporation or the other shareholders by a shareholder who wishes to sell his or her shares. In some cases, the corporation or the other shareholders have an option, rather than an obligation,

Figure 15–4, continued

Notice is hereby given that the shares of stock represented by this certificate are held subject to, and may not be transferred except in accordance with, the provisions of that certain Shareholders' Agreement, dated November 27, 1994, between the Corporation and the Shareholders, a copy of which is on file at the registered office of the Corporation, where it may be inspected.

For Value Received, _____ hereby sell, assign and transfer
unto _____
_____ Shares
represented by the within Certificate, and do hereby
irrevocably constitute and appoint
_____ Attorney
to transfer the said Shares on the books of the within named
Corporation with full power of substitution in the premises.
Dated _____ 19___
    In presence of
_____   _____

Back

to purchase the shares of a deceased shareholder or a shareholder who is disabled, is bankrupt or insolvent, or has been terminated from employment. However, under these circumstances, the corporation or the other shareholders may have a mandatory obligation to purchase the shares.

15–5 Mechanisms for Pricing Shares

One of the greatest difficulties with shareholders' agreements is determining the price at which shares are to be purchased, whether an option is being exercised or a mandatory obligation is being enforced. As we have just discussed, a shareholders' agreement generally provides an option or imposes a mandatory obligation on the corporation or the other shareholders or both to purchase shares from a shareholder under certain circumstances. The circumstances provided in the sample shareholders' agreement in Figure 15–3 include (1) death of a shareholder, (2) bankruptcy or insolvency of a shareholder, (3) total disability or insanity of a shareholder, and (4) termination of employment of a shareholder. These circumstances are typical of those that activate the option or mandatory obligation of the corporation or the other shareholders to purchase the shares.

In these circumstances, how much should the shareholder (or the deceased shareholder's estate) be paid for his or her shares?

Whatever pricing mechanism is chosen, the parties to the shareholders' agreement determine that mechanism, and it is specifically defined in the shareholders' agreement. One method that is virtually impossible to use is the market value of the shares. Because shares of the closely held corporation have no market, the market value is indeterminable. However, in lieu of setting a specific price for the shares, a formula is usually specified in the agreement. That formula will be used to calculate a price for the shares.

The different pricing mechanisms or formulas used to set the price of shares include the following:

1. **Stipulated value**—The stipulated value method is used in Section 8 of our sample shareholders' agreement in Figure 15–3 and is probably the only one of the mechanisms described here that does not fall into the category of a formula.

   Using this method, the board of directors uses its best judgment to establish from time to time, generally annually, the price at which shares may be purchased by the corporation or the other shareholders. Note that this section reduces the stipulated value by 50 percent in the case of the shareholder who is also an officer or employee of the corporation and who willfully fails or refuses to perform his or her duties on behalf of the corporation. The stipulated value and any adjustment to that value are set and changed at the sole discretion of the board of directors. A problem arises with this pricing mechanism when the board of directors fails to set the value annually or semiannually, at whatever interval was agreed on in the shareholders' agreement. Years may have gone by without the board setting the stipulated value, and the deceased shareholder's estate or the terminated shareholder-employee is bound by the stipulated value last set by the board of directors.

2. **Book value**—Book value is determined by dividing the corporation's net worth (assets minus liabilities) by the total number of outstanding shares of the corporation. Care must be taken when using this method, as accounting procedures used by corporations can vary.

3. **Asset appraisal**—The asset appraisal method for determining the price of shares can be utilized in one of a couple of ways. Each party to the agreement can select an appraiser, and if the two appraisers cannot agree, the parties can select a third appraiser, whose determination will be final and binding on the parties. In the alternative, an average can be taken of the two appraisals, and that average can be deemed to be the stock's fair market value. The primary reason for using appraisers is the independent review they can conduct of the corporation.

4. **Capitalization of earnings**—Determining value by capitalizing the corporation's earnings is only fair for use in corporations whose earnings are fairly stable. The average of the earnings per share of the corporation over a specified period of time (usually three years) is calculated, and the value of the shares is based on the figure so derived.

As previously mentioned, the bona fide offer price is the price the corporation and the other shareholders must pay to purchase shares when exercising their right of first refusal. Generally, shareholders' agreements provide that when a bona fide offer is made by a third party, the bona fide offer price becomes the amount that the corporation or the other shareholders must pay for the shares. Review Section 3 of the shareholders' agreement in Figure 15–3. Note that this section provides that the price at which shares may be purchased in exercise of the right of first refusal is the price contained in the bona fide offer.

15–6   Practical Considerations

Drafting the shareholders' agreement can be one of the most rewarding responsibilities for the corporate paralegal. Drafting the agreement requires thought, imagination, and ingenuity because of the variety of provisions and options that can be contained in an agreement.

It is important that we discuss here again as we have in previous chapters, that models or forms of agreements, including shareholders' agreements, can be found in forms books and files retained in your firm's or office's library or central filing location. In addition, your local law library maintains books, manuals, and loose-leaf publications which contain forms of agreements. When you are asked to draft a shareholders' agreement, use your imagination and ingenuity in locating forms of agreements and specific provisions of agreements to use in preparing a draft of a shareholders' agreement. You should also make inquiries of the attorneys and paralegals in your office or call your paralegal colleagues working as corporate paralegals and review other client files in your office for forms of shareholders' agreements previously prepared by other attorneys and paralegals.

SUMMARY

15–1

Corporate statutes are designed to regulate both the publicly held corporation and the closely held corporation. The publicly held corporation usually has hundreds, thousands, or tens of thousands of shareholders, and its shares are freely transferable. Because the shares are traded on a national securities exchange or over the counter, the shareholders' ability to purchase and sell shares is facilitated. The closely held corporation has relatively few shareholders, and many of them are also directors or officers of the corporation, who usually conduct business without corporate formalities. Because shares of a closely held corporation are not readily available for purchase or sale, it is difficult for the shareholders to purchase and sell shares. A closely held corporation may or may not be a close corporation, which is managed like a partnership and operates without a board of directors.

15–2

A shareholders' agreement is a written agreement entered into by two or more shareholders and the corporation itself. It provides restrictions on the disposition of shares by the shareholders, both during their lifetimes and upon their deaths, and on the sale of shares by the corporation. The shareholders' agreement usually governs certain management aspects of the corporation. A court will not enforce an absolute restriction on the transfer of a corporation's shares. Agreements are usually entered into upon (1) incorporation, (2) the issuance of shares subsequent to incorporation, or (3) the resolution of a dispute among the shareholders. A typical shareholders' agreement includes procedures for the disposition of shares by a shareholder upon his or her death, disability, bankruptcy or insolvency, retirement, or termination of employment. The shareholders' agreement may contain both the option and the mandatory obligation to purchase shares or may contain only the option or only the mandatory obligation. Usually, both the

corporation and the shareholders are parties to the agreement. The board of directors must approve the action of the corporation if it is to be a party to the agreement.

15–3

Share transfer restrictions are limitations of the sale, transfer, or other disposition of shares by shareholders of the corporation. These restrictions are typically found in a shareholders' agreement, but they may be included in the articles of incorporation or the bylaws. Because share transfer restrictions cannot be absolute and unconditional, the corporation or the other shareholders or both have the right to purchase or refuse to purchase the shares that a shareholder wants to sell. The interests of both the majority and the minority shareholders are protected by the restrictions imposed in a shareholders' agreement. The agreement usually requires the corporation to imprint a share certificate legend on each certificate. The legend gives notice of the existence of a shareholders' agreement.

15–4

The mandatory obligation and option provisions in a shareholders' agreement can vary depending on the desires of the parties to the agreement. A shareholders' agreement will generally provide (1) the obligation of the corporation or the shareholders to purchase from a shareholder, (2) the obligation of the shareholder to sell to the corporation or the other shareholders or both, and (3) the option of the corporation or the shareholders or both to purchase from a shareholder. The mandatory obligation to purchase or sell and the option to purchase usually come into play only upon the happening of specific events, such as the death, disability, termination from employment, or bankruptcy or insolvency of a shareholder.

15–5

Determining the price at which shares may be purchased from the shareholders is difficult. Pricing methods include stipulated value, book value, asset appraisal, and capitalization of earnings. If a shareholder receives a bona fide offer, the price offered by the third party—the bona fide offer price—is the price to be paid by the corporation or the other shareholders.

15–6

Drafting shareholders' agreements requires thought, imagination, and ingenuity because of the variety of provisions and options that can be included in an agreement.

REVIEW GUIDE

Key Terms

Before proceeding, review the key terms listed below to be sure you understand each one. If necessary, read over the corresponding section of the chapter. When you are ready to test your understanding, answer the review questions.

publicly held corporation (p. 363)
closely held corporation (p. 363)
publicly traded (p. 363)
close corporation (p. 364)
shareholders' agreement (p. 364)
option (p. 366)
mandatory obligation (p. 366)
share transfer restrictions (p. 370)
right of first refusal (p. 371)
bona fide offer (p. 371)
bona fide offer price (p. 371)
share certificate legend (p. 372)
stipulated value (p. 376)
book value (p. 376)
asset appraisal (p. 376)
capitalization of earnings (p. 376)

Questions for Review and Discussion

1. What are the differences between the publicly held corporation and the closely held corporation?
2. Explain in detail the reasons shareholders would want to enter into a shareholders' agreement.
3. Must the corporation be party to a shareholders' agreement? Why or why not?
4. What is the corporation's and shareholders' right of first refusal?
5. Review the form of shareholders' agreement in Figure 15–3. Considering the information in the agreement and the information provided in this chapter, determine whether this agreement was entered into upon the incorporation of Genesis Garden Corporation or at some time after its incorporation. Explain your answer.
6. How would a potential purchaser of shares of a corporation know whether a shareholders' agreement existed?
7. Under what circumstances does the corporation or the other shareholders have the option to purchase shares?
8. When does the corporation or the other shareholders have a mandatory obligation to purchase shares?
9. How is the bona fide offer price determined?
10. What is the flaw in the stipulated value method of determining the price at which shares are to be purchased?

Activities

1. Draft a provision of a shareholders' agreement that provides for the right of first refusal to the corporation exclusively.
2. Visit the law library and review various forms of shareholder's agreements. Note the various ways in which different forms treat the obligations and options of the corporation upon the death of a shareholder.
3. Draft a resolution or resolutions of the board of directors approving the execution and delivery by the corporation of the shareholders' agreement in the example in Figure 15–3. Explain the two ways in which the resolution or resolutions you drafted may be adopted by the board of directors.

APPENDIX A Model Business Corporation Act (1984)

Approved by the Committee on
Corporate Laws (Section of
Business Law)
of the
American Bar Association

Chapter 1. General provisions

Subchapter A. Short title and reservation of power
§ 1.01. Short title
1.02. Reservation of power to amend or repeal

Subchapter B. Filing documents
§ 1.20. Filing requirements
1.21. Forms
1.22. Filing, service, and copying fees
1.23. Effective time and date of filing
1.24. Correcting filed document
1.25. Filing duty of secretary of state
1.26. Appeal from secretary of state's refusal to file document
1.27. Evidentiary effect of copy of filed document
1.28. Certificate of existence
1.29. Penalty for signing false document

Subchapter C. Secretary of State
§ 1.30. Powers

Subchapter D. Definitions
§ 1.40. Act definitions
1.41. Notice
1.42. Number of shareholders

Chapter 2. Incorporation

§ 2.01. Incorporators
2.02. Articles of incorporation
2.03. Incorporation
2.04. Liability for preincorporation transactions
2.05. Organization of corporation
2.06. Bylaws
2.07. Emergency bylaws

Chapter 3. Purposes and powers

§ 3.01. Purposes
3.02. General powers
3.03. Emergency powers
3.04. Ultra vires

Chapter 4. Name

§ 4.01. Corporate name
4.02. Reserved name
4.03. Registered name

Chapter 5. Office and agent

§ 5.01. Registered office and registered agent
5.02. Change of registered office or registered agent
5.03. Resignation of registered agent
5.04. Service on corporation

Chapter 6. Shares and distributions

Subchapter A. Shares
§ 6.01. Authorized shares
6.02. Terms of class or series determined by board of directors
6.03. Issued and outstanding shares
6.04. Fractional shares

Subchapter B. Issuance of shares
§ 6.20. Subscription for shares before incorporation
6.21. Issuance of shares
6.22. Liability of shareholders
6.23. Share dividends
6.24. Share options
6.25. Form and content of certificates
6.26. Shares without certificates
6.27. Restriction on transfer or registration of shares or other securities
6.28. Expense of issue

Subchapter C. Subsequent acquisition of shares by shareholders and corporation
§ 6.30. Shareholders' preemptive rights
6.31. Corporation's acquisition of own shares

Subchapter D. Distributions
§ 6.40. Distributions to shareholders

Chapter 7. Shareholders

Subchapter A. Meetings
§ 7.01. Annual meeting
7.02. Special meeting
7.03. Court-ordered meeting
7.04. Action without meeting
7.05. Notice of meeting
7.06. Waiver of notice
7.07. Record date

Subchapter B. Voting
§ 7.20. Shareholders' list for meeting
7.21. Voting entitlement of shares
7.22. Proxies
7.23. Shares held by nominees
7.24. Corporation's acceptance of votes
7.25. Quorum and voting requirements for voting groups
7.26. Action by single and multiple voting groups
7.27. Greater quorum or voting requirements
7.28. Voting for directors; cumulative voting

Subchapter C. Voting trusts and agreements
§ 7.30. Voting trusts
7.31. Voting agreements
7.32. Shareholder Agreements

Subchapter D. Derivative proceedings
7.40. Subchapter definitions
7.41. Standing
7.42. Demand
7.43. Stay of proceedings
7.44. Dismissal
7.45. Discontinuance or settlement
7.46. Payment of expenses
7.47. Applicability to foreign corporations

Chapter 8. Directors and Officers

Subchapter A. Board of directors
§ 8.01. Requirement for and duties of board of directors
8.02. Qualifications of directors
8.03. Number and election of directors
8.04. Election of directors by certain classes of shareholders
8.05. Terms of directors generally
8.06. Staggered terms for directors
8.07. Resignation of directors
8.08. Removal of directors by shareholders
8.09. Removal of directors by judicial proceeding
8.10. Vacancy on board
8.11. Compensation of directors

Subchapter B. Meetings and action of board of directors
§ 8.20. Meetings
8.21. Action without meeting
8.22. Notice of meeting
8.23. Waiver of notice

8.24. Quorum and voting
8.25. Committees
Subchapter C. Standards of conduct
§ 8.30. General standards for directors
8.31. Director or officer conflict of interest
8.32. Loans to directors
8.33. Liability for unlawful distributions
Subchapter D. Officers
§ 8.40. Required officers
8.41. Duties of officers
8.42. Standards of conduct for officers
8.43. Resignation and removal of officers
8.44. Contract rights of officers
Subchapter E. Indemnification
§ 8.50. Subchapter definitions
8.51. Authority to indemnify
8.52. Mandatory indemnification
8.53. Advance for expenses
8.54. Court-ordered indemnification
8.55. Determination and authorization of indemnification
8.56. Indemnification of officers, employees, and agents
8.57. Insurance
8.58. Application of subchapter
Subchapter F. Directors' conflicting interest transactions
§ 8.60. Subchapter definitions
8.61. Judicial action
8.62. Directors' action
8.63. Shareholders' action

Chapter 9. [Reserved]

Chapter 10. Amendment of articles of incorporation and bylaws
Subchapter A. Amendment of articles of incorporation
§ 10.01. Authority to amend
10.02. Amendment by board of directors
10.03. Amendment by board of directors and shareholders
10.04. Voting on amendments by voting groups
10.05. Amendment before issuance of shares
10.06. Articles of amendment
10.07. Restated articles of incorporation
10.08. Amendment pursuant to reorganization
10.09. Effect of amendment
Subchapter B. Amendment of bylaws
§ 10.20. Amendment by board of directors or shareholders
10.21. Bylaw increasing quorum or voting requirement for shareholders
10.22. Bylaw increasing quorum or voting requirement for directors

Chapter 11. Merger and share exchange
§ 11.01. Merger
11.02. Share exchange
11.03. Action on plan
11.04. Merger of subsidiary
11.05. Articles of merger or share exchange
11.06. Effect of merger or share exchange
11.07. Merger or share exchange with foreign corporation

Chapter 12. Sale of assets
§ 12.01. Sale of assets in regular course of business and mortgage of assets
12.02. Sale of assets other than in regular course of business

Chapter 13. Dissenters' rights
Subchapter A. Right to dissent and obtain payment for shares
§ 13.01. Definitions
13.02. Right to dissent
13.03. Dissent by nominees and beneficial owners
Subchapter B. Procedure for exercise of dissenters' rights
§ 13.20. Notice of dissenters' rights
13.21. Notice of intent to demand payment
13.22. Dissenters' notice
13.23. Duty to demand payment
13.24. Share restrictions
13.25. Payment
13.26. Failure to take action
13.27. After-acquired shares
13.28. Procedure if shareholder dissatisfied with payment or offer
Subchapter C. Judicial appraisal of shares
§ 13.30. Court action
13.31. Court costs and counsel fees

Chapter 14. Dissolution
Subchapter A. Voluntary dissolution
§ 14.01. Dissolution by incorporators or initial directors
14.02. Dissolution by board of directors and shareholders
14.03. Articles of dissolution
14.04. Revocation of dissolution

14.05. Effect of dissolution
14.06. Known claims against dissolved corporation
14.07. Unknown claims against dissolved corporation
Subchapter B. Administrative dissolution
§ 14.20. Grounds for administrative dissolution
14.21. Procedure for and effect of administrative dissolution
14.22. Reinstatement following administrative dissolution
14.23. Appeal from denial of reinstatement
Subchapter C. Judicial dissolution
§ 14.30. Grounds for judicial dissolution
14.31. Procedure for judicial dissolution
14.32. Receivership or custodianship
14.33. Decree of dissolution
14.34. Election to purchase in lieu of dissolution
Subchapter D. Miscellaneous
§ 14.40. Deposit with state treasurer

Chapter 15. Foreign corporations
Subchapter A. Certificate of authority
§ 15.01. Authority to transact business required
15.02. Consequences of transacting business without authority
15.03. Application for certificate of authority
15.04. Amended certificate of authority
15.05. Effect of certificate of authority
15.06. Corporate name of foreign corporation
15.07. Registered office and registered agent of foreign corporation
15.08. Change of registered office or registered agent of foreign corporation
15.09. Resignation of registered agent of foreign corporation
15.10. Service on foreign corporation
Subchapter B. Withdrawal
§ 15.20. Withdrawal of foreign corporation
Subchapter C. Revocation of certificate of authority
§ 15.30. Grounds for revocation
15.31. Procedure for and effect of revocation
15.32. Appeal from revocation

Chapter 16. Records and reports
Subchapter A. Records
§ 16.01. Corporate records
16.02. Inspection of records by shareholders
16.03. Scope of inspection right
16.04. Court-ordered inspection
Subchapter B. Reports
§ 16.20. Financial statements for shareholders
16.21. Other reports to shareholders
16.22. Annual report for secretary of state

Chapter 17. Transition provisions
§ 17.01. Application to existing domestic corporations
17.02. Application to qualified foreign corporations
17.03. Saving provisions
17.04. Severability
17.05. Repeal
17.06. Effective date

CHAPTER 1. GENERAL PROVISIONS

Subchapter A. Short Title and Reservation of Power

§ 1.01. **Short Title.**—This Act shall be known and may be cited as the "[name of state] Business Corporation Act."

§ 1.02. **Reservation of Power to Amend or Repeal.**—The [name of state legislature] has power to amend or repeal all or part of this Act at any time and all domestic and foreign corporations subject to this Act are governed by the amendment or repeal.

Subchapter B. Filing Documents

§ 1.20. **Filing Requirements.**—

(a) A document must satisfy the requirements of this section, and of any other section that adds to or varies these requirements, to be entitled to filing by the secretary of state.

(b) This Act must require or permit filing the document in the office of the secretary of state.

(c) The document must contain the information required by this Act. It may contain other information as well.

(d) The document must be typewritten or printed.

(e) The document must be in the English language. A corporate name need not be in English if written in English letters or Arabic or Roman numerals, and the certificate of existence required of foreign corporations need not be in English if accompanied by a reasonably authenticated English translation.

(f) The document must be executed:

(1) by the chairman of the board of directors of a domestic or foreign corporation, by its president, or by another of its officers;

(2) if directors have not been selected or the corporation has not been formed, by an incorporator; or

(3) if the corporation is in the hands of a receiver, trustee, or other court-appointed fiduciary, by that fiduciary.

(g) The person executing the document shall sign it and state beneath or opposite his signature his name and the capacity in which he signs. The document may but need not contain: (1) the corporate seal, (2) an attestation by the secretary or an assistant secretary, (3) an acknowledgement, verification, or proof.

(h) If the secretary of state has prescribed a mandatory form for the document under section 1.21, the document must be in or on the prescribed form.

(i) The document must be delivered to the office of the secretary of state for filing and must be accompanied by one exact or conformed copy (except as provided in sections 5.03 and 15.09), the correct filing fee, and any franchise tax, license fee, or penalty required by this Act or other law.

§ 1.21. Forms.—

(a) The secretary of state may prescribe and furnish on request forms for: (1) an application for a certificate of existence, (2) a foreign corporation's application for a certificate of authority to transact business in this state, (3) a foreign corporation's application for a certificate of withdrawal, and (4) the annual report. If the secretary of state so requires, use of these forms is mandatory.

(b) The secretary of state may prescribe and furnish on request forms for other documents required or permitted to be filed by this Act but their use is not mandatory.

§ 1.22. Filing, Service, and Copying Fees.—

(a) The secretary of state shall collect the following fees when the documents described in this subsection are delivered to him for filing:

Document	Fee
(1) Articles of incorporation	$ _____ .
(2) Application for use of indistinguishable name	$ _____ .
(3) Application for reserved name	$ _____ .
(4) Notice of transfer of reserved name	$ _____ .
(5) Application for registered name	$ _____ .
(6) Application for renewal of registered name	$ _____ .
(7) Corporation's statement of change of registered agent or registered office or both	$ _____ .
(8) Agent's statement of change of registered office for each affected corporation	$ _____ ,
not to exceed a total of	$ _____ .
(9) Agent's statement of resignation	No fee.
(10) Amendment of articles of incorporation	$ _____ .
(11) Restatement of articles of incorporation with amendment of articles	$ _____ ,
(12) Articles of merger or share exchange	$ _____ .
(13) Articles of dissolution	$ _____ .
(14) Articles of revocation of dissolution	$ _____ .
(15) Certificate of administrative dissolution	No fee.
(16) Application for reinstatement following administrative dissolution	$ _____ .
(17) Certificate of reinstatement	No fee.
(18) Certificate of judicial dissolution	No fee.
(19) Application for certificate of authority	$ _____ .
(20) Application for amended certificate of authority	$ _____ .
(21) Application for certificate of withdrawal	$ _____ .
(22) Certificate of revocation of authority to transact business	No fee.
(23) Annual report	$ _____ .
(24) Articles of correction	$ _____ .
(25) Application for certificate of existence or authorization	$ _____ .
(26) Any other document required or permitted to be filed by this Act.	$ _____ .

(b) The secretary of state shall collect a fee of $_____ each time process is served on him under this Act. The party to a proceeding causing service of process is entitled to recover this fee as costs if he prevails in the proceeding.

(c) The secretary of state shall collect the following fees for copying and certifying the copy of any filed document relating to a domestic or foreign corporation:

(1) $_____ a page for copying; and

(2) $_____ for the certificate.

§ 1.23. Effective Time and Date of Document.—

(a) Except as provided in subsection (b) and section 1.24(c), a document accepted for filing is effective:

(1) at the time of filing on the date it is filed, as evidenced by the secreatary of state's date and time endorsement on the original document; or

(2) at the time specified in the document as its effective time on the date it is filed.

(b) A document may specify a delayed effective time and date, and if it does so the document beomes effective at the time and date specified. If a delayed effective date but no time is specified, the document is effective at the close of business on that date. A delayed effective date for a document may not be later than the 90th day after the date it is filed.

§ 1.24. Correcting Filed Document.—

(a) A domestic or foreign corporation may correct a document filed by the secretary of state if the document (1) contains an incorrect statement or (2) was defectively executed, attested, sealed, verified, or acknowledged.

(b) A document is corrected:

(1) by preparing articles of correction that (i) describe the document (including its filing date) or attach a copy of it to the articles, (ii) specify the incorrect statement and the reason it is incorrect or the manner in which the execution was defective, and (iii) correct the incorrect statement or defective execution; and

(2) by delivering the articles to the secretary of state for filing.

(c) Articles of correction are effective on the effective date of the document they correct except as to persons relying on the uncorrected document and adversely affected by the correction. As to those persons, articles of correction are effective when filed.

§ 1.25. Filing Duty of Secretary of State.—

(a) If a document delivered to the office of the secretary of state for filing satisfies the requirements of section 1.20, the secretary of state shall file it.

(b) The secretary of state files a document by stamping or otherwise endorsing "Filed," together with his name and official title and the date and time of receipt, on both the original and the document copy and on the receipt for the filing fee. After filing a document, except as provided in sections 5.03 and 15.10, the secretary of state shall deliver the document copy, with the filing fee receipt (or acknowledgement of receipt if no fee is required) attached, to the domestic or foreign corporation or its representative.

(c) If the secretary of state refuses to file a document, he shall return it to the domestic or foreign corporation or its representative within five days after the document was delivered, together with a brief, written explanation of the reason for his refusal.

(d) The secretary of state's duty to file documents under this section is ministerial. His filing or refusing to file a document does not:

(1) affect the validity or invalidity of the document in whole or part;

(2) relate to the correctness or incorrectness of information contained in the document;

(3) create a presumption that the document is valid or invalid or that information contained in the document is correct or incorrect.

§ 1.26. Appeal from Secretary of State's Refusal to File Document.—

(a) If the secretary of state refuses to file a document delivered to his office for filing, the domestic or foreign corporation may appeal the refusal within 30 days after the return of the document to the [name or describe] court [of the country where the corporation's principal office (or, if none in this state, its registered office) is or will be located] [of _____ county]. The appeal is commenced by petitioning the court to compel filing the document and by attaching to the petition the document and the secretary of state's explanation of his refusal to file.

(b) The court may summarily order the secretary of state to file the document or take other action the court considers appropriate.

(c) The court's final decision may be appealed as in other civil proceedings.

§ 1.27. Evidentiary Effect of Copy of Filed Document.—A certificate attached to a copy of a document filed by the secretary of state, bearing his signature (which may be in fascimile) and the seal of this state, is conclusive evidence that the original document is on file with the secretary of state.

§ 1.28. Certificate of Existence.—

(a) Anyone may apply to the secretary of state to furnish a certificate of existence for a domestic corporation or a certificate of authorization for a foreign corporation.

(b) A certificate of existence or authorization sets forth:

(1) the domestic corporation's corporate name or the foreign corporation's corporate name used in this state;

(2) that (i) the domestic corporation is duly incorporated under the law of this state, the date of its incorporation, and the period of its duration if less than perpetual; or (ii) that the foreign corporation is authorized to transact business in this state;

(3) that all fees, taxes, and penalties owed to this state have been paid, if (i) payment is reflected in the records of the secretary of state and (ii) nonpayment affects the existence or authorization of the domestic or foreign corporation;

(4) that its most recent annual report required by section 16.22 has been delivered to the secretary of state;

(5) that articles of dissolution have not been filed; and

(6) other facts of record in the office of the secretary of state that may be requested by the applicant.

(c) Subject to any qualification stated in the certificate, a certificate of existence or authorization issued by the secretary of state may be relied upon as conclusive evidence that the domestic or foreign corporation is in existence or is authorized to transact business in this state.

§ 1.29. Penalty for Signing False Document.—

(a) A person commits an offense if he signs a document he knows is false in any material respect with intent that the document be delivered to the secretary of state for filing.

(b) An offense under this section is a [_____] misdemeanor [punishable by a fine of not to exceed $_____].

Subchapter C. Secretary of State

§ 1.30. Powers.—The secretary of state has the power reasonably necessary to perform the duties required of him by this Act.

Subchaper D. Definitions

§ 1.40. Act Definitions.—In this Act:

(1) "Articles of incorporation" include amended and restated articles of incorporation and articles of merger.

(2) "Authorized shares" means the shares of all classes a domestic or foreign corporation is authorized to issue.

(3) "Conspicuous" means so written that a reasonable person against whom the writing is to operate should have noticed it. For example, printing in italics or boldface or contrasting color, or typing in capitals or underlined, is conspicuous.

(4) "Corporation" or "domestic corporation" means a corporation for profit, which is not a foreign corporation, incorporated under or subject to the provisions of this Act.

(5) "Deliver" includes mail.

(6) "Distribution" means a direct or indirect transfer of money or other property (except its own shares) or incurrence of indebtedness by a corporation to or for the benefit of its shareholders in respect of any of its shares. A distribution may be in the form of a declaration or payment of a dividend; a purchase, redemption, or other acquisition of shares; a distribution of indebtedness; or otherwise.

(7) "Effective date of notice" is defined in section 1.41.

(8) "Employee" includes an officer but not a director. A director may accept duties that make him also an employee.

(9) "Entity" includes corporation and foreign corporation; not-for-profit corporation; profit and not-for-profit unincorporated association; business trust, estate, partnership, trust, and two or more persons having a joint or common economic interest; and state, United States, and foreign government.

(10) "Foreign corporation" means a corporation for profit incorporated under a law other than the law of this state.

(11) "Governmental subdivision" includes authority, county, district, and municipality.

(12) "Includes" denotes a partial definition.

(13) "Individual" includes the estate of an incompetent or deceased individual.

(14) "Means" denotes an exhaustive definition.

(15) "Notice" is defined in section 1.41.

(16) "Person" includes individual and entity.

(17) "Principal office" means the office (in or out of this state) so designated in the annual report where the principal executive offices of a domestic or foreign corporation are located.

(18) "Proceeding" includes civil suit and criminal, administrative, and investigatory action.

(19) "Record date" means the date established under chapter 6 or 7 on which a corporation determines the identity of its shareholders and their shareholdings for purposes of this Act. The determinations shall be made as of the close of business on the record date unless another time for doing so is specified when the record date is fixed.

(20) "Secretary" means the corporate officer to whom the board of directors has delegated responsibility under section 8.40(c) for custody of the minutes of the meetings of the board of directors and of the shareholders and for authenticating records of the corporation.

(21) "Share" means the unit into which the proprietary interests in a corporation are divided.

(22) "Shareholder" means the person in whose name shares are registered in the records of a corporation or the beneficial owner of shares to the extent of the rights granted by a nominee certificate on file with a corporation.

(23) "State," when referring to a part of the United States, includes a state and commonwealth (and their agencies and governmental subdivisions) and a territory and insular possession (and their agencies and governmental subdivisions) of the United States.

(24) "Subscriber" means a person who subscribes for shares in a corporation, whether before or after incorporation.

(25) "United States" includes district, authority, bureau, commission, department, and any other agency of the United States.

(26) "Voting group" means all shares of one or more classes or series that under the articles of incorporation or this Act are entitled to vote and be counted together collectively on a matter at a meeting of shareholders. All shares entitled by the articles of incorporation or this Act to vote generally on the matter are for that purpose a single voting group.

§ 1.41. Notice.—

(a) Notice under this Act must be in writing unless oral notice is reasonable under the circumstances.

(b) Notice may be communicated in person; by telephone, telegraph, teletype, or other form of wire or wireless communication; or by mail or private carrier. If these forms of personal notice are impracticable, notice may be communicated by a newspaper of general circulation in the area where published; or by radio, television, or other form of public broadcast communication.

(c) Written notice by a domestic or foreign corporation to its shareholder, if in a comprehensible form, is effective when mailed, if mailed postpaid and correctly addressed to the shareholder's address shown in the corporation's current record of shareholders.

(d) Written notice to a domestic or foreign corporation (authorized to transact business in this state) may be addressed to its registered agent at its registered office or to the corporation or its secretary at its principal office shown in its most recent annual report or, in the case of a foreign corporation that has not yet delivered an annual report, in its application for a certificate of authority.

(e) Except as provided in subsection (c), written notice, if in a comprehensible form, is effective at the earliest of the following:

(1) when received;

(2) five days after its deposit in the United States Mail, as evidenced by the postmark, if mailed postpaid and correctly addressed;

(3) on the date shown on the return receipt, if sent by registered or certified mail, return receipt requested, and the receipt is signed by or on behalf of the addressee.

(f) Oral notice is effective when communicated if communicated in a comprehensible manner.

(g) If this Act prescribes notice requirements for particular circumstances, those requirements govern. If articles of incorporation or bylaws prescribe notice requirements, not inconsistent with this section or other provisions of this Act, those requirements govern.

§ 1.42. Number of Shareholders.—

(a) For purposes of this Act, the following identified as a shareholder in a corporation's current record of shareholders constitutes one shareholder:

(1) three or fewer coowners;

(2) a corporation, partnership, trust, estate, or other entity;

(3) the trustees, guardians, custodians, or other fiduciaries of a single trust, estate, or account.

(b) For purposes of this Act, shareholdings registered in substantially similar names constitute one shareholder if it is reasonable to believe that the names represent the same person.

CHAPTER 2. INCORPORATION

§ 2.01. Incorporators.—One or more persons may act as the incorporator or incorporators of a corporation by delivering articles of incorporation to the secretary of state for filing.

§ 2.02. Articles of Incorporation.—

(a) The articles of incorporation must set forth:

(1) a corporate name for the corporation that satisfies the requirements of section 4.01;

(2) the number of shares the corporation is authorized to issue;

(3) the street address of the corporation's initial registered office and the name of its initial registered agent at that office; and

(4) the name and address of each incorporator.

(b) The articles of incorporation may set forth:

(1) the names and addresses of the individuals who are to serve as the initial directors;

(2) provisions not inconsistent with law regarding:

(i) the purpose or purposes for which the corporation is organized;

(ii) managing the business and regulating the affairs of the corporation;

(iii) defining, limiting, and regulating the powers of the corporation, its board of directors, and shareholders;

(iv) a par value for authorized shares or classes of shares;

(v) the imposition of personal liability on shareholders for the debts of the corporation to a specified extent and upon specified conditions;

(3) any provision that under this Act is required or permitted to be set forth in the bylaws; and

(4) a provision eliminating or limiting the liability of a director to the corporation or its shareholders for money damages for any action taken, or any failure to take any action, as a director, except liability for (A) the amount of a financial benefit received by a director to which he is not entitled; (B) an intentional infliction of harm on the corporation or the shareholders; (C) a violation of section 8.33; or (D) an intentional violation of criminal law.

(c) The articles of incorporation need not set forth any of the corporate powers enumerated in this Act.

§ 2.03. Incorporation.—

(a) Unless a delayed effective date is specified, the corporate existence begins when the articles of incorporation are filed.

(b) The secretary of state's filing of the articles of incorporation is conclusive proof that the incorporators satisfied all conditions precedent to incorporation except in a proceeding by the state to cancel or revoke the incorporation or involuntarily dissolve the corporation.

§ 2.04. Liability for Preincorporation Transactions.—All persons purporting to act as or on behalf of a corporation, knowing there was no incorporation under this Act, are jointly and severally liable for all liabilities created while so acting.

§ 2.05. Organization of Corporation.—

(a) After incorporation:

(1) if initial directors are named in the articles of incorporation, the initial directors shall hold an organizational meeting, at the call of a majority of the directors, to complete the organization of the corporation by appointing officers, adopting bylaws, and carrying on any other business brought before the meeting;

(2) if initial directors are not named in the articles, the incorporator or incorporators shall hold an organizational meeting at the call of a majority of the incorporators:

(i) to elect directors and complete the organization of the corporation; or

(ii) to elect a board of directors who shall complete the organization of the corporation.

(b) Action required or permitted by this Act to be taken by incorporators at an organizational meeting may be taken without a meeting if the action taken is evidenced by one or more written consents describing the action taken and signed by each incorporator.

(c) An organizational meeting may be held in or out of this state.

§ 2.06. Bylaws.—

(a) The incorporators or board of directors of a corporation shall adopt initial bylaws for the corporation.

(b) The bylaws of a corporation may contain any provision for managing the business and regulating the affairs of the corporation that is not inconsistent with law or the articles of incorporation.

§ 2.07. Emergency Bylaws.—

(a) Unless the articles of incorporation provide otherwise, the board of directors of a corporation may adopt bylaws to be effective only in an emergency defined in subsection (d). The emergency bylaws, which are subject to amendment or repeal by the shareholders, may make all provisions necessary for managing the corporation during the emergency, including:

(1) procedures for calling a meeting of the board of directors;

(2) quorum requirements for the meeting; and

(3) designation of additional or substitute directors.

(b) All provisions of the regular bylaws consistent with the emergency bylaws remain effective during the emergency. The emergency bylaws are not effective after the emergency ends.

(c) Corporate action taken in good faith in accordance with the emergency bylaws:

(1) binds the corporation; and

(2) may not be used to impose liability on a corporate director, officer, employee, or agent.

(d) An emergency exists for purposes of this section if a quorum of the corporation's directors cannot readily be assembled because of some catastrophic event.

CHAPTER 3. PURPOSES AND POWERS

§ 3.01. Purposes.—

(a) Every corporation incorporated under this Act has the purpose of engaging in any lawful business unless a more limited purpose is set forth in the articles of incorporation.

(b) A corporation engaging in a business that is subject to regulation under another statute of this state may incorporate under this Act only if permitted by, and subject to all limitations of, the other statute.

§ 3.02. General Powers.—Unless its articles of incorporation provide otherwise, every corporation has perpetual duration and succession in its corporate name and has the same powers as an individual to do all things necessary or convenient to carry out its business and affairs, including without limitation power:

(1) to sue and be sued, complain and defend in its corporate name;

(2) to have a corporate seal, which may be altered at will, and to use it, or a facsimile of it, by impressing or affixing it or in any other manner reproducing it;

(3) to make and amend bylaws, not inconsistent with its articles of incorporation or with the laws of this state, for managing the business and regulating the affairs of the corporation;

(4) to purchase, receive, lease, or otherwise acquire, and own, hold, improve, use, and otherwise deal with, real or personal property, or any legal or equitable interest in property, wherever located;

(5) to sell, convey, mortgage, pledge, lease, exchange, and otherwise dispose of all or any part of its property;

(6) to purchase, receive, subscribe for, or otherwise acquire; own, hold, vote, use, sell, mortgage, lend, pledge, or otherwise dispose of; and deal in and with shares or other interests in, or obligations of, any other entity;

(7) to make contracts and guarantees, incur liabilities, borrow money, issue its notes, bonds, and other obligations (which may be convertible into or include the option to purchase other securities of the corporation), and secure any of its obligations by mortgage or pledge of any of its property, franchises, or income;

(8) to lend money, invest and reinvest its funds, and receive and hold real and personal property as security for repayment;

(9) to be a promoter, partner, member, associate, or manager of any partnership, joint venture, trust, or other entity;

(10) to conduct its business, locate offices, and exercise the powers granted by this Act within or without this state;

(11) to elect directors and appoint officers, employees, and agents of the corporation, define their duties, fix their compensation, and lend them money and credit;

(12) to pay pensions and establish pension plans, pension trusts, profit sharing plans, share bonus plans, share option plans, and benefit or incentive plans for any or all of its current or former directors, officers, employees, and agents;

(13) to make donations for the public welfare or for charitable, scientific, or educational purposes;

(14) to transact any lawful business that will aid governmental policy;

(15) to make payments or donations, or do any other act, not inconsistent with law, that furthers the business and affairs of the corporation.

§ 3.03. Emergency Powers.—

(a) In anticipation of or during an emergency defined in subsection (d), the board of directors of a corporation may:

(1) modify lines of succession to accommodate the incapacity of any director, officer, employee, or agent; and

(2) relocate the principal office, designate alternative principal offices or regional offices, or authorize the officers to do so.

(b) During an emergency defined in subsection (d), unless emergency bylaws provide otherwise:

(1) notice of a meeting of the board of directors need be given only to those directors whom it is practicable to reach and may be given in any practicable manner, including by publication and radio; and

(2) one or more officers of the corporation present at a meeting of the board of directors may be deemed to be directors for the meeting, in order of rank and within the same rank in order of seniority, as necessary to achieve a quorum.

(c) Corporate action taken in good faith during an emergency under this section to further the ordinary business affairs of the corporation:

(1) binds the corporation; and

(2) may not be used to impose liability on a corporate director, officer, employee, or agent.

(d) An emergency exists for purposes of this section if a quorum of the corporation's directors cannot readily be assembled because of some catastrophic event.

§ 3.04. Ultra Vires.—

(a) Except as provided in subsection (b), the validity of corporate action may not be challenged on the ground that the corporation lacks or lacked power to act.

(b) A corporation's power to act may be challenged:

(1) in a proceeding by a shareholder against the corporation to enjoin the act;

(2) in a proceeding by the corporation, directly, derivatively, or through a receiver, trustee, or other legal representative, against an incumbent or former director, officer, employee, or agent of the corporation; or

(3) in a proceeding by the Attorney General under section 14.30.

(c) In a shareholder's proceeding under subsection (b)(1) to enjoin an unauthorized corporate act, the court may enjoin or set aside the act, if equitable and if all affected persons are parties to the proceeding, and may award damages for loss (other than anticipated profits) suffered by the corporation or another party because of enjoining the unauthorized act.

CHAPTER 4. NAME

§ 4.01. Corporate Name.—

(a) A corporate name:

(1) must contain the word "corporation," "incorporated," "company," or "limited," or the abbreviation "corp.," "inc.," "co.," or "ltd.," or words or abbreviations of like import in another language; and

(2) may not contain language stating or implying that the corporation is organized for a purpose other than that permitted by section 3.01 and its articles of incorporation.

(b) Except as authorized by subsections (c) and (d), a corporate name must be distinguishable upon the records of the secretary of state from:

(1) the corporate name of a corporation incorporated or authorized to transact business in this state;

(2) a corporate name reserved or registered under section 4.02 or 4.03;

(3) the fictitious name adopted by a foreign corporation authorized to transact business in this state because its real name is unavailable; and

(4) the corporate name of a not-for-profit corporation incorporated or authorized to transact business in this state.

(c) A corporation may apply to the secretary of state for authorization to use a name that is not distinguishable upon his records from one or more of the names described in subsection (b). The secretary of state shall authorize use of the name applied for if:

(1) the other corporation consents to the use in writing and submits an undertaking in form satisfactory to the secretary of state to change its name to a name that is distinguishable upon the records of the secretary of state from the name of the applying corporation; or

(2) the applicant delivers to the secretary of state a certified copy of the final judgment of a court of competent jurisdiction establishing the applicant's right to use the name applied for in this state.

(d) A corporation may use the name (including the fictitious name) of another domestic or foreign corporation that is used in this state if the other corporation is incorporated or authorized to transact business in this state and the proposed user corporation:

(1) has merged with the other corporation;

(2) has been formed by reorganization of the other corporation; or

(3) has acquired all or substantially all of the assets, including the corporate name, of the other corporation.

(e) This Act does not control the use of fictitious names.

§ 4.02. Reserved Name.—

(a) A person may reserve the exclusive use of a corporate name, including a fictitious name for a foreign corporation whose corporate name is not available, by delivering an application to the secretary of state for filing. The application must set forth the name and address of the applicant and the name proposed to be reserved. If the secretary of state finds that the corporate name applied for is available, he shall reserve the name for the applicant's exclusive use for a nonrenewable 120-day period.

(b) The owner of a reserved corporate name may transfer the reservation to another person by delivering to the secretary of state a signed notice of the transfer that states the name and address of the transferee.

§ 4.03. Registered Name.—

(a) A foreign corporation may register its corporate name, or its corporate name with any addition required by section 15.06, if the name is distinguishable upon the records of the secretary of state from the corporate names that are not available under section 4.01(b)(3).

(b) A foreign corporation registers its corporate name, or its corporate name with any addition required by section 15.06, by delivering to the secretary of state for filing an application:

(1) setting forth its corporate name, or its corporate name with any addition required by section 15.06, the state or country and date of its incorporation, and a brief description of the nature of the business in which it is engaged; and

(2) accompanied by a certificate of existence (or a document of similar import) from the state or country of incorporation.

(c) The name is registered for the applicant's exclusive use upon the effective date of the application.

(d) A foreign corporation whose registration is effective may renew it for successive years by delivering to the secretary of state for filing a renewal application, which complies with the requirements of subsection (b), between October 1 and December 31 of the preceding year. The renewal application renews the registration for the following calendar year.

(e) A foreign corporation whose registration is effective may thereafter qualify as a foreign corporation under that name or consent in writing to the use of that name by a corporation thereafter incorporated under this Act or by another foreign corporation thereafter authorized to transact business in this state. The registration terminates when the domestic corporation is incorporated or the foreign corporation qualifies or consents to the qualification of another foreign corporation under the registered name.

CHAPTER 5. OFFICE AND AGENT

§ 5.01. Registered Office and Registered Agent.—Each corporation must continuously maintain in this state:

(1) a registered office that may be the same as any of its places of business; and

(2) a registered agent, who may be:

(i) an individual who resides in this state and whose business office is identical with the registered office;

(ii) a domestic corporation or not-for-profit domestic corporation whose business office is identical with the registered office; or

(iii) a foreign corporation or not-for-profit foreign corporation authorized to transact business in this state whose business office is identical with the registered office.

§ 5.02. Change of Registered Office or Registered Agent.—

(a) A corporation may change its registered office or registered agent by delivering to the secretary of state for filing a statement of change that sets forth:

(1) the name of the corporation,

(2) the street address of its current registered office;

(3) if the current registered office is to be changed, the street address of the new registered office;

(4) the name of its current registered agent;

(5) if the current registered agent is to be changed, the name of the new registered agent and the new agent's written consent (either on the statement or attached to it) to the appointment; and

(6) that after the change or changes are made, the street addresses of its registered office and the business office of its registered agent will be identical.

(b) If a registered agent changes the street address of his business office, he may change the street address of the registered office of any corporation for which he is the registered agent by notifying the corporation in writing of the change and signing (either manually or in facsimile) and delivering to the secretary of state for filing a statement that complies with the requirements of subsection (a) and recites that the corporation has been notified of the change.

§ 5.03. Resignation of Registered Agent.—

(a) A registered agent may resign his agency appointment by signing and delivering to the secretary of state for filing the signed original and two exact or conformed copies of a statement of resignation. The statement may include a statement that the registered office is also discontinued.

(b) After filing the statement the secretary of state shall mail one copy to the registered office (if not discontinued) and the other copy to the corporation at its principal office.

(c) The agency appointment is terminated, and the registered office discontinued if so provided, on the 31st day after the date on which the statement was filed.

§ 5.04. Service on Corporation.—

(a) A corporation's registered agent is the corporation's agent for service of process, notice, or demand required or permitted by law to be served on the corporation.

(b) If a corporation has no registered agent, or the agent cannot with reasonable diligence be served, the corporation may be served by registered or certified mail, return receipt requested, addressed to the secretary of the corporation at its principal office. Service is perfected under this subsection at the earliest of:

(1) the date the corporation receives the mail;

(2) the date shown on the return receipt, if signed on behalf of the corporation; or

(3) five days after its deposit in the United States Mail as evidenced by the postmark, if mailed postpaid and correctly addressed.

(c) This section does not prescribe the only means, or necessarily the required means, of serving a corporation.

CHAPTER 6. SHARES AND DISTRIBUTIONS

Subchapter A. Shares

§ 6.01. Authorized Shares.

(a) The articles of incorporation must prescribe the classes of shares and the number of shares of each class that the corporation is authorized to issue. If more than one class of shares is authorized, the articles of incorporation must prescribe a distinguishing designation for each class, and prior to the issuance of shares of a class the preferences, limitations, and relative rights of that class must be described in the articles of incorporation. All shares of a class must have preferences, limitations, and relative rights identical with those of other shares of the same class except to the extent otherwise permitted by section 6.02.

(b) The articles of incorporation must authorize (1) one or more classes of shares that together have unlimited voting rights, and (2) one or more classes of shares (which may be the same class or classes as those with voting rights) that together are entitled to receive the net assets of the corporation upon dissolution.

(c) The articles of incorporation may authorize one or more classes of shares that:

(1) have special, conditional, or limited voting rights, or no right to vote, except to the extent prohibited by this Act;

(2) are redeemable or convertible as specified in the articles of incorporation (i) at the option of the corporation, the shareholder, or another person or upon the occurrence of a designated event; (ii) for cash, indebtedness, securities, or other property; (iii) in a designated amount or in an amount determined in accordance with a designated formula or by reference to extrinsic data or events;

(3) entitle the holders to distributions calculated in any manner, including dividends that may be cumulative, noncumulative, or partially cumulative;

(4) have preference over any other class of shares with respect to distributions, including dividends and distributions upon the dissolution of the corporation.

(d) The description of the designations, preferences, limitations, and relative rights of share classes in subsection (c) is not exhaustive.

§ 6.02. Terms of Class or Series Determined by Board of Directors.—

(a) If the articles of incorporation so provide, the board of directors may determine, in whole or part, the preferences, limitations, and relative rights (within the limits set forth in section 6.01) of (1) any class of shares before the issuance of any shares of that class or (2) one or more series within a class before the issuance of any shares of that series.

(b) Each series of a class must be given a distinguishing designation.

(c) All shares of a series must have preferences, limitations, and relative rights identical with those of other shares of the same series and, except to the extent otherwise provided in the description of the series, with those of other series of the same class.

(d) Before issuing any shares of a class or series created under this section, the corporation must deliver to the secretary of state for filing articles of amendment, which are effective without shareholder action, that set forth:

(1) the name of the corporation;

(2) the text of the amendment determining the terms of the class or series of shares;

(3) the date it was adopted; and

(4) a statement that the amendment was duly adopted by the board of directors.

§ 6.03. Issued and Outstanding Shares.—

(a) A corporation may issue the number of shares of each class or series authorized by the articles of incorporation. Shares that are isswed are outstanding shares until they are reacquired, redeemed, converted, or cancelled.

(b) The reacquisition, redemption, or conversion of outstanding shares is subject to the limitations of subsection (c) of this section and to section 6.40.

(c) At all times that shares of the corporation are outstanding, one or more shares that together have unlimited voting rights and one or more shares that together are entitled to receive the net assets of the corporation upon dissolution must be outstanding.

§ 6.04. Fractional Shares.—

(a) A corporation may:

(1) issue fractions of a share or pay in money the value of fractions of a share;

(2) arrange for disposition of fractional shares by the shareholders;

(3) issue scrip in registered or bearer form entitling the holder to receive a full share upon surrendering enough scrip to equal a full share.

(b) Each certificate representing scrip must be conspicuously labeled "scrip" and must contain the information required by section 6.25(b).

(c) The holder of a fractional share is entitled to exercise the rights of a shareholder, including the right to vote, to receive dividends, and to participate in the assets of the corporation upon liquidation. The holder of scrip is not entitled to any of these rights unless the scrip provides for them.

(d) The board of directors may authorize the issuance of scrip subject to any condition considered desirable, including:

(1) that the scrip will become void if not exchanged for full shares before a specified date; and

(2) that the shares for which the scrip is exchangeable may be sold and the proceeds paid to the scripholders.

Subchapter B. Issuance of Shares

§ 6.20. Subscription for Shares Before Incorporation.—

(a) A subscription for shares entered into before incorporation is irrevocable for six months unless the subscription agreement provides a longer or shorter period or all the subscribers agree to revocation.

(b) The board of directors may determine the payment terms of subscriptions for shares that were entered into before incorporation, unless the subscription agreement specifies them. A call for payment by the board of directors must be uniform so far as practicable as to all shares of the same class or series, unless the subscription agreement specifies otherwise.

(c) Shares issued pursuant to subscriptions entered into before incorporation are fully paid and nonassessable when the corporation receives the consideration specified in the subscription agreement.

(d) If a subscriber defaults in payment of money or property under a subscription agreement entered into before incorporation, the corporation may collect the amount owed as any other debt. Alternatively, unless the subscription agreement provides otherwise, the corporation may rescind the agreement and may sell the shares if the debt remains unpaid more than 20 days after the corporation sends written demand for payment to the subscriber.

(e) A subscription agreement entered into after incorporation is a contract between the subscriber and the corporation subject to section 6.21.

§ 6.21. Issuance of Shares.—

(a) The powers granted in this section to the board of directors may be reserved to the shareholders by the articles of incorporation.

(b) The board of directors may authorize shares to be issued for consideration consisting of any tangible or intangible property or benefit to the corporation, including cash, promissory notes, services performed, contracts for services to be performed, or other securities of the corporation.

(c) Before the corporation issues shares, the board of directors must determine that the consideration received or to be received for shares to be issued is adequate. That determination by the board of directors is conclusive insofar as the adequacy of consideration for the issuance of shares relates to whether the shares are validly issued, fully paid, and nonassessable.

(d) When the corporation receives the consideration for which the board of directors authorized the issuance of shares, the shares issued therefor are fully paid and nonassessable.

(e) The corporation may place in escrow shares issued for a contract for future services or benefits or a promissory note, or make other arrangements to restrict the transfer of the shares, and may credit distributions in respect of the shares against their purchase price, until the services are performed, the note is paid, or the benefits received. If the services are not performed, the note is not paid, or the benefits are not received, the shares escrowed or restricted and the distributions credited may be cancelled in whole or part.

§ 6.22. Liability of Shareholders.—

(a) A purchaser from a corporation of its own shares is not liable to the corporation or its creditors with respect to the shares except to pay the consideration for which the shares were authorized to be issued (section 6.21) or specified in the subscription agreement (section 6.20).

(b) Unless otherwise provided in the articles of incorporation, a shareholder of a corporation is not personally liable for the acts or debts of the corporation except that he may become personally liable by reason of his own acts or conduct.

§ 6.23. Share Dividends.—

(a) Unless the articles of incorporation provide otherwise, shares may be issued pro rata and without consideration to the corporation's shareholders or to the shareholders of one or more classes or series. An issuance of shares under this subsection is a share dividend.

(b) Shares of one class or series may not be issued as a share dividend in respect of shares of another class or series unless (1) the articles of incorporation so authorize, (2) a majority of the votes entitled to be cast by the class or series to be issued approve the issue, or (3) there are no outstanding shares of the class or series to be issued.

(c) If the board of directors does not fix the record date for determining shareholders entitled to a share dividend, it is the date the board of directors authorizes the share dividend.

§ 6.24. Share Options.—

A corporation may issue rights, options, or warrants for the purchase of shares of the corporation. The board of directors shall determine the terms upon which the rights, options, or warrants are issued, their form and content, and the consideration for which the shares are to be issued.

§ 6.25. Form and Content of Certificates.—

(a) Shares may but need not be represented by certificates. Unless this Act or another statute expressly provides otherwise, the rights and obligations of shareholders are identical whether or not their shares are represented by certificates.

(b) At a minimum each share certificate must state on its face:

(1) the name of the issuing corporation and that it is organized under the law of this state;

(2) the name of the person to whom issued; and

(3) the number and class of shares and the designation of the series, if any, the certificate represents.

(c) If the issuing corporation is authorized to issue different classes of shares or different series within a class, the designations, relative rights, preferences, and limitations applicable to each class and the variations in rights, preferences, and limitations determined for each series (and the authority of the board of directors to determine variations for future series) must be summarized on the front or back of each certificate. Alternatively, each certificate may state conspicuously on its front or back that the corporation will furnish the shareholder this information on request in writing and without charge.

(d) Each share certificate (1) must be signed (either manually or in facsimile) by two officers designated in the bylaws or by the board of directors and (2) may bear the corporate seal or its facsimile.

(e) If the person who signed (either manually or in facsimile) a share certificate no longer holds office when the certificate is issued, the certificate is nevertheless valid.

§ 6.26. Shares Without Certificates.—

(a) Unless the articles of incorporation or bylaws provide otherwise, the board of directors of a corporation may authorize the issue of some or all of the shares of any or all of its classes or series without certificates. The authorization does not affect shares already represented by certificates until they are surrendered to the corporation.

(b) Within a reasonable time after the issue or transfer of shares without certificates, the corporation shall send the shareholder a written statement of the information required on certificates by section 6.25(b) and (c), and, if applicable, section 6.27.

§ 6.27. Restriction on Transfer of Shares and Other Securities.—

(a) The articles of incorporation, bylaws, an agreement among shareholders, or an agreement between shareholders and the corporation may impose restrictions on the transfer or registration of transfer of shares of the corporation. A restriction does not affect shares issued before the restriction was adopted unless the holders of the shares are parties to the restriction agreement or voted in favor of the restriction.

(b) A restriction on the transfer or registration of transfer of shares is valid and enforceable against the holder or a transferee of the holder if the restriction is authorized by this section and its existence is noted conspicuously on the front or back of the certificate or is contained in the information statement required by section 6.26(b). Unless so noted, a restriction is not enforceable against a person without knowledge of the restriction.

(c) A restriction on the transfer or registration of transfer of shares is authorized:

(1) to maintain the corporation's status when it is dependent on the number or identity of its shareholders;

(2) to preserve exemptions under federal or state securities law;

(3) for any other reasonable purpose.

(d) A restriction on the transfer or registration of transfer of shares may:

(1) obligate the shareholder first to offer the corporation or other persons (separately, consecutively, or simultaneously) an opportunity to acquire the restricted shares;

(2) obligate the corporation or other persons (separately, consecutively, or simultaneously) to acquire the restricted shares;

(3) require the corporation, the holders of any class of its shares, or another person to approve the transfer of the restricted shares, if the requirement is not manifestly unreasonable;

(4) prohibit the transfer of the restricted shares to designated persons or classes of persons, if the prohibition is not manifestly unreasonable.

(e) For purposes of this section, "shares" includes a security convertible into or carrying a right to subscribe for or acquire shares.

§ 6.28. Expense of Issue.—

A corporation may pay the expenses of selling or underwriting its shares, and of organizing or reorganizing the corporation, from the consideration received for shares.

Subchapter C. Subsequent Acquisition of Shares
by Shareholders and Corporation

§ 6.30. Shareholders' Preemptive Rights.—

(a) The shareholders of a corporation do not have a preemptive right to acquire the corporation's unissued shares except to the extent the articles of incorporation so provide.

(b) A statement included in the articles of incorporation that "the corporation elects to have preemptive rights" (or words of similar import) means that the following principles apply except to the extent the articles of incorporation expressly provide otherwise:

(1) The shareholders of the corporation have a preemptive right, granted on uniform terms and conditions prescribed by the board of directors, to provide a fair and reasonable opportunity to exercise the right, to acquire proportional amounts of the corporation's unissued shares upon the decision of the board of directors to issue them.

(2) A shareholder may waive his preemptive right. A waiver evidenced by a writing is irrevocable even though it is not supported by consideration.

(3) There is no preemptive right with respect to:

(i) shares issued as compensation to directors, officers, agents, or employees of the corporation, its subsidiaries or affiliates;

(ii) shares issued to satisfy conversion or option rights created to provide compensation to directors, officers, agents, or employees of the corporation, its subsidiaries or affiliates;

(iii) shares authorized in articles of incorporation that are issued within six months from the effective date of incorporation;

(iv) shares sold otherwise than for money.

(4) Holders of shares of any class without general voting rights but with preferential rights to distributions or assets have no preemptive rights with respect to shares of any class.

(5) Holders of shares of any class with general voting rights but without preferential rights to distributions or assets have no preemptive rights with respect to shares of any class with preferential rights to distributions or assets unless the shares with preferential rights are convertible into or carry a right to subscribe for or acquire shares without preferential rights.

(6) Shares subject to preemptive rights that are not acquired by shareholders may be issued to any person for a period of one year after being offered to shareholders at a consideration set by the board of directors that is not lower than the consideration set for the exercise of preemptive rights. An offer at a lower consideration or after the expiration of one year is subject to the shareholders' preemptive rights.

(c) For purposes of this section, "shares" includes a security convertible into or carrying a right to subscribe for or acquire shares.

§ 6.31. Corporation's Acquisition of its Own Shares.—

(a) A corporation may acquire its own shares and shares so acquired constitute authorized but unissued shares.

(b) If the articles of incorporation prohibit the reissue of acquired shares, the number of authorized shares is reduced by the number of shares acquired, effective upon amendment of the articles of incorporation.

(c) The board of directors may adopt articles of amendment under this section without shareholder action, and deliver them to the secretary of state for filing. The articles must set forth:

(1) the name of the corporation;

(2) the reduction in the number of authorized shares, itemized by class and series; and

(3) the total number of authorized shares, itemized by class and series, remaining after reduction of the shares.

Subchapter D. Distributions

§ 6.40. Distributions to Shareholders.—

(a) A board of directors may authorize and the corporation may make distributions to its shareholders subject to restriction by the articles of incorporation and the limitation in subsection (c).

(b) If the board of directors does not fix the record date for determining shareholders entitled to a distribution (other than one involving a purchase redemption, or other acquisition of the corporation's shares), it is the date the board of directors authorizes the distribution.

(c) No distribution may be made if, after giving it effect:

(1) the corporation would not be able to pay its debts as they become due in the usual course of business; or

(2) the corporation's total assets would be less than the sum of its total liabilities plus (unless the articles of incorporation permit otherwise) the amount that would be needed, if the corporation were to be dissolved at the time of the distribution, to satisfy the preferential rights upon dissolution of shareholders whose preferential rights are superior to those receiving the distribution.

(d) The board of directors may base a determination that a distribution is not prohibited under subsection (c) either on financial statements prepared on the basis of accounting practices and principles that are reasonable in the circumstances or on a fair valuation or other method that is reasonable in the circumstances.

(e) Except as provided in subsection (g), the effect of a distribution under subsection (c) is measured:

(1) in the case of distribution by purchase, redemption, or other acquisition of the corporation's shares, as of the earlier of (i) the date money or other property is transferred or debt incurred by the corporation or (ii) the date the shareholder ceases to be a shareholder with respect to the acquired shares;

(2) in the case of any other distribution of indebtedness, as of the date the indebtedness is distributed; and

(3) in all other cases, as of (i) the date the distribution is authorized if the payment occurs within 120 days after the date of authorization or (ii) the date the payment is made if it occurs more than 120 days after the date of authorization.

(f) A corporation's indebtedness to a shareholder incurred by reason of a distribution made in accordance with this section is at parity with the corporation's indebtedness to its general, unsecured creditors except to the extent subordinated by agreement.

(g) Indebtedness of a corporation, including indebtedness issued as a distribution, is not considered a liability for purposes of determination under subsection (c) if its terms provide that payment of principal and interest are made only if and to the extent that payment of a distribution to shareholders could then be made under this section. If the indebtedness is issued as a distribution, each payment of principal or interest is treated as a distribution, the effect of which is measured on the date the payment is actually made.

CHAPTER 7. SHAREHOLDERS

Subchapter A. Meetings

§ 7.01. Annual Meeting.—

(a) A corporation shall hold annually at a time stated in or fixed in accordance with the bylaws a meeting of shareholders.

(b) Annual shareholders' meetings may be held in or out of this state at the place stated in or fixed in accordance with the bylaws. If no place is stated in or fixed in accordance with the bylaws, annual meetings shall be held at the corporation's principal office.

(c) The failure to hold an annual meeting at the time stated in or fixed in accordance with a corporation's bylaws does not affect the validity of any corporate action.

§ 7.02. Special Meeting.—

(a) A corporation shall hold a special meeting of shareholders:

(1) on call of its board of directors or the person or persons authorized to do so by the articles of incorporation or bylaws; or

(2) if the holders of at least 10 percent of all the votes entitled to be cast on any issue proposed to be considered at the proposed special meeting sign, date, and deliver to the corporation's secretary one or more written demands for the meeting describing the purpose or purposes for which it is to be held.

(b) If not otherwise fixed under sections 7.03 or 7.07, the record date for determining shareholders entitled to demand a special meeting is the date the first shareholder signs the demand.

(c) Special shareholders' meetings may be held in or out of this state at the place stated in or fixed in accordance with the bylaws. If no place is stated or fixed in accordance with the bylaws, special meetings shall be held at the corporation's principal office.

(d) Only business within the purpose or purposes described in the meeting notice required by section 7.05(c) may be conducted at a special shareholders' meeting.

§ 7.03. Court-Ordered Meeting.—

(a) The [name or describe] court of the county where a corporation's principal office (or, if none in this state, its registered office) is located may summarily order a meeting to be held:

(1) on application of any shareholder of the corporation entitled to participate in an annual meeting if an annual meeting was not held within the earlier of 6 months after the end of the corporation's fiscal year or 15 months after its last annual meeting; or

(2) on application of a shareholder who signed a demand for a special meeting valid under section 7.02 if:

(i) notice of the special meeting was not given within 30 days after the date the demand was delivered to the corporation's secretary; or

(ii) the special meeting was not held in accordance with the notice.

(b) The court may fix the time and place of the meeting, determine the shares entitled to participate in the meeting, specify a record date for determining shareholders entitled to notice of and to vote at the meeting, prescribe the form and content of the meeting notice, fix the quorum required for specific matters to be considered at the meeting (or direct that the votes represented at the meeting constitute a quorum for action on those matters), and enter other orders necessary to accomplish the purpose or purposes of the meeting.

§ 7.04. Action Without Meeting.—

(a) Action required or permitted by this Act to be taken at a shareholders' meeting may be taken without a meeting if the action is taken by all the shareholders entitled to vote on the action. The action must be evidenced by one or more written consents describing the action taken, signed by all the shareholders entitled to vote on the action, and delivered to the corporation for inclusion in the minutes or filing with the corporate records.

(b) If not otherwise determined under sections 7.03 or 7.07, the record date for determining shareholders entitled to take action without a meeting is the date the first shareholder signs the consent under subsection (a).

(c) A consent signed under this section has the effect of a meeting vote and may be described as such in any document.

(d) If this Act requires that notice of proposed action be given to nonvoting shareholders and the action is to be taken by unanimous consent of the voting shareholders, the corporation must give its nonvoting shareholders written notice of the proposed action at least 10 days before the action is takgn. The notice must contain or be accompanied by the same material that, under this Act, would have been required to be sent to nonvoting shareholders in a notice of meeting at which the proposed action would have been submitted to the shareholders for action.

§ 7.05. Notice of Meeting.—

(a) A corporation shall notify shareholders of the date, time, and place of each annual and special shareholders' meeting no fewer than 10 nor more than 60 days before the meeting date. Unless this Act or the articles of incorporation require otherwise, the corporation is required to give notice only to shareholders entitled to vote at the meeting.

(b) Unless this Act or the articles of incorporation require otherwise, notice of an annual meeting need not include a description of the purpose or purposes for which the meeting is called.

(c) Notice of a special meeting must include a description of the purpose or purposes for which the meeting is called.

(d) If not otherwise fixed under section 7.03 or 7.07, the record date for determining shareholders entitled to notice of and to vote at an annual or special shareholders' meeting is the day before the first notice is delivered to shareholders.

(e) Unless the bylaws require otherwise, if an annual or special shareholders' meeting is adjourned to a different date, time, or place, notice need not be given of the new date, time, or place if the new date, time, or place is announced at the meeting before adjournment. If a new record date for the adjourned meeting is or must be fixed under section 7.07, however, notice of the adjourned meeting must be given under this section to persons who are shareholders as of the new record date.

§ 7.06. Waiver of Notice.—
(a) A shareholder may waive any notice required by this Act, the articles of incorporation, or bylaws before or after the date and time stated in the notice. The waiver must be in writing, be signed by the shareholder entitled to the notice, and be delivered to the corporation for inclusion in the minutes or filing with the corporate records.

(b) A shareholder's attendance at a meeting:

(1) waives objection to lack of notice or defective notice of the meeting, unless the shareholder at the beginning of the meeting objects to holding the meeting or transacting business at the meeting;

(2) waives objection to consideration of a particular matter at the meeting that is not within the purpose or purposes described in the meeting notice, unless the shareholder objects to considering the matter when it is presented.

§ 7.07. Record Date.—
(a) The bylaws may fix or provide the manner of fixing the record date for one or more voting groups in order to determine the shareholders entitled to notice of a shareholders' meeting, to demand a special meeting, to vote, or to take any other action. If the bylaws do not fix or provide for fixing a record date, the board of directors of the corporation may fix a future date as the record date.

(b) A record date fixed under this section may not be more than 70 days before the meeting or action requiring a determination of shareholders.

(c) A determination of shareholders entitled to notice of or to vote at a shareholders' meeting is effective for any adjournment of the meeting unless the board of directors fixes a new record date, which it must do if the meeting is adjourned to a date more than 120 days after the date fixed for the original meeting.

(d) If a court orders a meeting adjourned to a date more than 120 days after the date fixed for the original meeting, it may provide that the original record date continues in effect or it may fix a new record date.

Subchapter B. Voting

§ 7.20. Shareholders' List for Meeting.—
(a) After fixing a record date for a meeting, a corporation shall prepare an alphabetical list of the names of all its shareholders who are entitled to notice of a shareholders' meeting. The list must be arranged by voting group (and within each voting group by class or series of shares) and show the address of and number of shares held by each shareholder.

(b) The shareholders' list must be available for inspection by any shareholder, beginning two business days after notice of the meeting is given for which the list was prepared and continuing through the meeting, at the corporation's principal office or at a place identified in the meeting notice in the city where the meeting will be held. A shareholder, his agent, or attorney is entitled on written demand to inspect and, subject to the requirements of section 16.02(c), to copy the list, during regular business hours and at his expense, during the period it is available for inspection.

(c) The corporation shall make the shareholders' list available at the meeting, and any shareholder, his agent, or attorney is entitled to inspect the list at any time during the meeting or any adjournment.

(d) If the corporation refuses to allow a shareholder, his agent, or attorney to inspect the shareholders' list before or at the meeting (or copy the list as permitted by subsection (b)), the [name or describe] court of the county where a corporation's principal office (or, if none in this state, its registered office) is located, on application of the shareholder, may summarily order the inspection or copying at the corporation's expense and may postpone the meeting for which the list was prepared until the inspection or copying is complete.

(e) Refusal or failure to prepare or make available the shareholders' list does not affect the validity of action taken at the meeting.

§ 7.21. Voting Entitlement of Shares.—
(a) Except as provided in subsections (b) and (c) or unless the articles of incorporation provide otherwise, each outstanding share, regardless of class, is entitled to one vote on each matter voted on at a shareholders' meeting. Only shares are entitled to vote.

(b) Absent special circumstances, the shares of a corporation are not entitled to vote if they are owned, directly or indirectly, by a second corporation, domestic or foreign, and the first corporation owns, directly or indirectly, a majority of the shares entitled to vote for directors of the second corporation.

(c) Subsection (b) does not limit the power of a corporation to vote any shares, including its own shares, held by it in a fiduciary capacity.

(d) Redeemable shares are not entitled to vote after notice of redemption is mailed to the holders and a sum sufficient to redeem the shares has been deposited with a bank, trust company, or other financial institution under an irrevocable obligation to pay the holders the redemption price on surrender of the shares.

§ 7.22. Proxies.—
(a) A shareholder may vote his shares in person or by proxy.

(b) A shareholder may appoint a proxy to vote or otherwise act for him by signing an appointment form, either personally or by his attorney-in-fact.

(c) An appointment of a proxy is effective when received by the secretary or other officer or agent authorized to tabulate votes. An appointment is valid for 11 months unless a longer period is expressly provided in the appointment form.

(d) An appointment of a proxy is revocable by the shareholder unless the appointment form conspicuously states that it is irrevocable and the appoint-

ment is coupled with an interest. Appointments coupled with an interest include the appointment of:

(1) a pledgee;

(2) a person who purchased or agreed to purchase the shares;

(3) a creditor of the corporation who extended it credit under terms requiring the appointment;

(4) an employee of the corporation whose employment contract requires the appointment; or

(5) a party to a voting agreement created under section 7.31.

(e) The death or incapacity of the shareholder appointing a proxy does not affect the right of the corporation to accept the proxy's authority unless notice of the death or incapacity is received by the secretary or other officer or agent authorized to tabulate votes before the proxy exercises his authority under the appointment.

(f) An appointment made irrevocable under subsection (d) is revoked when the interest with which it is coupled is extinguished.

(g) A transferee for value of shares subject to an irrevocable appointment may revoke the appointment if he did not know of its existence when he acquired the shares and the existence of the irrevocable appointment was not noted conspicuously on the certificate representing the shares or on the information statement for shares without certificates.

(h) Subject to section 7.24 and to any express limitation on the proxy's authority appearing on the face of the appointment form, a corporation is entitled to accept the proxy's vote or other action as that of the shareholder making the appointment.

§ 7.23. Shares Held by Nominees.—
(a) A corporation may establish a procedure by which the beneficial owner of shares that are registered in the name of a nominee is recognized by the corporation as the shareholder. The extent of this recognition may be determined in the procedure.

(b) The procedure may set forth:

(1) the types of nominees to which it applies;

(2) the rights or privileges that the corporation recognizes in a beneficial owner;

(3) the manner in which the procedure is selected by the nominee;

(4) the information that must be provided when the procedure is selected;

(5) the period for which selection of the procedure is effective; and

(6) other aspects of the rights and duties created.

§ 7.24. Corporation's Acceptance of Votes.—
(a) If the name signed on a vote, consent, waiver, or proxy appointment corresponds to the name of a shareholder, the corporation if acting in good faith is entitled to accept the vote, consent, waiver, or proxy appointment and give it effect as the act of the shareholder.

(b) If the name signed on a vote, consent, waiver, or proxy appointment does not correspond to the name of its shareholder, the corporation if acting in good faith is nevertheless entitled to accept the vote, consent, waiver, or proxy appointment and give it effect as the act of the shareholder if:

(1) the shareholder is an entity and the name signed purports to be that of an officer or agent of the entity;

(2) the name signed purports to be that of an administrator, executor, guardian, or conservator representing the shareholder and, if the corporation requests, evidence of fiduciary status acceptable to the corporation has been presented with respect to the vote, consent, waiver, or proxy appointment;

(3) the name signed purports to be that of a receiver or trustee in bankruptcy of the shareholder and, if the corporation requests, evidence of this status acceptable to the corporation has been presented with respect to the vote, consent, waiver, or proxy appointment;

(4) the name signed purports to be that of a pledgee, beneficial owner, or attorney-in-fact of the shareholder and, if the corporation requests, evidence acceptable to the corporation of the signatory's authority to sign for the shareholder has been presented with respect to the vote, consent, waiver, or proxy appointment;

(5) two or more persons are the shareholder as cotenants or fiduciaries and the name signed purports to be the name of at least one of the coowners and the person signing appears to be acting on behalf of all the coowners.

(c) The corporation is entitled to reject a vote, consent, waiver, or proxy appointment if the secretary or other officer or agent authorized to tabulate votes, acting in good faith, has reasonable basis for doubt about the validity of the signature on it or about the signatory's authority to sign for the shareholder.

(d) The corporation and its officer or agent who accepts or rejects a vote, consent, waiver, or proxy appointment in good faith and in accordance with the standards of this section are not liable in damages to the shareholder for the consequences of the acceptance or rejection.

(e) Corporate action based on the acceptance or rejection of a vote, consent, waiver, or proxy appointment under this section is valid unless a court of competent jurisdiction determines otherwise.

§ 7.25. Quorum and Voting Requirements for Voting Groups.—
(a) Shares entitled to vote as a separate voting group may take action on a matter at a meeting only if a quorum of those shares exists with respect to that matter. Unless the articles of incorporation or this Act provide otherwise, a majority of the votes entitled to be cast on the matter by the voting group constitutes a quorum of that voting group for action on that matter.

(b) Once a share is represented for any purpose at a meeting, it is deemed present for quorum purposes for the remainder of the meeting and for any adjournment of that meeting unless a new record date is or must be set for that adjourned meeting.

(c) If a quorum exists, action on a matter (other than the election of directors) by a voting group is approved if the votes cast within the voting group favoring the action exceed the votes cast opposing the action, unless the articles of incorporation or this Act require a greater number of affirmative votes.

(d) An amendment of articles of incorporation adding, changing, or deleting a quorum or voting requirement for a voting group greater than specified in subsection (b) or (c) is governed by section 7.27.

(e) The election of directors is governed by section 7.28.

§ 7.26. Action by Single and Multiple Voting Groups.—

(a) If the articles of incorporation or this Act provide for voting by a single voting group on a matter, action on that matter is taken when voted upon by that voting group as provided in section 7.25.

(b) If the articles of incorporation or this Act provide for voting by two or more voting groups on a matter, action on that matter is taken only when voted upon by each of those voting groups counted separately as provided in section 7.25. Action may be taken by one voting group on a matter even though no action is taken by another voting group entitled to vote on the matter.

§ 7.27. Greater Quorum or Voting Requirements.—

(a) The articles of incorporation may provide for a greater quorum or voting requirement for shareholders (or voting groups of shareholders) than is provided for by this Act.

(b) An amendment to the articles of incorporation that adds, changes, or deletes a greater quorum or voting requirement must meet the same quorum requirement and be adopted by the same vote and voting groups required to take action under the quorum and voting requirements then in effect or proposed to be adopted, whichever is greater.

§ 7.28. Voting for Directors; Cumulative Voting.—

(a) Unless otherwise provided in the articles of incorporation, directors are elected by a plurality of the votes cast by the shares entitled to vote in the election at a meeting at which a quorum is present.

(b) Shareholders do not have a right to cumulate their votes for directors unless the articles of incorporation so provide.

(c) A statement included in the articles of incorporation that "[all] [a designated voting group of] shareholders are entitled to cumulate their votes for directors" (or words of similar import) means that the shareholders designated are entitled to multiply the number of votes they are entitled to cast by the number of directors for whom they are entitled to vote and cast the product for a single candidate or distribute the product among two or more candidates.

(d) Shares otherwise entitled to vote cumulatively may not be voted cumulatively at a particular meeting unless:

(1) the meeting notice or proxy statement accompanying the notice states conspicuously that cumulative voting is authorized; or

(2) a shareholder who has the right to cumulate his votes gives notice to the corporation not less than 48 hours before the time set for the meeting of his intent to cumulate his votes during the meeting, and if one shareholder gives this notice all other shareholders in the same voting group participating in the election are entitled to cumulate their votes without giving further notice.

Subchapter C. Voting Trusts and Agreements

§ 7.30. Voting Trusts.—

(a) One or more shareholders may create a voting trust, conferring on a trustee the right to vote or otherwise act for them, by signing an agreement setting out the provisions of the trust (which may include anything consistent with its purpose) and transferring their shares to the trustee. When a voting trust agreement is signed, the trustee shall prepare a list of the names and addresses of all owners of beneficial interests in the trust, together with the number and class of shares each transferred to the trust, and deliver copies of the list and agreement to the corporation's principal office.

(b) A voting trust becomes effective on the date the first shares subject to the trust are registered in the trustee's name. A voting trust is valid for not more than 10 years after its effective date unless extended under subsection (c).

(c) All or some of the parties to a voting trust may extend it for additional terms of not more than 10 years each by signing an extension agreement and obtaining the voting trustee's written consent to the extension. An extension is valid for 10 years from the date the first shareholder signs the extension agreement. The voting trustee must deliver copies of the extension agreement and list of beneficial owners to the corporation's principal office. An extension agreement binds only those parties signing it.

§ 7.31. Voting Agreements.—

(a) Two or more shareholders may provide for the manner in which they will vote their shares by signing an agreement for that purpose. A voting agreement created under this section is not subject to the provisions of section 7.30.

(b) A voting agreement created under this section is specifically enforceable.

§ 7.32. Shareholder Agreements.—

(a) An agreement among the shareholders of a corporation that complies with this section is effective among the shareholders and the corporation even though it is inconsistent with one or more other provisions of this Act in that it:

(1) eliminates the board of directors or restricts the discretion or powers of the board of directors;

(2) governs the authorization or making of distributions whether or not in proportion to ownership of shares, subject the limitations in section 6.40;

(3) establishes who shall be directors or officers of the corporation, or their terms of office or manner of selection or removal;

(4) governs, in general or in regard to specific matters, the exercise or division of voting power by or between the shareholders and directors or by or among any of them, including use of weighted voting rights or director proxies;

(5) establishes the terms and conditions of any agreement for the transfer or use of property or the provision of services between the corporation and any shareholder, director, officer or employee of the corporation or among any of them;

(6) transfers to one or more shareholders or other persons all or part of the authority to exercise the corporate powers or to manage the business and affairs of the corporation, including the resolution of any issue about which there exists a deadlock among directors or shareholders;

(7) requires dissolution of the corporation at the request of one or more of the shareholders or upon the occurrence of a specified event or contingency; or

(8) otherwise governs the exercise of the corporate powers or the management of the business and affairs of the corporation or the relationship among the shareholders, the directors and the corporation, or among any of them, and is not contrary to public policy.

(b) An agreement authorized by this section shall be:

(1) set forth (A) in the articles of incorporation or bylaws and approved by all persons who are shareholders at the time of the agreement or (B) in a written agreement that is signed by all persons who are shareholders at the time of the agreement and is made known to the corporation;

(2) subject to amendment only by all persons who are shareholders at the time of the amendment, unless the agreement provides otherwise; and

(3) valid for 10 years, unless the agreement provides otherwise.

(C) The existence of an agreement authorized by this section shall be noted conspicuously on the front or back of each certificate for outstanding shares or on the information statement required by section 6.26(b). If at the time of the agreement the corporation has shares outstanding represented by certificates, the corporation shall recall the outstanding certificates and issue substitute certificates that comply with this subsection. The failure to note the existence of the agreement on the certificate or information statement shall not affect the validity of the agreement or any action taken pursuant to it. Any purchaser of shares who, at the time of purchase, did not have knowledge of the existence of the agreement shall be entitled to rescission of the purchase. A purchaser shall be deemed to have knowledge of the existence of the agreement if its existence is noted on the certificate or information statement for the shares in compliance with this subsection and, if the shares are not represented by a certificate, the information statement is delivered to the purchaser at or prior to the time of purchase of the shares. An action to enforce the right of rescission authorized by this subsection must be commenced within the earlier of 90 days after discovery of the existence of the agreement or two years after the time of purchase of the shares.

(d) An agreement authorized by this section shall cease to be effective when shares of the corporation are listed on a national securities exchange or regularly traded in a market maintained by one or more members of a national or affiliated securities association. If the agreement ceases to be effective for any reason, the board of directors may, if the agreement contained or referred to in the corporation's articles of incorporation or bylaws, adopt an amendment to the articles of incorporation or bylaws, without shareholder action, to delete the agreement and any references to it.

(e) An agreement authorized by this section that limits the discretion or powers of the board of directors shall relieve the directors of, and impose upon the person or persons in whom such discretion or powers are vested, liability for acts or omissions imposed by law on directors to the extent that the discretion or powers of the directors are limited by the agreement.

(f) The existence or performance of an agreement authorized by this section shall not be a ground for imposing personal liability on any shareholder for the acts or debts of the corporation even if the agreement or its performance treats the corporation as if it were a partnership or results in failure to observe the corporate formalities otherwise applicable to the matters governed by the agreement.

(g) Incorporators or subscribers for shares may act as shareholders with respect to an agreement authorized by this section if no shares have been issued when the agreement is made.

Subchapter D. Derivative Proceedings

§ 7.40. Subchapter Definitions.—In this subchapter:

(1) "Derivative proceeding" means a civil suit in the right of a domestic corporation or, to the extent provided in section 7.47, in the right of a foreign corporation.

(2) "Shareholder" includes a beneficial owner whose shares are held in a voting trust or held by a nominee on the beneficial owner's behalf.

§ 7.41. Standing.—A shareholder may not commence or maintain a derivative proceeding unless the shareholder:

(1) was a shareholder of the corporation at the time of the act or omission complained of or became a shareholder through transfer by operation of law from one who was a shareholder at that time; and

(2) fairly and adequately represents the interests of the corporation in enforcing the right of the corporation.

§ 7.42. Demand.—No shareholder may commence a derivative proceeding until:

(1) a written demand has been made upon the corporation to take suitable action; and

(2) 90 days have expired from the date the demand was made unless the shareholder has earlier been notified that the demand has been rejected by the corporation or unless irreparable injury to the corporation would result by waiting for the expiration of the 90 day period.

§ 7.43. Stay of Proceedings.—If the corporation commences an inquiry into the allegations made in the demand or complaint, the court may stay any derivative proceeding for such period as the court deems appropriate.

§ 7.44. Dismissal.—

(a) A derivative proceeding shall be dismissed by the court on motion by the corporation if one of the groups specified in subsections (b) or (f) has determined in good faith after conducting a reasonable inquiry upon which its conclusions are based that the maintenance of the derivative proceeding is not in the best interests of the corporation.

(b) Unless a panel is appointed pursuant to subsection (f), the determination in subsection (a) shall be made by:

(1) a majority vote of independent directors present at a meeting of the board of directors if the independent directors constitute a quorum; or

(2) a majority vote of a committee consisting of two or more independent directors appointed by majority vote of independent directors present at a meeting of the board of directors, whether or not such independent directors constituted a quorum.

(c) None of the following shall by itself cause a director to be considered not independent for purposes of this section:

(1) the nomination or election of the director by persons who are defendants in the derivative proceeding or against whom action is demanded;

(2) the naming of the director as a defendant in the derivative proceeding or as a person against whom action is demanded; or

(3) the approval by the director of the act being challenged in the derivative proceeding or demand if the act resulted in no personal benefit to the director.

(d) If a derivative proceeding is commenced after a determination has been made rejecting a demand by a shareholder, the complaint shall allege with particularity facts establishing either (1) that a majority of the board of directors did not consist of independent directors at the time the determination was made or (2) that the requirements of subsection (a) have not been met.

(e) If a majority of the board of directors does not consist of independent directors at the time the determination is made, the corporation shall have the burden of proving that the requirements of subsection (a) have been met. If a majority of the board of directors consists of independent directors at the time the determination is made, the plaintiff shall have the burden of proving that the requirements of subsection (a) have not been met.

(f) The court may appoint a panel of one or more independent persons upon motion by the corporation to make a determination whether the maintenance of the derivative proceeding is in the best interests of the corporation. In such case, the plaintiff shall have the burden of proving that the requirements of subsection (a) have not been met.

§ 7.45. Discontinuance or Settlement.—A derivative proceeding may not be discontinued or settled without the court's approval. If the court determines that a proposed discontinuance or settlement will substantially affect the interests of the corporation's shareholders or a class of shareholders, the court shall direct that notice be given to the shareholders affected.

§ 7.46. Payment of Expenses.—On termination of the derivative proceeding the court may:

(1) order the corporation to pay the plaintiff's reasonable expenses (including counsel fees) incurred in the proceeding if it finds that the proceeding has resulted in a substantial benefit to the corporation;

(2) order the plaintiff to pay any defendant's reasonable expenses (including counsel fees) incurred in defending the proceeding if it finds that the proceeding was commenced or maintained without reasonable cause or for an improper purpose; or

(3) order a party to pay an opposing party's reasonable expenses (including counsel fees) incurred because of the filing of a pleading, motion or other paper, if it finds that the pleading, motion or other paper was not well grounded in fact, after reasonable inquiry, or warranted by existing law or a good faith argument for the extension, modification or reversal of existing law and was interposed for an improper purpose, such as to harass or to cause unnecessary delay or needless increase in the cost of litigation.

§ 7.47. Applicability to Foreign Corporations.—In any derivative proceeding in the right of a foreign corporation, the matters covered by this subchapter shall be governed by the laws of the jurisdiction of incorporation of the foreign corporation except for sections 7.43, 7.45 and 7.46.

CHAPTER 8. DIRECTORS AND OFFICERS

Subchapter A. Board of Directors

§ 8.01. Requirement for and Duties of Board of Directors.—

(a) Except as provided in section 7.32, each corporation must have a board of directors.

(b) All corporate powers shall be exercised by or under the authority of, and the business and affairs of the corporation managed under the direction of, its board of directors, subject to any limitation set forth in the articles of incorporation or in an agreement authorized under section 7.32.

(c) A corporation having 50 or fewer shareholders may dispense with or limit the authority of a board of directors by describing in its articles of incorporation who will perform some or all of the duties of a board of directors.

§ 8.02. Qualifications of Directors.—The articles of incorporation or bylaws may prescribe qualifications for directors. A director need not be a resident of this state or a shareholder of the corporation unless the articles of incorporation or bylaws so prescribe.

§ 8.03. Number and Election of Directors.—

(a) A board of directors must consist of one or more individuals, with the number specified in or fixed in accordance with the articles of incorporation or bylaws.

(b) If a board of directors has power to fix or change the number of directors, the board may increase or decrease by 30 percent or less the number of directors last approved by the shareholders, but only the shareholders may increase or decrease by more than 30 percent the number of directors last approved by the shareholders.

(c) The articles of incorporation or bylaws may establish a variable range for the size of the board of directors by fixing a minimum and maximum number of directors. If a variable range is established, the number of directors may be fixed or changed from time to time, within the minimum and maximum, by the shareholders or the board of directors. After shares are issued, only the shareholders may change the range for the size of the board or change from a fixed to a variable-range size board or vice versa.

(d) Directors are elected at the first annual shareholders' meeting and at each annual meeting thereafter unless their terms are staggered under section 8.06.

§ 8.04. Election of Directors by Certain Classes of Shareholders.—If the articles of incorporation authorize dividing the shares into classes, the articles may also authorize the election of all or a specified number of directors by the holders of one or more authorized classes of shares. A class (or classes) of shares entitled to elect one or more directors is a separate voting group for purposes of the election of directors.

§ 8.05. Terms of Directors Generally.—

(a) The terms of the initial directors of a corporation expire at the first shareholders' meeting at which directors are elected.

(b) The terms of all other directors expire at the next annual shareholders' meeting following their election unless their terms are staggered under section 8.06.

(c) A decrease in the number of directors does not shorten an incumbent director's term.

(d) The term of a director elected to fill a vacancy expires at the next shareholders' meeting at which directors are elected.

(e) Despite the expiration of a director's term, he continues to serve until his successor is elected and qualifies or until there is a decrease in the number of directors.

§ 8.06. Staggered Terms for Directors.—If there are nine or more directors, the articles of incorporation may provide for staggering their terms by dividing the total number of directors into two or three groups, with each group containing one half or one-third of the total, as near as may be. In that event, the terms of directors in the first group expire at the first annual shareholders' meeting after their election, the terms of the second group expire at the second annual shareholders' meeting after their election, and the terms of the third group, if any, expire at the third annual shareholders' meeting after their election. At each annual shareholders' meeting held thereafter, directors shall be chosen for a term of two years or three years, as the case may be, to succeed those whose terms expire.

§ 8.07. Resignation of Directors.—

(a) A director may resign at any time by delivering written notice to the board of directors, its chairman, or to the corporation.

(b) A resignation is effective when the notice is delivered unless the notice specifies a later effective date.

§ 8.08. Removal of Directors by Shareholders.—

(a) The shareholders may remove one or more directors with or without cause unless the articles of incorporation provide that directors may be removed only for cause.

(b) If a director is elected by a voting group of shareholders, only the shareholders of that voting group may participate in the vote to remove him.

(c) If cumulative voting is authorized, a director may not be removed if the number of votes sufficient to elect him under cumulative voting is voted against his removal. If cumulative voting is not authorized, a director may be removed only if the number of votes cast to remove him exceeds the number of votes cast not to remove him.

(d) A director may be removed by the shareholders only at a meeting called for the purpose of removing him and the meeting notice must state that the purpose, or one of the purposes, of the meeting is removal of the director.

§ 8.09. Removal of Directors by Judicial Proceeding.—

(a) The [name or describe] court of the county where a corporation's principal office (or, if none in this state, its registered office) is located may remove a director of the corporation from office in a proceeding commenced either by the corporation or by its shareholders holding at least 10 percent of the outstanding shares of any class if the court finds that (1) the director engaged in fraudulent or dishonest conduct, or gross abuse of authority or discretion, with respect to the corporation and (2) removal is in the best interest of the corporation.

(b) The court that removes a director may bar the director from reelection for a period prescribed by the court.

(c) If shareholders commence a proceeding under subsection (a), they shall make the corporation a party defendant.

§ 8.10. Vacancy on Board.—

(a) Unless the articles of incorporation provide otherwise, if a vacancy occurs on a board of directors, including a vacancy resulting from an increase in the number of directors:

    (1) the shareholders may fill the vacancy;

    (2) the board of directors may fill the vacancy; or

    (3) if the directors remaining in office constitute fewer than a quorum of the board, they may fill the vacancy by the affirmative vote of a majority of all the directors remaining in office.

(b) If the vacant office was held by a director elected by a voting group of shareholders, only the holders of shares of that voting group are entitled to vote to fill the vacancy if it is filled by the shareholders.

(c) A vacancy that will occur at a specific later date (by reason of a resignation effective at a later date under section 8.07(b) or otherwise) may be filled before the vacancy occurs but the new director may not take office until the vacancy occurs.

§ 8.11. Compensation of Directors.—Unless the articles of incorporation or bylaws provide otherwise, the board of directors may fix the compensation of directors.

Subchapter B. Meetings and Action of the Board

§ 8.20. Meetings.—

(a) The board of directors may hold regular or special meetings in or out of this state.

(b) Unless the articles of incorporation or bylaws provide otherwise, the board of directors may permit any or all directors to participate in a regular or special meeting by, or conduct the meeting through the use of, any means of communication by which all directors participating may simultaneously hear each other during the meeting. A director participating in a meeting by this means is deemed to be present in person at the meeting.

§ 8.21. Action Without Meeting.—

(a) Unless the articles of incorporation or bylaws provide otherwise, action required or permitted by this Act to be taken at a board of directors' meeting may be taken without a meeting if the action is taken by all members of the board. The action must be evidenced by one or more written consents describing the action taken, signed by each director, and included in the minutes or filed with the corporate records reflecting the action taken.

(b) Action taken under this section is effective when the last director signs the consent, unless the consent specifies a different effective date.

(c) A consent signed under this section has the effect of a meeting vote and may be described as such in any document.

§ 8.22. Notice of Meeting.—

(a) Unless the articles of incorporation or bylaws provide otherwise, regular meetings of the board of directors may be held without notice of the date, time, place, or purpose of the meeting.

(b) Unless the articles of incorporation or bylaws provide for a longer or shorter period, special meetings of the board of directors must be preceded by at least two days' notice of the date, time, and place of the meeting. The notice need not describe the purpose of the special meeting unless required by the articles of incorporation or bylaws.

§8.23. Waiver of Notice.—

(a) A director may waive any notice required by this Act, the articles of incorporation, or bylaws before or after the date and time stated in the notice. Except as provided by subsection (b), the waiver must be in writing, signed by the director entitled to the notice, and filed with the minutes or corporate records.

(b) A director's attendance at or participation in a meeting waives any required notice to him of the meeting unless the director at the beginning of the meeting (or promptly upon his arrival) objects to holding the meeting or transacting business at the meeting and does not thereafter vote for or assent to action taken at the meeting.

§8.24. Quorum and Voting.—

(a) Unless the articles of incorporation or bylaws require a greater number, a quorum of a board of directors consists of:

    (1) a majority of the fixed number of directors if the corporation has a fixed board size; or

    (2) a majority of the number of directors prescribed, or if no number is prescribed the number in office immediately before the meeting begins, if the corporation has a variable-range size board.

(b) The articles of incorporation or bylaws may authorize a quorum of a board of directors to consist of no fewer than one-third of the fixed or prescribed number of directors determined under subsection (a).

(c) If a quorum is present when a vote is taken, the affirmative vote of a majority of directors present is the act of the board of directors unless the articles of incorporation or bylaws require the vote of a greater number of directors.

(d) A director who is present at a meeting of the board of directors or a committee of the board of directors when corporate action is taken is deemed to

have assented to the action taken unless: (1) he objects at the beginning of the meeting (or promptly upon his arrival) to holding it or transacting business at the meeting; (2) his dissent or abstention from the action taken is entered in the minutes of the meeting; or (3) he delivers written notice of his dissent or abstention to the presiding officer of the meeting before its adjournment or to the corporation immediately after adjournment of the meeting. The right of dissent or abstention is not available to a director who votes in favor of the action taken.

§ 8.25. Committees.—

(a) Unless the articles of incorporation or bylaws provide otherwise, a board of directors may create one or more committees and appoint members of the board of directors to serve on them. Each committee may have two or more members, who serve at the pleasure of the board of directors.

(b) The creation of a committee and appointment of members to it must be approved by the greater of (1) a majority of all the directors in office when the action is taken or (2) the number of directors required by the articles of incorporation or bylaws to take action under section 8.24.

(c) Sections 8.20 through 8.24, which govern meetings, action without meetings, notice and waiver of notice, and quorum and voting requirements of the board of directors, apply to committees and their members as well.

(d) To the extent specified by the board of directors or in the articles of incorporation or bylaws, each committee may exercise the authority of the board of directors under section 8.01.

(e) A committee may not, however:

    (1) authorize distributions;

    (2) approve or propose to shareholders action that this Act requires be approved by shareholders;

    (3) fill vacancies on the board of directors or on any of its committees;

    (4) amend articles of incorporation pursuant to section 10.02;

    (5) adopt, amend, or repeal bylaws;

    (6) approve a plan of merger not requiring shareholder approval;

    (7) authorize or approve reacquisition of shares, except according to a formula or method prescribed by the board of directors; or

    (8) authorize or approve the issuance or sale or contract for sale of shares, or determine the designation and relative rights, preferences, and limitations of a class or series of shares, except that the board of directors may authorize a committee (or a senior executive officer of the corporation) to do so within limits specifically prescribed by the board of directors.

(f) The creation of, delegation of authority to, or action by a committee does not alone constitute compliance by a director with the standards of conduct described in section 8.30.

Subchapter C. Standards of Conduct

§ 8.30. General Standards for Directors.—

(a) A director shall discharge his duties as a director, including his duties as a member of a committee:

    (1) in good faith;

    (2) with the care an ordinarily prudent person in a like position would exercise under similar circumstances; and

    (3) in a manner he reasonably believes to be in the best interests of the corporation.

(b) In discharging his duties a director is entitled to rely on information, opinions, reports, or statements, including financial statements and other financial data, if prepared or presented by:

    (1) one or more officers or employees of the corporation whom the director reasonably believes to be reliable and competent in the matters presented;

    (2) legal counsel, public accountants, or other persons as to matters the director reasonably believes are within the person's professional or expert competence; or

    (3) a committee of the board of directors of which he is not a member if the director reasonably believes the committee merits confidence.

(c) A director is not acting in good faith if he has knowledge concerning the matter in question that makes reliance otherwise permitted by subsection (b) unwarranted.

(d) A director is not liable for any action taken as a director, or any failure to take any action, if he performed the duties of his office in compliance with this section.

§ 8.31. Director Conflict of Interest.—

(a) A conflict of interest transaction is a transaction with the corporation in which a director of the corporation has a direct or indirect interest. A conflict of interest transaction is not voidable by the corporation solely because of the director's interest in the transaction if any one of the following is true:

    (1) the material facts of the transaction and the director's interest were disclosed or known to the board of directors or a committee of the board of directors and the board of directors or committee authorized, approved, or ratified the transaction;

    (2) the material facts of the transaction and the director's interest were disclosed or known to the shareholders entitled to vote and they authorized, approved, or ratified the transaction; or

    (3) the transaction was fair to the corporation.

(b) For purposes of this section, a director of the corporation has an indirect interest in a transaction if (1) another entity in which he has a material financial interest or in which he is a general partner is a party to the transaction or (2) another entity of which he is a director, officer, or trustee is a party to the transaction and the transaction is or should be considered by the board of directors of the corporation.

(c) For purposes of subsection (a)(1), a conflict of interest transaction is authorized, approved, or ratified if it receives the affirmative vote of a majority of the directors on the board of directors (or on the committee) who have no direct or indirect interest in the transaction, but a transaction may not be authorized, approved, or ratified under this section by a single director. If a majority of the directors who have no direct or indirect interest in the transaction vote to authorize, approve, or ratify the transaction, a quorum is present for the purpose of taking action under this section. The presence of, or a vote cast by, a director with a direct or indirect interest in the transaction does not affect the validity of any action taken under subsection (a)(1) if the transaction is otherwise authorized, approved, or ratified as provided in that subsection.

(d) For purposes of subsection (a)(2), a conflict of interest transaction is authorized, approved, or ratified if it receives the vote of a majority of the shares entitled to be counted under this subsection. Shares owned by or voted under the control of a director who has a direct or indirect interest in the transaction, and shares owned by or voted under the control of an entity described in subsection (b)(1), may not be counted in a vote of shareholders to determine whether to authorize, approve, or ratify a conflict of interest transaction under subsection (a)(2). The vote of those shares, however, is counted in determining whether the transaction is approved under other sections of this Act. A majority of the shares, whether or not present, that are entitled to be counted in a vote on the transaction under this subsection constitutes a quorum for the purpose of taking action under this section.

§ 8.32. Loans to Directors.—

(a) Except as provided by subsection (c), a corporation may not lend money to or guarantee the obligation of a director of the corporation unless:

(1) the particular loan or guarantee is approved by a majority of the votes represented by the outstanding voting shares of all classes, voting as a single voting group, except the votes of shares owned by or voted under the control of the benefited director; or

(2) the corporation's board of directors determines that the loan or guarantee benefits the corporation and either approves the specific loan or guarantee or a general plan authorizing loans and guarantees.

(b) The fact that a loan or guarantee is made in violation of this section does not affect the borrower's liability on the loan.

(c) This section does not apply to loans and guarantees authorized by statute regulating any special class of corporations.

§ 8.33. Liability for Unlawful Distributions.—

(a) A director who votes for or assents to a distribution made in violation of section 6.40 or the articles of incorporation is personally liable to the corporation for the amount of the distribution that exceeds what could have been distributed without violating section 6.40 or the articles of incorporation if it is established that he did not perform his duties in compliance with section 8.30. In any proceeding commenced under this section, a director has all of the defenses ordinarily available to a director.

(b) A director held liable under subsection (a) for an unlawful distribution is entitled to contribution:

(1) from every other director who could be liable under subsection (a) for the unlawful distribution; and

(2) from each shareholder for the amount the shareholder accepted knowing the distribution was made in violation of section 6.40 or the articles of incorporation.

(c) A proceeding under this section is barred unless it is commenced within two years after the date on which the effect of the distribution was measured under section 6.40(e) or (g).

Subchapter D. Officers

§ 8.40. Required Officers.—

(a) A corporation has the officers described in its bylaws or appointed by the board of directors in accordance with the bylaws.

(b) A duly appointed officer may appoint one or more officers or assistant officers if authorized by the bylaws or the board of directors.

(c) The bylaws or the board of directors shall delegate to one of the officers responsibility for preparing minutes of the directors' and shareholders' meetings and for authenticating records of the corporation.

(d) The same individual may simultaneously hold more than one office in a corporation.

§ 8.41. Duties of Officers.—Each officer has the authority and shall perform the duties set forth in the bylaws or, to the extent consistent with the bylaws, the duties prescribed by the board of directors or by direction of an officer authorized by the board of directors to prescribe the duties of other officers.

§ 8.42. Standards of Conduct for Officers.—

(a) An officer with discretionary authority shall discharge his duties under that authority:

(1) in good faith;

(2) with the care an ordinarily prudent person in a like position would exercise under similar circumstances; and

(3) in a manner he reasonably believes to be in the best interests of the corporation.

(b) In discharging his duties an officer is entitled to rely on information, opinions, reports, or statements, including financial statements and other financial data, if prepared or presented by:

(1) one or more officers or employees of the corporation whom the officer reasonably believes to be reliable and competent in the matters presented; or

(2) legal counsel, public accountants, or other persons as to matters the officer reasonably believes are within the person's professional or expert competence.

(c) An officer is not acting in good faith if he has knowledge concerning the matter in question that makes reliance otherwise permitted by subsection (b) unwarranted.

(d) An officer is not liable for any action taken as an officer, or any failure to take any action, if he performed the duties of his office in compliance with this section.

§ 8.43. Resignation and Removal of Officers.—

(a) An officer may resign at any time by delivering notice to the corporation. A resignation is effective when the notice is delivered unless the notice specifies a later effective date. If a resignation is made effective at a later date and the corporation accepts the future effective date, its board of directors may fill the pending vacancy before the effective date if the board of directors provides that the successor does not take office until the effective date.

(b) A board of directors may remove any officer at any time with or without cause.

§ 8.44. Contract Rights of Officers.—

(a) The appointment of an officer does not itself create contract rights.

(b) An officer's removal does not affect the officer's contract rights, if any, with the corporation. An officer's resignation does not affect the corporation's contract rights, if any, with the officer.

Subchapter E. Indemnification

§ 8.50. Subchapter Definitions.—In this subchapter:

(1) "Corporation" includes any domestic or foreign predecessor entity of a corporation in a merger or other transaction in which the predecessor's existence ceased upon consummation of the transaction.

(2) "Director" means an individual who is or was a director of a corporation or an individual who, while a director of a corporation, is or was serving at the corporation's request as a director, officer, partner, trustee, employee, or agent of another foreign or domestic corporation, partnership, joint venture, trust, employee benefit plan, or other enterprise. A director is considered to be serving an employee benefit plan at the corporation's request if his duties to the corporation also impose duties on, or otherwise involve services by, him to the plan or to participants in or beneficiaries of the plan. "Director" includes, unless the context requires otherwise, the estate or personal representative of a director.

(3) "Expenses" include counsel fees.

(4) "Liability" means the obligation to pay a judgment, settlement, penalty, fine (including an excise tax assessed with respect to an employee benefit plan), or reasonable expenses incurred with respect to a proceeding.

(5) "Official capacity" means: (i) when used with respect to a director, the office of director in a corporation; and (ii) when used with respect to an individual other than a director, as contemplated in section 8.56, the office in a corporation held by the officer or the employment or agency relationship undertaken by the employee or agent on behalf of the corporation. "Official capacity" does not include service for any other foreign or domestic corporation or any partnership, joint venture, trust, employee benefit plan, or other enterprise.

(6) "Party" includes an individual who was, is, or is threatened to be made a named defendant or respondent in a proceeding.

(7) "Proceeding" means any threatened, pending, or completed action, suit, or proceeding, whether civil, criminal, administrative, or investigative and whether formal or informal.

§ 8.51. Authority to Indemnify.—

(a) Except as provided in subsection (d), a corporation may indemnify an individual made a party to a proceeding because he is or was a director against liability incurred in the proceeding if:

(1) he conducted himself in good faith; and

(2) he reasonably believed:

(i) in the case of conduct in his official capacity with the corporation, that his conduct was in its best interests; and

(ii) in all other cases, that his conduct was at least not opposed to its best interests; and

(3) in the case of any criminal proceeding, he had no reasonable cause to believe his conduct was unlawful.

(b) A director's conduct with respect to an employee benefit plan for a purpose he reasonably believed to be in the interests of the participants in and beneficiaries of the plan is conduct that satisfies the requirement of subsection (a)(2)(ii).

(c) The termination of a proceeding by judgment, order, settlement, conviction, or upon a plea of nolo contendere or its equivalent is not, of itself, determinative that the director did not meet the standard of conduct described in this section.

(d) A corporation may not indemnify a director under this section:

(1) in connection with a proceeding by or in the right of the corporation in which the director was adjudged liable to the corporation; or

(2) in connection with any other proceeding charging improper personal benefit to him, whether or not involving action in his official capacity, in which he was adjudged liable on the basis that personal benefit was improperly received by him.

(e) Indemnification permitted under this section in connection with a proceeding by or in the right of the corporation is limited to reasonable expenses incurred in connection with the proceeding.

§ 8.52. **Mandatory Indemnification.**—Unless limited by its articles of incorporation, a corporation shall indemnify a director who was wholly successful, on the merits or otherwise, in the defense of any proceeding to which he was a party because he is or was a director of the corporation against reasonable expenses incurred by him in connection with the proceeding.

§ 8.53. **Advance for Expenses.**—

(a) A corporation may pay for or reimburse the reasonable expenses incurred by a director who is a party to a proceeding in advance of final disposition of the proceeding if:

(1) the director furnishes the corporation a written affirmation of his good faith belief that he has met the standard of conduct described in section 8.51;

(2) the director furnishes the corporation a written undertaking, executed personally or on his behalf, to repay the advance if it is ultimately determined that he did not meet the standard of conduct; and

(3) a determination is made that the facts then known to those making the determination would not preclude indemnification under this subchapter.

(b) The undertaking required by subsection (a)(2) must be an unlimited general obligation of the director but need not be secured and may be accepted without reference to financial ability to make repayment.

(c) Determinations and authorizations of payments under this section shall be made in the manner specified in section 8.55.

§ 8.54. **Court-Ordered Indemnification.**—Unless a corporation's articles of incorporation provide otherwise, a director of the corporation who is a party to a proceeding may apply for indemnification to the court conducting the proceeding or to another court of competent jurisdiction. On receipt of an application, the court after giving any notice the court considers necessary may order indemnification if it determines:

(1) the director is entitled to mandatory indemnification under section 8.52, in which case the court shall also order the corporation to pay the director's reasonable expenses incurred to obtain court-ordered indemnification; or

(2) the director is fairly and reasonably entitled to indemnification in view of all the relevant circumstances, whether or not he met the standard of conduct set forth in section 8.51 or was adjudged liable as described in section 8.51(d), but if he was adjudged so liable his indemnification is limited to reasonable expenses incurred.

§ 8.55. **Determination and Authorization of Indemnification.**—

(a) A corporation may not indemnify a director under section 8.51 unless authorized in the specific case after a determination has been made that indemnification of the director is permissible in the circumstances because he has met the standard of conduct set forth in section 8.51.

(b) The determination shall be made:

(1) by the board of directors by majority vote of a quorum consisting of directors not at the time parties to the proceeding;

(2) if a quorum cannot be obtained under subdivision (1), by majority vote of a committee duly designated by the board of directors (in which designation directors who are parties may participate), consisting solely of two or more directors not at the time parties to the proceeding;

(3) by special legal counsel:

(i) selected by the board of directors or its committee in the manner prescribed in subdivision (1) or (2); or

(ii) if a quorum of the board of directors cannot be obtained under subdivision (1) and a committee cannot be designated under subdivision (2), selected by majority vote of the full board of directors (in which selection directors who are parties may participate); or

(4) by the shareholders, but shares owned by or voted under the control of directors who are at the time parties to the proceeding may not be voted on the determination.

(c) Authorization of indemnification and evaluation as to reasonableness of expenses shall be made in the same manner as the determination that indemnification is permissible, except that if the determination is made by special legal counsel, authorization of indemnification and evaluation as to reasonableness of expenses shall be made by those entitled under subsection (b)(3) to select counsel.

§ 8.56. **Indemnification of Officers, Employees, and Agents.**—Unless a corporation's articles of incorporation provide otherwise:

(1) an officer of the corporation who is not a director is entitled to mandatory indemnification under section 8.52, and is entitled to apply for court-ordered indemnification under section 8.54, in each case to the same extent as a director;

(2) the corporation may indemnify and advance expenses under this subchapter to an officer, employee, or agent of the corporation who is not a director to the same extent as to a director; and

(3) a corporation may also indemnify and advance expenses to an officer, employee, or agent who is not a director to the extent, consistent with public policy, that may be provided by its articles of incorporation, bylaws, general or specific action of its board of directors, or contract.

§ 8.57. **Insurance.**—A corporation may purchase and maintain insurance on behalf of an individual who is or was a director, officer, employee, or agent of the corporation, or who, while a director, officer, employee, or agent of the corporation, is or was serving at the request of the corporation as a director, officer, partner, trustee, employee, or agent of another foreign or domestic corporation, partnership, joint venture, trust, employee benefit plan, or other enterprise, against liability asserted against or incurred by him in that capacity or arising from his status as a director, officer, employee, or agent, whether or not the corporation would have power to indemnify him against the same liability under section 8.51 or 8.52.

§ 8.58. **Application of Subchapter.**—

(a) A provision treating a corporation's indemnification of or advance for expenses to directors that is contained in its articles of incorporation, bylaws, a resolution of its shareholders or board of directors, or in a contract or otherwise, is valid only if and to the extent the provision is consistent with this subchapter. If articles of incorporation limit indemnification or advance for expenses, indemnification and advance for expenses are valid only to the extent consistent with the articles.

(b) This subchapter does not limit a corporation's power to pay or reimburse expenses incurred by a director in connection with his appearance as a witness in a proceeding at a time when he has not been made a named defendant or respondent to the proceeding.

Subchapter F. Directors' Conflicting Interest Transactions

§ 8.60. **Subchapter Definitions.**—In this subchapter:

(1) "Conflicting interest" with respect to a corporation means the interest a director of the corporation has respecting a transaction effected or proposed to be effected by the corporation (or by a subsidiary of the corporation or any other entity in which the corporation has a controlling interest) if

(i) whether or not the transaction is brought before the board of directors of the corporation for action, the director knows at the time of commitment that he or a related person is a party to the transaction or has a beneficial financial interest in or so closely linked to the transaction and of such financial significance to the director or a related person that the interest would reasonably be expected to exert an influence on the director's judgment if he were called upon to vote on the transaction; or

(ii) the transaction is brought (or is of such character and significance to the corporation that it would in the normal course be brought) before the board of directors of the corporation for action, and the director knows at the time of commitment that any of the following persons is either a party to the transaction or has a beneficial financial interest in or so closely linked to the transaction and of such financial significance to the person that the interest would reasonably be expected to exert an influence on the director's judgment if he were called upon to vote on the transaction: (A) an entity (other than the corporation) of which the director is a director, general partner, agent, or employee; (B) a person that controls one or more of the entities specified in subclause (A) or an entity that is controlled by, or is under common control with, one or more of the entities specified in subclause (A); or (C) an individual who is a general partner, principal, or employer of the director.

(2) "Director's conflicting interest transaction" with respect to a corporation means a transaction effected or proposed to be effected by the corporation (or by a subsidiary of the corporation or any other entity in which the corporation has a controlling interest) respecting which a director of the corporation has a conflicting interest.

(3) "Related person" of a director means (i) the spouse (or a parent or sibling thereof) of the director, or a child, grandchild, sibling, parent (or spouse of any thereof) of the director, or an individual having the same home as the director, or a trust or estate of which an individual specified in this clause (i) is a substantial beneficiary; or (ii) a trust, estate, incompetent, conservatee, or minor of which the director is a fiduciary.

(4) "Required disclosure" means disclosure by the director who has a conflicting interest of (i) the existence and nature of his conflicting interest, and (ii) all facts known to him respecting the subject matter of the transaction that an ordinarily prudent person would reasonably believe to be material to a judgment about whether or not to proceed with the transaction.

(5) "Time of commitment" respecting a transaction means the time when the transaction is consummated or, if made pursuant to contract, the time when the corporation (or its subsidiary or the entity in which it has a controlling interest) becomes contractually obligated so that its unilateral withdrawal from the transaction would entail significant loss, liability, or other damage.

§ 8.61. **Judicial Action.**—

(a) A transaction effected or proposed to be effected by a corporation (or by a subsidiary of the corporation or any other entity in which the corporation has a controlling interest) that is not a director's conflicting interest transaction may not be enjoined, set aside, or give rise to an award of damages or other sanctions, in a proceeding by a shareholder or by or in the right of the corporation, because a director of the corporation, or any person with whom or which he has a personal, economic, or other association, has an interest in the transaction.

(b) A director's conflicting interest transaction may not be enjoined, set aside, or give rise to an award of damages or other sanctions, in a proceeding by a shareholder or by or in the right of the corporation, because the director, or any person with whom or which he has a personal, economic, or other association, has an interest in the transaction, if:

(1) directors' action respecting the transaction was at any time taken in compliance with section 8.62;

(2) shareholders' action respecting the transaction was at any time taken in compliance with section 8.63; or

(3) the transaction, judged according to the circumstances at the time of commitment, is established to have been fair to the corporation.

§ 8.62. Directors' Action.—

(a) Directors' action respecting a transaction is effective for purposes of section 8.61(b)(1) if the transaction received the affirmative vote of a majority (but no fewer than two) of those qualified directors on the board of directors or on a duly empowered committee of the board who voted on the transaction after either required disclosure to them (to the extent the information was not known by them) or compliance with subsection (b); provided that action by a committee is so effective only if:

(1) all its members are qualified directors; and

(2) its members are either all the qualified directors on the board or are appointed by the affirmative vote of a majority of the qualified directors on the board.

(b) If a director has a conflicting interest respecting a transaction, but neither he nor a related person of the director specified in section 8.60(3)(i) is a party to the transaction, and if the director has a duty under law or professional canon, or a duty of confidentiality to another person, respecting information relating to the transaction such that the director may not make the disclosure described in section 8.60(4)(ii), then disclosure is sufficient for purposes of subsection (a) if the director (1) discloses to the directors voting on the transaction the existence and nature of his conflicting interest and informs them of the character and limitations imposed by that duty before their vote on the transaction, and (2) plays no part, directly or indirectly, in their deliberations or vote.

(c) A majority (but no fewer than two) of all the qualified directors on the board of directors, or on the committee, constitutes a quorum for purposes of action that complies with this section. Directors' action that otherwise complies with this section is not affected by the presence or vote of a director who is not a qualified director.

(d) For purposes of this section, "qualified director" means, with respect to a director's conflicting interest transaction, any director who does not have either (1) a conflicting interest respecting the transaction, or (2) a familial, financial, professional, or employment relationship with a second director who does have a conflicting interest respecting the transaction, which relationship would, in the circumstances, reasonably be expected to exert an influence on the first director's judgment when voting on the transaction.

§ 8.63. Shareholders' Action.—

(a) Shareholders' action respecting a transaction is effective for purposes of section 8.61(b)(2) if a majority of the votes entitled to be cast by the holders of all qualified shares were cast in favor of the transaction after (1) notice to shareholders describing the director's conflicting interest transaction, (2) provision of the information referred to in subsection (d), and (3) required disclosure to the shareholders who voted on the transaction (to the extent the information was not known by them).

(b) For purposes of this section, "qualified shares" means any shares entitled to vote with respect to the director's conflicting interest transaction except shares that, to the knowledge, before the vote, of the secretary (or other officer or agent of the corporation authorized to tabulate votes), are beneficially owned (or the voting of which is controlled) by a director who has a conflicting interest respecting the transaction or a related person of the director, or both.

(c) A majority of the votes entitled to be cast by the holders of all qualified shares constitutes a quorum for purposes of action that complies with this section. Subject to the provisions of subsections (d) and (e), shareholders' action that otherwise complies with this section is not affected by the presence or voting of holders, or the voting, of shares that are not qualified shares.

(d) For purposes of compliance with subsection (a), a director who has a conflicting interest respecting the transaction shall, before the shareholders' vote, inform the secretary (or other officer or agent of the corporation authorized to tabulate votes) of the number, and the identity of persons holding or controlling the vote, of all shares that the director knows are beneficially owned (or the voting of which is controlled) by the director or by a related person of the director, or both.

(e) If a shareholders' vote does not comply with subsection (a) solely because of a failure of a director to comply with subsection (d), and if the director establishes that his failure did not determine and was not intended by him to influence the outcome of the vote, the court may, with or without further proceedings respecting section 8.61(b)(3), take such action respecting the transaction and the director, and give such effect, if any, to the shareholders' vote, as it considers appropriate in the circumstances.

CHAPTER 9

[Reserved]

CHAPTER 10. AMENDMENT OF ARTICLES OF INCORPORATION AND BYLAWS

Subchapter A. Amendment of Articles of Incorporation

§ 10.01. Authority to Amend.—

(a) A corporation may amend its articles of incorporation at any time to add or change a provision that is required or permitted in the articles of incorporation or to delete a provision not required in the articles of incorporation. Whether a provision is required or permitted in the articles of incorporation is determined as of the effective date of the amendment.

(b) A shareholder of the corporation does not have a vested property right resulting from any provision in the articles of incorporation, including provisions relating to management, control, capital structure, dividend entitlement, or purpose or duration of the corporation.

§ 10.02. Amendment by Board of Directors.—Unless the articles of incorporation provide otherwise, a corporation's board of directors may adopt one or more amendments to the corporation's articles of incorporation without shareholder action:

(1) to extend the duration of the corporation if it was incorporated at a time when limited duration was required by law;

(2) to delete the names and addresses of the initial directors;

(3) to delete the name and address of the initial registered agent or registered office, if a statement of change is on file with the secretary of state;

(4) to change each issued and unissued authorized share of an outstanding class into a greater number of whole shares if the corporation has only shares of that class outstanding;

(5) to change the corporate name by substituting the word "corporation," "incorporated," "company," "limited," or the abbreviation "corp.," "inc.," "co.," or "ltd.," for a similar word or abbreviation in the name, or by adding, deleting, or changing a geographical attribution for the name; or

(6) to make any other change expressly permitted by this Act to be made without shareholder action.

§ 10.03. Amendment by Board of Directors and Shareholders.—

(a) A corporation's board of directors may propose one or more amendments to the articles of incorporation for submission to the shareholders.

(b) For the amendment to be adopted:

(1) the board of directors must recommend the amendment to the shareholders unless the board of directors determines that because of conflict of interest or other special circumstances it should make no recommendation and communicates the basis for its determination to the shareholders with the amendment; and

(2) the shareholders entitled to vote on the amendment must approve the amendment as provided in subsection (e).

(c) The board of directors may condition its submission of the proposed amendment on any basis.

(d) The corporation shall notify each shareholder, whether or not entitled to vote, of the proposed shareholders' meeting in accordance with section 7.05. The notice of meeting must also state that the purpose, or one of the purposes, of the meeting is to consider the proposed amendment and contain or be accompanied by a copy or summary of the amendment.

(e) Unless this Act, the articles of incorporation, or the board of directors (acting pursuant to subsection (c)) require a greater vote or a vote by voting groups, the amendment to be adopted must be approved by:

(1) a majority of the votes entitled to be cast on the amendment by any voting group with respect to which the amendment would create dissenters' rights; and

(2) the votes required by sections 7.25 and 7.26 by every other voting group entitled to vote on the amendment.

§ 10.04. Voting on Amendments by Voting Groups.—

(a) The holders of the outstanding shares of a class are entitled to vote as a separate voting group (if shareholder voting is otherwise required by this Act) on a proposed amendment if the amendment would:

(1) increase or decrease the aggregate number of authorized shares of the class;

(2) effect an exchange or reclassification of all or part of the shares of the class into shares of another class;

(3) effect an exchange or reclassification, or create the right of exchange, of all or part of the shares of another class into shares of the class;

(4) change the designation, rights, preferences, or limitations of all or part of the shares of the class;

(5) change the shares of all or part of the class into a different number of shares of the same class;

(6) create a new class of shares having rights or preferences with respect to distributions or to dissolution that are prior, superior, or substantially equal to the shares of the class;

(7) increase the rights, preferences, or number of authorized shares of any class that, after giving effect to the amendment, have rights or preferences with respect to distributions or to dissolution that are prior, superior, or substantially equal to the shares of the class;

(8) limit or deny an existing preemptive right of all or part of the shares of the class; or

(9) cancel or otherwise affect rights to distributions or dividends that have accumulated but not yet been declared on all or part of the shares of the class.

(b) If a proposed amendment would affect a series of a class of shares in one or more of the ways described in subsection (a), the shares of that series are entitled to vote as a separate voting group on the proposed amendment.

(c) If a proposed amendment that entitles two or more series of shares to vote as separate voting groups under this section would affect those two or more series in the same or a substantially similar way, the shares of all the series so affected must vote together as a single voting group on the proposed amendment.

(d) A class or series of shares is entitled to the voting rights granted by this section although the articles of incorporation provide that the shares are nonvoting shares.

§ 10.05. Amendment Before Issuance of Shares.—If a corporation has not yet issued shares, its incorporators or board of directors may adopt one or more amendments to the corporation's articles of incorporation.

§ 10.06. **Articles of Amendment.**—A corporation amending its articles of incorporation shall deliver to the secretary of state for filing articles of amendment setting forth:

(1) the name of the corporation;

(2) the text of each amendment adopted;

(3) if an amendment provides for an exchange, reclassification, or cancellation of issued shares, provisions for implementing the amendment if not contained in the amendment itself;

(4) the date of each amendment's adoption;

(5) if an amendment was adopted by the incorporators or board of directors without shareholder action, a statement to that effect and that shareholder action was not required;

(6) if an amendment was approved by the shareholders:

(i) the designation, number of outstanding shares, number of votes entitled to be cast by each voting group entitled to vote separately on the amendment, and number of votes of each voting group indisputably represented at the meeting;

(ii) either the total number of votes cast for and against the amendment by each voting group entitled to vote separately on the amendment or the total number of undisputed votes cast for the amendment by each voting group and a statement that the number cast for the amendment by each voting group was sufficient for approval by that voting group.

§ 10.07. **Restated Articles of Incorporation.**—

(a) A corporation's board of directors may restate its articles of incorporation at any time with or without shareholder action.

(b) The restatement may include one or more amendments to the articles. If the restatement includes an amendment requiring shareholder approval, it must be adopted as provided in section 10.03.

(c) If the board of directors submits a restatement for shareholder action, the corporation shall notify each shareholder, whether or not entitled to vote, of the proposed shareholders' meeting in accordance with section 7.05. The notice must also state that the purpose, or one of the purposes, of the meeting is to consider the proposed restatement and contain or be accompanied by a copy of the restatement that identifies any amendment or other change it would make in the articles.

(d) A corporation restating its articles of incorporation shall deliver to the secretary of state for filing articles of restatement setting forth the name of the corporation and the text of the restated articles of incorporation together with a certificate setting forth:

(1) whether the restatement contains an amendment to the articles requiring shareholder approval and, if it does not, that the board of directors adopted the restatement; or

(2) if the restatement contains an amendment to the articles requiring shareholder approval, the information required by section 10.06.

(e) Duly adopted restated articles of incorporation supersede the original articles of incorporation and all amendments to them.

(f) The secretary of state may certify restated articles of incorporation, as the articles of incorporation currently in effect, without including the certificate information required by subsection (d).

§ 10.08. **Amendment Pursuant to Reorganization.**—

(a) A corporation's articles of incorporation may be amended without action by the board of directors or shareholders to carry out a plan of reorganization ordered or decreed by a court of competent jurisdiction under federal statute if the articles of incorporation after amendment contain only provisions required or permitted by section 2.02.

(b) The individual or individuals designated by the court shall deliver to the secretary of state for filing articles of amendment setting forth:

(1) the name of the corporation;

(2) the text of each amendment approved by the court;

(3) the date of the court's order or decree approving the articles of amendment;

(4) the title of the reorganization proceeding in which the order or decree was entered; and

(5) a statement that the court had jurisdiction of the proceeding under federal statute.

(c) Shareholders of a corporation undergoing reorganization do not have dissenters' rights except as and to the extent provided in the reorganization plan.

(d) This section does not apply after entry of a final decree in the reorganization proceeding even though the court retains jurisdiction of the proceeding for limited purposes unrelated to consummation of the reorganization plan.

§ 10.09. **Effect of Amendment.**—An amendment to articles of incorporation does not affect a cause of action existing against or in favor of the corporation, a proceeding to which the corporation is a party, or the existing rights of persons other than shareholders of the corporation. An amendment changing a corporation's name does not abate a proceeding brought by or against the corporation in its former name.

Subchapter B. Amendment of Bylaws

§ 10.20. **Amendment by Board of Directors or Shareholders.**—

(a) A corporation's board of directors may amend or repeal the corporation's bylaws unless:

(1) the articles of incorporation or this Act reserve this power exclusively to the shareholders in whole or part; or

(2) the shareholders in amending or repealing a particular bylaw provide expressly that the board of directors may not amend or repeal that bylaw.

(b) A corporation's shareholders may amend or repeal the corporation's bylaws even though the bylaws may also be amended or repealed by its board of directors.

§ 10.21. **Bylaw Increasing Quorum or Voting Requirement for Shareholders.**—

(a) If authorized by the articles of incorporation, the shareholders may adopt or amend a bylaw that fixes a greater quorum or voting requirement for shareholders (or voting groups of shareholders) than is required by this Act. The adoption or amendment of a bylaw that adds, changes, or deletes a greater quorum or voting requirement for shareholders must meet the same quorum requirement and be adopted by the same vote and voting groups required to take action under the quorum and voting requirement then in effect or proposed to be adopted, whichever is greater.

(b) A bylaw that fixes a greater quorum or voting requirement for shareholders under subsection (a) may not be adopted, amended, or repealed by the board of directors.

§ 10.22. **Bylaw Increasing Quorum or Voting Requirement for Directors.**—

(a) A bylaw that fixes a greater quorum or voting requirement for the board of directors may be amended or repealed:

(1) if originally adopted by the shareholders, only by the shareholders;

(2) if originally adopted by the board of directors, either by the shareholders or by the board of directors.

(b) A bylaw adopted or amended by the shareholders that fixes a greater quorum or voting requirement for the board of directors may provide that it may be amended or repealed only by a specified vote of either the shareholders or the board of directors.

(c) Action by the board of directors under subsection (a)(2) to adopt or amend a bylaw that changes the quorum or voting requirement for the board of directors must meet the same quorum requirement and be adopted by the same vote required to take action under the quorum and voting requirement then in effect or proposed to be adopted, whichever is greater.

CHAPTER 11. MERGER AND SHARE EXCHANGE

§ 11.01. **Merger.**—

(a) One or more corporations may merge into another corporation if the board of directors of each corporation adopts and its shareholders (if required by section 11.03) approve a plan of merger.

(b) The plan of merger must set forth:

(1) the name of each corporation planning to merge and the name of the surviving corporation into which each other corporation plans to merge;

(2) the terms and conditions of the merger; and

(3) the manner and basis of converting the shares of each corporation into shares, obligations, or other securities of the surviving or any other corporation or into cash or other property in whole or part.

(c) The plan of merger may set forth:

(1) amendments to the articles of incorporation of the surviving corporation; and

(2) other provisions relating to the merger.

§ 11.02. **Share Exchange.**—

(a) A corporation may acquire all of the outstanding shares of one or more classes or series of another corporation if the board of directors of each corporation adopts and its shareholders (if required by section 11.03) approve the exchange.

(b) The plan of exchange must set forth:

(1) the name of the corporation whose shares will be acquired and the name of the acquiring corporation;

(2) the terms and conditions of the exchange;

(3) the manner and basis of exchanging the shares to be acquired for shares, obligations, or other securities of the acquiring or any other corporation or for cash or other property in whole or part.

(c) The plan of exchange may set forth other provisions relating to the exchange.

(d) This section does not limit the power of a corporation to acquire all or part of the shares of one or more classes or series of another corporation through a voluntary exchange or otherwise.

§ 11.03. **Action on Plan.**—

(a) After adopting a plan of merger or share exchange, the board of directors of each corporation party to the merger, and the board of directors of the corporation whose shares will be acquired in the share exchange, shall submit the plan of merger (except as provided in subsection (g)) or share exchange for approval by its shareholders.

(b) For a plan of merger or share exchange to be approved:

(1) the board of directors must recommend the plan of merger or share exchange to the shareholders, unless the board of directors determines that because of conflict of interest or other special circumstances it should make no recommendation and communicates the basis for its determination to the shareholders with the plan; and

(2) the shareholders entitled to vote must approve the plan.

(c) The board of directors may condition its submission of the proposed merger or share exchange on any basis.

(d) The corporation shall notify each shareholder, whether or not entitled to vote, of the proposed shareholders' meeting in accordance with section 7.05. The notice must also state that the purpose, or one of the purposes, of the meeting is to consider the plan of merger or share exchange and contain or be accompanied by a copy or summary of the plan.

(e) Unless this Act, the articles of incorporation, or the board of directors (acting pursuant to subsection (c)) require a greater vote or a vote by voting groups, the plan of merger or share exchange to be authorized must be approved by each voting group entitled to vote separately on the plan by a majority of all the votes entitled to be cast on the plan by that voting group.

(f) Separate voting by voting groups is required:

(1) on a plan of merger if the plan contains a provision that, if contained in a proposed amendment to articles of incorporation, would require action by one or more separate voting groups on the proposed amendment under section 10.04;

(2) on a plan of share exchange by each class or series of shares included in the exchange, with each class or series constituting a separate voting group.

(g) Action by the shareholders of the surviving corporation on a plan of merger is not required if:

(1) the articles of incorporation of the surviving corporation will not differ (except for amendments enumerated in section 10.02) from its articles before the merger;

(2) each shareholder of the surviving corporation whose shares were outstanding immediately before the effective date of the merger will hold the same number of shares, with identical designations, preferences, limitations, and relative rights, immediately after;

(3) the number of voting shares outstanding immediately after the merger, plus the number of voting shares issuable as a result of the merger (either by the conversion of securities issued pursuant to the merger or the exercise of rights and warrants issued pursuant to the merger), will not exceed by more than 20 percent the total number of voting shares of the surviving corporation outstanding immediately before the merger; and

(4) the number of participating shares outstanding immediately after the merger, plus the number of participating shares issuable as a result of the merger (either by the conversion of securities issued pursuant to the merger or the exercise of rights and warrants issued pursuant to the merger), will not exceed by more than 20 percent the total number of participating shares outstanding immediately before the merger.

(h) As used in subsection (g):

(1) "Participating shares" means shares that entitle their holders to participate without limitation in distributions.

(2) "Voting shares" means shares that entitle their holders to vote unconditionally in elections of directors.

(i) After a merger or share exchange is authorized, and at any time before articles of merger or share exchange are filed, the planned merger or share exchange may be abandoned (subject to any contractual rights), without further shareholder action, in accordance with the procedure set forth in the plan of merger or share exchange or, if none is set forth, in the manner determined by the board of directors.

§ 11.04. Merger of Subsidiary.—

(a) A parent corporation owning at least 90 percent of the outstanding shares of each class of a subsidiary corporation may merge the subsidiary into itself without approval of the shareholders of the parent or subsidiary.

(b) The board of directors of the parent shall adopt a plan of merger that sets forth:

(1) the names of the parent and subsidiary; and

(2) the manner and basis of converting the shares of the subsidiary into shares, obligations, or other securities of the parent or any other corporation or into cash or other property in whole or part.

(c) The parent shall mail a copy or summary of the plan of merger to each shareholder of the subsidiary who does not waive the mailing requirement in writing.

(d) The parent may not deliver articles of merger to the secretary of state for filing until at least 30 days after the date it mailed a copy of the plan of merger to each shareholder of the subsidiary who did not waive the mailing requirement.

(e) Articles of merger under this section may not contain amendments to the articles of incorporation of the parent corporation (except for amendments enumerated in section 10.02).

§11.05. Articles of Merger or Share Exchange.—

(a) After a plan of merger or share exchange is approved by the shareholders, or adopted by the board of directors if shareholder approval is not required, the surviving or acquiring corporation shall deliver to the secretary of state for filing articles of merger or share exchange setting forth:

(1) the plan of merger or share exchange;

(2) if shareholder approval was not required, a statement to that effect;

(3) if approval of the shareholders of one or more corporations party to the merger or share exchange was required:

(i) the designation, number of outstanding shares, and number of votes entitled to be cast by each voting group entitled to vote separately on the plan as to each corporation; and

(ii) either the total number of votes cast for and against the plan by each voting group entitled to vote separately on the plan or the total number of undisputed votes cast for the plan separately by each voting group and a statement that the number cast for the plan by each voting group was sufficient for approval by that voting group.

(b) A merger or share exchange takes effect upon the effective date of the articles of merger or share exchange.

§ 11.06. Effect of Merger or Share Exchange.—

(a) When a merger takes effect:

(1) every other corporation party to the merger merges into the surviving corporation and the separate existence of every corporation except the surviving corporation ceases;

(2) the title to all real estate and other property owned by each corporation party to the merger is vested in the surviving corporation without reversion or impairment;

(3) the surviving corporation has all liabilities of each corporation party to the merger;

(4) a proceeding pending against any corporation party to the merger may be continued as if the merger did not occur or the surviving corporation may be substituted in the proceeding for the corporation whose existence ceased;

(5) the articles of incorporation of the surviving corporation are amended to the extent provided in the plan of merger; and

(6) the shares of each corporation party to the merger that are to be converted into shares, obligations, or other securities of the surviving or any other corporation or into cash or other property are converted, and the former holders of the shares are entitled only to the rights provided in the articles of merger or to their rights under chapter 13.

(b) When a share exchange takes effect, the shares of each acquired corporation are exchanged as provided in the plan, and the former holders of the shares are entitled only to the exchange rights provided in the articles of share exchange or to their rights under chapter 13.

§ 11.07. Merger or Share Exchange with Foreign Corporation.—

(a) One or more foreign corporations may merge or enter into a share exchange with one or more domestic corporations if:

(1) in a merger, the merger is permitted by the law of the state or country under whose law each foreign corporation is incorporated and each foreign corporation complies with that law in effecting the merger;

(2) in a share exchange, the corporation whose shares will be acquired is a domestic corporation, whether or not a share exchange is permitted by the law of the state or country under whose law the acquiring corporation is incorporated;

(3) the foreign corporation complies with section 11.05 if it is the surviving corporation of the merger or acquiring corporation of the share exchange, and

(4) each domestic corporation complies with the applicable provisions of sections 11.01 through 11.04 and, if it is the surviving corporation of the merger or acquiring corporation of the share exchange, with section 11.05.

(b) Upon the merger or share exchange taking effect, the surviving foreign corporation of a merger and the acquiring foreign corporation of a share exchange is deemed:

(1) to appoint the secretary of state as its agent for service of process in a proceeding to enforce any obligation or the rights of dissenting shareholders of each domestic corporation party to the merger or share exchange; and

(2) to agree that it will promptly pay to the dissenting shareholder of each domestic corporation party to the merger or share exchange the amount, if any, to which they are entitled under chapter 13.

(c) This section does not limit the power of a foreign corporation to acquire all or part of the shares of one or more classes or series of a domestic corporation through a voluntary exchange or otherwise.

CHAPTER 12. SALE OF ASSETS

§ 12.01. Sale of Assets in Regular Course of Business and Mortgage of Assets.—

(a) A corporation may, on the terms and conditions and for the consideration determined by the board of directors:

(1) sell, lease, exchange, or otherwise dispose of all, or substantially all, of its property in the usual and regular course of business;

(2) mortgage, pledge, dedicate to the repayment of indebtedness (whether with or without recourse), or otherwise encumber any or all of its property whether or not in the ususal and regular course of business; or

(3) transfer any or all of its property to a corporation all the shares of which are owned by the corporation.

(b) Unless the articles of incorporation require it, approval by the shareholders of a transaction described in subsection (a) is not required.

§ 12.02. Sale of Assets Other Than in Regular Course of Business.—

(a) A corporation may sell, lease, exchange, or otherwise dispose of all, or substantially all, of its property (with or without the good will), otherwise than in the usual and regular course of business, on the terms and conditions and for the consideration determined by the corporation's board of directors, if the board of directors proposes and its shareholders approved the proposed transaction.

(b) For a transaction to be authorized:

(1) the board of directors must recommend the proposed transaction to the shareholders unless the board of directors determines that because of conflict of interest or other special circumstances it should make no recommendation and communicates the basis for its determination to the shareholders with the submission of the proposed transaction; and

(2) the shareholders entitled to vote must approve the transaction.

(c) The board of directors may condition its submission of the proposed transaction on any basis.

(d) The corporation shall notify each shareholder, whether or not entitled to vote, of the proposed shareholders' meeting in accordance with section 7.05. The notice must also state that the purpose, or one of the purposes, of the meeting is to consider the sale, lease, exchange, or other disposition of all, or substantially all, the property of the corporation and contain or be accompanied by a description of the transaction.

(e) Unless the articles of incorporation or the board of directors (acting pursuant to subsection (c)) require a greater vote or a vote by voting groups, the transaction to be authorized must be approved by a majority of all the votes entitled to be cast on the transaction.

(f) After a sale, lease, exchange, or other disposition of property is authorized, the transaction may be abandoned (subject to any contractual rights) without further shareholder action.

(g) A transaction that constitutes a distribution is governed by section 6.40 and not by this section.

CHAPTER 13. DISSENTERS' RIGHTS

Subchapter A.   Right to Dissent and Obtain Payment for Shares

§ 13.01.   Definitions.—In this chapter:

(1) "Corporation" means the issuer of the shares held by a dissenter before the corporate action, or the surviving or acquiring corporation by merger or share exchange of that issuer.

(2) "Dissenter" means a shareholder who is entitled to dissent from corporate action under section 13.02 and who exercises that right when and in the manner required by sections 13.20 through 13.28.

(3) "Fair value," with respect to a dissenter's shares, means the value of the shares immediately before the effectuation of the corporate action to which the dissenter objects, excluding any appreciation or depreciation in anticipation of the corporate action unless exclusion would be inequitable.

(4) "Interest" means interest from the effective date of the corporate action until the date of payment, at the average rate currently paid by the corporation on its principal bank loans or, if none, at a rate that is fair and equitable under all the circumstances.

(5) "Record shareholder" means the person in whose name shares are registered in the records of a corporation or the beneficial owner of shares to the extent of the rights granted by a nominee certificate on file with a corporation.

(6) "Beneficial shareholder" means the person who is a beneficial owner of shares held in a voting trust or by a nominee as the record shareholder.

(7) "Shareholder" means the record shareholder or the beneficial shareholder.

§ 13.02.   Right to Dissent.—

(a) A shareholder is entitled to dissent from, and obtain payment of the fair value of his shares in the event of, any of the following corporate actions:

(1) consummation of a plan of merger to which the corporation is a party (i) if shareholder approval is required for the merger by section 11.03 or the articles of incorporation and the shareholder is entitled to vote on the merger or (ii) if the corporation is a subsidiary that is merged with its parent under section 11.04;

(2) consummation of a plan of share exchange to which the corporation is a party as the corporation whose shares will be acquired, if the shareholder is entitled to vote on the plan;

(3) consummation of a sale or exchange of all, or substantially all, of the property of the corporation other than in the usual and regular course of business, if the shareholder is entitled to vote on the sale or exchange, including a sale in dissolution, but not including a sale pursuant to court order or a sale for cash pursuant to a plan by which all or substantially all of the net proceeds of the sale will be distributed to the shareholders within one year after the date of sale;

(4) an amendment of the articles of incorporation that materially and adversely affects rights in respect of a dissenter's shares because it:

(i) alters or abolishes a preferential right of the shares;

(ii) creates, alters, or abolishes a right in respect of redemption, including a provision respecting a sinking fund for the redemption or repurchase, of the shares;

(iii) alters or abolishes a preemptive right of the holder of the shares to acquire shares or other securities;

(iv) excludes or limits the right of the shares to vote on any matter, or to cumulate votes, other than a limitation by dilution through issuance of shares or other securities with similar voting rights; or

(v) reduces the number of shares owned by the shareholder to a fraction of a share if the fractional share so created is to be acquired for cash under section 6.04; or

(5) any corporate action taken pursuant to a shareholder vote to the extent the articles of incorporation, bylaws, or a resolution of the board of directors provides that voting or nonvoting shareholders are entitled to dissent and obtain payment for their shares.

(b) A shareholder entitled to dissent and obtain payment for his shares under this chapter may not challenge the corporate action creating his entitlement unless the action is unlawful or fraudulent with respect to the shareholder or the corporation.

§ 13.03.   Dissent by Nominees and Beneficial Owners.—

(a) A record shareholder may assert dissenters' rights as to fewer than all the shares registered in his name only if he dissents with respect to all shares beneficially owned by any one person and notifies the corporation in writing of the name and address of each person on whose behalf he asserts dissenters' rights. The rights of a partial dissenter under this subsection are determined as if the shares as to which he dissents and his other shares were registered in the names of different shareholders.

(b) A beneficial shareholder may assert dissenters' rights as to shares held on his behalf only if:

(1) he submits to the corporation the record shareholder's written consent to the dissent not later than the time the beneficial shareholder asserts dissenters' rights; and

(2) he does so with respect to all shares of which he is the beneficial shareholder or over which he has power to direct the vote.

Subchapter B.   Procedure for Exercise of Dissenters' Rights

§ 13.20.   Notice of Dissenters' Rights.—

(a) If proposed corporate action creating dissenters' rights under section 13.02 is submitted to a vote at a shareholders' meeting, the meeting notice must state that shareholders are or may be entitled to assert dissenters' rights under this chapter and be accompanied by a copy of this chapter.

(b) If corporate action creating dissenters' rights under section 13.02 is taken without a vote of shareholders, the corporation shall notify in writing all shareholders entitled to assert dissenters' rights that the action was taken and send them the dissenters' notice described in section 13.22.

§ 13.21.   Notice of Intent to Demand Payment.—

(a) If proposed corporate action creating dissenters' rights under section 13.02 is submitted to a vote at a shareholders' meeting, a shareholder who wishes to assert dissenters' rights (1) must deliver to the corporation before the vote is taken written notice of his intent to demand payment for his shares if the proposed action is effectuated and (2) must not vote his shares in favor of the proposed action.

(b) A shareholder who does not satisfy the requirements of subsection (a) is not entitled to payment for his shares under this chapter.

§ 13.22.   Dissenters' Notice.—

(a) If proposed corporate action creating dissenters' rights under section 13.02 is authorized at a shareholders' meeting, the corporation shall deliver a written dissenters' notice to all shareholders who satisfied the requirements of section 13.21.

(b) The dissenters' notice must be sent no later than 10 days after the corporate action was taken, and must:

(1) state where the payment demand must be sent and where and when certificates for certificated shares must be deposited;

(2) inform holders of uncertificated shares to what extent transfer of the shares will be restricted after the payment demand is received;

(3) supply a form for demanding payment that includes the date of the first announcement to news media or to shareholders of the terms of the proposed corporate action and requires that the person asserting dissenters' rights certify whether or not he acquired beneficial ownership of the shares before that date;

(4) set a date by which the corporation must receive the payment demand, which date may not be fewer than 30 nor more than 60 days after the date the subsection (a) notice is delivered; and

(5) be accompanied by a copy of this chapter.

§ 13.23.   Duty to Demand Payment.—

(a) A shareholder sent a dissenters' notice described in section 13.22 must demand payment, certify whether he acquired beneficial ownership of the shares before the date required to be set forth in the dissenters' notice pursuant to section 13.22(b)(3), and deposit his certificates in accordance with the terms of the notice.

(b) The shareholder who demands payment and deposits his shares under section (a) retains all other rights of a shareholder until these rights are cancelled or modified by the taking of the proposed corporate action.

(c) A shareholder who does not demand payment or deposit his share certificates where required, each by the date set in the dissenters' notice, is not entitled to payment for his shares under this chapter.

§ 13.24.   Share Restrictions.—

(a) The corporation may restrict the transfer of uncertificated shares from the date the demand for their payment is received until the proposed corporate action is taken or the restrictions released under section 13.26.

(b) The person for whom dissenters' rights are asserted as to uncertificated shares retains all other rights of a shareholder until these rights are cancelled or modified by the taking of the proposed corporate action.

§ 13.25.   Payment.—

(a) Except as provided in section 13.27, as soon as the proposed corporate action is taken, or upon receipt of a payment demand, the corporation shall pay each dissenter who complied with section 13.23 the amount the corporation estimates to be the fair value of his shares, plus accrued interest.

(b) The payment must be accompanied by:

(1) the corporation's balance sheet as of the end of a fiscal year ending not more than 16 months before the date of payment, an income statement for that year, a statement of changes in shareholders' equity for that year, and the latest available interim financial statements, if any;

(2) a statement of the corporation's estimate of the fair value of the shares;

(3) an explanation of how the interest was calculated;

(4) a statement of the dissenter's right to demand payment under section 13.28; and

(5) a copy of this chapter.

§ 13.26.   Failure to Take Action.—

(a) If the corporation does not take the proposed action within 60 days after the date set for demanding payment and depositing share certificates, the corporation shall return the deposited certificates and release the transfer restrictions imposed on uncertificated shares.

(b) If after returning deposited certificates and releasing transfer restrictions, the corporation takes the proposed action, it must send a new dissenters' notice under section 13.22 and repeat the payment demand procedure.

§ 13.27. After-acquired Shares.—

(a) A corporation may elect to withhold payment required by section 13.25 from a dissenter unless he was the beneficial owner of the shares before the date set forth in the dissenters' notice as the date of the first announcement to news media or to shareholders of the terms of the proposed corporate action.

(b) To the extent the corporation elects to withhold payment under subsection (a), after taking the proposed corporate action, it shall estimate the fair value of the shares, plus accrued interest, and shall pay this amount to each dissenter who agrees to accept it in full satisfaction of his demand. The corporation shall send with its offer a statement of its estimate of the fair value of the shares, an explanation of how the interest was calculated, and a statement of the dissenter's right to demand payment under section 13.28.

§ 13.28. Procedure if Shareholder Dissatisfied with Payment or Offer.—

(a) A dissenter may notify the corporation in writing of his own estimate of the fair value of his shares and amount of interest due, and demand payment of his estimate (less any payment under section 13.25), or reject the corporation's offer under section 13.27 and demand payment of the fair value of his shares and interest due, if:

(1) the dissenter believes that the amount paid under section 13.25 or offered under section 13.27 is less than the fair value of his shares or that the interest due is incorrectly calculated;

(2) the corporation fails to make payment under section 13.25 within 60 days after the date set for demanding payment; or

(3) the corporation, having failed to take the proposed action, does not return the deposited certificates or release the transfer restrictions imposed on uncertificated shares within 60 days after the date set for demanding payment.

(b) A dissenter waives his right to demand payment under this section unless he notifies the corporation of his demand in writing under subsection (a) within 30 days after the corporation made or offered payment for his shares.

Subchapter C. Judicial Appraisal of Shares

§ 13.30. Court Action.—

(a) If a demand for payment under section 13.28 remains unsettled, the corporation shall commence a proceeding within 60 days after receiving the payment demand and petition the court to determine the fair value of the shares and accrued interest. If the corporation does not commence the proceeding within the 60-day period, it shall pay each dissenter whose demand remains unsettled the amount demanded.

(b) The corporation shall commence the proceeding in the [name or describe] court of the county where a corporation's principal office (or, if none in this state, its registered office) is located. If the corporation is a foreign corporation without a registered office in this state, it shall commence the proceeding in the county in this state where the registered office of the domestic corporation merged with or whose shares were acquired by the foreign corporation was located.

(c) The corporation shall make all dissenters (whether or not residents of this state) whose demands remain unsettled parties to the proceeding as in an action against their shares and all parties must be served with a copy of the petition. Nonresidents may be served by registered or certified mail or by publication as provided by law.

(d) The jurisdiction of the court in which the proceeding is commenced under subsection (b) is plenary and exclusive. The court may appoint one or more persons as appraisers to receive evidence and recommend decision on the question of fair value. The appraisers have the powers described in the order appointing them, or in any amendment to it. The dissenters are entitled to the same discovery rights as parties in other civil proceedings.

(e) Each dissenter made a party to the proceeding is entitled to judgment (1) for the amount, if any, by which the court finds the fair value of his shares, plus interest, exceeds the amount paid by the corporation or (2) for the fair value, plus accrued interest, of his after-acquired shares for which the corporation elected to withhold payment under section 13.27.

§ 13.31. Court Costs and Counsel Fees.—

(a) The court in an appraisal proceeding commenced under section 13.30 shall determine all costs of the proceeding, including the reasonable compensation and expenses of appraisers appointed by the court. The court shall assess the costs against the corporation, except that the court may assess costs against all or some of the dissenters, in amounts the court finds equitable, to the extent the court finds the dissenters acted arbitrarily, vexatiously, or not in good faith in demanding payment under section 13.28.

(b) The court may also assess the fees and expenses of counsel and experts for the respective parties, in amounts the court finds equitable:

(1) against the corporation and in favor of any or all dissenters if the court finds the corporation did not substantially comply with the requirements of sections 13.20 through 13.28; or

(2) against either the corporation or a dissenter, in favor of any other party, if the court finds that the party against whom the fees and expenses are assessed acted arbitrarily, vexatiously, or not in good faith with respect to the rights provided by this chapter.

(c) If the court finds that the services of counsel for any dissenter were of substantial benefit to other dissenters similarly situated, and that the fees for those services should not be assessed against the corporation, the court may award to these counsel reasonable fees to be paid out of the amounts awarded the dissenters who were benefited.

CHAPTER 14. DISSOLUTION

Subchapter A. Voluntary Dissolution

§ 14.01. Dissolution by Incorporators or Initial Directors.—A majority of the incorporators or initial directors of a corporation that has not issued shares or has not commenced business may dissolve the corporation by delivering to the secretary of state for filing articles of dissolution that set forth:

(1) the name of the corporation;

(2) the date of its incorporation;

(3) either (i) that none of the corporation's shares has been issued or (ii) that the corporation has not commenced business;

(4) that no debt of the corporation remains unpaid;

(5) that the net assets of the corporation remaining after winding up have been distributed to the shareholders, if shares were issued; and

(6) that a majority of the incorporators or initial directors authorized the dissolution.

§ 14.02. Dissolution by Board of Directors and Shareholders.—

(a) A corporation's board of directors may propose dissolution for submission to the shareholders.

(b) For a proposal to dissolve to be adopted:

(1) the board of directors must recommend dissolution to the shareholders unless the board of directors determines that because of conflict of interest or other special circumstances it should make no recommendation and communicates the basis for its determination to the shareholders; and

(2) the shareholders entitled to vote must approve the proposal to dissolve as provided in subsection (e).

(c) The board of directors may condition its submission of the proposal for dissolution on any basis.

(d) The corporation shall notify each shareholder, whether or not entitled to vote, of the proposed shareholders' meeting in accordance with section 7.05. The notice must also state that the purpose, or one of the purposes, of the meeting is to consider dissolving the corporation.

(e) Unless the articles of incorporation or the board of directors (acting pursuant to subsection (c)) require a greater vote or a vote by voting groups, the proposal to dissolve to be adopted must be approved by a majority of all the votes entitled to be cast on that proposal.

§ 14.03. Articles of Dissolution.—

(a) At any time after dissolution is authorized, the corporation may dissolve by delivering to the secretary of state for filing articles of dissolution setting forth:

(1) the name of the corporation;

(2) the date dissolution was authorized;

(3) if dissolution was approved by the shareholders:

(i) the number of votes entitled to be cast on the proposal to dissolve; and

(ii) either the total number of votes cast for and against dissolution or the total number of undisputed votes cast for dissolution and a statement that the number cast for dissolution was sufficient for approval.

(4) If voting by voting groups was required, the information required by subparagraph (3) must be separately provided for each voting group entitled to vote separately on the plan to dissolve.

(b) A corporation is dissolved upon the effective date of its articles of dissolution.

§ 14.04. Revocation of Dissolution.—

(a) A corporation may revoke its dissolution within 120 days of its effective date.

(b) Revocation of dissolution must be authorized in the same manner as the dissolution was authorized unless that authorization permitted revocation by action of the board of directors alone, in which event the board of directors may revoke the dissolution without shareholder action.

(c) After the revocation of dissolution is authorized, the corporation may revoke the dissolution by delivering to the secretary of state for filing articles of revocation of dissolution, together with a copy of its articles of dissolution, that set forth:

(1) the name of the corporation;

(2) the effective date of the dissolution that was revoked;

(3) the date that the revocation of dissolution was authorized;

(4) if the corporation's board of directors (or incorporators) revoked the dissolution, a statement to that effect;

(5) if the corporation's board of directors revoked a dissolution authorized by the shareholders, a statement that revocation was permitted by action by the board of directors alone pursuant to that authorization; and

(6) if shareholder action was required to revoke the dissolution, the information required by section 14.03(a)(3) or (4).

(d) Revocation of dissolution is effective upon the effective date of the articles of revocation of dissolution.

(e) When the revocation of dissolution is effective, it relates back to and takes effect as of the effective date of the dissolution and the corporation resumes carrying on its business as if dissolution had never occurred.

§ 14.05. Effect of Dissolution.—

(a) A dissolved corporation continues its corporate existence but may not carry on any business except that appropriate to wind up and liquidate its business and affairs, including:

(1) collecting its assets;

(2) disposing of its properties that will not be distributed in kind to its shareholders;

(3) discharging or making provision for discharging its liabilities;

(4) distributing its remaining property among its shareholders according to their interests; and

(5) doing every other act necessary to wind up and liquidate its business and affairs.

(b) Dissolution of a corporation does not:

(1) transfer title to the corporation's property;

(2) prevent transfer of its shares or securities, although the authorization to dissolve may provide for closing the corporation's share transfer records;

(3) subject its directors or officers to standards of conduct different from those prescribed in chapter 8;

(4) change quorum or voting requirements for its board of directors or shareholders; change provisions for selection, resignation, or removal of its directors or officers or both; or change provisions for amending its bylaws;

(5) prevent commencement of a proceeding by or against the corporation in its corporate name;

(6) abate or suspend a proceeding pending by or against the corporation on the effective date of dissolution; or

(7) terminate the authority of the registered agent of the corporation.

§ 14.06. Known Claims Against Dissolved Corporation.—

(a) A dissolved corporation may dispose of the known claims against it by following the procedure described in this section.

(b) The dissolved corporation shall notify its known claimants in writing of the dissolution at any time after its effective date. The written notice must:

(1) describe information that must be included in a claim;

(2) provide a mailing address where a claim may be sent;

(3) state the deadline, which may not be fewer than 120 days from the effective date of the written notice, by which the dissolved corporation must receive the claim; and

(4) state that the claim will be barred if not received by the deadline.

(c) A claim against the dissolved corporation is barred:

(1) if a claimant who was given written notice under subsection (b) does not deliver the claim to the dissolved corporation by the deadline;

(2) if a claimant whose claim was rejected by the dissolved corporation does not commence a proceeding to enforce the claim within 90 days from the effective date of the rejection notice.

(d) For purposes of this section, "claim" does not include a contingent liability or a claim based on an event occurring after the effective date of dissolution.

§ 14.07. Unknown Claims Against Dissolved Corporation.—

(a) A dissolved corporation may also publish notice of its dissolution and request that persons with claims against the corporation present them in accordance with the notice.

(b) The notice must:

(1) be published one time in a newspaper of general circulation in the county where the dissolved corporation's principal office (or, if none in this state, its registered office) is or was last located;

(2) describe the information that must be included in a claim and provide a mailing address where a claim may be sent; and

(3) state that a claim against the corporation will be barred unless a proceeding to enforce the claim is commenced within five years after the publication of the notice.

(c) If the dissolved corporation publishes a newspaper notice in accordance with subsection (b), the claim of each of the following claimants is barred unless the claimant commences a proceeding to enforce the claim against the dissolved corporation within five years after the publication date of the newspaper notice:

(1) a claimant who did not receive written notice under section 14.06;

(2) a claimant whose claim was timely sent to the dissolved corporation but not acted on;

(3) a claimant whose claim is contingent or based on an event occurring after the effective date of dissolution.

(d) A claim may be enforced under this section:

(1) against the dissolved corporation, to the extent of its undistributed assets; or

(2) if the assets have been distributed in liquidation, against a shareholder of the dissolved corporation to the extent of his pro rata share of the claim or the corporate assets distributed to him in liquidation, whichever is less, but a shareholder's total liability for all claims under this section may not exceed the total amount of assets distributed to him.

Subchapter B. Administrative Dissolution

§ 14.20. Grounds for Administrative Dissolution.—

The secretary of state may commence a proceeding under section 14.21 to administratively dissolve a corporation if:

(1) the corporation does not pay within 60 days after they are due any franchise taxes or penalties imposed by this Act or other law;

(2) the corporation does not deliver its annual report to the secretary of state within 60 days after it is due;

(3) the corporation is without a registered agent or registered office in this state for 60 days or more;

(4) the corporation does not notify the secretary of state within 60 days that its registered agent or registered office has been changed, that its registered agent has resigned, or that its registered office has been discontinued; or

(5) the corporation's period of duration stated in its articles of incorporation expires.

§ 14.21. Procedure for and Effect of Administrative Dissolution.—

(a) If the secretary of state determines that one or more grounds exist under section 14.20 for dissolving a corporation, he shall serve the corporation with written notice of his determination under section 5.04.

(b) If the corporation does not correct each ground for dissolution or demonstrate to the reasonable satisfaction of the secretary of state that each ground determined by the secretary of state does not exist within 60 days after service of the notice is perfected under section 5.04, the secretary of state shall administratively dissolve the corporation by signing a certificate of dissolution that recites the ground or grounds for dissolution and its effective date. The secretary of state shall file the original of the certificate and serve a copy on the corporation under section 5.04.

(c) A corporation administratively dissolved continues its corporate existence but may not carry on any business except that necessary to wind up and liquidate its business and affairs under section 14.05 and notify claimants under sections 14.06 and 14.07.

(d) The administrative dissolution of a corporation does not terminate the authority of its registered agent.

§ 14.22. Reinstatement Following Administrative Dissolution.—

(a) A corporation administratively dissolved under section 14.21 may apply to the secretary of state for reinstatement within two years after the effective date of dissolution. The application must:

(1) recite the name of the corporation and the effective date of its administrative dissolution;

(2) state that the ground or grounds for dissolution either did not exist or have been eliminated;

(3) state that the corporation's name satisfies the requirements of section 4.01; and

(4) contain a certificate from the [taxing authority] reciting that all taxes owed by the corporation have been paid.

(b) If the secretary of state determines that the application contains the information required by subsection (a) and that the information is correct, he shall cancel the certificate of dissolution and prepare a certificate of reinstatement that recites his determination and the effective date of reinstatement, file the original of the certificate, and serve a copy on the corporation under section 5.04.

(c) When the reinstatement is effective, it relates back to and takes effect as of the effective date of the administrative dissolution and the corporation resumes carrying on its business as if the administrative dissolution had never occurred.

§ 14.23. Appeal From Denial of Reinstatement.—

(a) If the secretary of state denies a corporation's application for reinstatement following administrative dissolution, he shall serve the corporation under section 5.04 with a written notice that explains the reason or reasons for denial.

(b) The corporation may appeal the denial of reinstatement to the [name or describe] court within 30 days after service of the notice of denial is perfected. The corporation appeals by petitioning the court to set aside the dissolution and attaching to the petition copies of the secretary of state's certificate of dissolution, the corporation's application for reinstatement, and the secretary of state's notice of denial.

(c) The court may summarily order the secretary of state to reinstate the dissolved corporation or may take other action the court considers appropriate.

(d) The court's final decision may be appealed as in other civil proceedings.

Subchapter C. Judicial Dissolution

§ 14.30. Grounds for Judicial Dissolution.—

The [name or describe court or courts] may dissolve a corporation:

(1) in a proceeding by the attorney general if it is established that:

(i) the corporation obtained its articles of incorporation through fraud; or

(ii) the corporation has continued to exceed or abuse the authority conferred upon it by law;

(2) in a proceeding by a shareholder if it is established that:

(i) the directors are deadlocked in the management of the corporate affairs, the shareholders are unable to break the deadlock, and irreparable injury to the corporation is threatened or being suffered, or the business and affairs of the corporation can no longer be conducted to the advantage of the shareholders generally, because of the deadlock;

(ii) the directors or those in control of the corporation have acted, are acting, or will act in a manner that is illegal, oppressive, or fraudulent;

(iii) the shareholders are deadlocked in voting power and have failed, for a period that includes at least two consecutive annual meeting dates, to elect successors to directors whose terms have expired; or

(iv) the corporate assets are being misapplied or wasted;

(3) in a proceeding by a creditor if it is established that:

(i) the creditor's claim has been reduced to judgment, the execution on the judgment returned unsatisfied, and the corporation is insolvent; or

(ii) the corporation has admitted in writing that the creditor's claim is due and owing and the corporation is insolvent; or

(4) in a proceeding by the corporation to have its voluntary dissolution continued under court supervision.

§ 14.31. Procedure for Judicial Dissolution.—

(a) Venue for a proceeding by the attorney general to dissolve a corporation lies in [name the county or counties]. Venue for a proceeding brought by any other party named in section 14.30 lies in the county where a corporation's principal office (or, if none in this state, its registered office) is or was last located.

(b) It is not necessary to make shareholders parties to a proceeding to dissolve a corporation unless relief is sought against them individually.

(c) A court in a proceeding brought to dissolve a corporation may issue injunctions, appoint a receiver or custodian pendente lite with all powers and duties the court directs, take other action required to preserve the corporate assets wherever located, and carry on the business of the corporation until a full hearing can be held.

(d) Within 10 days of the commencement of a proceeding under section 14.30(2) to dissolve a corporation that has no shares listed on a national securities exchange or regularly traded in a market maintained by one or more members of a national securities exchange, the corporation must send to all shareholders, other than the petitioner, a notice stating that the shareholders are entitled to avoid the dissolution of the corporation by electing to purchase the petitioner's shares under section 14.34 and accompanied by a copy of section 14.34.

§ 14.32. Receivership or Custodianship.—

(a) A court in a judicial proceeding brought to dissolve a corporation may appoint one or more receivers to wind up and liquidate, or one or more custodians to manage, the business and affairs of the corporation. The court shall hold a hearing, after notifying all parties to the proceeding and any interested persons designated by the court, before appointing a receiver or custodian. The court appointing a receiver or custodian has exclusive jurisdiction over the corporation and all of its property wherever located.

(b) The court may appoint an individual or a domestic or foreign corporation (authorized to transact business in this state) as a receiver or custodian. The court may require the receiver or custodian to post bond, with or without sureties, in an amount the court directs.

(c) The court shall describe the powers and duties of the receiver or custodian in its appointing order, which may be amended from time to time. Among other powers:

(1) the receiver (i) may dispose of all or any part of the assets of the corporation wherever located, at a public or private sale, if authorized by the court; and (ii) may sue and defend in his own name as receiver of the corporation in all courts of this state;

(2) the custodian may exercise all of the powers of the corporation, through or in place of its board of directors or officers, to the extent necessary to manage the affairs of the corporation in the best interests of its shareholders and creditors.

(d) The court during a receivership may redesignate the receiver a custodian, and during a custodianship may redesignate the custodian a receiver, if doing so is in the best interests of the corporation, its shareholders, and creditors.

(e) The court from time to time during the receivership or custodianship may order compensation paid and expense disbursements or reimbursements made to the receiver or custodian and his counsel from the assets of the corporation or proceeds from the sale of the assets.

§ 14.33. Decree of Dissolution.—

(a) If after a hearing the court determines that one or more grounds for judicial dissolution described in section 14.30 exist, it may enter a decree dissolving the corporation and specifying the effective date of the dissolution, and the clerk of the court shall deliver a certified copy of the decree to the secretary of state, who shall file it.

(b) After entering the decree of dissolution, the court shall direct the winding up and liquidation of the corporation's business and affairs in accordance with section 14.05 and the notification of claimants in accordance with sections 14.06 and 14.07.

§ 14.34. Election to Purchase in Lieu of Dissolution.—

(a) In a proceeding under section 14.30(2) to dissolve a corporation that has no shares listed on a national securities exchange or regularly traded in a market maintained by one or more members of a national or affiliated securities association, the corporation may elect or, if it fails to elect, one or more shareholders may elect to purchase all shares owned by the petitioning shareholder at the fair value of the shares. An election pursuant to this section shall be irrevocable unless the court determines that it is equitable to set aside or modify the election.

(b) An election to purchase pursuant to this section may be filed with the court at any time within 90 days after the filing of the petition under section 14.30(2) or at such later time as the court in its discretion may allow. If the election to purchase is filed by one or more shareholders, the corporation shall, within 10 days thereafter, give written notice to all shareholders, other than the petitioner. The notice must state the name and number of shares owned by the petitioner and the name and number of shares owned by each electing shareholder and must advise the recipients of their right to join in the election to purchase shares in accordance with this section. Shareholders who wish to participate must file notice of their intention to join in the purchase no later than 30 days after the effective date of the notice to them. All shareholders who have filed an election or notice of their intention to participate in the election to purchase thereby become parties to the proceeding and shall participate in the purchase in proportion to their ownership of shares as of the date the first election was filed, unless they otherwise agree or the court otherwise directs. After an election has been filed by the corporation or one or more shareholders, the proceeding under section 14.30(2) may not be discontinued or settled, nor may the petitioning shareholder sell or otherwise dispose of his shares, unless the court determines that it would be equitable to the corporation and the shareholders, other than the petitioner, to permit such discontinuance, settlement, sale, or other disposition.

(c) If, within 60 days of the filing of the first election, the parties reach agreement as to the fair value and terms of purchase of the petitioner's shares, the court shall enter an order directing the purchase of petitioner's shares upon the terms and conditions agreed to by the parties.

(d) If the parties are unable to reach an agreement as provided for in subsection (c), the court, upon application of any party, shall stay the section 14.30(2) proceedings and determine the fair value of the petitioner's shares as of the day before the date on which the petition under section 14.30(2) was filed or as of such other date as the court deems appropriate under the circumstances.

(e) Upon determining the fair value of the shares, the court shall enter an order directing the purchase upon such terms and conditions as the court deems appropriate, which may include payment of the purchase price in installments, where necessary in the interest of equity, provision for security to assure payment of the purchase price and any additional costs, fees, and expenses as may have been awarded, and, if the shares are to be purchased by shareholders, the allocation of shares among them. In allocating petitioner's shares among holders of different classes of shares, the court should attempt to preserve the existing distribution of voting rights among holders of different classes insofar as practicable and may direct that holders of a specific class or classes shall not participate in the purchase. Interest may be allowed at the rate and from the date determined by the court to be equitable, but if the court finds that the refusal of the petitioning shareholder to accept an offer of payment was arbitrary or otherwise not in good faith, no interest shall be allowed. If the court finds that the petitioning shareholder had probable grounds for relief under paragraphs (ii) or (iv) of section 14.30(2), it may award to the petitioning shareholder reasonable fees and expenses of counsel and of any experts employed by him.

(f) Upon entry of an order under subsections (c) or (e), the court shall dismiss the petition to dissolve the corporation under section 14.30, and the petitioning shareholder shall no longer have any rights or status as a shareholder of the corporation, except the right to receive the amounts awarded to him by the order of the court which shall be enforceable in the same manner as any other judgment.

(g) The purchase ordered pursuant to subsection (e), shall be made within 10 days after the date the order becomes final unless before that time the corporation files with the court a notice of its intention to adopt articles of dissolution pursuant to sections 14.02 and 14.03, which articles must then be adopted and filed within 50 days thereafter. Upon filing of such articles of dissolution, the corporation shall be dissolved in accordance with the provisions of section 14.05 through .07, and the order entered pursuant to subsection (e) shall no longer be of any force or effect, except that the court may award the petitioning shareholder reasonable fees and expenses in accordance with the provisions of the last sentence of subsection (e) and the petitioner may continue to pursue any claims previously asserted on behalf of the corporation.

(h) Any payment by the corporation pursuant to an order under subsections (c) or (e), other than an award of fees and expenses pursuant to subsection (e), is subject to the provisions of section 6.40.

Subchapter D. Miscellaneous

§ 14.40. Deposit With State Treasurer.—Assets of a dissolved corporation that should be transferred to a creditor, claimant, or shareholder of the corporation who cannot be found or who is not competent to receive them shall be reduced to cash and deposited with the state treasurer or other appropriate state official for safekeeping. When the creditor, claimant, or shareholder furnishes satisfactory proof of entitlement to the amount deposited, the state treasurer or other appropriate state official shall pay him or his representative that amount.

CHAPTER 15. FOREIGN CORPORATIONS

Subchapter A. Certificate of Authority

§ 15.01. Authority to Transact Business Required.—

(a) A foreign corporation may not transact business in this state until it obtains a certificate of authority from the secretary of state.

(b) The following activities, among others, do not constitute transacting business within the meaning of subsection (a):

(1) maintaining, defending, or settling any proceeding;

(2) holding meetings of the board of directors or shareholders or carrying on other activities concerning internal corporate affairs;

(3) maintaining bank accounts;

(4) maintaining offices or agencies for the transfer, exchange, and registration of the corporation's own securities or maintaining trustees or depositaries with respect to those securities;

(5) selling through independent contractors;

(6) soliciting or obtaining orders, whether by mail or through employees or agents or otherwise, if the orders require acceptance outside this state before they become contracts;

(7) creating or acquiring indebtedness, mortgages, and security interests in real or personal property;

(8) securing or collecting debts or enforcing mortgages and security interests in property securing the debts;

(9) owning, without more, real or personal property;

(10) conducting an isolated transaction that is completed within 30 days and that is not one in the course of repeated transactions of a like nature;

(11) transacting business in interstate commerce.

(c) The list of activities in subsection (b) is not exhaustive.

§ 15.02. Consequences of Transacting Business Without Authority.—

(a) A foreign corporation transacting business in this state without a certificate of authority may not maintain a proceeding in any court in this state until it obtains a certificate of authority.

(b) The successor to a foreign corporation that transacted business in this state without a certificate of authority and the assignee of a cause of action arising out of that business may not maintain a proceeding based on that cause of action in any court in this state until the foreign corporation or its successor obtains a certificate of authority.

(c) A court may stay a proceeding commenced by a foreign corporation, its successor, or assignee until it determines whether the foreign corporation or its successor requires a certificate of authority. If it so determines, the court may further stay the proceeding until the foreign corporation or its successor obtains the certificate.

(d) A foreign corporation is liable for a civil penalty of $_____ for each day, but not to exceed a total of $_____ for each year, it transacts business in this state without a certificate of authority. The attorney general may collect all penalties due under this subsection.

(e) Notwithstanding subsections (a) and (b), the failure of a foreign corporation to obtain a certificate of authority does not impair the validity of its corporate acts or prevent it from defending any proceeding in this state.

§ 15.03. Application for Certificate of Authority.—

(a) A foreign corporation may apply for a certificate of authority to transact business in this state by delivering an application to the secretary of state for filing. The application must set forth:

(1) the name of the foreign corporation or, if its name is unavailable for use in this state, a corporate name that satisfies the requirements of section 15.06;

(2) the name of the state or country under whose law it is incorporated;

(3) its date of incorporation and period of duration;

(4) the street address of its principal office;

(5) the address of its registered office in this state and the name of its registered agent at that office; and

(6) the names and usual business addresses of its current directors and officers.

(b) The foreign corporation shall deliver with the completed application a certificate of existence (or a document of similar import) duly authenticated by the secretary of state or other official having custody of corporate records in the state or country under whose law it is incorporated.

§ 15.04. Amended Certificate of Authority.—

(a) A foreign corporation authorized to transact business in this state must obtain an amended certificate of authority from the secretary of state if it changes:

(1) its corporate name;

(2) the period of its duration; or

(3) the state or country of its incorporation.

(b) The requirements of section 15.03 for obtaining an original certificate of authority apply to obtaining an amended certificate under this section.

§ 15.05. Effect of Certificate of Authority.—

(a) A certificate of authority authorizes the foreign corporation to which it is issued to transact business in this state subject, however, to the right of the state to revoke the certificate as provided in this Act.

(b) A foreign corporation with a valid certificate of authority has the same but no greater rights and has the same but no greater privileges as, and except as otherwise provided by this Act is subject to the same duties, restrictions, penalties, and liabilities now or later imposed on, a domestic corporation of like character.

(c) This Act does not authorize this state to regulate the organization or internal affairs of a foreign corporation authorized to transact business in this state.

§ 15.06. Corporate Name of Foreign Corporation.—

(a) If the corporate name of a foreign corporation does not satisfy the requirements of section 4.01, the foreign corporation to obtain or maintain a certificate of authority to transact business in this state:

(1) may add the word "corporation," "incorporated," "company," or "limited," or the abbreviation "corp.," "inc.," "co.," or "ltd.," to its corporate name for use in this state; or

(2) may use a fictitious name to transact business in this state if its real name is unavailable and it delivers to the secretary of state for filing a copy of the resolution of its board of directors, certified by its secretary, adopting the fictitious name.

(b) Except as authorized by subsections (c) and (d), the corporate name (including a fictitious name) of a foreign corporation must be distinguishable upon the records of the secretary of state from:

(1) the corporate name of a corporation incorporated or authorized to transact business in this state;

(2) a corporate name reserved or registered under section 4.02 or 4.03;

(3) the fictitious name of another foreign corporation authorized to transact business in this state; and

(4) the corporate name of a not-for-profit corporation incorporated or authorized to transact business in this state.

(c) A foreign corporation may apply to the secretary of state for authorization to use in this state the name of another corporation (incorporated or authorized to transact business in this state) that is not distinguishable upon his records from the name applied for. The secretary of state shall authorize use of the name applied for if:

(1) the other corporation consents to the use in writing and submits an undertaking in form satisfactory to the secretary of state to change its name to a name that is distinguishable upon the records of the secretary of state from the name of the applying corporation; or

(2) the applicant delivers to the secretary of state a certified copy of a final judgment of a court of competent jurisdiction establishing the applicant's right to use the name applied for in this state.

(d) A foreign corporation may use in this state the name (including the fictitious name) of another domestic or foreign corporation that is used in this state if the other corporation is incorporated or authorized to transact business in this state and the foreign corporation:

(1) has merged with the other corporation;

(2) has been formed by reorganization of the other corporation; or

(3) has acquired all or substantially all of the assets, including the corporate name, of the other corporation.

(e) If a foreign corporation authorized to transact business in this state changes its corporate name to one that does not satisfy the requirements of section 4.01, it may not transact business in this state under the changed name until it adopts a name satisfying the requirements of section 4.01 and obtains an amended certificate of authority under section 15.04.

§ 15.07. Registered Office and Registered Agent of Foreign Corporation.—

Each foreign corporation authorized to transact business in this state must continuously maintain in this state:

(1) a registered office that may be the same as any of its places of business; and

(2) a registered agent, who may be:

(i) an individual who resides in this state and whose business office is identical with the registered office;

(ii) a domestic corporation or not-for-profit domestic corporation whose business office is identical with the registered office; or

(iii) a foreign corporation or foreign not-for-profit corporation authorized to transact business in this state whose business office is identical with the registered office.

§ 15.08. Change of Registered Office or Registered Agent of Foreign Corporation.—

(a) A foreign corporation authorized to transact business in this state may change its registered office or registered agent by delivering to the secretary of state for filing a statement of change that sets forth:

(1) its name;

(2) the street address of its current registered office;

(3) if the current registered office is to be changed, the street address of its new registered office;

(4) the name of its current registered agent;

(5) if the current registered agent is to be changed, the name of its new registered agent and the new agent's written consent (either on the statement or attached to it) to the appointment; and

(6) that after the change or changes are made, the street addresses of its registered office and the business office of its registered agent will be identical.

(b) If a registered agent changes the street address of his business office, he may change the street address of the registered office of any foreign corporation for which he is the registered agent by notifying the corporation in writing of the change and signing (either manually or in facsimile) and delivering to the secretary of state for filing a statement of change that complies with the requirements of subsection (a) and recites that the corporation has been notified of the change.

§ 15.09. Resignation of Registered Agent of Foreign Corporation.—

(a) The registered agent of a foreign corporation may resign his agency appointment by signing and delivering to the secretary of state for filing the original and two exact or conformed copies of a statement of resignation. The statement of resignation may include a statement that the registered office is also discontinued.

(b) After filing the statement, the secretary of state shall attach the filing receipt to one copy and mail the copy and receipt to the registered office if not discontinued. The secretary of state shall mail the other copy to the foreign corporation at its principal office address shown in its most recent annual report.

(c) The agency appointment is terminated, and the registered office discontinued if so provided, on the 31st day after the date on which the statement was filed.

§ 15.10. Service on Foreign Corporation.—

(a) The registered agent of a foreign corporation authorized to transact business in this state is the corporation's agent for service of process, notice, or demand required or permitted by law to be served on the foreign corporation.

(b) A foreign corporation may be served by registered or certified mail, return receipt requested, addressed to the secretary of the foreign corporation at its principal office shown in its application for a certificate of authority or in its most recent annual report if the foreign corporation:

(1) has no registered agent or its registered agent cannot with reasonable diligence be served;

(2) has withdrawn from transacting business in this state under section 15.20; or

(3) has had its certificate of authority revoked under section 15.31.

(c) Service is perfected under subsection (b) at the earliest of:

(1) the date the foreign corporation receives the mail;

(2) the date shown on the return receipt, if signed on behalf of the foreign corporation; or

(3) five days after its deposit in the United States Mail, as evidenced by the postmark if mailed postpaid and correctly addressed.

(d) This section does not prescribe the only means, or necessarily the required means, of serving a foreign corporation.

Subchapter B. Withdrawal

§ 15.20. Withdrawal of Foreign Corporation.—

(a) A foreign corporation authorized to transact business in this state may not withdraw from this state until it obtains a certificate of withdrawal from the secretary of state.

(b) A foreign corporation authorized to transact business in this state may apply for a certificate of withdrawal by delivering an application to the secretary of state for filing. The application must set forth:

(1) the name of the foreign corporation and the name of the state or country under whose law it is incorporated;

(2) that it is not transacting business in this state and that it surrenders its authority to transact business in this state;

(3) that it revokes the authority of its registered agent to accept service on its behalf and appoints the secretary of state as its agent for service of process in any proceeding based on a cause of action arising during the time it was authorized to transact business in this state;

(4) a mailing address to which the secretary of state may mail a copy of any process served on him under subdivision (3); and

(5) a commitment to notify the secretary of state in the future of any change in its mailing address.

(c) After the withdrawal of the corporation is effective, service of process on the secretary of state under this section is service on the foreign corporation. Upon receipt of process, the secretary of state shall mail a copy of the process to the foreign corporation at the mailing address set forth under subsection (b).

Subchapter C. Revocation of Certificate of Authority

§ 15.30. Grounds for Revocation.—

The secretary of state may commence a proceeding under section 15.31 to revoke the certificate of authority of a foreign corporation authorized to transact business in this state if:

(1) the foreign corporation does not deliver its annual report to the secretary of state within 60 days after it is due;

(2) the foreign corporation does not pay within 60 days after they are due any franchise taxes or penalties imposed by this Act or other law;

(3) the foreign corporation is without a registered agent or registered office in this state for 60 days or more;

(4) the foreign corporation does not inform the secretary of state under section 15.08 or 15.09 that its registered agent or registered office has changed, that its registered agent has resigned, or that its registered office has been discontinued within 60 days of the change, resignation, or discontinuance;

(5) an incorporator, director, officer, or agent of the foreign corporation signed a document he knew was false in any material respect with intent that the document be delivered to the secretary of state for filing;

(6) the secretary of state receives a duly authenticated certificate from the secretary of state or other official having custody of corporate records in the state or country under whose law the foreign corporation is incorporated stating that it has been dissolved or disappeared as the result of a merger.

§ 15.31. Procedure for and Effect of Revocation.—

(a) If the secretary of state determines that one or more grounds exist under section 15.30 for revocation of a certificate of authority, he shall serve the foreign corporation with written notice of his determination under section 15.10.

(b) If the foreign corporation does not correct each ground for revocation or demonstrate to the reasonable satisfaction of the secretary of state that each ground determined by the secretary of state does not exist within 60 days after service of the notice is perfected under section 15.10, the secretary of state may revoke the foreign corporation's certificate of authority by signing a certificate of revocation that recites the ground or grounds for revocation and its effective date. The secretary of state shall file the original of the certificate and serve a copy on the foreign corporation under section 15.10.

(c) The authority of a foreign corporation to transact business in this state ceases on the date shown on the certificate revoking its certificate of authority.

(d) The secretary of state's revocation of a foreign corporation's certificate of authority appoints the secretary of state the foreign corporation's agent for service of process in any proceeding based on a cause of action which arose during the time the foreign corporation was authorized to transact business in this state. Service of process on the secretary of state under this subsection is service on the foreign corporation. Upon receipt of process, the secretary of state shall mail a copy of the process to the secretary of the foreign corporation at its principal office shown in its most recent annual report or in any subsequent communication received from the corporation stating the current mailing address of its principal office, or, if none are on file, in its application for a certificate of authority.

(e) Revocation of a foreign corporation's certificate of authority does not terminate the authority of the registered agent of the corporation.

§ 15.32. Appeal From Revocation.—

(a) A foreign corporation may appeal the secretary of state's revocation of its certificate of authority to the [name or describe] court within 30 days after service of the certificate of revocation is perfected under section 15.10. The foreign corporation appeals by petitioning the court to set aside the revocation and attaching to the petition copies of its certificate of authority and the secretary of state's certificate of revocation.

(b) The court may summarily order the secretary of state to reinstate the certificate of authority or may take any other action the court considers appropriate.

(c) The court's final decision may be appealed as in other civil proceedings.

CHAPTER 16. RECORDS AND REPORTS

Subchapter A. Records

§ 16.01. Corporate Records.—

(a) A corporation shall keep as permanent records minutes of all meetings of its shareholders and board of directors, a record of all actions taken by the shareholders or board of directors without a meeting, and a record of all actions taken by a committee of the board of directors in place of the board of directors on behalf of the corporation.

(b) A corporation shall maintain appropriate accounting records.

(c) A corporation or its agent shall maintain a record of its shareholders, in a form that permits preparation of a list of the names and addresses of all shareholders, in alphabetical order by class of shares showing the number and class of shares held by each.

(d) A corporation shall maintain its records in written form or in another form capable of conversion into written form within a reasonable time.

(e) A corporation shall keep a copy of the following records at its principal office:

(1) its articles or restated articles of incorporation and all amendments to them currently in effect;

(2) its bylaws or restated bylaws and all amendments to them currently in effect;

(3) resolutions adopted by its board of directors creating one or more classes or series of shares, and fixing their relative rights, preferences, and limitations, if shares issued pursuant to those resolutions are outstanding;

(4) the minutes of all shareholders' meetings, and records of all action taken by shareholders without a meeting, for the past three years;

(5) all written communications to shareholders generally within the past three years, including the financial statements furnished for the past three years under section 16.20;

(6) a list of the names and business addresses of its current directors and officers; and

(7) its most recent annual report delivered to the secretary of state under section 16.22.

§ 16.02. Inspection of Records by Shareholders.—

(a) A shareholder of a corporation is entitled to inspect and copy, during regular business hours at the corporation's principal office, any of the records of the corporation described in section 16.01(e) if he gives the corporation written notice of his demand at least five business days before the date on which he wishes to inspect and copy.

(b) A shareholder of a corporation is entitled to inspect and copy, during regular business hours at a reasonable location specified by the corporation, any of the following records of the corporation if the shareholder meets the requirements of subsection (c) and gives the corporation written notice of his demand at least five business days before the date on which he wishes to inspect and copy:

(1) excerpts from minutes of any meeting of the board of directors, records of any action of a committee of the board of directors while acting in place of the board of directors on behalf of the corporation, minutes of any meeting of the shareholders, and records of action taken by the shareholders or board of directors without a meeting, to the extent not subject to inspection under section 16.02(a);

(2) accounting records of the corporation; and

(3) the record of shareholders.

(c) A shareholder may inspect and copy the records described in subsection (b) only if:

(1) his demand is made in good faith and for a proper purpose;

(2) he describes with reasonable particularity his purpose and the records he desires to inspect; and

(3) the records are directly connected with his purpose.

(d) The right of inspection granted by this section may not be abolished or limited by a corporation's articles of incorporation or bylaws.

(e) This section does not affect:

(1) the right of a shareholder to inspect records under section 7.20 or, if the shareholder is in litigation with the corporation, to the same extent as any other litigant;

(2) the power of a court, independently of this Act, to compel the production of corporate records for examination.

(f) For purposes of this section, "shareholder" includes a beneficial owner whose shares are held in a voting trust or by nominee on his behalf.

§ 16.03. Scope of Inspection Right.—

(a) A shareholder's agent or attorney has the same inspection and copying rights as the shareholder he represents.

(b) The right to copy records under section 16.02 includes, if reasonable, the right to receive copies made by photographic, xerographic, or other means.

(c) The corporation may impose a reasonable charge, covering the costs of labor and material, for copies of any documents provided to the shareholder. The charge may not exceed the estimated cost of production or reproduction of the records.

(d) The corporation may comply with a shareholder's demand to inspect the record of shareholders under section 16.02(b)(3) by providing him with a list of its shareholders that was compiled no earlier than the date of the shareholder's demand.

§ 16.04. Court-ordered Inspection.—

(a) If a corporation does not allow a shareholder who complies with section 16.02(a) to inspect and copy any records required by that subsection to be available for inspection, the [name or describe court] of the county where the corporation's principal office (or, if none in this state, its registered office) is located may summarily order inspection and copying of the records demanded at the corporation's expense upon application of the shareholder.

(b) If a corporation does not within a reasonable time allow a shareholder to inspect and copy any other record, the shareholder who complies with section 16.02(b) and (c) may apply to the [name or describe court] in the county where the corporation's principal office (or, if none in this state, its registered office) is located for an order to permit inspection and copying of the records demanded. The court shall dispose of an application under this subsection on an expedited basis.

(c) If the court orders inspection and copying of the records demanded, it shall also order the corporation to pay the shareholder's costs (including reasonable counsel fees) incurred to obtain the order unless the corporation proves that it refused inspection in good faith because it had a reasonable basis for doubt about the right of the shareholder to inspect the records demanded.

(d) If the court orders inspection and copying of the records demanded, it may impose reasonable restrictions on the use or distribution of the records by the demanding shareholder.

Subchapter B. Reports

§ 16.20. Financial Statements for Shareholders.—

(a) A corporation shall furnish its shareholders annual financial statements, which may be consolidated or combined statements of the corporation and one or more of its subsidiaries, as appropriate, that include a balance sheet as of the end of the fiscal year, an income statement for that year, and a statement of changes in shareholders' equity for the year unless that information appears elsewhere in the financial statements. If financial statements are prepared for the corporation on the basis of generally accepted accounting principles, the annual financial statements must also be prepared on that basis.

(b) If the annual financial statements are reported upon by a public accountant, his report must accompany them. If not, the statements must be accompanied by a statement of the president or the person responsible for the corporation's accounting records:

(1) stating his reasonable belief whether the statements were prepared on the basis of generally accepted accounting principles and, if not, describing the basis of preparation; and

(2) describing any respects in which the statements were not prepared on a basis of accounting consistent with the statements prepared for the preceding year.

(c) A corporation shall mail the annual financial statements to each shareholder within 120 days after the close of each fiscal year. Thereafter, on written request from a shareholder who was not mailed the statements, the corporation shall mail him the latest financial statements.

§ 16.21. Other Reports to Shareholders.—

(a) If a corporation indemnifies or advances expenses to a director under section 8.51, 8.52, 8.53, or 8.54 in connection with a proceeding by or in the right of the corporation, the corporation shall report the indemnification or advance in writing to the shareholders with or before the notice of the next shareholders' meeting.

(b) If a corporation issues or authorizes the issuance of shares for promissory notes or for promises to render services in the future, the corporation shall report in writing to the shareholders the number of shares authorized or issued, and the consideration received by the corporation, with or before the notice of the next shareholders' meeting.

§ 16.22. Annual Report for Secretary of State.—

(a) Each domestic corporation, and each foreign corporation authorized to transact business in this state, shall deliver to the secretary of state for filing an annual report that sets forth:

(1) the name of the corporation and the state or country under whose law it is incorporated;

(2) the address of its registered office and the name of its registered agent at that office in this state;

(3) the address of its principal office;

(4) the names and business addresses of its directors and principal officers;

(5) a brief description of the nature of its business;

(6) the total number of authorized shares, itemized by class and series, if any, within each class; and

(7) the total number of issued and outstanding shares, itemized by class and series, if any, within each class.

(b) Information in the annual report must be current as of the date the annual report is executed on behalf of the corporation.

(c) The first annual report must be delivered to the secretary of state between January 1 and April 1 of the year following the calendar year in which a domestic corporation was incorporated or a foreign corporation was authorized to transact business. Subsequent annual reports must be delivered to the secretary of state between January 1 and April 1 of the following calendar years.

(d) If an annual report does not contain the information required by this section, the secretary of state shall promptly notify the reporting domestic or foreign corporation in writing and return the report to it for correction. If the report is corrected to contain the information required by this section and delivered to the secretary of state within 30 days after the effective date of notice, it is deemed to be timely filed.

CHAPTER 17. TRANSITION PROVISIONS

§ 17.01. Application to Existing Domestic Corporations.—This Act applies to all domestic corporations in existence on its effective date that were incorporated under any general statute of this state providing for incorporation of corporations for profit if power to amend or repeal the statute under which the corporation was incorporated was reserved.

§ 17.02. Application to Qualified Foreign Corporations.—A foreign corporation authorized to transact business in this state on the effective date of this Act is subject to this Act but is not required to obtain a new certificate of authority to transact business under this Act.

§ 17.03. Saving Provisions.—

(a) Except as provided in subsection (b), the repeal of a statute by this Act does not affect:

(1) the operation of the statute or any action taken under it before its repeal;

(2) any ratification, right, remedy, privilege, obligation, or liability acquired, accrued, or incurred under the statute before its repeal;

(3) any violation of the statute, or any penalty, forfeiture, or punishment incurred because of the violation, before its repeal;

(4) any proceeding, reorganization, or dissolution commenced under the statute before its repeal, and the proceeding, reorganization, or dissolution may be completed in accordance with the statute as if it had not been repealed.

(b) If a penalty or punishment imposed for violation of a statute repealed by this Act is reduced by this Act, the penalty or punishment if not already imposed shall be imposed in accordance with this Act.

§ 17.04. Severability.—If any provision of this Act or its application to any person or circumstance is held invalid by a court of competent jurisdiction, the invalidity does not affect other provisions or applications of the Act that can be given effect without the invalid provision or application, and to this end the provisions of the Act are severable.

§ 17.05. Repeal.—The following laws and parts of laws are repealed: [to be inserted].

§ 17.06. Effective Date.—This Act takes effect _____

APPENDIX B   Uniform Partnership Act (1914)*

Commissioners' Prefatory Note

Part I.   Preliminary Provisions
§1   Name of Act
§2   Definition of Terms
§3   Interpretation of Knowledge and Notice
§4   Rules of Construction
§5   Rules for Cases Not Provided for in This Act

Part II.   Nature of a Partnership
§6   Partnership Defined
§7   Rules for Determining the Existence of a Partnership
§8   Partnership Property

Part III.   Relations of Partners to Persons Dealing with the Partnership
§9   Partner Agent of Partnership as to Partnership Business
§10   Conveyance of Real Property of the Partnership
§11   Partnership Bound by Admission of Partner
§12   Partnership Charged with Knowledge of or Notice to Partner
§13   Partnership Bound by Partner's Wrongful Act
§14   Partnership Bound by Partner's Breach of Trust

§15   Nature of Partner's Liability
§16   Partner by Estoppel
§17   Liability of Incoming Partner

Part IV.   Relations of Partners to One Another
§18   Rules Determining Rights and Duties of Partners
§19   Partnership Books
§20   Duty of Partners to Render Information
§21   Partner Accountable as a Fiduciary
§22   Right to an Account
§23   Continuation of Partnership Beyond Fixed Term

Part V.   Property Rights of a Partner
§24   Extent of Property Rights of a Partner
§25   Nature of a Partner's Right in Specific Partnership Property
§26   Nature of Partner's Interest in the Partnership
§27   Assignment of Partner's Interest
§28   Partner's Interest Subject to Charging Order

Part VI.   Dissolution and Winding Up
§29   Dissolution Defined
§30   Partnership Not Terminated by Dissolution
§31   Causes of Dissolution
§32   Dissolution by Decree of Court
§33   General Effect of Dissolution on Authority of Partner
§34   Right of Partner to Contribution from Co-partners after Dissolution
§35   Power of Partner to Bind Partnership to Third Persons after Dissolution
§36   Effect of Dissolution on Partner's Existing Liability
§37   Right to Wind Up
§38   Rights of Partners to Application of Partnership Property
§39   Rights Where Partnership Is Dissolved for Fraud or Misrepresentation
§40   Rules for Distribution
§41   Liability of Persons Continuing the Business in Certain Cases
§42   Rights of Retiring or Estate of Decreased Partner When the Business Is Continued
§43   Accrual of Actions

Part VII.   Miscellaneous Provisions
§44   When Act Takes Effect
§45   Legislation Repealed

*Copies of this act may be ordered from the National Conference of Commissioners on Uniform State Laws, 676 North St. Clair St., Suite 1700, Chicago, Illinois 60611, 312–915–0195.

COMMISSIONERS' PREFATORY NOTE

The subject of a uniform law on partnership was taken up by the Conference of Commissioners on Uniform State Laws in 1902, and the Committee on Commercial Law was instructed to employ an expert and prepare a draft to be submitted to the next annual Conference. (See Am. Bar Assn. Report for 1902, p. 477.) At the meeting in 1903 the committee reported that it had secured the services of James Barr Ames, Dean of the Law School of Harvard University, as expert to draft the act. (See Am. Bar Assn. Report for 1903, p. 501.)

In 1905 the Committee on Commercial Law reported progress on this subject, and a resolution was passed by the Conference, directing that a draft be prepared upon the mercantile theory. (See Am. Bar Assn. Reports, 1905, pp. 731-738.) And in 1906 the committee reported that it had in its hands a draft of an act on this subject, which draft was recommitted to the committee for revision and amendment, with directions to report to the next Conference for discussion and action. (See Report, C.U.S.L, 1906, p. 40.)

In 1907 the matter was brought before the Conference and postponed until the 1908 meeting. (See Report, C.U.S.L, 1907, p. 93.) In 1908 the matter was discussed by the Conference. (See Am. Bar Assn. Reports, 1908, pp. 983, 1048.) And in 1909 the Second Tentative Draft of the Partnership Act was introduced and discussed. (See p. 1081 of Am. Bar Assn. Reports for 1909.)

In 1910 the committee reported that on account of the death of Dean Ames no progress had been made, but that Dr. Wm. Draper Lewis, then Dean and now Professor of Law at the Law School of the University of Pennsylvania, and Mr. James B. Lichtenberger, of the Philadelphia Bar, had prepared a draft of a partnership act on the so-called entity idea, with the aid of the various drafts and notes of Dean Ames, and that they had also submitted a draft of a proposed uniform act, embodying the theory that a partnership is an aggregate of individuals associated in business, which is that at present accepted in nearly all the states of the Union. (See Report C.U.S.L., 1910, p. 142.) Dean Lewis expressed his belief that with certain modifications the aggregate or common law theory should be adopted. A resolution was passed by the Conference that any action that might have theretofore been adopted by it, tending to limit the Committee on Commercial Law in its consideration of the partnership law to what is known as the entity theory, be rescinded and that the committee be allowed and directed to consider the subject of partnership at large as though no such resolution had been adopted by the Conference. (See p. 52.)

In the fall of 1910 the committee invited to a Conference, held in Philadelphia, all the teachers of, and writers on, partnerships, besides several other lawyers known to have made a special study of the subject. There was a large attendance. For two days the members of the committee and their guests discussed the theory on which the proposed act should be drawn. At the conclusion of the discussion the experts present recommended that the act be drawn on the aggregate or common law theory, with the modification that the partners be treated as owners of partnership property holding by a special tenancy which should be called tenancy in partnership. (See section 25 of the act recommended.) Accordingly, at the meeting of the Conference in the summer of 1911, the committee reported that, after hearing the discussion of experts, it had voted that Dean Lewis be requested to prepare a draft of a partnership act on the so-called common law theory. (See Report, C.U.S.L, 1911, p. 149.)

The committee reported another draft of the act to the Conference at its session in 1912, drawn on the aggregate or common law theory, with the modification referred to. At this session the Conference spent several days in the discussion of the act, again referring it to the Committee on Commercial Law for their further consideration. (See Report, C.U.S.L., 1912, p. 67.)

The Committee on Commercial Law held a meeting in New York on March 29, 1913, and took up the draft of the act referred back to it by the Conference, and after careful consideration of the amendments suggested by the Conference, prepared their seventh draft, which was, at their annual session in the summer of 1913, submitted to the Conference. The Conference again spent several days in discussing the act and again referred it to the Committee on Commercial Law, this time mainly for protection in form.

The Committee on Commercial Law assembled in the City of New York, September 21, 1914, and had before them a new draft of the act, which had been carefully prepared by Dr. Wm. Draper Lewis with valuable suggestions submitted by Charles E. Shepard, Esq., one of the commissioners from the State of Washington, and others interested in the subject. The committee reported the Eighth Draft to the Conference which, on October 14, 1914, passed a resolution recommending the act for adoption to the legislatures of all the States.

Uniformity of the law of partnerships is constantly becoming more important, as the number of firms increases which not only carry on business in more than one state, but have among the members residents of different states.

It is however, proper here to emphasize the fact that there are other reasons, in addition to the advantages which will result from uniformity, for the adoption of the act now issued by the Commissioners. There is probably no other subject connected with our business law in which a greater number of instances can be found where, in matters of almost daily occurrence, the law is uncertain. This uncertainty is due, not only to conflict between the decisions of different states, but more to the general lack of consistency in legal theory. In several of the sections, but especially in those which relate to the rights of the partner and his separate creditors in partnership property, and to the rights of firm creditors where the personnel of the partnership has been changed without liquidation of partnership affairs, there exists an almost hopeless confusion of theory and practice, making the actual administration of the law difficult and often inequitable.

Another difficulty of the present partnership law is the scarcity of authority on matters of considerable importance in the daily conduct and in the winding up of partnership affairs. In any one state it is often impossible to find an authority on a matter of comparatively frequent occurrence, while not infrequently an exhaustive research of the reports of the decisions of all the states and the federal courts fails to reveal a single authority throwing light on the question. The existence of a statute stating in detail the rights of the partners inter se during the carrying on of the partnership business, and on the winding up of partnership affairs, will be a real practical advantage of moment to the business world.

The notes which are printed in connection with this edition of the Act were prepared by Dr. Wm. Draper Lewis, the draftsman. They are designed to point out the few changes in the law which the adoption of the act will effect, and the many confusions and uncertainties which it will end. [Notes not reprinted here.]

Walter George Smith

PART I.   PRELIMINARY PROVISIONS

§1.   Name of Act

This act may be cited as Uniform Partnership Act.

§2.   Definition of Terms

In this act, "Court" includes every court and judge having jurisdiction in the case.

"Business" includes every trade, occupation, or profession.

"Person" includes individuals, partnerships, corporations, and other associations.

"Bankrupt" includes bankrupt under the Federal Bankruptcy Act or insolvent under any state insolvent act.

"Conveyance" includes every assignment, lease, mortgage, or encumbrance.

"Real property" includes land and any interest or estate in land.

§3.   Interpretation of Knowledge and Notice

(1) A person has "knowledge" of a fact within the meaning of this act not only when he has actual knowledge thereof, but also when he has knowledge of such other facts as in the circumstances shows bad faith.

(2) A person has "notice" of a fact within the meaning of this act when the person who claims the benefit of the notice:

    (a) States the fact to such person, or

    (b) Delivers through the mail, or by other means of communication, a written statement of the fact to such person or to a proper person at his place of business or residence.

§4. Rules of Construction

(1) The rule that statutes in derogation of the common law are to be strictly construed shall have no application to this act.

(2) The law of estoppel shall apply under this act.

(3) The law of agency shall apply under this act.

(4) This act shall be so interpreted and construed as to effect its general purpose to make uniform the law of those states which enact it.

(5) This act shall not be construed so as to impair the obligations of any contract existing when the act goes into effect, nor to affect any action or proceedings begun or right accrued before this act takes effect.

§5. Rules for Cases Not Provided for in This Act

In any case not provided for in this act the rules of law and equity, including the law merchant, shall govern.

PART II. NATURE OF A PARTNERSHIP

§6. Partnership Defined

(1) A partnership is an association of two or more persons to carry on as co-owners a business for profit.

(2) But any association formed under any other statute of this state, or any association formed by authority, other than the authority of this state, is not a partnership under this act, unless such associa-tion would have been a partnership in this state prior to the adoption of this act; but this act shall apply to limited partnerships except in so far as the statutes relating to such partnerships are inconsistent herewith.

§7. Rules for Determining the Existence of a Partnership

In determining whether a partnership exists, these rules shall apply:

(1) Except as provided by section 16 persons who are not partners as to each other are not partners as to third persons.

(2) Joint tenancy, tenancy in common, tenancy by the entireties, joint property, common property, or part ownership does not of itself establish a partnership, whether such co-owners do or do not share any profits made by the use of the property.

(3) The sharing of gross returns does not of itself establish a partnership, whether or not the persons sharing them have a joint or common right or interest in any property from which the returns are derived.

(4) The receipt by a person of a share of the profits of a business is prima facie evidence that he is a partner in the business, but no such inference shall be drawn if such profits were received in payment:

    (a) As a debt by installments or otherwise,

    (b) As wages of an employee or rent to a landlord,

    (c) As an annuity to a widow or representative of a deceased partner,

    (d) As interest on a loan, though the amount of payment vary with the profits of the business,

    (e) As the consideration for the sale of the good-will of a business or other property by installments or otherwise.

§8. Partnership Property

(1) All property originally brought into the partnership stock or subsequently acquired by purchase or otherwise, on account of the partnership, is partnership property.

(2) Unless the contrary intention appears, property acquired with partnership funds is partnership property.

(3) Any estate in real property may be acquired in the partnership name. Title so acquired can be conveyed only in the partnership name.

(4) A conveyance to a partnership in the partnership name, though without words of inheritance, passes the entire estate of the grantor unless a contrary intent appears.

PART III. RELATIONS OF PARTNERS TO PERSONS DEALING WITH THE PARTNERSHIP

§9. *Partner Agent of Partnership as to Partnership Business*

(1) Every partner is an agent of the partnership for the purpose of its business, and the act of every partner, including the execution in the partnership name of any instrument, for apparently carrying on in the usual way the business of the partnership of which he is a member binds the partnership, unless the partner so acting has in fact no authority to act for the partnership in the particular matter, and the person with whom he is dealing has knowledge of the fact that he has no such authority.

(2) An act of a partner which is not apparently for the carrying on of the business of the partnership in the usual way does not bind the partnership unless authorized by the other partners.

(3) Unless authorized by the other partners or unless they have abandoned the business, one or more but less than all the partners have no authority to:

(a) Assign the partnership property in trust for creditors or on the assignee's promise to pay the debts of the partnership,

(b) Dispose of the good-will of the business,

(c) Do any other act which would make it impossible to carry on the ordinary business of a partnership,

(d) Confess a judgment,

(e) Submit a partnership claim or liability to arbitration or reference.

(4) No act of a partner in contravention of a restriction on authority shall bind the partnership to persons having knowledge of the restriction.

§10. *Conveyance of Real Property of the Partnership*

(1) Where title to real property is in the partnership name, any partner may convey title to such property by a conveyance executed in the partnership name; but the partnership may recover such property unless the partner's act binds the partnership under the provisions of paragraph (1) of section 9, or unless such property has been conveyed by the grantee or a person claiming through such grantee to a holder for value without knowledge that the partner, in making the conveyance, has exceeded his authority.

(2) Where title to real property is in the name of the partnership, a conveyance executed by a partner, in his own name, passes the equitable interest of the partnership, provided the act is one within the authority of the partner under the provisions of paragraph (1) of section 9.

(3) Where title to real property is in the name of one or more but not all the partners, and the record does not disclose the right of the partnership, the partners in whose name the title stands may convey title to such property, but the partnership may recover such property if the partners' act does not bind the partnership under the provisions of paragraph (1) of section 9, unless the purchaser or his assignee, is a holder for value, without knowledge.

(4) Where the title to real property is in the name of one or more or all the partners, or in a third person in trust for the partnership, a conveyance executed by a partner in the partnership name, or in his own name, passes the equitable interest of the partnership, provided the act is one within the authority of the partner under the provisions of paragraph (1) of section 9.

(5) Where the title to real property is in the names of all the partners a conveyance executed by all the partners passes all their rights in such property.

§11. Partnership Bound by Admission of Partner

An admission or representation made by any partner concerning partnership affairs within the scope of his authority as conferred by this act is evidence against the partnership.

§12. Partnership Charged with Knowledge of or Notice to Partner

Notice to any partner of any matter relating to partnership affairs, and the knowledge of the partner acting in the particular matter, acquired while a partner or then present to his mind, and the knowledge of any other partner who reasonably could and should have communicated it to the acting partner, operate as notice to or knowledge of the partnership, except in the case of a fraud on the partnership committed by or with the consent of that partner.

§13. Partnership Bound by Partner's Wrongful Act

Where, by any wrongful act or omission of any partner acting in the ordinary course of the business of the partnership or with the authority of his co-partners, loss or injury is caused to any person, not being a partner in the partnership, or any penalty is incurred, the partnership is liable therefor to the same extent as the partner so acting or omitting to act.

§14. Partnership Bound by Partner's Breach of Trust

The partnership is bound to make good the loss:

(a) Where one partner acting within the scope of his apparent authority receives money or property of a third person and misapplies it; and

(b) Where the partnership in the course of its business receives money or property of a third person and the money or property so received is misapplied by any partner while it is in the custody of the partnership.

§15. Nature of Partner's Liability

All partners are liable

(a) Jointly and severally for everything chargeable to the partnership under sections 13 and 14.

(b) Jointly for all other debts and obligations of the partnership; but any partner may enter into a separate obligation to perform a partnership contract.

§16. Partner by Estoppel

(1) When a person, by words spoken or written or by conduct, represents himself, or consents to another representing him to any one, as a partner in an existing partnership or with one or more persons not actual partners, he is liable to any such person to whom such representation has been made, who has, on the faith of such representation, given credit to the actual or apparent partnership, and if he has made such representation or consented to its being made in a public manner he is liable to such person, whether the representation has or has not been made or communicated to such person so giving credit by or with the knowledge of the apparent partner making the representation or consenting to its being made.

(a) When a partnership liability results, he is liable as though he were an actual member of the partnership.

(b) When no partnership liability results, he is liable jointly with the other persons, if any, so consenting to the contract or representation as to incur liability, otherwise separately.

(2) When a person has been thus represented to be a partner in an existing partnership, or with one or more persons not actual partners, he is an agent of the persons consenting to such representation to bind them to the same extent and in the same manner as

though he were a partner in fact, with respect to persons who rely upon the representation. Where all the members of the existing partnership consent to the representation, a partnership act or obligation results; but in all other cases it is the joint act or obligation of the person acting and the persons consenting to the representation.

§17. Liability of Incoming Partner

A person admitted as a partner into an existing partnership is liable for all the obligations of the partnership arising before his admission as though he had been a partner when such obligations were incurred, except that this liability shall be satisfied only out of partnership property.

PART IV. RELATIONS OF PARTNERS TO ONE ANOTHER

§18. Rules Determining Rights and Duties of Partners

The rights and duties of the partners in relation to the partnership shall be determined, subject to any agreement between them, by the following rules:

(a) Each partner shall be repaid his contributions, whether by way of capital or advances to the partnership property and share equally in the profits and surplus remaining after all liabilities, including those to partners, are satisfied; and must contribute towards the losses, whether of capital or otherwise, sustained by the partnership according to his share in the profits.

(b) The partnership must indemnify every partner in respect of payments made and personal liabilities reasonably incurred by him in the ordinary and proper conduct of its business, or for the preservation of its business or property.

(c) A partner, who in aid of the partnership makes any payment or advance beyond the amount of capital which he agreed to contribute, shall be paid interest from the date of the payment or advance.

(d) A partner shall receive interest on the capital contributed by him only from the date when repayment should be made.

(e) All partners have equal rights in the management and conduct of the partnership business.

(f) No partner is entitled to remuneration for acting in the partnership business, except that a surviving partner is entitled to reasonable compensation for his services in winding up the partnership affairs.

(g) No person can become a member of a partnership without the consent of all the partners.

(h) Any difference arising as to ordinary matters connected with the partnership business may be decided by a majority of the partners; but no act in contravention of any agreement between the partners may be done rightfully without the consent of all the partners.

§19. Partnership Books

The partnership books shall be kept, subject to any agreement between the partners, at the principal place of business of the partnership, and every partner shall at all times have access to and may inspect and copy any of them.

§20. Duty of Partners to Render Information

Partners shall render on demand true and full information of all things affecting the partnership to any partner or the legal representative of any deceased partner or partner under legal disability.

§21. Partner Accountable as a Fiduciary

(1) Every partner must account to the partnership for any benefit, and hold as trustee for it any profits derived by him without

the consent of the other partners from any transaction connected with the formation, conduct, or liquidation of the partnership or from any use by him of its property.

(2) This section applies also to the representatives of a deceased partner engaged in the liquidation of the affairs of the partnership as the personal representatives of the last surviving partner.

§22. Right to an Account

Any partner shall have the right to a formal account as to partnership affairs:

(a) If he is wrongfully excluded from the partnership business or possession of its property by his co-partners,

(b) If the right exists under the terms of any agreement,

(c) As provided by section 21,

(d) Whenever other circumstances render it just and reasonable.

§23. Continuation of Partnership Beyond Fixed Term

(1) When a partnership for a fixed term or particular undertaking is continued after the termination of such term or particular undertaking without any express agreement, the rights and duties of the partners remain the same as they were at such termination, so far as is consistent with a partnership at will.

(2) A continuation of the business by the partners or such of them as habitually acted therein during the term, without any settlement or liquidation of the partnership affairs, is prima facie evidence of a continuation of the partnership.

PART V. PROPERTY RIGHTS OF A PARTNER

§24. Extent of Property Rights of a Partner

The property rights of a partner are (1) his rights in specific partnership property, (2) his interest in the partnership, and (3) his right to participate in the management.

§25. Nature of a Partner's Right in Specific Partnership Property

(1) A partner is co-owner with his partners of specific partnership property holding as a tenant in partnership.

(2) The incidents of this tenancy are such that:

(a) A partner, subject to the provisions of this act and to any agreement between the partners, has an equal right with his partners to possess specific partnership property for partnership purposes; but he has no right to possess such property for any other purpose without the consent of his partners.

(b) A partner's right in specific partnership property is not assignable except in connection with the assignment of rights of all the partners in the same property.

(c) A partner's right in specific partnership property is not subject to attachment or execution, except on a claim against the partnership. When partnership property is attached for a partnership debt the partners, or any of them, or the representatives of a deceased partner, cannot claim any right under the homestead or exemption laws.

(d) On the death of a partner his right in specific partnership property vests in the surviving partner or partners, except where the deceased was the last surviving partner, when his right in such property vests in his legal representative. Such surviving partner or partners, or the legal representative of the last surviving partner, has no right to possess the partnership property for any but a partnership purpose.

(e) A partner's right in specific partnership property is not subject to dower, curtesy, or allowances to widows, heirs, or next of kin.

§26. *Nature of Partner's Interest in the Partnership*

A partner's interest in the partnership is his share of the profits and surplus, and the same is personal property.

§27. *Assignment of Partner's Interest*

(1) A conveyance by a partner of his interest in the partnership does not of itself dissolve the partnership, nor, as against the other partners in the absence of agreement, entitle the assignee, during the continuance of the partnership, to interfere in the management or administration of the partnership business or affairs, or to require any information or account of partnership transactions, or to inspect the partnership books; but it merely entitles the assignee to receive in accordance with his contract the profits to which the assigning partner would otherwise be entitled.

(2) In case of a dissolution of the partnership, the assignee is entitled to receive his assignor's interest and may require an account from the date only of the last account agreed to by all the partners.

§28. *Partner's Interest Subject to Charging Order*

(1) On due application to a competent court by any judgment creditor of a partner, the court which entered the judgment, order, or decree, or any other court, may charge the interest of the debtor partner with payment of the unsatisfied amount of such judgment debt with interest thereon; and may then or later appoint a re-ceiver of his share of the profits, and of any other money due or to fall due to him in respect of the partnership, and make all other orders, directions, accounts and inquiries which the debtor partner might have made, or which the circumstances of the case may require.

(2) The interest charged may be redeemed at any time before foreclosure, or in case of a sale being directed by the court may be purchased without thereby causing a dissolution:

(a) With separate property, by any one or more of the partners, or

(b) With partnership property, by any one or more of the partners with the consent of all the partners whose interests are not so charged or sold.

(3) Nothing in this act shall be held to deprive a partner of his right, if any, under the exemption laws, as regards his interest in the partnership.

PART VI. DISSOLUTION AND WINDING UP

§29. *Dissolution Defined*

The dissolution of a partnership is the change in the relation of the partners caused by any partner ceasing to be associated in the carrying on as distinguished from the winding up of the business.

§30. *Partnership Not Terminated by Dissolution*

On dissolution the partnership is not terminated, but continues until the winding up of partnership affairs is completed.

§31. *Causes of Dissolution*

Dissolution is caused:

(1) Without violation of the agreement between the partners,

(a) By the termination of the definite term or particular undertaking specified in the agreement,

(b) By the express will of any partner when no definite term or particular undertaking is specified,

(c) By the express will of all the partners who have not assigned their interests or suffered them to be charged for their separate debts, either before or after the termination of any specified term or particular undertaking.

(d) By the expulsion of any partner from the business bona fide in accordance with such a power conferred by the agreement between the partners;

(2) In contravention of the agreement between the partners, where the circumstances do not permit a dissolution under any other provision of this section, by the express will of any partner at any time;

(3) By any event which makes it unlawful for the business of the partnership to be carried on or for the members to carry it on in partnership;

(4) By the death of any partner;

(5) By the bankruptcy of any partner or the partnership;

(6) By decree of court under section 32.

§32. Dissolution by Decree of Court

(1) On application by or for a partner the court shall decree a dissolution whenever:

(a) A partner has been declared a lunatic in any judicial proceeding or is shown to be of unsound mind,

(b) A partner becomes in any other way incapable of performing his part of the partnership contract,

(c) A partner has been guilty of such conduct as tends to affect prejudicially the carrying on of the business,

(d) A partner wilfully or persistently commits a breach of the partnership agreement, or otherwise so conducts himself in matters relating to the partnership business that it is not reasonably practicable to carry on the business in partnership with him,

(e) The business of the partnership can only be carried on at a loss,

(f) Other circumstances render a dissolution equitable.

(2) On the application of the purchaser of a partner's interest under sections 28 or 29 [should read 27 or 28];

(a) After the termination of the specified term or particular undertaking,

(b) At any time if the partnership was a partnership at will when the interest was assigned or when the charging order was issued.

§33. General Effect of Dissolution on Authority of Partner

Except so far as may be necessary to wind up partnership affairs or to complete transactions begun but not then finished, dissolution terminates all authority of any partner to act for the partnership,

(1) With respect to the partners,

(a) When the dissolution is not by the act, bankruptcy or death of a partner; or

(b) When the dissolution is by such act, bankruptcy or death of a partner, in cases where section 34 so requires.

(2) With respect to persons not partners, as declared in section 35.

§34. Rights of Partner to Contribution from Co-partners after Dissolution

Where the dissolution is caused by the act, death or bankruptcy of a partner, each partner is liable to his co-partners for his share of any liability created by any partner acting for the partnership as if the partnership had not been dissolved unless

(a) The dissolution being by act of any partner, the partner acting for the partnership had knowledge of the dissolution, or

(b) The dissolution being by the death or bankruptcy of a

partner, the partner acting for the partnership had knowledge or notice of the death or bankruptcy.

§35. Power of Partner to Bind Partnership to Third Persons after Dissolution

(1) After dissolution a partner can bind the partnership except as provided in Paragraph (3).

(a) By any act appropriate for winding up partnership affairs or completing transactions unfinished at dissolution;

(b) By any transaction which would bind the partnership if dissolution had not taken place, provided the other party to the transaction

(I) Had extended credit to the partnership prior to dissolution and had no knowledge or notice of the dissolution; or

(II) Though he had not so extended credit, had nevertheless known of the partnership prior to dissolution, and, having no knowledge or notice of dissolution, the fact of dissolution had not been advertised in a newspaper of general circulation in the place (or in each place if more than one) at which the partnership business was regularly carried on.

(2) The liability of a partner under Paragraph (1b) shall be satisfied out of partnership assets alone when such partner had been prior to dissolution

(a) Unknown as a partner to the person with whom the contract is made; and

(b) So far unknown and inactive in partnership affairs that the business reputation of the partnership could not be said to have been in any degree due to his connection with it.

(3) The partnership is in no case bound by any act of a partner after dissolution

(a) Where the partnership is dissolved because it is unlawful to carry on the business, unless the act is appropriate for winding up partnership affairs; or

(b) Where the partner has become bankrupt; or

(c) Where the partner has no authority to wind up partnership affairs; except by a transaction with one who

(I) Had extended credit to the partnership prior to dissolution and had no knowledge or notice of his want of authority; or

(II) Had not extended credit to the partnership prior to dissolution, and; having no knowledge or notice of his want of authority, the fact of his want of authority has not been advertised in the manner provided for advertising the fact of dissolution in Paragraph (1b II).

(4) Nothing in this section shall affect the liability under Section 16 of any person who after dissolution represents himself or consents to another representing him as a partner in a partnership engaged in carrying on business.

§36. Effect of Dissolution on Partner's Existing Liability

(1) The dissolution of the partnership does not of itself discharge the existing liability of any partner.

(2) A partner is discharged from any existing liability upon dissolution of the partnership by an agreement to that effect between himself, the partnership creditor and the person or partnership continuing the business; and such agreement may be inferred from the course of dealing between the creditor having knowledge of the dissolution and the person or partnership continuing the business.

(3) Where a person agrees to assume the existing obligations of a dissolved partnership, the partners whose obligations have been assumed shall be discharged from any liability to any creditor of the partnership who, knowing of the agreement, consents to a material alteration in the nature or time of payment of such obligations.

(4) The individual property of a deceased partner shall be liable for all obligations of the partnership incurred while he was a partner but subject to the prior payment of his separate debts.

§37. Right to Wind Up

Unless otherwise agreed the partners who have not wrongfully dissolved the partnership or the legal representative of the last surviving partner, not bankrupt, has the right to wind up the partnership affairs; provided, however, that any partner, his legal representative or his assignee, upon cause shown, may obtain winding up by the court.

§38. Rights of Partners to Application of Partnership Property

(1) When dissolution is caused in any way, except in contravention of the partnership agreement, each partner, as against his co-partners and all persons claiming through them in respect of their interests in the partnership, unless otherwise agreed, may have the partnership property applied to discharge its liabilities, and the surplus applied to pay in cash the net amount owing to the respective partners. But if dissolution is caused by expulsion of a partner, bona fide under the partnership agreement and if the expelled partner is discharged from all partnership liabilities, either by payment or agreement under section 36(2), he shall receive in cash only the net amount due him from the partnership.

(2) When dissolution is caused in contravention of the partnership agreement the rights of the partners shall be as follows:

(a) Each partner who has not caused dissolution wrongfully shall have,

I. All the rights specified in paragraph (1) of this section, and

II. The right, as against each partner who has caused the dissolution wrongfully, to damages for breach of the agreement.

(b) The partners who have not caused the dissolution wrongfully, if they all desire to continue the business in the same name, either by themselves or jointly with others, may do so, during the agreed term for the partnership and for that purpose may possess the partnership property, provided they secure the payment by bond approved by the court, or pay to any partner who has caused the dissolution wrongfully, the value of his interest in the partnership at the dissolution, less any damages recoverable under clause (2a II) of this section, and in like manner indemnify him against all present or future partnership liabilities.

(c) A partner who has caused the dissolution wrongfully shall have:

I. If the business is not continued under the provisions of paragraph (2b) all the rights of a partner under paragraph (1), subject to clause (2a II), of this section,

II. If the business is continued under paragraph (2b) of this section the right as against his co-partners and all claiming through them in respect of their interests in the partnership, to have the value of his interest in the partnership, less any damages caused to his co-partners by the dissolution, ascertained and paid to him in cash, or the payment secured by bond approved by the court, and to be released from all existing liabilities of the partnership; but in ascertaining the value of the partner's interest the value of the good-will of the business shall not be considered.

§39. Rights Where Partnership Is Dissolved for Fraud or Misrepresentation

Where a partnership contract is rescinded on the ground of the fraud or misrepresentation of one of the parties thereto, the party entitled to rescind is, without prejudice to any other right, entitled,

(a) To a lien on, or a right of retention of, the surplus of the partnership property after satisfying the partnership liabilities to third persons for any sum of money paid by him for the purchase of an interest in the partnership and for any capital or advances contributed by him; and

(b) To stand, after all liabilities to third persons have been satisfied, in the place of the creditors of the partnership for any payments made by him in respect of the partnership liabilities; and

(c) To be indemnified by the person guilty of the fraud or making the representation against all debts and liabilities of the partnership.

§40.   Rules for Distribution

In settling accounts between the partners after dissolution, the following rules shall be observed, subject to any agreement to the contrary:

(a) The assets of the partnership are:
I. The partnership property,
II. The contributions of the partners necessary for the payment of all the liabilities specified in clause (b) of this paragraph.

(b) The liabilities of the partnership shall rank in order of payment, as follows:
I. Those owing to creditors other than partners,
II. Those owing to partners other than for capital and profits,
III. Those owing to partners in respect of capital,
IV. Those owing to partners in respect of profits.

(c) The assets shall be applied in the order of their declaration in clause (a) of this paragraph to the satisfaction of the liabilities.

(d) The partners shall contribute, as provided by section 18 (a) the amount necessary to satisfy the liabilities; but if any, but not all, of the partners are insolvent, or, not being subject to process, refuse to contribute, the other partners shall contribute their share of the liabilities, and, in the relative proportions in which they share the profits, the additional amount necessary to pay the liabilities.

(e) An assignee for the benefit of creditors or any person appointed by the court shall have the right to enforce the contributions specified in clause (d) of this paragraph.

(f) Any partner or his legal representative shall have the right to enforce the contributions specified in clause (d) of this paragraph, to the extent of the amount which he has paid in excess of his share of the liability.

(g) The individual property of a deceased partner shall be liable for the contributions specified in clause (d) of this paragraph.

(h) When partnership property and the individual properties of the partners are in possession of a court for distribution, partnership creditors shall have priority on partnership property and separate creditors on individual property, saving the rights of lien or secured creditors as heretofore.

(i) Where a partner has become bankrupt or his estate insolvent the claims against his separate property shall rank in the following order:
I. Those owing to separate creditors,
II. Those owing to partnership creditors,
III. Those owing to partners by way of contribution.

§41.   Liability of Persons Continuing the Business in Certain Cases

(1) When any new partner is admitted into an existing partnership, or when any partner retires and assigns (or the representative of the deceased partner assigns) his rights in partnership property to two or more of the partners, or to one or more of the partners and one or more third persons, if the business is continued without liquidation of the partnership affairs, creditors of the first or dissolved partnership are also creditors of the partnership so continuing the business.

(2) When all but one partner retire and assign (or the representative of a deceased partner assigns) their rights in partnership property to the remaining partner, who continues the business without liquidation of partnership affairs, either alone or with others, creditors of the dissolved partnership are also creditors of the person or partnership so continuing the business.

(3) When any partner retires or dies and the business of the dissolved partnership is continued as set forth in paragraphs (1) and (2) of this section, with the consent of the retired partners or the representative of the deceased partner, but without any assignment of his right in partnership property, rights of creditors of the dissolved partnership and of the creditors of the person or partnership continuing the business shall be as if such assignment had been made.

(4) When all the partners or their representatives assign their rights in partnership property to one or more third persons who promise to pay the debts and who continue the business of the dissolved partnership, creditors of the dissolved partnership are also creditors of the person or partnership continuing the business.

(5) When any partner wrongfully causes a dissolution and the remaining partners continue the business under the provisions of section 38(2b), either alone or with others, and without liquidation of the partnership affairs, creditors of the dissolved partnership are also creditors of the person or partnership continuing the business.

(6) When a partner is expelled and the remaining partners continue the business either alone or with others, without liquidation of the partnership affairs, creditors of the dissolved partnership are also creditors of the person or partnership continuing the business.

(7) The liability of a third person becoming a partner in the partnership continuing the business, under this section, to the creditors of the dissolved partnership shall be satisfied out of partnership property only.

(8) When the business of a partnership after dissolution is continued under any conditions set forth in this section the creditors of the dissolved partnership, as against the separate creditors of the retiring or deceased partner or the representative of the deceased partner, have a prior right to any claim of the retired partner or the representative of the deceased partner against the person or partnership continuing the business, on account of the retired or deceased partner's interest in the dissolved partnership or on account of any consideration promised for such interest or for his right in partnership property.

(9) Nothing in this section shall be held to modify any right of creditors to set aside any assignment on the ground of fraud.

(10) The use by the person or partnership continuing the business of the partnership name, or the name of a deceased partner as part thereof, shall not of itself make the individual property of the deceased partner liable for any debts contracted by such person or partnership.

§42. *Rights of Retiring or Estate of Deceased Partner When the Business Is Continued*

When any partner retires or dies, and the business is continued under any of the conditions set forth in section 41 (1, 2, 3, 5, 6), or section 38(2b) without any settlement of accounts as between him or his estate and the person or partnership continuing the business, unless otherwise agreed, he or his legal representative as against such persons or partnership may have the value of his interest at the date of dissolution ascertained, and shall receive as an ordinary creditor an amount equal to the value of his interest in the dissolved partnership with interest, or, at his option or at the option of his legal representative, in lieu of interest, the profits attributable to the use of his right in the property of the dissolved partnership; provided that the creditors of the dissolved partnership as against the separate creditors, or the representative of the retired or deceased partner, shall have priority on any claim arising under this section, as provided by section 41(8) of this act.

§43. *Accrual of Actions*

The right to an account of his interest shall accrue to any partner, or his legal representative, as against the winding up partners or the surviving partners or the person or partnership continuing the business, at the date of dissolution, in the absence of any agreement to the contrary.

PART VII. MISCELLANEOUS PROVISIONS

§44. *When Act Takes Effect*

This act shall take effect on the _____ day of _____ one thousand nine hundred and _____.

§45. *Legislation Repealed*

All acts or parts of acts inconsistent with this act are hereby repealed.

APPENDIX C Uniform Limited Partnership Act (1976) with the 1985 Amendments*

Article 1. General Provisions

§101 Definitions
§102 Name
§103 Reservation of Name
§104 Specified Office and Agent
§105 Records to Be Kept
§106 Nature of Business
§107 Business Transactions of Partner with Partnership

Article 2. Formation: Certificate of Limited Partnership

§201 Content of Certificate
§202 Amendment to Certificate
§203 Cancellation of Certificate
§204 Execution of Certificates
§205 Execution by Judicial Act
§206 Filing in Office of Secretary of State
§207 Liability for False Statement in Certificate
§208 Scope of Notice
§209 Delivery of Certificates to Limited Partners

Article 3. Limited Partners

§301 Admission of Limited Partners
§302 Voting
§303 Liability to Third Parties
§304 Person Erroneously Believing Himself Limited Partner
§305 Information

Article 4. General Partners

§401 Admission of Additional General Partners
§402 Events of Withdrawal
§403 General Powers and Liabilities
§404 Contributions by General Partner
§405 Voting

Article 5. Finance

§501 Form of Contribution
§502 Liability for Contribution
§503 Sharing of Profits and Losses
§504 Sharing of Distributions

Article 6. Distributions and Withdrawal

§601 Interim Distributions
§602 Withdrawal of General Partner
§603 Withdrawal of Limited Partner
§604 Distribution upon Withdrawal
§605 Distribution in Kind
§606 Right to Distribution
§607 Limitations on Distribution
§608 Liability upon Return of Contribution

Article 7. Assignment of Partnership Interests

§701 Nature of Partnership Interest
§702 Assignment of Partnership Interest
§703 Rights of Creditor
§704 Right of Assignee to Become Limited Partner
§705 Power of Estate of Deceased or Incompetent Partner

Article 8. Dissolution

§801 Nonjudicial Dissolution
§802 Judicial Dissolution
§803 Winding Up
§804 Distribution of Assets

*Copies of this act may be ordered from the National Conference of Commissioners on Uniform State Laws, 676 North St. Clair St., Suite 1700, Chicago, Illinois 60611, 312–915–0195.

Article 9.   Foreign Limited Partnerships
§901   Law Governing
§902   Registration
§903   Issuance of Registration
§904   Name
§905   Changes and Amendments
§906   Cancellation of Registration
§907   Transaction of Business Without Registration
§908   Action by [Appropriate Official]

Article 10.   Derivative Actions
§1001   Right of Action
§1002   Proper Plaintiff
§1003   Pleading
§1004   Expenses

Article 11.   Miscellaneous
§1101   Construction and Application
§1102   Short Title
§1103   Severability
§1104   Effective Date, Extended Effective Date and Repeal
§1105   Savings Clause
§1106   Rules for Cases Not Provided for in This Act

ARTICLE 1.   GENERAL PROVISIONS

§101.   Definitions

As used in this [Act], unless the context otherwise requires:

(1) "Certificate of limited partnership" means the certificate referred to in Section 201, and the certificate as amended or restated.

(2) "Contribution" means any cash, property, services rendered, or a promissory note or other obligation to contribute cash or property or to perform services, which a partner contributes to a limited partnership in his capacity as a partner.

(3) "Event of withdrawal of a general partner" means an event that causes a person to cease to be a general partner as provided in Section 402.

(4) "Foreign limited partnership" means a partnership formed under the laws of another state and having as partners one or more general partners and one or more limited partners.

(5) "General partner" means a person who has been admitted to a limited partnership as a general partner in accordance with the partnership agreement and named in the certificate of limited partnership as a general partner.

(6) "Limited partner" means a person who has been admitted to a limited partnership as a limited partner in accordance with the partnership agreement.

(7) "Limited partnership" and "domestic limited partnership" means a partnership formed by two or more persons under the laws of this State and having one or more general partners and one or more limited partners.

(8) "Partner" means a limited or general partner.

(9) "Partnership agreement" means a valid agreement, written or oral, of the partners as to the affairs of a limited partnership and the conduct of its business.

(10) "Partnership interest" means a partner's share of the profits and losses of a limited partnership and the right to receive distributions of partnership assets.

(11) "Person" means an individual, corporation, business trust, estate, trust, partnership, association, joint venture, [government, governmental subdivision or agency,] or any other legal or commercial entity.

(12) "State" means a state, territory, or possession of the United States, the District of Columbia, or the Commonwealth of Puerto Rico.

§102.   Name

The name of each limited partnership as set forth in its certificate of limited partnership:

(1) must contain without abbreviation the words "limited partnership";

(2) may not contain the name of a limited partner unless (i) it is also the name of a general partner or the corporate name of a

corporate general partner, or (ii) the business of the limited partnership had been carried on under that name before the admission of that limited partner;

(3) may not be the same as, or deceptively similar to, the name of a corporation or limited partnership organized under the laws of this State or licensed or registered as a foreign corporation or limited partnership in this State; and

(4) may not contain the following words [here insert prohibited words].

§103. Reservation of Name

(a) The exclusive right to the use of a name may be reserved by:

(1) a person intending to organize a limited partnership under this [Act] and to adopt that name;

(2) a domestic limited partnership or a foreign limited partnership registered in this State which, in either case, intends to adopt that name;

(3) a foreign limited partnership intending to register in this State and adopt that name; and

(4) a person intending to organize a foreign limited partnership and intending to have it register in this State and adopt that name.

(b) The reservation must be made by filing with the Secretary of State an application, executed by the applicant, to reserve a specified name. If the Secretary of State finds that the name is available for use by a domestic or foreign limited partnership, he [or she] shall reserve the name for the exclusive use of the applicant for a period of 120 days. Once having so reserved a name, the applicant may not again reserve the same name until more than 60 days after the expiration of the last 120-day period for which that applicant reserved that name. The right to the exclusive use of a reserved name may be transferred to any other person by filing in the office of the Secretary of State a notice of the transfer, executed by the applicant for whom the name was reserved and specifying the name and address of the transferee.

§104. Specified Office and Agent

(a) Each limited partnership shall continuously maintain in this State:

(1) an office, which may but need not be a place of its business in this State, at which must be kept the records required by Section 105 to be maintained; and

(2) an agent for service of process on the limited partnership.

(b) An agent for service of process must be an individual resident of this State, a domestic corporation, or a foreign corporation authorized to do business in this State.

§105. Records to Be Kept

(a) Each limited partnership shall keep at the office referred to in Section 104(a)(1) the following:

(1) a current list of the full name and last known business address of each partner, separately identifying in alphabetical order the general partners and the limited partners;

(2) a copy of the certificate of limited partnership and all certificates of amendment thereto, together with executed copies of any powers of attorney pursuant to which any certificate has been executed;

(3) copies of the limited partnership's federal, state and local income tax returns and reports, if any, for the three most recent years;

(4) copies of any then effective written partnership agreements and of any financial statements of the limited partnership for the three most recent years; and

(5) unless contained in a written partnership agreement, a writing setting out:

(i) the amount of cash and a description and statement of the agreed value of the other property or services contributed by each partner and which each partner has agreed to contribute;

(ii) the times at which or events on the happening of

which any additional contributions agreed to be made by each partner are to be made;

(iii) any right of a partner to receive, or of a general partner to make, distributions to a partner which include a return of all or any part of the partner's contribution; and

(iv) any events upon the happening of which the limited partnership is to be dissolved and its affairs wound up.

(b) Records kept under this section are subject to inspection and copying at the reasonable request and at the expense of any partner during ordinary business hours.

§106. Nature of Business

A limited partnership may carry on any business that a partnership without limited partners may carry on except [here designate prohibited activities].

§107. Business Transactions of Partner with Partnership

Except as provided in the partnership agreement, a partner may lend money to and transact other business with the limited partnership and, subject to other applicable law, has the same rights and obligations with respect thereto as a person who is not a partner.

ARTICLE 2. FORMATION: CERTIFICATE OF LIMITED PARTNERSHIP

§201. Content of Certificate

(a) In order to form a limited partnership, a certificate of limited partnership must be executed and filed in the office of the Secretary of State. The certificate must set forth:

(1) the name of the limited partnership;

(2) the address of the office and the name and address of the agent for service of process required to be maintained by Section 104;

(3) the name and the business address of each general partner;

(4) the latest date upon which the limited partnership is to dissolve; and

(5) any other matters the general partners determine to include therein.

(b) A limited partnership is formed at the time of the filing of the certificate of limited partnership in the office of the Secretary of State or at any later time specified in the certificate of limited partnership if, in either case, there has been substantial compliance with the requirements of this section.

§202. Amendment to Certificate

(a) A certificate of limited partnership is amended by filing a certificate of amendment thereto in the office of the Secretary of State. The certificate must set forth:

(1) the name of the limited partnership;

(2) the date of filing the certificate; and

(3) the amendment to the certificate.

(b) Within 30 days after the happening of any of the following events, an amendment to a certificate of limited partnership reflecting the occurrence of the event or events must be filed:

(1) the admission of a new general partner;

(2) the withdrawal of a general partner; or

(3) the continuation of the business under Section 801 after an event of withdrawal of a general partner.

(c) A general partner who becomes aware that a statement in a certificate of limited partnership was false when made or that arrangements or other facts described have changed, making the certificate inaccurate in any respect, shall promptly amend the certificate.

(d) A certificate of limited partnership may be amended at any time for any other proper purpose the general partners determine.

(e) If an amendment to a certificate of limited partnership is filed in compliance with subsection (b), no person is subject to liability because the amendment was not filed earlier.

(f) A restated certificate of limited partnership may be executed and filed in the same manner as a certificate of amendment.

203. Cancellation of Certificate

A certificate of limited partnership must be cancelled upon the dissolution and the commencement of winding up of the partnership or when there are no limited partners. A certificate of cancellation must be filed in the office of the Secretary of State and set forth:

(1) the name of the limited partnership;

(2) the date of filing of its certificate of limited partnership;

(3) the reason for filing the certificate of cancellation;

(4) the effective date of cancellation, which must be a date certain unless it is effective upon the filing of the certificate; and

(5) any other information the general partners filing the certificate determine.

§204. Execution of Certificates

(a) Each certificate required by this Article to be filed in the office of the Secretary of State must be executed in the following manner:

(1) an original certificate of limited partnership must be signed by all general partners;

(2) a certificate of amendment must be signed by at least one general partner and by each other general partner designated in the certificate as a new general partner; and

(3) a certificate of cancellation must be signed by all general partners.

(b) Any person may sign a certificate by an attorney-in-fact, but a power of attorney to sign a certificate relating to the admission of a general partner must specifically describe the admission.

(c) The execution of a certificate by a general partner constitutes an affirmation under the penalties of perjury that the facts stated are true.

§205. Execution by Judicial Act

If a person required by Section 204 to execute a certificate fails or refuses to do so, any other person who is adversely affected by the failure or refusal may petition the [designate the appropriate court] to direct the execution of the certificate. If the court finds that it is proper for the certificate to be executed and that any person so designated has failed or refused to execute the certificate, it shall order the Secretary of State to record an appropriate certificate.

§206. Filing in Office of Secretary of State

(a) Two signed copies of the certificate of limited partnership and of any certificates of amendment or cancellation, or of any judicial decree of amendment or cancellation, must be delivered to the Secretary of State. A person who executes a certificate as an agent or fiduciary need not exhibit evidence of his [or her] authority as a prerequisite to filing. Unless the Secretary of State finds that a certificate does not conform to law, upon receipt of all filing fees required by law he [or she] shall:

(1) endorse on each duplicate original the word "Filed" and the day, month, and year of the filing thereof;

(2) file one duplicate original in his [or her] office; and

(3) return the other duplicate original to the person who filed it or his representative.

(b) Upon the filing of a certificate of amendment or judicial decree of amendment in the office of the Secretary of State, the certificate of limited partnership must be amended as set forth therein, and upon the effective date of a certificate of cancellation or a judicial decree thereof, the certificate of limited partnership is cancelled.

§207. Liability for False Statement in Certificate

If a certificate of limited partnership or certificate of amendment or cancellation contains a false statement, one who suffers loss by reliance on the statement may recover damages for the loss from:

(1) a person who executed the certificate, or caused another to execute it on his behalf, and knew, and a general partner who knew or should have known, the statement to be false at the time the certificate was executed; and

(2) a general partner who thereafter knew or should have known that an arrangement or other fact described in the certificate has changed, making the statement inaccurate in any respect within a sufficient time before the statement was relied upon reasonably to have enabled that general partner to cancel or amend the certificate or to file a petition for its cancellation or amendment under Section 205.

§208. Scope of Notice

The fact that a certificate of limited partnership is on file in the office of the Secretary of State is notice that the partnership is a limited partnership and that a person designated as a general partner is a general partner, but it is not notice of any other fact.

§209. Delivery of Certificates to Limited Partners

Upon the return by the Secretary of State pursuant to Section 206 of a certificate marked "Filed," the general partners shall promptly deliver or mail a copy of the certificate of limited partnership and each certificate of amendment or cancellation to each limited partner unless the partnership agreement provides otherwise.

ARTICLE 3. LIMITED PARTNERS

§301. Admission of Limited Partners

(a) A person becomes a limited partner on the later of:

(1) the date the original certificate of limited partnership is filed; or

(2) the date stated in the records of the limited partnership as the date that person becomes a limited partner.

(b) After the filing of a limited partnership's original certificate of limited partnership, a person may be admitted as an additional limited partner:

(1) in the case of a person acquiring a partnership interest directly from the limited partnership, upon compliance with the partnership agreement or, if the partnership agreement does not so provide, upon the written consent of all partners; and

(2) in the case of an assignee of a partnership interest of a partner who has the power, as provided in Section 704, to grant the assignee the right to become a limited partner, upon the exercise of that power and compliance with any conditions limiting the grant or exercise of the power.

§302. Voting

Subject to Section 303, the partnership agreement may grant to all or a specified group of the limited partners the right to vote upon any matter on a per capita or other basis.

§303. Liability to Third Parties

(a) Except as provided in subsection (d), a limited partner is not liable for the obligations of a limited partnership unless be [or she] is also a general partner or, in addition to the exercise of his [or her] rights and powers as a limited partner, he [or she] participates in the control of the business. However, if the limited partner participates in the control of the business, he [or she] is liable only to persons who transact business with the limited partnership reasonably believing, based upon the limited partner's conduct, that the limited partner is a general partner.

(b) A limited partner does not participate in the control of the business within the meaning of subsection (a) solely by doing one or more of the following:

(1) being a contractor for or an agent or employee of the limited partnership or of a general partner or being an officer, director, or shareholder of a general partner that is a corporation;

(2) consulting with and advising a general partner with respect to the business of the limited partnership;

(3) acting as surety for the limited partnership or guaranteeing or assuming one or more specific obligations of the limited partnership;

(4) taking any action required or permitted by law to bring or pursue a derivative action in the right of the limited partnership;

(5) requesting or attending a meeting of partners;

(6) proposing, approving, or disapproving, by voting or otherwise, one or more of the following matters:

(i) the dissolution and winding up of the limited partnership;

(ii) the sale, exchange, lease, mortgage, pledge, or other transfer of all or substantially all of the assets of the limited partnership;

(iii) the incurrence of indebtedness by the limited partnership other than in the ordinary course of its business;

(iv) a change in the nature of the business;

(v) the admission or removal of a general partner;

(vi) the admission or removal of a limited partner;

(vii) a transaction involving an actual or potential conflict of interest between a general partner and the limited partnership or the limited partners

(viii) an amendment to the partnership agreement or certificate of limited partnership; or

(ix) matters related to the business of the limited partnership not otherwise enumerated in this subsection, which the partnership agreement states in writing may be subject to the approval or disapproval of limited partners;

(7) winding up the limited partnership pursuant to Section 803; or

(8) exercising any right or power permitted to limited partners under this [Act] and not specifically enumerated in this subsection.

(c) The enumeration in subsection (b) does not mean that the possession or exercise of any other powers by a limited partner constitutes participation by him [or her] in the business of the limited partnership.

(d) A limited partner who knowingly permits his [or her] name to be used in the name of the limited partnership, except under circumstances permitted by Section 102(2), is liable to creditors who extend credit to the limited partnership without knowledge that the limited partner is not a general partner.

§304. Person Erroneously Believing Himself Limited Partner

(a) Except as provided in subsection (b), a person who makes a contribution to a business enterprise and erroneously but in good faith believes that he [or she] has become a limited partner in the enterprise is not a general partner in the enterprise and is not bound by its obligations by reason of making the contribution, receiving distributions from the enterprise, or exercising any right of a limited partner, if, on ascertaining the mistake, he [or she]:

(1) causes an appropriate certificate of limited partnership or a certificate of amendment to be executed and filed; or

(2) withdraws from future equity participation in the enterprise by executing and filing in the office of the Secretary of State a certificate declaring withdrawal under this section.

(b) A person who makes a contribution of the kind described in subsection (a) is liable as a general partner to any third party who transacts business with the enterprise (i) before the person withdraws and an appropriate certificate is filed to show withdrawal, or (ii) before an appropriate certificate is filed to show that he [or she] is not a general partner, but in either case only if the third party believed in good faith that the person was a general partner at the time of the transaction.

§305. *Information*

A limited partner may:

(1) inspect and copy any partnership record required to be maintained by Section 105; and

(2) obtain from the general partners from time to time upon reasonable demand (i) true and full information regarding the state of the business and financial condition of the limited partnership, (ii) promptly after becoming available, a copy of the limited partnership's federal, state, and local income tax returns for each year, and (iii) other information regarding the affairs of the limited partnership as is just and reasonable.

ARTICLE 4. GENERAL PARTNERS

§401. *Admission of Additional General Partners*

After the filing of a limited partnership's original certificate of limited partnership, additional general partners may be admitted as provided in writing in the partnership agreement or, if the partnership agreement does not provide in writing for the admission of additional general partners, with the written consent of all partners.

§402. *Events of Withdrawal*

Except as approved by written consent of all partners at the time, a person ceases to be a general partner of a limited partnership upon the occurrence of one or more of the following events:

(1) the general partner withdraws from the limited partnership as provided in Section 602;

(2) the general partner ceases to be a member of the limited partnership as provided in Section 702;

(3) the general partner is removed as a general partner in accordance with the partnership agreement;

(4) unless otherwise provided in writing in the partnership agreement, the general partner: (i) makes an assignment for the benefit of creditors; (ii) files a voluntary petition in bankruptcy; (iii) is adjudicated a bankrupt or insolvent; (iv) files a petition or answer seeking for himself [or herself] any reorganization, arrangement, composition, readjustment, liquidation, dissolution, or similar relief under any statute, law, or regulation; (v) files an answer or other pleading admitting or failing to contest the material allegations of a petition filed against him [or her] in any proceeding of this nature; or (vi) seeks, consents to, or acquiesces in the appointment of a trustee, receiver, or liquidator of the general partner or of all or any substantial part of his [or her] properties;

(5) unless otherwise provided in writing in the partnership agreement, [120] days after the commencement of any proceeding against the general partner seeking reorganization, arrangement, composition, readjustment, liquidation, dissolution, or similar relief under any statute, law, or regulation, the proceeding has not been dismissed, or if within [90] days after the appointment without his [or her] consent or acquiescence of a trustee, receiver, or liquidator of the general partner or of all or any substantial part of his [or her] properties, the appointment is not vacated or stayed or within [90] days after the expiration of any stay, the appointment is not vacated;

(6) in the case of a general partner who is an individual,

(i) his [or her] death; or

(ii) the entry of an order by a court of competent jurisdiction adjudicating him [or her] incompetent to manage his [or her] person or his [or her] estate;

(7) in the case of a general partner who is acting as such by virtue of being a trustee of a trust, the termination of the trust, but not merely the substitution of a new trustee;

(8) in the case of a general partner that is a separate partnership, the dissolution and commencement of winding up of the separate partnership;

(9) in the case of a general partner that is a corporation, the filing of a certificate of its dissolution or the equivalent or the revocation of its charter; or

(10) in the case of an estate, the distribution by the fiduciary of the estate's entire interest in the partnership.

ARTICLE 5. FINANCE

§501. Form of Contribution

The contribution of a partner may be in cash, property, services rendered, or a promissory note or other obligation to contribute cash or property or to perform services.

§502. Liability for Contribution

(a) A promise by a limited partner to contribute to the limited partnership is not enforceable unless set out in a writing signed by the limited partner.

(b) Except as provided in the partnership agreement, a partner is obligated to the limited partnership to perform an enforceable promise to contribute cash or property or to perform services, even if he [or she] is unable to perform because of death, disability, or any other reason. If a partner does not make the required contribution of property or services, he [or she] is obligated at the option of the limited partnership to contribute cash equal to that portion of the value, as stated in the partnership records required to be kept pursuant to Section 105, of the stated contribution which has not been made.

(c) Unless otherwise provided in the partnership agreement, the obligation of a partner to make a contribution or return money or other property paid or distributed in violation of this [Act] may be compromised only by consent of all partners. But, a creditor of a limited partnership who extends credit or otherwise acts in reliance on that obligation after the partner signs a writing that reflects the obligation and before the amendment or cancellation thereof to reflect the compromise may enforce the original obligation.

§503. Sharing of Profits and Losses

The profits and losses of a limited partnership must be allocated among the partners, and among classes of partners, in the manner provided in the partnership agreement. If the partnership

§403. General Powers and Liabilities

(a) Except as provided in this [Act] or in the partnership agreement, a general partner of a limited partnership has the rights and powers and is subject to the restrictions of a partner in a partnership without limited partners.

(b) Except as provided in this [Act], a general partner of a limited partnership has the liabilities of a partner in a partnership without limited partners to persons other than the partnership and the other partners. Except as provided in this [Act] or in the partnership agreement, a general partner of a limited partnership has the liabilities of a partner in a partnership without limited partners to the partnership and to the other partners.

§404. Contributions by General Partner

A general partner of a limited partnership may make contributions to the partnership and share in the profits and losses of, and in distributions from, the limited partnership as a general partner. A general partner also may make contributions to and share in profits, losses, and distributions as a limited partner. A person who is both a general partner and a limited partner has the rights and powers and is subject to the restrictions and liabilities of a general partner and, except as provided in the partnership agreement, also has the powers and is subject to the restrictions of a limited partner to the extent of his [or her] participation in the partnership as a limited partner.

§405. Voting

The partnership agreement may grant to all or certain identified general partners the right to vote, on a per capita or any other basis and separately or with all or any class of the limited partners, on any matter.

agreement does not so provide in writing, profits and losses must be allocated on the basis of the value, as stated in the partnership records required to be kept pursuant to Section 105, of the contributions made by each partner to the extent they have been received by the partnership and have not been returned.

§504. Sharing of Distributions

Distributions of cash or other assets of a limited partnership must be allocated among the partners and among classes of partners in the manner provided in writing in the partnership agreement. If the partnership agreement does not so provide in writing, distributions must be made on the basis of the value, as stated in the partnership records required to be kept pursuant to Section 105, of the contributions made by each partner to the extent they have been received by the partnership and have not been returned.

ARTICLE 6. DISTRIBUTIONS AND WITHDRAWAL

§601. Interim Distributions

Except as provided in this Article, a partner is entitled to receive distributions from a limited partnership before his [or her] withdrawal from the limited partnership and before the dissolution and winding up thereof to the extent and at the times or upon occurrence of the events specified in the partnership agreement.

§602. Withdrawal of General Partner

A general partner may withdraw from a limited partnership at any time by giving written notice to the other partners, but if the withdrawal violates the partnership agreement, the limited partnership may recover from the withdrawing general partner damages for breach of the partnership agreement and offset the damages against the amount otherwise distributable to him [or her].

§603. Withdrawal of Limited Partner

A limited partner may withdraw from a limited partnership at the time or upon the occurrence of events specified in writing in the partnership agreement. If the agreement does not specify in writing the time or the events upon the occurrence of which a limited partner may withdraw or a definite time for the dissolution and winding up of the limited partnership, a limited partner may withdraw upon not less than six months' written notice to each general partner at his [or her] address on the books of the limited partnership at its office in this State.

§604. Distribution upon Withdrawal

Except as provided in this Article, upon withdrawal any withdrawing partner is entitled to receive any distribution to which he [or she] is entitled under the partnership agreement and, if not otherwise provided in the agreement, he [or she] is entitled to receive, within a reasonable time after withdrawal, the fair value of his [or her] interest in the limited partnership as of the date of withdrawal based upon his [or her] right to share in distributions from the limited partnership.

§605. Distribution in Kind

Except as provided in writing in the partnership agreement, a partner, regardless of the nature of his [or her] contribution, has no right to demand and receive any distribution from a limited partnership in any form other than cash. Except as provided in writing in the partnership agreement, a partner may not be compelled to accept a distribution of any asset in kind from a limited partnership to the extent that the percentage of the asset distributed to him [or her] exceeds a percentage of that asset which is equal to the percentage in which he [or she] shares in distributions from the limited partnership.

§606. Right to Distribution

At the time a partner becomes entitled to receive a distribution, he [or she] has the status of, and is entitled to all remedies available to, a creditor of the limited partnership with respect to the distribution.

§607. Limitations on Distribution

A partner may not receive a distribution from a limited partnership to the extent that, after giving effect to the distribution, all liabilities of the limited partnership, other than liabilities to partners on account of their partnership interests, exceed the fair value of the partnership assets.

§608. Liability upon Return of Contribution

(a) If a partner has received the return of any part of his [or her] contribution without violation of the partnership agreement or this [Act], he [or she] is liable to the limited partnership for a period of one year thereafter for the amount of the returned contribution, but only to the extent necessary to discharge the limited partnership's liabilities to creditors who extended credit to the limited partnership during the period the contribution was held by the partnership.

(b) If a partner has received the return of any part of his [or her] contribution in violation of the partnership agreement or this [Act], he [or she] is liable to the limited partnership for a period of six years thereafter for the amount of the contribution wrongfully returned.

(c) A partner receives a return of his [or her] contribution to the extent that a distribution to him [or her] reduces his [or her] share of the fair value of the net assets of the limited partnership below the value, as set forth in the partnership records required to be kept pursuant to Section 105, of his [or her] contribution which has not been distributed to him [or her].

ARTICLE 7. ASSIGNMENT OF PARTNERSHIP INTERESTS

§701. Nature of Partnership Interest

A partnership interest is personal property.

§702. Assignment of Partnership Interest

Except as provided in the partnership agreement, a partnership interest is assignable in whole or in part. An assignment of a partnership interest does not dissolve a limited partnership or entitle the assignee to become or to exercise any rights of a partner. An assignment entitles the assignee to receive, to the extent assigned, only the distribution to which the assignor would have been entitled. Except as provided in the partnership agreement, a partner ceases to be a partner upon assignment of all of his [or her] partnership interest.

§703. Rights of Creditor

On application to [designate appropriate court] by a judgment creditor of a partner, the court may charge the partnership interest of the partner with payment of the unsatisfied amount of the judgment, with interest. To the extent so charged, the judgment creditor has only the rights of an assignee of the partnership interest. This [Act] does not deprive any partner of the benefit of any exemption laws applicable to his [or her] partnership interest.

§704. Right of Assignee to Become Limited Partner

(a) An assignee of a partnership interest, including an assignee of a general partner, may become a limited partner if and to the extent that (i) the assignor gives the assignee that right in accordance with authority provided in the partnership agreement, or (ii) all other partners consent.

(b) An assignee who has become a limited partner has, to the extent assigned, the rights and powers and is subject to the restrictions and liabilities of a limited partner under the partnership agreement and this [Act]. An assignee who becomes a limited partner also is liable for the obligations of his [or her] assignor to make and return contributions as provided in Articles 5 and 6. However, the assignee is not obligated for liabilities unknown to the assignee at the time he [or she] became a limited partner.

(c) If an assignee of a partnership interest becomes a limited partner, the assignor is not released from his [or her] liability to the limited partnership under Sections 207 and 502.

§705. Power of Estate of Deceased or Incompetent Partner

If a partner who is an individual dies or a court of competent jurisdiction adjudges him [or her] to be incompetent to manage his [or her] person or his [or her] property, the partner's executor, administrator, guardian, conservator, or other legal representative may exercise all the partner's rights for the purpose of settling his [or her] estate or administering his [or her] property, including any power the partner had to give an assignee the right to become a limited partner. If a partner is a corporation, trust, or other entity and is dissolved or terminated, the powers of that partner may be exercised by its legal representative or successor.

ARTICLE 8.   DISSOLUTION

§801.   Nonjudicial Dissolution

A limited partnership is dissolved and its affairs must be wound up upon the first of the following to occur:

(1) at the time specified in the certificate of limited partnership;

(2) upon the occurrence of events specified in writing in the partnership agreement;

(3) written consent of all partners;

(4) an event of withdrawal of a general partner unless at the time there is at least one other general partner and the written provisions of the partnership agreement permit the business of the limited partnership to be carried on by the remaining general partner and that partner does so, but the limited partnership is not dissolved and is not required to be wound up by reason of any event of withdrawal if, within 90 days after the withdrawal, all partners agree in writing to continue the business of the limited partnership and to the appointment of one or more additional general partners if necessary or desired; or

(5) entry of a decree of judicial dissolution under Section 802.

§802.   Judicial Dissolution

On application by or for a partner, the [designate the appropriate court] court may decree dissolution of a limited partnership if it is not reasonably practicable to carry on the business in conformity with the partnership agreement.

§803.   Winding Up

Except as provided in the partnership agreement, the general partners who have not wrongfully dissolved a limited partnership or, if none, the limited partners, may wind up the limited partnership's affairs; but the [designate the appropriate court] court may wind up the limited partnership's affairs upon application of a partner, his [or her] legal representative, or assignee.

§804. Distribution of Assets

Upon the winding up of a limited partnership, the assets must be distributed as follows:

(1) to creditors, including partners who are creditors, to the extent permitted by law, in satisfaction of liabilities of the limited partnership other than liabilities for distributions to partners under Section 601 or 604;

(2) except as provided in the partnership agreement, to partners and former partners in satisfaction of liabilities for distributions under Section 601 or 604; and

(3) except as provided in the partnership agreement, to partners first for the return of their contributions and secondly respecting their partnership interests, in the proportions in which the partners share in distribution.

ARTICLE 9.   FOREIGN LIMITED PARTNERSHIPS

§901.   Law Governing

Subject to the Constitution of this State, (i) the laws of the state under which a foreign limited partnership is organized govern its organization and internal affairs and the liability of its limited partners, and (ii) a foreign limited partnership may not be denied registration by reason of any difference between those laws and the laws of this State.

§902.   Registration

Before transacting business in this State, a foreign limited partnership shall register with the Secretary of State. In order to register, a foreign limited partnership shall submit to the Secretary of State an application in duplicate for registration as a foreign limited partnership, signed and sworn to by a general partner and setting forth:

(1) the name of the foreign limited partnership and, if different, the name under which it proposes to register and transact business in this State;

(2) the State and date of its formation;

(3) the name and address of any qualified agent for service of process on the foreign limited partnership whom the foreign limited partnership elects to appoint; the agent must be an individual resident of this State, a domestic corporation, or a foreign corporation having a place of business and authorized to do business in this State;

(4) a statement that the Secretary of State is appointed the agent of the foreign limited partnership for service of process if no agent has been appointed under paragraph (3) or, if appointed, the agent's authority has been revoked or if the agent cannot be found or served with the exercise of reasonable diligence;

(5) the address of the office required to be maintained in the state of its organization by the laws of that state or, if not so required, of the principal office of the foreign limited partnership;

(6) the name and business address of each general partner; and

(7) the address of the office at which is kept a list of the names and addresses of the limited partners and their capital contributions, together with an undertaking by the foreign limited partnership to keep those records until the foreign limited partnership's registration in this State is cancelled or withdrawn.

§903.   Issuance of Registration

(a) If the Secretary of State finds that an application for registration conforms to law and all requisite fees have been paid, he [or she] shall:

(1) endorse on the application the word "Filed," and the month, day, and year of the filing;

(2) file in his [or her] office a duplicate original of the application; and

(3) issue a certificate of registration to transact business in this State.

(b) The certificate of registration, together with a duplicate original of the application, must be returned to the person who filed the application or his [or her] representative.

§904. Name

A foreign limited partnership may register with the Secretary of State under any name, whether or not it is the name under which it is registered in its state of organization, that includes without abbreviation the words "limited partnership" and that could be registered by a domestic limited partnership.

§905. Changes and Amendments

If a statement in the application for registration of a foreign limited partnership was false when made or any arrangements or other facts described have changed, making the application inaccurate in any respect, the foreign limited partnership shall promptly file in the office of the Secretary of State a certificate, signed and sworn to by a general partner, correcting the statement.

§906. Cancellation of Registration

A foreign limited partnership may cancel its registration by filing with the Secretary of State a certificate of cancellation signed and sworn to by a general partner. A cancellation does not terminate the authority of the Secretary of State to accept service of process on the foreign limited partnership with respect to [claims for relief] [causes of action] arising out of the transactions of business in this State.

§907. Transaction of Business Without Registration

(a) A foreign limited partnership transacting business in this State may not maintain an action, suit, or proceeding in a court of this State until it has registered in this State.

(b) The failure of a foreign limited partnership to register in this State does not impair the validity of any contract or act of the foreign limited partnership or prevent the foreign limited partnership from defending any action, suit, or proceeding in any court of this State.

(c) A limited partner of a foreign limited partnership is not liable as a general partner of the foreign limited partnership solely by reason of having transacted business in this State without registration.

(d) By transacting business in this State without registration, a foreign limited partnership appoints the Secretary of State as its agent for service of process with respect to a [claim for relief] [cause of action] arising out of the transaction of business in this State.

§908. Action by [Appropriate Official]

The [designate the appropriate official] may maintain an action to restrain a foreign limited partnership from transacting business in this State in violation of this Article.

ARTICLE 10. DERIVATIVE ACTIONS

§1001. Right of Action

A limited partner may maintain an action in the right of a limited partnership to recover a judgment in its favor if general partners with authority to do so have refused to bring the action or an effort to cause those general partners to bring the action is not likely to succeed.

§1002. Proper Plaintiff

In a derivative action, the plaintiff must be a partner at the time of bringing the action and (i) must have been a partner at the time of the transaction of which he [or she] complains or (ii) his [or her] status as a partner must have devolved upon him [or her] by operation of law or pursuant to the terms of the partnership agreement from a person who was a partner at the time of the transaction.

§1003. Pleading

In a derivative action, the complaint must set forth with particularity the effort of the plaintiff to secure commencement of the action by a general partner or the reasons for not making the effort.

§1004. Expenses

If a derivative action is successful, in whole or in part, or if anything is received by the plaintiff as a result of a judgment, compromise, or settlement of an action or claim, the court may award the plaintiff reasonable expenses, including reasonable attorney's fees, and shall direct him [or her] to remit to the limited partnership the remainder of those proceeds received by him [or her].

ARTICLE 11. MISCELLANEOUS

§1101. Construction and Application

This [Act] shall be so applied and construed to effectuate its general purpose to make uniform the law with respect to the subject of this [Act] among states enacting it.

§1102. Short Title

This [Act] may be cited as the Uniform Limited Partnership Act (1985).

§1103. Severability

If any provision of this [Act] or its application to any person or circumstance is held invalid, the invalidity does not affect other provisions or applications of the [Act] which can be given effect without the invalid provision or application, and to this end the provisions of this [Act] are severable.

§1104. Effective Date, Extended Effective Date and Repeal

Except as set forth below, the effective date of this [Act] is _____ and the following acts [list existing limited partnership acts] are hereby repealed:

(1) The existing provisions for execution and filing of certificates of limited partnerships and amendments thereunder and cancellations thereof continue in effect until [specify time required to create central filing system], the extended effective date, and Sections 102, 103, 104, 105, 201, 202, 203, 204 and 206 are not effective until the extended effective date.

(2) Section 402, specifying the conditions under which a general partner ceases to be a member of a limited partnership, is not effective until the extended effective date, and the applicable provisions of existing law continue to govern until the extended effective date.

(3) Sections 501, 502 and 608 apply only to contributions and distributions made after the effective date of this [Act].

(4) Section 704 applies only to assignments made after the effective date of this [Act].

(5) Article 9, dealing with registration of foreign limited partnerships, is not effective until the extended effective date.

(6) Unless otherwise agreed by the partners, the applicable provisions of existing law governing allocation of profits and losses (rather than the provisions of Section 503), distributions to a withdrawing partner (rather than the provisions of Section 604), and distribution of assets upon the winding up of a limited partnership (rather than the provisions of Section 804) govern limited partnerships formed before the effective date of this [Act].

§1105. Savings Clause

The repeal of any statutory provision by this [Act] does not impair, or otherwise affect, the organization or the continued existence of a limited partnership existing at the effective date of this [Act], nor does the repeal of any existing statutory provision by this [Act] impair any contract or affect any right accrued before the effective date of this [Act].

§1106. Rules for Cases Not Provided for in This Act

In any case not provided for in this [Act] the provisions of the Uniform Partnership Act govern.

GLOSSARY

Accredited investors: Banks, insurance companies, investment companies, registered dealers, directors, executive officers, or general partners of the issuer; individuals with net worth exceeding $1,000,000; trusts with total assets exceeding $5,000,000; certain natural persons with income exceeding $200,000; and entities of which all the owners are accredited investors.

Acquiring corporation: Corporation desiring to purchase shares of another corporation.

Administrative dissolution: Termination of a corporation's existence initiated by the state of incorporation.

Affidavit of assumed name: Another term for fictitious name registration.

Affidavit of lost certificate: Document provided by a shareholder to the corporation when a shareholder's share certificate has been lost, destroyed, or stolen. The affidavit (1) certifies that the shareholder is a record owner of certain shares of the corporation and (2) provides indemnification against any loss the corporation incurs because of the reissuance of the shares represented by the lost share certificate.

Agent for service of process: Person designated by a business organization to accept service on behalf of the business organization; often called a registered agent.

Agreement of trust: Written document, often called articles of agreement, that forms a business trust by identifying the responsibilities, duties, and powers of the trustee and the interests of the beneficiaries of the business trust.

Alter ego doctrine: Doctrine under which the shareholders of a corporation are denied the protection of limited liability when a court determines that an individual performed certain acts for personal purposes in the name of the corporation.

Amended certificate of authority: Document issued by the secretary of state upon its receipt of an application for amended certificate of authority, all other proper documentation, and filing fee.

Amendment to certificate of limited partnership: Document required to be filed by a limited partnership upon the change to any information contained in the certificate of limited partnership.

Annual franchise tax: Type of tax imposed on corporations that is generally calculated on the authorized capital of the corporation.

Annual meeting: Meeting held once a year by the shareholders or board of directors.

Annual report: Document usually containing the name of the corporation; the state of incorporation; addresses of the registered and principal offices; names and business addresses of the directors and officers; a description of the corporation's business; and the total number of authorized and issued shares of the corporation.

Application for amended certificate of authority: Document required to be filed with the secretary of state by a foreign corporation upon any change to information contained in the certificate of authority.

Application for certificate of authority: Document required to be filed with the secretary of state upon a corporation's determination that it must register or qualify to do business in a particular state.

Application for certificate of withdrawal: Document required to be filed with the secretary of state upon a foreign corporation's desire to cease doing business in that state.

Articles of amendment: Document required to be filed with the secretary of state upon any change to the information contained in the articles of incorporation.

Articles of consolidation: Document required to be filed with the secretary of state that includes details of effecting a consolidation.

Articles of dissolution: Document filed with the secretary of state upon the approval by the shareholders to dissolve the corporation.

Articles of incorporation: Document required to be filed with the secretary of state where the corporation is being formed, upon which the corporation's existence as a separate legal entity begins; referred to as certificate of incorporation by some states.

Articles of merger: Document required to be filed with the secretary of state that includes details of effecting a merger.

Articles of revocation of dissolution: Document prepared by the corporation and filed with the secretary of state because of the corporation's desire to rescind a voluntary dissolution.

Articles of share exchange: Document required to be filed with the secretary of state that includes details of effecting a share exchange.

Asset appraisal: Evaluation by two or more appraisers of a corporation's assets, used to determine the fair market value of the corporation's stock.

Asset purchase agreement: Agreement between the acquiring corporation and the selling corporation for the purchase and sale of certain assets of the selling corporation.

Asset transaction: Event in which the selling corporation sells all or substantially all its assets to a buyer in exchange for a form of consideration.

Assignment: Document through which the ownership of intangible personal property, such as accounts receivable, leases, and contracts, is transferred or sold.

Assumed name: Another term for fictitious name.

Authorized shares: Total number of shares that the corporation has the authority to issue to shareholders. This number must be included in the articles of incorporation.

Beneficial ownership: Ability to vote, or the ability to dispose of, transfer, or receive income from the ownership of a security.

Bill of sale: Document through which the ownership of tangible property, such as inventory, equipment, motor vehicles, and machinery, is transferred or sold.

Blue sky laws: State laws that provide for the regulation of the offer and sale of securities.

Bona fide offer: Good faith offer to purchase shares from a shareholder.

Bona fide offer price: Price at which a shareholder receives from another shareholder a good faith offer to purchase shares.

Bond: Long-term, secured or unsecured, written promise to pay a specified amount of money at a specified time.

Book value: Value of shares derived from dividing the corporation's net worth by the total number of outstanding shares of the corporation.

Bulk transfer law: Specific provisions of the Uniform Commercial Code designed to protect creditors.

Business corporation: Form of business organization created under state statute. The business corporation is the most common type of business organization, which includes privately held and publicly held corporations.

Business judgment rule: Rule that protects the directors and officers from liability for their decisions resulting from poor judgment or honest mistakes, as long as they do not violate their fiduciary duties of care and loyalty.

Business trust: Noncorporate form of business organization that shares some features of the corporation and some features of the partnership. The business trust may be organized without filing a document with the secretary of state.

Bylaws: Rules and regulations that govern the internal affairs of the corporation and specifically define the rights, powers, and duties of the shareholders, directors, and officers of the corporation.

C corporation: Type of corporation that, for federal income tax purposes, pays tax on its own income and realizes its own losses as a separate entity from the shareholders of the corporation.

Call of a meeting: Procedure for bringing a meeting of the incorporators, shareholders, or board of directors into existence.

Capital: Source of funds available to the corporation to enable it to operate its business successfully.

Capital surplus: Total amount of consideration received by a corporation for the sale of shares minus the par value of the shares sold.

Capitalization: Financial structure of the corporation. A combination of reinvestment of profits, equity securities, and debt securities compose the capitalization of the corporation.

Capitalization of earnings: Average earnings of the corporation calculated over a specified period and divided by the number of outstanding shares.

Cash dividend: Distribution of a corporation's profits to its shareholders in the form of cash.

Certificate of amendment: Document issued by the secretary of state upon its receipt of articles of amendment, all other proper documentation, and filing fee.

Certificate of authority: Document issued by the secretary of state upon its receipt of an application for certificate of authority, all other proper documentation, and filing fee.

Certificate of cancellation of limited partnership: Document required to be filed by a limited partnership on the dissolution or termination of the business.

Certificate of consolidation: Document issued by the secretary of state on the corporation's filing of articles of consolidation.

Certificate of dissolution: Document issued by the secretary of state upon its receipt of articles of dissolution, all other proper documentation, and filing fee.

Certificate of existence: Document issued by the secretary of state that evidences that a corporation has not filed an application to merge, liquidate, or dissolve the corporation or had paid all taxes due to the state, or both; also referred to as a good standing certificate.

Certificate of foreign limited partnership: Document required to be filed in the foreign state in which a limited partnership desires to transact business.

Certificate of incorporation: Document required to be filed with the secretary of state where the corporation is being formed, upon which the corporation comes into legal existence; referred to as articles of incorporation by some states.

Certificate of limited partnership: Document required to be filed with the secretary of state where a limited partnership is being formed, upon which the legal formation of a limited partnership occurs.

Certificate of merger: Document issued by the secretary of state upon a corporation's filing of articles of merger.

Certificate of reinstatement: Document issued by the secretary of state upon its determination that a corporation should be reinstated as a legal entity.

Certificate of revocation: Document issued by the secretary of state upon the revocation of a foreign corporation's certificate of authority.

Certificate of share exchange: Document issued by the secretary of state on the corporation's filing of articles of share exchange.

Certificate of withdrawal: Document issued by the secretary of state upon its receipt of an application for certificate of withdrawal, all other proper documentation, and filing fee.

Classes: Designation of various types of shares that a corporation has the authority to issue.

Clearance certificate: Document issued by the secretary of state evidencing the corporation's filing of all annual reports.

Clearance certificates: Types of documents issued by state revenue and state employment departments that evidence the timely and proper payment of taxes by a corporation.

Close corporation: Special form of corporation in which the shares are held by a small number of shareholders. The shareholders, in lieu of a board of directors, take an active role in the management of the corporation.

Closely held corporation: Corporation that has relatively few shareholders, and many of its shareholders are also directors or officers of the corporation. Shareholders are often related.

Common stock: Shares evidencing an ownership interest in a corporation. Corporations that authorize and issue only one type of stock usually identify it as common stock.

Conference telephone meetings: Meetings of the shareholders or board of directors at which special telephone equipment is used so that all participants can simultaneously hear each other.

Consideration: Cash, promissory notes, services performed, contracts for services to be performed, or other form of payment for shares of a corporation. The board of directors has the power to determine the amount and form of consideration to be paid for shares of a corporation.

Consolidation: Combination of two or more corporations into one entirely new legal entity, where none of the consolidating corporations remains after the consolidation.

Conversion privilege (debt security): Right of a holder of a debt security to convert such debt security to equity security.

Conversion rights (preferred shares): Option provided to the holder of shares with conversion rights to convert his or her shares to shares of another class of stock in the corporation.

Corporate actions: Deeds and proceedings taken by the corporation that must be approved at, and conducted through, meetings of the incorporators, the shareholders, and the board of directors.

Corporate designators: Certain words that identify the business organization as a corporation, one of which must be contained in the corporate name, such as "corporation," "incorporated," "company," or "limited," or the abbreviation "corp.," "inc.," "co.," or "ltd."

Corporate existence: Ability of the corporation to exist as a separate legal entity, which begins when the articles of incorporation are filed with the secretary of state.

Corporate name: One or more words used to identify a corporation. The corporate name must comply with the statutes of the state of incorporation.

Corporate seal: Device that imprints a mark that includes the corporation's name and state and year of incorporation.

Corporation: Form of business organization that involves a legal, separate, and distinct entity from its shareholders, the board of directors, officers, and employees. It is liable for its own obligations and debts, it can sue and be sued, and it can be fined for violating the law.

Creditor: A person that loans money or funds.

Cumulative dividends: Right to receive dividends or a distribution of a corporation's profit that will cumulate each year until the board of directors determines that a dividend may be paid.

Cumulative voting: Special procedure used only in the election of directors by the shareholders of a corporation. Under cumulative voting a shareholder is entitled to a number of votes equal to the number of shares he or she owns, multiplied by the number of directors to be elected.

Debenture: Long-term, unsecured, written promise to pay a specified amount of money at a specified time.

Debt holders: Owners or holders of debt securities issued by a corporation.

Debt securities: Evidence of a corporation's obligation to repay money borrowed from a creditor or lender.

Debtor: A person that owes money or funds.

Deed: Document through which the ownership of real property or real estate is transferred or sold.

Designation statement: Document that must be filed with the secretary of state and spells out the preferences, limitations, and relative rights of a newly created series of preferred stock.

Directors: Individuals elected by the shareholders of the corporation who are responsible for its management.

Directors' meetings: Vehicle through which the directors conduct business and approve corporate actions. Meetings are held annually, quarterly, monthly, weekly, or as often as the business of the corporation dictates.

Directors' organizational meeting: First meeting of the initial directors of the corporation after its incorporation.

Dissenter's rights: The right afforded a shareholder to dissent from a transaction under certain circumstances and to have his or her shares appraised and purchased by the corporation.

Dissolution: Formal termination of the existence of a business organization.

Dividend: Form in which a distribution of the corporation's earnings is made to its shareholders.

Dividend right: Shareholder's right to receive a return on his or her investment in the corporation.

Document of public record: Any document that has been filed with the secretary of state and becomes available for inspection by the general public.

Domestic corporation: A corporation incorporated and organized under the statutes of a particular state.

Domesticate: Act of incorporating in a state in which the corporation intends to operate its business.

Double taxation: The payment of tax by the corporation on its profits and the payment of tax by a shareholder on those same profits, which are subsequently distributed to the shareholders in the form of dividends.

Downstream merger: Combination by merger of a parent corporation and a subsidiary corporation whereby the parent corporation merges into the subsidiary corporation.

Due diligence process: Procedure of conducting a review of the selling corporation to uncover its potential liabilities, to identify contracts that require third-party approval, and to confirm the accuracy and validity of the representations made in the agreement.

Duty of care: Obligation of the directors and officers of the corporation to be assiduous in conducting the corporate affairs and to use prudent business judgment.

Duty of loyalty: Obligation of the directors and officers of the corporation to be faithful to their obligations and duties and to serve the best interests of the corporation.

Earned surplus: Cumulation of net profits, income, and gains, taking into account losses of the corporation from the date of incorporation, minus distributions and dividends paid; also referred to as retained earnings.

Effective date: Date on which a particular action of the corporation is effective. For example, the date on which a registration statement is declared by the Securities and Exchange Commission to be in effect is the effective date of the registration statement.

EIN: Abbreviation for employer identification number.

Employer identification number: A nine-digit number assigned by the Internal Revenue Service, upon the filing of Form SS-4, Application for Employer Identification Number, to a business organization or other person for tax filing and reporting purposes.

Equity holders: Owners of equity securities issued by a corporation.

Equity securities: Evidence of an ownership interest or investment in a corporation.

Exchange Act company: Corporation that has filed a registration statement under the rules and regulations of the Securities Exchange Act of 1934, and thus must comply with the numerous reporting and disclosure requirements of this act.

Express partnership: Partnership evidenced by the existence of a written or oral agreement.

Federal securities laws: Statutes regulating the offer and sale of securities that make use of interstate commerce or of the mails to sell such securities.

Fictitious name: Name, other than its own name, under which a sole proprietor, general or limited partnership, corporation, or other form of business organization conducts business.

Fictitious name registration: Document filed by a sole proprietor, general or limited partnership, corporation, or other form of business organization to register the name under which it intends to conduct business.

Fiduciaries: Persons who act for another in a position of trust and confidence.

Foreign corporation: A corporation transacting business in a state other than the one in which it was incorporated.

Foreign jurisdictions: States other than a corporation's home state in which the corporation conducts business.

Foreign limited partnership: Limited partnership transacting business in a state other than the one in which it initially registered.

Foreign state: State other than the state in which the business organization initially registered or incorporated.

Form 3:   SEC form Initial Statement of Beneficial Ownership of Securities, which must be filed by an insider within ten days after an event that triggers the requirement to file such form.

Form 4:   SEC form Statement of Changes of Beneficial Ownership of Securities, which must be filed by an insider on or before the tenth day of the month following the month in which the change occurred.

Form 5:   SEC form Annual Statement of Changes of Beneficial Ownership of Securities, which is required to be filed annually by an insider before the forty-fifth day after the end of the issuer's fiscal year, if certain disclosures were not made on Form 3 and Form 4.

Form 8-K: Current report that must be filed with the SEC within five days after a change in the corporation's certifying accountant or the resignation of a director of the corporation, or within fifteen days after the occurrence of other changes in the control or business of the corporation.

Form 10-K: Annual report that must be filed with the SEC within ninety days after the end of the issuer's fiscal year.

Form 10-Q: Quarterly report that must be filed with the SEC within forty-five days after the end of each of the first three quarters of the issuer's fiscal year.

Form 966:   Internal Revenue Service form Corporation Dissolution or Liquidation, which is required to be filed by a corporation within thirty days of the approval of the resolutions adopting the plan of dissolution or liquidation by the shareholders.

Form 1065:   Internal Revenue Service form U.S. Partnership Return of Income, filed by a partnership to report income or loss, deductions, and credits of the partnership.

Form 1120:   Internal Revenue Service form U.S. Corporation Income Tax Return, which is required to be filed by business organizations qualifying as corporations for tax purposes.

Form 1120-A: Internal Revenue Service form U.S. Corporation Short-Form Income Tax Return, required to be filed by business organizations qualifying as corporations for tax purposes whose gross receipts and total assets are under $500,000.

Freeze out: Attempt by a corporation to reduce the number of shareholders of the corporation and eliminate minority shareholders.

Fully paid and nonassessable: Condition of shares of a corporation when the corporation has received the consideration for those shares as determined by the board of directors.

General partner: Person who has active responsibility for the management and operation of the partnership and has unlimited liability for the debts and obligations of the partnership.

General partnership: Form of business organization owned and managed by two or more persons.

General partnership agreement: Written or oral agreement between the partners of a general partnership. A written agreement should contain all the provisions needed to carry on the management, operation, and liquidation of the partnership.

General proxy: Written document given by the holder of stock to another person granting the other person (the proxyholder) the right to vote on behalf of the shareholder as the proxyholder deems appropriate.

Good standing: The condition of a corporation that has not filed an application to merge, liquidate, or dissolve the corporation or that has paid all taxes due to the state, or both.

Good standing certificate: Document issued by the secretary of state that evidences that a corporation has not filed an application to merge, liquidate, or dissolve the corporation or has paid all taxes due to the state, or both; also referred to as a certificate of existence.

Holders of record: Shareholders listed in the stock records of the corporation as owning shares of the corporation.

Home state: State in which a corporation was incorporated; often called state of domicile.

Implied partnership: Partnership evidenced by the inferred acts and intent of the partners.

Income tax: Type of tax imposed on corporations that is usually calculated on the dollar amount of revenues, and in some cases on the value of property, number of employees, or type of business activities conducted.

Incorporator: Person who executes the articles of incorporation on behalf of the corporation and delivers them to the secretary of state for filing.

Incorporators' organizational meeting: First meeting of the corporation after its incorporation, held by the incorporators if directors were not named in the articles of incorporation.

Indemnification: Corporation's reimbursement of directors and officers for any expenses incurred by them in defending any threatened or pending suits or criminal proceedings stemming from actions they took in their capacities as directors and officers of the corporation.

Initial directors: Individuals who serve as the first directors of the corporation, who may or may not be named in the articles of incorporation.

Initial franchise tax: Type of tax imposed on corporations at the time of filing of the application for certificate of authority.

Insider trading: Sales or purchases of securities by persons who have access to and take advantage of information about an issuer or a security when the information is not available to the public.

Insiders: Owners of more than 10 percent of the shares of any one class of securities of an issuer and the issuer's directors and officers.

Insolvent: Inability of a business organization to pay its debts and obligations as they become due.

Interpretative letters: Responses issued by the SEC to individual inquiries by members of the public, attorneys, issuers, or other persons, interpreting the statutes or application of the statutes with regard to a particular transaction; also referred to as no-action letters.

Intrastate offering: Exempted offering where any security is offered and sold only to persons resident within a single state and where the issuer is a person resident and doing business within, or, if a corporation, incorporated by and doing business within that same state.

Investment Advisers Act of 1940: Statute that requires persons or organizations who are in the business of rendering investment advice to others to register with the SEC.

Investment Company Act of 1940: Statute enacted to regulate publicly owned companies, such as mutual funds, that engage in the business of investing and trading securities on behalf of others.

Involuntary dissolution: Cessation or termination of a corporation imposed on the corporation and accomplished without the approval of the corporation's shareholders and board of directors.

Issued and outstanding shares: Total number of shares that have been issued or sold to investors. Shares remain issued and outstanding until the corporation repurchases, redeems, or converts them into another type of equity security.

Issuer: Individual, corporation, partnership, association, trust, or unincorporated organization that issues or proposes to issue any security.

Jointly and severally liable: Obligation of two or more persons where the parties may be held liable either together (jointly) or individually (severally) for the entire obligation.

Jointly liable: Obligations of two or more persons where they are together held liable and share any debts or liabilities equally, regardless of ownership interest, up to the equity held in the partnership, and after that, in proportion to their respective ownership interest in the partnership.

Judicial dissolution: Termination of a corporation's existence initiated by the state of incorporation, shareholders of the corporation, or creditors of the corporation, accomplished through the court system.

Legal advertisement: Notice advising the general public of the corporation's desire to incorporate, qualify, or dissolve its business.

Legal capital: Sum of the par value of all par-value shares that have been issued and the amount of consideration received by a corporation for shares without par value that have been issued. No portion of legal capital may be distributed to the corporation's shareholders; also referred to as stated capital.

Legal notice: Announcement or advertisement placed in a legal journal or other publication that identifies that a corporation has been incorporated, has qualified to do business, or desires to dissolve.

Letter of intent: Document or agreement that spells out the general terms and conditions agreed upon by the parties to a transaction.

Limited liability company: Noncorporate form of business organization that is created as a separate legal entity under state statute. The limited liability company is managed similarly to the general partnership, and its owners enjoy both limited liability and favorable federal tax treatment.

Limited partner: Person who is a passive investor in a limited partnership, whose liability is limited to the amount invested in the partnership, and who is restricted from participating in the management of the partnership.

Limited partnership: Form of business organization having one or more general partners and one or more limited partners.

Limited partnership agreement: Comprehensive agreement that governs the principal aspects of the business relationship among the partners of a limited partnership; may be referred to as agreement of limited partnership or articles of partnership.

Limited partnership name: One or more words used to identify a limited partnership that must contain the words *limited partnership* or the abbreviation *L.P.*

Limited proxy: Written document given by the holder of stock to another person (the proxyholder) to vote on behalf of the shareholder in the manner in which the proxyholder is directed by the shareholder.

Liquidated: Result of process by which the assets of a business organization are sold, liabilities and bills are paid and satisfied, and any remaining cash or property is distributed to the owner or owners.

Liquidation: Winding-up process where assets are converted to cash, contracts are completed and terminated, creditors are paid and all debts satisfied, and any remaining cash is distributed to the owner or owners of the business organization.

Listed securities: Securities traded on an organized securities exchange.

Long-term debt: Loan by a creditor for which the debtor will repay the principal more than one year after such funds were loaned to the debtor.

Looseleaf service: Reference material contained in a book or volume whose pages can be replaced easily as the state statutes are amended.

Majority: Any number greater than 50 percent.

Majority vote: A corporate action approved by the affirmative vote of more than 50 percent of those shares entitled to vote.

Managing committee: Two or more partners appointed by all partners of a partnership to perform specific duties on behalf of the partnership.

Managing partner: One partner appointed by all partners of a partnership to manage the daily operations of the partnership.

Mandatory obligation: The duty to purchase shares from the corporation or other shareholders.

Market price: Price at which the corporation or a shareholder offers to sell a share.

Market value: Price a person is willing to pay for a share.

Meeting minutes: Record of proceedings and actions taken at a shareholders' or board of directors' meeting.

Merged corporations: Corporations that cease to exist as separate legal entities after a merger.

Merger: Combination of two or more corporations into one legal entity, in which only one of the merging corporations remains after, or survives, the merger.

Minute book: Depository of all corporate organizational documents, including the articles of incorporation, all amendments to the articles, all statutory filings required under the state's corporate statute, and the minutes of meetings of the board of directors and shareholders.

Model Act: Abbreviated form of the Model Business Corporation Act.

Model Business Corporation Act: Model statute originally drafted in 1950 by the Committee on Corporate Laws (Section of Business Law) of the American Bar Association for use by states in drafting their own corporate statutes. This act is continually being revised.

Model Non-Profit Corporation Law: Model statute that governs the formation and operation of nonprofit corporations.

Model Professional Corporation Supplement: Model statute that is part of the Model Business Corporation Act and that governs the incorporation and operation of professional corporations.

National Conference of Commissioners on Uniform State Laws: Organization responsible for preparing model statutes such as the Uniform Partnership Act and the Revised Uniform Limited Partnership Act.

Net worth: Amount by which total assets exceed total liabilities.

New issue: First instance when a corporation's board of directors determines to sell shares.

No-action letters: Responses issued by the SEC to individual inquiries by members of the public, attorneys, issuers, or other persons, interpreting the statutes or application of the statutes with regard to a particular transaction; also referred to as interpretative letters.

Noncumulative dividends: Right to receive a dividend or a distribution of a corporation's profit only on the declaration by the board of directors that a dividend is to be paid.

Nonprofit corporation: Type of corporation formed for the purpose of conducting a charitable, athletic, political, educational, religious, fraternal, or social service organization that does not contemplate pecuniary gain or profit.

Nonprofit nonstock corporation: Nonprofit corporation that issues no shares to its members.

Nonprofit stock corporation: Nonprofit corporation authorized by its articles of incorporation to issue shares to its members. No dividends are permitted to be paid on the shares issued by a nonprofit stock corporation.

Nontaxed entity: Business organization that reports revenues and expenses derived from the operation of the business but does not pay tax. The owner or owners of the business personally pay tax on the income of the business.

Notice of intent to dissolve: Document that provides notice to the secretary of state of the corporation's intent to dissolve.

Notice of meeting: Document that identifies the date, time, and place of meetings proposed to be held by the shareholders and directors.

Notice to claimants: Document that provides notice to all creditors and taxing authorities of the corporation's intent to dissolve.

Officers: Agents of the corporation who are appointed by the directors and who are responsible for the day-to-day operation and administration of the corporation.

Option: The right to purchase shares from the corporation or other shareholders prior to the shares being offered to other persons.

Organization: Performance of all the tasks necessary to bring the corporation into legal existence and to permit it to conduct business.

Organizational meeting: First meeting of the corporation held after its incorporation.

Organize: Procedures followed by the incorporators or the directors named in the articles to enable the corporation to transact the business for which it was incorporated. These procedures may include the appointment of officers, adoption of bylaws, and designation of registered agent and office.

Organized securities exchanges: Physical locations where securities are sold and purchased, for example, the New York Stock Exchange.

OTC: Abbreviation for "over the counter."

Over-the-counter market: Network of dealers through which securities are traded and who are linked by telecommunications equipment through the National Association of Securities Dealers Automated Quotation (NASDAQ) System.

Par value: Minimum consideration that is required to be paid for shares of stock sold by a corporation.

Partners: Persons who own and manage a partnership.

Partnership property: Cash, real property, personal property, or intellectual property acquired through contributions by the partners of the partnership.

Perpetual existence: The unlimited life of a corporation. A corporation will continue to exist regardless of the death or withdrawal of any one, or all, shareholders, directors, officers, or employees of the corporation, unless action is taken to terminate the corporate entity.

Personally liable: The extent to which an individual may be held legally responsible and at risk for the losses incurred by a business organization.

Persons: Individuals, partnerships, corporations, or other associations.

Piercing the corporate veil: Process by which the protection normally accorded the shareholders of a corporation from being held personally liable for the actions of the corporation is disregarded.

Plan of consolidation: Document or agreement that provides specific details of the agreement between the corporations that are parties to the consolidation, including, among other things, characteristics of the newly formed corporation, method of share distribution to shareholders of the combining corporation, and designation of individuals who are to act as the directors and officers of the newly formed corporation.

Plan of liquidation and dissolution: Outline of the procedures for the board of directors and officers to follow in the winding up and liquidating of the business and affairs of the corporation.

Plan of merger: Document or agreement that provides specific details of the agreement between the corporations that are parties to the merger.

Plan of share exchange: Document or agreement that provides specific details of the agreement between the corporations that are parties to the share exchange.

Powers: Authority granted by state statute that enables the corporation to carry out the purposes for which it was formed.

Preemptive right: Shareholder's right to purchase newly issued shares of the corporation before outsiders are allowed to purchase the shares. Shareholders may purchase new shares in the same proportion as their then-current ownership.

Preferred stock: Shares evidencing an ownership interest in a corporation and that have specific preferences over shares of common stock.

Private placement: Sale of substantial amounts of a security to an institutional investor, such as an insurance company or a pension fund, or a small group of individuals.

Professional corporation: Type of corporation organized by lawyers, physicians, dentists, architects, accountants, engineers, or other members of professions.

Profit/loss-sharing scheme: Plan agreed upon by all the partners of a partnership that identifies the percentage of profit and loss to which each partner is entitled to participate.

Promissory note: Written promise to pay a specified amount of money at a specified time.

Proof of publication: Evidence issued by the publisher of a legal journal or other publication that a legal notice was placed by a corporation.

Property dividend: Distribution of a corporation's profits to its shareholders in the form of property.

Prospectus: Document that contains information about the issuer and its business, the security being offered by the issuer, the finances of the issuer, risk factors in purchasing the security, and other information required to enable the investor to make an informed decision about purchasing the security.

Proxy: Written document given by the holder of stock to another person to authorize that person to exercise the shareholder's voting rights. The person authorized to exercise a shareholder's voting rights is often called a proxy or proxyholder.

Proxyholder: Person authorized by a shareholder to exercise that shareholder's voting rights; sometimes referred to as a proxy.

Public corporation: A corporation whose securities are registered under the federal securities laws and traded on one or more of the securities markets.

Public offering: Process of registering a security with the Securities and Exchange Commission and offering such security for sale to the public.

Public Utility Holding Company Act: Statute enacted by Congress in 1935 in response to manipulative practices in the public utilities industry.

Publicly held corporation: 1. Corporation that conducts a large amount of business and has numerous shareholders. Its shares are easily transferable and are traded on a national securities exchange or over the counter. 2. Corporation whose shares are held by the general public and that must comply with federal and state securities laws.

Publicly traded: Corporation whose shares are readily available for purchase or sale publicly.

Purposes: Corporation's goals and pursuits.

Qualify: The act of registering to do business in a state or states other than a corporation's home state or state of incorporation.

Quorum: Minimum number of shareholders or directors required to be present in order to transact business legally.

Record date: Date on which the stock transfer records of the corporation are reviewed to determine the persons entitled to vote as record owners of shares of the corporation.

Red-herring prospectus: Preliminary (not the final) prospectus of an issuer on which must be printed a red legend identifying it as preliminary and subject to change.

Registered agent: Person designated by a business organization to accept service on behalf of the business organization; often called an agent for service of process.

Registered office: Address designated by the corporation in its articles of incorporation or in an application for certificate of authority as the place where service of process may be effected.

Registration by coordination: Procedure under state statutes for registration by an issuer desiring to offer securities for which a registration statement has been filed under the Securities Act of 1933; does not require compliance with certain financial and qualifications tests.

Registration by filing: Procedure under state statutes for registration by an issuer desiring to offer securities for which a registration statement has been filed under the Securities Act of 1933 and that meets certain financial and qualifications tests.

Registration by qualification: Procedure under state statutes for registration by issuers who have not met or cannot meet the most stringent requirements for registration by filing and registration by coordination.

Registration statement: Document required to be filed with the Securities and Exchange Commission that includes the prospectus and other information and exhibits required under the rules and regulations of the federal securities laws.

Regular meetings: Meetings held on a specified day each week or month, usually with the day designated in the corporation's bylaws.

Regulation A: Rules 251–264 of the Securities Act of 1933, which require the issuer to file an "offering statement," including a "notification" and an "offering circular," at least ten days prior to the commencement of an offering.

Regulation D: Rules 501–508 of the Securities Act of 1933, which exempt accredited investors from certain filing requirements.

Resolution: Statement documenting an action taken or the authorization of an action to be taken. A resolution names the corporate person authorized to take the action and identifies the action to be taken.

Restated articles of incorporation: Document that contains a consolidation of the original articles of incorporation and all amendments to the articles of incorporation.

Retained earnings: Cumulation of net profits, income, and gains, taking into account losses of the corporation from the date of incorporation, minus distributions and dividends paid; also referred to as earned surplus.

Reverse stock split: Combination of a corporation's issued and outstanding shares into a lesser number of shares.

Reverse triangular merger: Combination by merger of three corporations (a parent corporation, a subsidiary corporation, and a target corporation) whereby the subsidiary corporation is merged into the target corporation.

Revised Uniform Limited Partnership Act: Model statute prepared by the National Conference of Commissioners on Uniform State Laws that clarified vague provisions and provided practical solutions to problems arising out of the Uniform Limited Partnership Act. This act was issued in 1976 and substantially amended in 1985.

Revocation of dissolution: To rescind the voluntary dissolution proceedings previously approved by the shareholders and board of directors of the corporation.

Right of first refusal: The privilege of having the first chance to purchase shares from shareholders desiring to sell their shares or from the corporation.

Right of redemption (debt security):   Right of a corporation to redeem bonds or debentures at the discretion of the board of directors of the corporation.

Right of redemption (preferred shares):   Agreement between the corporation and the preferred shareholder that the corporation has the right to redeem, or repurchase, the shares held by the preferred shareholder at some point in the future.

RULPA: Abbreviation for the Revised Uniform Limited Partnership Act.

S corporation: Type of corporation, for federal income tax purposes, that is a nontaxable entity whose shareholders personally report the income and losses of the S corporation on their personal income tax returns in the proportions of their ownership of the corporation; also referred to as a Subchapter S corporation.

Schedule K-1:   Internal Revenue Service form Partner's Share of Income, Credits, Deductions, etc., prepared and provided by the partnership to each partner, that shows each partner's distributive share of the partnership's income or loss, credit, and deduction.

SEC: Abbreviation for the Securities and Exchange Commission.

SEC releases: Statements distributed by the SEC that set forth the views of the SEC on certain issues.

Secured debt: Debt that requires the pledge of real property, personal property, equipment, inventory, or other property of the debtor.

Securities Act of 1933: First federal securities law enacted by Congress in 1933; it regulates the initial issuance of securities by corporations, requires broad disclosure of corporate and financial information to potential investors, prohibits fraudulent and deceptive practices in the sale of securities, and provides remedies for violations of any provisions of this statute.

Securities and Exchange Commission: Federal agency responsible for evaluating the sufficiency of the information disclosed to investors.

Securities Exchange Act of 1934: Statute that regulates the trading of securities already issued by corporations and requires brokers and dealers to register with the SEC.

Securities Investor Protection Act of 1970: Statute enacted as an amendment to the Securities Act of 1933 and that created the Securities Investor Protection Corporation.

Securities markets: Mechanisms that allow the sellers of securities (issuers) and the investors to consummate transactions.

Security: Evidence of (1) an ownership interest in the property of the corporation or (2) an obligation of the corporation to repay a loan or debt.

Selling corporation: Corporation desiring to sell its shares.

Series: Designation of various classes of shares that a corporation has the authority to issue.

Service companies: Organizations that offer to act as registered agent or agent for service of process on behalf of other business organizations and that provide document filing and retrieval services.

Share: Unit into which proprietary interests of a corporation are divided.

Share certificate: Tangible evidence of a shareholder's ownership in a corporation; referred to by some states as a stock certificate.

Share certificate legend: Statement printed on a share certificate that identifies the rights and restrictions imposed on the shares or holders of those shares and that provides a summary of the corporation's capitalization provisions; also referred to as a share legend.

Share dividend: Distribution of a corporation's own shares to the shareholders.

Share exchange: Combination of two or more corporations whereby one corporation (the purchasing corporation) acquires all the outstanding shares of one or more classes or series of the stock of another corporation (the target corporation), and both corporations remain in existence after the share exchange is consummated.

Share legend: Statement printed on a share certificate that identifies the rights and restrictions imposed on the shares or holders of those shares and that provides a summary of the corporation's capitalization provisions; also referred to as a share certificate legend.

Share transfer restriction: Limits placed on the sale, transfer, or other disposition of shares by shareholders of a corporation. These limits may be found in the articles of incorporation, bylaws, or shareholders' agreement.

Shareholder: Owner of the corporation.

Shareholders' agreement: Written agreement entered into by two or more shareholders and usually the corporation itself, whereby the corporation and the shareholders are restricted from selling shares of the corporation.

Shareholders' meetings: Vehicle through which the shareholders participate in the operation and management of the corporation, even though the shareholders have little or no control over the day-to-day operations of the corporation.

Shell corporation: Corporation that has sold all of its assets and is therefore unable to engage in its normal business.

Short-form merger: Combination by merger of a parent corporation and a subsidiary corporation, whereby the subsidiary corporation merges into the parent corporation (also known as an upstream merger). The procedure for merging a parent and a subsidiary is simplified.

Short-swing profit: Profit derived by an insider on the sale and purchase or purchase and sale of a security in any six-month period, which profit reverts back to the corporation.

Short-term debt: Loan by a creditor for which the debtor will repay the principal within one year or less from the date the loan was originally made.

Sinking fund: Account into which regular amounts are deposited for eventual use by the corporation in redeeming shares.

SIPC: Abbreviation for the Securities Investor Protection Corporation.

Small business corporation: Corporation that meets special requirements of the Internal Revenue Service.

Sole proprietor: Individual with ultimate responsibility for the operation, management, and liability of a business and all decisions affecting it.

Sole proprietorship: Form of business organization owned and managed by one individual.

Special meetings: Meetings held by the shareholders or board of directors whenever the corporation's activities require approval by the shareholders or directors.

Staggered terms: Alternate periods of time for which directors of the corporation may be elected to serve.

State of domestication: State in which the corporation was incorporated; also called the home state or state of domicile.

State of domicile: State in which a corporation was incorporated; often called the home state or state of domestication.

State statute: Law enacted by a state.

Stated capital: Sum of the par value of all par-value shares that have been issued and the amount of consideration received by a corporation for shares without par value that have been issued. No portion of stated capital may be distributed to the corporation's shareholders; also referred to as legal capital.

Statutory Close Corporation Supplement: Model statute that governs the formation and operation of close corporations.

Statutory provisions: Specific statements that are required by state statute to be contained in the articles of incorporation or other document filed with the secretary of state.

Stipulated value: The price at which shares may be purchased; it is determined by the board of directors in its best judgment.

Stock book: Depository where information on the issuance of shares (including the number of shares issued, the type of shares issued, the date of issuance, and the shareholders' names) is maintained.

Stock certificate: Tangible evidence of a shareholder's ownership of shares of a corporation; referred to by some states as a share certificate.

Stock purchase agreement: Agreement between the acquiring corporation and the shareholders of the selling corporation for the purchase and sale of shares.

Stock split: Distribution of a corporation's own shares to the shareholders.

Stock transaction: Event in which the shareholders of a selling corporation agree to sell or transfer their shares to an acquiring corporation or other person in exchange for a form of consideration.

Straight voting: Procedure for voting used by the shareholders of a corporation where each shareholder is entitled to cast the number of votes equal to the number of shares he or she owns.

Subchapter S corporation: Type of corporation, for federal income tax purposes, that is a nontaxable entity whose shareholders personally report the income and losses of the S corporation on their personal income tax returns in the proportions of their ownership of the corporation; also referred to as an S corporation.

Subordinated debt: Debt for which the holders have agreed to permit the repayment of other debts prior to the debt that has been subordinated.

Subscriber: Individual who agrees to purchase shares of the corporation prior to incorporation.

Subscription agreement: Written agreement by which the subscriber agrees to purchase shares of the corporation.

Surplus: Total of earned surplus, capital surplus, and the portion of the consideration for shares without par value that is treated as surplus rather than as stated capital.

Surviving corporation: Corporation that continues to exist after the merger of two or more corporations.

Tax clearance certificate: Document issued by the revenue department of the state evidencing the corporation's filing of its final income or franchise tax returns.

Tenancy in partnership: Type of ownership in which all the partners are co-owners of partnership assets or property in which they have limited ownership rights.

Termination: Ceasing to exist.

Tombstone ad: Notice that contains information about a proposed securities offering.

Transfer agent: Organization or entity that maintains a corporation's stock ledger.

Treasury shares: Shares that have been repurchased by the corporation from shareholders.

Triangular merger: Combination by merger of three corporations (a parent corporation, a subsidiary corporation, and a target corporation) whereby the target corporation is merged into the subsidiary corporation.

Trust indenture: Agreement between a corporation and a trustee pursuant to which debentures are issued by a corporation.

Trust Indenture Act of 1939: Statute designed to protect investors purchasing bonds, debentures, notes, and other debt securities by regulating the terms and conditions of the trust indenture under which debt securities are sold and the actions of the trustee of the trust indenture.

ULPA: Abbreviation for the Uniform Limited Partnership Act.

Underwriter: Person or organization that purchases securities from an issuer with a view to offer or sell such securities to the public.

Uniform Commercial Code: Statute designed to protect creditors; often referred to as the bulk transfer law.

Uniform Limited Partnership Act: Model statute prepared in 1916 by the National Conference of Commissioners on Uniform State Laws.

Uniform Partnership Act (UPA):   Model statute governing partnerships that was prepared by the National Conference of Commissioners on Uniform State Laws.

Uniform Securities Act: Form of statute prepared by the Commissioners on Uniform State Laws to provide uniform provisions of securities law adopted by states.

Unlisted securities: Securities traded in the over-the-counter market.

Unsecured debt: Debt that requires no pledge of any property of the debtor as security to ensure the repayment of the debt.

Upstream merger: Combination by merger of a parent corporation and a subsidiary corporation whereby the subsidiary corporation merges into the parent corporation.

Voluntary dissolution: Termination of the existence of a corporation at the recommendation of the board of directors and after approval by the shareholders of the corporation.

Voluntary termination: Intentional, deliberate cessation of the existence of a business organization.

Voting agreement: Agreement between two or more shareholders to combine their shares and vote as a unit to maximize the effect of their combined votes.

Voting right: Shareholder's right to vote his or her shares, through which the shareholder exercises control of the corporation.

Voting trust: Agreement between the shareholders of the corporation and a trustee in which the shareholders confer their right to vote on a trustee by transferring their shares to the trustee.

Waiver of notice: Document executed by a shareholder or director and delivered to the corporation evidencing a waiver of that shareholder's or director's right to receive proper and timely notice of a meeting.

Winding up: Process of completing unfinished business, converting assets to cash, paying outstanding debts and obligations, and collecting outstanding accounts.

Written consent: Document that evidences the actions taken by the shareholders or board of directors without the formality of holding a meeting.

INDEX

Accredited investor, 289
Acquiring corporation, 323
Administrative dissolution, 355–356
Advertisement. *See* Legal notice
Affidavit of assumed name, 3
Affidavit of lost certificate, 229, 230
Agent for service of process, 41–42
Agreement of trust, for business trust, 67
Alley v. Miramon, 185
Alter ego doctrine, 84
Amended certificate of authority, 204–206
American Association of Individual Investors,
　123
AmeriFirst Bank v. Bomar, 86
Annual meetings
　of directors, 149
　of shareholders, 153–154
Annual reports
　failure to file, 355
　of foreign corporation, 204
Appraisal (dissenters') rights, 333–334
Articles of agreement, for business trust, 67
Articles of amendment, 183–184
Articles of consolidation, 321
Articles of dissolution, 343–346
Articles of incorporation, 101
　amendments to
　　directors' approval, 181–182
　　effectiveness of, 185
　　preparation and filing of articles, 183–184
　　public record of, 184–185
　　publication and notice of, 185–186
　　purpose of, 180–181
　　shareholders' approval, 182–183
　of close corporation, 134
　filing procedures, 103–105
　of nonprofit corporation, 130
　optional provisions, 116–120
　of professional corporation, 128
　restated, 186
　statutory provisions, 112–115

Articles of merger, 321, 322
Articles of organization, for limited-liability
　company, 132–133, 136
Articles of revocation of dissolution, 354
Articles of share exchange, 321
Asset appraisal, 376
Asset purchase agreement, 330–333
Asset transaction
　bulk transfer law, 329–330
　defined, 327
　negotiation of, 328
　procedures for, 328–329
　purchase agreement, 330–333
Assignment, 330, 331, 332
Assumed name. *See* Fictitious name
Authorized shares, 113, 222

Balance sheet, 257–259
Bill of sale, 330, 331, 332
Blue Sky Law Reports, 304
Blue sky laws, 123, 279, 300–304
Board of directors. *See also* Directors
　committees, 79, 162
　functions and responsibilities, 78–81
　　amendments to articles of incorporation,
　　　181–182
　　approval of combinations, 318–321
　　approval of foreign status, 198–199
　　asset transactions, 328–329
　　debt security issuance, 241–242
　　dissolution of corporation, 347–348
　　dividend declaration, 76, 77, 255, 263
　　preferred stock redemption, 238, 239
　　reverse stock split, 269–270
　　share issuance, 227–228, 263
　　shareholders' agreements, 364–365
　　stock sale and purchase, 325
　　stock split, 266–267
　meetings of. *See* Directors' meetings
　officers, appointment of, 81
Bona fide offer, 371

Bona fide offer price, 371
Bonds, 244–245
Book value, 376
Bryan v. Western Pac. R. Corporation, 156
Bulk transfer law, 329–330
Business corporations, 61. *See also*
  Corporations
  actions requiring approval, 142
  balance sheet, 257–259
  bylaws, 124–126
  dissolution and liquidation. *See* Dissolution;
    Liquidation
  financing of. *See* Financing
  foreign jurisdiction qualification, 193–195
  insiders, 294
  management structure of, 56, 72–73
  mergers of. *See* Mergers
  optional provisions, 116–120
  organizing checklist, 102
  postincorporation activities, 121–124
  publicly held, 55, 363
  S corporation. *See* S corporations
  state of incorporation, 107–108
  statutory provisions, 112–115
  subscription for shares, 105–106
  taxation of, 58, 88–95
Business judgment rule, 84, 85, 86
Business trust, 66–67
Buy-sell agreement. *See* Shareholders'
  agreement
Bylaws, 124–126
  amendments to, 186–188

C corporation, taxation of, 88–95
Call of a meeting, 161–162
Capital, 121–122, 217, 257
Capital surplus, 259
Capitalization, 217. *See also* Financing
Capitalization of earnings, 376
Cash dividends, 260
CCH (Commerce Clearing House, Inc.), 135,
  304
Certificate of amendment, 185
Certificate of authority
  for foreign corporation, 196–198, 199
    amendments to, 204–206
    revocation of, 210–211
    withdrawal of, 208–210
Certificate of cancellation of limited
  partnership, 49–50
Certificate of consolidation, 321
Certificate of dissolution, 351
Certificate of existence, 196
Certificate of foreign limited partnership, 45
Certificate of incorporation. *See* Articles of
  incorporation
Certificate of limited partnership, 40–43
Certificate of merger, 321
Certificate of reinstatement, 355
Certificate of revocation, 210
Certificate of share exchange, 321

Certificate of withdrawal, 208–210
Clark Boardman Callaghan, 135, 174
Clearance certificates, 210, 349
Close corporations
  characteristics of, 63–64, 364
  difference from closely held corporation,
    364
  share certificate of, 64, 132–134
  state governing of, 129–131
Closely held corporations. *See also*
  Shareholders' agreements
  characteristics of, 63–64, 363–364
  difference from close corporation, 364
  stock sale and purchase, 323–327
  stock trading, 283
Commerce Clearing House, Inc. (CCH), 135,
  304
Common law trust, 66–67
Common stock, 113, 231–234
Computer research services, 135
Conference telephone meetings, 162
Consideration, 73
Consolidation
  approval procedures, 318–321
  defined, 45, 314
  dissenters' or appraisal rights, 333–334
  filing requirements, 321–323
  plan of, 318
Conversion rights
  debt securities, 246, 247
  preferred stock, 239–240
Corporate actions, 141–143. *See also* Meetings
Corporate designators, 108
Corporate existence, 141
Corporate name, 108–112
  change of, 182, 205
  fictitious or assumed. *See* Fictitious name
  for foreign corporations, 200–201, 205
  limited partnership, 41–42
Corporate seal, 122
Corporations
  advantages and disadvantages, 56–58
  asset sale and purchase, 327–333
  business. *See* Business corporations
  changes requiring shareholder approval,
    309–310
  characteristics of, 55–56
  closely held. *See* Close corporations; Closely
    held corporations
  defined, 55
  domestic, 59
  foreign, 59
  limited liability of, 57
  mergers and consolidation of. *See*
    Consolidation; Mergers
  nonprofit, 62–63, 128–129, 130
  organization costs, 58
  professional, 61–62, 126–128
  publicly held, 55, 363
  share exchange, 313
  statutory creation and powers, 59–61

stock sale and purchase, 323–327
types of, 61–64
Court cases
  business judgment rule, 86
  business trust, 66, 68
  corporate name change, 185
  dividend distribution, 262
  fictitious name, 5
  foreign jurisdiction qualification, 202
  limited partnership dissolution, 51
  merged corporation employee rights, 318
  partnership liability, 24
  piercing the corporate veil, 86
  preferred shareholders' rights, 233
  proxy vote, 156
  securities regulation, 287
  shareholders of closely held corporation, 371
  stockholders' meeting, 156
  voluntary liquidation, 352
Creditors, 241, 357
Criminal activity
  corporate indemnification, 87–88, 120
  partnership liability, 24
Cumulative dividends, 237
Cumulative voting, 74, 75, 118–119

Debentures, 245
Debt holders, 221
Debt securities
  conversion privilege, 246, 247
  defined, 218
  length of term, 243
  provisions of, 245–247
  redemption rights, 245–246
  secured and unsecured, 242–243
  subordination, 247
  types of, 243–245
  use of, 241–242
Debtor, 241
Deed, 330, 332
Delaware corporate statutes, 107–108
Designation statement, 241, 242
DeWitt Truck Brokers, Inc. v. W. Ray Flemming Fruit Company, 86
Directors. *See also* Board of directors
  authority of, 78
  election of, 74–75, 79, 118–119
  indemnification to, 87–88, 120
  initial, 116, 121
  liability of, 84–86
  number of, 80
  organizational meeting, 121
  removal of, 80
  responsibilities of, 72, 78, 84–85
  terms of, 79, 80
Directors' meetings. *See also* Meetings; Shareholders' meetings
  by conference telephone, 162
  location of, 149–150
  minutes of, 168–170
  notice of, 150–151
  purpose of, 143–144
  quorum and voting, 152–153
  requirements of, 148–149
  written consent in lieu of, 170–172
Directors' organizational meeting, 145, 147
Dissenters' (appraisal) rights, 333–334
Dissolution. *See also* Liquidation
  of corporation, 94–95
    articles of, 343–346
    directors' approval, 347–348
    filing requirements, 349–351
    involuntary, 354–357
    revocation of, 353–354
    shareholders' approval, 348–349
    tax considerations, 352–353
    voluntary, 343–346
  defined, 342
  of general partnership, 29–32
  of limited partnership, 49–50
Distributions of corporation
  dividends. *See* Dividends
  reverse stock split, 269–271
  stock split, 265–268
Dividend rights, 75–76, 77, 260
  common shareholders, 232–233
  preferred shareholders, 237–238
Dividends
  accounting procedures, 261, 264
  authorization for, 254–255, 263
  cash, 260
  criteria for, 256–259
  defined, 254
  payment of, 75–76, 77
  payment preferences for classes of stock, 260–261
  for preferred stock, 237, 260–261
  property, 260
  shares as, 262–265
  sources of payment, 259–260
  tax implications, 262, 265
Document of public record, 184
Domestic corporation, 59, 107, 193
Domesticate, 107
Double taxation, 89–91, 262
Downstream merger, 312
Due diligence process, 324, 335–336
Duty of care, 84–85
Duty of loyalty, 85
Dye, Alan L., 304

Earned surplus, 259
Effective date
  of dissolution, 351
  for securities sale, 281
Employer identification number (EIN)
  application for, 6–7
  for partnerships, 25, 47
Equity holders. *See* Shareholders
Equity securities
  authorized shares, 113, 222

classes and series of, 224–225
common stock, 113, 231–234
defined, 218
issuance authorization and certificate, 227–229
issued and outstanding shares, 223
market value, 227
par value, 225–226
payment for, 229–231
preferred stock. *See* Preferred stock
treasury shares, 223–224
Exchange Act company, 293
Express partnership, 14

Federal Securities Law Reports, 304
Federal securities laws, 278–280
terminology in, 280–281
Fictitious name
corporation, 111–112
change of, 182, 205
for foreign corporations, 200–201, 205
defined, 3
general partnership, 16
sole proprietorship, 4–6
Fiduciaries, 84
Financing. *See also* Debt securities; Equity securities of corporations
capital structure, 113–114, 216–217
payment of capital, 121–122
security issuance, 217–221
sole proprietorships, 3
First National Bank of Boston v. Nichols, 352
Fitsimmons v. Western Airlines, Inc., 312, 318
Foreign corporations
annual report requirement, 204
board of directors' approval, 198–199
certificate of authority, 196–198, 199
defined, 59, 107, 193
dissolution and liquidation, 351
failure to qualify penalties, 207–208
good standing requirement, 196–198
mergers of, 206
registered office and agent for, 202
revocation of authority, 210–211
tax requirements, 203
withdrawal of authority, 208–210
Foreign jurisdictions, 193
Foreign limited partnerships, 45
Foreign state, 45
Form 720 (excise tax), 25
Form 966 (corporate dissolution or liquidation), 352–353
Form 1065 (partnerships), 24–25, 26–29, 47
Form 1120 (corporation income tax), 89
Form 1120-A (corporation short-form income tax), 89, 90–91
Form 2553 (small business corporation), 92–94, 95, 124
Form books, 135
Form SS-4 (EIN), 6–7, 25, 47
Franchise tax, 95, 203, 226, 355

Freeze out of shareholders, 270
Fully paid and nonassessable shares, 106, 230

Galler v. Galler, 371
General partner of limited partnership, 38
addition and withdrawal of, 48
liability of, 47
General partnerships
advantages and disadvantages (list), 13
characteristics of, 13–15
defined, 13
dissolution and winding up, 29–32
express or implied, 14
fictitious name registration, 16
liability of partners, 23–24
management of, 20–21
partnership agreement
checklist, 16
drafting aids, 15–16
filing requirement, 15
importance, 13
sample written agreement, 17–19
profit and loss sharing, 26–28
property ownership, 22
regulatory filing requirements, 19–20
taxation of partners, 24–25
termination of, 29–32
Goldboss v. Reimann, 156
Good standing certificate, 196–198
Goodwyne v. Moore, 185
Greater-than-majority vote, 182
Gross receipts tax, 95

Hall v. Geiger-Jones Company, 300
Hecht v. Malley, 66
Holders of record, 154
Home state, for corporation, 59, 107, 193

Implied partnership, 14
Income taxes. *See* Taxes and taxation
Incorporator, 115
Incorporators' organizational meeting, 145, 146
Indemnification, 87–88, 120
Initial directors, 116, 121
Insider trading, 281
Insiders of corporation, 294
Insolvency, 259
Insurance, liability, 7
Internal Revenue Service
Form 720 (excise tax), 25
Form 966 (corporate dissolution or liquidation), 352–353
Form 1065 (partnerships), 24–25, 26–29, 47
Form 1120 (corporation income tax), 89
Form 1120-A (corporation short-form income tax), 89, 90–91
Form 2553 (small business corporation), 92–94, 95, 124
Form SS-4 (EIN), 6–7, 25, 47
Schedule K-1 (partnerships), 25, 30, 47

International Inventors Incorporated, East v. Martin Berger, 5
Interpretative letters, 304
Intrastate offering, 289
Investment Advisers Act of 1940, 279
Investment Company Act of 1940, 279
Involuntary dissolution, 354–357
Issued and outstanding shares, 223
Issuer, 281

Jointly and severally liable, 23
Jointly liable, 23
Judicial dissolution, 356–357

Landreth Timber Co. v. Landreth, 287
Legal advertisement. *See* Legal notice
Legal links. *See* Court cases
Legal notice
    of foreign corporation, 206–207
    of incorporation, 122–123
      amendments to articles, 185
    intent to dissolve, 349, 350
    tombstone ad, 281, 282, 287
Letter of intent, 324
Liability
    of corporations, 57
    of directors and officers, 84–86
    of general partners, 23–24
    indemnification for costs, 87–88
    insurance, 7
    of limited partners, 46–47
    of shareholders, 83–84
    of sole proprietor, 2, 7–8
Limited liability company, 64–66, 131–133
Limited partner, 38
    addition and withdrawal of, 48
    limited liability status, 46–47
    rights of, 45–46
Limited partnerships
    advantages and disadvantages (list), 40
    agent for service of process, 41–42
    certificate of, 40–43
    changes in partnership interests, 48
    characteristics of, 38–39
    defined, 39
    dissolution and termination, 49–50
    foreign limited partnerships, 45
    management of, 45–46
    mergers and consolidations, 45
    name of, 41–42
    partnership agreement, 43–44
      checklist, 44
    taxation of partners, 47–48
Liquidation. *See also* Dissolution
    of business, 8, 351–353
    of corporation, 76–77, 94–95, 351–353
    defined, 342
Liquidation rights
    common stock, 232
    preferred stock, 236–237
Listed securities, 283

Long-term debt, 243
Looseleaf services, 135, 304

Majority, 152
Majority vote, 182
Managing committee, 20
Managing partner, 20
Mandatory obligation
    to purchase shares, 366, 373–374
    to sell shares, 373
Market price, 227
Market value of shares, 227
Massachusetts trust, 66–67
Matthew Bender & Co., 174
Meetings. *See also* Directors' meetings;
    Shareholders' meetings
    of board committees, 162
    by conference telephone, 162
    call and notice of, 161–162
    documentation of, 162–163
    minutes of, 168–170
    resolutions, 164–168
    types of, 141–142
    written consent in lieu of, 170–172
Merged corporations, 311
Merger agreement, 315
Mergers
    approval procedures, 318–321
    defined, 45, 311
    dissenters' or appraisal rights, 333–334
    filing requirements, 321–323
    of foreign corporations, 206
    plan of, 315, 316–317
    types of, 312–313
Minute book, 122, 163. *See also* Meetings
    amendment document filing in, 185
    organization of, 172–173
Model Business Corporation Act (1984), 59
    corporate rights and powers, 59–60
    Model Professional Corporation
      Supplement, 61, 126
    Statutory Close Corporation Supplement,
      63, 129–130
    text, 381–404
Model Non-Profit Corporation Law, 62, 129
Moseley v. Commercial State Bank, 24

Name, corporate. *See* Corporate name
National Association of Securities Dealers
    Automated Quotation (NASDAQ)
    System, 283
National Conference of Commissioners on
    Uniform State Laws (NCCUSL), 39
Net income tax, 95. *See also* Taxes and taxation
Net worth, 217, 257
New issue of shares, 227
No-action letters, 304
Noncumulative dividends, 237
Nonprofit corporations, 62–63, 128–129, 130
Nonprofit nonstock corporations, 62
Nonprofit organizations, and partnerships, 15

Nonprofit stock corporations, 62–63
Nontaxed entity, 8
Notice of intent to dissolve, 349, 350
Notice of meeting, 150, 156–157, 161
Notice to claimants, 349, 350

Officers, corporate
  contract execution duty, 81
  indemnification to, 87–88, 120
  liability of, 84–86
  number and terms of, 83
  removal of, 83
  responsibilities of, 72, 81–83, 84–85
Option, to purchase shares, 366, 374–375
Organization, of corporation, 102
Organizational meetings
  call of, 147–148
  of directors, 145, 147
  of incorporators, 145, 146
  location of, 147
  purpose of, 143, 144–145
  quorum requirements, 147
Organized security exchanges, 283
Over-the-counter market (OTC), 283

Par value of shares, 114, 225–226
Paralegal tasks
  business incorporation, 96
    amending and restating, 188–189
  business organization form, 68
  bylaws, amending, 189
  dissolution and liquidation, 357–358
  dividends and distributions, 271–272
  financing, 247–248
  foreign corporations, 211
  general partnerships, 32–33
  limited partnerships, 50–51
  meetings, 173–174
  mergers and consolidations, 334–336
  research of state statutes, 135
  securities regulations, 304
  shareholders' agreements, 377
  sole proprietorships, 9
Partners
  of general partnership, 13
  of limited partnerships, 38
Partnership property, 22
Partnerships. See General partnerships;
    Limited partnerships
Perpetual existence, 95, 117
Personal liability. See also Liability
  of general partners, 13
  of sole proprietor, 7–8
Persons, in UPA, 14, 15
Piercing the corporate veil, 84, 86
Plan of consolidation, 318
Plan of liquidation and dissolution, 347, 348
Plan of merger, 315, 316–317
Plan of share exchange, 317
Powers of the corporation, 116–117

Preemptive rights, of shareholders, 77–78,
    117–118, 233
Preferred stock. See also Equity securities
  conversion rights, 239–240
  creation of, 240–241
  defined, 113, 234
  dividend rights, 237–238
  liquidation rights, 236–237
  redemption rights, 238
  sinking fund for, 238
  voting rights, 234–236
Prentice-Hall, 135, 174
Private placement, 288
Professional corporations, 61–62, 126–128
  foreign jurisdiction qualification, 194
Profit/loss-sharing scheme, 27
Promissory notes, 243–244
Proofs of publication, 185, 207
Property dividend, 260
Property tax, 95
Prospectus, 281
  red-herring, 287
Proxy, 158–159
Proxyholder, 158–159
Public corporation, 281
Public offering, 281
Public Utility Holding Company Act of 1935,
    279
Publicly held corporations, 55, 363
Publicly traded shares, 363
Purposes of the corporation, 116

Qualify
  as foreign corporation, 193
    penalties for failure, 207–208
Quorum, 119–112
  for directors' meeting, 152–153
  for organizational meeting, 147
  for shareholders' meeting, 159–160

Record date, 154–155
Red-herring prospectus, 287
Redemption rights
  debt securities, 245–246
  preferred stock, 238
Registered agent, of corporation, 114, 202, 355
Registered office, of corporation, 114, 202, 355
Registration, of fictitious name, 4–6, 111–112
Registration statement, 281
Regular meetings, of directors, 149
Research aids
  corporate meetings and actions, 174
  securities laws, 304
  state and local laws, 135
  types of, 135, 174
Resolutions, 164–168
Restated articles of incorporation, 186
Restrictive transfer agreement. See
    Shareholders' agreement
Retained earnings, 259
Reverse stock split, 269–271

Reverse triangular merger, 312
Revised Uniform Limited Partnership Act
       (RULPA), 39
   addition and withdrawal of partners, 48
   certificate of limited partnership filing, 40, 42
   dissolution, 49–50
   foreign limited partnerships, 45
   liability of limited partner, 46–47
   limited partnership name, 41–42
   voting rights, 45
Revocation of dissolution, 353–354
Right of first refusal, 371
Right of redemption. *See* Redemption rights
Rock-Ola Manufacturing Corporation v. Wertz,
       202
Roeschlein v. Watkins, 51
Romeo, Peter J., 304
RULPA. *See* Revised Uniform Limited
       Partnership Act (RULPA)

S corporations, 55
   election as, 124
   taxation of, 58, 92–95
Sales and use tax, 95
Schedule K-1 (partnerships), 25, 30, 47
SEC. *See* Securities and Exchange Commission
       (SEC)
SEC releases, 304
Section 16 Treatise and Reporting Guide, 304
Secured debt, 242
   bonds, 244–245
Securities. *See also* Debt securities; Equity
       securities; Financing
   beneficial ownership of, 294–295
       statement, 296–298
   defined, 217, 281–283
   as evidence of ownership interest, 277–278
   markets for, 283
   private placement, 288
   short-swing profit, 295, 299
Securities Act of 1933, 278–279
   liability and antifraud provisions, 290
   purposes of, 283–284
   registration exemption provisions, 288–290
   registration process, 286–288
   registration statement, 284–286
Securities and Exchange Commission (SEC),
       279
   beneficial ownership statements, 294–298
   organization of, 291–292
   Regulation A, 289
   Regulation D, 289
   SEC releases, 304
Securities Exchange Act of 1934, 279
   insider short-swing profits, 295, 299
   liability and antifraud provisions, 299–300
   purposes of, 291
   reporting and disclosure requirements,
       293–295
Securities Investor Protection Act of 1970
       (SIPC), 279

Securities markets, 283
Securities regulation
   blue sky laws, 123, 279, 300–304
   federal securities laws, 278–281
   importance, 277–278
Selling corporation, 323
Service companies, 202
Share certificates
   of close corporation, 64, 132–134
   as evidence of ownership, 73, 123, 218
   example of, 219–220
   issuance of, 227–229
   legend on, 228, 372–373, 374–375
   of nonprofit organization, 63
   vs. book-entry ownership, 123
Share dividends, 262–265
Share exchange
   approval procedures, 318–321
   defined, 313
   dissenters' or appraisal rights, 333–334
   filing requirements, 321–323
   plan of, 317
Share legend, 228, 372–373, 374–375
Share transfer restrictions, 370–373
Shareholders
   defined, 73, 218
   dissenters' or appraisal rights, 333–334
   dividend rights, 75–76, 77, 232–233, 237–238,
       260
   freeze out, 270
   limited liability of, 83–84
   liquidation right to assets, 76–77, 232,
       236–237
   minority dissolution action, 357
   preemptive rights, 77–78, 117–118, 233
   responsibilities of, 72
       amendments to articles of incorporation,
           182–183
       approval of corporate combinations,
           318–321
       changes requiring approval, 309–310
       dissolution of corporation, 348–349
   share transfer restrictions on, 370–373
   taxation of, 89–91
   voting rights, 74–75, 118–119, 158–159,
       231–232, 234–236
Shareholders' agreements. *See also* Closely
       held corporations
   characteristics of, 364–366
   components of, 367
   defined, 364
   example of, 367–370
   function of, 366
   pricing shares, 375–377
   purpose of, 365
   share sale procedures, 373–375
   share transfer restrictions, 370–373
Shareholders' equity, 257
Shareholders' meetings. *See also* Directors'
       meetings; Meetings
   annual and special, 153–154

location of, 154
minutes of, 168–170
notice and waiver of notice, 155–158
purpose of, 144, 153
quorum requirements, 159–160
record date, 154–155
voting of shares, 160–161
written consent in lieu of, 170–172
Shares. *See also* Shareholders
authorized shares, 113, 222
book-entry system of ownership, 123
certificates. *See* Share certificates
classes of, 113–114
common stock, 113, 231–234
corporate repurchase of, 223–224, 256
defined, 218
as dividend, 262–265
dividend payment. *See* Dividends
fully paid and nonassessable, 106, 230
issued and outstanding shares, 223
market value, 227
new issue, 227
par value, 114, 225–226
payment for, 229–231
preferred stock. *See* Preferred stock
publicly traded, 363
reverse stock split, 269–271
sale and purchase by corporations, 323–327
sales restrictions. *See* Shareholders'
   agreements
stock split, 265–268
transfer restrictions, 370–373
Shell corporation, 327
Short-form (upstream) merger, 312, 313, 321
Short-swing profit, 299
Short-term debt, 243
Sinking fund, 238
SIPC (Securities Investor Protection Act of
   1970), 279
Small business corporation, 92. *See also*
   S corporations
Sole proprietor
defined, 2
estimated tax payment requirement, 8
personal liability for losses, 7–8
Sole proprietorship
advantages and disadvantages (list), 2
defined, 2
financing of, 3
formation and operation of, 3
liability of, 2, 7–8
name registration, 3–6
personal nature of, 3
taxation of, 8
termination of, 8
Special meetings
of directors, 149
of shareholders, 153–154
Staggered terms, 79, 80
State and local laws
articles of incorporation, 101–102

filing procedures, 103–105
   optional provisions, 116–120
   statutory provisions, 112–115
blue sky laws, 123, 279, 300–304
certificate of limited partnership, 40–43
corporate governance, 59–61
corporate name selection, 108–112, 182
Delaware corporate statutes, 107–108
dissolution of corporation, 343–346,
   349–351, 355–356
fictitious name registration, 4, 16, 111–112,
   182, 200–201, 205
for foreign corporations, 193–195
partnership filing requirements, 19–20
preemptive rights of shareholders, 77–78
research of, 125
taxes on corporations, 94–95, 203
State of domestication, 107, 193
State of domicile, 59
State Street Trust Co. v. Hall, 68
Stated capital, 258–259
Statutory Close Corporation Supplement, 63,
   129–130
Statutory provisions, 112–115
Stipulated value, 376
Stock book, 122
Stock certificate. *See* Share certificate
Stock exchanges, 283
Stock purchase agreement, 325–327. *See also*
   Shareholders' agreement
Stock redemption agreement. *See*
   Shareholders' agreement
Stock split, 265–268
Stock transaction, 323
Stocks. *See* Shares
Straight voting, 74, 118
Subchapter S corporations. *See* S Corporations
Subordinated debt, 247
Subscriber, 105
Subscription agreement, 105–106
Surplus, 259
Surviving corporation, 206, 311

Tax clearance certificate, 349
Taxes and taxation
after stock split, 268
C corporation, 88–95
of corporations, 58, 88–91
in dissolution, 352–353
double taxation, 89–91, 262
of foreign corporations, 203
of general partners, 24–25
limited liability companies, 65
nonprofit corporations, 62
on dividend income, 262, 265
property, 95
S corporation, 58, 92–94
of sole proprietorship, 8
state income taxes, 94–95, 203
Tenancy in partnership, 22
Termination. *See also* Dissolution; Liquidation

of general partnership, 29–32
of limited partnership, 49–50
Tombstone ad, 281, 282, 287. *See also* Legal
 notice
Transfer agent, 229
Treasury shares, 223–224, 256
Triangular merger, 312
Trust Indenture Act of 1939, 279

Underwriter, 281
Uniform Commercial Code, 329–330
Uniform Limited Partnership Act (ULPA), 39.
 See also Revised Uniform Limited
 Partnership Act (RULPA)
 text, 419–434
Uniform Partnership Act (UPA), 14–15
 compensation of partners, 26–27
 dissolution and termination, 29–31
 liability of partners, 23–24
 management issues, 20–21
 property ownership, 22
 text, 405–418
Uniform Securities Act, 280
 antifraud provisions and enforcement,
 303–304
 blue sky provisions, 300–304
 purposes of, 300–301
 registration exemptions, 302–303
 registration process, 301–302
Unlisted securities, 283
Unsecured debt, 243
 bonds, 244–245
 debentures, 245
 promissory note, 243–244
Upstream (short-form) merger, 312, 313, 321

Voluntary dissolution, 343–346
Voluntary termination, 8
Voting
 by directors, 152–153
 by proxy, 158–159
 procedures, 160–161
Voting agreement, 75
Voting rights, of shareholders, 74–75
 common stock, 231–232
 preferred stock, 234–236
Voting trust, 74, 75

Wabash Railway Company v. Barclay, 262
Waiver of notice, 151, 157–158
Warren Gorham Lamont, 135
West Publishing Co., 135, 174
Winding up of business, 29, 351–352
Wood v. Coastal States Gas Corporation, 233
Written consent, 170–172